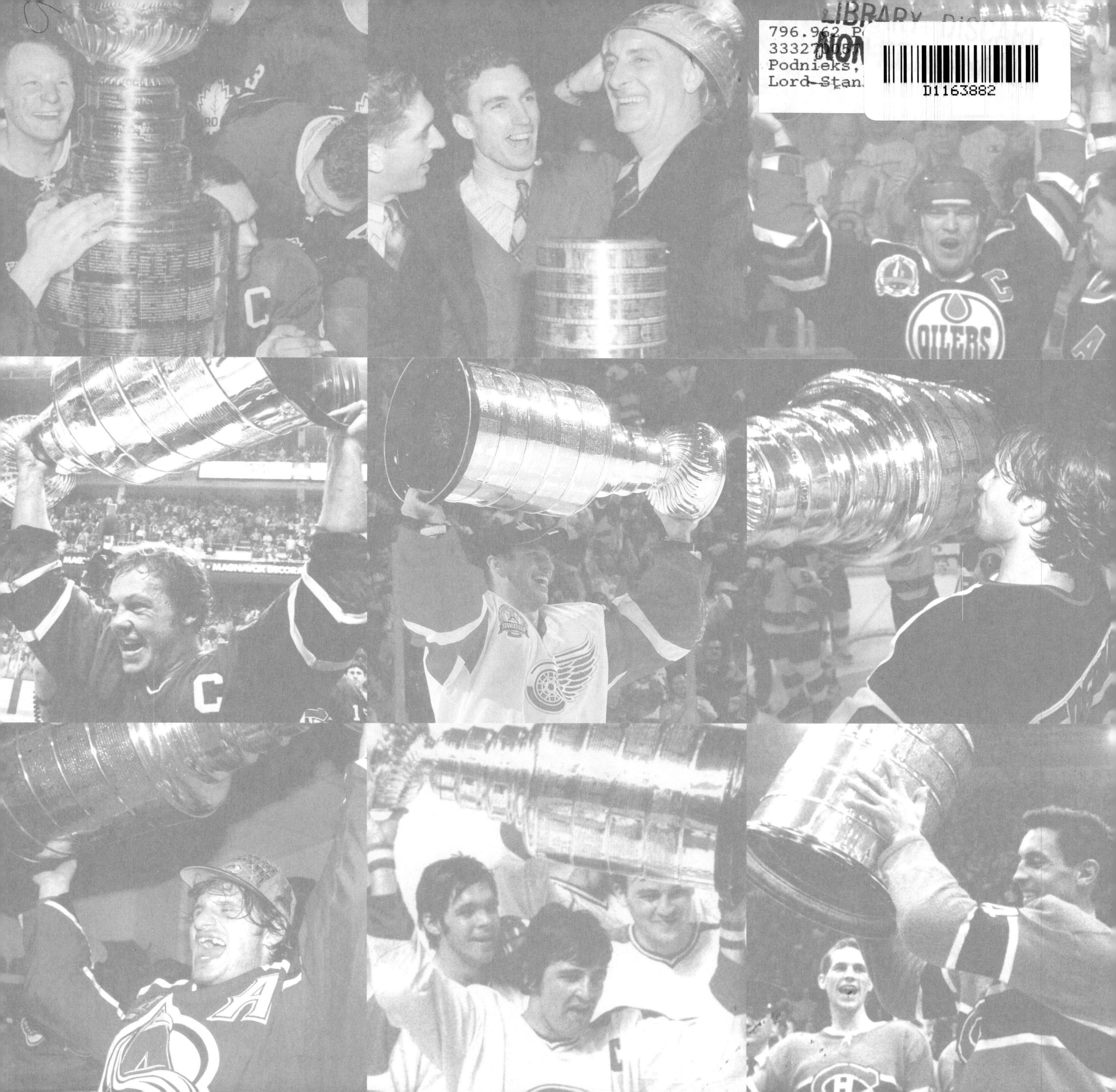

LORD STANLEY'S CUP
A Fenn Publishing Book / First Published in 2004

Fenn Publishing Company Ltd.
Bolton, Ontario, Canada

Distributed in Canada by H. B. Fenn and Company Ltd.
Bolton, Ontario, Canada, L7E 1W2
www.hbfenn.com

Library and Archives Canada Cataloguing in Publication

Podnieks, Andrew
Lord Stanley's cup / Andrew Podnieks.

"Hockey Hall of Fame".
ISBN 1-55168-261-3

Stanley Cup (Hockey) 1. Hockey Hall of Fame. II Title.

GV847.7.P619 2004 796.962'648
C2004-903142-2

Lord Stanley's Cup

Andrew Podnieks

Fenn Publishing Company Ltd.
Bolton, Ontario

Contents

1892-93	Montreal AAA
1893-94	Montreal AAA
1894-95	Montreal Victorias
1895-96Feb	Winnipeg Victorias
1895-96Dec	Montreal Victorias
1896-97	Montreal Victorias
1897-98	Montreal Victorias
1898-99Feb	Montreal Victorias
1898-99Mar	Montreal Shamrocks
1899-1900	Montreal Shamrocks
1900-01	Winnipeg Victorias
1901-02Jan	Winnipeg Victorias
1901-02Mar	Montreal AAA
1902-03Feb	Montreal AAA
1902-03Mar	Ottawa Silver Seven
1903-04	Ottawa Silver Seven
1904-05	Ottawa Silver Seven
1905-06Feb	Ottawa Silver Seven
1905-06Mar	Montreal Wanderers
1906-07Jan	Kenora Thistles
1906-07Mar	Montreal Wanderers
1907-08	Montreal Wanderers
1908-09	Ottawa Senators
1909-10	Montreal Wanderers
1910-11	Ottawa Senators
1911-12	Quebec Bulldogs
1912-13	Quebec Bulldogs
1913-14	Toronto Blueshirts
1914-15	Vancouver Millionaires
1915-16	Montreal Canadiens
1916-17	Seattle Metropolitans
1917-18	Toronto Arenas
1918-19	*Series Cancelled*
1919-20	Ottawa Senators
1920-21	Ottawa Senators
1921-22	Toronto St. Pats
1922-23	Ottawa Senators
1923-24	Montreal Canadiens
1924-25	Victoria Cougars
1925-26	Montreal Maroons
1926-27	Ottawa Senators
1927-28	New York Rangers
1928-29	Boston Bruins
1929-30	Montreal Canadiens
1930-31	Montreal Canadiens
1931-32	Toronto Maple Leafs
1932-33	New York Rangers
1933-34	Chicago Black Hawks
1934-35	Montreal Maroons
1935-36	Detroit Red Wings
1936-37	Detroit Red Wings
1937-38	Chicago Black Hawks
1938-39	Boston Bruins
1939-40	New York Rangers
1940-41	Boston Bruins
1941-42	Toronto Maple Leafs
1942-43	Detroit Red Wings
1943-44	Montreal Canadiens
1944-45	Toronto Maple Leafs
1945-46	Montreal Canadiens
1946-47	Toronto Maple Leafs
1947-48	Toronto Maple Leafs
1948-49	Toronto Maple Leafs
1949-50	Detroit Red Wings
1950-51	Toronto Maple Leafs
1951-52	Detroit Red Wings
1952-53	Montreal Canadiens
1953-54	Detroit Red Wings
1954-55	Detroit Red Wings
1955-56	Montreal Canadiens
1956-57	Montreal Canadiens
1957-58	Montreal Canadiens
1958-59	Montreal Canadiens
1959-60	Montreal Canadiens
1960-61	Chicago Black Hawks
1961-62	Toronto Maple Leafs
1962-63	Toronto Maple Leafs
1963-64	Toronto Maple Leafs
1964-65	Montreal Canadiens
1965-66	Montreal Canadiens
1966-67	Toronto Maple Leafs
1967-68	Montreal Canadiens
1968-69	Montreal Canadiens
1969-70	Boston Bruins
1970-71	Montreal Canadiens
1971-72	Boston Bruins
1972-73	Montreal Canadiens
1973-74	Philadelphia Flyers
1974-75	Philadelphia Flyers
1975-76	Montreal Canadiens
1976-77	Montreal Canadiens
1977-78	Montreal Canadiens
1978-79	Montreal Canadiens
1979-80	New York Islanders
1980-81	New York Islanders
1981-82	New York Islanders
1982-83	New York Islanders
1983-84	Edmonton Oilers
1984-85	Edmonton Oilers
1985-86	Montreal Canadiens
1986-87	Edmonton Oilers
1987-88	Edmonton Oilers
1988-89	Calgary Flames
1989-90	Edmonton Oilers
1990-91	Pittsburgh Penguins
1991-92	Pittsburgh Penguins
1992-93	Montreal Canadiens
1993-94	New York Rangers
1994-95	New Jersey Devils
1995-96	Colorado Avalanche
1996-97	Detroit Red Wings
1997-98	Detroit Red Wings
1998-99	Dallas Stars
1999-2000	New Jersey Devils
2000-01	Colorado Avalanche
2001-02	Detroit Red Wings
2002-03	New Jersey Devils
2003-04	Tampa Bay Lightning

ACKNOWLEDGEMENTS AND PHOTO CREDITS

ACKNOWLEDGEMENTS

So many people helped to a lesser and greater extent—providing information, photographs, leads, miscellaneous assistance of one sort or another—to get this book done. This is a small attempt to thank one and all for their kindness and generosity.

First, to the many people at archives and museums who provided photographs and textual information needed to make this book as complete as possible: Denis Brodeur, Glenn Levy, Patricia Desjardins, Donald Bowden, Tina Poitras, David Poremba, Jocelyn Robert, Myron Momryk, Ed Sweeney, Mac MacDermott, Len Kotylo, Greg Innis, Angela Wheelock, Michelle Purcell, John Halligan, Stephen Coutts, Antoine Pelletier, Carole Ritchot, Bruce Bennett, Glenn Levy, Richard Johnson, Aaron Schmidt, Paul Banfield, Bill Swift, Phil Norton, Richard Bak, Michelle Pilon, Kelly McKay, and Doug McLellan.

To others who were kind with their time and provided information that hopefully has made this book superior than what it would have been without their assistance, notably Frank Selke, Dick Irvin, Brian O'Neill, Billy Harris, Dr. Hugh Smythe, Al Ruelle, Denis Brodeur, and Kerry Day.

To Amanda Askari and the present Earl of Derby, for valuable information on the lineage of that family.

To Mike Bolt, Walt Neubrand, and Bill Wellman, for stories and photos of recent Cup adventures during the summertimes of celebration.

To those who have helped me personally gather and prepare the book, namely Greig Cowan (finally!), Stephanie Hicks, Kyle Laframboise, and Paul Patskou.

To everyone at the Hockey Hall of Fame for their support and assistance: Phil Pritchard for his enthusiasm and support for the book from the get-go, Tyler Wolosewich for being the go-to guy for so very much, Kevin Shea for a close edit of the text, Craig Campbell for invaluable assistance with photos, and everyone else at the Hall, namely: Bill Hay, Jeff Denomme, Craig Baines, Kelly Masse, Marilyn Robbins, Anthony Fusco, Darren Boyko, Ron Ellis, Peter Jagla, Steve Poirier, Steve Ozimec, Jackie Boughazale, Sylvia Lau, Izak Westgate, Craig Beckim, Tome Geneski, Mike Gouglas, Carmil Guspie, Joanne Laird, Patrick Minogue, Ray Paquet, Pearl Rajwanth, Dave Stubbs, Sanrda Walters, Greg Martin, Wendy Cramer, and all the part-timers in the Museum and store who make the Hall a great place to visit.

In particular, to Dave Dahms and (posthumously) Ed Moffett in Chicago, collectors who appreciate the history of hockey as much as any two people on the face of the earth, men who revere the game, respect it, worship it, and, insodoing, have become an important part of its history and upkeep. To Nicole Langlois for patient and perfect editing.

And to everyone at Fenn Publishing, primarily Jordan Fenn for his continued support of my projects (which will hopefully continue to continue!) and his designer, Kathryn Del Borrello who has poured imagination and determination and plenty of patience into these pages to produce what I hope readers will regard as a worthy work. To my agent Dean Cooke and his associates Samantha North and Suzanne Brendreth for their faithful and loyal support.

Lastly, to those who have been with me through thick and thin: me mum, Liz & Ian, the amazing Zack and M.

To one and all, a great thanks with fingers crossed that we can do it all again soon.

SHOOTING THE STANLEY CUP

Over a period of about a week, Dave Sandford secluded himself in a room at the Hockey Hall of Fame, set up the necessary lighting to shoot the Cup, and then captured every square inch of every part of the Cup on digital film. In all, he took more than 2,000 photographs, the best and most appropriate appearing in these pages. Each shot presented a new and special problem, for in addition to silver being the most difficult colour to photograph, the light was constantly changing because of the curves and lines of the Cup itself. Along with his devoted and incapable assistant, the author, Dave became the first man to photograph every piece of the Cup—the original bowl and base, the Presentation Cup, the Replica Cup, and the various bands and pieces currently housed in the vault at the Hockey Hall of Fame. The result is the most thorough photographic examination of the world's most important sports trophy ever undertaken.

To Dave Sandford goes a special thanks, and to his sister, Linda, goes a special toast to good health.

Andrew Podnieks

PHOTO CREDITS

All Cup photos (except the 2001-02 and 2002-03 engravings) taken by Dave Sandford

Hockey Hall of Fame Archives: p. 3, 6 (middle, top & bottom, right), 7 (left, both, middle, right top), 9 (left), 10 (left, top), 19 (team), 24 (team, bottom), 26, 30 (team), 31 (team), 32 (team), 33 (team), 36 (team, top), 37 (team, cartoon), 38 (team), 42 (bottom right), 43 (team, top & bottom), 44 (team & cartoon), 45 (team), 48 (bottom right), 49 (team), 50 (team), 51 (top left, bottom right), 52 (team), 54 (team & bottom right), 55 (team & bottom left), 57 (team), 58 (team), 59 (team), 60 (team), 62 (team), 64 (top right), 66 (top right, top middle), 68 (middle), 70 (top right, bottom left), 74 (top right), 76 (top right), 88 (cartoon), 98 (bottom left), 100 (top right, bottom right), 106 (bottom left, top right), 108 (team), 120 (left, top right), 132 (bottom right), 136 (left), 140 (top right), 142 (team), 168 (top right), 198 (top right)
Dave Sandford/Hockey Hall of Fame: p. 11 (left, bottom), 22 (bottom right), 23 (stick), 27 (three stick details), 29 (puck), 38 (jug), 41 (sticks), 46 (crest), 66 (middle, bottom), 88 (bottom left), 90 (cartoon), 120 (top middle), 200 (both), 202 (left), 204 (bottom left), 206 (left, bottom middle, top right), 208 (top left, middle, top right), 210 (top left, bottom left, top right), 213
Doug MacLellan/Hockey Hall of Fame: p. 11 (middle column, right column, top & bottom), 19 (ring), 31 (program), 94 (bottom right), 190 (top right) 192 (top left, bottom left, bottom middle, top right), 194 (both), 196 (top right, top left), 198 (top left, middle)
Imperial Oil/Turofsky Collection—Hockey Hall of Fame: p. 68 (team, top left, bottom left), 88 (team, top left), 94 (team), 98 (top left, top right), 100 (top left), 102 (all), 124 (top right, top middle, bottom middle)
Paul Bereswill/Hockey Hall of Fame: p. 164 (all), 166 (all), 168 (left), 170 (both), 172 (both), 174 (both), 176 (top left), 178 (all), 180 (all), 182 (all), 184 (both), 186 (all), 188 (all), 190 (top left, bottom left, top right)
Graphic Artists/Hockey Hall of Fame: p. 128 (all), 130 (top left, bottom left, top right), 132 (top right, top left, bottom left, bottom middle), 138 (bottom middle)
Richard Bak Collection: p. 78 (both), 90 (team), 112 (all), 114 (all)
Mike Bolt/Hockey Hall of Fame: p. 204 (right, top left), 206 (top middle), 212 (top right)
Fred Keenan/Hockey Hall of Fame: p. 144 (top middle)
Dr. Jeffrey Markowitz/Hockey Hall of Fame: p. 192 (top middle)
James McCarthy/Hockey Hall of Fame: p. 7 (bottom right)
Walt Neubrand/Hockey Hall of Fame: p. 198 (bottom left), 202 (right), 208, 210
Phil Pritchard/Hockey Hall of Fame: p. 212 (middle)
Frank Prazak/Hockey Hall of Fame: p. 138 (left, top middle, top right)
Craig Campbell/Hockey Hall of Fame: p.209, 211
National Archives of Canada: p. 2, 4 (both), 5, 6 (left), 19 (both ads), 32 (text), 53 (team), 74 (left), 96 (top right, bottom right), 118 (left), 122 (top right, bottom right)
McCord Museum: p. 20 (team), 21 (team, game), 22 (team), 23 (team), 24 (team, top), 25 (team), 26 (team), 27 (team), 28 (team), 39 (team), 46 (team)
Dave Dahms/Ed Moffett Collection: p. 66 (program, bottom right), 72 (all), 80 (all), 92 (all), 126 (all)
City of Montreal Archives: p. 56 (team), 96 (left), 110 (bottom left), 116 (top middle, top right), 124 (left), 134 (middle), 140 (top left, bottom left, middle), 142 (top left, bottom left), 146 (middle), 150 (top middle, bottom middle), 156 (left), 158 (top right), 160 (top left, bottom left), 162 (left), 176 (bottom left, middle)
City of Toronto Archives: p. 60 (Cup with team), 70 (top left, bottom right), 76 (both left, bottom right), 84 (all), 85 (bottom left & right), 98 (middle), 104 (all), 106 (top left, middle)
Charlotte Grahame/Colorado Avalanche: p. 196 (bottom left)
Al Ruelle: p. 144 (top right, left, middle bottom), 146 (top left, bottom left), 148 (all)
Boston Public Library: p. 82 (all), 86 (both), 87 (bottom right)
Bruce Bennett Studios (BBS): p. 142 (middle), 146 (top right), 150 (left, top right), 152 (both), 154 (all), 160 (middle), 162 (top right), 164 (top middle)
Denis Brodeur: p. 156 (right), 158 (left, top middle, bottom middle), 160 (top right), 176 (top right), 190 (middle)
Archives Nationales de Quebec: p. 64 (panorama & individual players)
Montreal Gazette: p. 110 (top right, top left, middle), 118 (top right), 134 (left), 136 (top right)
Burton Historical Collection: p. 76 (middle), 108 (left), 116 (bottom left), 122 (left)
Archives of Ontario: p. 94 (left), 100 (bottom left)
New England Sports Hall of Fame: p. 87 (bottom left)
B.C. Sports Hall of Fame: p. 47 (team)
City of Ottawa Archives: p. 41 (team)
City of Victoria Archives: p. 58 (bottom right)
Manitoba Sports Hall of Fame: p. 29
Earl of Derby: p. 2
Queen's University Archives: p. 36 (team, bottom)
Author's Collection: p. 52 (bottom right)

REIGNS OF ALL STANLEY CUP CHAMPIONS

Team	Won Cup	Champs Until	Reign
Tampa Bay Lightning	**June 7, 2004**	**Present**	
Montreal Canadiens	April 10, 1956	April 16, 1961	1,832 days
Montreal Canadiens	May 16, 1976	May 24, 1980	1,469 days
New York Islanders	May 24, 1980	May 19, 1984	1,456 days
Toronto Maple Leafs	April 22, 1962	May 1, 1965	1,105 days
Ottawa Silver Seven	March 10, 1903	March 17, 1906	1,103 days
Toronto Maple Leafs	April 19, 1947	April 23, 1950	1,100 days
Montreal Victorias	December 30, 1896	March 4, 1899	795 days
Pittsburgh Penguins	May 25, 1991	June 9, 1993	746 days
Detroit Red Wings	June 7, 1997	June 19, 1999	742 days
Montreal Canadiens	April 3, 1930	April 9, 1932	737 days
Quebec Bulldogs	March 5, 1912	March 11, 1914	736 days
Edmonton Oilers	May 19, 1984	May 24, 1986	735 days
Toronto Arenas	March 30, 1918	April 1, 1920	733 days
Detroit Red Wings	April 11, 1936	April 12, 1938	731 days
Montreal Canadiens	May 1, 1965	May 2, 1967	731 days
Montreal Canadiens	May 11, 1968	May 10, 1970	729 days
Philadelphia Flyers	May 19, 1974	May 16, 1976	728 days
Ottawa Senators	April 1, 1920	March 28, 1922	727 days
Detroit Red Wings	April 16, 1954	April 10, 1956	725 days
Edmonton Oilers	May 31, 1987	May 25, 1989	725 days
Montreal AAA	March 17, 1893	March 9, 1895	722 days
Montreal Wanderers	March 25, 1907	March 6, 1909	712 days
Montreal Shamrocks	March 4, 1899	January 31, 1901	699 days
Winnipeg Victorias	January 31, 1901	March 17, 1902	410 days
Toronto Blueshirts	March 11, 1914	March 26, 1915	380 days
Montreal Canadiens	April 9, 1946	April 19, 1947	375 days
Toronto Maple Leafs	May 2, 1967	May 11, 1968	375 days
New York Rangers	June 14, 1994	June 24, 1995	375 days
Ottawa Senators	March 6, 1909	March 15, 1910	374 days
Montreal Canadiens	April 13, 1944	April 22, 1945	374 days
Montreal Canadiens	May 10, 1973	May 19, 1974	374 days
Boston Bruins	May 10, 1970	May 18, 1971	373 days
Victoria Cougars	March 30, 1925	April 6, 1926	372 days
Montreal Maroons	April 6, 1926	April 13, 1927	372 days
Montreal Canadiens	May 24, 1986	May 31, 1987	372 days
Boston Bruins	March 28, 1929	April 3, 1930	371 days
Boston Bruins	April 12, 1941	April 18, 1942	371 days
Detroit Red Wings	April 8, 1943	April 13, 1944	371 days
Chicago Black Hawks	April 16, 1961	April 22, 1962	371 days

Team	Won Cup	Champs Until	Reign
Vancouver Millionaires	March 26, 1915	March 30, 1916	370 days
Seattle Metropolitans	March 25, 1917	March 30, 1918	370 days
Montreal Canadiens	March 25, 1924	March 30, 1925	370 days
Montreal Canadiens	June 9, 1993	June 14, 1994	370 days
Toronto Maple Leafs	April 9, 1932	April 13, 1933	369 days
Chicago Black Hawks	April 12, 1938	April 16, 1939	369 days
Colorado Avalanche	June 9, 2001	June 13, 2002	369 days
Toronto St. Pats	March 28, 1922	March 31, 1923	368 days
Montreal Maroons	April 9, 1935	April 11, 1936	368 days
Ottawa Senators	April 13, 1927	April 14, 1928	367 days
Detroit Red Wings	April 15, 1952	April 16, 1953	366 days
Edmonton Oilers	May 24, 1990	May 25, 1991	366 days
Montreal Canadiens	April 16, 1953	April 16, 1954	365 days
Chicago Black Hawks	April 10, 1934	April 9, 1935	364 days
New York Rangers	April 13, 1940	April 12, 1941	364 days
Boston Bruins	May 11, 1972	May 10, 1973	364 days
Calgary Flames	May 25, 1989	May 24, 1990	364 days
New Jersey Devils	June 10, 2000	June 9, 2001	364 days
New Jersey Devils	June 9, 2003	June 7th 2004	364 days
Boston Bruins	April 16, 1939	April 13, 1940	363 days
Detroit Red Wings	April 23, 1950	April 21, 1951	363 days
New York Rangers	April 13, 1953	April 10, 1934	362 days
Colorado Avalanche	June 10, 1996	June 7, 1997	362 days
Ottawa Senators	March 10, 1911	March 5, 1912	361 days
Detroit Red Wings	June 13, 2002	June 9, 2003	361 days
Montreal Wanderers	March 15, 1910	March 10, 1911	360 days
Montreal Canadiens	March 30, 1916	March 25, 1917	360 days
Ottawa Senators	March 31, 1923	March 25, 1924	360 days
Toronto Maple Leafs	April 21, 1951	April 15, 1952	360 days
Montreal Canadiens	May 18, 1971	May 11, 1972	359 days
Montreal AAA	March 17, 1902	March 10, 1903	358 days
Dallas Stars	June 19, 1999	June 10, 2000	357 days
Toronto Maple Leafs	April 18, 1942	April 8, 1943	355 days
Toronto Maple Leafs	April 22, 1945	April 9, 1946	352 days
New Jersey Devils	June 24, 1995	June 10, 1996	352 days
New York Rangers	April 14, 1928	March 28, 1929	348 days
Montreal Victorias	March 9, 1895	February 14, 1896	329 days
Winnipeg Victorias	February 14, 1896	December 30, 1896	320 days
Montreal Wanderers	March 17, 1906	January 21, 1907	310 days
Kenora Thistles	January 21, 1907	March 25, 1907	63 days

the history

Frederick Arthur Stanley 16th Earl of Derby

FREDERICK ARTHUR STANLEY, 16th Earl of Derby

b. London, England, January 15, 1841
d. London, England, June 14, 1908

Frederick Stanley's ancestry can be traced back to Thomas Stanley, who was born in 1435 and became the 1st Earl of Derby in 1485. Thomas was a steward in the household of both Edward IV and Richard III and purportedly betrayed Richard III at a critical moment during the Battle of Bosworth, on August 22nd, 1485. According to some accounts, he placed the crown on Henry VII's head shortly thereafter.

Frederick's father, Edward Geoffrey Smith-Stanley, was the premier of England on three occasions and produced a capable translation of Homer's *Iliad* in 1852. He had two sons: Edward, born in 1826, and Frederick, born fifteen years later, in 1841. Frederick was educated at Eton, entered the army in 1858 with the Grenadier Guards, and retired from service seven years later in order to stand for Parliament representing first Preston (1865-68), and then Lancashire (1868-85) and Blackpool (1885-86). During these years, Frederick also served as Civil Lord of the Admiralty (in 1868), Financial Secretary to the War Office (1874-77), and Secretary to the Treasury (1877-78). In 1878, he was made Secretary of State for War for two years and later Colonial Secretary (1885-86).

On May 31, 1864, Frederick married Lady Constance Villiers, daughter to George, fourth Earl of Clarendon. Together they had eight children: Edward George Villiers (who later became the 17th Earl upon Frederick's death), Victor Albert, Arthur, Geoffrey, Ferdinand Charles, George Frederick, Algernon Francis, and Frederick William. It was on August 27, 1886, that Frederick officially took the title Baron Stanley of Preston, and two years later he was named Canada's Governor General, England's highest official representative in Canada. He arrived in Ottawa with his wife and four of his children and fell in love with the city and the country's winter activities, as did a number of his sons. It was out of his love for hockey that his inspirational gift of the Stanley Cup came (see The Birth of the Stanley Cup).

Lord Stanley used his family's coat of arms, dating to 1485, in the design of the Stanley Cup, clear indication this was not simply some London-store bought piece of silverware but a commissioned work for the governor general.

The position of Governor General lasts five years, and in 1893 the Earl of Aberdeen replaced Baron Stanley. He returned to England that April, never to set foot in Canada again, never to see a hockey game contested for the trophy he established. Stanley became the Lord Mayor of Liverpool in 1895 and of Preston in 1901, and served as Chancellor of Liverpool University from 1903 until his death in 1908.

For much of the rest of his life, Frederick lived at Knowsley Hall, which has been the family's 2,500-acre estate in Merseyside since the 14th century (below). Its features include a log cabin, given to Frederick by the people of Canada in appreciation for his term as Governor General.

Besides the Cup, Lord Stanley left two other visible marks of his time in Canada, one in the name of the eponymous Stanley Park in Vancouver, that city's largest and most majestic green space, and the other, Stanley House, Lord Stanley's summer residence in New Richmond, Quebec. Stanley built the eleven-bedroom country house during his first summer in Ottawa on a beautiful eight-hectare piece of property on the south Gaspé coast. Stanley sold the house to an American in 1892 shortly before leaving the country, and in the first half of the 20th century its ownership passed through many hands. In 1961, Olivia Terrell, a Bostonian who had inherited the house through her Montreal-born step-father, donated the property to the Canada Council, and from 1975 to 1984 arts and cultural programmers used it regularly. However, budget cuts during the Brian Mulroney years forced the Council to board up the house and abandon the property. In 1994, efforts were made to upgrade the federal status of the house to one of national historic significance, but this proposal was rejected by the Historic Sites and Monuments Board of Canada.

Each Governor General is entrusted with creating a coat of arms, which becomes his identifiable symbol within the country. Lord Stanley used his family's coat of arms, parts of which date back to 1485 and the crest of which, unknown to almost anyone in hockey circles, is replicated on the bowl of the Stanley Cup (see photo below, left). The "blazon" is the official heraldic description of the arms and is as old as the arms itself. It reads as follows:

> "Arms: Argent on a bend azure three stag's heads cabossed or. Crest: On a chapeau gules doubled ermine an eagle, wings extended or, preying on an infant in its cradle proper, swaddled gules, the cradle laced or. Supporters: Dexter, a griffin, wings elevated or, ducally collared and line reflexed over the back azure; sinister, a stag or, collared and lined as the dexter. Motto: Sans changer ('Unchanging')."

An explanation for the origin of the arms follows the blazon:

> "The armorial bearings are said to have been first assumed by William (II) de Stanley in the late 13th century. The origin of the crest is more problem-atical and the subject of two legends (both of which, however, are almost certainly only legends). One tells of how the Isabel who married Sir John Stanley was daughter of a foundling discovered in an eagle's nest and made by the childless octoge-narian Thomas, Lord of Lathom (d. 1370), his heir. The other tells of how Thomas had an illegit-imate son who was discovered under a tree near an eagle's nest and subsequently bequeathed a trifling part of the Lathom properties, the lion's share going to the aforesaid Isabel and her Stanley descendants, who commemorated the picturesque incident in their own adoptive crest. Actually the crest in question was used by two members of the Lathom family a couple of generations before Isabel's time."

And so it is that the Lathom family of the 1300s designed the crest, which was adopted by the Derbys and used by Lord Stanley, which made its way onto the Stanley Cup. The remarkable image of an eagle plucking a baby from its crib also confirms that the Stanley Cup (the original bowl) was a commissioned work and not simply a bowl bought in a London store for a sum of money in 1892.

The Birth of the Stanley Cup

Queen Victoria appointed Sir Frederick Arthur Stanley as the sixth Governor General of Canada on June 11, 1888. The First Baron Stanley of Preston arrived at Government House (Rideau Hall) with four of his ten children (two boys and two girls) and his wife, Constance, and almost immediately every member of the family fell in love with hockey. Isobel, a daughter, played for a Government House ladies team in a game against the Rideau ladies, and the two boys—Arthur and Algernon—also played for a Government House team.

The Governor General's official title was a breathful: Right Honourable Sir Frederick Arthur Stanley, Baron Stanley of Preston, in the county of Lancaster, in the peerage of Great Britain, Knight Grand Cross of the Most Honourable Order of the Bath. At the seventh annual Winter Carnival in Montreal in the winter of 1888, Lord Stanley, as he was more commonly called, witnessed his first hockey game in his capacity as Governor General, the Vics versus the Montreal Amateur Athletic Association (MAAA). The *Montreal Gazette* proudly reported his attendance: "Lord Stanley expressed his great delight with the game of hockey and the expertise of the players."

At this time, organized hockey was truly in its infancy. Montreal and Ottawa, in fact, were the only two cities in Canada that could boast anything resembling leagues and teams playing a fixed schedule with a consistent set of rules in front of paying fans. The Amateur Hockey Association of Canada (AHA) had been formed in 1886 and centred around these two cities, so Lord Stanley was seeing hockey at its most sophisticated (it was not until 1890 that the Ontario Hockey Association—OHA—was formed).

Shortly after Carnival, Arthur and Algernon Stanley became part of the Ottawa Rideau Rebels, a hockey team that endured for several seasons (see photo below). They wore red sweaters and the team was composed of aides de camp and Members of Parliament. The Rebels played exhibition games against other teams in Ontario on an outdoor rink provided by Lord Stanley each winter on the grounds of Government House. Opponents included the St. James club of Montreal, the Lindsay skating club of Ontario, Queen's University in Kingston, and numerous teams from Toronto, notably the Granites.

Although these hockey matches were serious sporting competitions, they were equally important as social affairs, and visiting teams were treated with great respect by their host, Lord Stanley. Special lunches and dinners were arranged around the playing of the games, and each team invited the Rebels for a return match in their home city, offers the Rebels gracefully accepted whenever possible. Lord Stanley was always in attendance and followed play with the keen interest of a true fan.

In early 1892, Ottawa won the OHA championship, and on March 18 a banquet was held in the nation's capital to honour the team. Unable to attend, Lord Stanley prepared an important letter for his aide-de-camp, Lord Kilcoursie, to read to the banqueters. It changed the course of Canadian culture and sporting pursuits:

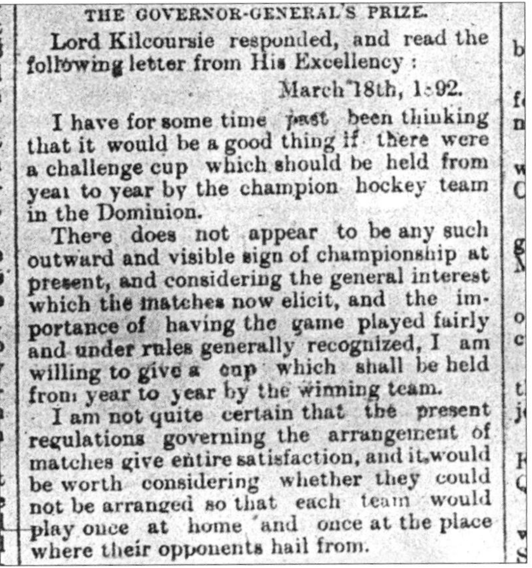

THE GOVERNOR-GENERAL'S PRIZE.

Lord Kilcoursie responded, and read the following letter from His Excellency :

March 18th, 1892.

I have for some time past been thinking that it would be a good thing if there were a challenge cup which should be held from year to year by the champion hockey team in the Dominion.

There does not appear to be any such outward and visible sign of championship at present, and considering the general interest which the matches now elicit, and the importance of having the game played fairly and under rules generally recognized, I am willing to give a cup which shall be held from year to year by the winning team.

I am not quite certain that the present regulations governing the arrangement of matches give entire satisfaction, and it would be worth considering whether they could not be arranged so that each team would play once at home and once at the place where their opponents hail from.

The story in the Montreal Gazette *as it appeared the morning of March 19, 1892, announcing the creation of a trophy for Canada's hockey champions.*

Lieutenant Viscount Frederick Rudolph Lambart Kilcoursie, son of the 9th Earl and Baron of Cavan and a part-time playing member of the Rideau Hall Rebels, was given a tremendous cheer upon reading the letter, and the proposals were instantly accepted. Thus, Lord Stanley gave birth not only to the Stanley Cup, but also to the modern schedule, with teams playing an equal number of "home" and "away" games.

Lord Stanley now had to deliver the goods, as it were. He contacted Captain Colville, an aide in London, England, and gave orders to find the finest silversmith in the city to make a small silver bowl. Colville was allowed to expend ten guineas for the commission. He retained a silversmith in Sheffield whose work was retailed by G.H. Collis, Regent Street, London, and using Lord Stanley's coat of arms crafted what was asked of him. The Dominion Challenge trophy, as it was engraved, arrived in Ottawa in early 1893 ready for competition.

Having appointed Sir John Thompson to take over as Governor General when he would return to England in 1893, Lord Stanley now had the responsibility to make one final provision. He appointed two trustees to oversee all matters pertaining to the Cup after his imminent departure: John Sweetland, Ottawa's sheriff, and Philip Ross, a former member of the Rideau Rebels. It was up to these two eximious men to award the Cup each year and to ensure that any worthy opponent in the country had the opportunity to challenge the Cup-winning team for possession of the trophy. Indeed, Lord Stanley set down a thorough constitution by which Sweetland and Ross should govern the Cup:

> (1) The winners shall give bond for the return of the cup in good order, when required by the trustees for the purpose of being handed over to any other team that may in turn win;
> (2) Each winning team shall have at their own charge, engraved on a silver ring fitted on the cup for that purpose, the name of the team and the year won;
> (3) The cup shall remain a challenge cup, and should not become the property of any team, even if won more than once;
> (4) In case of any doubt as to the title of any club to claim the position of champions, the cup shall be held or awarded by the trustees as they may think right, their decision being absolute;
> (5) Should either trustee resign or otherwise drop out, the remaining trustee shall nominate a substitute.

Almost as important as the Cup itself is Stanley's reference to a "silver ring" to be fitted onto the Cup, giving clear direction for the evolution of the trophy as an annual award that would continue for some time. He not only donated the trophy, he also proposed a design for its future.

Terms of victory, however, were still nebulous by the time the AHA season opened at the start of 1893. Lord Stanley's only wishes were that the Cup go to "the leading hockey club in Canada," and to this end he believed the AHA to be the most important league in the country. The AHA consisted of five teams: the Ottawa Generals, the Quebec Hockey Club, and three from Montreal—the Victorias, the Crystals, and the MAAA. A 20-game league schedule was drawn up such that each team played eight games, one at home and one away against each team, between January 7 and March 17. All games were played outdoors on natural ice, usually on Friday nights, starting at 8:30 p.m.

The league featured seven-man hockey. The three forward positions existed—left wing, right wing, centre—as did the goalie, of course. But there was also a rover, who stationed himself behind the centre and who became a forward or defence player depending on the circumstance. A point and coverpoint were early incarnations of modern defencemen, though the point stayed closer to the goalie and the coverpoint a little farther ahead. Games consisted of two, thirty-minute halves, and the small ring of boards around the perimeter of the rink was only six inches to a foot high. The goal nets consisted of two poles a few feet high (like the boards, their height was irrelevant because pucks rarely were raised more than a few inches off the ice). Interestingly, goals scored were often referred to as "games," as in: "The Vics returned the attack only to be taken up by Low[e] who scored the first game." The season's play was primitive compared to hockey a century later. Referees were often players from other teams in the league; there were no playoffs; and, one game, Ottawa at Quebec, was played under protest by the latter because the referee was a native Ottawan.

The finest team in the AHA was the MAAA, champions of the league each year since the AHA formed in 1886. The MAAA was a Montreal social and sporting club that had been established in 1881. It was devoted to the "encouragement of athletic sports, the promotion of physical and mental culture among men, and the providing of rational amusements and recreation for its members." The club promoted three activities in particular—lacrosse, snowshoeing, and bicycling. It became known informally as the "Winged Wheel" because its logo featured a large wheel with wings to encourage the use of the bicycle, a new innovation to North America that same year. (Today, the MAAA is the world's oldest bicycle club.) The MAAA's motto was inscribed in the rim of the wheel: jungor ut implear—"I am joined in order that I may be complete." The wings symbolized progress.

Hockey in Montreal was often called winter lacrosse during the 1880s because of the similarity of rules of play between the two sports. The Montreal Hockey Club (MHC) was formed in 1884 and acquired "connected club status" with the MAAA as the club's hockey representatives. Thus, the MAAA hockey club was really the MHC operating under the aegis of the bicycle club (although in order to play for the MHC, one first had to be a member of the MAAA). The Montreal Hockey Club was pioneering for its coherent system of player development. Even though hockey was in its infancy, the MHC had an Intermediate team in 1893. It also inaugurated a Junior team the year after to ensure that when members of the MHC team retired or grew too old to play there would be adequately prepared replacements at the ready. Thus, the MHC introduced the farm system to the game.

MONTREAL TOBOGGAN
—CLUB—
SKATING RINK
(M.A.A.A. GROUNDS).
A : FANCY : DRESS : CARNIVAL
Will be held in the above rink,
ON TUESDAY EV'G, FEB. 10th INST.,
At 8 o'clock P.M.
Members wishing to take part in above will kindly register their names with representation, in books provided for the purpose, at Club House, Cote St. Antoine.
Admission to grounds (for non-subscribers), 25c.
WILL BRUCE, Hon. Sec.
Next Fortnightly Hop, Thursday Ev'g, February 5th inst. 28 3eod

The Montreal AAA, as the team was officially called, played its home games at the gas-lit Victoria Skating Rink near Dorchester and Stanley streets in downtown Montreal. The smoke congestion in the rink proved to be a constant problem for players and fans alike.

The Ottawa Generals and the MAAA were the class of the 1893 AHA season, and by the end of the schedule only one victory separated the two teams. The MAAA lost only once, to the Generals early in the season, and Ottawa lost twice, once to the Victorias on the first day of the season. The most important game of the year came the night of February 18 when the MAAA beat Ottawa 7-1, and that loss was, in effect, the difference in the standings at the end of the eight-game schedule. Arguably, however, the last game of the year—March 9, 1893—for the MAAA was equally significant because that was the match that confirmed a first-place finish for the team. It was also a victory clouded by controversy.

Officially, Montreal AAA won a close 2-1 victory over cross-town rivals the Crystals at the eponymous Crystal Rink. But what actually happened that night was a different story. The Crystals abandoned their game against Montreal AAA when one of their players, Murray, was given a game misconduct during the second half of a game that ended 2-2 after regulation time. As the teams prepared for overtime, the Crystals assumed they could use Murray now that regulation time had expired. Referee Lewis refused to allow the banished player to return, but the Crystals refused to play without him. Lewis awarded the game to Montreal, and so the Stanley Cup was won, indirectly, as a result of this controversial, incomplete game. Had the overtime been played, there is every reason to believe that the MAAA might have lost. The headline the next day in the *Montreal Gazette* said it all: "An Unsatisfactory Game."

As a result of the season's play, trustees Sweetland and Ross named the Montreal AAA winners of the Stanley Cup, believing first place in the AHA entitled the team to be called the best in Canada. And, of course, they welcomed any other league-champion team in the country to challenge the MAAA for the trophy. The Ottawa club was upset with the decision because there had been no playoffs scheduled and because conditions for winning the Cup had not been made clear prior to the start of the season. However, since these matters were left to the discretion of the trustees, the MAAA were named the first winners of the Dominion Challenge trophy and no more could be done.

The Stanley Cup, as it became known almost from the day it was brought out of its crate, was shipped off to Montreal AAA headquarters. All seemed in order until Sweetland travelled to Montreal to present the trophy to the directors of the MAAA, and not to the Montreal Hockey Club itself. The MHC players quickly found out about Sweetland's visit—of which they had not been apprised—and were enraged. They argued that the MHC was completely autonomous from the MAAA, save for a symbolic connection, and wanted to be presented the trophy directly, as minutes from an MHC meeting reveal:

> "Mr. Freeman [of the MAAA] suggested that if the Directors handed over the Cup to the [Montreal] Hockey Club would the Club accept the same. Mr. Stewart [of the MHC] replied that the Club would not." Instead, the MHC demanded that the Stanley Cup be sent back to Ottawa, an action the MAAA refused to take: "it was moved...that the Governor General's Hockey Trophy be retained by this Assn, in trust, subject to the order of the Governor General's Trustees." The Hockey Club contacted the trustees to inform them that they felt slighted by how the Cup had been presented. Ross replied to the MHC, suggesting he and Sweetland "may have misunderstood the relations existing between the MAAA and the MHC Club, and that if any misunderstanding occurred the Trustees would be glad to have further information and suggestions to aid in the proper execution of Lord Stanley's wishes to present this Cup to the Champions of the Dominion." The trustees then contacted the MAAA and asked the Club to hand over the trophy to the MHC, which it did.

Initially, the MHC intended to engrave its name for three years' worth of championships, having won the league title also in 1891 and 1892, but eventually decided to have only their 1893 victory acknowledged on the Cup. Ironically, the MHC then wanted to further commemorate this first victory of the Stanley Cup by giving all its players rings with the MAAA emblem on it, something the jeweller charged with the crafting of the rings would not properly execute without consent from the parent club:

> "...a letter from Mr. Hemsley who stated that he had been favoured with an order for eleven gold watch chain charms by the Comtee [Committee] of the Montreal Hockey Club, and requested that authority be given to him to use the Winged Wheel emblem thereon, as requested, by said Comtee."

Not wanting further fuss, the MAAA consented, providing they received a list of the players to whom this honour would be conferred so that each might be acknowledged to be a member of the MAAA as per the MHC constitution.

In the short time left in the winter season, no team challenged the Montreal Hockey Club for possession of the Cup and the team was able to keep the trophy for the year, though under the formal appellation Montreal AAA and not their own MHC!

"I cannot say how deeply I shall feel the severance of my connection with Canada," Lord Stanley wrote in a letter to friend Sir John Thompson upon leaving for England. It was a severance, however, that was purely physical, and one hundred years later his spirit, words, and influence are as much a part of Canadian culture as if he had never left at all. In 1893, the Stanley Cup was born.

Stanley of Preston

Stanley Cup Trust

THE STANLEY CUP TRUST

The Stanley Cup Trust lay down in words the means by which the trophy should be awarded. The Trust also acted as a constitution of sorts for the Trustees' conduct. Divided into four sections, the Trust was the foundation for the operation of hockey more or less until the National Hockey League took control of the Cup in 1927.

HIS EXCELLENCY'S CONDITIONS

(1.) The winners to give bond for the return of the Cup in good order when required by the trustees for any reason.

(2.) Each winning team to have at their own charge engraved, on a silver ring fitted on the Cup for the purpose, the name of the team and the team won.

(3.) The cup to remain a challenge cup, and not to become the property of any team, even if won more than once.

(4.) In case of any doubt as to the title of any club to claim the position of champions, the Cup to be held or awarded by the trustees as they may think right, their decision being absolute.

(5.) Should either trustee resign or otherwise drop out, the remaining trustee to nominate a substitute.

TRUSTEES' PRESENT REGULATIONS

In dealing with challenges and matches the trustees observe the following principles:

(1.) So far as any league or association in which the Cup is held is concerned, the Cup goes with the championship of that league each year without the necessity of any special or extra contest.

(2.) Challenges are recognized by the trustees only from champion clubs of senior hockey leagues.

(3.) When a challenge is accepted the trustees desire the competing clubs to arrange by mutual agreement all terms of the contest themselves, such as choice of date or dates for matches, choice of rink, division of the gate money, selection of officials, etc., etc. The trustees do not wish to interfere in any way, shape or form if it can be avoided.

WHERE CLUBS DISAGREE

Where competing clubs fail to agree the trustees have observed and will continue to observe as far as practicable the following principles:

(a) Cup to be awarded by the result of one match, or of the most goals in two matches, as the trustees may consider fair.

(b) Contest to take place on ice in the home city, the date and dates and choice of rink to be made or approved by the trustees.

(c) The net gate money obtained by the arrangements with the rink to be divided equally between the competing teams.

(d) If the clubs fail to agree on a referee, the trustees shall appoint him. The two clubs to share any expense equally.

(e) If the clubs fail to agree on other officials the trustees shall either appoint them or authorize the referee to appoint them, the expense, if any, to be shared equally by the competing clubs.

(f) No second challenge recognized in one season from the same hockey association.

(g) Except where the club which holds the Cup is willing to agree to an earlier contest, the trustees do not undertake to require a contest in any league season on a date earlier than February 28th in any year, so as to allow the league in which the Cup is held to complete its season before being called on to defend the Cup.

STATUS OF PLAYERS

The trustees do not consider eligible to play in a contest for the Stanley Cup at the close of the ordinary hockey season players who during that season were not regular members of the teams concerned. In the case of challenges accepted for matches to be played at or prior to the opening of the regular hockey season, the trustees will consider requests for the authorization of bona fide changes rendered necessary in the teams since the preceding season.

The above agreement governed the handling of the Stanley Cup until June 30, 1947, when P.D. Ross felt that the regulations needed to be updated. He cited his own age, the total control of the NHL over the Cup, and the arrival of Cooper Smeaton as new Trustee and Clarence Campbell as the new NHL president as reasons to prepare a modern constitution. The agreement was set down in new language honouring the spirit and ethical merits of the original:

1. The Trustees hereby delegate to the League full authority to determine and amend from time to time the conditions for competition of the Stanley Cup, including the qualifications of challengers, the appointment of officials, the apportionment and distribution of all gate receipts, provided always that the winners of the trophy shall be the acknowledged World's Professional Hockey Champions.

2. The Trustees agree that during the currency of this agreement they will not acknowledge or accept any challenge for the Stanley Cup unless such a challenge is in conformity with the condition specified in paragraph one (1) hereof.

3. The League undertakes the responsibility for the care and safe custody of the Stanley Cup including all necessary repairs and alterations to the cup and sub-structure as may be required from time to time, and further undertakes to insure the Stanley Cup for its full insurable value.

4. The League hereby acknowledges itself to be bound to the Trustees in the sum of One Thousand Dollars, which bond is conditioned upon the safe return of the Stanley Cup to the Trustees in accordance with the terms of this Agreement, and it is agreed that the League shall have the right to return the trophy to the Trustees at any time.

5. This agreement shall remain in force so long as the League continues to be the world's leading professional hockey league as determined by its playing calibre, and in the event of dissolution or other termination of the National Hockey League, the Stanley Cup shall revert to the custody of the trustees.

6. In the event of default in the appointment of a new trustee by the surviving trustee, the "Trustees" hereby delegate and appoint the Governors of the International Hockey Hall of Fame in Kingston, Ontario, to name two Canadian trustees to carry on under the terms of the original trust, and in conformity with this Agreement.

7. And it is further mutually agreed that any disputes arising as to the interpretation of this Agreement or the facts upon which such interpretation is to be made, shall be settled by an Arbitration Board of three, one member to be appointed by each of the parties, and the third to be selected by the two appointees. The decision of the Arbitration Board shall be final.

This agreement has not been altered since its introduction in 1947, with the exception of section 6. On November 22, 1961, at the suggestion of Clarence Campbell, the term "Governors of the International Hockey Hall of Fame in Kingston" was changed to the "Committee of the Hockey Hall of Fame in Toronto," in recognition of the Hockey Hall of Fame's recent opening on the grounds of the Canadian National Exhibition.

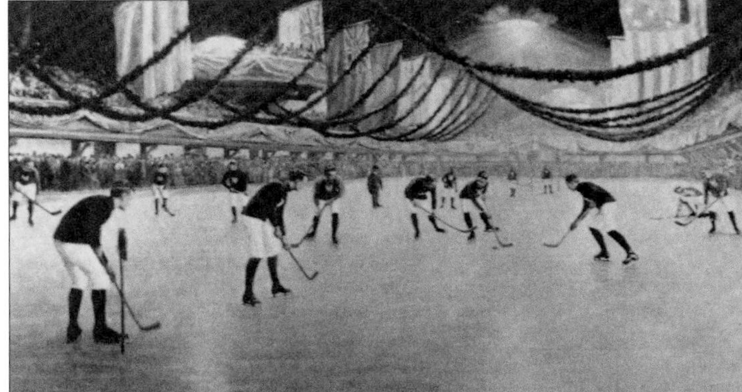

Early hockey played at the Victoria Skating rink in Montreal.

Stanley Cup Trustees

By the time Lord Stanley left Canada, on July 15, 1893, never to return, he had ensured that his new hockey trophy would live past the term of his duties as governor general. Stanley enlisted the services of two men—P.D. Ross and John Sweetland—to oversee the awarding of the Cup on an annual basis and to resolve any disputes over who was the champion or who might challenge the champion to become Cup holders. Ross and Sweetland adjudicated everything from type of series (best two-of-three, two games-total goals) to who would be the referee to where the games were to be played. The life of a trustee has become simpler in more recent years, but to this day the trustee is as much a part of the tradition of the Stanley Cup as the bowl itself.

SHERIFF JOHN SWEETLAND

b. Kingston, Ontario, August 15, 1835
d. Ottawa, Ontario, May 5, 1907
Appointed 1893 by Lord Stanley

A graduate of Queen's University (M.D. 1858), Sweetland practiced medicine in Pakenham, Ontario, until he settled in Ottawa in 1867. He was made Sheriff for the county of Carleton in 1880, having previously been a coroner in the area and later surgeon for the County Carleton prison. As sheriff of Carleton, Sweetland was also titular sheriff of the Supreme Court of Canada. A Liberal and Anglican, he helped oversee the building of the Ottawa water-works and became president of many associations and businesses including the Ottawa Ladies' College, the St. George's Association of Ottawa, and the Associated Charities of Ottawa. Along with P.D. Ross, Sweetland became the first trustee of the Stanley Cup in 1893 until his death some 14 years later.

PHILIP DANSKEN ROSS

b. Montreal, Quebec, January 1, 1858
d. Ottawa, Ontario, July 5, 1949
Appointed 1893 by Lord Stanley

P.D. Ross earned a B.Sc. in engineering from McGill University in 1878. The following year he began working for the *Montreal Star*. During the next six years, he worked for, variously, the *Toronto Mail* and *Toronto News*, and by 1891 his involvement in journalism reached new heights when he bought the *Ottawa Journal*. An avid athlete, Ross played for

the Ottawa Rebels Hockey Club from 1891 to 1895, one of his teammates being Lord Stanley's son, Edward. During this time he was appointed by Lord Stanley as one of the Cup's trustees. He also captained the McGill football team and the Toronto Rowing Club and later refereed in both football and hockey. Ross became trustee of the Minto Cup (for lacrosse), but turned down the opportunity to act as trustee for the Grey Cup. He was elected an alderman in Ottawa (1902) and after establishing Ottawa Hydro sat on that company's board until 1934. Ross remained a trustee of the Cup until his death in 1949, a period stretching some 56 years. At the time, he gave the NHL "full authority to determine and amend...conditions of competition for the Stanley Cup...providing always that the winners...shall be acknowledged World's Professional Hockey Champions." He was inducted into the Hockey Hall of Fame on August 16, 1976.

WILLIAM A. FORAN

b. Ottawa, Ontario, February 4, 1871
d. Ottawa, Ontario, November 30, 1945
Appointed May 6, 1907, on the nomination of P.D. Ross

A trustee of the Stanley Cup for 38 years, Foran was famous for his "sharp, crisp speech," according to the *Ottawa Citizen*. He was an alderman and athlete, an avid golfer who took the Ottawa Capitals, Canada's national lacrosse team, to a gold medal at the 1908 Olympics. He remained active in lacrosse most of his life as a coach, and from 1908 to his death he was secretary for the Civil Service Commission, the year the CSC was first established.

J. COOPER SMEATON

b. Carleton Place, Ontario, July 22, 1890
d. Montreal, Quebec, October 3, 1978
Appointed February 24, 1946, on the nomination of P.D. Ross

Cooper Smeaton had a long and active life in hockey, but as a referee rather than a player. After playing for the New York Wanderers with the Cleghorn brothers, he turned down several offers to turn pro during his youth, deciding instead to serve overseas in France and Belgium during World War I and for which he received the Military Medal "for bravery on the field of battle." Upon returning home to Canada, he continued his fledgling career as a hockey official and served the game in this capacity more or less non-stop until 1937. The brief ellipsis to this streak occurred in 1930-31 when he coached the ill-fated Philadelphia Quakers franchise to a dismal 4-36-4 record in the team's only NHL season. At season's end, he was appointed the NHL's referee-in-chief. In a letter to Smeaton from P.D. Ross, dated February 11, 1946, the surviving trustee wrote: "You are probably aware of the recent death of William Foran, my valued colleague in the Stanley Cup Trust. I am writing you herewith to invite you to take his place." Two days later, Smeaton forwarded his acceptance of the offer. He remained a trustee until his death, and he was inducted into the Hockey Hall of Fame as a referee in 1961.

NORMAN ALEXANDER "MERVYN" ("RED") DUTTON

b. Russell, Manitoba, July 23, 1898
d. Calgary, Alberta, March 15, 1987
Appointed March 30, 1950, on the nomination of Cooper Smeaton

Red's favourite expression was "keep punching," a motto he acquired as an 18-year-old severely wounded at Farbus Wood in 1917 in World War I when doctors had him on the operating table after both his legs were badly smashed. He survived, and after being discharged in 1919 pursued a career in hockey, playing first with Calgary in the Big Four League and working his way up to the Montreal Maroons in the NHL in 1926. A decade later, he took over as manager of the New York Americans and stayed with the team until it folded seven years later. He became the league's president in 1944 after the sudden death of Frank Calder, a position he accepted only at the behest of the NHL's six owners. Within two years, however, the business in western Canada that he started many years

previously with his brother had become a profitable and burgeoning pursuit, and he stepped down as president to focus solely on these interests. Dutton became a Stanley Cup trustee in 1950 and was duly inducted into the Hockey Hall of Fame in 1958, but his relationship with the game was strained. For some 35 years, he refused to enter an NHL rink, though he maintained his trusteeship until the day he died. This bitter paradox was not lost on Frank Selke, managing director of the Montreal Canadiens, who objected to Dutton's appointment as soon as it was announced. He wrote Cooper Smeaton: "Everyone in hockey has always had the highest regard for Red Dutton. Unfortunately, he seems to have soured on the game and has refused to go to hockey games here and in other cities when I have promised to leave tickets for him. This being so, I am wondering whether the appointment has been a wise one after all. I just cannot reconcile myself to the idea that Red Dutton has forgotten what he has done for hockey and what hockey has done for him."

CLARENCE SUTHERLAND CAMPBELL

b. Fleming, Saskatchewan, July 9, 1905
d. Montreal, Quebec, June 24, 1984
Appointed January 19, 1979, on the nomination of Red Dutton

After becoming the youngest graduate in the history of the University of Alberta in 1924, Clarence Campbell was named a Rhodes scholar and studied at Oxford University. Already in possession of degrees in law and arts, he earned two more in England before returning to Canada to practise law. He also became a hockey referee, eventually moving up to the NHL. In 1940, Campbell enlisted in the Canadian army, serving as a major for the Fourth Canadian Armoured Division Headquarters Squadron. In 1945, he transferred to the War Crimes Unit where he was promoted to lieutenant colonel. During this time, he was awarded the Order of the British Empire, made King's Counsel, and joined the NHL as assistant to the president. When incumbent Red Dutton resigned in the summer of 1946, Campbell became the league's new leader, a position he held for an unprecedented 31 years. During his time as president, the league expanded from its original six teams to 18. Still, he is likely remembered best for suspending superstar Maurice Richard in 1955, which caused the infamous Richard Riot in Montreal. In 1977, Campbell retired as NHL president, and two years later he was named a Stanley Cup trustee, a responsibility he maintained until the day he died.

WILLARD ZEBEDEE "BUD" ESTEY, Q.C.

b. Saskatoon, Saskatchewan, October 10, 1919
d. Toronto, Ontario, January 25, 2002
Appointed August 16, 1984, on the nomination of Red Dutton

Bud Estey graduated from the University of Saskatchewan with a B.A. and LL.B. and earned another LL.B. from Harvard a few years later. After serving in the Canadian Army in World War II, he taught Law at the University of Saskatchewan and lectured at Osgoode Hall in Toronto for four years, from 1947 to 1951. For the next quarter century he practiced law privately in Toronto before moving first to the Supreme Court of Ontario and then the Supreme Court of Canada. He was a Companion of the Order of Canada and was awarded numerous honorary law degrees throughout the country.

BRIAN FRANCIS O'NEILL

b. Montreal, Quebec, January 25, 1929
Appointed May 5, 1988, on the nomination of Willard Estey

O'Neill is an unlikely participant in the Stanley Cup's history since little from his early years reveals a connection to the game. Although he played some hockey, he graduated from Loyola College in Montreal with a B.A. and shortly thereafter from McGill with a Bachelor of Commerce. In 1962, he joined the *Financial Times of Canada*, but four years later he

applied for a job as an administrative director for a "sports organization," as the advertisement vaguely put it. He got the job, and only then discovered the organization was the NHL. In time, he became the second-most knowledgeable man in the game behind president Clarence Campbell, and over time O'Neill assumed the title of executive director. He has been the league disciplinarian, and initiated various programs and rule changes. His understanding of the league's constitution remains without compare, and he has served on virtually every important league committee during the last thirty years. One of two active trustees, O'Neill was inducted into the Hockey Hall of Fame as a Builder in 1994.

IAN "SCOTTY" MORRISON

b. Montreal, Quebec, April 22, 1930
Appointed March 18, 2002, on the nomination of Brian O'Neill

Scotty Morrison knew he was made for hockey at an early age, but he also knew it wasn't going to be as a player. He focused his on-ice pursuits as an official, and in 1954, at age 24, he became the youngest member of the NHL's crew.

Morrison left the game for the most part just two years later to pursue business opportunities, though he still officiated in a part-time capacity. In 1965 he was named referee-in-chief to replace the retiring Carl Voss, and under his aegis the officiating crew grew larger and more sophisticated. In 1986, Morrison was asked by NHL president John Ziegler to oversee the important job of finding a new and permanent home for the Hockey Hall of Fame, which had outgrown its home at the CNE in Toronto. Morrison moved the Hall to its present location in downtown Toronto at Yonge and Front streets, and in 1991 was named its chairman and CEO. He retired in 1998 and was inducted into the Hockey Hall of Fame as a Builder a year later. He became a Cup trustee upon the death of Bud Estey in early 2002.

Stanley Cup Traditions

THE PARADE

Winnipeg gave its Victorias a parade in 1896 after their stunning win over the Montreal Victorias; Ottawa had a parade in 1921 and 1923; and, Toronto had its first Bay Street victory dance in 1948. After that, parades grew more frequent but it was not until the 1960s with Toronto and Montreal that it became a de rigueur part of the celebrations.

SIPPING CHAMPAGNE FROM THE CUP

One of the longest-standing traditions, champagne was drunk from the Cup as early as 1896 in Winnipeg's celebration of its unexpected victory. To this day, it is symbolic of victory, and even the teetotalling Toronto coach Happy Day stuck his finger in the champers and sucked on it in victory toast.

ON ICE PRESENTATION

It is almost certain that during the 1920s and earlier the Cup was not presented on ice immediately after victory, though today this is regarded as tradition. Possibly the first time this occurred was at Maple Leaf Gardens in 1932, but for many years thereafter the practice was sporadic at best. In 1947, Conn Smythe refused to allow the Cup to travel to Toronto from Montreal for fear of making his team over-confident.

In 1958, the young tradition of the on-ice presentation almost came to an end for good. That year, Montreal won the Cup at the Boston Garden, and during the presentation to the Canadiens the local fans became unruly. It spurred Cup trustee Cooper Smeaton to write co-trustee Red Dutton: "The disgraceful behaviour of the fans at the end of the final game for the Stanley Cup in Boston last Sunday when the President of the League, Mr. Clarence Campbell, endeavoured to present the Cup, confirmed my thinking in connection with the presentation of the Cup and that is that no presentation should ever be made on the ice at the conclusion of any Cup series. After all, the Cup is the emblem of the World Championship and there should be some dignity in connection with the presentation."

Nonetheless, when Montreal won at home in the spring of 1959, the Cup was there for the Habs to enjoy with their fans.

ON-ICE TEAM PORTRAIT

It wasn't until the Edmonton Oilers gathered near centre ice after their 1988 victory that the team portrait was executed on ice, for fans and all to witness and, sometimes, take part in.

CARRYING THE CUP AROUND THE ICE

The on-ice Cup presentation was a formal and stiff affair until the night of April 23, 1950, when Ted Lindsay accepted the Cup from NHL president Clarence Campbell, and then lifted the Cup off the presentation table and skated around the boards so fans in all corners could share in the magic. Since then, a lap around the ice with the Cup has become an essential and memorable event at every Cup-clinching game.

STANLEY CUP RINGS

This tradition began the first year of the Cup, 1893, but although it is now an annual present—made by the club to its players—it didn't really catch on as a tradition until Toronto and Montreal began to dominate the game, first in the late '40s, then in the late '50s. Alternately, some winning teams have been given commemorative coins. The '32 Leafs were given gold coins that Conn Smythe promised would act as lifetime passes for that player to the Gardens. Ditto for the '39 Bruins and '42 Leafs. In the case of the five-Cup Montreal Canadiens (1956-60), players were given a ring with a new diamond each season the team won the Cup, a cost-saving tradition the Leafs replicated for their four Cups in the 1960s.

A DAY WITH THE CUP

The honour of each player getting the Cup for a day during the summer of their victory began only in 1993. Previously, it would make brief appearances at team parties, or occasionally a mischievous player would kidnap the Cup for a day, but no official schedule had been made as occurs today.

WHERE THE CUP IS KEPT

For many years, the Cup remained in Montreal year-round with Carl Pedersen, the engraver. The league would take possession of it in the days leading up to the finals series, but it was returned to him after a winner so that he could engrave the newest names. When the Hockey Hall of Fame opened in 1961, the Cup was put on permanent display there.

ENGRAVER'S INITIALS

The Cup has been engraved by only four people since World War II. A tradition that few people know about is that when the job is handed down, the new engraver carves into the inside of the Cup the initials of the outgoing engraver.

CUP BANNERS

The Kenora Thistles made a banner to celebrate their remarkable Cup win in 1907, and almost every team has been doing so ever since.

MINI CUPS

Each player on a Cup-winning team receives a 13-inch replica Stanley Cup, engraved with the same names that are on the real Cup. The tradition started informally about half a century ago to honour great men such as Conn Smythe and Jack Adams, and likely became a regular part of the Cup history in the 1950s with Montreal.

STANLEY CUP THEFTS

In the spring of 1962, Montreal and Chicago met in the semi-finals of that year's playoffs. The Hawks had won the Cup the previous year after upsetting the Canadiens in the semi-finals. They lost the first two games in Montreal, but returned home for games three and four. During these days, the team displayed the Cup in a glass case in the lobby of the Chicago Stadium. Kenneth Kilander, 25, an ardent Habs fan, followed his team everywhere, supporting himself by playing the piano at after-game parties during the winter and as a beach patrol in Atlantic City in the summer.

On the night of April 1, 1962, he picked the lock of the glass case housing the Cup while the game was in progress and proceeded to walk out of the building. He offered a guard and usher $250 to let him go, his destination being a hotel in the Loop where he would present the trophy to a group of Montreal sportswriters covering the series. Kilander was arrested on charges of disorderly conduct and placed in jail. "A newspaperman from Quebec said he thought it would be fun to swipe the Cup and bring it back to the hotel and take some pictures of it," Kilander explained. "I was elected to do it. I wasn't really trying to steal it. They said it would be funny." Kilander was fined ten dollars and released.

A more serious theft occurred in January 1970 at the Hockey Hall of Fame in Toronto when the original silver collar was stolen while the Hall's curator, Lefty Reid, was in St. Louis for the All-Star game. A woman phoned police shortly after the theft and promised the collar's safe return if the thieves were given lenient sentences, but the law refused to negotiate with the perpetrators. The collar was not recovered until September 18, 1977, when police received an anonymous phone call to go to the basement of a drycleaning store on Toronto's Woodbine Avenue, where they would find a package of interest. Sure enough, in a brown parcel, was the collar, a bit scratched but otherwise in good condition. Police charged Diomed Karrys with theft.

A short time before the collar was recovered, another attempt to steal the Cup occurred at the Hall's CNE location. On March 9, 1977, seven people entered the Hall and tried to make off with the Cup. Hall employee Ray Paquet alerted curator Lefty Reid to the suspicious behaviour of these people and called the police, who detained the group outside the Hall. Searching the seven individuals, officers found photographs and drawings detailing every aspect of the Hall's interior and the Cup casing, and the suspects admitted they were, in fact, trying to steal the Cup. It turned out the six men and one woman were students at the University of Montreal. They were on a scavenger hunt for the best "find" possible and concluded the Cup was the best candidate. After detailed questioning, they were released without being charged.

The Ever-Changing Stanley Cup

Although the Stanley Cup has been a symbol of hockey supremacy for more than a century, it has changed size and shape many times during its life. Originally, it was simply a bowl, and the victorious team had its name engraved in the bowl. In some years, winning teams added a ring to the base as Lord Stanley himself had suggested; other times, the team name was engraved in the bowl itself. Eventually, space ran out, and more and more rings were added to the base in a simple "stovepipe" continuation. Interestingly, during the stovepipe years (1930-45), rings were added above the previous year's, so that the final year, 1944-45, was nearest the original bowl and the first band, the 1927-28 Rangers, was at the base of the stovepipe Stanley Cup.

Over time, the stovepipe Stanley Cup, too, reached the limit of its design. The stovepipe became full in 1944-45 while the NHL considered what to do next, and as a result there was no engraving for the 1945-46 team when the Canadiens won the Cup! The modern Cup design originated in 1947, was redesigned a decade later in 1957, and has remained more or less the same ever since. Now, when the bottom of the five rings of the body of the Cup is filled, the top ring is taken off and installed in the Hockey Hall of Fame. All the rings are moved up, and a new ring at the bottom begins. Thus, a player's name will remain on the Cup for between 50 and 63 years. The current band will be filled with the 2003-04 team, after which the top band containing the teams from 1940-41 to 1952-53 will be retired to the Hockey Hall of Fame. The top ring (which is currently the second-from-the-top) will begin with the 1953-54 team, and remain until the new band is filled 13 years later, with the 2016-17 team.

While the perfection of the Cup makes its evolution seem almost predestined, there was a time when its future design was very much in doubt. The period just after WWII was one of great change and uncertainty: the war had recently ended; NHL president Red Dutton had just resigned; and the stovepipe Cup was beginning to look ungainly. On April 23, 1946, Cooper Smeaton, the newest Cup trustee, wrote a letter to his colleague, P.D. Ross, in which he made the following observations: "As you know, the Cup now rests on a very ugly-looking, elongated base [the stovepipe] and it occurred to me that it might be possible to get Henry Birks for instance, to design a nice big base which would permit space for sufficient shields, on which could be engraved the name of the Club and the year and have a sort of Golden Book made up with perhaps a copy of the Deed of Gift in it, along with some history of the Cup, in which the names of the players on each Team winning the cup could be inscribed rather than have their names on the silver bands now placed around the base. In this way the Cup would look very much more dignified and would be a Cup instead of a long, ugly base with the Cup perched on it, as it is today."

Six days later, Ross replied: "Regarding the Cup itself, I make this suggestion: — In preference to encumbering it with more shields, and in order to get rid of the tower structure, why not have Birks make a new base, with a receptacle in the base for a "golden book" to record all the past and prospective winnings of the Cup? The book would only need to be of moderate size, a hundred pages or so, with the base detachable from the cup of course, for purpose of transportation."

Fortunately, the NHL Board of Governors did not approve the suggestion! Indeed, in 1947 they offered the job of remodelling the Cup to engraver Carl Pedersen, and it has remained that shape ever since (amazingly, Petersen is not in the Hall of Fame as a Builder, despite the fact it was he who created, literally, the world's most famous trophy). In 1968, Pedersen made a replica of the bowl itself because the Hall of Fame feared the original was becoming too fragile from wear and tear. In 1970, the original bowl atop the Cup was officially retired to the Hall and the replacement installed in its place. In 1994, the Hockey Hall of Fame made a replica of the entire Stanley Cup so that when the original travelled with the players and teams there would always be a version at the Hall of Fame itself for visitors to admire. (Yes, the original is always presented to the players after victory and is always the one that they are given for a day during their victory summer.)

Stanley Cup Existing Pieces

The original Stanley Cup bowl (on permanent display at the Hockey Hall of Fame)

The 1927-28 to 1944-45 bands from the stovepipe design of the Cup (on permanent display)

The bands from the redesigned Cup (1945-46 to 1956-57; on permanent display)

The first retired band from the current Stanley Cup design (1927-28 to 1939-40, on permanent display)

The abandoned band (1978-79 to 1990-91, held in storage—see "The Abandoned Ring")

The replica Stanley Cup (always at the Hockey Hall of Fame, and always on display when the original is travelling)

The Stanley Cup itself (also called the Presentation Cup)

The Presentation Stanley Cup

Here is the makeup of the actual Stanley Cup as it exists today and when its various parts were created.

BOWL 1970 (made 1968 to replace the fragile original)
NECK BRACE added for support between the bowl and the body of the neck (1994)
NECK AND SHOULDER crafted by Carl Pedersen for the final re-design of the Cup (1957)
BODY

BAND 1: 1940-41 to 1952-53	engraved in 1957 for the final Cup re-design
BAND 2: 1953-54 to 1964-65	1953-57 engraved for final re-design in 1957; rest engraved year by year
BAND 3: 1965-66 to 1977-78	engraved annually with each new winner
BAND 4: 1978-79 to 1990-91	engraved annually with each new winner
BAND 5: 1991-92 to 2003-04	engraved annually with each new winner

BASE added for support (1984)

Photographed together for the first time, here are the presentation Cup (left), the original bowl and base (centre), and the replica Cup.

The Abandoned Ring

In 1993, after the Montreal Canadiens won the Stanley Cup, the trophy was dutifully sent, as usual, to Montreal to have the new players' names engraved. But the NHL also requested that the Cup be fixed to take care of the most prominent error on the Cup—the x'd out name of Basil Pocklington for the 1983-84 Oilers' team. The engraver removed that ring and re-engraved an entire new band, eliminating the name and x's of Basil Pocklington altogether!

When officials at the Hall of Fame received the Stanley Cup, complete with new band on the Cup and the old band in a plastic bag, they were surprised. For, in correcting the one Basil error, new errors had been made and the lore and historical fact of the Basil entry had been completely eliminated. The 1980-81 New York Islanders, for instance, spelled correctly at the time of its original engraving (top, far right), was now badly misspelled as "Ilanders" (bottom, far right). The old band, however, could not be re-used because the narrow steel ring used to connect each band had been rendered useless. The Hall, in short, was stuck with the new version of the band.

The Cup was re-sent to Montreal, though, with orders to re-engrave the name of Basil Pocklington and then x it out, as had been done on the original (because Basil, the father of Oilers' owner Peter Pocklington, had no formal affiliation at all with the Cup-winning team). Thus, the original band for the years 1978-79 to 1990-91 sits in storage at the Hockey Hall of Fame, while the current band on the Cup has been fixed, with new mistakes, and then corrected —to include an old mistake!).

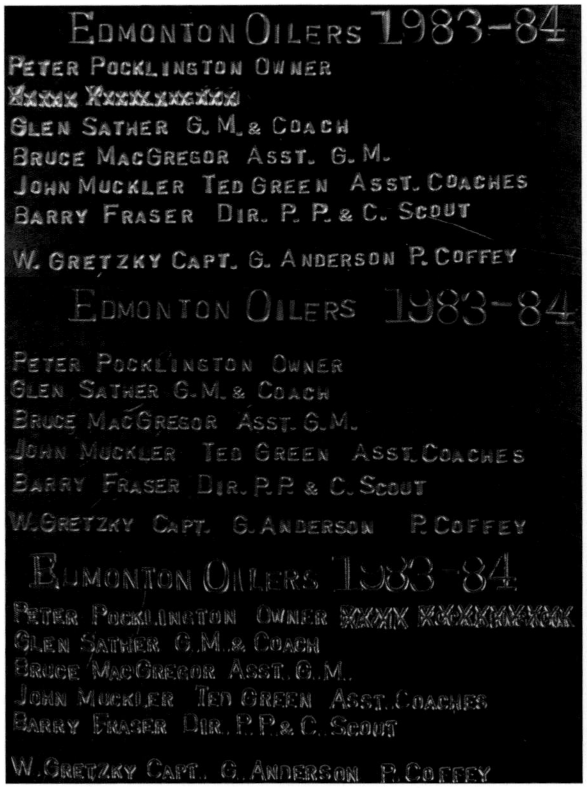

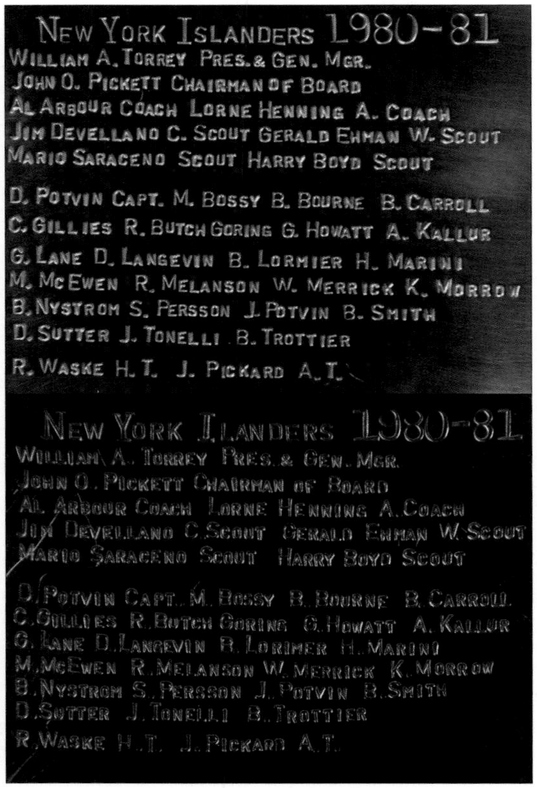

(above left) the abandoned, replica, and current stampings for the contentious Oilers; (above right) the original Islanders spelled correctly, and the "revised" name misspelled; (below) the entire abandoned ring.

THE MELTED BAND

When Toe Blake retired as coach of the Montreal Canadiens in 1968, he had won nine Stanley Cups in just 13 years behind the bench, a record of success not likely to be matched. The Canadiens wanted to hold a dinner in his honour, but for years he refused such a night of personal glory. Finally, in 1972, he agreed, and the team's top executives fêted their greatest coach. Claude Mouton later wrote in his book on the Canadiens that Blake was given a trophy that evening made in part with silver from the original Stanley Cup!

While no one connected with the Canadiens will admit knowledge of the story or confirm its veracity, the fact is that the 1928-29 Boston Bruins band from the original stovepipe Stanley Cup is missing. Myth has it that the Canadiens so detested the Bruins that they were able to get this band and happily melted it down to help create Blake's special trophy.

Stanley Cup Engravers

Carl Poul Petersen (pictured below) came to Canada from Denmark, settling with his wife in Montreal in 1929. A silversmith, he found employment with Henry Birks & Sons Ltd. He opened his own studio in 1937 for two years, until the war rendered the purchasing of silver almost impossible. After the war he again struck out on his own, becoming financially stable thanks to early commissions from Saidye and Samuel Bronfman. Petersen ran the studio with his three sons—Arno, Ole, and John Paul—who had apprenticed under their father and master.

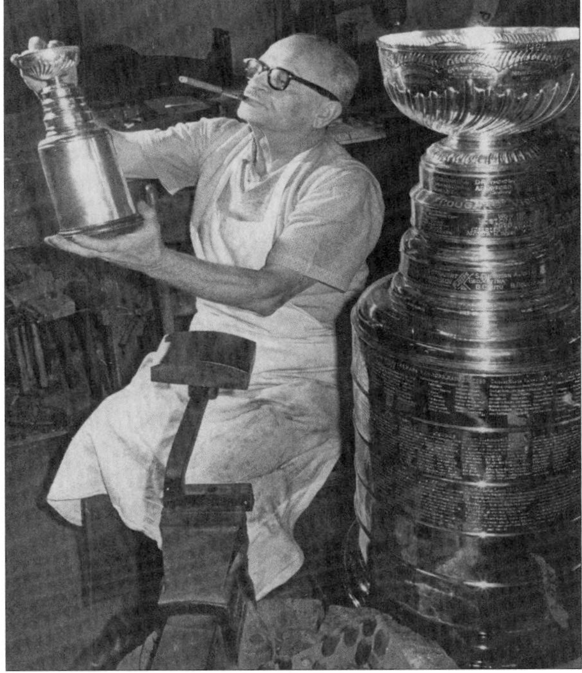

By the mid-1940s, Petersen had established an enviable reputation. He was commissioned by the NHL to engrave the names of the Stanley Cup winners on a trophy he alone would re-design to replace the stovepipe Cup. In 1968, when the league decided the original Cup was becoming too frail, it was Pedersen again who struck a new Stanley Cup bowl in case of permanent damage or theft to the original.

Pedersen died in 1977, but the Cup engraving remained in his family until 1979 when the business closed. At that point, bids were solicited by the league, and Doug Boffey of Boffey Inc. of Montreal won the contract. The engraving contract has been in his family and business ever since. The current engraver is Boffey's wife, Louise St. Jacques, who has worked professionally with Boffey since 1978 and started engraving the Cup in 1989. It was she who struck the complete replica Cup in 1994. Boffey also makes the miniature 13-inch replica Cups which each player gets, a tradition that started informally more than half a century ago but one that has become an annual tradition since the early 1960s.

The engravers have always adhered to a ritual when they receive the Cup. The first task is to clean the entire trophy. To do this, it must be dismantled (see photo below). The five barrel rings slide off and are dipped in solvent to remove the protective lacquer. They are then re-lacquered and buffed. Although the Cup is hollow inside, there is a round, plastic plate within to prevent current players from scratching their names into the Cup or denting it badly. Only the top inside of the bowl isn't lacquered because the players drink champagne from it each year. The bottom ring is then mounted onto a specially-designed steel back to allow the engraving, after which the entire Cup is re-assembled.

PROCEDURES: WHAT HAPPENS TODAY

So a team wins the Stanley Cup. Then what? There is, of course, a procedure that ensures the proper engraving of the team and its members. First, the team general manager prepares a list of those names he wants to go on the Cup. There has been no minimum or maximum number of names permitted, though 52 is currently the most allowed to ensure the list of non-players does not become ridiculous. For a player, the rules are pretty clear: he must have played in 41 regular season games or have been on the active roster by the 26th day preceding the end of the regular season or else have played one shift during the best-of-seven Stanley Cup finals. Management names are limited only to those who are part of the actual operations of the team (no wives or relatives with superfluous connections qualify). This list is then submitted to Jim Gregory at the NHL offices in Toronto. Once he approves the list, it is sent to Phil Pritchard at the Hockey Hall of Fame, and he sends this with the Cup to Louise St. Jacques at Boffey Inc. in Montreal. (In recent years many names have been submitted that don't qualify, and despite objections from the Hall of Fame, the names have been accepted by the NHL.) St. Jacques engraves only what is on the list she receives and is not responsible for spelling errors. She will take about a week to finish the work. Once the Presentation Cup is finished, she will do the same work on the Replica Cup.

(far left) Carl Petersen at work; (below and left) tools of the trade for stamping names into the Cup; (above) current engraver Louise St. Jacques.

For common understanding, the word "engraved" is always used to describe the process of putting names on the Cup, but, technically, this is not correct. The NHL trophies (Art Ross, Hart, etc.) have engraved names on their plates. The Cup names are "stamped": each letter is individually punched using a letter and a small hammer (seel tools of the trade, below left). The letters used on the Cup are the original letters used with the original tools from the Petersen redesign in 1947. These come in three sizes: one, the large size for team names at the top of each entry; two, a smaller size for the initials of first and last names; and three, an even smaller size to differentiate from initials. All letters are capitals and are never used for any other project during the year—their exclusive domain is the Stanley Cup. The mini-Cup each player receives includes all names that are on the Stanley Cup. These are prepared during the summer while the players have the Cup.

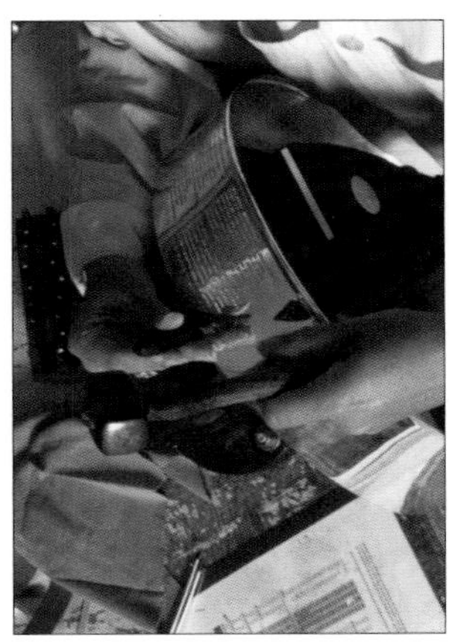

Chronology of Engravings

1892 The Stanley Cup is minted with the words "DOMINION HOCKEY CHALLENGE CUP" on one side of the outside rim and "From Stanley of Preston" on the other side.
1893 "MONTREAL AAA" engraved as AHA league champions.
1894 "MONTREAL 1894" engraved, the same AAA team as the year previous.
1895 "VICTORIAS OF MONTREAL 1895" engraved as AHA champions.
1896 "VICTORIAS OF WINNIPEG 1895" engraved for the team that won a challenge from Montreal in February 1896, before the end of the '96 season.
1896 "VICTORIAS OF MONTREAL 1896" engraved for the December '96 challenge win over Winnipeg prior to the start of the 1897 season.
1897 "VICTORIAS OF MONTREAL 1897" engraved as AHA champions and victors from Ottawa in a challenge.
1898 "VICTORIAS OF MONTREAL 1898" engraved as league champions.
1899 "VICTORIAS OF MONTREAL 1899" engraved for the February '99 challenge victory over Winnipeg.
1899 "SHAMROCKS OF MONTREAL 1899" engraved for their CAHL league title and March '99 challenge win over Queen's University.
1900 "SHAMROCKS OF MONTREAL 1900" engraved for February 1900 challenge victory over Winnipeg, but after another challenge win in March another engraving was not added.
1901 "VICTORIAS OF WINNIPEG 1901" engraved after defeating the Shamrocks in a challenge.
1902 "VICTORIAS OF WINNIPEG 1902" engraved for January '02 challenge win over Toronto Wellingtons.
1902 "MONTREAL 1902" engraved for Montreal AAA challenge win in March 1902 over Winnipeg.
1903 "MONTREAL 1903" engraved for February '03 challenge win by Montreal AAA over Winnipeg Victorias.
1903 "OTTAWA 1903" engraved for March '03 win over Montreal Vics in two-game challenge.
1903 "OTTAWA 1903" engraved for January '03 challenge win over Rat Portage.
1904 "OTTAWA 1904" engraved for March 1903 challenge victory over Rat Portage.
1904 "Ottawa 1904" engraved again for January '04 win vs. Toronto Marlboros.
1904 "OTTAWA 1904" engraved a third time for victory vs. Wanderers.
1904 "OTTAWA 1904" engraved a fourth time for win over Brandon in two-game challenge.
1905 "OTTAWA 1905" engraved for challenge win over Dawson City in January '05.
1905 "OTTAWA 1905 OTTAWA VS. KENORA" engraved for win over Rat Portage.
1906 "OTTAWA 1906" engraved for wins in February and March vs. Queen's University and Smiths Falls.
1906 "Ottawa March 15-17 Wanderers vs. Ottawa Score 12-10" engraved for Silver Seven victory in two-game, total-goals challenge.
1906 "Montreal December 27-29 Wanderers vs New Glasgow 10-3 6-2" engraved for Wanderer's two-game, total-goals challenge victory.
1907 Although Kenora defeated Wanderers in January 1907, there is no Cup engraving to memorialize the victory.
1907 "WANDERERS DEFEATED KENORA 12 TO 8 MARCH 25TH 1907" engraved for win to avenge challenge defeat two months earlier. For the first time, all the players' names are engraved, inside the Cup bowl.
1908 Although the Wanderers won four successive challenges—one in January 1908, two in March, and a last in December—there is no mention of these wins on the Cup.
1909 "OTTAWA 1909" engraved for ECHA league champions.
1910 "OTTAWA 1910/OTTAWA VS GALT/OTTAWA VS EDMONTON" engraved for these two challenge wins in January 1910. However, the Wanderers took possession of the Cup in March based on its NHA title and defeated Berlin in a challenge, but no mention of this exists on the Cup.
1911 Ottawa won the NHA title and twice beat challenges (vs. Galt and Port Arthur), but no mention of any of these three Cup achievements is engraved.
1912 "QUEBEC/1911-1912/DEFEATED MONCTON/9-2 & 8-0" engraved after challenge victory.
1913 "QUEBEC/1912-1913/DEFEATED—SYDNEY/14-3 & 6-2" engraved after challenge victory.
1914 "TORONTOS/1913-14/DEFEATED VICTORIAS B.C./3 STRAIGHT GAMES" refers to the Blueshirts' best-of-five win over the Victoria Cougars.
1915 "VANCOUVER. B.C./1914-15./DEFEATED OTTAWA/3 STRAIGHT GAMES" engraved after finals between the two league champions (PCHA and NHA). All players' names are engraved inside the bowl, along the fluted sides, accompanying the 1907 Wanderers' names.
1916 "PORTLAND.ORE./P.C.H.A. CHAMPIONS./1915-16" engraved, the first time a non-Cup winning team is acknowledged for earning a chance to play for the Cup. Beside it comes the champions' engraving: "CANADIAN/N.H.A. & WORLD'S CHAMPIONS/DEFEATED PORTLAND /1915-16"
1917 "SEATTLE/WORLD'S CHAMPIONS/ DEFEATED CANADIANS" engraved (note, as above, the anglicized spelling of the "Canadiens").
1918 "VANCOUVER/DEFEATED SEATTLE/1917-18 /SCORE 1-0" engraved to honour the Millionaires' appearance in the Cup final, but the Toronto Arenas, who beat Vancouver in five games to win the Cup, are not represented!
1919 No winner.
1920 There is no mention of the Cup-winning Ottawa Senators on the Cup.
1921 There is no mention of the Cup-winning Ottawa Senators on the Cup.
1922 There is no mention of the Cup-winning Toronto St. Pats on the Cup.
1923 There is no mention of the Cup-winning Ottawa Senators on the Cup.
1924 A new ring is added. "CANADIENS of MONTREAL /WORLD'S CHAMPIONS /DEFEATED / OTTAWA VANCOUVER CALGARY / TWO STRAIGHT/GAMES EACH" is engraved along with the full roster.
1925 A new, angled ring is added above the original first ring of the base, directly below the base of the Cup bowl: "WON/BY/"COUGARS" VICTORIA, B.C. 1925"
1926 A new ring is added above the previous, again directly underneath the Cup bowl: "WON/BY MONTREAL "MAROONS" 1925-26". The names of the players are also engraved, the first time since Vancouver in 1915, and for the first time includes non-players (i.e., members of the executive) and the specific identification of the team captain.
1927 A new ring is added underneath the Cougars': "WON BY/OTTAWA SENATORS/1926-27" and includes the full team roster.
1928 A new ring is added for the Rangers, above the top-most ring sitting directly below the Cup base: "NEW YORK RANGERS/1927-28" in which the full roster is listed. Frank Boucher and Lester Patrick are the only full names. When the Cup was redesigned in 1957, the list was made into two columns, mostly with the players' first initials, and ordered identically from the original.
1929 "WON BY/BOSTON BRUINS/1928-29" is added to the open half of the ring started by the 1926-27 Maroons. When the Cup was redesigned in 1957, the first ring began with the 1927-28 Rangers. Thus, for many years, this Bruins team was represented on the Cup twice, once on the base of the original Cup, and once on the barrel.
1930 The beginning of an annual ring and the start of the stovepipe Cup, with each addition being added to the top, so the progression is upward rather than the present downward style. "WORLD'S CHAMPIONS/CANADIENS OF MONTREAL/1930" including full names and, for the first time, all playoff scores from three playoff rounds the Canadiens played. The directors and team doctors are also listed and the redesign uses mostly full names as well.
1931 A new ring added above: "WORLD'S CHAMPIONS /CANADIENS OF MONTREAL/1931" including full names and dates and scores from both playoff rounds won by

Montreal. Full names and similar order mark the redesigned Cup for this year.

1932 A new ring added above: "TORONTO MAPLE LEAFS/1931-32/WORLD'S CHAMPIONS" including team rosters with first initials and last names and playoff game scores from all three rounds played by the Leafs. Also engraved for the first time is a team mascot. The team is listed in perfect order from goalie to defencemen to forwards (listed first as line combinations, then spares). The engraving consists of 16 players and 27 non-players. For the redesigned Cup, only eleven players and nine non-players are listed.

1933 A new ring added above: "NEW YORK RANGERS PROFESSIONAL HOCKEY CLUB/WORLD'S CHAMPIONS AND WINNERS OF THE/STANLEY CUP-1932-33" including the full team roster. For the first time, the captain is listed first, and although most first names are written in full, some players have only a first initial. The redesign is almost identical to the original.

1934 A new ring added above: "CHICAGO NATIONAL HOCKEY TEAM INC./THE BLACK HAWKS/1933-34" including full team roster: 12 players, a spare goalie, and a trainer. The redesign uses full names but different order.

1935 A new ring added above: "MONTREAL PROFESSIONAL HOCKEY CLUB/WINNERS/1934-35" including full team roster. For the first time, the list is alphabetical, though Blake and Blinco are out of order. The redesign features initials only for first names and is not in alphabetical order.

1936 A new ring added above: "DETROIT RED WINGS/1935-36" including full team roster and playoff scores. Full names are inscribed, as well as players' positions. The redesign also has full names but not in the same sequence.

1937 A new ring added above: "DETROIT RED WINGS/1936-37" including full team roster and scores from the finals. Full names and players' positions are engraved, but again the redesign doesn't follow the same order.

1938 A new ring added above: "CHICAGO NATIONAL HOCKEY TEAM INC./THE BLACK HAWKS/1937-38" including full team roster and all Chicago playoff scores from three rounds. Full names are used, though the listing is random. The redesign follows the original exactly.

1939 A new ring added above: "BOSTON BRUINS/1938-39" including full team roster and all Boston playoff scores from the semi-finals and finals. Names with first initials are used, and players' positions are also listed. The redesign bears no relation to the original.

1940 A special, much larger ring is added to the top of the stovepipe Cup, one that could accommodate six winning teams in a more organized fashion. Scores are not listed, and teams have two symmetrical columns to honour their personnel: "THE NEW YORK RANGERS 1939-40". The list starts with the goalie, then the captain, then the rest of the team in random order. The redesign is almost identical to the original.

1941 A second entry on the wide ring at the top: "BOSTON BRUINS 1940-1" including full roster. The captain is the first player listed, then everyone else follows in alphabetical order. The redesign is identical.

1942 A third entry on the wide ring at the top of the stovepipe Cup: "TORONTO MAPLE LEAFS 1941-2" including full roster. Full names are used, in random order, and the captain is identified but placed arbitrarily in the middle. The redesign lists the captain first and the rest of the players follow in random order.

1943 A fourth entry on the wide ring at the top of the stovepipe Cup: "DETROIT RED WINGS 1942-3" including full roster. The goalie is listed first, then all other players, in no particular order. On the redesign, the trainer is listed after the captain and before the rest of the team.

1944 A fifth entry on the wide ring at the top of the stovepipe Cup: "CANADIENS OF MONTREAL 1943-4" including full roster. The goalie is listed first, then the rest of the team in alphabetical order. On the redesign, the captain in listed first, then the rest of the team, full names, in random order.

1945 A sixth entry on the wide ring at the top of the stovepipe Cup: "TORONTO MAPLE LEAFS 1944-45" including full roster. Full names are used, and the captain is listed second, the rest of the team following in random order. On the redesign, the captain is listed first, then the rest of the team, full names, in random order.

1946 A seventh entry on the wide ring at the top of the stovepipe Cup: "CANADIENS OF MONTREAL 1945-46" including full roster. The captain is listed before the coach, and full names are engraved.

1947 The 1946-47 entry is added at the same time the 1947-48 entry (see below), on the redesigned Cup that looks like today's Cup, though the bands on the first redesign featured a hodge-podge of sizes, many coming from the stovepipe Cup: "TORONTO MAPLE LEAFS 1946-47" including full roster. The captain is listed first, then all other players, full names, in alphabetical order.

1948 The Stanley Cup underwent a revolutionary design change, shifting away from the impracticality of the stovepipe Cup, to a more economical use of space. The bowl at the top remained unchanged, of course. The base of the stovepipe Cup, which was the oldest part of the Cup, was moved from the bottom to the top, directly under the original bowl. Underneath this came a new shoulder onto which only the names of winning teams were engraved (and which filled to capacity in 1992—it will remain unchanged in perpetuity). Below this came a vastly expanded trunk or body, the rings from the stovepipe being combined so that two bands fitted onto one new and wider band. This lower trunk was completely separate from the top of the Cup, which came apart, literally, at the shoulder (when the current Cup was designed in 1957, it was still in two pieces that were screwed together—it became one piece only when the collar was retired, in 1962, and the two pieces were soldered). Six such new rings were created, five formed from the various and previous stovepipe bands, one left blank for future years. Under this came the wide, previous top band from the stovepipe Cup, now expanded to allow room for six more teams. And finally, at the bottom, came two more expanded, narrow stovepipe-like strips of rings for future teams. The additional team entries now moved down, away from the bowl. "TORONTO MAPLE LEAFS 1947-48" including full team roster. The order of non-players/players is reversed this year. The captain is the first name on the Cup, then all other players, full names, in alphabetical order, and then non-players. On the redesign, the captain is listed first but not identified as captain. He is followed by all other players, full names, in alphabetical order.

1949 Added to the new, wider, expansive former stovepipe band near the base: "TORONTO MAPLE LEAFS 1948-49" including full team roster. Off-ice personnel listed first, then players (captain, then others, full names, alphabetical order), then the team's executive. On the redesign, the players are listed with full names and alphabetically, so although the captain is identified as such his name appears in alphabetical order, not first among players.

1950 Added to the new stovepipe band: "DETROIT RED WINGS 1949 50" including full team roster. Like the '47-'48 Leafs team, the players are listed first, then the executive. Players are listed captain first, then all others in alphabetical order, with full names. On the redesign, the captain is listed first, then the rest of the team in no particular order, full names used except for two only whose initials are used.

1951 The last team is added to the new stovepipe band: "TORONTO MAPLE LEAFS 1950-51" including full team roster. The list is alphabetical, followed by off-ice and executive members of the team. On the redesign, the list again is perfectly alphabetical and the captain is not identified as such.

1952 The first team is engraved on the narrow ring below the stovepipe band, second band from the bottom: "DETROIT RED WINGS/1951-52" including full team roster. The captain is listed first, then all other players in alphabetical order, but written right to left, moving away from the centre of the band with the team name. On the other side of the team name is listed the executive and off-ice members of the team. On the redesign, names are listed in full, in no particular order, and the captain is listed last.

1953 Added to the narrow ring, second from the bottom: "CANADIENS OF MONTREAL 1952-53" including full team roster. The captain is listed first, then all other players, full names but in no particular order. On the redesign, the players are listed in no particular order, full names, and the captain is listed arbitrarily in the middle.

1954 The first name is engraved on the last, bottom-most band on the Cup: "DETROIT RED WINGS 1953-54" including full team roster. As with 1951-52, players are listed alphabetically right to left (the captain in order, not listed first). On the redesign, the players are listed randomly, full names, and the captain is listed arbitrarily in the middle.

1955 Added to the last ring: "DETROIT RED WINGS 1954-55" including full team roster. As with the previous year, players' names are engraved right to left in alphabetical order (the captain in order, not listed first). On the redesign, the players are listed in no particular order, full names, but the captain is listed last.

1956 The only space now left on the Cup is on the narrow band immediately above the expanded stovepipe band: "MONTREAL "CANADIENS" 1955-56" including full team roster. The list is perfectly alphabetical, but only players' initials for first names are engraved. Also, only players and two trainers are on this year's Cup team. On the redesign, the captain is listed before the trainer, and all other players follow, initials only for first names, in no particular order.

1957 The Stanley Cup undergoes its final transformation. From the shoulder up, nothing alters, but the various narrow and wide bands of inconsistent width below are replaced by five symmetrical bands, each capable of holding 13 Stanley Cup winners. Screws are inserted between the shoulder and body so that the Cup is a single, non-detachable unit. Although the 1956-57 Montreal team is the first to win the Cup in the new incarnation, the league fills more than two of the five newly-designed bands with previous winners, so that the lower half of the Cup doesn't look altogether void. The first band lists winners from 1927-28 to 1939-40. The second includes 1940-41 to 1952-53. The third begins with 1953-54 and continues to this '56-'57 team: "MONTREAL CANADIENS 1956-57" including full roster listed in alphabetical order, some with full first names, others initials only.

1958 Added to the third band on the body: "MONTREAL CANADIENS 1957-58" including full team roster in alphabetical order. Some names are listed in full, others initials only for first names.

1959 A sixth team is added to the third band: "MONTREAL CANADIENS 1958-59" including full team roster. First names are a preposterous range of initials (A Provost) to formal, first name (Richard Moore) to bizarre shortenings of first names (Alb Langlois, Ch Hodge). Names are listed alphabetically, except for Beliveau who is listed out of sequence after Bonin.

1960 A seventh team is added to the third band: "MONTREAL CANADIENS 1959-60" including full team roster. The names are listed alphabetically, with four discrepancies.

1961 An eighth team is added to the third band: "CHICAGO BLACK HAWKS 1960-61" including full team roster. The point size for Arthur Wirtz's name is greater than the rest of the entries and the list of player names is not alphabetical.

1962 A ninth team is added to the third band: "TORONTO MAPLE LEAFS 1961-62" including full team roster listed alphabetically, except Horton.

1963 A tenth team is added to the third band: "TORONTO MAPLE LEAES 1962-63" ("Leafs" misspelled) including full team roster in alphabetical order.

1964 An eleventh team is added to the third band: "TORONTO MAPLE LEAFS 1963-64" including full team roster in alphabetical order.

1965 A twelfth team is added to the third band: "MONTREAL CANADIENS 1964-65" including full team roster. All players' names appear in full, but the engraver took up space for two teams.

1966 The last team is engraved on the third band of the body of the Cup: "MONTREAL CANADIENS 1965-66" including full team roster in random order.

1967 The first team on the fourth ring on the body of the trunk is engraved: "TORONTO MAPLE LEAFS 1966-67" including full team roster. For the second time (after the 1931-32 Leafs) the space allocated to non-players is equal to that allocated to players (six and a half lines each), though the number of names favours the players (21-11).

1968 Another team is added to the fourth ring on the trunk: "CLUB DE HOCKEY CANADIEN 1967-68" including full team roster. The use of full first names or initials is evenly divided. Goalies are listed separately at the bottom.

1969 Another team is added to the fourth ring: "CLUB DE HOCKEY CANADIEN 1968-69" including full team roster. Every player is listed by initial only for first names.

1970 Another team is added to the fourth ring: "BOSTON BRUINS 1969-70" including full team roster. Only four first names are spelled out: Don Awrey, John Bucyk, Ted Green and Bobby Orr.

1971 Another team is added to the fourth ring: "CLUB. DE. HOCKEY. CANADIEN. 1970.71" including full team roster. Most first names are identified by initials only, and this is the "year of the period"—there are 54 periods used on this year's team engraving.

1972 Another team is added to the fourth ring: "BOSTON BRUINS 1971-72" including full team roster. Likely to acknowledge Orr's superiority, the engraving has a particular order this year: Orr, the two goalies, then the rest of the team in random order. All first names appear in full.

1973 Another team is added to the fourth ring: "CLUB DE HOCKEY CANADIEN 1972-73" including full team roster with full first names.

1974 Another team is added to the fourth ring: "PHILADELPHIA FLYERS 1973-74" including full team roster with full first names.

1975 Another team is added to the fourth ring: "PHILADELPHIA FLYERS 1974-75" including full team roster with full first names.

1976 Another team is added to the fourth ring: "CLUB DE HOCKEY CANADIEN 1975-76" including full team roster with full first names.

1977 Another team is added to the fourth ring: "CLUB DE HOCKEY CANADIEN 1976-77" including full team roster with full first names.

1978 Another team is added to the fourth ring: "CLUB DE HOCKEY CANADIEN 1977-78" including full team roster with full first names.

1979 The last team on the fourth ring in engraved: "CLUB DE HOCKEY CANADIEN 1978-79" including full team roster with initials only for first names.

1980 The first team on the fifth and bottom ring is engraved: "NEW YORK ISLANDERS 1979-80" including full team roster in alphabetical order after the captain. Only initials for first names are used with the exception of R. Butch Goring.

1981 Another team is added to the fifth ring: "NEW YORK ISLANDERS 1980-81" including full team roster in alphabetical order after the captain. Only initials for first names are used with the exception of R Butch Goring. ("Islanders" is later misspelled when this band is replaced—see "The Abandoned Ring.")

1982 Another team is added to the fifth ring: "NEW YORK ISLANDERS 1981-82" including full team roster in alphabetical order after the captain. Only initials for first names are used with the exception of R Butch Goring.

1983 Another team is added to the fifth ring: "NEW YORK ISLANDERS 1982-83" including full team roster in alphabetical order after the captain. Only initials for first names are used with the exception of R Butch Goring.

1984 Another team is added to the fifth ring: "EDMONTON OILERS 1983-84" including full team roster in alphabetical order after the captain. Only initials for first names are used, and the space allotted to non-players is greater than that taken up by players (seven lines to six).

1985 Another team is added to the fifth ring: "EDMONTON OILERS 1984-85" including full team roster in alphabetical order after the captain. Only initials for first names are used.

1986 Another team is added to the fifth ring: "CLUB DE HOCKEY CANADIEN 1985-86" including full team roster, starting with the captain, then goalies, then all other players in no particular order. Only initials for first names are used.

1987 Another team is added to the fifth band: "EDMONTON OILERS 1986-87" including full team roster listed alphabetically after the captain. Only initials for first names are used.

1988 Another team is added to the fifth band: "EDMONTON OILERS 1987-88" including full team roster listed alphabetically after the captain. Only initials for first names are used.

1989 Another team is added to the fifth band: "CALGARY FLAMES 1988-89" including full team roster starting with the captain, co-captain, and assistant captains listed for the first time, followed by goalies, then all other players in random order. Only initials for first names are used.

1990 Another team is added to the fifth band: "EDMONTON OILERS 1989-90" including full team roster. The captain and assistant captains are listed first, followed by the rest of the team in random order.

1991 Another team is added to the fifth band: "PITTSBURGH PENGUINS 1990-91" including full team roster starting with the captain then the rest of the team in random order. Only initials are used for first names.

1992 The last name on the bottom ring of the Cup is engraved: "PITTSBURGH PENGUINS 1991-92" including full team roster starting with the captain and followed by the rest of the team in random order. A record 31 player names are included, including some who don't technically qualify for the honour (not having played half a season or a game in the finals). The Cup is now full.

1993 The top ring of the Cup is retired. The Cup-winning teams 1927-28 to 1939-40 from this ring are taken to the

Hockey Hall of Fame. A new, empty band is added to the bottom of the Cup, and the first team is honoured: "MONTREAL CANADIENS 1992-93" including full team roster listing the captain, then goalies, then the rest of the team in random order.

1994 Another team is added to the lowest band: "NEW YORK RANGERS 1993-94" including full team roster starting with the captain then the rest of the team in inconsistent alphabetical order. Only initials are used for first names.

1995 Another team is added to the lowest band: "NEW JERSEY DEVILS 1994-95" including full team roster. For the first time since 1952-53, the captain is not listed first among the players. The names appear in perfect alphabetical order.

1996 Another team is added to the lowest band: "COLORADO AVALANCHE 1995-96" including full team roster in perfect alphabetical order. Joe Sakic is not identified as captain, the first such occurrence since 1951-52.

1997 Another team is added to the lowest band: "DETROIT RED WINGS 1996-97" including full team roster in perfect alphabetical order.

1998 Another team is added to the lowest band: "DETROIT RED WINGS 1997-98" including full team roster. For only the second time (after Toronto 1931-32), non-players outnumber players (29-26) and take up eight lines compared to just five for the players. Non-players are listed using full names; players with first-name initials only, listed alphabetically after the captain.

1999 Another team is added to the lowest band: "DALLAS STARS 1998-99" including full team roster. The captain and assistant captains are listed first followed by the rest of the team in alphabetical order with full names.

2000 Another team is added to the lowest band: "NEW JERSEY DEVILS 1999-2000" including full team roster in perfect alphabetical order. Scott Stevens is not identified as captain, and this is the year of the middle initial. Some eight players have both their first name in full and an initial before their surname.

2001 Another team is added to the lowest band: "COLORADO AVALANCHE 2000-01" including full team roster. Players are listed alphabetically, full first names

2002 Another team is added to the lowest band: "DETROIT RED WINGS 2001-02" including full roster. The captain is listed first, followed by the goalies, then the rest of the roster in alphabetical order. Full first names are used throughout.

2003 Another team is added to the lowest band: "NEW JERSEY DEVILS 2002-03" including full roster. Roster is in perfect alphabetical order with the exception of lines 3 and 4 of player names. There is particular reference to the captain, and most players have a middle initial.

2004 Another team will be added to fill the lowest band: "TAMPA BAY LIGHTNING 2003-04" including full roster. This will occur in October 2004.

Names by Section on the Stanley Cup

Section	Names
INSIDE BOWL (1907 & 1915)	29
OUTSIDE BOWL	0
FIRST BAND (1924-25 & 1925-26)	30
SECOND BAND (1926-27 & 1928-29)	33
THIRD BAND	0
FOURTH BAND (1923-24)	21
COLLAR Teams only (1893-1992)	
BAND 1 (1940-41 to 1952-53)	363
BAND 2 (1953-54 to 1964-65)	340
BAND 3 (1965-66 to 1977-78)	400
BAND 4 (1978-79 to 1990-91)	463
BAND 5 (1991-92 to 2002-03)	581 (up to 2003)
Total	**2,260**

DIMENSIONS

Total weight	34 1/2 lbs.
Total height	35 1/4"
Bowl	height 7 1/2" diameter 11 1/4" circumference 35"
Collar	height 6 1/4"
Shoulder	height 3 1/4"
Barrel	height 18 1/4"
Base	diameter 17 1/4"

Stanley Cup Records

MOST STANLEY CUPS BY A PLAYER

There is no official, complete list of Stanley Cup winners by player name and team in large measure because the names that are on the Stanley Cup often differ from the criteria which, technically, dictate which names should be engraved. It was not until 1977 that the NHL decreed that a player must have played for half a season (or, a goalie dressed for half a season) to qualify for engraving. The list below consists of all player names that are on the Cup, regardless whether they have met any necessary criteria.

11 Henri Richard
10 Jean Beliveau, Yvan Cournoyer
9 Claude Provost
8 Red Kelly, Maurice Richard, Jacques Lemaire
7 Serge Savard, Jean-Guy Talbot

CONSECUTIVE CUPS WITH DIFFERENT TEAMS

Jack Marshall	1901 Winnipeg Victorias 1902 Montreal AAA
Art Ross	1907 Kenora Thistles 1908 Montreal Wanderers
Bruce Stuart	1908 Montreal Wanderers 1909 Ottawa Senators
Harry Holmes	1917 Seattle Metropolitans 1918 Toronto Arenas
Eddie Gerard	1921 Ottawa Senators 1922 Toronto St. Pats
Eddie Gerard	1922 Toronto St. Pats 1923 Ottawa Senators
Lionel Conacher	1934 Chicago Black Hawks 1935 Montreal Maroons
Ab McDonald	1960 Montreal Canadiens 1961 Chicago Black Hawks
Al Arbour	1961 Chicago Black Hawks 1962 Toronto Maple Leafs
Ed Litzenberger	1961 Chicago Black Hawks 1962 Toronto Maple Leafs
Claude Lemieux	1995 New Jersey Devils 1996 Colorado Avalanche

CUPS WON WITH THE MOST TEAMS

4 Jack Marshall, Claude Lemieux*
** won twice with the New Jersey franchise, but at different times*
3 Al Arbour, Frank Foyston, Larry Hillman, Harry Holmes, Mike Keane, Gord Pettinger, Jack Walker, Scotty Bowman (coach), Dick Irvin (player & coach), Bryan Trottier (player & coach)

MOST STANLEY CUPS BY A PLAYER NOT IN THE HOCKEY HALL OF FAME

9 Claude Provost
6 Glenn Anderson, Ralph Backstrom, Dick Duff, Kevin Lowe, Jean-Guy Talbot

LONGEST TIME BETWEEN FIRST AND SECOND STANLEY CUP WINS

21 years Lester Patrick
16 years Chris Chelios
15 years Dutch Gainor

LONGEST TIME BETWEEN FIRST AND LAST CUP

(not necessarily second)
21 years Lester Patrick
17 years Red Kelly, Marcel Pronovost, Henri Richard
16 years Maurice Richard, Chris Chelios

OLDEST PLAYER ON THE CUP

42 Johnny Bower (1967)

OLDEST PERSON ON THE CUP

87 Walter Crossman (1998)

YOUNGEST PLAYER ON THE CUP

18 years, 2 months, 9 days Larry Hillman
18 years, 9 months, 21 days Gaye Stewart

YOUNGEST PERSON ON THE CUP

11 Stafford Smythe

MOST TIMES NAME ON THE STANLEY CUP

(all players, coaches, trainers, etc.)
17 Jean Beliveau
12 Sam Pollock
11 Toe Blake, Jacques Lemaire, Henri Richard
10 Yvan Cournoyer, Eddie Palchak, Scotty Bowman

GREATEST TIME BETWEEN FIRST AND LAST TIME NAME ON THE CUP

53 years Marcel Pronovost
46 years Wally Crossman
40 years King Clancy
37 years Jack Adams, Jean Beliveau, Lorne Davis, Glenn Hall

ONLY STANLEYS ON THE CUP

Lord Stanley, Stanley Jaffe, Stan Mikita, Stan Smith, Allan Stanley, Barney Stanley, E. Stanley Kroenke

OFFICIALS IN STANLEY CUP SERIES (1893-2004)

R = referee, L = linesman *(the number after the R or L indicates career number of games officiated in that capacity)*
(1893-1925, one referee; 1926 to 1938, two referees; 1939 to 1941, one referee, one linesman; 1942 to 1998, one referee, two linesmen; since 1999, two referees, two linesmen)

Neil Armstrong (L-48), John Ashley (R-14), Sammy Babcock (L-41), Hugh Baird (R-7), Claude Bechard (L-27), William Bell (R-10), Wayne Bonney (L-11), Russell Bowie (R-14), Gord Broseker (L-13), Vern Buffey (R-9), Ernie Butterworth (R-1), Clarence Campbell (R-2), Brent Casselman (L-5), Bill Chadwick (R-41, L-2), Fred Chittick (R-4), King Clancy (R-20), Odie Cleghorn (R-12), Kevin Collins (L-31), John D'Amico (L-53), Doug Davies (L-11), Happy Day (L-1), Paul Devorski (R-6), Loring Dolittle (L-2), Scott Driscoll (L-3), Babe Dye (R-2), Ron Ego (L-2), Jack Findlay (R-3), Ron Finn (L-34), Kerry Fraser (R-21), Bill Friday (R-9), Gerard Gauthier (L-10), Ray Getliffe (L-3), Lloyd Gilmour (R-5), Mike Grant (R-2), Georges Gravel (R-7, L-12), Terry Gregson (R-14), Wally Harris (R-8), Mel Harwood (R-1), George Hayes (L-58), Bert Hedges (L-6), Bobby Hewitson (R-13), Tom Hodge (R-2), Bob Hodges (L-7), Bruce Hood (R-9), Mickey Ion (R-30), George Irvine (R-4), Aurel Joliat (L-5), Billy Kean (R-2), Doc Kearns (R-1), Butch Keeling (L-4), Chauncey Kirby (R-3), Swede Knox (L-12), Don Koharski (R-19), Jerry Laflamme (R-4), Norm Lamport (R-4), Brad Lazarowich (L-11), Bryan Lewis (R-7), William MacFarlane (R-5), George Mallinson (R-7), Mush March (L-6), Dan Marouelli (R-13), Lou Marsh (R-7), Jack Marshall (R-2), Alex Martin (R-1), Stan McCabe (L-2), Bert McCaffery (R-1), Bill McCreary (R-30), Hartland McDougall (R-1), Don McFayden (L-7), Hugh McLean (L-4), Charles McVeigh (L-5), Jack Mehlenbacher (R-2), Bob Meldrum (R-7), Eddie Mepham (L-4), John Mitchell (R-4), Randy Mitton (L-3), Denis Morel (R-4), Jean Morin (L-2), Bill Morrison (L-35), Ken Mullins (L-2), Brian Murphy (L-15), Bob Myers (R-6, L-2), Dave Newell (R-10), Tim Nowak (L-3), Frank Patrick (R-2), Matt Pavelich (L-55), Tom Phillips (R-4), Joe Power (R-3), Eddie Powers (R-14), Jim Primeau (L-4), Harvey Pulford (R-7), Percy Quinn (R-4), Mike Rodden (R-5), Alex Romeril (R-5), Art Ross (R-6), Ray Scapinello (L-53), Dan Schachte (L-13), Herbert Scott (R-1), Jay Sharrers (L-6), Pat Shetler (L-5), Rob Shick (R-2), Bruce Sims (L-4), Art Skov (R-17, L-5), Cooper Smeaton (R-14), Ag Smith (R-11, L-2), Brian Sopp (L-3), William Stewart (R-12), Leon Stickle (L-15), Harlow Stiles (R-1), Red Storey (R-14), Harry Trihey (R-5), Frank Udvari (R-25), Andy Van Hellemond (R-35), Stephen Walkom (R-7), Brad Watson (R-5), Mark Wheler (L-9), Ron Wicks (R-4, L-9), Archie Wilcox (L-5), Doug Young (L-2), Weldy Young (R-2)

the champions

FROM STANLEY OF PRESTON

Montreal AAA 1892 1893

Montreal AAA was awarded the Stanley Cup even though the Montreal Hockey Club, which had recently become affiliated with the AAA, formed the basis of the team. The MHC, in fact, at first refused the awarding of the Cup unless it was the acknowledged winner, but the players were later placated by gifts, notably rings, recognizing their achievement. The MAAA's motto was "jungor ut implear"— "I am joined [in the club] in order that I may compete." Today, the Peel St. club has a thriving membership of 2,400 and is one of the more popular centres for exercise and entertainment in the city.

The first Cup winners, Montreal AAA of 1893.

STANLEY CUP AWARDED

Montreal AAA win Stanley Cup based on first place finish

MONTREAL AAA: Tom Paton, James Stewart, Allan Cameron, Haviland Routh, Archie Hodgson, Billy Barlow, Alex Kingan, George Low, Alex Irving

A.H.A. FINAL STANDINGS	GP	W	L	T	GF	GA	Pts*
Montreal AAA	8	7	1	0	38	18	14
Ottawa Generals	8	6	2	0	49	22	12
Montreal Crystals	8	3	5	0	25	34	6
Quebec Hockey Club	8	2	5	1	23	46	5
Montreal Victorias	8	1	6	1	20	35	3

** points are listed here for consistency; such a column did not appear in the standings regularly until 1914*

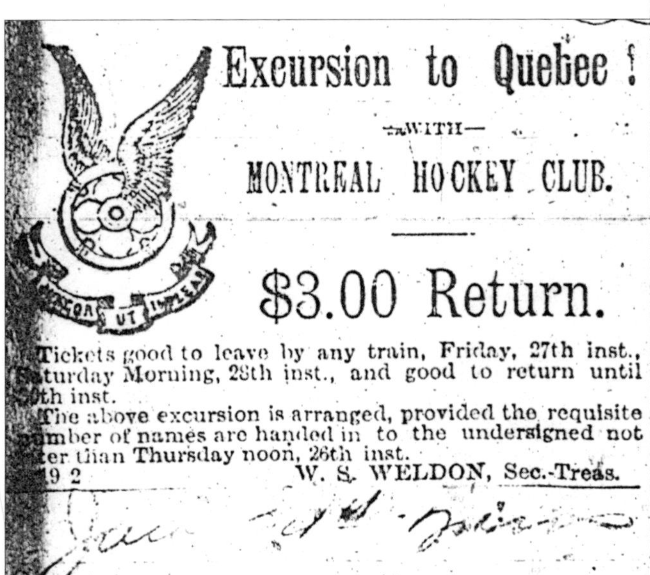

Excursion to Quebec !

—WITH—

MONTREAL HOCKEY CLUB.

$3.00 Return.

Tickets good to leave by any train, Friday, 27th inst., Saturday Morning, 28th inst., and good to return until [illegible]th inst.

The above excursion is arranged, provided the requisite number of names are handed in to the undersigned not later than Thursday noon, 26th inst.

W. S. WELDON, Sec.-Treas.

Advertisement for fans to see their team play on the road.

TOM PATON led all goalies in this AHA season with a 2.30 goals-against average in eight games. By day he was a manufacturer's agent. By night, he was active in the MAAA and was credited with introducing quoits to the club.

JAMES STEWART played point, similar to modern defence. In seven games, he didn't score.

Cover point **ALLAN CAMERON** was a tea and butter merchant for the makers of "Liebling's liquid extract and tonic invigorator."

HAVILAND (HAVIE) ROUTH led the league in goals with 12 in just seven games.

ARCHIE HODGSON ranked second on the team in scoring over the year with eight goals in six games.

BILLY BARLOW was outstanding in the AAA's late-season victory over Ottawa to secure first place.

ALEX KINGAN kept a job as a book-keeper. A forward, he was a seldom-used sub.

GEORGE LOW (a bank clerk) and **ALEX IRVING** (a bookkeeper) were substitute forwards.

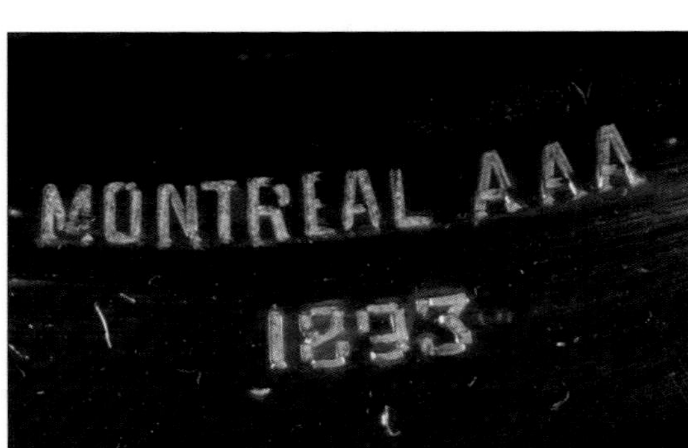

Team engraving from the base of the original Cup

Hockey Championship !

THE DECIDING MATCH!

OTTAWA

vs.

MONTREAL

(Champions),

Victoria Skating Rink,

SATURDAY EVENING, FEBRUARY 18, 1893,

Commencing at 8.30 o'clock.

Admission (to non-subscribers), 25 cents.

39 3 H. L. SHAW, Hon. Sec. M. H. C.

"FAMILY JARS," and "THE APOTHECARY'S MISTAKE" at THE POP to-night. 10 cts.

41 1

(above) An ad for the game that decided the first winner of the Stanley Cup; (left) Billy Barlow's ring.

1893 THE CHAMPIONS
1894 Montreal AAA

Winners for the second year in a row, Montreal won and lost a game to Ottawa during the regular schedule. After the final victory, fans carried the players off the ice triumphantly. A challenge by a team from Osgoode Hall in Toronto, champions of the OHA, was accepted then cancelled because of lack of ice.

STANLEY CUP CHAMPIONSHIP GAME

Montreal AAA win one-game Stanley Cup playoff

*March 23, 1894 Ottawa Capitals 1 at Montreal AAA 3 {Billy Barlow 9:00 2nd half}
Montreal AAA win one-game Stanley Cup playoff

** played at Victoria Rink, Montreal*

MONTREAL AAA: Herbert Collins, Allan Cameron, George James, Billy Barlow, Clare Mussen, Archie Hodgson, Edward O'Brien, Havie Routh, Alex Irving, Arthur "Toad" Waud, Alex Kingan

Montreal AAA, 1893-94

Team engraving from the base of the original Cup

Team engraving from the shoulder of the original Cup

HERBERT COLLINS played in goal every minute this year for the AAA and led the league with only 15 goals allowed in eight games (1.88 GAA).

ALLAN CAMERON was the team's point for the balance of the season.

GEORGE JAMES played cover-point for the AAA in his only Stanley Cup victory.

Weighing only 125 pounds, **BILLY BARLOW** was the Stanley Cup's first hero with his game-winning goal.

CLARE MUSSEN scored once in the two league games he played this season. "Barlow, Hodgson, and Mussen rushed that puck around in a way to make the Ottawa men nervous," according to game reports from the finals.

ARCHIE HODGSON scored two goals in as many playoff games this Stanley Cup season.

EDWARD O'BRIEN was a bank clerk when he wasn't playing hockey.

HAVIE ROUTH scored five goals in the team's season opener, a 7-0 win over Quebec on January 5, 1894.

ARTHUR "TOAD" WAUD and **ALEX IRVING** played but one game with the AHA this year.

ALEX KINGAN scored four goals in as many games during the AHA regular season.

JAMES STEWART was the team's president.

HARRY SHAW was the acting secretary of the club. He took minutes and organized activities, and he later became honourary secretary-treasurer for the CAHL.

A.H.A. FINAL STANDINGS	GP	W	L	T	GF	GA	Pts
Montreal AAA	8	5	3	0	25	15	10*
Ottawa Capitals+	8	5	3	0	24	16	10*
Montreal Victorias	8	5	3	0	36	20	10*
Quebec Hockey Club~	8	5	3	0	26	27	10*
Montreal Crystals	8	0	8	0	10	43	0

** four-way tie forced a playoff to decide a league champion and, additionally, Stanley Cup champion (Montreal AAA beat Montreal Victorias 3-2 in the semi-finals)*
~ withdrew from playoffs
+ as only away (i.e., non-Montreal) team, Ottawa given bye to Stanley Cup finals game

Team engraving from the shoulder of the replica Cup

Montreal Victorias 1894 1895

Montreal Victorias won the Stanley Cup based on first place finish in AHA league play. However, Cup trustees Sweetland and Ross had already accepted a challenge by Queen's against reigning champions MAAA. They ruled that had Queen's defeated MAAA, the University would be declared Cup champs; if MAAA won, the Vics, as league champs, would be declared Stanley Cup holders! The Vics clinched the league title when they beat second-place Ottawa 3-2 on the final day of the schedule. MAAA won its challenge in large part because three Queen's goals were ruled offside by the Quebec referee (the offside rule differed in Ontario and Quebec). The larger Montreal ice surface also caused problems for the Kingston, Ontario representatives.

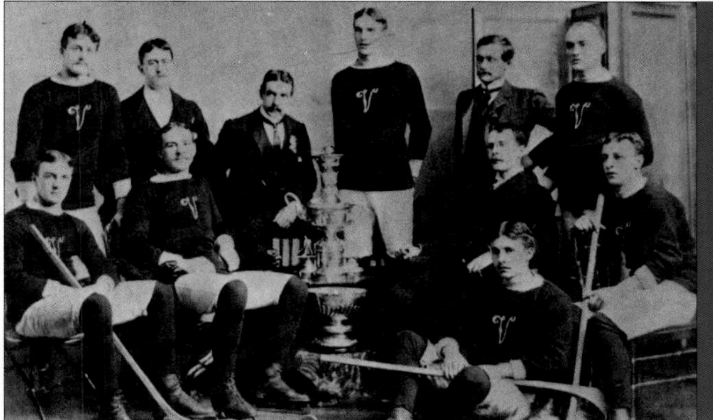

Montreal Victorias, 1894-95

STANLEY CUP CHAMPIONSHIP GAME

Montreal Victorias win Stanley Cup based on first place finish

*March 9, 1895 Queen's University 1 at Montreal AAA 5

** played at Victoria Rink, Montreal*

MONTREAL VICTORIAS: Robert Jones, Harold Henderson, Mike Grant, Shirley Davidson, Bob McDougall, Norman Rankin, Graham Drinkwater, Roland Elliot, William Pullan, Hartland McDougall, Jim Fenwick, A. McDougall

A.H.A. FINAL STANDINGS	GP	W	L	T	GF	GA	Pts
Montreal Victorias	8	6	2	0	35	20	12
Montreal AAA	8	4	4	0	33	22	8
Ottawa Capitals	8	4	4	0	25	24	8
Montreal Crystals*	7	3	4	0	21	39	6
Quebec Hockey Club*+	7	2	5	0	18	27	4

** Crystals-Quebec game voided after Quebec protest that Crystals had used ineligible players*

+ team suspended after players assaulted officials

The Vics in action out of doors in early 1895.

ROBERT JONES played in net for four of the team's eight games, allowing just eight goals.

HAROLD HENDERSON played just three games during the season as a point, not scoring a goal.

Captain **MIKE GRANT** was a brilliant and champion speed skater as well as a fine hockeyist.

SHIRLEY DAVIDSON scored the game-winner in a 3-2 Montreal victory over Ottawa that gave the Vics first place in the league standings. He had been captain and quarterback of the McGill football team.

BOB McDOUGALL scored ten goals this season, second best on the team.

The leading scorer for the Vics, **NORMAN RANKIN** had eleven goals in eight games.

GRAHAM DRINKWATER attended McGill University where he starred in football as well as hockey.

ROLAND ELLIOT played fiercely on defence for a team that allowed just 20 goals in eight games.

Defenceman **WILLIAM PULLAN** appeared in only one game for the Vics and wasn't really considered a member of the team proper.

HARTLAND McDOUGALL was one of four goalies used by the Vics. He gave up nine goals in his two games.

Team engraving from the base of the original Cup

Goalie **JIM FENWICK** played just one game all year, allowing two goals.

One of three McDougalls on the team (though not all brothers), **A.** allowed one goal in his only game in net, a 5-1 win over Ottawa.

G.R. HOOPER was an executive with William Dow & Co. in the city.

W. JACK was the Vics' team president.

P.M. DeSTERNEAK was the team's honourary secretary-treasurer and a bank clerk as well.

FRED MEREDITH, honourary president for Montreal AAA, was a lawyer and partner in Abbotts, Campbell, Meredith.

1895 1896 Winnipeg Victorias

THE CHAMPIONS

February '95

Upon returning to Winnipeg a few days after their challenge victory, the Vics were given a parade, complete with the Stanley Cup travelling in one of the cabs. After many speeches, there was a private party for the team and the Cup was "filled to the brim with champagne." Reports from the *Winnipeg Daily Tribune* were, naturally, slanted for Western readers: "This was the first time the eastern men had to submit to a defeat at the hands of comparative babes in the sport of hockey, and yet it was not only a defeat but a complete whitewash." The Winnipeg fans sung their team song over and over: "Hobble Gobble Razzle Dazzle Sis Boom Bah/Victoria Victoria Rah Rah Rah."

STANLEY CUP CHALLENGE GAME

Winnipeg Victorias win one-game Stanley Cup challenge

*February 14, 1896 Winnipeg Victorias 2 at Montreal Victorias 0 [Whitey Merritt] {Jack Armytage, 1st}

* *played at Victoria Rink, Montreal*

WINNIPEG VICTORIAS: "Whitey" Merritt, Rod Flett, Fred Higginbotham, Jack Armytage, C.J. (Toat) Campbell, Dan Bain, Charles Johnstone, "Attie" Howard

Winnipeg Victorias, 1895-96

A.H.A. FINAL STANDINGS	GP	W	L	T	GF	GA	Pts
Montreal Victorias	8	7	1	0	41	24	14
Ottawa Capitals	8	6	2	0	22	16	12
Quebec Hockey Club	8	4	4	0	23	23	8
Montreal AAA	8	2	6	0	24	33	4
Montreal Shamrocks	8	1	7	0	16	30	2

Team engraving from the base of the original Cup

Born in Goderich in 1862, goalie **GEORGE "WHITEY" MERRITT** was a great lacrosse star and member of Winnipeg's first hockey team. He appeared in the challenge game wearing white cricket pads, the first goalie adorned with leg equipment in hockey's early history. His superb play in the second half as Montreal pressed for a tie proved the key to Winnipeg's victory.

ROD FLETT was a superb athlete who played baseball, football, and lacrosse with skill. A quick stickhandler, he was Winnipeg's cover point, even though the 23-year old had been playing hockey for just four years!

FRED HIGGINBOTHAM was a heavy hitter and a good "lifter," the primary means of getting the puck out of the defensive end. Just a few months later, he was killed while playing with Joe Hall's children. He was riding a pony in the back yard when a clothesline caught him around the neck. The fall killed Higginbotham.

Captain and forward, **JACK ARMYTAGE** was among the fittest of the game's early stars and as a result was a great second half player. In the first challenge, his rushes were so impressive even the Montreal fans cheered him. The 25-year old Fergus, Ontario native also acted as the team's coach.

"TOAT" CAMPBELL scored the insurance goal in Winnipeg's stunning 2-0 win over Montreal. Born in Erin, Ontario in 1874, he was famous for his bank shots, considered the best in the game, and for shooting hard from a long way out or in full flight.

A superb cyclist and lacrossist, **DAN BAIN** was often called Manitoba's greatest athlete. He was heart and soul of the team's Cup victory, though he was expelled with Henderson of Montreal early in the second half of the challenge. He kept his stick from the game and recorded other names of non-playing teammates: "Bobby, spare/Joe, mascot/Abe, manager/Redmond, guide."

CHARLES JOHNSTONE was a seldom-used spare who had little impact on the outcome of either challenge. He was a member of Winnipeg's champion team at the Canadian and National Regatta and had been skating for only two seasons.

"ATTIE" HOWARD had a quiet game in the Cup-winning challenge but scored twice in a losing cause in the re-match. Born in St. Andrews, Manitoba in 1871, he had a superb shot noted for its accuracy, and had been playing with the Vics since 1891.

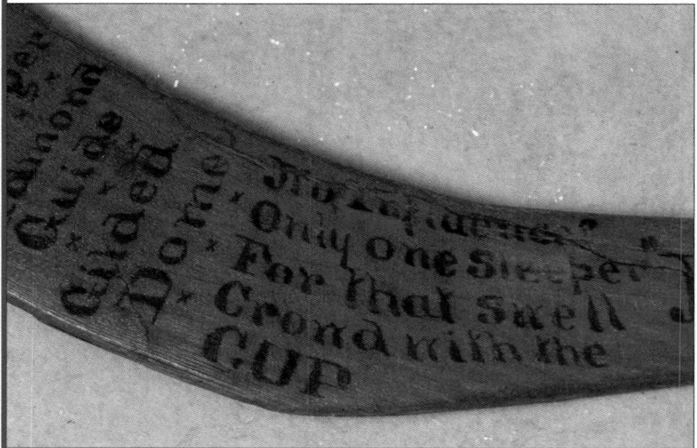

Detail of Whitey Merritt's goal stick used in the 1896 challenge game vs. Montreal.

Montreal Victorias 1895 1896

December '96

After losing the Cup in a challenge but winning the league championship at the end of the season, the Montreal Vics challenged Winnipeg right back. The match, played prior to the start of the following season, returned the Cup to Montreal. There was a celebration at the Victoria Rink, with a band in attendance and the Cup on display. After the game, players from both teams met at the Manitoba Hotel where captain Grant was officially presented the Cup.

Montreal Victorias, Cup champs in December 1896

STANLEY CUP CHALLENGE GAME

Montreal Victorias win one-game Stanley Cup challenge

*December 30, 1896 Montreal Victorias 6 at Winnipeg Victorias 5 {Ernie McLea, 2nd}

** played at Granite Rink, Winnipeg*

MONTREAL VICTORIAS: Harold Henderson, Mike Grant, Bob McDougall, Graham Drinkwater, Shirley Davidson, Ernie McLea, Robert Jones, Cam Davidson, David Gillelan, Stanley Willett, William Wallace, Gordon Lewis, Hartland McDougall

== McIntyre ==

Skating Rink.

W. H SEACH, Manager.

RESERVE SEAT SALE

for the championship match will open in the rink at 10.30 a. m. sharp, on Thursday, December 24.

(above) detail of Whitey Merritt's stick commemorating the challenge game: newspaper ad for tickets to the Cup challenge of December 1896.

HAROLD HENDERSON was a reliable player whose excellence as a skater and fearless competitor was rarely highlighted, though he was always respected by opponents.

Known for his end-to-end rushes from defence, captain **MIKE GRANT** was brilliant in the challenge game. He started playing organized hockey at age nine, with the Junior Crystals, in Montreal.

BOB McDOUGALL led the AHA in scoring with ten goals in six games. Just twenty years of age, he attended McGill University for a year before securing a job at the Bank of Montreal.

GRAHAM DRINKWATER scored the go-ahead goal in the second half. He teamed with Davidson and McDougall to form a deadly combination.

At 5'6" 150 lbs., **SHIRLEY DAVIDSON** was the outstanding player of the first challenge loss and scored twice to help Montreal recover the Cup later in the season.

The 20-year old **ERNIE McLEA** also played football for McGill this season. He scored the Cup-winning goal late in what was quickly called the finest hockey game ever played.

Goalie **ROBERT JONES** played every game for his team this season. In Montreal's successful re-match the *Winnipeg Daily Tribune* said: "He is certainly a splendid custodian...He had many shots to stop, and he acquitted himself in such a manner that nothing else can be said but that he did his duty well."

Team engraving from the base of the replica Cup

CAM DAVIDSON was a forward with the team.

A spare, **DAVID GILLELAN** played in neither challenge.

Like Gillelan, **STANLEY WILLETT** appeared only in league play. He was the owner of Richelieu Woollen Mills as well as Chambly Shovel Works.

WILLIAM WALLACE played only one league game. In the first challenge, he was injured and had to remove himself from play.

GORDON LEWIS became the team's number-one goalie after the challenge victory.

HARTLAND McDOUGALL, although no relation to Bob, was also born in Lennoxville, Quebec and, like his namesake, worked at the Bank of Montreal.

1896 THE CHAMPIONS

1897 Montreal Victorias

The Vics accepted a challenge from the Ottawa Capitals, champions of the Central Canada Association league, after finishing first in the AHA with an impressive 7-1 record. Intended to be a best-of-three series, the challenge was curtailed after one lop-sided victory.

STANLEY CUP CHALLENGE GAME

Montreal Victorias win one-game Stanley Cup challenge

*December 27, 1897 Ottawa Capitals 2 at Montreal Victorias 15

** played at Victoria Rink, Montreal*

MONTREAL VICTORIAS: Gordon Lewis, Harold Henderson, Mike Grant, Cam Davidson, Graham Drinkwater, Bob McDougall, Ernie McLea, Shirley Davidson, Hartland McDougall, Jack Ewing, Percy Molson, David Gillelan, Dan McLellan

Montreal Victorias, 1896-97

Team engraving from the base of the original Cup

Team engraving from the shoulder of the original Cup

Goaler **GORDON LEWIS** played every game this year for the Vics in leading the team to their third straight league championship.

Point man **HAROLD HENDERSON** didn't miss a game this year, his third Cup-winning season with the Vics.

After retiring in 1902, **MIKE GRANT** turned to officiating, causing a stir in one series when he refereed wearing a derby hat.

CAM DAVIDSON played all year with Vics, league play and Cup challenge both.

Injuries limited **GRAHAM DRINKWATER** to four games of AHA play, but he was front and centre during the challenge game in combination with Davidson and Bob McDougall.

BOB McDOUGALL was one of many Montrealers who had learned the game at Lennoxville school. McDougall had been a half back with Montreal's provincial championship football team but quit two years' previous because of a shoulder injury.

After scoring eight goals in as many games in AHA play, **ERNIE McLEA** found himself on the bench for the challenge. The four-year Vics veteran had also played at McGill while still in school.

Like Hartland McDougall, **SHIRLEY DAVIDSON** played only in the lop-sided challenge. He was a swift skater noted for his ability to dodge, and his father was the Honourable Mr. Justice Davidson.

Defenceman **HARTLAND McDOUGALL** was brought in as a ringer for the challenge game. A "general utility man," he was a good skater who had played one season as goalie before finding his true calling as a defenceman.

JACK EWING, PERCY MOLSON, DAVID GILLELAN, and **DAN McLELLAN** were spares who saw limited action during the season.

A.H.A. FINAL STANDINGS	GP	W	L	T	GF	GA	Pts
Montreal Victorias	8	7	1	0	48	26	14
Ottawa Capitals	8	5	3	0	25	18	10
Montreal AAA	8	5	3	0	31	26	10
Quebec Hockey Club	8	2	6	0	22	46	4
Montreal Shamrocks	8	1	7	0	27	37	2

Team photo of the Victorias later in the season after having won the Stanley Cup.

Montreal Victorias 1897 1898

The Vics went undefeated in league play and again led the MAAA in goal scoring by a wide margin to retain the Cup for another year without challenge.

The Victorias of Montreal, repeat champions

STANLEY CUP FINALS

Montreal Victorias win Stanley Cup based on first place finish and were not challenged by any team.

MONTREAL VICTORIAS: Gordon Lewis, Hartland McDougall, Mike Grant, Graham Drinkwater, Cam Davidson, Bob McDougall, Ernie McLea, Frank Richardson, Jack Ewing

A.H.A. FINAL STANDINGS	GP	W	L	T	GF	GA	Pts
Montreal Victorias	8	8	0	0	53	33	16
Montreal AAA	8	5	3	0	34	21	10
Montreal Shamrocks	8	3	5	0	25	36	6
Quebec Hockey Club	8	2	6	0	29	35	4
Ottawa Capitals	8	2	6	0	28	44	4

GORDON LEWIS played three games in goal, surrendering a respectable nine goals.

A point not noted for his scoring, **HARTLAND McDOUGALL** had three goals in eight league games.

MIKE GRANT played in his fourth Stanley Cup in as many winters. The captain of his third team (after Crystals and Shamrocks), he was likely the first defenceman to rush the puck.

After retiring, **GRAHAM DRINKWATER** became a stockbroker in Montreal with the firm Oswald, Drinkwater, and Graham, a prosperous business which continued to flourish long after his death in 1946.

CAM DAVIDSON led all scorers in the AHA with 14 goals in seven games, one more than Clare McKerrow of Montreal AAA.

A forward, **BOB McDOUGALL** placed third in league scoring with 12 goals in eight games. He was admired for his great speed and accurate shot.

ERNIE McLEA had four goals in seven league games.

The Vics' other goaler, **FRANK RICHARDSON**, played five games in leading his team to a perfect season.

A spare, **JACK EWING** played just one game all year.

Team engraving from the base of the original Cup.

Team engraving from the shoulder of the replica Cup

Others: **W. JACK** (honourary president), **F.H. WILSON** (honourary vice-president), **P.M. DeSTERNEAK** (president), **J.S. BISHOP** (honourary secretary-treasurer)

Team engraving from the shoulder of the original Cup

1898
1899 Montreal Victorias

THE CHAMPIONS

February '99

The Montreal Vics withstood a challenge from Winnipeg, but not without incident. Late in the second game with the score 3-2, Bob McDougall of the Vics slashed Gingras of Winnipeg violently. Gingras was carried from the ice, but referee Findlay called only a two-minute minor after assessing Gingras' condition. Incensed, the Winnipeggers left the ice. Insulted, Findlay went home. Officials took a sleigh to the official's house and persuaded him to return to the rink. Once there, he gave Winnipeg players fifteen minutes to return to the ice themselves, and when they refused he disqualified the team and declared the Vics winners.

STANLEY CUP CHALLENGE

Montreal Victorias win best-of-two total-goals Stanley Cup challenge 5-3

*February 15, 1899 Winnipeg Victorias 1 at Montreal Victorias 2
*February 18, 1899 Winnipeg Victorias 2 at Montreal Victorias 3 {B. McDougall, 2nd half}

** played at Westmount Arena, Montreal*

MONTREAL VICTORIAS: Gordon Lewis, Mike Grant, Graham Drinkwater, Cam Davidson, Bob McDougall, Ernie McLea, Frank Richardson, Jack Ewing, Russell Bowie, Douglas Acer, Fred McRobie

The Montreal Victorias, victors for a fourth successive time

Team engraving from the base of the original Cup

Team engraving from the base of the replica Cup

In his three games in goal, **GORDON LEWIS** allowed just seven goals. He recorded a shutout and had a record of 2-1 during the half a season he played.

After retiring, **MIKE GRANT**, the 5'10" 170 lbs. native of Montreal, organized hockey exhibitions in the United States to help promote the qualities of the game.

Captain **GRAHAM DRINKWATER** scored the winner in game one of the February '99 challenge with just seconds left to play, sending the crowd into a collective delirium.

CAM DAVIDSON later became a practising doctor, but this year he was a scorer for the Vics with nine goals in seven games.

BOB McDOUGALL tied game one with a goal in the final minute, and scored the Cup-winner in game two. During the regular season, he scored all his seven goals on the season in one game, February 11 vs. Ottawa.

ERNIE McLEA scored four times in four games.

Goaltender **FRANK RICHARDSON** split the duties this year with Lewis, allowing 16 goals in four games (3-1 record) to start the season.

JACK EWING scored seven goals in five games.

A great stick-handler, **RUSSELL BOWIE** turned down a grand piano as inducement to turn pro with the Montreal Wanderers. This was his first year of senior hockey.

DOUGLAS ACER scored four goals in two games.

FRED McROBIE played three games but didn't score a goal.

Others: **J.S. BISHOP** (honourary secretary-treasurer), **F.H. WILSON** (honourary president), **F.C. BUDDEN** (president)

OFFICERS VICTORIA HOCKEY CLUB
1899-1900.

HON. H. J. MACDONALD, PATRON. E. L. DREWRY, HON. PRES.
J. C. G. ARMYTAGE, PRES. J. S. CARTER, VICE-PRES.
D. H. BAIN, CAPTAIN. W. E. ROBINSON, SEC.-TREAS.

EXECUTIVE COMMITTEE.
E. B. NIXON. A. CODE. G. H. MERRITT.

SENIOR TEAM
THAT VISITED MONTREAL LAST FEBRUARY, AND IN THEIR ATTEMPT TO SECURE ONCE MORE FOR WINNIPEG THE STANLEY CHAMPIONSHIP CUP, PLAYED THE FINEST HOCKEY EVER WITNESSED

D. BAIN. G. H. MERRITT. R. M. FLETT. A. GINGRAS.
CHAS. JOHNSTON. W. R. ROXBOROUGH. T. CAMPBELL.
SPARE MEN: M. FLETT. S. MACDONALD. TRAINER: M. HOOPER.

DINNER GIVEN BY MR. E. L. DREWRY
TO THE
PLAYERS WHO VISITED MONTREAL.

Notice of a dinner given the Winnipeg Victorias in honour of their noble efforts to wrest the Cup from their Montreal counterparts.

Montreal Shamrocks 1898 1899

March '99

The Montreal Shamrocks changed their name from Crystals prior to the 1895-96 season as they became affiliated with the Shamrock AAA. In order to keep the senior league Ottawa Capitals out the AHA, teams formed a new league called the Canadian Amateur Hockey League. They won the league title after a ferocious 1-0 win over Vics on March 1 before some 8,000 fans. The Shamrocks defeated a team of students in their only challenge of the winter. It was an odd game in that it was played under Ontario rules for the first half and Quebec rules for the second half. This came about under a provision for all Cup challenges—in a case where both teams could not come to terms on which regulations to play under, both would be used.

The Montreal Shamrocks, 1898-99

STANLEY CUP CHALLENGE GAME

Montreal Shamrocks win one-game Stanley Cup challenge

*March 14, 1899 Queen's University 2 at Montreal Shamrocks 6 {Trihey}

* *played at Westmount Arena, Montreal*

MONTREAL SHAMROCKS: Jim McKenna, Frank Tansey, Frank Wall, Harry Trihey, Art Farrell, Fred Scanlon, Jack Brannen, John Dobby, Charles Hoerner

A.H.A. FINAL STANDINGS	GP	W	L	T	GF	GA	Pts
Montreal Shamrocks	8	7	1	0	40	21	14
Montreal Victorias	8	6	2	0	44	23	12
Ottawa Capitals	8	4	4	0	21	43	8
Montreal AAA	8	3	5	0	30	29	6
Quebec Hockey Club	8	0	8	0	12	31	0

Shamrocks win Stanley Cup based on first place finish

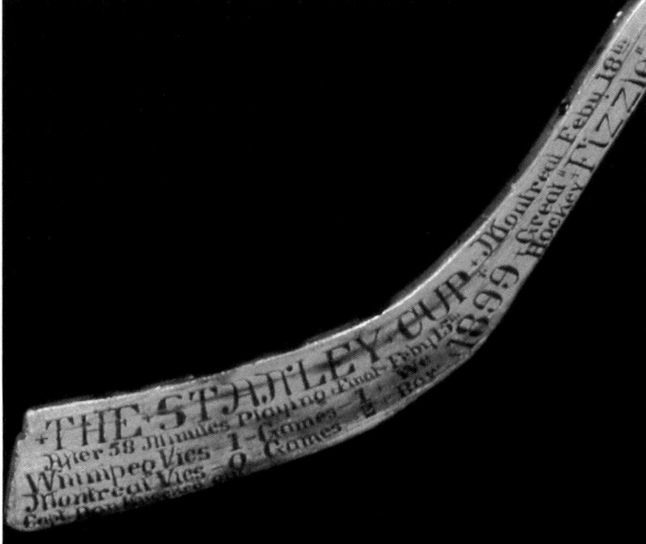

Detail of a Winnipeg Victorias stick decorated with results of the hockey season leading to the Stanley Cup.

JIM McKENNA played goal all year, including the challenge game versus Queen's.

FRANK TANSEY played point, a reliable rock on defence even though he didn't score a goal all season.

FRANK WALL was the team's cover point, easily outclassing his Queen's counterpart Merrill during the challenge.

Captain **HARRY TRIHEY** scored ten goals in one regular season game, vs. Quebec on February 4, 1899. He played just five seasons, retiring in 1900 to become president of the Canadian Amateur Hockey League (CAHL).

ART FARRELL played on a line with Trihey and Scanlon, one of the first times an entire line was used as an entity rather than just a group of individual stars. Later this year he wrote *Hockey: Canada's Royal Winter Game*, the earliest extant book devoted to the game.

FRED SCANLON had a terrific shot and possessed remarkable endurance during games, known to play an entire game without substitution or loss of effectiveness.

JACK BRANNEN received his degree in medicine from McGill University in 1901.

JOHN DOBBY and **CHARLES HOERNER** were seldom-used subs.

Team engraving from the base of the original Cup

Details from a Winnipeg Victorias stick with a complete summary of games and players handwritten on it.

1899 THE CHAMPIONS

1900 Montreal Shamrocks

Only a meaningless loss to Quebec on the final day of the season sullied an otherwise perfect record for the Irishmen. In the challenge against the Vics, the Shamrocks concentrated on defence to shut down the high-scoring Western seven led by Dan Bain and Tony Gingras. They defeated the "Noble Seven" of Winnipeg in three games, though the next year the results would be reversed.

STANLEY CUP CHALLENGES

Montreal Shamrocks win Stanley Cup based on first place finish

*February 12, 1900	Winnipeg Victorias 4 at Montreal Shamrocks 3
*February 14, 1900	Winnipeg Victorias 2 at Montreal Shamrocks 3
*February 15, 1900	Winnipeg Victorias 4 at Montreal Shamrocks 5 {Harry Trihey, 2nd half}
	Montreal Shamrocks win best-of-three Stanley Cup challenge 2-1
*March 5, 1900	Halifax Crescents 2 at Montreal Shamrocks 10
*March 7, 1900	Halifax Crescents 0 at Montreal Shamrocks 11 [Joe McKenna]
	Montreal Shamrocks win best-of-three Stanley Cup challenge 2-0

** played at Westmount Arena, Montreal*

MONTREAL SHAMROCKS: Joe McKenna, Frank Tansey, Frank Wall, Art Farrell, Fred Scanlon, Harry Trihey, Jack Brannen

Montreal Shamrocks, 1899-1900

C.A.H.L. FINAL STANDINGS	GP	W	L	T	GF	GA	Pts
Montreal Shamrocks	8	7	1	0	49	26	14
Montreal AAA	8	5	3	0	34	36	10
Ottawa Capitals	8	4	4	0	28	19	8
Montreal Victorias	8	2	6	0	44	55	4
Quebec Hockey Club	8	2	6	0	33	52	4

Team engraving from the base of the original Cup

Team engraving from the shoulder of the replica Cup

JOE McKENNA played in goal all seven league games this year. The previous season, he won the provincial championship of British Columbia as a lacrosse player.

A jeweller by trade, **FRANK TANSEY** was the low scorer on the team, though he was a superb defender. He missed next year's challenge because of illness, and not coincidentally Montreal lost.

Cover-point **FRANK WALL** scored four goals in five challenge games and then retired to become a referee. He also worked in a wholesale house during his playing days.

ART FARRELL scored four goals in both games of the challenge vs. Halifax and later scored five in a single game, March 2, 1901 vs. Quebec. He worked in his father's store in the daytime, but in 1906 he contracted tuberculosis and died in a sanatorium three years later.

FRED SCANLON formed one of the great forward lines of the era, with Trihey and Farrell, and was inducted into the Hockey Hall of Fame because of his great shot, endurance, and remarkable play on this line.

While leading the league with 17 goals, Shamrocks captain **HARRY TRIHEY** also scored seven times in the Winnipeg challenge and five more against Halifax. After retiring in 1901, he opened a law practise in Montreal and was a Lieutenant Colonel in the Irish Rangers during WWI.

A forward, **JACK BRANNEN** received his doctor of medicine from McGill University the following year.

As with last year, **CHARLES HOERNER** was a spare, but this season he didn't play a single minute with the team.

Others: **W.H. KEARNEY** (director), **H. McLAUGHLIN** (president), **C.F. SMITH** (director), **C.M. HART** (vice-president), **B. DUNPHY** (trainer), **C. FOLEY** (trainer)

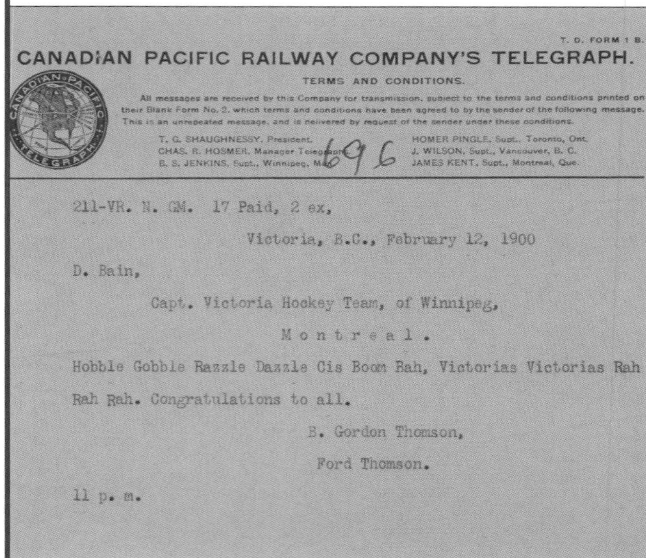

T. D. FORM 1 B.

CANADIAN PACIFIC RAILWAY COMPANY'S TELEGRAPH.

TERMS AND CONDITIONS.

All messages are received by this Company for transmission, subject to the terms and conditions printed on their Blank Form No. 2, which terms and conditions have been agreed to by the sender of the following message. This is an unrepeated message, and is delivered by request of the sender under these conditions.

T. G. SHAUGHNESSY, President. CHAS. R. HOSMER, Manager Telegraphs. B. S. JENKINS, Supt., Winnipeg, Man.
HOMER PINGLE, Supt., Toronto, Ont. J. WILSON, Supt., Vancouver, B. C. JAMES KENT, Supt., Montreal, Que.

696

211-VR. N. GM. 17 Paid, 2 ex,

Victoria, B.C., February 12, 1900

D. Bain,

Capt. Victoria Hockey Team, of Winnipeg,

Montreal.

Hobble Gobble Razzle Dazzle Cis Boom Bah, Victorias Victorias Rah Rah Rah. Congratulations to all.

E. Gordon Thomson,

Ford Thomson.

11 p. m.

Telegram of support to Dan Bain and the Winnipeg Victorias from friends back home on the eve of their challenge series in Montreal

Winnipeg Victorias 1900 1901

The challenge games were broadcast back to Winnipeg and throngs of fans listened in rapture in the Clarendon, Queen's, and Leland Hotels as the game's drama unfolded. The only player missing from the previous championship team was Frank Tansey who was sick and forced to watch in street clothes. Prior to the challenge, all Vics players were given a rabbit's foot in a silver case for good luck, provided by a local Winnipeg jeweller. Game two, won in overtime, was considered the most exciting in Cup history. The Cup was in the hands of Andrew McKerrow, one of the umpires, but he could not be found after the game and the Vics' late-night celebrations were tainted by the Cup's absence.

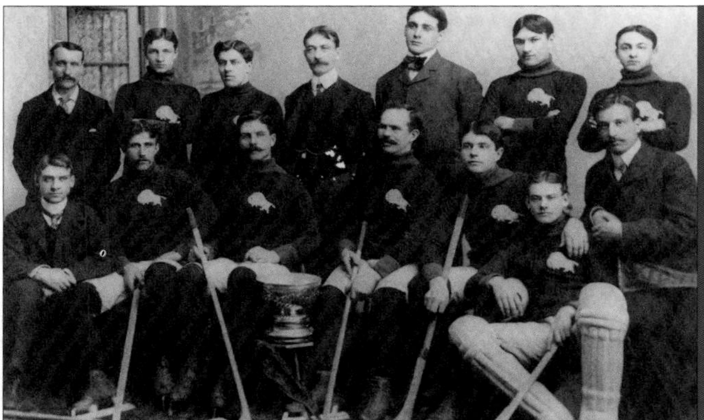

Winnipeg Victorias, 1900-01

STANLEY CUP CHALLENGE

Winnipeg Victorias win best-of-three Stanley Cup challenge 2-0

*January 29, 1901 Winnipeg Victorias 4 at Montreal Shamrocks 3
*January 31, 1901 Winnipeg Victorias 2 at Montreal Shamrocks 1 {Dan Bain 4:00 OT}

** played at Westmount Arena, Montreal*

WINNIPEG VICTORIAS: Burke Wood, Jack Marshall, Tony Gingras, Charlie Johnstone, Rod Flett, Magnus Flett, Dan Bain, Art Brown

C.A.H.L. FINAL STANDINGS	GP	W	L	T	GF	GA	Pts
Ottawa Capitals	8	7	0	1	33	20	15
Montreal Victorias	8	4	3	1	45	32	9
Montreal Shamrocks	8	4	4	0	30	25	8
Montreal AAA	8	3	5	0	28	37	6
Quebec Hockey Club	8	1	7	0	21	43	2

A puck used during the CAHL season in 1901, virtually identical to that which is used today.

After Harry Trihey was forced out of game two with an injured hand, Winnipeg put **BURKE WOOD** to the bench to even the sides, as per the rules of the day. He was the youngest player on the team and had scored the winner in game one in the dying moments.

Although **JACK MARSHALL** was a spare for the Vics, Montreal AAA recruited him and convinced him to stay in that city where he became a regular the following winter.

TONY GINGRAS had been the unequivocal star the previous year in defeat, receiving a floral bouquet prior to game three in respect of his great stick-handling skills. His great rushes set up four of Winnipeg's six goals, though leagues didn't officially count assists.

CHARLIE JOHNSTONE was born in Ontario in 1873 but moved to Winnipeg at age four. He became a noted oarsman, helping Winnipeg win gold in the Canadian and National regattas. After retiring from hockey, he coached at the Winnipeg Rowing Club for many years.

A veteran of hockey since 1891, **ROD FLETT** twice ventured East to fight Montreal for the Cup but came up short both times before this victory. He, Bain, and Johnstone are the only three to have won the Cup in 1896.

MAGNUS FLETT, cover-point, was new to the team. Paired with his brother, Rod, he proved efficient as a checker and lifter.

Team engraving from the base of the original Cup

Captain **DAN BAIN** played the entire first game of the series wearing a mask to protect an eye injury, though he ran into Farrell near the end of a game and had to retire. He skated like the wind and held both the mile and half-mile bike records in Manitoba.

An able successor to Whitey Merritt, goalie **ART BROWN** appeared nervous at first but settled down to make some big saves at critical times during the challenge games.

JACK ARMYTAGE was a former Cup champ as a player for the 1896 Winnipeg Vics who retired to become the team's president for this year's Cup win.

1901 THE CHAMPIONS

1902 Winnipeg Victorias

January '02

Chummy Hill of Toronto scored a goal in the challenge versus the Winnipeg Vics in which the puck split in two and only half went in the net. The goal counted! Though they lost, the Torontos certainly did not embarrass themselves in the face of inferior preparation. "It seemed ridiculous a week ago for a team from Toronto, a city where the ice is really not fit for practise purposes until January, to anticipate a victory over seven men in a position to get into training at the end of November and keep to shape without soft spells to interfere with them," suggested one report. After defeating the Wellingtons, the Vics held a banquet at the Queen's Hotel in Winnipeg with the Cup on display.

STANLEY CUP CHALLENGE

Winnipeg Victorias win best-of-three Stanley Cup challenge 2-0

*January 21, 1902 Toronto Wellingtons 3 at Winnipeg Victorias 5
*January 23, 1902 Toronto Wellingtons 3 at Winnipeg Victorias 5 {Scanlon 9:00 2nd half}

** played at Winnipeg Auditorium*

WINNIPEG VICTORIAS: Burke Wood, Tony Gingras, Charlie Johnstone, Rod Flett, Magnus Flett, Dan Bain, Fred Scanlon, Dr. Fred Cadham, Art Brown

Team engraving from the base of the original Cup

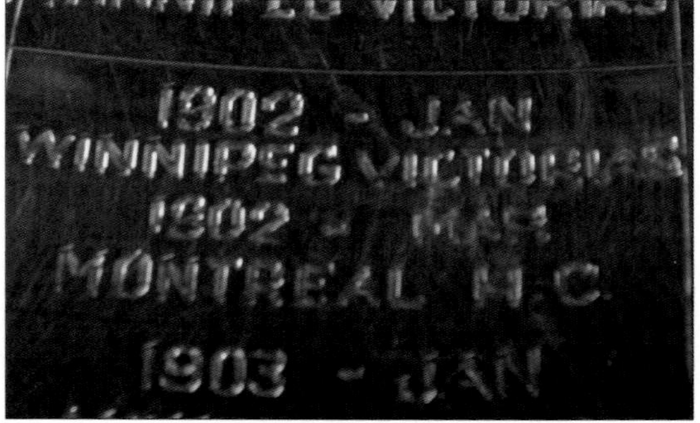

Team engraving from the shoulder of the replica Cup

BURKE WOOD had been a new addition to the team the previous season. He proved to be a spectacular scoring forward who had two goals in the Vics' 5-3 win in game one of the challenge against Toronto.

Again the outstanding player of the challenge versus the Toronto Wellingtons, **TONY GINGRAS**, the "Flying Frenchman," skated faster and longer than anyone else on ice. He scored two game-winning goals in the Montreal AAA challenge.

CHARLES JOHNSTONE dislocated his shoulder in practise leading up to the challenge and didn't play at all vs. Toronto. He later worked at a wholesale house for years.

The ignominious **ROD FLETT** deflected the puck into his own net in game one of the challenge against the Wellingtons.

MAGNUS FLETT played the entire second half of game one against Toronto with damaged ribs, one in a long line of hockey players who battled through short-term pain for the eternal glory of the Stanley Cup. "Magnus is of the right kind of grit, however, and is a hard man to kill, and he pluckily stayed out the fight," according to accounts.

Captain **DAN BAIN** was a lifelong member of the Vics, the team's leader who was in his final season as a player.

This represented **FRED SCANLON'S** third Cup (1899, 1900). He had played for the Shamrocks the previous year.

In 1901, the 18-year-old, 120-lbs. future doctor, **FRED CADHAM**, went with the Vics to Montreal as a spare. This time, he was a star, and a year later he became team captain. After retiring, he became a noted bacteriologist.

Goalie **ART BROWN** shut out the AAA in game one (a rare feat in hockey's early days) and almost stole a victory for the team in game three of the return challenge. He ended his career with the Winnipeg Rowing Club.

Team president **JACK ARMYTAGE** and his wife were presented a large bouquet of flowers by the players after the victory.

C.A.H.L. FINAL STANDINGS	GP	W	L	T	GF	GA	Pts
Montreal AAA	8	6	2	0	39	15	12
Ottawa Capitals	8	5	3	0	35	15	10
Montreal Victorias	8	4	4	0	36	25	8
Quebec Hockey Club	8	4	4	0	26	34	8
Montreal Shamrocks	8	1	7	0	15	62	2

Montreal AAA wins league title and right to challenge Winnipeg for the Stanley Cup

The Toronto Wellingtons, unsuccessful challengers in January 1902

1901–1902 Montreal AAA

March '02

It was from their play during the third game of the finals that this Montreal AAA team earned the nickname "Little Men of Iron," after fending off the bigger and more violent Westerners and inspiring *Montreal Star* reporter Peter Spanjaardt to refer to them in those terms. The sobriquet later transferred to the Wanderers, where numerous members of this team later played. Upon their return, they were accorded a great reception at Windsor Station. Upon stepping off the train, the players were "drawn in sleighs by man-power from the station to the MAAA club-house when thousands of admirers refused to allow the horses to pull their heroes. They unhitched the horses and pulled the sleighs themselves, through the snow and slush."

Montreal AAA, 1901-02

STANLEY CUP CHALLENGE

Montreal AAA win best-of-three Stanley Cup challenge 2-1

*March 13, 1902 Montreal AAA 0 at Winnipeg Victorias 1
(Tony Gingras, 12:00 1st half) [Art Brown]
*March 15, 1902 Montreal AAA 5 at Winnipeg Victorias 0 [Billy Nicholson]
*March 17, 1902 Montreal AAA 2 at Winnipeg Victorias 1
{Jack Marshall, 1st half}

** played at Winnipeg Auditorium*

MONTREAL AAA: Tom Hodge, Dickie Boon, Billy Nicholson, Archie Hooper, Billy Bellingham, Charles Liffiton, Jack Marshall, Roland Elliott, Jim Gardner

Auditorium Rink

Monday Night
Wednesday Night.
Friday Night
Saturday Afternoon
Saturday Night

General admission tickets for Stanley Cup Matches now on sale at 435 Main street.
Reserved seats for Stanley Cup Matches now on sale at 435 Main street.

AUDITORIUM RINK CO. LTD.

Newspaper ad in support of ticket sales for the Montreal-Winnipeg Stanley Cup series

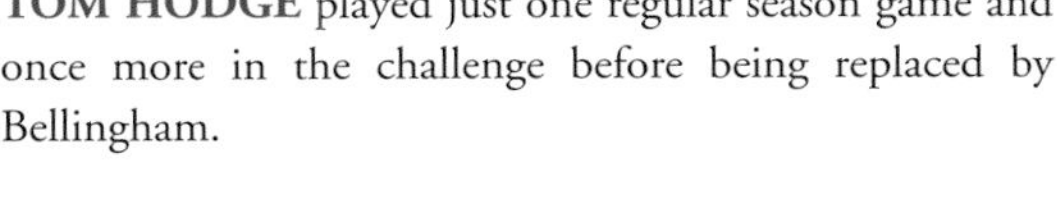

TOM HODGE played just one regular season game and once more in the challenge before being replaced by Bellingham.

Weighing only 130 pounds, **DICKIE BOON** was nonetheless a great rusher and poke-checker. He played the last half of the final game with one eye shut from a bad cut. After retiring, he became manager of the Wanderers.

One of the heaviest goalies of all time, **BILLY NICHOLSON** barely touched the puck in game two of the challenge, such was his team's dominance.

Playing on a line with Marshall and Gardner, **ARCHIE HOOPER** led the league with 17 goals, including nine in one game against the Shamrocks.

BILLY BELLINGHAM replaced Hodge for game two of the challenge after the latter proved ineffectual in the opening contest.

CHARLES LIFFITON played with the Wanderers in 1905, a team that valued his play so much that it once chartered a private train to get him to a road game on time after he missed the regular train because of work duties.

Recruited from the Cup-winning Winnipeg team of the previous year, **JACK MARSHALL** led the Montrealers to the Cup, scoring the winning goal in the deciding game.

ROLAND ELLIOTT went scoreless in seven games during the season and didn't play at all in the challenge.

Team engraving from the base of the original Cup

JIM GARDNER played in one game with Montreal the previous year and was just beginning a long and distinguished career in hockey.

Trainer **PAUL LEFEBVRE** practised his craft for more than half a century in Montreal with many teams at many levels of organized sport.

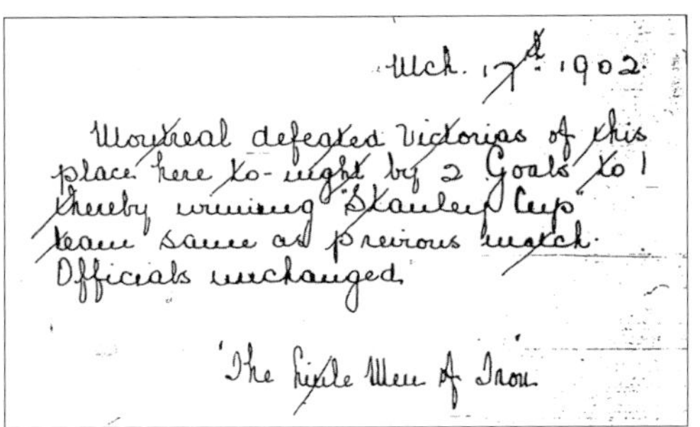

Mch. 17th 1902

Montreal defeated Victorias of this place here to-night by 2 Goals to 1 thereby winning Stanley Cup. Team same as previous match. Officials unchanged.

'The Little Men of Iron.

Notes from the minute-book of the Montreal AAA recording the team's Cup victory the night of March 17, 1902.

1902 THE CHAMPIONS
1903 Montreal AAA

February '03

This was the last year of the great Winnipeg-Montreal rivalry that had been maintained for the better part of a decade and some 15 challenge games, though it ended with a bang and what was thought to be one of the great series of early hockey. The victorious AAA players, as well as the coach and secretary, were given "diamond rings to the value of one hundred dollars each" and also photographs for their triumphs.

STANLEY CUP CHALLENGE

Montreal AAA win best-of-three Stanley Cup challenge 2-1

*January 29, 1903	Winnipeg Victorias 1 at Montreal AAA 8
*January 31, 1903	Winnipeg Victorias 2 at Montreal AAA 2 (27:00 OT—suspended by curfew and result discarded)
*February 2, 1903	Winnipeg Victorias 4 at Montreal AAA 2
*February 4, 1903	Winnipeg Victorias 1 at Montreal AAA 4 {Phillips 6:00 1st half}

** played at Westmount Arena, Montreal*

MONTREAL AAA: Tom Hodge, Dickie Boon, Billy Nicholson, Tom Phillips, Art Hooper, Billy Bellingham, Charles Liffiton, Jack Marshall, Jim Gardner, Cecil Blachford, George Smith

Team engraving from the bowl of the Stanley Cup

C.A.H.L. FINAL STANDINGS	GP	W	L	T	GF	GA	Pts
Ottawa Senators+	8	6	2	0	47	26	12~
Montreal Victorias	8	6	2	0	48	33	12~
Montreal AAA*	7	4	3	0	34	19	8
Quebec Hockey Club*	7	3	4	0	30	46	6
Montreal Shamrocks	8	0	8	0	21	56	0

** one Quebec-MAAA league game postponed but never re-played*
+ team became known as Silver Seven after winning Stanley Cup
~ because of a tie in the standings, a home-and-home playoff was held to determine both league and Stanley Cup champions

The question of challenging for the Stanley
Cup was then discussed at length. It was finally
moved by Mr. Cameron, seconded by Mr. Chitty and
unanimously ~~carried~~ agreed that a challenge
be sent at once to the Trustees of the Cup, suggesting
March 13th and 15th as dates for the matches and
should a third game be necessary, March 17th.
It was moved by Mr Andrews. Seconded by Mr
Boon, that Mr Chitty be authorized to leave for
Ottawa to-night with the challenge and to get
what information he could regarding financial

Notes from the minute-book of the Montreal AAA discussing possible challenge for the Cup at the end of the 1903 season.

TOM HODGE played point in two of the four challenge games against the Vics and only four regular season games.

DICKIE BOON became the team's director and coach two years later and then the director of the Wanderers until their building burned down in 1917. He was inducted into the Hockey Hall of Fame in 1952.

Of the 20 games that made up this year's entire league schedule, **BILLY NICHOLSON** was the only goaler to record a shutout, 10-0 vs. Shamrocks in Montreal's first game of the year.

TOM PHILLIPS replaced **CHARLES LIFFITON** on the team after Liffiton left to play pro with Pittsburgh before the start of the season.

ART HOOPER led the team in scoring even though he had only six goals in nine games. He died in October 1904.

BILLY BELLINGHAM played point for most of the season with the MAAA but just two challenge games.

JACK MARSHALL was a champion football and soccer player as well. This was his third Cup in a row, of a total of six he won during his outstanding career. He retired at age 40 in 1917 just before the formation of the NHL.

After dominating the first game of the challenge, **JIM GARDNER** suffered a broken collarbone during the suspended game two, the result of a fierce check from Kean of Winnipeg.

Along with Phillips, **CECIL BLACHFORD** and **GEORGE SMITH** were the only new additions to the team that had won the Cup ten months previous.

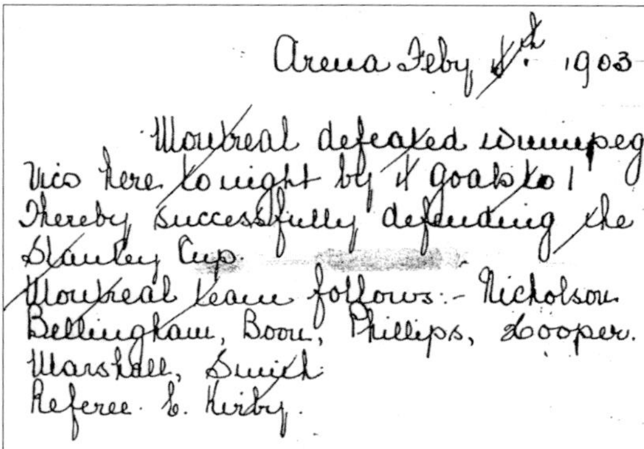

Arena Feby 4th 1903
Montreal defeated Winnipeg
Vics here tonight by 4 goals to 1
thereby successfully defending the
Stanley Cup.
Montreal team follows:- Nicholson.
Bellingham, Boon, Phillips, Hooper.
Marshall, Smith
Referee. E. Kirby.

Notes from the minute-book of the Montreal AAA recording the team's Cup victory the night of February 4, 1903.

Taken on the Grand Trunk Dock in Detroit, Michigan, as the train was being loaded onto the ferry to Windsor, Ontario, the Winnipeg Victorias are seen en route to Montreal for their Stanley Cup challenge series in January 1903.

Ottawa Silver Seven 1902 1903

The Ottawa challenge against Rat Portage was played on ice so bad that the speedier, younger Thistles could not play to their strength. Ottawa was the more physical team. After the victory, each member of the Silver Seven received a box of La Fortuna cigars.

March '03

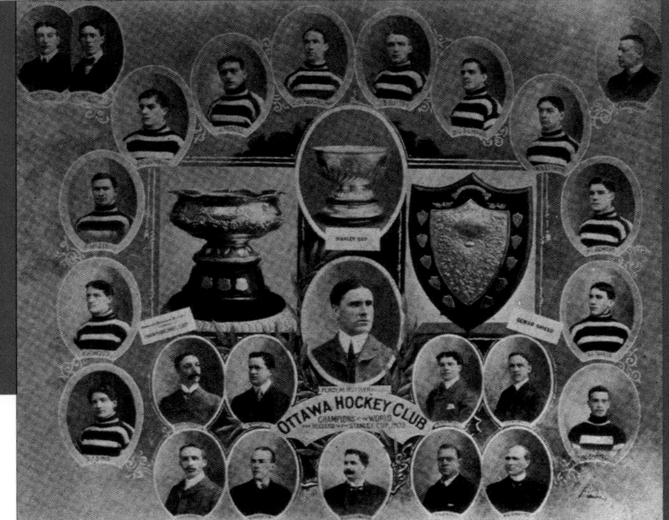

Ottawa Silver Seven, 1902-03

STANLEY CUP PLAYOFFS

Ottawa Silver Seven win best-of-two total-goals Stanley Cup playoffs 9-1

*March 7, 1903 Ottawa Silver Seven 1 at Montreal Victorias 1
**March 10, 1903 Montreal Victorias 0 at Ottawa Silver Seven 8 [Bouse Hutton]

STANLEY CUP CHALLENGE

Ottawa Silver Seven win best-of-three Stanley Cup challenge 2-0

**March 12, 1903 Rat Portage Thistles 2 at Ottawa Silver Seven 6
**March 14, 1903 Rat Portage Thistles 2 at Ottawa Silver Seven 4 {McGee 8:20 1st half}

** played at Westmount Arena, Montreal ** played at Dey's Arena, Ottawa*

OTTAWA SILVER SEVEN: Suddy Gilmour, Percy Sims, Bouse Hutton, Dave Gilmour, Billy Gilmour, Harry Westwick, Frank McGee, Fred Wood, Arthur Fraser, Charles Spittal, Harvey Pulford, Arthur Moore, Alf Smith (coach)

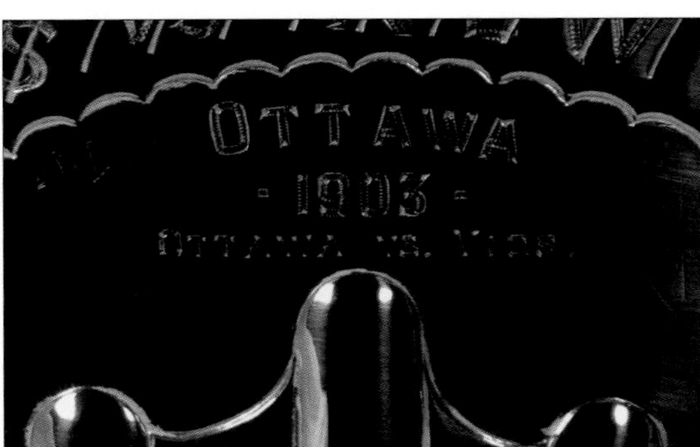

Team engraving from the bowl of the Stanley Cup

Team engraving from the bowl of the Stanley Cup

Brother of Dave and Billy, **SUDDY GILMOUR** averaged a goal a game during the CAHL season but was unable to play in the challenge games.

PERCY SIMS played just one challenge game, the last of the Rat Portage series, in place of Suddy Gilmour who was in the stands with a bad arm.

A fine goalie in lacrosse as well as a star football player, **BOUSE HUTTON** won all three championships in one season.

The three **GILMOURS** (**DAVE**, **BILLY**, and **SUDDY**) and McGee combined to score every goal for Ottawa in the four challenge games this year.

A pure goal scorer, **BILLY GILMOUR** won his first of three consecutive Stanley Cups.

After breaking a bone in his ankle from a vicious slash from Bert Strachan of Montreal Vics, **HARRY WESTWICK** was out of commission for the rest of the season. Nor could he even attend the Rat Portage games, owing to the illness of his wife.

The core of the first Stanley Cup victory, "One-eyed" **FRANK McGEE** played only four seasons with Ottawa, averaging more than three goals a game both regular season and Cup challenge. He had been working for the Department of Indian Affairs in Ottawa, but quit to pursue his passion—hockey. McGee lost an eye in an exhibition game that was in support of Canada's efforts in the Boer War, and he was out of action for two years recovering from the accident.

FRED WOOD was also a clerk at Woods Ltd., a grocery store in Ottawa.

ARTHUR FRASER was a student at Perkins, Fraser, and Burbridge, a law firm in the city.

CHARLES SPITTAL was a seldom-used sub this season.

A natural, all-round athlete, equally talented in lacrosse, football, and rowing, captain **HARVEY PULFORD** was a vicious and dangerous player. He played his whole career in Ottawa.

ART MOORE was the only core member of the historic Silver Seven team not in the Hockey Hall of Fame.

Coach **ALF SMITH** had been a demon of a player in Ottawa and Pittsburgh before retiring in 1900. He returned to coach the team this season, but resumed his playing career the following year with Ottawa, playing on a line with Frank McGee.

1903 THE CHAMPIONS 1904 Ottawa Silver Seven

Ottawa resigned from the CAHL in mid-season after being told to replay a game against the Montreal Victorias that they were leading 4-1 when the midnight curfew arrived. This was due to the Vics late arrival. Ottawa refused, withdrew from the league, and took on all challenges for the Cup, winning all of them. They were in tough against Winnipeg because the Rowing Club had its pot sweetened when a fan, one T.J. Porter, promised to give each player from any Western team that won the Cup a gold charm in the shape of the famous trophy which could be attached to any watch chain. That Ottawa-Winnipeg series marked the first time that goal lines were drawn from post to post to more clearly identify a puck crossing the goal line.

STANLEY CUP CHALLENGES

Ottawa Silver Seven win series of Stanley Cup challenges

*December 30, 1903 Winnipeg Rowing Club 1 at Ottawa Silver Seven 9
*January 1, 1904 Winnipeg Rowing Club 6 at Ottawa Silver Seven 2
*January 4, 1904 Winnipeg Rowing Club 0 at Ottawa Silver Seven 2 {McGee 11:00 2nd half} [Bouse Hutton]
Ottawa Silver Seven win best-of-three Stanley Cup challenge 2-1

*February 23, 1904 Toronto Marlboros 3 at Ottawa Silver Seven 6
*February 25, 1904 Toronto Marlboros 2 at Ottawa Silver Seven 11 {Moore 9:38 1st half}
Ottawa Silver Seven win best-of-three Stanley Cup challenge 2-0

**March 2, 1904 Ottawa Silver Seven 5 at Montreal Wanderers 5
Wanderers disqualified for refusing to play two away games in Ottawa after the challenge tie; Silver Seven awarded Stanley Cup

*March 9, 1904 Brandon 3 at Ottawa Silver Seven 6
*March 11, 1904 Brandon 3 at Ottawa Silver Seven 9
Ottawa Silver Seven win best-of-three Stanley Cup challenge 2-0

** played at Aberdeen Pavilion, Ottawa ** played at Westmount Arena, Montreal*

OTTAWA SILVER SEVEN: Suddy Gilmour, Arthur Moore, Frank McGee, Bouse Hutton, Billy Gilmour, Jim McGee, Harry Westwick, Harvey Pulford, Scott, Alf Smith (playing coach)

SUDDY GILMOUR had averaged two goals a game before Ottawa withdrew from the league.

When Pete Charlton of the Marlies was injured in game two, **ARTHUR MOORE** was the Ottawa player removed to equalize players as per the rules.

On the cusp of greatness, "One-eyed" **FRANK McGEE** scored five goals in game two against Toronto, a Cup challenge record for the time and one he equalled in the first game against Brandon a few nights later. Though one-eyed, he received little sympathy from opponents who regularly were butt-ended by him.

After retiring in 1911, goalie **BOUSE HUTTON** coached local teams in Ottawa for a number of years.

The Silver Seven was such a strong outfit that star player **BILLY GILMOUR** was but a sub and part-time player this season.

JIM McGEE replaced the injured Art Moore for the Wanderers series and acquitted himself honourably, though he was badly bruised and battered by the Wanderers.

HARRY WESTWICK started his career with Ottawa in 1895 as a goalie but was soon replaced and moved to forward. Later in life he had his left leg amputated above the knee as a result of numerous injuries incurred during his playing days.

Master of the "lift," captain **HARVEY PULFORD** played seven years before scoring his first goal!

SCOTT scored once in two regular season appearances and didn't play at all in the challenge games.

Player and coach **ALF SMITH** filled the breach when Harvey Pulford went down with an injury during the end of the challenge against Toronto. In one game he hit Joe Hall from behind squarely over the head with his stick, earning the wrath of even his own fans.

MAC McGILTON was the Silver Seven trainer.

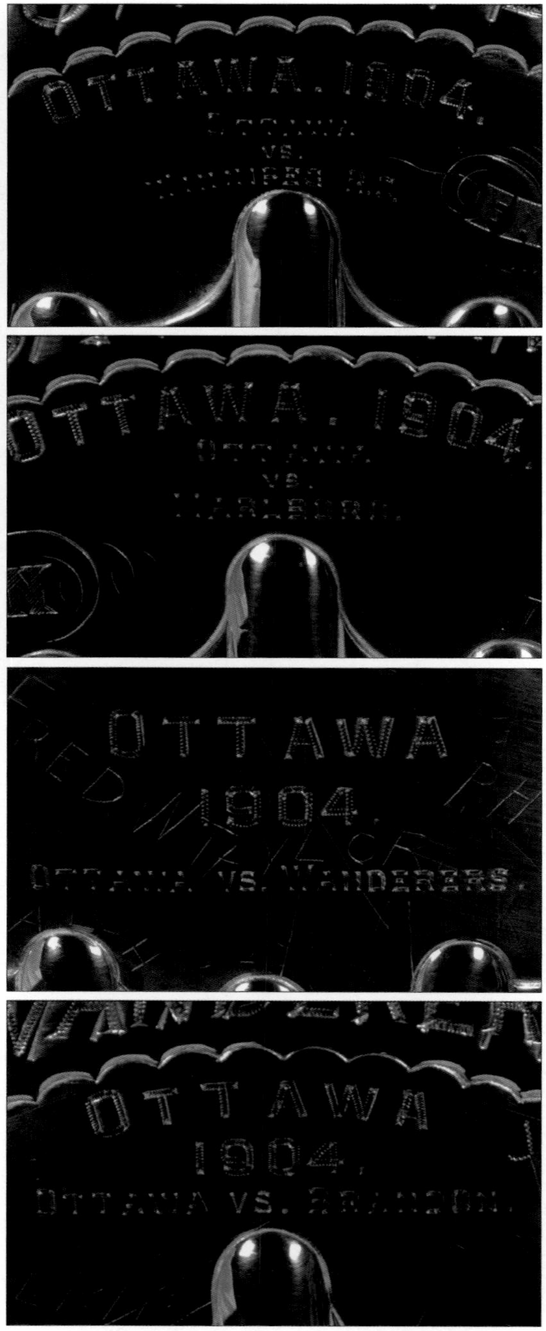

The most engraved team in Cup history for one year, Ottawa has all four of its challenge victories noted on the bowl of the Stanley Cup.

Ottawa Silver Seven 1904 1905

The Silver Seven played in the FAHL and finished in first place. They scored a record 23 goals in a game against a team from Dawson City that had travelled some 6,400 kilometres from the Yukon for the Cup challenge. Dawson goalie Albert Forrest was, at 17, the youngest player ever to participate in a Stanley Cup game. The series was supposed to be a best-of-five affair, but the rest of the series was cancelled after the shellacking the Yukoners received in game two. Two weeks after the Rat Portage series, the Ottawa Hockey Club gave a banquet for the team at the Russell Hotel. Several of the Silver Seven players got drunk and drop-kicked the Cup onto the frozen Rideau Canal later that night.

Team engraving from the bowl of the Stanley Cup

STANLEY CUP CHALLENGES

Ottawa Silver Seven win Stanley Cup based on first place finish

*January 13, 1905 Dawson City 2 at Ottawa Silver Seven 9
*January 16, 1905 Dawson City 2 at Ottawa Silver Seven 23 {Westwick 12:15 1st half}
Ottawa Silver Seven win best-of-three Stanley Cup challenge 2-0

*March 7, 1905 Rat Portage Thistles 9 at Ottawa Silver Seven 3
*March 9, 1905 Rat Portage Thistles 2 at Ottawa Silver Seven 4
*March 11, 1905 Rat Portage Thistles 4 at Ottawa Silver Seven 5 {McGee 2nd half}
Ottawa Silver Seven win best-of-three Stanley Cup challenge 2-1

** played at Dey's Arena, Ottawa*

OTTAWA SILVER SEVEN: Dave Finnie, Harvey Pulford, Arthur Moore, Harry Westwick, Frank McGee, Alf Smith (playing coach), Billy Gilmour, Frank White, Horace Gaul, Hamby Shore, Bones Allen, Billy Bawlf

F.A.H.L. FINAL STANDINGS	GP	W	L	T	GF	GA	Pts
Ottawa Silver Seven	8	7	1	0	60	19	14
Montreal Wanderers	8	6	2	0	44	27	12
Brockville Hockey Club	8	4	4	0	34	30	8
Cornwall Hockey Club	8	3	5	0	18	37	6
Ottawa Montagnards	8	0	8	0	19	62	0

Montreal Vics won the right to challenge, but bickering over game dates prevented such a series from materializing

Team engraving from the bowl of the Stanley Cup

DAVE FINNIE wasn't the team's first choice in goal—Bouse Hutton was. But Hutton, miffed that he hadn't been used all year, indignantly refused to play.

Captain **HARVEY PULFORD** was the heavyweight boxing champ of Eastern Canada from 1898 to 1908. It was he who kicked the Cup onto the frozen Rideau.

ARTHUR MOORE was hit over the head by Norm Watt of Dawson. Watt was given a game misconduct.

HARRY WESTWICK acquired his nickname "Rat" after Ottawa played in Quebec in 1896 and a local reporter gave sinister nicknames to all Ottawa players.

FRANK McGEE scored 14 goals the night of January 16, 1905, a Stanley Cup record that will surely never be broken.

The oldest of seven hockey-playing brothers, playing-coach **ALF SMITH** played all his 14 years with Ottawa.

BILLY GILMOUR missed game one vs. Rat Portage because he was still attending university in Montreal.

In one game against Dawson City, Watts cut **FRANK WHITE** over the head with his stick. Nonetheless, White scored twice.

HORACE GAUL played only once in the regular season and once more in the challenges.

HAMBY SHORE played on a forward line with Alf Smith and Harry Westwick in his first year of pro hockey.

BONES ALLEN played but irregularly during the winter.

BILLY BAWLF scored one goal in his only game played for the season.

SAM ROSENTHAL kept the Cup in his safe for the balance of the year.

PETE GREEN and **MAC McGILTON** were the team trainers.

T. D'ARCY McGEE was the team's secretary and worked for Fripp & McGee, barristers on Sparks St. in Ottawa.

CHARLES SPARKS, a director, was partner in Sparks & Legatt, a law firm.

HALDER KIRBY was the team's physician.

G.P. MURPHY, Ottawa's president, was also secretary-treasurer of the Ottawa Transportation Company.

It was manager **BOB SHILLINGTON** who gave the players silver nuggets after winning the Cup in 1903.

J.P. DICKSON was secretary-treasurer of the Canadian Railway Accident Insurance Co.

PATRICK JEROME BASKERVILLE, Ottawa's treasurer, was a 29-year-old businessman in Ottawa.

DAVID H. BAIRD was the team dentist.

LLEWELLYN BATE, a director, worked in town for Bate & Co.

1905 THE CHAMPIONS

1906 Ottawa Silver Seven

February '06

The length of the Ottawa rink and its round corners hampered the visitors from Queen's University in their challenge. The Silver Seven proved to be the better team around the net as a result of rebounds. Ottawa relied on short passes for success and skated with the puck close to their skates, both unique features of their play at this time. Their narrow victory over Smiths Falls in game one was the result of the play of Smiths Falls goalie, Percy LeSueur, who so impressed Ottawa management that his services were acquired in time for the challenge against Wanderers less than a week later.

STANLEY CUP CHALLENGES

Ottawa Silver Seven win series of Stanley Cup challenges

*February 27, 1906 Queen's University 7 at Ottawa Silver Seven 16
*February 28, 1906 Queen's University 7 at Ottawa Silver Seven 12 {Pulford 10:00 2nd half}
Ottawa Silver Seven win best-of-three Stanley Cup challenge 2-0

*March 6, 1906 Smiths Falls 5 at Ottawa Silver Seven 6
*March 8, 1906 Smiths Falls 2 at Ottawa Silver Seven 8 {McGee 17:45 1st half}
Ottawa Silver Seven win best-of-three Stanley Cup challenge 2-0

** played at Dey's Arena, Ottawa*

OTTAWA SILVER SEVEN: Harvey Pulford, Arthur Moore, Harry Westwick, Frank McGee, Alf Smith (playing coach), Billy Gilmour, Billy Hague, Percy LeSueur, Harry Smith, Tommy Smith, Dion, Ebbs

Ottawa Silver Seven, 1905-06

E.C.A.H.A. FINAL STANDINGS	GP	W	L	GF	GA	Pts
Ottawa Silver Seven	10	9	1	90	42	18
Montreal Wanderers	10	9	1	74	38	18
Montreal Victorias	10	6	4	76	73	12
Quebec Hockey Club	10	3	7	57	70	6
Montreal AAA	10	3	7	49	63	6
Montreal Shamrocks	10	0	10	30	90	0

Team engraving from the bowl of the Stanley Cup

Captain **HARVEY PULFORD** also played football for the Ottawa Rough Riders and later won a city squash championship at age 49, twenty years after retiring from hockey.

ARTHUR MOORE went goalless in ten league games but was named team captain ahead of more likely candidates such as Pulford and Smith.

This was the last of three straight Cups for **HARRY WESTWICK**, though he played in one more finals, with Kenora in 1907 vs. Wanderers, even though he had skated all season with Ottawa. Bill Westwick, a relative, would later become one of hockey's finest writers and chroniclers of the success of the 1920s Senators.

FRANK McGEE continued his scoring dominance, scoring 15 times in the four challenge games with Queen's and Smiths Falls. He was later killed on September 23, 1916 in action in Courcellette, France during the height of World War I.

A Hall of Famer (as is brother Tommy), **ALF SMITH** was one of seven hockey-playing brothers. The playing coach skated on a line with McGee and later played for Kenora during its unsuccessful challenge in 1907.

A native of Ottawa and a McGill University graduate, **BILLY GILMOUR** retired after this Cup win but a year later returned to action as a member of the Montreal Vics.

BILLY HAGUE played every minute in goal for the team.

HARRY SMITH led all league scorers with 31 goals, including individual games with eight, six, and five. He had taken the Cup home after recovering it the previous year from the Rideau. When the Wanderers won the Cup, they had to come to his house to get it!

Brother of Harry, **TOMMY SMITH** saw limited action in this his first season with the Silver Seven, though he showed great skill and potential.

DION played two regular season games and none during the challenges.

EBBS scored a hat trick in his only league game but never played in the challenge.

MAC McGILTON remained the team's trainer.

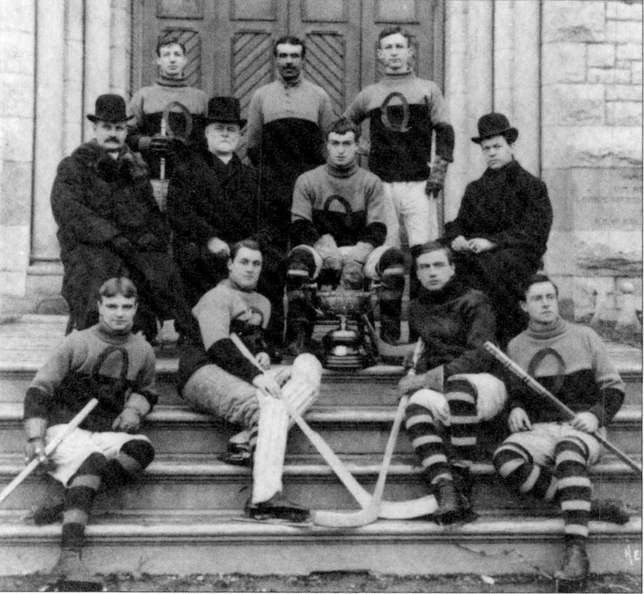

The team from Queen's University that put up an unsuccessful challenge to the Ottawas in February 1906.

Montreal Wanderers 1905 1906

March '06

This year was an oddity in that Ottawa accepted challenges from two teams prior to the conclusion of the current hockey season. Although the Silver Seven won the challenges, they lost the Stanley Cup just a few days later. They tied in the standings with the Wanderers, and in a two-game, total-goals playoffs it was Montreal that emerged from the league as champions. In that series, the "Redbands" were leading 10-1 in total goals early in game two only to see Ottawa score nine in a row and tie the score! Montreal then went on the attack to score two more and win the Cup. The Wanderers had a far easier time of it against New Glasgow, although their own fans cheered for the visitors early in game one. The matches were marked by heavy checking.

Montreal Wanderers, 1905-06

STANLEY CUP PLAYOFFS

Montreal Wanderers win best-of-two total-goals Stanley Cup playoffs 12-10

*March 14, 1906 Ottawa Silver Seven 1 at Montreal Wanderers 9
**March 17, 1906 Montreal Wanderers 3 at Ottawa Silver Seven 9

STANLEY CUP CHALLENGE

Montreal Wanderers win best-of-two total-goals Stanley Cup challenge 17-5

*December 27, 1906 New Glasgow Cubs 3 at Montreal Wanderers 10
*December 29, 1906 New Glasgow Cubs 2 at Montreal Wanderers 7

** played at Westmount Arena, Montreal ** played at Dey's Arena, Ottawa*

MONTREAL WANDERERS: Henri Menard, Billy Strachan, Rod Kennedy, Lester Patrick, Pud Glass, Ernie Russell, Moose Johnson, Cecil Blachford, John Arnold, Dickie Boon (manager)

Cartoon from the Montreal Daily Star poking fun at Montreal's victory over the Silver Seven to capture the Stanley Cup.

Goaltender **HENRI MENARD** led the league with a GAA of 3.80 and appeared in all ten league games.

BILLY STRACHAN on point didn't score a goal all year but was as reliable as he was unspectacular.

ROD KENNEDY at cover point played only in the two challenge games against Ottawa.

LESTER PATRICK was famous for his patented end-to-end rushes, the first defenceman (rover) so accomplished. It was his two late goals on great solo dashes that gave the Wanderers their win over Ottawa in game one.

"FRANK" THE SCOT, usually called **"PUD" GLASS**, won four Stanley Cups in five years with the Wanderers, playing most of the time with two Ernies, Russell and Johnson. He signed with the Wanderers as a pro, and, as a result, Montreal AAA demanded that he be expelled. Two-thirds majority of league officials voted in his favour and he was allowed to play.

ERNIE RUSSELL also played football for the Montreal AAA. He rose through the hockey ranks by playing junior with the Starlings before coming to the AAA.

During one bit of action along the boards, **MOOSE**

Team engraving from the shoulder of the replica Cup

JOHNSON'S stick came up and struck the Governor General on his hatted head! This was not surprising given that the master of the poke check used a stick that was 75" long and his reach was an unparalleled 99".

Captain **CECIL BLACHFORD** suffered from blood poisoning in his arm during the season and didn't play during the challenge vs. Ottawa.

JOHN ARNOLD played just one regular season game all year (and scored a goal).

Manager **DICKIE BOON** was a player on the Montreal AAA team that beat Winnipeg in the 1902 challenge. He remained the team manager until 1917 when the Westmount arena burned down.

1906–1907 Kenora Thistles

THE CHAMPIONS

January '07

Kenora was formerly known as Rat Portage until the city changed its name. The Thistles had advanced the game fundamentally the previous year when they lined their defencemen side by side rather than up and back. The nickname Thistles was the result of a contest to name the team, won by one Bill Dunsmore, a local carpenter who had emigrated to the area from Scotland.

STANLEY CUP CHALLENGE

Kenora Thistles win best-of-two total-goals Stanley Cup challenge 12-8

*January 17, 1907 Kenora Thistles 4 at Montreal Wanderers 2
*January 21, 1907 Kenora Thistles 8 at Montreal Wanderers 6

** played at Westmount Arena, Montreal*

KENORA THISTLES: Eddie Geroux, Art Ross, Si Griffis, Tom Hooper, Billy McGimsie, Roxy Beaudro, Tom Phillips, R. Phillips, Joe Hall, Fred Hudson (manager)

Kenora Thistles, Cup champs for the shortest time ever

E.C.A.H.A. FINAL STANDINGS	GP	W	L	T	GF	GA	Pts
Montreal Wanderers	10	10	0	0	105	39	20
Ottawa Silver Seven	10	7	3	0	76	54	14
Montreal Victorias	10	6	4	0	101	70	12
Montreal AAA	10	3	7	0	58	83	6
Quebec Hockey Club	10	2	8	0	62	88	4
Montreal Shamrocks	10	2	8	0	52	120	4

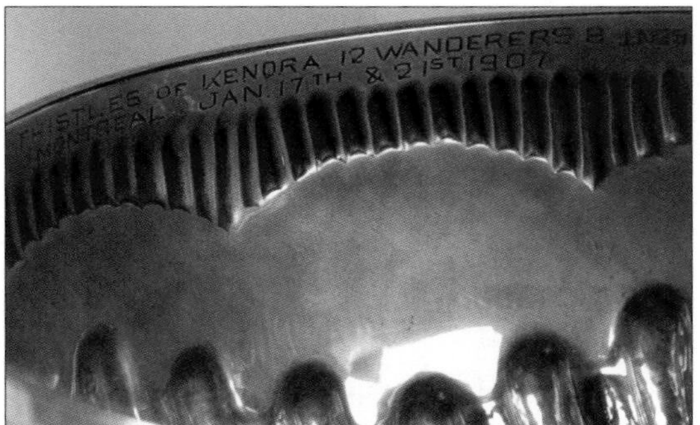

Detail from inside the bowl of the replica Cup

Team engraving from the shoulder of the replica Cup

Goaler **EDDIE GEROUX** kept the Wanderers, particularly the dangerous forwards, at bay during this tremendous upset for the Stanley Cup, stopping many "hot ones" during the dramatic win in game two.

A ringer, **ART ROSS** had been a member of the Brandon Kings and played for Kenora only during this challenge (for a fee of $1,000) and starring with his great rushes from his point position. He later played for Ottawa and ran the most successful sporting goods store in the city.

After this win, **SILAS SETH (SOX) GRIFFIS** retired from hockey for five full seasons before returning to the game in 1912 in the PCHA. Born in Kansas in 1883, he moved to Rat Portage with his family at a young age and won another Cup in Vancouver in 1915.

Called "vice-captain" of the team, **TOM HOOPER** scored five power-play goals—two in the first half and three more in the second half—in their 8-6 win over the Wanderers, all coming with Art Ross in the penalty box.

BILLY McGIMSIE had been badly bruised and cut in his first challenge against the Silver Seven two years previous. He was known for his skating and "dribbling" (i.e., stickhandling).

ROXY BEAUDRO was a replacement for Bellefeuille. His late goal in game two broke a 6-6 tie and proved to be the game winner for the Thistles.

Arguably the greatest left-winger of his era, captain **TOM PHILLIPS** scored all four goals in the first game, then had a hat trick in the Cup clincher. "His Nibs" had been on the Marlboro team that had challenged in '04 and with Rat Portage in '05. Fans used to chant, "Never a man like Phillips; never another like he."

The 25-year-old **JOE HALL** was a member of the team but did not play.

R. PHILLIPS was a spare and did not play.

This commemorative mug was given to star Billy McGimsie in honour of his heroic contributions to this most unlikely Cup victory.

Montreal Wanderers 1906 1907

March '07

Although Kenora no longer had Art Ross, the Thistles used Alf Smith and Harry Westwick from Ottawa, ringers the Wanderers objected to but who nonetheless didn't affect the outcome. After their victory, the Montrealers were given a long parade on March 30 upon returning home, finishing at the Savoy Hotel. They had their portrait made at a photographer's home, but left the Cup behind. It was subsequently stolen, but as no one was prepared to pay a ransom for it, the thief shamefacedly returned the Cup to the photographer.

Montreal Wanderers, 1906-07

STANLEY CUP CHALLENGE

Montreal Wanderers win Stanley Cup based on first place finish

*March 23, 1907 Montreal Wanderers 7 Kenora Thistles 2
*March 25, 1907 Kenora Thistles 6 Montreal Wanderers 5
Wanderers win best-of-two total-goals Stanley Cup challenge 12-8

** played at Winnipeg Arena*

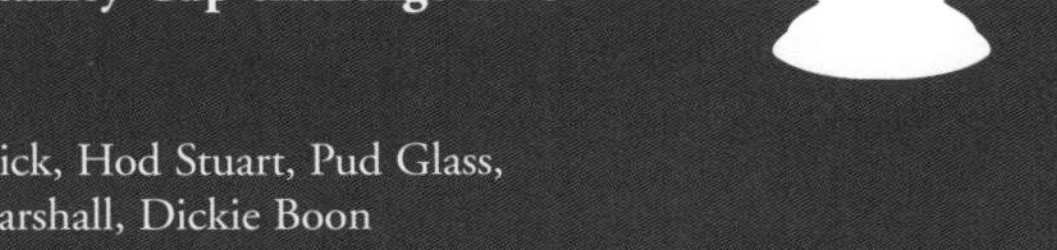

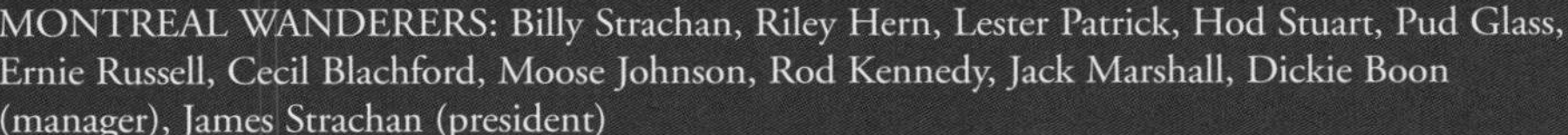

MONTREAL WANDERERS: Billy Strachan, Riley Hern, Lester Patrick, Hod Stuart, Pud Glass, Ernie Russell, Cecil Blachford, Moose Johnson, Rod Kennedy, Jack Marshall, Dickie Boon (manager), James Strachan (president)

Detail inside the bowl of the original Cup

Point **BILLY STRACHAN** played only in the challenge games in his second of two straight Cup-winning seasons.

Goalie **RILEY HERN'S** name is misspelled "RIELY" on the Cup. He led the league in GAA by a wide margin, allowing just 39 goals.

In one strange way or another, **LESTER PATRICK** had one of the longest careers in hockey, beginning in 1903 and ending in 1928 as a goalie with the New York Rangers as an emergency replacement.

HOD STUART was a late-arriving refugee from Pittsburgh and was one of the first to sign a pro contract in the ECAHA which for the first time was mixing amateurs with pros in their lineups.

Accused of signing pro contracts with both Wanderers and Montreal AAA, **PUD GLASS** eventually was allowed to play for the Cup-winners.

ERNIE RUSSELL produced an amazing season of scoring with 42 goals in just nine games, twice getting eight in a game and three other times scoring at least five.

Captain **CECIL BLACHFORD'S** career was nearly ended after he was bludgeoned by Charlie Spittal during the challenge.

Although known as a defence player, **MOOSE JOHNSON** played left wing on a line with Pud Glass and Ernie Russell on the team that won three Cups in succession. His name here is misspelled "JOHNSTON."

Called one of the team's "amateurs" by the Wanderers, **ROD KENNEDY** was nonetheless openly paid.

JACK MARSHALL had tremendous speed and was physically intimidating to play against.

Manager **DICKIE BOON** was considered the first man to pokecheck an opponent off the puck.

JAMES STRACHAN was involved in a bread-manufacturing business in Montreal for thirty years. He was president of the Wanderers for five years.

BOB AHERN was the team's executive and its honourary vice-president.

GEORGE GUILE was the team's honourary secretary-treasurer and president of the Savoy Hotel.

CLARENCE McKERROW, the honourary president, soon after won a gold medal with Canada's lacrosse team at the 1908 Olympics in London.

TOM HODGE was the honourary secretary-treasurer and executive vice-president.

BERT STRACHAN served as an executive for the team.

MR. CHIPCHASE is an unknown member of this Wanderers team but has his name on the Cup.

BOB STEPHENSON was the executive honourary-treasurer and manager of the Quebec Bank.

WILLIAM JENNINGS was the 2nd vice-president of the league.

PAUL LEFEBVRE worked as Montreal's trainer.

DR. WALTER DORION was the team physician.

1907

THE CHAMPIONS

1908 Montreal Wanderers

The Wanderers won the league title on the final day of the schedule with a 6-4 win over the Shamrocks. In their challenge against Toronto, they almost forfeited the Cup before the series began. Toronto had insisted on a two-game challenge, but Montreal couldn't fathom another drawn-out series. Said Montreal president Jennings: "They don't seem to appreciate in Toronto that the Montreal public are weary of hockey. ..The second Maple Leaf match will be the twenty-second in which our players have figured this season...we will leave it to the players to decide, but most of us feel inclined to send the Cup to Toronto, and let them have it, and be done with it."

STANLEY CUP CHALLENGES

Montreal Wanderers win Stanley Cup based on first place finish

*January 9, 1908 Ottawa Victorias 3 at Montreal Wanderers 9
*January 13, 1908 Ottawa Victorias 1 at Montreal Wanderers 13
Montreal Wanderers win best-of-two total-goals Stanley Cup challenge 22-4

*March 10, 1908 Winnipeg Maple Leafs 5 at Montreal Wanderers 11
*March 12, 1908 Winnipeg Maple Leafs 3 at Montreal Wanderers 9
Montreal Wanderers win best-of-two total-goals Stanley Cup challenge 20-8

*March 14, 1908 Toronto 4 at Montreal Wanderers 6 {Johnson 2nd half}
Montreal Wanderers win one-game Stanley Cup challenge

*December 28, 1908 Edmonton Eskimos 3 at Montreal Wanderers 7
*December 30, 1908 Edmonton Eskimos 7 at Montreal Wanderers 6
Montreal Wanderers win best-of-two total-goals Stanley Cup challenge 13-10

** played at Westmount Arena, Montreal*

MONTREAL WANDERERS: Riley Hern, Art Ross, Walter Smaill, Pud Glass, Bruce Stuart, Ernie Russell, Moose Johnson, Cecil Blachford, Tom Hooper, Larry Gilmour, Ernie Liffiton, Dickie Boon (manager)

Team engraving from the shoulder of the original Cup

E.C.A.H.A. FINAL STANDINGS	GP	W	L	T	GF	GA	Pts
Montreal Wanderers	10	8	2	0	63	52	16
Ottawa Capitals	10	7	3	0	86	51	14
Quebec Hockey Club	10	5	5	0	81	74	10
Montreal Shamrocks	10	5	5	0	53	49	10
Montreal Victorias	10	4	6	0	73	78	8
Montreal AAA	10	1	9	0	53	105	2

Team engraving from the shoulder of the replica Cup

Goalie **RILEY HERN** allowed a goal against Toronto when he was talking to friends and didn't notice a faceoff.

ART ROSS became only the second man to win Cups in consecutive years with two different teams.

WALTER SMAILL played in three Cup challenges for the Wanderers.

PUD GLASS became involved in a contract controversy, allegedly signing with the AAA for $400 more than his Wanderers' contract. The AAA signing was quickly voided.

BRUCE STUART became a star during the challenges, scoring seven times in three games.

After promising himself to Montreal AAA, **ERNIE RUSSELL** promptly signed with the cross-town Wanderers, earning expulsion from MAAA membership.

ERNIE JOHNSON earned the nickname "Moose" because of his ability to play with, and cause injury.

Upon retirement, the league presented Captain **CECIL BLACHFORD** with the Arena Cup (awarded to league champions) in honour of his career achievements.

TOM HOOPER signed a contract with Montreal AAA that paid $400 more than his Wanderers contract, though he was eventually reeled in by his rightful team.

LARRY GILMOUR played just one game during the season and not at all in the challenges.

ERNIE LIFFITON and older brother, Charles, who won the Cup in 1902 as a player, also ran their father's jewellery business in Montreal.

Manager **DICKIE BOON** won the Cup the previous two years as well as as a player in 1902.

ALF SMITH played the two games against Edmonton which were held at the start of the '08-'09 season. Technically, he was part of the new year's team, but equally he played in a challenge game for the Cup.

HARRY SMITH was new to the team but played both challenges against Edmonton.

JOHNSTON played only the December games and played right wing rather than his usual spot on the left.

JIMMY GARDNER had been with the Shamrocks the previous year. His great rush led to Alf Smith's goal in game one to make the score 4-3.

Ottawa Senators 1908 1909

Ottawa beat the Wanderers 6-3 on the second last day of the season to finish first in the league and wrest the Cup from the Montrealers.

Ottawa Senators, 1908-09

STANLEY CUP FINALS

Ottawa Senators win Stanley Cup based on first place finish and received a challenge only from the Winnipeg Shamrocks that was too late in the season to accept.

OTTAWA SENATORS: Fred Lake, Percy LeSueur, Cyclone Taylor, Billy Gilmour, Dubbie Kerr, Edgar Dey, Marty Walsh, Bruce Stuart

E.C.A.H.A. FINAL STANDINGS	GP	W	L	T	GF	GA	Pts
Ottawa Senators	12	10	2	0	117	63	20
Montreal Wanderers	12	9	3	0	82	61	18
Quebec Bulldogs	12	3	9	0	78	106	6
Montreal Shamrocks	12	2	10	0	56	103	4

Details of Cyclone Taylor's stick giving specifics of the Senators' Cup-winning season

FRED LAKE replaced the retired Harvey Pulford. Lake lost an eye in an accident earlier in his career.

PERCY LESUEUR started playing hockey as a forward with Quebec but fell back to goal with Smiths Falls in 1906.

FRED TAYLOR was named "Cyclone" when playing with Renfrew due to his speed.

BILLY GILMOUR retired after this season though he made a brief comeback with the Senators seven years later.

ALBERT "DUBBY" KERR'S career almost ended when a skate caught his eye, forcing him to miss two months.

EDGAR DEY scored eleven goals in just six games.

A superb skater, **MARTY WALSH** played for Queen's in the 1906 challenge before joining the Senators this season.

After transferring from the Wanderers, captain **BRUCE STUART** brought his winning formula to the Senators.

D'ARCY MCGEE, president and lawyer, King's Counsel, was the son of another McGee who was a Father of Confederation at Canada's birth as a nation in 1867.

LLEWELLYN BATE, vice-president, was managing director of Gloucester Trading Co. Ltd.

CHARLES BRYSON, an executive with the team, was president of Bryson-Graham Ltd., a department store.

Team engraving from the base of the original Cup

PERCIVAL BUTTLER, an executive, worked as a city passenger and ticket agent for the Grand Trunk Railway.

M. ROSENTHAL, executive, worked as a jeweller at A. Rosenthal & Sons, a prominent store in the city.

Executive **PATRICK BASKERVILLE** entered politics in 1879 and was elected to the Legislature of Ontario.

N.C. SPARKS, executive, worked as manager of N.C. Sparks Co., a stock broker house in the city that made Sparks St. the famous street it is today in Ottawa.

MULLIGAN studied law at Osgoode Hall. He later became managing director of the Windsor Hotel in Montreal, where the NHL was formed in 1917.

Others: **MAC MCGILTON** (trainer), **PETE GREEN** (coach), **H.M. MERRILL** (spare)

1909 THE CHAMPIONS

1910 Montreal Wanderers

Prior to the start of the new season, Ottawa had to finish a bit of old business by first of all accepting challenges from Galt and Edmonton. The Senators won these handily, but during the NHA season they finished second to the Wanderers and lost the Cup. The Montrealers had time to accept only one challenge before winter ended, and they defeated a team from Berlin with little difficulty. The Wanderers were part of the new NHA, formed December 2, 1909 as a thoroughly pro league. The team moved from the Wood Ave. arena to the Jubilee Arena, where the Canadiens would also play. They won the O'Brien Trophy as league champs, a trophy that also transferred to the NHL.

STANLEY CUP CHALLENGES

Montreal Wanderers win Stanley Cup based on first place finish

*January 5, 1910 Galt 3 at Ottawa Senators 12
*January 7, 1910 Galt 1 at Ottawa Senators 3 {Bruce Ridpath 2nd half}
Ottawa Senators win best-of-two total-goals Stanley Cup challenge 15-4

*January 18, 1910 Edmonton Eskimos 4 at Ottawa Senators 8
*January 20, 1910 Edmonton Eskimos 7 at Ottawa Senators 13 {Bruce Stuart 23:45 1st half}
Ottawa Senators win best-of-two total-goals Stanley Cup challenge 21-11

**March 12, 1910 Berlin Union Jacks 3 at Montreal Wanderers 7 {Harry Hyland 22:00 1st half}
Montreal Wanderers win one-game Stanley Cup challenge

** played at Dey's Arena, Ottawa ** played at Jubilee Rink, Montreal*

MONTREAL WANDERERS: Cecil Blachford, Moose Johnson, Ernie Russell, Riley Hern, Harry Hyland, Jack Marshall, Pud Glass, Jimmy Gardner, Dickie Boon (manager)

Team engraving from the base of the original Cup

N.H.A. FINAL STANDINGS	GP	W	L	T	GF	GA	Pts
Montreal Wanderers	12	11	1	0	91	41	22
Ottawa Senators	12	9	3	0	89	66	18
Renfrew Creamery Kings	12	8	3	1	96	54	17
Cobalt Silver Kings	12	4	8	0	79	104	8
Haileybury Hockey Club	12	4	8	0	77	83	8
Montreal Shamrocks	12	3	8	1	52	95	7
Montreal Canadiens	12	2	10	0	59	100	4

Team engraving from the base of the replica Cup

CECIL BLACHFORD missed much of the season with injuries and didn't play in the challenge vs. Berlin. He was also employed by the Bell Telephone Company.

MOOSE JOHNSON filed a lawsuit with Jimmy Gardner against owner P.J. Doran saying their contracts called for a $200 bonus for winning the Stanley Cup. Doran argued that team manager Boon signed the contract without proper authority, thus invalidating the promise. The players lost their case. After retiring, Johnson became a railway trainman at Portland.

ERNIE RUSSELL scored four goals to lead the Wanderers to victory in the only challenge game of the season against Berlin. By day he worked in a wool importing business.

Goalie **RILEY HERN** opened a clothing store in Ottawa during his playing days and became the Montreal representative for Spaulding Sporting Goods when he retired.

HARRY HYLAND was in his second year of pro having entered the game the previous season with the Shamrocks. In daytime, he worked for the Hudson Bay Knitting Company.

JACK MARSHALL suffered a serious eye injury early the next season and missed two years. After retiring, he worked at the McDonald's Tobacco Company in Montreal.

Captain **PUD GLASS** joined the Canadiens in 1912 even though league rules stipulated that the Habs could sign only French-Canadian players. He was also a jeweller.

After retiring in 1915, **JIMMY GARDNER** became a referee for many years. During his playing days he also worked as a machinist.

"The Boon Trophy" is renowned in Montreal curling circles as the major bonspiel at Outremont curling club in honour of manager **DICKIE BOON**.

This interior photograph of the Jubilee Rink in Montreal shows part of the ice surface which was lit by 240 incandescent lights and could accommodate 4,000 spectators for hockey games. It played host to the Cup challenge on March 12, 1910.

Ottawa Senators 1910 1911

This was the year the NHA changed games from two, 30-minute halves to three, 20-minute periods. Ottawa had a record of 3-1 against the Cup-champion Wanderers during the NHA season. The challenge team from Galt boasted five Ottawa-born players: Billy Hague, Billy Baird, Rae Murphy, Tommy Smith, and Louis "Dutch" Berlinquette. Prior to the game, trustee William Foran escorted His Excellency Earl Grey to centre ice to face off the opening puck. The game would have been even more lopsided than 7-4 but for the play of goalie Hague.

Ottawa Senators, 1910-11

STANLEY CUP CHALLENGES

Ottawa Senators win Stanley Cup based on first place finish

*March 13, 1911 Galt 4 at Ottawa Senators 7 {Marty Walsh 5:00 3rd}
Ottawa Senators win one-game Stanley Cup challenge

*March 16, 1911 Port Arthur Seniors 4 at Ottawa Senators 14 {Marty Walsh 4:30 2nd}
Ottawa Senators win one-game Stanley Cup challenge

** played at Dey's Arena, Ottawa*

OTTAWA SENATORS: Hamby Shore, Percy LeSueur, Jack Darragh, Bruce Stuart, Marty Walsh, Bruce Ridpath, Fred Lake, Dubbie Kerr, Alex Currie, Horace Gaul

N.H.A. FINAL STANDINGS	GP	W	L	T	GF	GA	Pts
Ottawa Senators	16	13	3	0	122	69	26
Montreal Canadiens	16	8	8	0	66	62	16
Renfrew Creamery Kings	16	8	8	0	91	101	16
Montreal Wanderers	16	7	9	0	73	88	14
Quebec Bulldogs	16	4	12	0	65	97	8

The Galt team that lost its one-game challenge to the Senators

Although he was to play for Ottawa for seven more years, after missing a year with illness in 1908, **HAMBY SHORE** died in 1918 during the influenza epidemic.

Hemp guardian **PERCY LeSUEUR** produced a design for a goal net that was accepted by the NHA and adopted for the 1911-12 season. Later an original member of the Hot Stove League on radio, he also developed the goal glove and a statistic for shots on goal, and he remained in hockey the rest of his life.

A 19-year old rookie, **JACK DARRAGH** played right wing on a line with Marty Walsh and Dubbie Kerr, this his first of 13 seasons with Ottawa. He went off in the second period to even the teams after McDonagh of Port Arthur hurt his knee and had to retire.

The Senators' team captain **BRUCE STUART** became so upset with the NHA's proposal for a salary cap that he retired from the game for good and opened a shoe store in downtown Ottawa.

MARTY WALSH led all scorers with 37 goals in 16 league games. In game two of the challenge, he scored ten goals vs. Port Arthur. Later this year he moved to Edmonton in the hope that the weather would improve his health, but four years later he died in a sanatorium in Northern Ontario.

BRUCE RIDPATH was a member of Toronto's Cup challenge team of 1908. Shortly after this win he was hit by a car in Toronto and never played again.

Team engraving from the shoulder of the replica Cup

One of the team's professional players, **FRED LAKE** was being paid just $600, half what he made the year before, as owners cracked down on runaway salaries.

DUBBIE KERR finished second in league scoring with 32 goals, including a consecutive-games streak that reached 12. He was famous for playing with a white feather in his hair when in Quebec City.

ALEX CURRIE had one goal in five games and saw no action in challenge play.

HORACE GAUL played just two regular season games all season. He had served in the Canadian Army in South Africa before joining the Ottawas as one of the finest stick-handlers around.

1911 THE CHAMPIONS
1912 Quebec Bulldogs

This was the first year teams in the east played six men aside instead of seven. The Bulldogs defeated Ottawa on the last day of the season in league play, a thrilling 6-5 overtime victory, leaving Ottawa's final game, against the Wanderers, to decide first place. The Senators lost 5-2, thus giving the Bulldogs first place and the Stanley Cup. A banquet was held on March 5 at the Victoria Hotel while the Cup-deciding Ottawa-Montreal game was played. The challenging Moncton team was almost man for man the same as the previous year's entry from Galt.

STANLEY CUP CHALLENGE

Quebec Bulldogs win Stanley Cup based on first place finish

*March 11, 1912 Moncton Victorias 3 at Quebec Bulldogs 9
*March 13, 1912 Moncton Victorias 0 at Quebec Bulldogs 8 [Paddy Moran]
Quebec Bulldogs win best-of-three Stanley Cup challenge 2-0

** played at Quebec Rink, Quebec City*

QUEBEC BULLDOGS: Goldie Prodgers, Joe Hall, Walter Rooney, Paddy Moran, Jack Marks, Jack MacDonald, Eddie Oatman, George Leonard, Joe Malone, Charlie Nolan (coach), Mike Quinn (manager)

Quebec Bulldogs, 1911-12

N.H.A. FINAL STANDINGS	GP	W	L	T	GF	GA	Pts
Quebec Bulldogs	18	10	8	0	81	79	20
Ottawa Senators	18	9	9	0	99	93	18
Montreal Wanderers	18	9	9	0	95	96	18
Montreal Canadiens	18	8	10	0	59	66	16

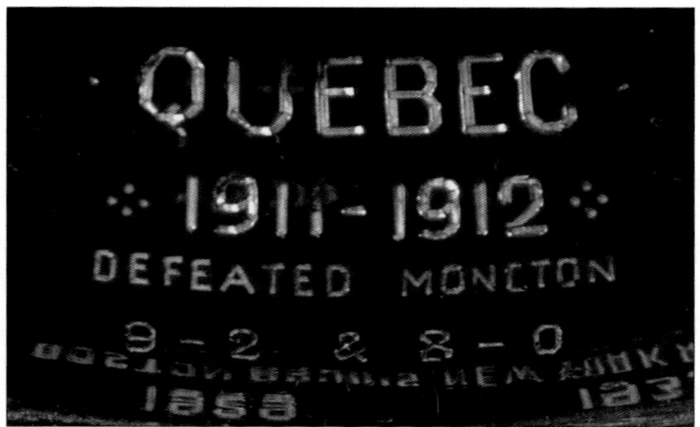

Team engraving, with scores, from the base of the original Cup

GEORGE "GOLDIE" PRODGERS was, at 20, a great defenceman, a heavy hitter with a good shot. At season's end, he jumped to the PCHA, signing with Victoria.

JOE HALL tied the score 5-5 with 20 seconds to play and then scored the winner after 24:00 of overtime in the final game of the regular season.

WALTER ROONEY played only one game with Quebec all year, the final challenge game against Moncton, and he scored a goal in the 8-0 rout.

PADDY MORAN played every minute in goal for the Bulldogs this year. His shutout in game two of the Moncton challenge was the first in Stanley Cup history.

JACK MARKS had formerly played in the Ontario Pro League. Marks replaced Eddie Oatman who suffered a foot injury and the grippe during the 9-3 win over Moncton.

JACK MacDONALD scored five goals in game two of the challenge but left the Bulldogs to accept a pro contract offer from Vancouver of the PCHA.

EDDIE OATMAN missed game two because of the grippe, and although he played pro for 17 seasons, he never played in the NHL.

GEORGE LEONARD played only one challenge game.

A scoring star in both the NHA and NHL, team captain **JOE MALONE** was a draughtsman for the Ross Rifle Company factory.

In his youth, coach **CHARLIE NOLAN** played for the Quebec Crescents, an intermediate team that won the local championship.

Manager **MIKE QUINN** began playing hockey and lacrosse as a teen, but like many a successful manager his talents were greater in a suit than in equipment.

Trainer **DAVE BELAND** was one of Canada's first successful, competitive runners and a member of the country's 1908 Olympic team.

Team president **SENATOR CHOQUETTE** was later awarded the Jacques Cartier Medal for service to France.

Spare goalie **JOE SAVARD** played against the Wanderers in his major league debut this year.

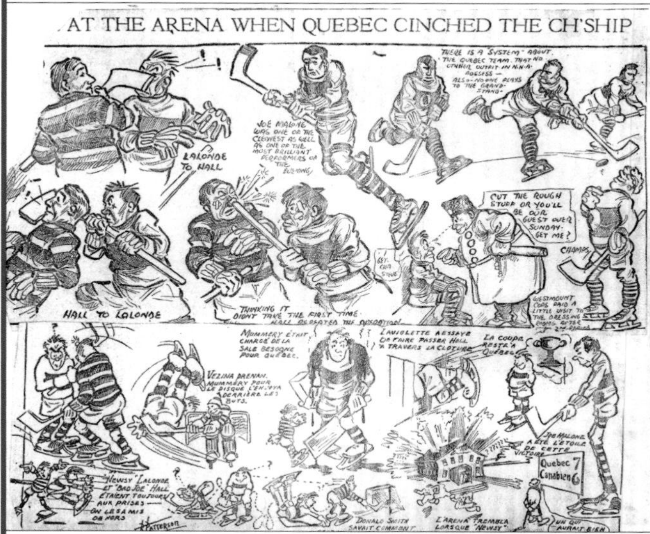

Detail from a drawn game story featuring caricatures and descriptions of play in the days before photography

Quebec Bulldogs 1912 1913

Quebec's lone challenge came from Sydney, Nova Scotia, winners of the Maritime Professional League and a team notorious for vicious, dirty play. After clinching first place in the standings and, by extension, the Stanley Cup in the 17th game of the season, in Montreal, the Bulldogs were greeted by thousands of well-wishers at the train station upon their return. Leading the welcoming was the QOCH band, the Mayor, and other dignitaries to give the players a parade to the Victoria Hotel.

Quebec Bulldogs, 1912-13

STANLEY CUP CHALLENGE

Quebec Bulldogs win Stanley Cup based on first place finish

*March 8, 1913 Sydney Millionaires 3 at Quebec Bulldogs 14
*March 10, 1913 Sydney Millionaires 2 at Quebec Bulldogs 6
Quebec Bulldogs win two-game total-goals Stanley Cup challenge 20-5

** played at Quebec Rink, Quebec City*

QUEBEC BULLDOGS: Joe Malone, Joe Hall, Paddy Moran, Harry Mummery, Tommy Smith, Jack Marks, Rusty Crawford, Billy Creighton, Jeff Malone, Rocket Power, Eddie Oatman, Georges Leonard, Walter Rooney, Jack MacDonald, George Carey, Goldie Prodgers, Mike Quinn (vice-president & manager)

N.H.A. FINAL STANDINGS	GP	W	L	T	GF	GA	Pts
Quebec Bulldogs	20	16	4	0	112	75	32
Montreal Wanderers	20	10	10	0	93	90	20
Ottawa Senators	20	9	11	0	87	81	18
Toronto Blueshirts	20	9	11	0	86	95	18
Montreal Canadiens	20	9	11	0	83	81	18
Toronto Tecumsehs	20	7	13	0	59	98	14

Team engraving, with scores, from the base of the original Cup

JOE MALONE scored nine goals in game one of the challenge.He was also a crack sprinter in the 100-yard dash and quarter-mile.

JOE HALL pushed a peanut with a toothpick from the Victoria Hotel to the Auditorium after the Bulldogs won.

Goalie **PADDY MORAN** played the full season and led the league in goals against.

HARRY MUMMERY, "Big Mum," was the heaviest player of his era and was making his debut with Quebec.

TOMMY SMITH finished second in league scoring behind linemate Joe Malone.

During the first intermission of game two of the challenge, **JACK MARKS** presented coach Quinn with a locket on behalf of the players.

A tireless backchecker, **RUSTY CRAWFORD** won this Cup in his rookie season.

A part-timer and sub, **BILLY CREIGHTON** played just three regular season games.

JEFF MALONE was the lesser brother of Joe. He and Billy Creighton replaced Hall and Smith for parts of game one.

ROCKET POWER was the brother of Charles and Joe Power. His father was MP for Quebec West.

To celebrate, **GOLDIE PRODGERS**, rolled Joe Savard in a wheel-barrow from the Victoria Hotel to the Auditorium.

GEORGE CAREY was a spare on last year's team after graduating from the Crescents.

WALTER ROONEY was a practising dentist in Quebec City, though a sub on the team.

JACK MacDONALD worked as a tool-maker at the Ross Rifle Company factory which also employed Joe Malone.

EDDIE OATMAN was born in Belleville, Ontario, and thought of as the best young right winger in the game.

A utility forward, **GEORGES LEONARD** had been a rising star until he injured his knee playing indoor baseball.

Manager **MIKE QUINN**, Lieutenant in the 8th Royal Rifles, was a city assessor when out of his gala garb.

Trainer **DAVE BELAND** was himself a former player in and around Quebec.

The team's coach, **CHARLIE NOLAN**, worked as a typographer by day.

Senator **CHOQUETTE** rode in a sleigh from the train station to the Victoria Hotel after his team won the Cup.

BARNEY KAINE, the team secretary, made a terrific speech after the Cup-winning parade.

All players wore white sweaters with "QUEBEC" printed across the chest. **JOE SAVARD'S** had a simple "Q".

T.B. O'NEIL, C. LOCKWELL, LOUIS LAGEUEX, C. FREEMONT, FRED HILL were all committee members.

A. DEROME was Quebec's commissioner.

JOE HALL JR. was the team's mascot.

1913 1914 THE CHAMPIONS Toronto Blueshirts

On the final day of the regular season, Toronto lost its game and the Canadiens won theirs, thus creating a tie for first place and forcing a two-game, total-goals playoff to determine the Stanley Cup winner. On the fast, artificial ice of Mutual Street Arena, Toronto prevailed, 6-2. During the challenge series against Victoria, the Cup was on display at Eaton's on Yonge St. in downtown Toronto.

STANLEY CUP FINALS

Toronto Blueshirts (NHA champions) defeat Victoria (PCHA champions) in best-of-five Stanley Cup finals 3-0

*March 14, 1914 Victoria Cougars 2 at Toronto Blueshirts 5
*March 17, 1914 Victoria Cougars 5 at Toronto Blueshirts 6 (Roy McGiffen 15:00 OT)
*March 19, 1914 Victoria Cougars 1 at Toronto Blueshirts 2 {Harry Cameron 6:00 3rd}

** played at Arena Gardens (Mutual St. Arena), Toronto*

TORONTO BLUESHIRTS: Con Corbeau, Roy McGiffen, Jack Walker, George McNamara, Cully Wilson, Frank Foyston, Harry Cameron, Harry Holmes, Alan Davidson, James Harriston, Jack Marshall (playing manager)

Toronto Blueshirts, 1913-14

Team engraving from the base of the original Cup

Signed during the season, **CON CORBEAU** was with Toronto for the final six games of the regular season.

ROY "MINNIE" McGIFFEN scored the OT winner in game two of the challenge, despite a bloody gash over his eye. This was not surprising. During the season he was fined a total of $116 for numerous infractions and violations.

The master of the hook check, **JACK WALKER** won this Cup with his third team, the only man to accomplish this peripatetic feat to date.

GEORGE McNAMARA and his equally ferocious brother were known as the "Dynamite Twins." He began the season with the Ontarios before arriving with the Blueshirts in time for the playoffs.

CAROL "CULLY" WILSON was a nasty bit of business who used his stick for swinging as much as stick-handling. He was known as the "Wild Man of the West" in this his first year of pro.

FRANK FOYSTON played centre on a line with Davidson and Walker and scored 16 goals in 18 regular season games. He was the scoring star of the finals as well.

HARRY CAMERON was the highest-scoring defenceman of the pre-1926 era of hockey.

HARRY "HAP" HOLMES' career GAA of 3.12 was second only to Clint Benedict during this era of the game.

Captain **ALAN DAVIDSON** missed one game of the challenge with grippe (replaced by Cully Wilson). Davidson later lost his life in Belgium, in 1915.

JAMES HARRISTON was a spare who worked as a bricklayer by day.

At age 37, playing manager **JACK MARSHALL** was partnered with Harry Cameron on defence and the pair was impregnable in the deciding playoff game against the Canadiens. Prior to game one of the finals the team held a dinner in his honour—it was his birthday—and gave him a diamond ring as a token of their admiration.

Owner **PERCY QUINN** had been goalie with the famous Montreal Shamrocks lacrosse team, world champs in 1896. He had officiated Stanley Cup games and was a key player in bringing artificial ice to Toronto a few years later. (His brother, Raphael, was a monk in Jerusalem.)

N.H.A. FINAL STANDINGS	GP	W	L	T	GF	GA	Pts
Toronto Blueshirts	20	13	7	0	93	65	26*
Montreal Canadiens	20	13	7	0	85	65	26*
Quebec Bulldogs	20	12	8	0	111	73	24
Ottawa Senators	20	11	9	0	65	71	22
Montreal Wanderers	20	7	13	0	102	125	14
Toronto Ontarios	20	4	16	0	61	118	8

* Toronto Blueshirts won two-game total-goals playoffs with Montreal 6-2 to break the tie in the standings

Patch worn by the team on their sweaters the season following the Blueshirts' Cup victory

Vancouver Millionaires 1914–1915

Some Cup historians argue that Ottawa should have been acknowledged as Cup winners in 1915 for winning the NHA title, though such a fact was never made at the time and present argument has no business trying to alter past event. The PCHL had become such a formidable league that the hockey year wasn't finished until the champions of it and the NHA met for the Stanley Cup. Clearly, after the Vancouver victory, play out West in the Patricks' league was equal to, if not superior to, the NHA. During their trip out West, the Senators visited Stanley Park in Vancouver, named for the same Lord Stanley as the eponymous trophy.

Vancouver Millionaires, 1914-15

STANLEY CUP FINALS

Vancouver Millionaires (PCHL champions) beat Ottawa Senators (NHA champions) to win best-of-five Stanley Cup finals 3-0

*March 22, 1915 Ottawa Senators 2 at Vancouver Millionaires 6
*March 24, 1915 Ottawa Senators 3 at Vancouver Millionaires 8
*March 26, 1915 Ottawa Senators 3 at Vancouver Millionaires 12 {Barney Stanley 5:10 2nd}

** played at Denman Street Arena, Vancouver*

VANCOUVER	GP	G	A	P	Pim
Cyclone Taylor	3	6	—	6	—
Mickey MacKay	3	5	—	5	—
Frank Nighbor	3	5	—	5	—
Barney Stanley	3	5	—	5	—
Lloyd Cook	3	3	—	3	—
Frank Patrick	3	2	—	2	—
Si Griffis	3	0	—	0	—
Hugh Lehman	3	0	—	0	—
Kenny Mallen	3	0	—	0	—
Jean Matz	3	0	—	0	—
Jim Seaborn	3	0	—	0	—

In Goal	GP	W-L	Mins	GA	SO	Avg
Hugh Lehman	3	3-0	180	8	0	2.67

Even though Ottawa didn't win the Cup this year, its name is still on the base of the original Cup for having won the league title in the NHA!

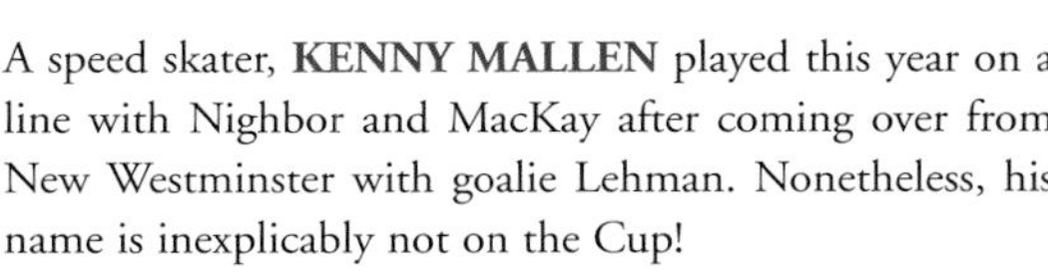

A speed skater, **KENNY MALLEN** played this year on a line with Nighbor and MacKay after coming over from New Westminster with goalie Lehman. Nonetheless, his name is inexplicably not on the Cup!

The Bob Gainey of his day, **FRANK NIGHBOR** was a superb poke-checker and two-way player who could both score and play defence. He was soon to join the Air Force, stationed in Toronto.

Called "Fred" on this Cup engraving, **CYCLONE TAYLOR** once scored a goal skating backward through the entire opposition, though the goal is more myth than substantiated report.

HUGHIE LEHMAN had played goal for Berlin and Galt in the challenges of 1910, and although he had been playing pro since 1909 he didn't make his NHL debut until 1926.

As a rookie, **LLOYD COOK** was a sub until Si Griffis broke his leg near the end of the season. Cook came in and shone during the Ottawa series and returned to his ranch in Tabor, Saskatchewan, after the victory.

Name misspelled "McKay," **MICKEY MACKAY**, the 145 lbs. "Wee Scot," was new to the PCHL from the Boundary League. Nonetheless, he led the league in scoring.

BARNEY STANLEY scored four goals in the deciding game of the Ottawa series—including three in the second period—to clinch the Stanley Cup.

Team engraving from the base of the original Cup

JIM SEABORN played the first game of the year as a member of Portland, then left the team and signed with Vancouver.

One of the fastest big men of his era, captain **SI GRIFFIS** did not appear in the playoffs because of a broken left ankle. But when Vancouver proposed Lester Patrick to be his substitute, Ottawa, knowing Lester's abilities, refused the request, allowing only the weaker Lloyd Cook to fill the roster.

JEAN MATZ played only one game during the season, not enough to get his name on the Cup in the eyes of team officials.

Teamed with Lloyd Cook on defence for the challenge, **FRANK PATRICK** once scored six goals from defence in a 1912 game.

1915 THE CHAMPIONS
1916 Montreal Canadiens

As was the case the previous year with Ottawa, many historians felt that Portland, by virtue of their league win over Vancouver, should have been named Cup champions prior to the challenge against the Canadiens (or, "Canadian," as the engraving misspells the name). After finishing last the previous year, the Montreals completely revamped their lineup to produce this winning roster. This was the last year the team was referred to as the "Club Athletique Canadien."

STANLEY CUP FINALS

Montreal Canadiens (NHA champions) beat Portland Rosebuds (PCHL champions) to win best-of-five Stanley Cup finals 3-2

*March 20, 1916 Portland Rosebuds 2 at Montreal Canadiens 0 [Tom Murray]
*March 22, 1916 Portland Rosebuds 1 at Montreal Canadiens 2
*March 25, 1916 Portland Rosebuds 3 at Montreal Canadiens 6
*March 28, 1916 Portland Rosebuds 6 at Montreal Canadiens 5
*March 30, 1916 Portland Rosebuds 1 at Montreal Canadiens 2 {Goldie Prodgers 16:45 3rd}

** played at Westmount Arena, Montreal*

WHEN ROSEBUDS FOOLED CANADIENS IN LAST NIGHT'S STANLEY CUP MATCH

Newspaper story covering the Portland-Montreal fight for the Cup.

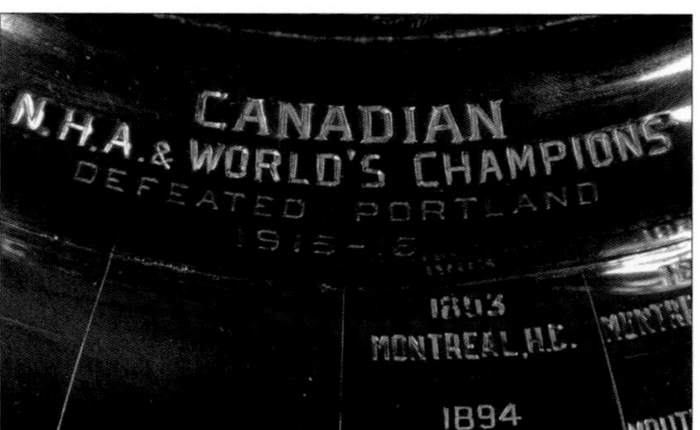

Team engraving from the shoulder of the original Cup

GEORGES VEZINA never missed a game until illness resulted in his death from a game on March 27, 1926.

BERTHAM "BERT" CORBEAU, drowned September 21, 1942 when his boat capsized.

Captain **JACK LAVIOLETTE** missed game two of the finals with a broken nose. He was also a race car driver.

Although he was one of the greatest players of his era, this was to be **NEWSY LALONDE'S** only Stanley Cup.

LOUIS BERLINQUETTE played in more games than any other skater of the pre-NHL era during a career that lasted from 1912 to '23.

GOLDIE PRODGERS was the hero at the last dance, scoring the Cup-winner on a superb end-to-end rush.

A new defencemen, **HOWARD McNAMARA** represented an integral part of the revamped Habs' lineup.

The first-ever member of the Canadiens (in 1909), **DIDIER PITRE** often drank champagne between periods.

SKENE RONAN arrived from Toronto and retired after this win. He later made a brief comeback with Ottawa.

ARMOS ARBOUR was struck over the head with a stick at the end of a game on February 26, and a brawl erupted.

GEORGES POULIN was born in Smiths Falls, Ontario and captained that OHA team to titles in 1904 and '05.

A sub, **JACQUES FOURNIER** didn't score once in the nine games he played during the regular schedule.

Secretary **NAPOLEON DORVAL** had been co-owner of the Nationals with Adolphe Lecours, but the team had been refused entry into the NHA in 1909.

U.P. BOUDIER was the team president.

One of the owners, **GEORGES KENDALL** later changed his name to George Kennedy.

Georges Vezina was scouted by manager **GEORGE McNAMARA** and signed on the spot.

ALDRIE OUIMET and **S. NEWSWORTHY** were members of the Montreal directorate.

MONTREAL	GP	G	A	P	Pim
Didier Pitre	5	4	—	4	—
Armos Arbour	4	3	—	3	—
Newsy Lalonde	4	3	—	3	—
Goldie Prodgers	4	3	—	3	—
Georges Poulin	3	1	—	1	—
Skene Ronan	2	1	—	1	—
Bert Corbeau	5	0	—	0	—
Howard McNamara	5	0	—	0	—
Georges Vezina	5	0	—	0	—
Jack Laviolette	4	0	—	0	—
Louis Berlinquette	1	0	—	0	—

In Goal	GP	W-L	Mins	GA	SO	Avg
Georges Vezina	5	3-2	300	13	0	2.60

Montreal goalie Georges Vezina celebrates the Cup victory by being almost certainly the first man to put his son into the bowl, a tradition that has gone on strong ever since.

Seattle Metropolitans 1916 1917

This Seattle team was stacked with former Toronto Blueshirts from the 1914 Cup win (Holmes, Walker, Foyston, Wilson). Although the Mets were not amateurs, were not playing in Canada, and were not challengers, the trustees of the Cup allowed an American team to compete for the Cup. Seattle won for the first time because it had proved its superiority.

Seattle (left) and Montreal pose inside the Seattle Ice Arena

STANLEY CUP FINALS

Seattle Metropolitans (PCHL champions) beat Montreal Canadiens (NHA champions) to win best-of-five Stanley Cup finals 3-1

*March 17, 1917 Montreal Canadiens 8 at Seattle Metropolitans 4
*March 20, 1917 Montreal Canadiens 1 at Seattle Metropolitans 6
*March 23, 1917 Montreal Canadiens 1 at Seattle Metropolitans 4
*March 26, 1917 Montreal Canadiens 1 at Seattle Metropolitans 9 {Morris 7:55 2nd}

** played at Seattle Ice Arena*

SEATTLE	GP	G	A	P	Pim
Bernie Morris	4	14	—	14	0
Frank Foyston	4	7	—	7	3
Cully Wilson	4	1	—	1	6
Jack Walker	4	1	—	1	0
Roy Rickey	4	0	—	0	23
Ed Carpenter	4	0	—	0	3
Jim Riley	4	0	—	0	3
Hap Holmes	4	0	—	0	0
Bobby Rowe	3	0	—	0	0

In Goal	GP	W-L	Mins	GA	SO	Avg
Hap Holmes	4	3-1	240	11	0	2.90

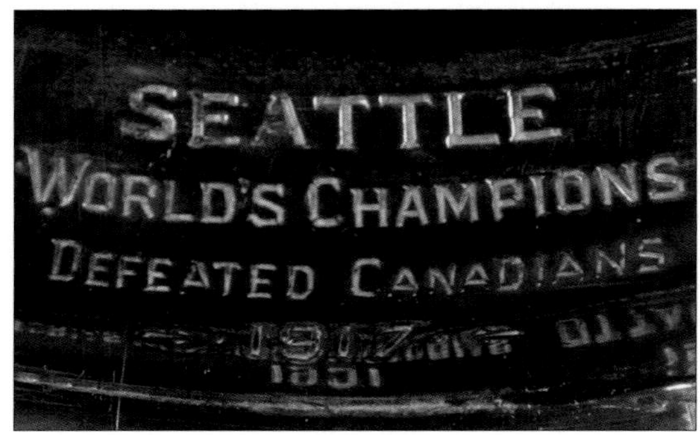

Team engraving from the base of the original Cup

Cover point **EVERAR "ED" CARPENTER** played all season without missing a game, scoring five goals in Seattle's 24 league games. He played only two pro seasons, both with the Mets.

Despite playing professionally until 1928, **HAP HOLMES** played only two years in the NHL. He recorded the only two shutouts in PCHL play this year and allowed just 80 goals, 32 fewer than the next best cage guardian, Tommy Murray of Portland.

CULLY WILSON was one of the first to leave the established NHA for the upstart PCHA yet was later banned from the West Coast league for a vicious cross-check on Mickey MacKay. He was famed for being able to hook a shot from behind the goal line into the net.

JACK WALKER spent nine years with Seattle, won three Cups, each with a different team, and retired in 1932 at the age of 43.

The goal-scoring star of the year, **BERNIE MORRIS** scored goals with the greatest ease since Frank McGee. In four games of the Stanley Cup finals, he scored three, two, three, and six goals. Two years later, the Canadian citizen was convicted of being a deserter from the U.S. army and sentenced to two years' hard labour.

In his second year with Seattle, captain **FRANK FOYSTON** became one of the PCHA's greatest scorers.

Team engraving from the base of the replica Cup

During the finals, **ROY RICKEY** got into a nasty fight with Billy Coutu that saw Harry Mummery come out of the penalty box to help Coutu. Mummery was given a misconduct for his actions.

A sub, this was **JIM RILEY'S** first year with the team. A native of Bayfield, New Brunswick, he played with Seattle until retiring in 1924.

BOBBY ROWE played just four NHL games in a 17-year pro career, and equally surprising was that this was his only Stanley Cup.

PETE MULDOON started athletics as a boxer, then disappeared for many years and resurfaced as manager of the Metropolitans.

1917–1918 THE CHAMPIONS Toronto Arenas

So reviled was previous Toronto owner Eddie Livingstone that the NHA disbanded in 1917 and reformed as the NHL a few months later to ensure the city's entry would not have him as the man in charge. On November 26, 1917, at the Windsor Hotel in Montreal, the National Hockey League was born. "Don't get us wrong, Elmer," Montreal Wanderers owner Sam Lichtenheim told reporter Elmer Ferguson. "We didn't throw Livingstone out. He's still got his franchise in the old National Hockey Association...The only problem is, he's playing in a one-team league."

STANLEY CUP FINALS

Toronto Arenas (NHL champions) beat Vancouver Millionaires (PCHL champions) to win best-of-five Stanley Cup finals 3-2

*March 20, 1918 Vancouver Millionaires 3 at Toronto Arenas 5
*March 23, 1918 Vancouver Millionaires 6 at Toronto Arenas 4
*March 26, 1918 Vancouver Millionaires 3 at Toronto Arenas 6
*March 28, 1918 Vancouver Millionaires 8 at Toronto Arenas 1
*March 30, 1918 Vancouver Millionaires 1 at Toronto Arenas 2 {Corb Denneny 10:30 3rd}

** played at Arena Gardens (Mutual St. Arena), Toronto*

Toronto Arenas, 1917-18

Team engraving from the shoulder of the original Cup

ALF SKINNER and **JOE HALL** were charged by Toronto police following a stick-swinging duel on January 28.

HARRY MUMMERY was selected by the Arenas at the start of the season in the dispersal of Quebec players.

Earlier in the season, **HARRY CAMERON** was fined $100 by coach Querrie for not trying hard enough!

CORB DENNENY scored the Cup-winning goal on a spectacular individual rush before beating goalie Lehman.

REG NOBLE finished the previous year with the Habs before rejoining Toronto at the start of this season.

Harry's lesser-known brother, **GORDON MEEKING**, played 1916-22 in the NHA as well as leagues out West.

In game two of the finals, **KEN RANDALL** was fined $15 for abusive language.

One of Charlie Querrie's first moves as manager was to sign the veteran **HAP HOLMES** for goal.

CHARLIE QUERRIE agreed to be team manager on condition Eddie Livingstone not interfere in any way.

A scorer in the NHA during his prime, **JACK MARKS** played just seven games over three years in the NHL.

Because he arrived late in the season, **JACK ADAMS** was not eligible to play in the finals.

RUSTY CRAWFORD, like Adams, arrived too late to be eligible for the finals.

JACK COUGHLIN played the first six games of the season before being released outright on January 6, 1918.

MIKE NEVILLE scored a goal in his one and only game this year.

SAMMY HEBERT had also been a spare with Ottawa during its Cups of the early 1920s.

ARTHUR BROOKS was with the Arenas in December 1917, until the team signed Hap Holmes.

Brothers **DICK** and **FRANK CARROLL** were alternately trainers and coaches with the Arenas.

TORONTO	GP	G	A	P	Pim
Alf Skinner	5	8	2	10	18
Harry Mummery	5	0	6	6	21
Harry Cameron	5	3	1	4	12
Corb Denneny	5	3	1	4	0
Reg Noble	5	2	1	3	12
Harry Meeking	5	1	2	3	18
Ken Randall	5	1	0	1	21
Hap Holmes	5	0	0	0	0

In Goal	GP	W-L	Mins	GA	SO	Avg
Hap Holmes	5	3-2	300	21	0	4.20

Although Vancouver lost to Toronto for the Stanley Cup, it's the Millionaires, and not the Arenas, that are on the replica Cup (above) as well as the Stanley Cup and original base!

1918 Series Cancelled 1919

PNEUMONIA TAKES JOE HALL, OLDEST PLAYER IN HOCKEY

Veteran Star of Great Winter Game Succumbs to Disease Following "Flu" Attack.

"TRADE MARK OF HOCKEY"

Born in England 38 Years Ago Deceased Was One of Best Known Men in Sportdom.

Newspaper announcement of the death of Joe Hall

STANLEY CUP FINALS

Series cancelled when tied 2-2-1 because of influenza epidemic

*March 19, 1919 Montreal Canadiens 0 at Seattle Metropolitans 7 [Hap Holmes]
*March 22, 1919 Montreal Canadiens 4 at Seattle Metropolitans 2
*March 24, 1919 Montreal Canadiens 2 at Seattle Metropolitans 7
*March 26, 1919 Montreal Canadiens 0 at Seattle Metropolitans 0 (20:00 OT) [Georges Vezina/Hap Holmes]
*March 30, 1919 Montreal Canadiens 4 at Seattle Metropolitans 3 {(Jack McDonald 15:57 OT)}

** played at Seattle Ice Arena*

MONTREAL	GP	G	A	P	Pim
Newsy Lalonde	5	6	0	6	3
Didier Pitre	5	0	3	3	0
Odie Cleghorn	5	2	0	2	9
Jack MacDonald	5	1	1	2	3
Louis Berlinquette	5	1	1	2	0
Bert Corbeau	5	0	1	1	3
Billy Coutu	5	0	1	1	0
Joe Hall	5	0	0	0	6
Georges Vezina	5	0	0	0	0

In Goal	GP	W-L	Mins	GA	SO	Avg
Georges Vezina	5	2-2-1	336	19	1	3.39

SEATTLE	GP	G	A	P	Pim
Frank Foyston	5	9	1	10	0
Cully Wilson	5	1	3	4	6
Jack Walker	5	3	0	3	9
Muzz Murray	5	3	0	3	3
Roy Rickey	5	1	2	3	0
Ran McDonald	5	1	1	2	3
Bobby Rowe	5	1	0	1	6
Hap Holmes	5	0	0	0	0

In Goal	GP	W-L	Mins	GA	SO	Avg
Hap Holmes	5	2-2-1	336	10	2	1.79

The year 1919 marked the only time in Stanley Cup history that no winner was named. The finals was tied when the series was cancelled because literally every Montreal player, except Odie Cleghorn, had fallen ill as a result of the influenza epidemic. Joe Hall, the baddest and oldest professional hockey player, died of pneumonia in the Columbus sanatorium in Seattle, and manager George Kennedy recovered only to die a few weeks later. As a result, his wife sold the team, and the introduction of the NHL Montreal Canadiens franchise was at hand.

Many Seattle players were also felled by the flu, but the extraordinary number of Canadiens being laid low was attributed to their having just been in Victoria, where many players from that team had only recently recovered from bouts of the illness. That the series was tied at the time of cancellation was in many ways fitting. The teams were playing what might otherwise have been a sensational hockey finals, and the Canadiens had only just tied the series after a second lengthy overtime. Prior to the sixth game, the series was cancelled and the ill Montreal players returned home, all except Lalonde, Couture, and Berlinquette who travelled to Manitoba to act as pallbearers at Hall's funeral.

Team engraving from the shoulder of the original Cup

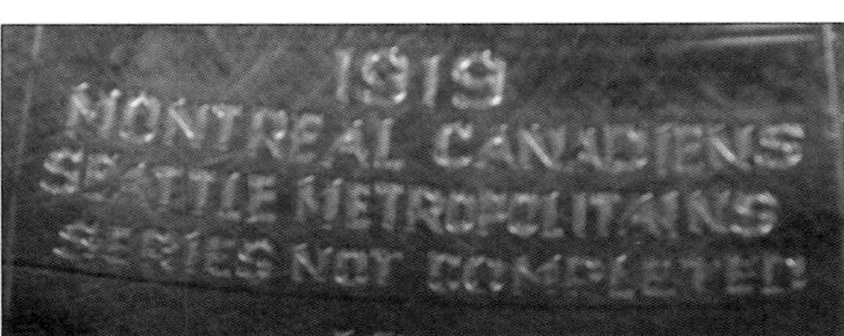

Team engraving from the shoulder of the replica Cup, including misspelling of "Metroplitains"

Influenza Knocks Out World's Hockey Match

Bunch of Visiting Canadiens Sick in Bed—Looks as If Stanley Series Was Off.

THE hockey game for tonight has been called off and from all appearances the Stanley cup series for 1919 will have to be abandoned.

Influenza has within the past forty-eight hours laid out five of the Canadiens, while a sixth, Corbeau, is so badly banged up that he cannot play. But three men are left capable of handling a stick.

Newspaper story reports on the cancellation of the Stanley Cup series for the first and only time in Cup history

1919 THE CHAMPIONS

1920 Ottawa Senators

During the finals, the Cup was on display in Ottawa at R.J. Devlin Co., a furrier on Sparks Street. The Senators won both halves of the NHL schedule, thus eliminating the need for a league playoff. However, the ice was so bad in Ottawa that the final two games of the Stanley Cup playoffs were re-located to Toronto where artificial ice was available.

STANLEY CUP FINALS

Ottawa Senators win best-of-five Stanley Cup finals 3-2

*March 22, 1920	Seattle Metropolitans 2 at Ottawa Senators 3
*March 24, 1920	Seattle Metropolitans 0 at Ottawa Senators 3 [Clint Benedict]
*March 27, 1920	Seattle Metropolitans 3 at Ottawa Senators 1
**March 30, 1920	Seattle Metropolitans 5 Ottawa Senators 2
**April 1, 1920	Ottawa Senators 6 Seattle Metropolitans 1 {Jack Darragh 5:00 3rd}

** played at Dey's Arena, Ottawa ** played at Arena Gardens (Mutual St. Arena), Toronto (artificial ice) because of poor ice conditions in Ottawa (natural ice)*

Ottawa Senators, 1919-20

OTTAWA	GP	G	A	P	Pim
Frank Nighbor	5	6	1	7	2
Jack Darragh	5	5	2	7	3
Eddie Gerard	2	2	1	3	3
George Boucher	5	2	0	2	3
Cy Denneny	5	0	2	2	3
Sprague Cleghorn	5	0	1	1	4
Clint Benedict	5	0	0	0	0
Morley Bruce	5	0	0	0	0
Jack Mackell	5	0	0	0	0
Punch Broadbent	4	0	0	0	0

In Goal	GP	W-L	Mins	GA	SO	Avg
Clint Benedict	5	3-2	300	11	1	2.20

Team engraving from the shoulder of the replica Cup

FRANK NIGHBOR led the teams in playoff scoring with his six goals and became the winner of the first Hart Trophy.

JACK DARRAGH was in his tenth season with Ottawa and he scored three goals in the Cup-winning contest.

At age 17, **EDDIE GERARD** had played for the Ottawa Vics in January 1908 against the Wanderers in a challenge. He was a government employee in the daytime.

Left winger **GEORGE BOUCHER** possessed tremendous strength gained largely from his playing days as a running back with a battery team in Petawawa during WWI.

CY DENNENY had been acquired from Toronto in 1917 for goalie Sammy Hebert and $750.

SPRAGUE CLEGHORN'S end-to-end rushes were spectacular, outdone only by his violent temper.

CLINT BENEDICT'S five shutouts this season were incredible not just for leading the league but because he was the only goalie to record even one!

Back from overseas service during the war, **MORLEY BRUCE** didn't score a goal all season.

JACK MACKELL was making NHL debut. His son, Fleming, later played on Cup-winning Leafs teams in 1949 and '51.

PUNCH BROADBENT had been awarded the Military Cross during WWI before embarking on an NHL career.

Defenceman **HORACE MERRILL** was also a member of the successful printing business of Kuhn and Merrill.

Manager **TOMMY GORMAN** was one of the founders of the NHL. He later managed the Agua Caliente Racetrack in Mexico (1929-52).

PETE GREEN had earlier coached Ottawa to the Cup in 1908-09 before returning to the club this year.

"TED" DEY was one of three brothers (William and Frank) active in hockey. He was club president, 1918-23.

TOMMY AHEARN worked at the Western Union Telegraph Co. in New York (1873-75) before returning to Ottawa.

FRANK "COZY" DOLAN was the Ottawa trainer.

Dey's Arena (right) on Laurier Ave. between Canal and Elgin Streets in Ottawa

Ottawa Senators 1920 1921

Ottawa won the first half of the schedule to qualify for the NHL playoffs, but during the second half the Senators had a stretch of seven losses in a row. They recovered in time for the playoffs. The Senators adopted a team defence that came to be known as "Kitty Bar the Door" for its stifling success. In the NHL finals series, a two-game, total-goals playoffs, the Sens didn't allow a single St. Pats goal, winning 5-0 and 2-0 to advance to the Cup finals where they allowed just 12 goals in five games. On April 10, the city hosted a grand parade for the victors, culminating with a banquet at the Chateau Laurier Hotel in downtown Ottawa.

Ottawa Senators, 1920-21

STANLEY CUP FINALS

Ottawa Senators win best-of-five Stanley Cup finals 3-2

*March 21, 1921 Ottawa Senators 1 at Vancouver Millionaires 3
*March 24, 1921 Ottawa Senators 4 at Vancouver Millionaires 3
*March 28, 1921 Ottawa Senators 3 at Vancouver Millionaires 2
*March 31, 1921 Ottawa Senators 2 at Vancouver Millionaires 3
*April 4, 1921 Ottawa Senators 2 at Vancouver Millionaires 1 {Jack Darragh 9:40 2nd}

** played at Denman Street Arena, Vancouver*

OTTAWA	GP	G	A	P	Pim
Jack Darragh	5	5	0	5	7
Cy Denneny	5	2	2	4	10
George Boucher	5	2	0	2	9
Punch Broadbent	5	2	0	2	0
Sprague Cleghorn	5	1	1	2	36
Frank Nighbor	2	0	1	1	0
Eddie Gerard	2	0	0	0	44
Clint Benedict	5	0	0	0	0
Jack Mackell	4	0	0	0	0

In Goal	GP	W-L	Mins	GA	SO	Avg
Clint Benedict	5	3-2	300	12	0	2.40

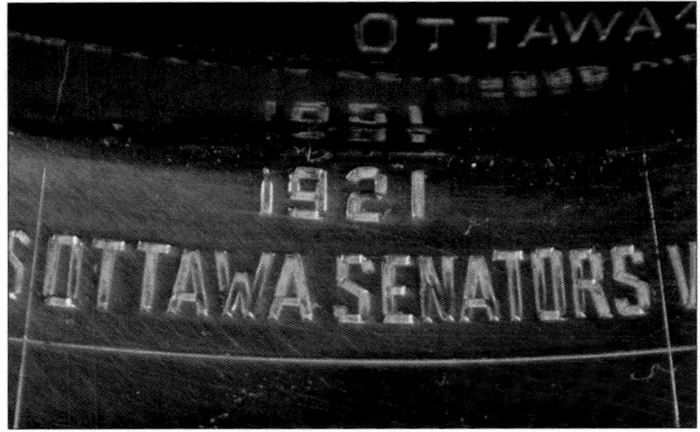

Team engraving from the shoulder of the original Cup

In order for **JACK DARRAGH** to play in the finals, Ottawa mayor Frank Plant had to convince Darragh's employers, the Ottawa Dairy Company, to grant him the necessary time off. Darragh scored the Cup-winner for the second year in a row.

CY DENNENY faced his brother Corb in the NHL finals series, the first time brothers had opposed each other in the playoffs.

Teamed with Gerard, **GEORGE BOUCHER** formed the best defensive tandem in the league and was the nucleus of the "Kitty Bar the Door" style of play.

PUNCH BROADBENT got married just a few hours before the team boarded the train for Vancouver, bringing the bride, Leda Fitzsimmons, along for a hockey honeymoon.

After three regular season games, **SPRAGUE CLEGHORN** was dumped by Ottawa and played the second half of the schedule with Toronto. He then played for the St. Pats in the playoffs against the Sens, but when Toronto was eliminated Cleghorn re-joined Ottawa!

FRANK NIGHBOR spent more than 12 years with the Sens, winning four Cups.

EDDIE GERARD incurred six penalties in game five, including a match penalty near the end of the game.

Called "Praying Benny" because he fell to the ice so often during an era when this was not permitted, goalie **CLINT BENEDICT** almost single-handedly forced the league to change rules about this practise.

Sub **JACK MACKELL** played just 45 NHL games with the Senators over two seasons but won a Cup each year.

Utility forward **LETH GRAHAM** worked for the Ottawa Electric Company by day.

A sub, **MORLEY BRUCE** played in the regular season and NHL playoffs but not in the Cup finals.

The well-liked **PETE GREEN** coached the Senators to his third Stanley Cup.

Ted Dey's cousin (brother Frank's son, **EDGAR**) died three years later from injuries suffered during a vicious stick-swinging battle during a game in Halifax.

Executive **TOMMY AHEARN**, in partnership with Warren Soper, started an incandescent lighting system in Ottawa which made electronic service on wheels possible throughout the winter months.

TOMMY GORMAN quit school at age nine and found work as a parliamentary page boy and later became a spot reporter for the *Ottawa Citizen.*

FRANK "COZY" DOLAN was still the team's trainer.

1921 THE CHAMPIONS
1922 Toronto St. Pats

The Toronto Blueshirts had been purchased in 1919 and the new owners changed the team's name to St. Pats in the hope of attracting the large Irish population in the city to their home games. This was the first year the NHL played a full season that counted as a whole. Previously, the schedule was split in two, the winners of the first half playing the winners of the second half to advance to the Cup finals. Now, the top two teams met in a playoffs, Toronto beating Ottawa 5-4 in a two-game, total-goals series that saw the second game end in a scoreless tie.

STANLEY CUP FINALS

Toronto St. Pats win best-of-five Stanley Cup finals 3-2

*March 17, 1922 Vancouver Millionaires 4 at Toronto St. Pats 3
*March 20, 1922 Vancouver Millionaires 1 at Toronto St. Pats 2 (Babe Dye 4:50 OT)
*March 23, 1922 Vancouver Millionaires 3 at Toronto St. Pats 0 [Hugh Lehman]
*March 25, 1922 Vancouver Millionaires 0 at Toronto St. Pats 6 [John Ross Roach]
*March 28, 1922 Vancouver Millionaires 1 at Toronto St. Pats 5 {Babe Dye 4:20 1st}

** played at Arena Gardens (Mutual St. Arena), Toronto*

Toronto St. Pats, 1921-22

Team engraving from the shoulder of the Stanley Cup

BABE DYE'S nine goals in the finals set a record that stands to this day. In game two, he was awarded the first-ever penalty shot—he missed.

CORB DENNENY was traded to Vancouver for Jack Adams shortly after winning the Cup.

DR. ROD SMYLIE won this Cup while interning at St. Mike's Hospital and after retiring as a player in 1924 he specialized in chest medicines and allergies.

Forward **LLOYD ANDREWS** was signed midway through the season after playing senior hockey.

HARRY CAMERON hurt his shoulder in game two but rallied to play most of the deciding game.

RED STUART was a rock on defence. He was one of the reasons Vancouver managed only nine goals.

KEN RANDALL played both defence (with Cameron) and right wing (on a line with Noble and Dye).

REG NOBLE broke training numerous times and aggravated coach Querrie to no end.

Nervous and restless, **JOHN ROSS ROACH** twitched and fidgeted in goal whenever play moved up ice.

TED STACKHOUSE was a new recruit who saw only limited action in the playoffs.

The great Ottawa captain **EDDIE GERARD** played one game on loan from the Senators as an emergency replacement for the injured Cameron.

IVAN "MIKE" MITCHELL played two games in goal with the St. Pats this season, winning both.

STANTON "STAN" JACKSON played only on December 24, 1921.

PAT NOLAN played only two career NHL games and was long gone from the city by the time the St. Pats won.

WILLY POPP and **H. McILORY** were the team's trainers.

GEORGE DONAHUE was the team's business manager.

Manager **CHARLIE QUERRIE** later ran a movie house in the city and wrote for the Leafs' souvenir programme.

TORONTO	GP	G	A	P	Pim
Babe Dye	5	9	1	10	3
Corb Denneny	5	3	2	5	2
Rod Smylie	5	1	3	4	0
Lloyd Andrews	5	2	0	2	3
Harry Cameron	4	0	2	2	11
Red Stuart	5	0	2	2	6
Ken Randall	4	1	0	1	19
Reg Noble	5	0	1	1	9
John Ross Roach	5	0	0	0	0
Ted Stackhouse	4	0	0	0	0
Eddie Gerard	1	0	0	0	0

In Goal	GP	W-L	Mins	GA	SO	Avg
John Ross Roach	5	3-2	305	9	1	1.77

Three members of this Cup-winning team—star defenceman Babe Dye, goalie John Ross Roach, and forward Lloyd Andrews

Ottawa Senators 1922 1923

Playoff rules were simple. In the case of a tie, teams would play sudden death or two, ten-minute periods, whichever came first. Ottawa qualified for the Stanley Cup playoffs by beating the Canadiens 3-2 in a two-game, total-goals NHL playoffs before beating two teams out West for the Cup. On their way home, the Sens stopped off in Winnipeg to play an exhibition game. They arrived in the 'Peg a day early and went rabbit hunting in the afternoon before playing that night. Upon arriving in Ottawa on April 5 after the Cup victory, the Senators were greeted by thousands of fans and were given a parade through the city. Players each received a record $700 for their win.

Ottawa Senators, 1922-23

STANLEY CUP FINALS

Ottawa Senators win best-of-three Stanley Cup finals 2-0

*March 16, 1923	Ottawa Senators 1 at Vancouver Maroons 0
	(Punch Broadbent 15:00 3rd) [Clint Benedict]
*March 19, 1923	Ottawa Senators 1 at Vancouver Maroons 4
*March 23, 1923	Ottawa Senators 3 at Vancouver Maroons 2
*March 26, 1923	Ottawa Senators 5 at Vancouver Maroons 1
	Ottawa Senators (NHL champs) beat Vancouver Millionaires (PCHL champs) 3-1 to face Edmonton Eskimos (WCHL champs) for the Stanley Cup
*March 29, 1923	Ottawa Senators 2 Edmonton Eskimos 1 (Cy Denneny 2:08 OT)
*March 31, 1923	Ottawa Senators 1 Edmonton Eskimos 0
	{(Punch Broadbent 11:23 1st)} [Clint Benedict]

** played at Denman Street Arena, Vancouver*

OTTAWA	GP	G	A	P	Pim
Punch Broadbent	6	6	1	7	12
George Boucher	6	2	1	3	6
Frank Nighbor	6	1	1	2	10
Cy Denneny	6	1	1	2	8
King Clancy	6	1	0	1	4
Eddie Gerard	6	1	0	1	4
Lionel Hitchman	5	1	0	1	4
Jack Darragh	2	1	0	1	2
Clint Benedict	6	0	0	0	2
Harry Helman	2	0	0	0	0

In Goal	GP	W-L	Mins	GA	SO	Avg
King Clancy	1	0-0	2	0	0	0.00
Clint Benedict	6	5-1	360	8	1	1.33

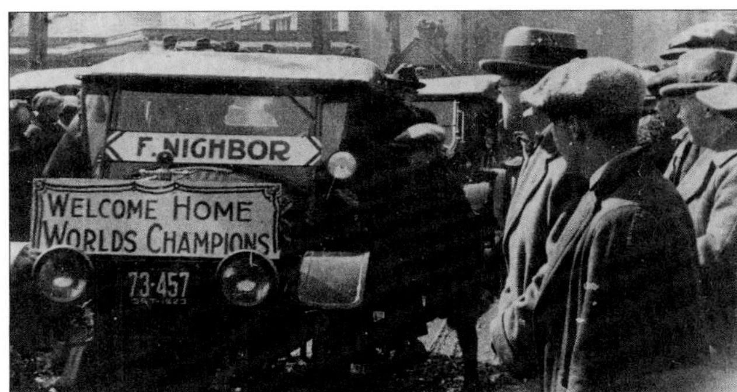

A car moves slowly through the streets of Ottawa during the Senators' Cup parade, each player getting his own transportation. The capped lad on the car is Sam Macli, a 14-year-old newspaper seller who became caught up in the celebrations.

In game one against Vancouver, **PUNCH BROADBENT** was stymied repeatedly by Lehman leading up to Broadbent's late, game-winning goal.

GEORGE BOUCHER played against his brother, Frank, versus Vancouver, as did Cy Denneny face his brother, Corb.

In the finals, it was **FRANK NIGHBOR'S** checking of Edmonton star Duke Keats that shut down the Eskimos' offense.

CY DENNENY suffered a concussion after being hit on the head by Billy Coutu during the regular season, though he recovered to play an important role against Edmonton.

KING CLANCY played every position in a game against Vancouver. He took the Cup home and it stayed in his house the entire year until president Calder came looking for it in 1924!

Captain **EDDIE GERARD** won his fourth straight Cup in his last season.

LIONEL HITCHMAN scored the only goal of the deciding match of the NHL playoffs.

In game two against Edmonton, **CLINT BENEDICT** was penalized for slashing and had to serve the infraction himself.

Team engraving from the shoulder of the original Cup

HARRY HELMAN suffered a serious cut to his face from a teammate's skate in practise. He played only two games of the playoffs.

When **FRANK BOUCHER** left Ottawa to play out West, the Sens talked Jack Darragh out of retirement. He spent much of the season as a sub for Harry Broadbent.

PETE GREEN, the coach, won his third Cup in four years with the Senators.

Manager **TOMMY GORMAN** won a gold medal with Canada's lacrosse team at the 1908 London Olympics and abandoned a career in journalism to focus on management.

TED DEY was one of the first men to install red lights above the nets to signal goals, improving on his earlier method of having goal judges use flashlights with red bulbs!

1923 THE CHAMPIONS

1924 Montreal Canadiens

A group of players, entrusted with the Cup, drove over to manager Leo Dandurand's house for a celebration party. En route, they suffered a flat tire, and while they changed wheels they placed the Cup by the side of the road. They drove on to Dandurand's, only later discovering that they had left the Cup on the road. They drove back and recovered the trophy which had remained, untouched and unscathed, where it had been forgotten!
To mark the victory, the Habs drastically altered their sweaters for the '24-'25 season, replacing the sacred "C H" crest with a two-dimensional globe to indicate their place as world's champions.

STANLEY CUP FINALS

Montreal Canadiens defeat Calgary Tigers 2-0 in best two-of-three Stanley Cup finals

*March 18, 1924 Vancouver Maroons 2 at Montreal Canadiens 3
*March 20, 1924 Vancouver Maroons 1 at Montreal Canadiens 2

Montreal Canadiens (NHL champs) defeat Vancouver Maroons (PCHL champs) 2-0 in best two-of-three to face Calgary Tigers (WCHL champs) for the Stanley Cup

*March 22, 1924 Calgary Tigers 1 at Montreal Canadiens 6
**March 25, 1924 Montreal Canadiens 3 Calgary Tigers 0 {Morenz 1:16 1st} [Georges Vezina]

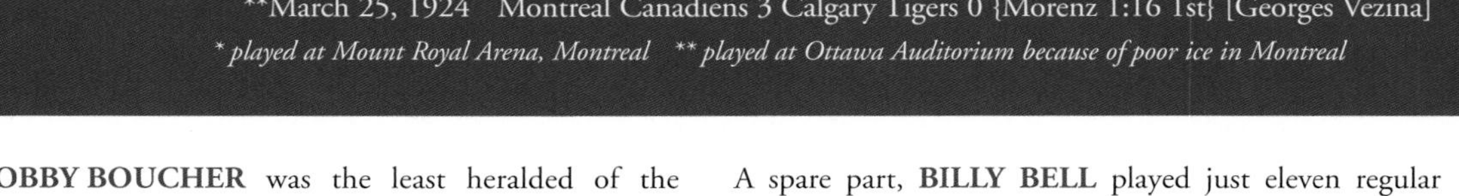

** played at Mount Royal Arena, Montreal ** played at Ottawa Auditorium because of poor ice in Montreal*

Montreal Canadiens, 1923-24

BOBBY BOUCHER was the least heralded of the Boucher brothers and, at 140 lbs., the lightest and least successful. He played on a line with Joliat and Morenz, one of the best threesomes of any era.

HOWARTH "HOWIE" MORENZ turned pro when his father signed a contract for him to join the Canadiens.

Weighing just 135 pounds, **AUREL JOLIAT** arrived in Montreal in a trade from Saskatoon for Newsy Lalonde.

SPRAGUE CLEGHORN was reviled by all. He was also considered one of the greatest daredevil motorcycle racers in North America.

When Couture went down with an injury, coach Dandurand used the deadly, vicious, violent **ODIE CLEGHORN** and his brother as a defensive pairing.

Although he played just 45 total NHL games, **BILLY CAMERON** has his name on the Cup from this year.

This was **BILLY COUTU'S** only Cup. In the 1927 playoffs, he assaulted a referee after the final game while playing for Boston and was suspended for life.

This was **SYLVIO MANTHA'S** first of three Cups with Montreal during his distinguished 14-year NHL career.

Today's Vezina Trophy is named after **GEORGES VEZINA**, the greatest goalie of his era.

A spare part, **BILLY BELL** played just eleven regular season games in this his final NHL season.

From hockey to lacrosse, **JOE MALONE** spent all his adult life in pro sports, much of it as a champion.

CHARLES FORTIER worked at the Bell Telephone Company for forty years.

ED DUFOUR was the team's trainer.

Executive the Honourable **LOUIS ATHANASE DAVID** was called to the Senate in February 1940.

CATTARINICH, LETOURNEAU, and **DANDURAND** were nicknamed the "Three Musketeers" after buying the team on November 3, 1921 for $11,000.

In addition to his affiliation with the Canadiens, **NAPOLEON DORVAL** was an iron worker in the city.

"EDDIE" ST. PERE was a member of parliament for Quebec and also a lieutenant.

HENRY ELLIOTT, King's Council, was partner in Elliott & David, barristers and solicitors.

A team director, **DR. HART** had long been associated with Dandurand in semi-pro baseball and city hockey.

FERNAND RINFRET and **H.A. LETOURNEAU** were members of the board of directors.

MONTREAL	GP	G	A	P	Pim
Howie Morenz	4	4	2	6	4
Aurel Joliat	4	3	1	4	6
Sprague Cleghorn	4	2	2	4	2
Odie Cleghorn	4	0	1	1	0
Billy Cameron	4	0	0	0	0
Billy Coutu	4	0	0	0	0
Sylvio Mantha	4	0	0	0	0
Georges Vezina	4	0	0	0	0
Billy Bell	3	0	0	0	0
Bobby Boucher	3	0	0	0	0

In Goal	GP	W-L	Mins	GA	SO	Avg
Georges Vezina	4	4-0	240	4	1	1.00

Team engraving from the base of the Stanley Cup

Victoria Cougars 1924 1925

Although Victoria finished in third place in the WCHL standings, the Cougars beat the Saskatoon Crescents and Calgary Tigers to advance to the finals. The games were broadcast on radio, with play-by-play coming from Dr. Clem Davies. In a fit of superstition, the Cougars came off the ice first in the final game after the warmup. They had done so in the first two games (wins) but were beaten to it by the Canadiens in game three (a loss). Much like today's hockey, the team that scored first won every game of the series. Victoria Mayor Pendray hosted a banquet in the Chamber of Commerce in his city two days after victory, April 1, 1925.

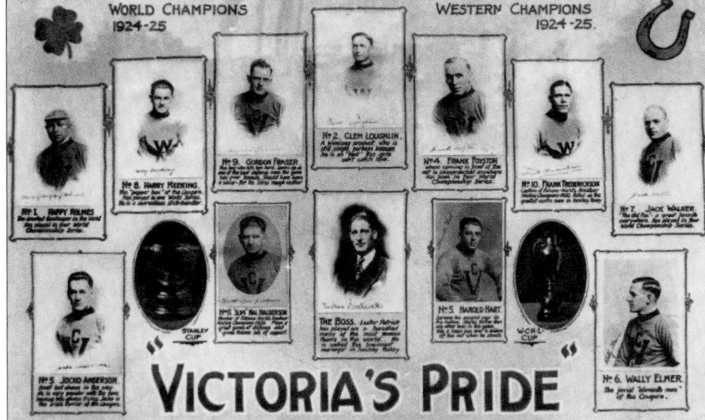

Victoria Cougars, 1924-25

STANLEY CUP FINALS

Victoria Cougars win best-of-five Stanley Cup finals 3-1

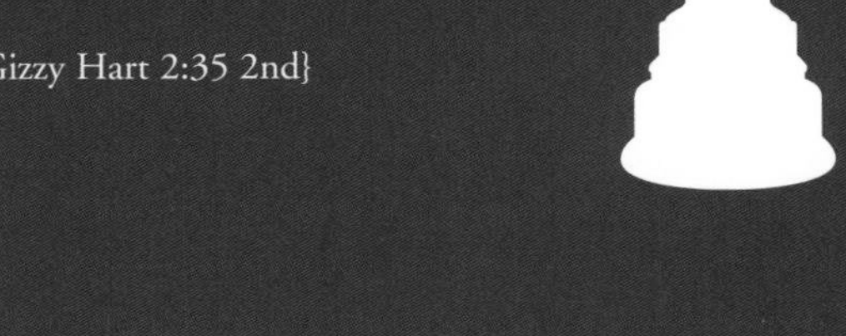

*March 21, 1925 Montreal Canadiens 2 at Victoria Cougars 5
*March 23, 1925 Montreal Canadiens 1 at Victoria Cougars 3
*March 27, 1925 Montreal Canadiens 4 at Victoria Cougars 2
*March 30, 1925 Montreal Canadiens 1 at Victoria Cougars 6 {Gizzy Hart 2:35 2nd}

** played at Victoria Arena*

VICTORIA	GP	G	A	P	Pim
Jack Walker	4	4	2	6	0
Frank Fredrickson	4	3	3	6	6
Slim Halderson	4	2	1	3	8
Gord Fraser	4	2	1	3	6
Gizzy Hart	4	2	1	3	0
Jocko Anderson	4	1	0	1	10
Clem Loughlin	4	1	0	1	4
Frank Foyston	4	1	0	1	0
Harry Meeking	4	0	1	1	2
Hap Holmes	4	0	0	0	0
Wally Elmer	2	0	0	0	0

In Goal	GP	W-L	Mins	GA	SO	Avg
Hap Holmes	4	3-1	240	8	0	2.00

Detail of the base of the original Cup with the name of the team

JACK WALKER signed with Victoria after Seattle withdrew from the league. The goal-scoring star of the team, he had goals in six straight playoff games.

FRANK FREDRICKSON joined the Vics in 1920 after leading Canada to gold at the 1920 Olympics and led the team in scoring with 21 goals.

A teammate of Fredrickson's on Canada's 1920 Olympic squad, **SLIM HALDERSON** played pro for more than twenty years, but only one, 1926-27, in the NHL.

GORD FRASER was one of four Seattle players acquired during the off season (along with Holmes, Foyston, and Walker) and scored two important goals in game one of the finals. Like Foyston, he received a gold locket for his help in securing the Cup.

GIZZY HART played on a line with Walker and Fredrickson. In recognition of his scoring the winning goal, the Mayor had the puck from the final game engraved and decorated in the team's blue and gold colours for him.

A sub most of the year, **JOCKO ANDERSON** was the Manitoba-born brother of Ernie. He played this year in combination with Meeking and Foyston.

Captain **CLEM LOUGHLIN** played eight years with the Vics, then when Detroit bought the team and transferred the players to an NHL franchise, he moved east and played for the Cougars (which later became the Red Wings).

Names on the base of the original Cup which extend around the full circumference of the Cup

FRANK FOYSTON received a gold locket from Mayor Pendray at the victory banquet in appreciation of his efforts.

HARRY MEEKING played every minute between NHL stops in 1919 and 1926 with the Vics, having won the Cup with the Toronto Arenas in 1918.

Goaler **HAP HOLMES** outplayed Vezina in the finals, particularly the deciding game.

A late addition to the team, **WALLY ELMER** appeared in just four games during the season and one in the playoffs and retired after this Cup win.

Manager **LESTER PATRICK** was likely the first man in hockey to use three lines, so the forwards were always stronger and fresher than their opponents.

L. BRUNELL was the Cougars' trainer.

1925 THE CHAMPIONS
1926 Montreal Maroons

This marked the last time a non-NHL team competed for the Cup. The Maroons were the English team in Montreal, with not a single Frenchman on the roster. The next year, the Cup became the sole proprietorship of the NHL, a remarkable change of events from the purely amateur competition Lord Stanley had envisioned back in 1892 to what was now an entirely professional series of playoff games in which money dictated so much of the fate of players and teams. In fact, the entire Maroons team had received thirty dollars in gold the previous season to celebrate the team's first season in the NHL.

STANLEY CUP FINALS

Montreal Maroons win best-of-five Stanley Cup finals 3-1

*March 30, 1926 Victoria Cougars 0 at Montreal Maroons 3 [Clint Benedict]
*April 1, 1926 Victoria Cougars 0 at Montreal Maroons 3 [Clint Benedict]
*April 3, 1926 Victoria Cougars 3 at Montreal Maroons 2
*April 6, 1926 Victoria Cougars 0 at Montreal Maroons 2
{Nels Stewart 2:50 2nd} [Clint Benedict]

** played at the Forum, Montreal*

Montreal Maroons, 1925-26

Detail of the base of the original Cup. The engraving for this year extends around the full circumference of the Cup.

Victoria manager Lester Patrick cursed the Maroons for putting goal scorer **NELS STEWART** on defence.

BABE SIEBERT is identified by his initials on the Cup, "A" for Albert, "C" for Charles.

Although he was called Bill by one and all, his given name was **MERLYN PHILLIPS**.

HARRY "PUNCH" BROADBENT won the Art Ross Trophy in 1921-22 and was a Hall of Fame inductee in 1962.

Captain **DUNC MUNRO'S** father rubbed each player's back with a lucky rabbit's foot before each game.

REG NOBLE played only sporadically in the finals, still recovering from a fractured skull suffered earlier in the year.

"DINNY" DINSMORE was the team's premier puck ragger during man shortages.

CLINT BENEDICT championed the wearing of wider goal pads and helped develop a proper catcher and blocker.

Brother of Bill, **FRANK CARSON** had an NHL career that was sporadic and peripatetic.

SAMMY ROTHSCHILD played semi-pro in his native Sudbury for many years.

They called him Toots, but his real name was **ALBERT ROBERT HOLWAY**.

Maroons manager **EDDIE GERARD** had acquired many former Senators he had previously known as teammates.

President **JAMES STRACHAN** came from a family that made its fortune in the baking business.

Owner of Ekers Brewery, vice-president **GORDON CUSHING** made his living as a stockbroker.

Vice-president **TOM ARNOLD** was also president of Taylor & Arnold and Manitoba Steel Foundries.

DONAT RAYMOND was a driving force behind the building of the Forum.

ART CAYFORD was the team's secretary-treasurer.

BILL O'BRIEN was the team's trainer.

MONTREAL	GP	G	A	P	Pim
Nels Stewart	4	6	1	7	14
Babe Siebert	4	1	2	3	2
Bill Phillips	4	1	1	2	0
Punch Broadbent	4	1	0	1	22
Dunc Munro	4	1	0	1	6
Reg Noble	4	0	0	0	4
Chuck Dinsmore	4	0	0	0	2
Clint Benedict	4	0	0	0	0
Frank Carson	4	0	0	0	0
Sammy Rothschild	4	0	0	0	0
Toots Holway	2	0	0	0	0

In Goal	GP	W-L	Mins	GA	SO	Avg
Clint Benedict	4	3-1	240	3	3	0.75

A lineup snakes around the block in downtown Victoria, B.C., as tickets go on sale for the Western finals between the Cougars and Edmonton Eskimos.

Ottawa Senators 1926 1927

The Stanley Cup was now officially an NHL trophy. Save for the addition of Jack Adams, this was virtually the same Senators team as last year. Before home games in Boston, the Bruins' band played "Tessie," the song which had helped the Red Sox win the '03 World Series. It didn't work for the B's. At the end of the final game, Billy Coutu assaulted a referee in the corridor and was subsequently suspended for life by NHL president Frank Calder. After the series, all Sens were given an 18-carat gold ring with fourteen small diamonds in the shape of an "O." This was the team's last Cup. The Senators transferred to St. Louis in 1934 and folded a year later.

Ottawa Senators, 1926-27

STANLEY CUP FINALS

Ottawa wins best-of-five Stanley Cup finals 2-0-2

*April 7, 1927	Ottawa Senators 0 at Boston Bruins 0 (20:00 OT) [Alec Connell/Hal Winkler]
*April 9, 1927	Ottawa Senators 3 at Boston Bruins 1
**April 11, 1927	Boston Bruins 1 at Ottawa Senators 1 (20:00 OT)+
**April 13, 1927	Boston Bruins 1 at Ottawa Senators 3 {Cy Denneny 7:30 2nd}

** played at Boston Arena ** played at Ottawa Auditorium*
+ game halted at 20:00 OT because of bad ice

OTTAWA	GP	G	A	P	Pim
Cy Denneny	4	4	0	4	0
Frank Finnigan	4	2	0	2	0
King Clancy	4	1	1	2	4
Hooley Smith	4	0	1	1	12
Hec Kilrea	4	0	1	1	2
Frank Nighbor	4	0	1	1	0
George Boucher	4	0	0	0	27
Alex Smith	4	0	0	0	8
Jack Adams	4	0	0	0	2
Alec Connell	4	0	0	0	0
Ed Gorman	4	0	0	0	0
Milt Halliday	4	0	0	0	0

In Goal	GP	W-L	Mins	GA	SO	Avg
Alec Connell	4	2-0-2	240	3	1	0.75

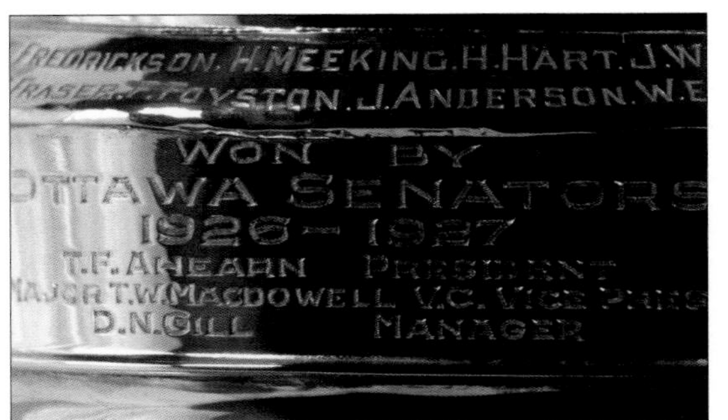

Detail of the base of the Stanley Cup featuring the team and some of the names engraved for this year which extend around half the circumference of the Cup.

CY DENNENY later became a coach and referee after a distinguished 12-year NHL career, all but one of which were with the Sens (his last, 1928-29, was with Boston).

FRANK FINNIGAN had his number 8 retired by the new Sens when they re-entered the NHL in 1992.

One of the most determined players of all time, **KING CLANCY** was small in height and weight but big in spirit.

It was **HOOLEY SMITH** who clobbered Harry Oliver over the face with his stick that inflamed Boston teammate Billy Coutu to hit referee Jerry Laflamme at game's end.

As a 19-year old rookie, **HEC KILREA** saw little ice time in the finals.

FRANK NIGHBOR, the legendary "Pembroke Peach," won his fourth Cup with Ottawa in seven years in the 1920s, one of hockey's earliest dynasties.

GEORGE BOUCHER played in the NHL's first 15 years of existence, and when he retired in 1932 was, naturally, the all-time leader in games played.

Born in England, **ALEX SMITH** came to Canada with his family as a boy and learned the game in Ottawa.

JACK ADAMS retired as a player to coach Detroit the next year, beginning one of hockey's greatest and longest executive careers.

Goaler **ALEC CONNELL** so impressed the Senators management as an amateur that they traded Clint Benedict to give him the starting job.

ED GORMAN'S brief playing career culminated in this Cup win.

In this his rookie season, **MILT HALLIDAY** played defence for the Sens.

Owner and team president as of 1924, **THOMAS FRANKLIN AHEARN** spent much of the '30s as an MP. He enlisted with the Canadian Expeditionary Force in World War I and was made first lieutenant in the First Canadian Division.

MAJOR W. MACDOWELL was the team's vice president.

A veteran of World War I, **DAVE GILL** began as an office boy under Tommy Ahearn with the Ottawa Electric Railway. Gill later became the director of the Ottawa Rough Riders for whom he had played (1912-23).

ED GLEESON was the team trainer while **DON HUGHES** and **B. DEVINE** acted as his assistants this season.

Other players to appear for the Senators this season: **STAN JACKSON**

1927 THE CHAMPIONS
1928 New York Rangers

Conn Smythe built this team prior to being fired by Col. John Hammond and returning to Toronto to form the Maple Leafs. This was just the Rangers' second season of play in the NHL, and the team was often called by the media "the classiest team in hockey" or the "Park Avenue Rangers" because of their grand entry into the league. Controversy erupted early in the third period of the final game when Russell Oatman scored a goal to tie the game. Referee Rodden disallowed the score, insisting he blew the play dead on an offside well before the goal was scored. After the victory, the Rangers held a huge party at the Windsor Hotel in Montreal which was attended by many of the Maroons players and officials.

STANLEY CUP FINALS

New York Rangers win best-of-five Stanley Cup finals 3-2

*April 5, 1928 New York Rangers 0 at Montreal Maroons 2 [Clint Benedict]
*April 7, 1928 New York Rangers 2 at Montreal Maroons 1 (Frank Boucher 7:05 OT)
*April 10, 1928 New York Rangers 0 at Montreal Maroons 2 [Clint Benedict]
*April 12, 1928 New York Rangers 1 at Montreal Maroons 0 (Frank Boucher 6:15 2nd) [Joe Miller]
*April 14, 1928 New York Rangers 2 at Montreal Maroons 1 {Frank Boucher 3:35 3rd}

** all games played at the Forum, Montreal because Madison Square Garden previously booked for the circus*

New York Rangers, 1927-28

NY RANGERS	GP	G	A	P	Pim
Frank Boucher	5	4	0	4	2
Bill Cook	5	1	2	3	16
Ching Johnson	5	0	2	2	26
Taffy Abel	5	0	1	1	10
Bun Cook	5	0	1	1	4
Paul Thompson	3	0	0	0	19
Murray Murdoch	5	0	0	0	10
Leo Bourgeault	5	0	0	0	6
Bill Boyd	5	0	0	0	2
Patsy Callighen	5	0	0	0	0
Alex Gray	5	0	0	0	0
Joe Miller	3	0	0	0	0
Lorne Chabot	2	0	0	0	0
Lester Patrick	1	0	0	0	0

In Goal	GP	W-L	Mins	GA	SO	Avg
Joe Miller	3	2-1	180	3	1	1.00
Lester Patrick	1	1-0	47	1	0	1.28
Lorne Chabot	2	0-1	80	2	0	1.50

Players gather around Col. John Hammond who stands before the Cup.

Team engraving from the shoulder of the replica Cup

FRANK BOUCHER was one of the great playmakers of the era and a rarity for having recorded more than 200 goals and assists. He led these playoffs with eight points, including three game-winning goals. Boucher opened the scoring of the final game with a clever shot through Dutton's legs and past Benedict.

BILL COOK played with brother Bun in Saskatoon for two years before Smythe signed him to a Rangers' contract.

The behemoth defenceman **CHING JOHNSON** was acquired by Smythe from Minneapolis along with Taffy Abel and led the league with 146 penalty minutes. He was bleeding over the left eye for most of the last game from a deep cut.

Christened Clarence at birth, **TAFFY ABEL** got his nickname because of his fondness for saltwater taffy. On ice, he was one of the game's hardest hitters and a man to be avoided at all costs.

FRED "BUN" COOK was not the scorer and skater his older brother Bill was, but he played with the Rangers for a decade until a throat condition forced him to retire. He finished the finals heroically, despite having a long, deep gash in one leg.

PAUL THOMPSON didn't record a point in these playoffs, though he did lead the way with 30 penalty minutes.

MURRAY MURDOCH'S name is misspelled "Murdock" on the Cup. After his playing days, the Lucknow, Ontario native coached at Yale University for 27 years and was given the Lester Patrick Award in 1974 for his contribution to the game in the United States.

LEO BOURGEAULT had a respectable eight-year NHL career that included three Canadian stops: Toronto, Ottawa, and Montreal. He was the first player to wear number 99, with the Habs in 1935-36.

BILL BOYD played defence for the "Garden Horsemen" during 1926-28, his first two years in the league, before moving up to forward to start 1928-29.

Amazingly, **PATSY CALLIGHEN** played every game with the team, never registered a goal or assist, won the Stanley Cup, and never played again in the NHL.

Strangely, although he played the full regular season and playoffs with the Rangers, **ALEX GRAY** name never made the engraver's list for this Cup season.

JOE MILLER came on to replace goalie Lorne Chabot in game three after Chabot's eye was so badly swollen he couldn't see. Miller himself suffered a bad cut in game five from Hooley Smith's skate blade but after ten minutes with the doctor managed to finish the game and series. He returned to the game and was allowed to wipe his face when he needed to, keeping a towel on top of the net for that purpose. "Red Light" refused to go to the team's victory party for fear of taking any of Chabot's glory.

Team engraving from the original band, later retired to the Hockey Hall of Fame

Details from the engraving of the stovepipe Cup

Team engraving from the shoulder of the Stanley Cup

Arguably the best goalie not in the Hockey Hall of Fame, **LORNE CHABOT** retired with 73 career shutouts. However, the Rangers felt an eye injury he suffered during this season would mark the end of his career. They gave up on him, and his play in the ensuing nine years elsewhere in the league ensured the Blueshirts rued their hasty decision. Chabot nearly lost his eye from a Nels Stewart shot in game two and was lost for the series.

Team manager **LESTER PATRICK** made his goaltending debut at age 44 under emergency circumstances. Early in the second period of game two, Chabot was injured and couldn't continue. With no one else on hand, Patrick put on the equipment, played the rest of the game into overtime, and emerged with a win. "I tell you, these boys have all the courage in the world," he said of his banged-up, victorious crew.

COL. JOHN S. HAMMOND ran a tight ship at MSG, in contrast to the cross-town, high-flying Amerks whose behaviour on the town was legendary. Hammond had been responsible both for the hiring and firing of Conn Smythe, the man who built this team the previous season.

TEX RICKARD was born in Kansas City and ran saloons in Alaska and Nevada before trying his hand at promoting boxing in New York City. He was president of MSG.

In his youth, trainer **HARRY WESTERBY** played for the Granite Hockey Club and Aura Lee, and the Argos football team, all in Toronto, before joining the Rangers in 1926. He also acted as trainer for the Toronto Maple Leafs baseball club in the summers.

BILL CAREY was president of Madison Square Garden. In 1933, he hosted a sumptuous banquet at the Astor Hotel for the victorious Rangers at which time he introduced the players to the team's new president, General John Reed Kilpatrick.

RICHARD HOYT worked for Hayden, Stone and Company, a New York investment house. He was part of the syndicate formed by Tex Rickard to build a new Madison Square Garden.

Other players to appear for the Rangers this season: **LAURIE SCOTT**

1928–1929 Boston Bruins

THE CHAMPIONS

This was the first all-American finals, Boston having eliminated the Canadiens, Detroit ousting Toronto, and Ottawa not qualifying at all for the post-season. It was also the first time the playoffs were held at the new Boston Garden. After the victory, the players held a party the next night at the Copleys Plaza at which time each member of the team received $500 in $20 gold coins.

STANLEY CUP FINALS

Boston Bruins win best-of-three Stanley Cup finals 2-0

*March 28, 1929 New York Rangers 0 at Boston Bruins 2 [Tiny Thompson]
**March 29, 1929 Boston Bruins 2 at New York Rangers 1 {Bill Carson 18:02 3rd}

** played at Boston Garden ** played at Madison Square Garden, New York*
+ series made best-of-three because Madison Square Garden was booked for the circus and the Boston Garden was hosting a track meet

Boston Bruins, 1928-29

BOSTON	GP	G	A	P	Pim
Harry Oliver	2	1	1	2	2
Bill Carson	2	1	0	1	2
Dit Clapper	2	1	0	1	0
Dutch Gainor	2	1	0	1	0
Lionel Hitchman	2	0	0	0	10
Eddie Shore	2	0	0	0	8
Percy Galbraith	2	0	0	0	2
Myles Lane	2	0	0	0	0
George Owen	2	0	0	0	0
Mickey MacKay	2	0	0	0	0
Tiny Thompson	2	0	0	0	0
Cooney Weiland	2	0	0	0	0
Cy Denneny	1	0	0	0	0
Red Green	1	0	0	0	0

In Goal	GP	W-L	Mins	GA	SO	Avg
Tiny Thompson	2	2-0	120	1	1	0.50

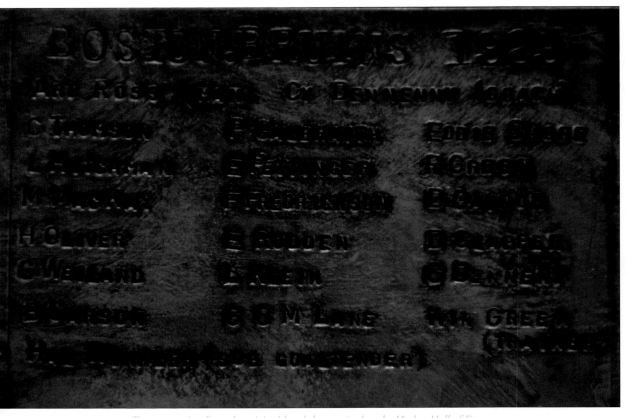

Team engraving from the original band, later retired to the Hockey Hall of Fame

An unsung hero, **HARRY OLIVER** played on a line with Carson and Galbraith and this threesome carried the team to victory. Oliver started Boston on the road to victory with a great solo rush to open the scoring in the deciding game.

The usual formalization of names for engraving was eschewed in favour of the diminutive "Doc" for **DR. BILL CARSON** who had been purchased from Toronto during the season. He scored the Cup winner with less than two minutes to play.

VICTOR "DIT" CLAPPER later became the first man in the NHL to play 20 years for one team. His childhood lisp transformed his name "Vic" to "Dit" and the name stuck for the rest of his life.

DUTCH GAINOR was the best passer in the league and key to the explosive offensive abilities of the Dynamite Line which dominated the NHL the following season.

Fearless, with a high threshold for pain, **LIONEL HITCHMAN** played with Eddie Shore as the best and most ferocious defensive combination in the league. In the summers, he was an RCMP officer.

Outside Boston, he was detested; inside Boston, revered. Everywhere, he was respected. **EDDIE SHORE** was a force in the series, incurring penalties for vicious checks but generating offense and starring on the Boston blueline.

PERCY "PERK" GALBRAITH made his NHL debut with the Bruins in 1926 at age 27 and played all but two of his 347 career games with the Bruins.

MYLES LANE attended Dartmouth College and after graduating in 1928 joined the Rangers. The Blueshirts sold him to Boston on January 21, 1929, and so the rookie won the Cup just two months later.

GEORGE OWEN was born in Ontario but his dad moved the family to Massachusetts to become a professor at MIT. George went to Harvard where he was an outstanding football player.

After more than a decade with Vancouver in the PCHA, **MICKEY MacKAY** won his second Cup, his first coming way back in 1915. In the interim, he had suffered a serious jaw break thanks to a Cully Wilson swing of the stick to his face, requiring a year to recover fully.

TINY THOMPSON replaced the retired Hal Winkler and allowed just three goals in five games while recording three shutouts during the '29 NHL playoffs.

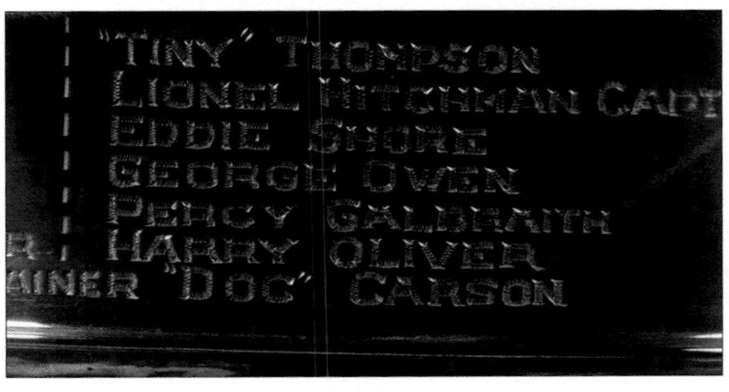

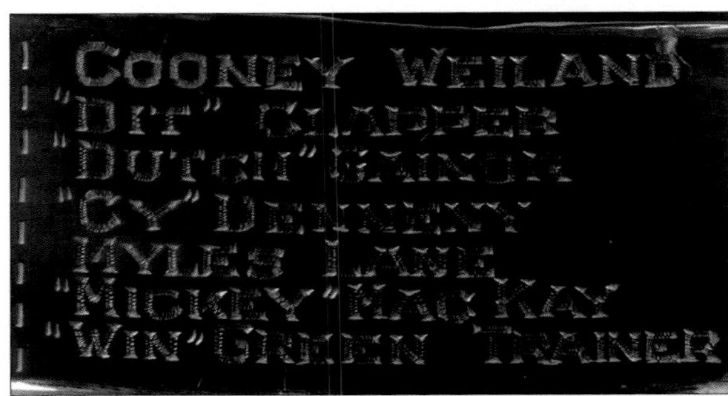

Three details of engravings from the Stanley Cup base, underneath the bowl and above the rings

In his first year with the team, **COONEY WEILAND** played with Clapper and Gainor to form the newly-coined Dynamite Line.

In a Cup anomaly, **CY DENNENY'S** name appears twice on this Cup, once as a player, once as a coach (the second reference in misspelled).

RED, short for "Redvers," **GREEN** actually finished the season with the Detroit Cougars after a late trade, yet his name still appears on the Cup, a rarity indeed in Stanley Cup engraving history.

As a boy, **CHARLES ADAMS** spent his winters with the woodsmen of Quebec. As he grew up, he got a job in a grocery store, gained control of a racetrack and ballclub, and later bought the Bruins.

A referee after his playing days, vice-president and manager **ART ROSS** was at one time the only active official to use a bell instead of a whistle to blow play dead. He was the genius behind the team, a coach who would smoke in the dressing room between periods, giving guilty players the evil eye and then tapping his head and offering two short words of advice—USE IT.

"WIN" GREEN was the team's long-time trainer who worked in like capacity for the Red Sox during the summer months.

Although he had retired the previous season, **HAL WINKLER** was so popular that his teammates ensured his name went on this Cup win in memory of his contributions to the team.

Other players to appear for the Bruins this season: **FRANK FREDRICKSON, LLOYD KLEIN, ERIC PETTINGER, EDDIE RODDEN**

1929 THE CHAMPIONS

1930 Montreal Canadiens

One of the great Cup upsets featured Montreal (which had finished with 56 points) beating Boston (with 77 points) to win the 1930 championship. The two losses by the Bruins in the finals were the only back-to-back losses the team had suffered all season. The Canadiens' success was fortified by the team's adopting of an old French song that had been first used by the Montagnards, a snow-shoeing club, and taken over by Montreal fans, the word "Canadiens" replacing "Montagnards" so the line came out: "Halte-la, halte-la, les Canadiens sont la!"

STANLEY CUP FINALS

Montreal Canadiens win best-of-three Stanley Cup finals 2-0

*April 1, 1930 Montreal Canadiens 3 at Boston Bruins 0 [George Hainsworth]
**April 3, 1930 Boston Bruins 3 at Montreal Canadiens 4 {Howie Morenz 1:00 2nd}

** played at Boston Garden ** played at the Forum, Montreal*

LE CLUB DE HOCKEY CANADIEN INC
1929
1930

Montreal Canadiens, 1929-30

(above) team photo taken outside the Forum; (left, left to right) three of the greatest Canadiens of all time—goalie George Hainsworth, Aurel Joliat, and Howie Morenz.

MONTREAL	GP	G	A	P	Pim
Albert Leduc	2	1	2	3	0
Sylvio Mantha	2	2	0	2	2
Nick Wasnie	2	1	1	2	6
Pit Lepine	2	1	1	2	0
Howie Morenz	2	1	0	1	6
Bert McCaffery	2	1	0	1	0
Marty Burke	2	0	1	1	0
Aurel Joliat	2	0	1	1	0
Wildor Larochelle	2	0	0	0	8
Armand Mondou	2	0	0	0	2
Gerry Carson	2	0	0	0	0
George Hainsworth	2	0	0	0	0
Georges Mantha	2	0	0	0	0
Gus Rivers	2	0	0	0	0

In Goal	GP	W-L	Mins	GA	SO	Avg
George Hainsworth	2	2-0	120	3	1	1.50

Detail from the stovepipe Cup

Called "Battleship," **ALBERT LEDUC** skated awkwardly but was a wrecker when he built up steam. He later coached at Providence and is credited with discovering Toe Blake as a player.

In this year, the first of the new offside rule which allowed for players to "hang" near the other goal, few players scored as consistently as **SYLVIO MANTHA**.

NICK WASNIE replaced Art Gagne on the big line with Morenz and Joliat. He played more than 200 consecutive games with the Habs, New York Americans, and Ottawa before finishing his career with St. Louis in '34-'35.

ALFRED "PIT" LEPINE, prematurely grey, played in combination with Mantha and Larochelle.

HOWIE MORENZ'S Cup-winning goal gave Boston two losses in a row for the first time all season. Morenz was apprenticing as a machinist when he was discovered by one Ernie Sauve who saw him score nine goals for Stratford in a game against the Montreal CNR team.

BERT McCAFFERY played many years of amateur hockey in Toronto, culminating with a gold medal at the 1924 Olympics in Chamonix, France, while playing with Canada's representatives, the Toronto Granites.

MARTY BURKE later coached the Saskatoon Quakers and then took the Calgary Stampeders to the Memorial Cup finals where they lost to the Kirkland Lake Blue Devils.

AUREL JOLIAT was a shifty, small player who was difficult to catch or knock off the puck. He wore a black cap to cover his baldness and became violent when players purposefully knocked said hat off (which they did often!).

WILDOR LAROCHELLE played every game this year, scoring 14 goals and 25 points in the 44-game season.

ARMAND MONDOU was the first to experiment with something akin to the slapshot, though it resulted in just three goals all year.

GERRY CARSON had finished the previous season with the Rangers, on loan from the Habs. He returned to the bleu, blanc, et rouge for this season and stayed in Montreal the rest of his career, playing for the Maroons in '36-'37, his last year of hockey.

GEORGE HAINSWORTH was acquired by the Habs on the recommendation of Newsy Lalonde. He allowed just six goals in six games while recording three shutouts during these playoffs.

Defenceman **GEORGES MANTHA** went scoreless in six playoff games, although in '37-'38 he had a career-high 23 in the regular season playing as a left-winger.

GUS RIVERS came out of the Winnipeg city leagues to replace George Patterson who had been sold outright to Boston.

Detail from the stovepipe Cup

Team engraving from the original band, later retired to the Hockey Hall of Fame

ED DUFOUR and **JIM McKENNA** were the team's trainers.

HON. LOUIS ATHANASE DAVID acted as the team's honourary president. A graduate of Laval University, he was a powerful member of Quebec's Legislative Assembly who espoused education and helped establish technical schools in that province.

Vice-president **JOE CATTARINICH** had been the Canadiens' first goalie ever, back in 1909, but after seeing Georges Vezina play he urged the team to sign the future great. Cattarinich's playing career was over, but his executive life in hockey was just beginning. He was also a director of the Canadian Arena Company, owner of the cross-town rival Maroons, in the days before conflict of interest held sway in the NHL.

In 1924, **LEO DANDURAND** sold half of Montreal's territorial rights to James Strachan and the Canadian Arena Company so the Maroons could play: "I figured," Dandurand said, "that having an English team to compete with the French Canadiens would make for a great rivalry. And I was proven right."

CECIL HART had been manager of both the Habs and Maroons previously and got his start with Leo Dandurand in semi-pro baseball before getting into hockey as a lifelong profession.

FERNAND RINFRET later became Montreal's mayor (1932-34) after having been the Dominion Secretary of State under Prime Minister Mackenzie King.

DR. HENRY McILLREE WILLIAMSON GRAY was born in Aberdeen, Scotland, studied medicine at Bonn, Leipzig, and London, and became a distinguished physician and surgeon in Montreal.

DR. J.A. CORRIGAN was one of the team's physicians.

Others: **H.A.LETOURNEAU, AMEDEE MONET JUGE, EDDIE ST. PERE, GEORGES RICHER**

Other players to appear for the Canadiens this season: **GORD FRASER, MICKEY MURRAY, ROY WORTERS**

1930 THE CHAMPIONS
1931 Montreal Canadiens

This was the first year the finals were a best-of-five and, appropriately, the series went the distance. To offset the Habs' tremendous speed, Chicago coach Dick Irvin utilized four lines, hoping quick shifts of energy would counter Montreal's superiority of skill. But the Habs also had the better goaltending in George Hainsworth who gave up just eight goals in five games.

STANLEY CUP FINALS

Montreal Canadiens win best-of-five Stanley Cup finals 3-2

*April 3, 1931 Montreal Canadiens 2 at Chicago Black Hawks 1
*April 5, 1931 Montreal Canadiens 1 at Chicago Black Hawks 2 (Johnny Gottselig 24:50 OT)
**April 9, 1931 Chicago Black Hawks 3 at Montreal Canadiens 2 (Cy Wentworth 53:50 OT)
**April 11, 1931 Chicago Black Hawks 2 at Montreal Canadiens 4
**April 14, 1931 Chicago Black Hawks 0 at Montreal Canadiens 2 {Johnny Gagnon 9:59 2nd} [George Hainsworth]

** played at Chicago Stadium ** played at the Forum, Montreal*

Montreal Canadiens, 1930-31

MONTREAL	GP	G	A	P	Pim
Johnny Gagnon	5	4	2	6	2
Pit Lepine	5	3	1	4	4
Georges Mantha	5	2	1	3	4
Nick Wasnie	5	1	1	2	2
Aurel Joliat	5	0	2	2	2
Howie Morenz	5	1	0	1	6
Wildor Larochelle	5	0	1	1	6
Marty Burke	5	0	1	1	2
Albert Leduc	2	0	1	1	2
Sylvio Mantha	5	0	0	0	16
Art Lesieur	5	0	0	0	4
George Hainsworth	5	0	0	0	0
Gus Rivers	5	0	0	0	0
Armand Mondou	3	0	0	0	0
Jean Pusie	3	0	0	0	0

In Goal	GP	W-L	Mins	GA	SO	Avg
George Hainsworth	5	3-2	379	8	1	1.27

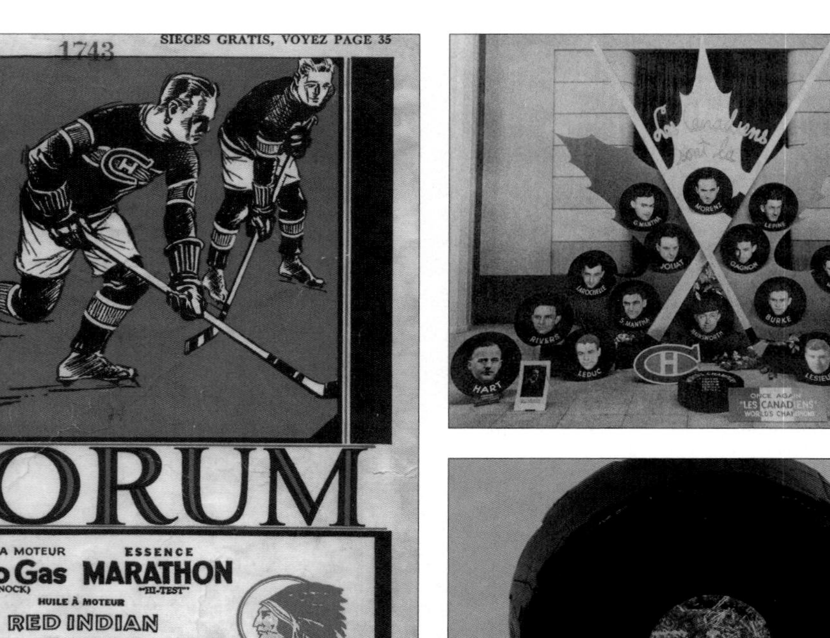

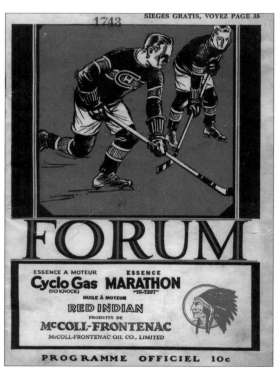

(clockwise) A program from the finals series; a window display at the Forum of the Cup-winning team; a game puck from the Cup-clinching game; (far right) members of the Chicago Black Hawks arrive in Montreal on April 8, 1931, for game five of the Stanley Cup finals.

JOHNNY GAGNON, "the Black Cat," was added to the team as a new forward to play alongside Morenz and Joliat. The rookie scored 18 goals and a league-leading six more in the playoffs, including the Cup winner.

PIT LEPINE played all his 526 NHL games and 13 seasons with the Canadiens. He suffered through the finals with a broken finger.

GEORGES MANTHA, lesser-known brother of Sylvio, scored five of the team's 24 goals this playoffs, notably the overtime winner in game three of the semi-finals against Boston to give the Habs a 2-1 series lead.

NICK WASNIE started his career with Chicago but after just 14 games was released. He spent the next year and a half in the Can-Am league before the Habs signed him as a free agent.

Called the "Mighty Atom" or "Little Giant," **AUREL JOLIAT** played on a line most of his career with Morenz after being acquired in a controversial trade in 1922 for the great and popular Newsy Lalonde.

"HOWARD" is incorrectly formalized for **HOWIE MORENZ'S** real name Howarth, though French Montrealers called him "l'homme eclair." Although he won the scoring championship this year, he went eight games without a goal in the playoffs, though his only goal came at a critical time in the Cup-clinching game.

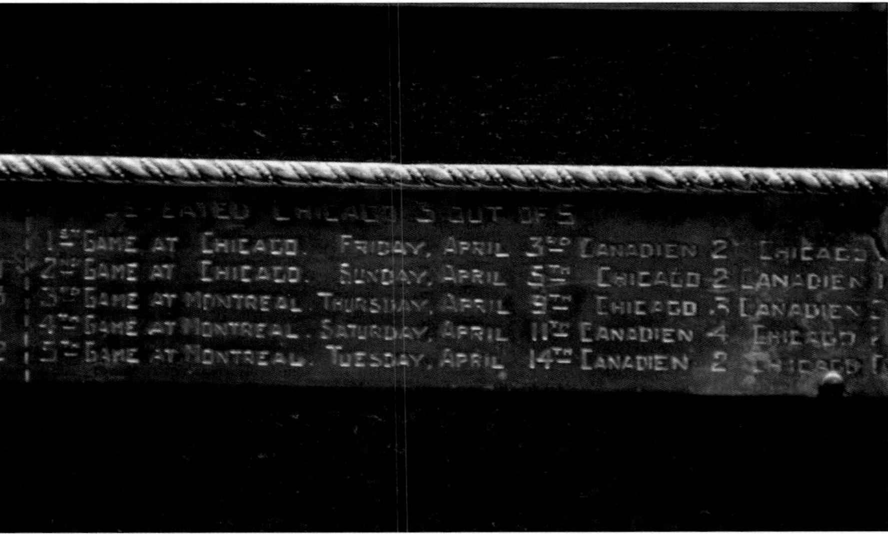

Detail from the stovepipe Cup showing scores of finals games

After retiring, **WILDOR LAROCHELLE** went into the hotel business with his father, though he spent the last 13 years of his life in a convalescent home where he died of tuberculosis in 1964.

Like many a hockey player before and since, **MARTY BURKE** entered the hotel business after retiring, in his case as manager of the Victoria Hotel in Calgary from 1939 on.

ALBERT LEDUC played only part of the finals after having suffered a concussion and spending several days in hospital.

Nearing the end of his playing career, **SYLVIO MANTHA** was named the Habs' playing coach in 1935-36 and later became an NHL official as both a linesman and referee.

ART LESIEUR arrived mid-season to replace Bert McCaffery whom the Habs had placed on waivers.

In 1928-29, **GEORGE HAINSWORTH** posted a record 22 shutouts in 44 games during an era when forward passing was permitted only between the bluelines. He is second all-time in shutouts to Terry Sawchuk with 94.

Rookie **GUS RIVERS** made it to the NHL just after his 20th birthday, but although his career lasted all of three years and 88 games, he won two Cups.

ARMAND MONDOU played with an injured rib and shoulder and scored just one goal in a reduced capacity during this successful playoff run.

ED DUFOUR and **JIM McKENNA** were back for another year and another Cup as the Canadiens' trainers.

Detail from the stovepipe Cup showing victorious team

DR. J.A. CORRIGAN was the team physician.

JULES DUGAL was the team's business manager, though he became the GM for 1939-40 during a period of transition when Dandurand was selling the Canadiens and Cecil Hart was out as manager.

President **LOUIS ATHANASE DAVID** later headed a consortium that revived the Montreal Royals of the International League (baseball) and built Delorimier Stadium. He had been called to the bar in 1905 at just 23 years of age and later established the David prize for excellence in writing to both English and French writers.

Called "Catta" or "the Quiet One," **GEORGE CATTARINICH** was part owner of the Blue Bonnets racetrack. He also purchased a large tract of land on the Ottawa River, just east of Rigaud, fenced in the property, and turned it into a park for deer and other animals of the wild.

LEO DANDURAND introduced pari-mutuel betting machines to Chicago, Tampa, New Orleans, and Cleveland. He also controlled racetracks in Montreal, handling $75 million in annual wagers.

Manager **CECIL HART** was credited with finding Herb Gardiner, playing for the Calgary Tigers, and bringing him to the Canadiens in '26-'27 where the defenceman won the Hart Trophy in his rookie season.

FERNAND RINFRET died of a heart attack while on vacation in Los Angeles in 1939, and his reputation was so great that King George and Queen Elizabeth offered their condolences.

ALPHONSE RAYMOND got his start in Montreal with his brother, Joe, operating a grocery store that became one of the largest makers of jam in the country. His success grew to the point that Premier Duplessis made Raymond president of the Legislative Council.

DR. GRAY was a Surgeon Colonel during World War I and in 1923 became the Surgeon-in-Chief at the Royal Victoria Hospital in Montreal.

Others: **EDDIE ST. PERE, M.P., AMEDEE MONET JUGE, GEORGES RICHER**

Other players to appear for the Canadiens this season: **BERT McCAFFERY, JEAN PUSIE**

1931–1932 Toronto Maple Leafs

This was first Cup for the Maple Leafs, in the newly-built Gardens, and the first for the city in a decade. After the final game, a microphone was set up on ice near the penalty box for Irvin, Day, and Smythe to make speeches and Rangers players shook hands on ice with the victorious Leafs. In the Toronto dressing room afterward, fans crowded for autographs and souvenirs of the historic victory. This series has been dubbed the "Tennis Series" because of the scores of the games—6-4, 6-2, 6-4. The AHL officially challenged for the Stanley Cup, but trustee William Foran rejected the bid.

STANLEY CUP FINALS

Toronto Maple Leafs win best-of-five Stanley Cup finals 3-0

*April 5, 1932 Toronto Maple Leafs 6 at New York Rangers 4
**April 7, 1932 Toronto Maple Leafs 6 New York Rangers 2
***April 9, 1932 New York Rangers 4 at Toronto Maple Leafs 6 {Ace Bailey 15:07 3rd}

** played at Madison Square Garden, New York ** played at Boston Garden because of circus at MSG*
**** played at Maple Leaf Gardens, Toronto*

Toronto Maple Leafs, 1931-32

(clockwise) The Leafs and Rangers at Maple Leaf Gardens the night of April 9, 1932, in one of the earliest game action photos of NHL play; cartoon created by the legendary Lou Skuce for the Leafs' game-night program; game action from the Cup-clinching game.

TORONTO	GP	G	A	P	Pim
Busher Jackson	3	5	2	7	9
Charlie Conacher	3	3	2	5	2
Happy Day	3	1	3	4	4
Joe Primeau	3	0	4	4	0
King Clancy	3	2	0	2	8
Andy Blair	3	2	0	2	2
Baldy Cotton	3	1	1	2	10
Frank Finnigan	3	1	1	2	8
Red Horner	3	1	1	2	6
Bob Gracie	3	1	1	2	0
Ace Bailey	3	1	0	1	0
Alex Levinsky	3	0	0	0	2
Lorne Chabot	3	0	0	0	0
Harry Darragh	3	0	0	0	0
Fred Robertson	3	0	0	0	0
Earl Miller	2	0	0	0	0

In Goal	GP	W-L	Mins	GA	SO	Avg
Lorne Chabot	3	3-0	180	10	0	3.33

HARVEY JACKSON scored three goals in the second period of game one of the finals, the first player to record a one-period hat trick in the playoffs.

From the great **CONACHER** family, **CHARLIE**, Lionel, and Roy all won Stanley Cups during this era.

His given name of "Clarence" graces the Cup. **HAP DAY** was discovered by Smythe while playing hockey at the University of Toronto and studying Pharmacy.

"You have this sense of accomplishment after reaching what you have been driving for for so long, and you have this feeling of relief." **JOE PRIMEAU** on his first Cup.

KING CLANCY was acquired by the Leafs after owner Conn Smythe won a large bet at the track and insodoing was able to afford Clancy's $35,000 price tag.

The only mustachioed player of his era, **ANDY BLAIR** played on a line with Ace Bailey and Baldy Cotton.

Acquired for Gerry Lowrey, **BALDY COTTON** later became a member of the Hot Stove League on the radio and a scout for the Boston Bruins.

FRANK FINNIGAN was one in a long line of great Senators to be sold over the years by perpetually cash-strapped owner Frank Ahearn.

RED HORNER epitomized tough hockey, leading the league in penalties for eight straight seasons (1932-40).

BOB GRACIE may have made his living in big-time hockey cities, but after the war he moved out to California to coach.

The great Leafs scorer of the pre-Kid Line era, **ACE BAILEY** suffered a career-ending injury in December 1933, resulting in the beginnings of the NHL's All-Star Game.

ALEX LEVINSKY was nicknamed "Mine Boy" by his team-mates because his father would come to all games and practises and shout out, "That's mine boy!"

The number-one goalie for Toronto for five years, **CHABOT** was traded to Montreal in 1933 for George Hainsworth.

HARRY DARRAGH suffered a serious leg injury with Boston toward the end of the '30-'31 season, so the Bruins put him on waivers figuring his career was over. They were wrong.

Born in England, **FRED ROBERTSON** was a solid, sturdy defenceman much admired by coach Dick Irvin.

EARL MILLER started the year in Chicago but was sold outright to the Leafs in February.

STAFFORD SMYTHE is included on the Cup as the team mascot. He was Conn's son, and at eleven years of age remains the youngest person to have his name on the Cup.

DICK IRVIN left Toronto immediately after the victory to be with his sick son in Calgary.

TIM DALY was perhaps the funniest dressing-room man of all time, and a former national boxing champion to boot.

CONN SMYTHE has his name appear twice on this Cup.

Team engraving from the original band, later retired to the Hockey Hall of Fame

FRANK SELKE was Smythe's right-hand man and partner until 1946 when he left for Montreal.

The first president of Maple Leaf Gardens and a good friend of Conn Smythe, **JACK (J.P.) BICKELL** was a driving force behind raising the funds necessary to build Maple Leaf Gardens.

HARRY McGEE was a member of the board of directors.

GEORGE COTTRELLE, a colleague of Bickell's at the Bank of Commerce in Toronto, was the team's financial watchdog. He believed the team had to spend money to make money.

ED BICKLE arranged the mortgage for Maple Leaf Gardens through the Sun Life Insurance Company.

A director, **SIR JOHN AIRD** was the president of the Canadian Bank of Commerce.

J.E. BIRKS was a member of the prestigious Birks family, owners of the finest jewellery stores in Toronto.

BOB LAIDLAW was the man behind Laidlaw Lumber. He got to know Conn Smythe through the sand pits.

FRED MORROW had lost a leg in World War I and owned property near Smythe up around Lake Simcoe.

A former financial editor of the *Toronto Globe*, **VICTOR ROSS** became a director and later vice-president of Imperial Oil Limited.

WILLIAM DONALD ROSS was just finishing his term as lieutenant-governor of Ontario (1927-32).

JOHN A. TORY was one of the founders of Tory & Tory, one of the city's largest firms.

ALBERT LeROY ELLSWORTH established the British-America Oil Company in 1906, which he served until 1943.

GEORGE GOODERHAM was the son of George Sr., who built Gooderham and Worts Distilleries.

McCARTHY was great friends with Franklin Roosevelt owing to a mutual interest in helping victims of infantile paralysis.

Lieutenant-Colonel **BILL MacBRIEN** was presently the honourary Colonel of the Toronto Scottish Regiment.

JAMES YOUNG MURDOCH founded Noranda Mines, one of the world's richest copper and gold mines.

Senator **FRANK O'CONNOR** was the president of Laura Secord candy stores and owner of the prosperous Maryvale Farms.

ALFRED ROGERS received a call personally from J.P. Bickell to invest in the team, and on this alone he agreed.

A member of the Canadian War Mission to Washington during WWI, **ROLPH** was chairman of the board for the Imperial Bank of Canada.

ROBERT HOME SMITH was vital to the development of land around the Humber Valley, in particular the Old Mill.

DR. SAMUEL gave much of his fortune to the University of Toronto and the Royal Ontario Museum.

Other players to appear for the Leafs this season: **BENNY GRANT, SYD HOWE**

1932 THE CHAMPIONS

1933 New York Rangers

The Rangers took no short cuts this year, beating the Habs, Red Wings, and Leafs to win the Cup. They became the first team to win the Cup in overtime, and on the power-play to boot. Toronto had been softened for the series after their five-game series with Boston which featured the longest OT in league history to date, a six-overtime marathon in the deciding game. After the victory, the Rangers displayed the Cup in the lobby of MSG for the public to admire and the players were later banqueted at the Astor Hotel hosted by MSG president William Carey. They never received the Cup, however, until November 11, 1933, some six months after the victory, leading many to call this the "Forgotten Cup."

STANLEY CUP FINALS

New York Rangers win best-of-five Stanley Cup finals 3-1

*April 4, 1933	Toronto Maple Leafs 1 at New York Rangers 5
**April 8, 1933	New York Rangers 3 at Toronto Maple Leafs 1
**April 11, 1933	New York Rangers 2 at Toronto Maple Leafs 3
**April 13, 1933	New York Rangers 1 at Toronto Maple Leafs 0 {(Bill Cook 7:33 OT)} [Andy Aitkenhead]

** played at Madison Square Garden, New York*

*** all remaining games played at Maple Leaf Gardens because Madison Square Garden previously booked for circus*

Members of the Rangers pose with the Cup on November 11, 1933.

NY RANGERS	GP	G	A	P	Pim
Cecil Dillon	4	3	1	4	4
Bill Cook	4	2	1	3	4
Art Somers	4	0	3	3	4
Ott Heller	4	2	0	2	4
Butch Keeling	4	1	1	2	6
Murray Murdoch	4	1	1	2	2
Bun Cook	4	1	0	1	4
Earl Seibert	4	1	0	1	2
Frank Boucher	4	0	1	1	4
Ossie Asmundson	4	0	1	1	2
Babe Siebert	4	0	0	0	10
Ching Johnson	4	0	0	0	8
Doug Brennan	4	0	0	0	2
Andy Aitkenhead	4	0	0	0	0
Gord Pettinger	4	0	0	0	0

In Goal	GP	W-L	Mins	GA	SO	Avg
Andy Aitkenhead	4	3-1	248	5	1	1.21

(clockwise) Toronto goalie Lorne Chabot makes a save at Maple Leaf Gardens, April 11, 1933; Rangers' goalie Andy Aitkenhead finds himself scrambling but the puck has moved out of harm's way; the full Rangers team takes the train home: top row (left to right) Harry Westerby (trainer), Murray Murdoch, Ossie Asmundson, Earl Seibert, Gord Pettinger, Bun Cook, Lester Patrick, Doug Brennan, Bill Cook, Butch Keeling, Ott Heller/kneeling (left to right) Frank Boucher, Cecil Dillon, Art Somers, Andy Aitkenhead, Babe Siebert.

Playing in combination with Keeling and Murdoch, **CECIL DILLON** led the playoffs in scoring with eight goals and ten points.

BILL COOK'S Cup-winning goal came on a power-play, the only time in Cup history this has occurred. By the time he retired, Cook's 321 career goals were second only to Nels Stewart on the all-time list.

ART SOMERS exacted revenge on a Leaf team that had beaten his Rangers in the previous year's finals. "Toronto had the one great line of Conacher, Jackson, and Primeau, and all we had to do was check them," he said, in understatement, of the team's heroics this year.

"Erhardt" is his first name, and **HELLER'S** 15 years of service to the Rangers has yet to be eclipsed. He was often called the Pepper Martin of hockey for his enthusiasm for the team and game.

Lester Patrick described **BUTCH KEELING** as "one of the best money players" in the game. Years later, in Winnipeg, Keeling proved Patrick's point by preventing a purse snatcher from robbing his neighbour as she walked home.

MURRAY MURDOCH played eleven seasons in the NHL, all with the Rangers. Incredibly, he never missed a single game, regular season or playoffs, the only player whose career was without blemish!

FRED COOK at birth, Bunny got his nickname (shortened to Bun) because of his style of taking short, hopping strides to gain momentum when skating.

At 6'2" 200 lbs. **EARL SEIBERT** was one of the biggest players in the league and the only player the feared Eddie Shore was himself afraid to fight for sheer strength and mean streak.

In spite of the violent reputations of his brothers Billy and George, **FRANK BOUCHER** won the Lady Byng seven times. In his last seven years in the league, he incurred just 21 penalty minutes.

OSSIE ASMUNDSON won this Cup as a rookie, but after one more season he became a fringe NHLer and was down in minor pro for another decade.

Team engraving from the original band, later retired to the Hockey Hall of Fame

Purchased from Montreal, **BABE SIEBERT** became an important player, though he was a holdout the first three games of the season in a contract dispute.

CHING JOHNSON survived poison gas and two years' combat in WWI to become the hardest hitter of his generation. He was discovered by Conn Smythe in the Central Hockey League.

DOUG BRENNAN came from out of the PCHL, and after three NHL years (1931-34) was back in the minors to stay.

Called the "Glasgow Gabber" because of his place of birth and his penchant for talking all game, **ANDY AITKENHEAD** replaced John Ross Roach in goal.

LESTER PATRICK became president of the Rangers and vice-president of MSG only on December 22 when Colonel John Hammond resigned. After the win he was presented with a replica Stanley Cup made of sugar!

GORD PETTINGER was born in England but came to Canada at a young age, playing on two Memorial Cup winners with Regina before joining the Rangers this year as a rookie.

An ex-boxer, trainer **HARRY WESTERBY** frequently had lunch with manager Frank Boucher and world champion Jack Dempsey at "Dempsey's," the eponymous restaurant kitty corner to Madison Square Garden.

Other players to appear for the Rangers this season: **CARL VOSS**

Details from the stovepipe Cup showing players' names as well as team information

1933 THE CHAMPIONS
1934 Chicago Black Hawks

This was the team's first Cup in its second finals appearance. The Hawks had lost to Montreal in the '31 finals 3-2 in the best-of-five. For the second year in a row, the Cup was won in overtime. After the last game, president Calder presented the Cup to owner Fred McLaughlin on ice.

STANLEY CUP FINALS

Chicago Black Hawks win best-of-five Stanley Cup finals 3-1

*April 3, 1934 Chicago Black Hawks 2 at Detroit Red Wings 1 (Paul Thompson 21:10 OT)
*April 5, 1934 Chicago Black Hawks 4 at Detroit Red Wings 1
**April 8, 1934 Detroit Red Wings 5 at Chicago Black Hawks 2
**April 10, 1934 Detroit Red Wings 0 at Chicago Black Hawks 1 {(Mush March 30:05 OT)} [Gardiner]

** played at the Olympia, Detroit ** played at the Chicago Stadium*

Replica Cup given to team owner Major McLaughlin

CHICAGO	GP	G	A	P	Pim
Doc Romnes	4	1	3	4	0
Johnny Gottselig	4	2	1	3	4
Paul Thompson	4	2	1	3	0
Rosie Couture	4	1	1	2	2
Mush March	4	1	1	2	2
Art Coulter	4	1	0	1	4
Lionel Conacher	4	1	0	1	2
Don McFadyen	4	0	1	1	2
Taffy Abel	4	0	0	0	2
Tom Cook	4	0	0	0	0
Chuck Gardiner	4	0	0	0	0
Leroy Goldsworthy	4	0	0	0	0
Roger Jenkins	4	0	0	0	0
Louis Trudel	4	0	0	0	0
Johnny Sheppard	3	0	0	0	0
Bill Kendall	1	0	0	0	0

In Goal	GP	W-L	Mins	GA	SO	Avg
Chuck Gardiner	4	3-1	291	7	1	1.44

(clockwise) Game action from game three of the Chicago-Detroit finals; keeping his promise, Roger Jenkins (left) puts goalie great Charlie Gardiner in a wheelbarrow and takes him for a celebration ride through the downtown streets of Chicago; game action from game two of the finals; Major McLaughlin holds the Cup while surrounded by his triumphant players.

FRED McLAUGHLIN named his team after the Black Hawk regiment of World War I. He was owner and president from the club's inception in 1926 to his death in 1944. McLaughlin married Irene Castle, an internationally famous dancer who was renowned for spicing up the sartorial appearance of both players and executives on the Hawks.

Despite taking the team to the Cup, and despite having won the Cup three times previous as coach (with Ottawa), **TOMMY GORMAN** was fired shortly after this victory.

One of the few goalie-captains in league history, **CHARLIE GARDINER** suffered a brain hemorrhage and died just two months after leading his Hawks to the Cup.

Trainer for most of his adult life, **ED FROELICH** deserved the inscription as much as any player. A native of Chicago, he graduated from the local National College of Physiotherapy with honours.

A veteran of nine seasons over 349 games with the Hawks and Maroons, this was **TOMMY COOK'S** only Stanley Cup triumph.

In a fit of triumphant insanity, **LOUIS TRUDEL** skated wildly around the ice with the Cup as soon as it was brought out.

The inscription reads **"ELVIN" ROMNES** but everyone called him **DOC**. He later became one of the first inductees of the U.S. Hockey Hall of Fame.

JACK LESWICK played just three regular season games with the Hawks this year, but in those days that was good enough to get his name on the Cup.

In this his last year in the NHL, **TAFFY ABEL** won his second Cup, the first coming with the Rangers during their second year in business, 1927-28.

Born in Wisconsin, **ROGER JENKINS** was a journeyman who played for every Original Six team except Detroit, in addition to a brief stint with the defunct Montreal Maroons. He promised to wheel goalie Gardiner in a wheelbarrow through the Chicago Loop if the Hawks won the Cup. They did, and he kept his word!

DON McFADYEN had probably not been called Donald since his childhood, but no matter. He played only eleven career playoff games and won a Stanley Cup.

JOE STARK was the team's backup, or, practise, goalie. Not only did he not play a minute during the season, he never played in the NHL at all! Yet his name is on the Cup.

Details from the stovepipe Cup showing both players and team

Team engraving from the original band, later retired to the Hockey Hall of Fame

BILL "COWBOY" KENDALL'S rookie season ended perfectly in what would be his only career Stanley Cup.

Right winger **MUSH MARCH** scored the Cup winner in double OT this year.

JOHNNY SHEPPARD'S eighth and last year in the NHL started in Boston, but he was released by the Bruins and happily signed with Chicago as a free agent in November.

His surname misspelled, **"THOMPSON," TINY** won his second of three Cups during a superb 13-year career with Chicago and the Rangers.

"Rosario" was quickly shortened to "Rosie" which in turn gave way to the equally effeminate "Lola," but nicknames have a way of sticking and **COUTURE** won his second Cup with the Hawks nonetheless.

LEROY GOLDSWORTHY got his name on the Cup even though he wasn't even with the team at the end of the year. After just seven games with Chicago at the start of the season, he was sold to London of the IAHL and later moved on to the Canadiens.

Born in Odessa, Soviet Union, **JOHNNY GOTTSELIG** played all his 17 NHL years with the Hawks before going on to coach the team from 1944 to '48.

That looks like a "T" but it should be an "L" for **LIONEL CONACHER**. A career given up for dead a few years earlier because of the bottle, the Big Train got himself on track and won his first Cup in his first year with Chicago.

ART COULTER, like many a Hawk, won a Cup with both Chicago and the Rangers, in his case a 1940 win on Broadway following this Windy City triumph.

Other players to appear for the Hawks this season: **DUKE DUTKOWSKI, JACK LESWICK**

1934 THE CHAMPIONS
1935 Montreal Maroons

This was the first all-Canadian finals since 1926. In seven playoff games, the Maroons were undefeated (5-0-2), though they were heavy underdogs going into the finals against a Toronto team noted for its speed. The Maroons were feted at City Hall in Montreal with their own Mayor Houde hosting the celebrations. Toronto Mayor Simpson and many of the Leafs players were also in attendance. Alderman W.S. Weldon also made a speech, at which time he revealed that he had been secretary of the MAAA in 1893 and as a result was actually one of the first men to hold the Stanley Cup upon its arrival from England.

STANLEY CUP FINALS

Montreal Maroons win best-of-five Stanley Cup finals 3-0

*April 4, 1935	Montreal Maroons 3 at Toronto Maple Leafs 2 (Dave Trottier 5:28 OT)
*April 6, 1935	Montreal Maroons 3 at Toronto Maple Leafs 1
**April 9, 1935	Toronto Maple Leafs 1 at Montreal Maroons 4 {Baldy Northcott 16:18 2nd}

** played at Maple Leaf Gardens, Toronto   ** played at the Forum, Montreal*

Montreal Maroons, 1934-35

MONTREAL	GP	G	A	P	Pim
Cy Wentworth	3	2	2	4	0
Baldy Northcott	3	2	1	3	0
Earl Robinson	3	2	1	3	0
Russ Blinco	3	1	1	2	0
Jimmy Ward	3	1	1	2	0
Dave Trottier	3	1	0	1	4
Gus Marker	3	1	0	1	0
Allan Shields	3	0	1	1	2
Lionel Conacher	3	0	0	0	8
Stewart Evans	3	0	0	0	4
Hooley Smith	3	0	0	0	4
Herb Cain	3	0	0	0	0
Alec Connell	3	0	0	0	0
Bob Gracie	3	0	0	0	0

In Goal	GP	W-L	Mins	GA	SO	Avg
Alec Connell	3	3-0	185	4	0	1.30

NHL president Frank Calder makes a formal presentation of the Cup to the Maroons hockey club on April 11, 1935, two days after victory. (left to right) Herbert Molson, Tommy Gorman, Ken Dawes, Frank Calder, Thomas Arnold, Robert MacDougall, and A.D. McTier.

Team engraving from the shoulder of the original Cup

CY WENTWORTH was great at checking with both his body and stick, but he remained under-rated because he never did anything fancily.

Big and tough, **BALDY NORTHCOTT** played on a line with Ward and Smith and led all playoff scorers with four goals.

After working his way up through the minors, **EARL ROBINSON** scored some timely goals, including both markers in the decisive 2-1 win to eliminate the Rangers from the 1934 quarter-finals and the opening goal of the Maroons 3-1 win over Toronto in game two of this year's finals.

RUSS BLINCO centred the "Blue Line" with Trottier and Robinson. The dazzling blonde won the Calder Trophy and the hearts of many women fans, yet off ice he wore thick glasses! The next year he experienced such a bad scoring slump that he started to wear the glasses on ice, thus becoming the first NHLer to do so (Hal Laycoe and Al Arbour later did likewise).

Reminiscent of the Shore-Bailey incident the previous year, **JIMMY WARD** suffered a serious concussion during the season. Shore knocked him violently to the ice and then Conacher kayoed Nels Stewart because he thought Stewart had been the culprit. Ward didn't miss any action, but tragedy was narrowly averted a second time.

DAVE TROTTIER was a member of Canada's 1928 Olympic team and a hero in game one of the finals, scoring the game-winner after overcoming a bad fever that felled him prior to the playoffs.

GUS MARKER scored a career-high eleven goals during the regular season and also accounted for the last goal of the year, the fourth in the 4-1 Cup-winning game.

ALLAN SHIELDS, or, the "Big A" to his teammates, led a full life in hockey, starting with the Montagnards in Ottawa, continuing in the NHL and on to RCAF hockey, and then to refereeing in the AHL after the war.

The Big Train, **LIONEL CONACHER**, won the Cup the previous year with Chicago, one of only a few men to win consecutive Cups with different teams.

Captain and member of the "S" Line with Stewart and Siebert, **HOOLEY SMITH** broke his thumb during the regular season but recovered in time for the playoffs.

In the 1937 playoffs, **STEWART EVANS** was the goat in game one versus the Rangers. The defenceman lost control of the puck in his own end, and Babe Pratt swooped in and scored. The Rangers won the game 1-0 and eliminated the Maroons the next game.

HERB CAIN played with Gracie and Marker and was, quite literally, a gift from the Habs. "The Montreal Maroons were wobbling badly at that time," Canadiens manager Leo Dandurand later explained, "so when I signed Cain, I turned him over to the Maroons for development."

Coach Gorman replaced incumbent Kerr in goal with **ALEC CONNELL** who had retired to the Ottawa Fire Department for civilian life away from the rink.

Details from the stovepipe Cup showing both players and team

Team engraving from the original band, later retired to the Hockey Hall of Fame

BOB GRACIE was carried from the ice unconscious after hitting his head on the ice following a Red Horner check. Luckily, he was back for the next game.

TOMMY GORMAN had won the Cup with Chicago the previous year but was summarily fired. He earned his measure of revenge and justice with this second win with a new team. "When they want open hockey, our team gives it to them. When they want defensive hockey, we have that, too. What a team! What a team!" he enthused.

TOE BLAKE signed with the team on February 22 and played the end of the regular season, though he saw action in only one playoff game.

Born in Belfast, Ireland, **SAM McMANUS** played half a season with the Maroons this year and one game with Boston in '36-'37 in a lengthy career spent mostly outside the NHL.

NORM "DUTCH" GAINOR played with Boston for four years (1927-31) with Cooney Weiland and Dit Clapper on the Dynamite Line.

BILL MacKENZIE (correct spelling) was a rarity. He played five games with the Maroons then was *loaned* to the Rangers for the rest of the season. Technically, he was a member of the Maroons because he hadn't been traded per se.

The next season **BILL MILLER** would be traded to crosstown rivals the Canadiens with Toe Blake and Ken Gravel for Lorne Chabot, a deal that had ramifications for the Habs for the next thirty years (Blake became the winningest coach in the game with the Habs).

As a member of the Maroons' executive, Senator **DONAT RAYMOND** happily collected a $500 bet from a Canadiens' associate upon winning the Cup.

THOMAS ARNOLD, an executive with the team, was an industrialist. He had the foresight to ensure that Tommy Gorman managed the team, a decision that helped win the Maroons the Cup.

Executive **KENNETH DAWES** was a beer magnate (with National Breweries) and horse breeder (Black Horse Stables). He promised Hooley Smith a horse if the team won the Cup. When the victorious team held a lavish ceremony at the Brewery, he indeed gave Smith a mare. Dawes was a powerful member within the English community of Montreal.

ROBERT MacDOUGALL (no relation to Hartland MacDougall) was another of the team's directors who didn't get his name on the Cup! Nonetheless, the two—Robert and Hartland—were partners of a brokerage firm and had been teammates on the Montreal Vics Cup-winning team of 1898.

Other players to appear for the Maroons this season: **PAUL HAYNES, AUBREY WEBSTER**

1935 1936 Detroit Red Wings

THE CHAMPIONS

After the final bell, the Leafs players dropped their sticks to the ice and skated over to the Wings to offer congratulations. This was a remarkable victory given that Detroit's first playoff game went 116:30 into overtime against the Maroons, the longest game ever (won by the Wings 1-0). Detroit had finished in last place the previous year but was presented the Cup later that night by president Calder to owner James Norris at the Royal York Hotel in Toronto. The Cup was filled with champagne, and even Adams himself had a sip. Each player was later given a ring to commemorate the victory. On April 18, the festivities continued with a lavish banquet at the Masonic Temple in Detroit.

STANLEY CUP FINALS

Detroit Red Wings win best-of-five Stanley Cup finals 3-1

*April 5, 1936 Toronto Maple Leafs 1 at Detroit Red Wings 3
*April 7, 1936 Toronto Maple Leafs 4 at Detroit Red Wings 9
**April 9, 1936 Detroit Red Wings 3 at Toronto Maple Leafs 4 (Buzz Boll 0:31 OT)
**April 11, 1936 Detroit Red Wings 3 at Toronto Maple Leafs 2 {Pete Kelly 9:45 3rd}

** played at the Olympia, Detroit ** played at Maple Leaf Gardens, Toronto*

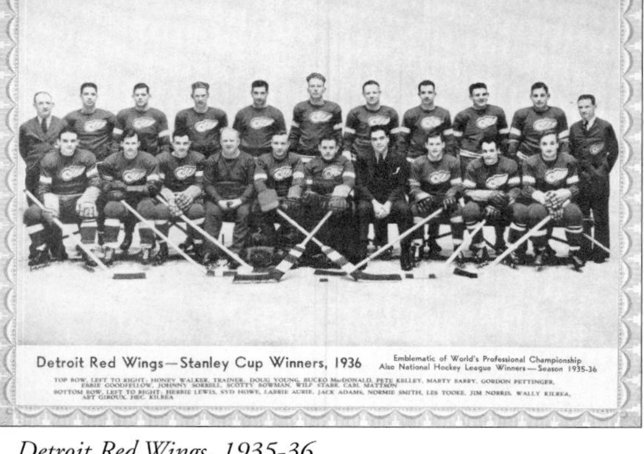

Detroit Red Wings, 1935-36

DETROIT	GP	G	A	P	Pim
Syd Howe	4	2	3	5	2
John Sorrell	4	2	3	5	0
Marty Barry	4	2	2	4	2
Gord Pettinger	4	2	2	4	0
Bucko McDonald	4	3	0	3	4
Wally Kilrea	4	2	1	3	0
Mud Bruneteau	4	1	2	3	0
Herbie Lewis	4	1	2	3	0
Scotty Bowman	4	1	1	2	2
Pete Kelly	4	1	1	2	0
Hec Kilrea	4	0	2	2	0
Doug Young	4	0	2	2	0
Ebbie Goodfellow	4	1	0	1	2
Larry Aurie	4	0	1	1	2
Normie Smith	4	0	0	0	0

In Goal	GP	W-L	Mins	GA	SO	Avg
Normie Smith	4	3-1	241	11	0	2.74

(clockwise) The jubilant Detroit dressing room the night of victory, April 11, 1936; owner James Norris takes a sip from the Cup as GM and coach Jack Adams tips the bowl for his boss; two photos taken at Maple Leaf Gardens from game three, April 9, 1936, won by the Leafs 4-3 in overtime.

His name is spelled the correct "**SID**" on Cup, which was how he liked his name written during his playing days (though he changed to Syd later). **HOWE** was the first player to score six goals in a game—February 3, 1944—and was on the ice when the winning goal was scored to end that longest game in NHL history against the Maroons.

In his sixth year with the Detroit organization, **JOHN SORRELL** didn't play in the NHL until he was 24 years old. He was a slim 5'11" 155 lbs.

MARTY BARRY was acquired from Boston for Cooney Weiland and played well on a line with Lewis and Aurie. After the war, he coached St. Mary's junior team in Halifax and died of a heart attack in 1969.

In his four seasons with Detroit, **GORD PETTINGER** won two Stanley Cups. His brother, Eric, also played briefly in the NHL, 1928 to '31.

BUCKO McDONALD had been a pro lacrosse player and minor league hockeyist until the league folded. At 21, and with no other options, he tried out for the Red Wings and made the team his first year.

Brother of Hec, **WALLY KILREA** missed playing with a second brother, Ken, by one year. Wally retired after '37-'38, and Ken joined the Wings for '38-'39.

MODERE "MUD" BRUNETEAU scored the historic 1-0 goal in the longest game ever played. The following morning, Maroons goaler Lorne Chabot presented him with the historic puck, a terrific sporting gesture that Bruneteau remembered the rest of his life.

HERBIE LEWIS played in the Ace Bailey Benefit Game in February 1934. "Lewis is a sportsman of the highest type," said Jack Adams. "I defy baseball or football or boxing or any other sport to produce an individual who can eclipse Herbie Lewis as a perfect model of what an athlete should stand for."

RALPH "SCOTTY" BOWMAN was claimed by Jack Adams from St. Louis when the Eagles disbanded prior to the start of the season after having played kid hockey with Parkdale and Niagara Falls. (He has no relation to modern-day coach William "Scotty" Bowman.)

PETE KELLY'S Cup-winning goal came serendipitously. "It wasn't my shift," he admitted. "But Larry Aurie, who was the right winger on our scoring line, was limping to the bench at the end of a long shift and I jumped over the boards without waiting for Jack Adams to tell me to go. I got a pass from Herbie Lewis and I just shot it into the top left corner of the net." The victim was George Hainsworth.

Called "General" on the original Cup band, **HEC KILREA** received special congrats from Jack Adams, the two having won the Cup with Ottawa nine years previous as teammates.

In a game February 24, 1935, against Toronto, at the Olympia, captain **DOUG YOUNG** swung at a puck near the boards and missed, hitting instead a fan, Mrs. Doris Geldhart. The stick broke her nose and blackened both her eyes, and she sued him, unsuccessfully, for $25,000.

Details from the stovepipe Cup showing both players and team

Team engraving from the original band, later retired to the Hockey Hall of Fame

After six years as a forward, **EBBIE GOODFELLOW** moved back to defence where he proved equally skilled. He tied the final game 1-1 in the second period, taking a pass from Johnny Sorrell and going through the Blair-Horner defence to beat Hainsworth with a shot.

LARRY AURIE broke his collarbone February 18 and seemed gone for the rest of the season. However, after missing just four games, he was back in the lineup.

Goaler **NORMIE SMITH** played all 48 games during the regular season, allowing just 103 goals and recording a shutout sequence lasting 248:32.

Trainer **FRANK "HONEY" WALKER** was highly regarded and known for making his own 'liniments,' that is, concoctions to cure various ailments that befell players (cuts, sores, bruises, etc.).

LOU GIFFELLS was called the business manager by the team though he was general manager of the Olympia as opposed to Adams who was called the hockey manager.

JACK ADAMS began his career as a player with Toronto in 1917, winning the Cup in the NHL's inaugural season. He began his affiliation with Detroit in 1927, one that lasted some 35 years and seven Stanley Cups.

Team president **JAMES NORRIS** made his fortune via the Norris Grain Co. of Chicago, a worldwide enterprise. He had wanted to buy an NHL team for that city, but when rebuffed settled for Detroit in 1933. He changed the name from Falcons to Red Wings, a symbol of the Montreal Winged Wheels hockey team of his youth in Quebec. Later, in an era without conflict of interest bylaws, he held simultaneous power over the Olympia, Madison Square Garden, and the Chicago Stadium, giving rise to jokes of the Norris Hockey League (NHL).

As the owner's son, **JAMES D. NORRIS**, Jr. held a privileged position with the Red Wings. "Meet my son, Jim," his dad began. "He doesn't seem to belong in my business world. He eats and sleeps sport. I'm putting him under Jack Adams' care. He'll probably want to play, but he's a lousy hockey player."

A Chicago native, **ARTHUR MICHAEL WIRTZ** began his adult life as a commercial leasing broker, and at the height of the Great Depression partnered with James Norris in grain speculation and became a millionaire.

Other players to appear for the Wings this season: **LORNE DUGUID, ART GIROUX, ORVILLE "ROLLY" ROULSTON, JOHN SHERF, WILF STARR, EDDIE WISEMAN**

1936 / 1937 Detroit Red Wings

THE CHAMPIONS

This was virtually the same team as last year's winning roster, Jack Adams refusing to tamper with success. The only difference was having to overcome serious injuries to Young and Aurie, but the Wings were aided by playing four of the five games of the finals on home ice thanks again to MSG booking the more profitable and reliable circus and leaving the Rangers in the lurch.

STANLEY CUP FINALS

Detroit Red Wings win best-of-five Stanley Cup finals 3-2

*April 6, 1937	Detroit Red Wings 1 at New York Rangers 5
**April 8, 1937	New York Rangers 2 at Detroit Red Wings 4
**April 11, 1937	New York Rangers 1 at Detroit Red Wings 0 (Neil Colville 0:23 2nd) [Dave Kerr]
**April 13, 1937	New York Rangers 0 at Detroit Red Wings 1 (Marty Barry 12:43 3rd) [Earl Robertson]
**April 15, 1937	New York Rangers 0 at Detroit Red Wings 3 {Marty Barry 19:22 1st} [Earl Robertson]

** played at Madison Square Garden, New York*
*** all remaining games played at the Olympia, Detroit because Madison Square Garden previously booked for circus*

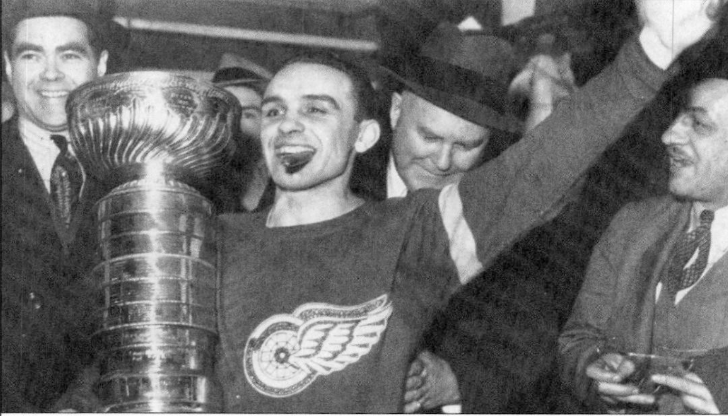

Herbie Lewis chews on a cigar and cradles the Cup.

Detroit goalie Earl Robertson makes a save off the shaft of his stick during a Cup finals game at the Olympia in Detroit.

DETROIT	GP	G	A	P	Pim
Syd Howe	5	1	4	5	0
Marty Barry	5	3	1	4	0
John Sorrell	5	2	2	4	2
Ebbie Goodfellow	4	0	2	2	12
John Gallagher	5	1	0	1	8
Herbie Lewis	5	1	0	1	4
Mud Bruneteau	5	1	0	1	2
Wally Kilrea	5	0	1	1	4
Gord Pettinger	5	0	1	1	2
John Sherf	5	0	1	1	2
Hec Kilrea	5	0	1	1	0
Scotty Bowman	5	0	0	0	2
Bucko McDonald	5	0	0	0	0
Earl Robertson	5	0	0	0	0
Pete Kelly	3	0	0	0	0
Howie Mackie	3	0	0	0	0
Normie Smith	1	0	0	0	0

In Goal	GP	W-L	Mins	GA	SO	Avg
Normie Smith	1	1-0	20	0	0	0.00
Earl Robertson	5	2-2	280	8	2	1.71

After retiring in 1946, **SYD HOWE** later got a job with the civil service, becoming a purchasing officer in the aircraft branch in the Department of Defense Production in Ottawa.

Although ornery early in his career, **MARTY BARRY** mellowed as he got older. This year, incredibly, he won the Lady Byng as well as leading the playoffs in scoring with eleven points.

JOHN SORRELL played every game this year for Detroit but midway through '37-'38 was traded to the New York Americans for Hap Emms.

Possessed of a hard shot, **EBBIE GOODFELLOW** was a top scorer, first as a forward, then as a defenceman. A knee injury eventually ended his career at the end of 1940-41.

LARRY AURIE broke his ankle late in the regular season and missed the rest of the year. "Pound for pound," Jack Adams said, "he has more courage than any player hockey has ever known." After this Cup win, Aurie raced into the dressing room, threw down his crutches, and performed a victory dance for the boys.

JOHN GALLAGHER started the year with the Americans, was sold to Detroit after just nine games, and re-sold to the Amerks in the off season.

Shortly after being inducted into the Hockey Hall of Fame in 1989, **HERBIE LEWIS** suffered a mild stroke and soon after broke his pelvis in a fall. When, for safety reasons, nurses tried to remove his Stanley Cup and Hall of Fame rings, he said simply, "over my dead body."

After retiring, **MUD BRUNETEAU** was selected by Jack Adams to coach the team's minor league affiliate Omaha Knights, featuring goaler Terry Sawchuk.

After just five games with Detroit the next year, **WALLY KILREA** was sent to Hershey where he played for a number of years, setting an AHL record with 99 points in 1942-43.

Younger brother of Eric, **GORD PETTINGER** ended his career in Boston in 1940 after which he joined the Army for two years and resumed playing, in the minors, upon being discharged into civvy street.

JOHN SHERF'S NHL career was brief though protracted. In '35-'36 he played one game, another game this Cup-winning season (plus five in the playoffs), and nine games over the next two years.

HEC KILREA was promoted to the number-one line with Barry and Lewis after Aurie broke his ankle. He responded well, scoring the OT winner in game five of the semi-finals vs. the Canadiens.

Winnipeg native **RALPH "SCOTTY" BOWMAN** played '33-'34 with Ottawa and went with the team when it transferred to St. Louis. Bowman was soon traded to Detroit, and it was with the Wings that he spent the final 197 games of his career.

After his NHL days, **BUCKO McDONALD** played Intermediate hockey in Sundridge, Ontario. Once, when his team was in nearby Georgetown, a woman pulled a corset over his head while he was in the penalty box. McDonald adjusted it, and when he came out of the box he had it on his head for all to see. "I didn't think it was fair that only one side of the rink could see it," he explained with a grin.

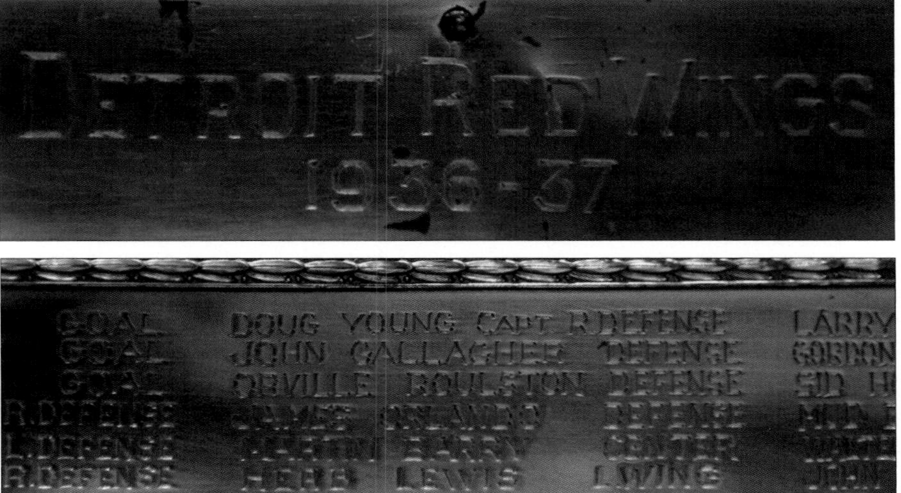

Details from the stovepipe Cup showing both players and team

The rookie **EARL ROBERTSON** stopped Alex Shibicky of the Rangers on a penalty shot, only the second in playoff history. He had been called up March 28 to replace the injured Smith who was not expected to recover from his elbow injury.

After the war, when his career was over, **PETE KELLY** accepted a job offer to coach the University of New Brunswick hockey team. Unsure what he wanted to do with the rest of his life, he accepted. He remained thirty years.

A career minor leaguer, **HOWIE MACKIE** played just 13 games this season and eight more in the playoffs. He played seven the following year, and then another decade in the AHL.

NORMIE SMITH hurt his elbow March 27, an injury that began the downward spiral of his career. He returned briefly to the Wings during the war when the team was short on goaltending.

A rookie, there was little room for **JIMMY ORLANDO** on a team laden with talent on the blueline, though he was to become one of the league's hardest hitters and "baddest men on ice."

Captain **DOUG YOUNG** suffered a broken leg on December 6 and was gone for the year.

Another accident victim, **ORVILLE ROULSTON** also broke his leg during the regular season and missed the rest of the year.

JIMMY FRANKS replaced Smith the night of March 27 when the starter hurt his elbow in a game vs. the Habs.

Prior to game five, **JACK ADAMS** brought the Cup into the dressing room to inspire the team. Earlier, he had made his team's plan against the Rangers very simple: "Hit Neil Colville hard. His jaw is busted. Give him lumps early and he won't be so strong later on." So excited was Adams afterward by the win that he fainted in the Detroit dressing room and had to be revived before the players could relax and continue their celebrations.

JAMES NORRIS joined into a hockey partnership with Arthur Wirtz and together they helped establish Sonja Henie as a skating attraction. They also owned the Cole Brothers circus.

Shortly before his death in 1966, **"YOUNG JIM" NORRIS** suggested that the NHL adopt a new trophy for the league's yearly goal-scoring champion.

One of **ARTHUR WIRTZ'S** great brainstorms was to bring Sonja Henie to the U.S. under an excuse called the Hollywood Ice Revue. She alone made the show a terrific success, and Wirtz's entrepreneurial escapades were just beginning.

Like many trainers of the early days, **FRANK "HONEY" WALKER** also acted as a snoop for GM Jack Adams, ratting out any players who had been out drinking or carousing the night before and compromising their playing ability.

Other players to appear for the Red Wings this season: **DON DEACON, BURR WILLIAMS**

1937 1938 THE CHAMPIONS Chicago Black Hawks

A most improbable Cup victory for Chicago, won with a roster that was fully half American-born players and with a team that had the worst regular season record for a Cup winner: 14-25-9. They finished in third place in the American Division, just two points ahead of Detroit and 23 behind second place Rangers. So certain was the NHL that Chicago wouldn't win game four that the Cup was never sent to Chicago and the Hawks had no trophy to hold in celebration!

STANLEY CUP FINALS

Chicago Black Hawks win best-of-five Stanley Cup finals 3-1

*April 5, 1938 Chicago Black Hawks 3 at Toronto Maple Leafs 1
*April 7, 1938 Chicago Black Hawks 1 at Toronto Maple Leafs 5
**April 10, 1938 Toronto Maple Leafs 1 at Chicago Black Hawks 2
**April 12, 1938 Toronto Maple Leafs 1 at Chicago Black Hawks 4
{Carl Voss 16:45 2nd}

** played at Maple Leaf Gardens, Toronto ** played at Chicago Stadium*

Members of the Hawks....

CHICAGO	GP	G	A	P	Pim
Johnny Gottselig	4	2	2	4	0
Doc Romnes	4	1	2	3	2
Paul Thompson	4	1	2	3	2
Carl Voss	4	2	0	2	0
Earl Seibert	4	1	1	2	8
Mush March	3	1	1	2	6
Jack Shill	4	1	1	2	4
Cully Dahlstrom	4	1	1	2	0
Roger Jenkins	4	0	2	2	6
Louis Trudel	4	0	1	1	0
Bill MacKenzie	4	0	0	0	9
Art Wiebe	4	0	0	0	2
Alex Levinsky	4	0	0	0	0
Pete Palangio	3	0	0	0	0
Virgil Johnson	2	0	0	0	0
Mike Karakas	2	0	0	0	0
Paul Goodman	1	0	0	0	0
Alfie Moore	1	0	0	0	0

In Goal	GP	W-L	Mins	GA	SO	Avg
Mike Karakas	2	2-0	120	2	0	1.00
Alfie Moore	1	1-0	60	1	0	1.00
Paul Goodman	1	0-1	60	5	0	5.00

(top) Players start pouring off the bench after the horn to end game four, giving the Hawks their second Stanley Cup in five years; (left) Bill Stewart gives the Cup a celebratory kiss while (left to right) Doc Romnes, Alfie Moore, and Jack Shill look on with delight.

A 16-year Hawks player, **JOHNNY GOTTSELIG** later coached the team for three and a half years (1944-48), making the playoffs only once when the Habs swept them in four straight games in 1946.

Anyone who tangles with Red Horner had better be prepared. **DOC ROMNES** got his stick up on the tough Leaf, and in exchange had his nose broken by rough Red.

PAUL THOMPSON scored the winner to eliminate the Habs from the quarter-finals and the next year became the team's playing coach.

CARL VOSS signed during the season after the Maroons gave him his outright release three games into the schedule.

Although he had been an all-star defenceman for a decade, **EARL SEIBERT** was moved up to right wing by coach Stewart to excellent effect this finals.

HAROLD "MUSH" MARCH scored the first-ever goal at Maple Leaf Gardens on November 12, 1931. He kept the puck, and at the final game in the league's oldest building—February 13, 1999, in Toronto—he used it at the ceremonial faceoff.

Sold by the New York Americans to Chicago on January 26, 1938, **JACK SHILL** arrived just in time to join in the Hawks' Stanley Cup run.

In his rookie season, **CULLY DAHLSTROM** scored the only goal, in overtime, to give the Hawks a 1-0 win in game two of the series versus the Americans. He was later elected to the United States Hockey Hall of Fame.

ROGER JENKINS was a native of Wisconsin who made his reputation by being a good hitter and puck carrier. He played with four Original Six teams, as well as the defunct Maroons and Americans, during his eight-year career.

LOUIS TRUDEL was a French-Canadian whose middle name was Napoleon, though his last name is misspelled on the Cup.

After eleven games with the Canadiens, **BILL MacKENZIE** was sent by Montreal to Chicago for Marty Burke. After two more years with Chicago, he went to the minors and never made it back to the NHL.

ART WEIBE retired in 1942 and returned home to Vermilion, Alberta to open a bakery. But each of the next two seasons owner Bill Tobin and Wiebe's great defense partner, Earl Siebert, called and begged him to return to the team, which he did, while newspapers carried headlines such as, "Art Kneads Dough, Hawks Need Art."

A hard hitter, **ALEX LEVINSKY** was one of many players Toronto boss Conn Smythe immortalized by naming one of his horses after, in Alex's case, Mine Boy. After retiring, Levinsky returned to Toronto to run a bowling alley, car dealership, and furniture warehouse.

PETE PALANGIO'S name appears twice on this year's Cup entry, the second time misspelled "Palagio."

Team engraving from the original band, later retired to the Hockey Hall of Fame

Team engraving from the shoulder of the original Cup

Details from the stovepipe Cup showing both players and team

VIRGIL JOHNSON played 25 regular season games and all of the playoffs as a 25-year old rookie, though he did not make it back to the NHL until 1943 when the war depleted the Chicago defense corps.

MIKE KARAKAS played games three and four of the finals with a special toe guard in his skate boot to protect his injured and tender foot.

PAUL GOODMAN was called up from the minors after Karakas's injury, but he thought Moore would start game two. He went off to the movies, and had to be pulled from the theatre to get to the game!

In perhaps the most famous playoff appearance of all time, **ALFIE MOORE** had been drinking with friends in a Toronto bar when Karakas couldn't play game one of the finals because of a broken toe. Moore, played a remarkable game that staked the Chicagos to a 1-0 series lead they never relinquished.

Team president McLaughlin fired coach Clem Laughlin and brought in a former referee, **BILL STEWART**, to boss the Black Hawks bench this season!

FREDERIC McLAUGHLIN owned Chicago's Manor House Coffee. The Major experimented with coaches, to varying degrees of success, hiring and firing with little regard for merit and experience. It was his idea to stack the team with U.S.-born players.

McLaughlin became so upset with NHL officials at one point that he resigned as the team's governor and delegated his authority at league meetings to **BILL TOBIN**. Tobin later acquired a majority interest in the team.

THORNE DONNELLY was a wealthy friend of the Major's and became one of two trustees to McLaughlin's will.

Trainer **ED FROELICH** got his first job, in 1931, with the Chicago Cubs baseball team. Since then he had been oilman for the Hawks in the winter and, variously, the Cubs, Brooklyn Dodgers, New York Yankees, and Chicago White Sox in the summer.

Other players to appear for the Black Hawks this season: **GLEN BRYDSON, MARTY BURKE, BERT CONNELLY, OSCAR HANSON, VIC HEYLIGER, HAL JACKSON, BILL KENDALL, IVAN NICHOLSON**

1938 THE CHAMPIONS
1939 Boston Bruins

For the first time, the playoffs adopted a best-of-seven format, but it was the semi-finals, not the finals, that produced the greater story. The Boston-Rangers series went the full seven games, four going into overtime and the B's winning three on goals by Mel Hill, who now became known as "Sudden Death." President Calder brought the Cup with him for game five in Boston, and after victory presented the trophy to captain Cooney Weiland as firecrackers went off in the Garden and the band played "Paree."

STANLEY CUP FINALS

Boston Bruins win best-of-seven Stanley Cup finals 4-1

*April 6, 1939	Toronto Maple Leafs 1 at Boston Bruins 2
*April 9, 1939	Toronto Maple Leafs 3 at Boston Bruins 2 (Doc Romnes 10:38 OT)
**April 11, 1939	Boston Bruins 3 at Toronto Maple Leafs 1
**April 13, 1939	Boston Bruins 2 at Toronto Maple Leafs 0 [Frank Brimsek]
*April 16, 1939	Toronto Maple Leafs 1 at Boston Bruins 3 {Roy Conacher 17:54 2nd}

** played at Boston Garden ** played at Maple Leaf Gardens, Toronto*

Boston Bruins in the dressing room after victory

(top) Boston goalie Frank Brimsek comes out of his goal to make a save off an oncoming Leafs forward; (left) Mel Hill (left) and Bill Cowley both have reasons to smile after winning the Cup. Hill scored three overtime goals in the first round of the playoffs against the Rangers, and Cowley set records for the post season with eleven assists and 14 points.

BOSTON	GP	G	A	P	Pim
Roy Conacher	5	5	2	7	6
Bill Cowley	5	0	7	7	2
Mel Hill	5	2	2	4	4
Bobby Bauer	5	2	1	3	0
Eddie Shore	5	0	3	3	6
Jack Crawford	5	1	1	2	4
Milt Schmidt	5	0	2	2	0
Woody Dumart	5	1	0	1	2
Flash Hollett	5	1	0	1	0
Ray Getliffe	5	0	0	0	2
Red Hamill	5	0	0	0	2
Jack Portland	5	0	0	0	2
Frank Brimsek	5	0	0	0	0
Dit Clapper	5	0	0	0	0
Gord Pettinger	5	0	0	0	0
Cooney Weiland	5	0	0	0	0

In Goal	GP	W-L	Mins	GA	SO	Avg
Frank Brimsek	5	4-1	311	6	1	1.16

Team engraving from the shoulder of the original Cup

ROY CONACHER set finals records for goals (five) and points (seven) by a rookie and also scored the Cup winner.

BILL COWLEY started his career with the doomed St. Louis franchise but led all players with 14 points in these playoffs despite missing several weeks during the regular season with an injured knee.

MEL HILL scored three overtime goals in the semi-finals against the Rangers to earn his nickname "Sudden Death." The goals were all the sweeter for Hill who had been released by Lester Patrick in New York in 1937 with the parting advice that he find some other form of employment!

BOBBY BAUER'S first NHL game came on the final day of the '36-'37 season when he scored a goal playing with Kraut Line teammates Schmidt and Dumart.

EDDIE SHORE missed the first two weeks of the season in a contract dispute before signing for the league maximum of $7,000, but only after president Calder intervened in the negotiations between player and management (Weston Adams and Art Ross). After the victory, Shore went straight to the dressing room as a form of protest, but the crowd would not allow the Cup presentation to begin without their great number 2 on ice to accept the trophy.

JACK CRAWFORD was the number one defenceman during Shore's earlier absence in the regular season. He wore a helmet to cover his baldness, a state that resulted from an infection from paint off his high school football helmet.

MILT SCHMIDT and Dumart were even closer friends than Lindsay and Howe in Detroit. They negotiated their contracts together, roomed together, and when they were married lived across the street from each other for thirty years.

The key to **WODDY DUMART'S** longevity was off-ice discipline. He kept proper hours, maintained a healthy diet, and trained in the off season to keep his weight steady at 190.

FLASH HOLLETT proved the veracity of his nickname each night, the best rushing defenceman of his era who later scored 15 or more goals in four straight seasons.

Demoted during the regular season, **RAY GETLIFFE** was recalled for the playoffs and provided invaluable play to the Cup victory.

RED HAMILL later lost a leg because of illness but continued to coach and ref kids games. When doctors told him his other leg had to go, he promised to keep active in hockey, but he passed away before he could make good on that promise.

In his youth, **JACK PORTLAND** was a champion high jumper at Collingwood Collegiate Institute, clearing as much as 6'4 1/8" before settling into a hockey career.

In a wildly prophetic, though initially unpopular move, GM Art Ross sold goalie Tiny Thompson to Detroit and brought up **FRANK BRIMSEK** from Providence. Frankie's brilliant play almost single-handedly won the Cup although he was at first jeered by local fans because he was replacing the hugely popular Thompson.

Details from the stovepipe Cup showing both players and team

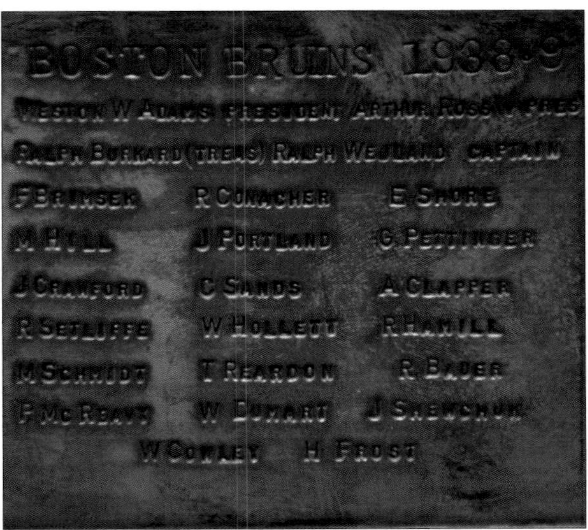

Team engraving from the original band, later retired to the Hockey Hall of Fame

The team's policeman, **DIT CLAPPER** won his first Cup in ten years and made the first all-star team on defence for the first of three successive years after earning berths at right wing earlier in his career.

GORD PETTINGER was no superstar, but he played for four Cup winners spread over three teams between 1932 and '39.

COONEY WEILAND (and later Claude Provost) won the Cup in both his first and last years in the NHL (1929 and '39). He later coached hockey at Harvard for twenty years.

"This is the greatest team ever assembled," opined builder and lifetime member of the Bruins, **ART ROSS**.

CHARLIE SANDS played for four Original Six teams (Toronto, Montreal, the Rangers) before retiring and moving out to sunny California with his family and working at the Rose Bowl in Pasadena.

Brother of Hall of Famer Ken, **TERRY REARDON** interrupted his career to join the army, then played an extended period in the AHL before becoming a longtime coach and general manager.

PAT McREAVY had been a member of Canada's gold medal team at the 1938 World Championships before joining the Bruins a year later. Even though he played only six regular season games and none in the playoffs, his name is still on the Cup.

JACK SHEWCHUK played only three regular season games, but like McReavy made the engraver's list.

HARRY FROST'S only NHL time came this year (four regular season games and one against the Rangers in the semi-finals) though his minor pro career lasted almost two decades.

WESTON ADAMS had recently replaced his dad as team owner, in 1936. He had been a goalie of note during his years at Harvard, but he learned the art of managing from his dad.

RALPH BURHARD was the team trainer.

Other players to appear for the Bruins this season: **TINY THOMPSON**

1939–1940 New York Rangers

A quick-skating team with a ferocious defence, the Rangers went undefeated in 19 games during one stretch of the regular season before knocking off Cup champions Boston in the semi-finals. After the win, in Toronto, the team went to a restaurant with the Cup to celebrate. During the party, one Toronto fan tried to steal the Cup but was caught. The "dinner" bill came to $3,700. After, the party continued at the Royal York Hotel and again the next morning on the train back to Manhattan.

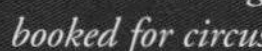

STANLEY CUP FINALS

New York Rangers win best-of-seven Stanley Cup finals 4-2

*April 2, 1940	Toronto Maple Leafs 1 at New York Rangers 2 (Alf Pike 15:30 OT)
*+April 3, 1940	Toronto Maple Leafs 2 at New York Rangers 6
**April 6, 1940	New York Rangers 1 at Toronto Maple Leafs 2
**April 9, 1940	New York Rangers 0 at Toronto Maple Leafs 3 [Turk Broda]
**April 11, 1940	New York Rangers 2 at Toronto Maple Leafs 1 (Muzz Patrick 31:43 OT)
**April 13, 1940	New York Rangers 3 at Toronto Maple Leafs 2 {(Bryan Hextall 2:07 OT)}

** played at Madison Square Garden, New York + played a day early because of the circus*
*** all remaining games played at Maple Leaf Gardens, Toronto because Madison Square Garden previously booked for circus*

Players joke with Lester Patrick, placing the Cup on his head like a hat.

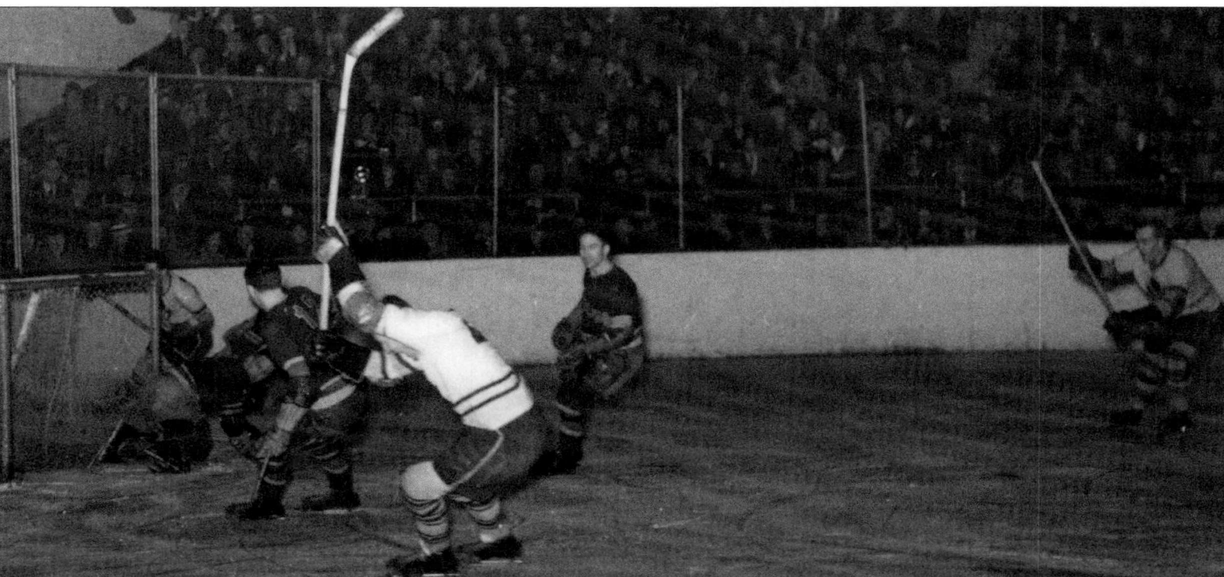

(top) The Leafs beat goalie Dave Kerr for a goal in game six at the Gardens, but by the end of the night it was Kerr and teammates who were celebrating a Cup win; (left) Lester Patrick (second from right) examines the Cup bowl in detail with members of the Rangers.

NY RANGERS	GP	G	A	P	Pim
Bryan Hextall	6	4	1	5	7
Neil Colville	6	2	3	5	12
Phil Watson	6	1	4	5	8
Dutch Hiller	6	1	2	3	0
Alf Pike	6	2	0	2	4
Babe Pratt	6	1	1	2	6
Lynn Patrick	6	1	1	2	0
Ott Heller	6	0	2	2	8
Alex Shibicky	5	0	2	2	2
Art Coulter	6	1	0	1	8
Muzz Patrick	6	1	0	1	6
Mac Colville	6	0	1	1	6
Clint Smith	6	0	1	1	2
Kilby MacDonald	6	0	0	0	4
Dave Kerr	6	0	0	0	0

In Goal	GP	W-L	Mins	GA	SO	Avg
Dave Kerr	6	4-2	394	11	0	1.68

Team engraving from the shoulder of the original Cup

After going scoreless in the first seven games of the playoffs, **BRYAN HEXTALL** had a hat trick in game two of the finals to ignite a key victory.

NEIL COLVILLE and brother Mac signed with the Rangers at the same time. Neil joined the army in 1942 and later became coach on Broadway.

The Rangers and Habs had competed bitterly to sign **PHIL WATSON**. He played on a line with Hextall and Hiller that was key to the win.

In the '41 playoffs, **DUTCH HILLER** got into hot water with his boss Lester Patrick. He showed up for the final game of the Rangers-Detroit semis with all his bags packed, a sign Patrick took to mean that Hiller thought the team would lose and he wanted to get out of town right away. "I never packed my bags because I thought we would lose," he tried to explain. "I thought we would win." Regardless, two days after the win Patrick traded him to Detroit.

ALF PIKE scored on his own goal in game one to tie the score 1-1 but made amends in the overtime by scoring the game winner.

Tall, dark, and handsome, a great player who loved trouble off ice, **BABE PRATT** knew the whereabouts of every emergency exit in every hotel room in the city.

Son of Lester, brother of Muzz, and nephew of Frank, **LYNN PATRICK** was part of hockey's royal family represented today by Craig Patrick, Pittsburgh GM and son of Lynn.

OTT HELLER was the only player left from the '33 Cup win and the only man after Dit Clapper to appear in 15 consecutive NHL seasons (1931-46). He was paired on defence with the even larger Babe Pratt.

Lester Patrick (left) examines the Cup with members of his Rangers' executive.

Pulled from his job in Winnipeg making boxes used for packing fish, **ALEX SHIBICKY** impressed Lester Patrick who signed him to the NHL. Shibicky played game five with his broken ankle frozen.

ART COULTER joined the army in 1942 and never played again. Prior to a game against Boston in the semis, he put a message at every player's stall in the dressing room: "Determination was the predominating factor in last year's Stanley Cup champions. We have it too. Let's go. Art Coulter."

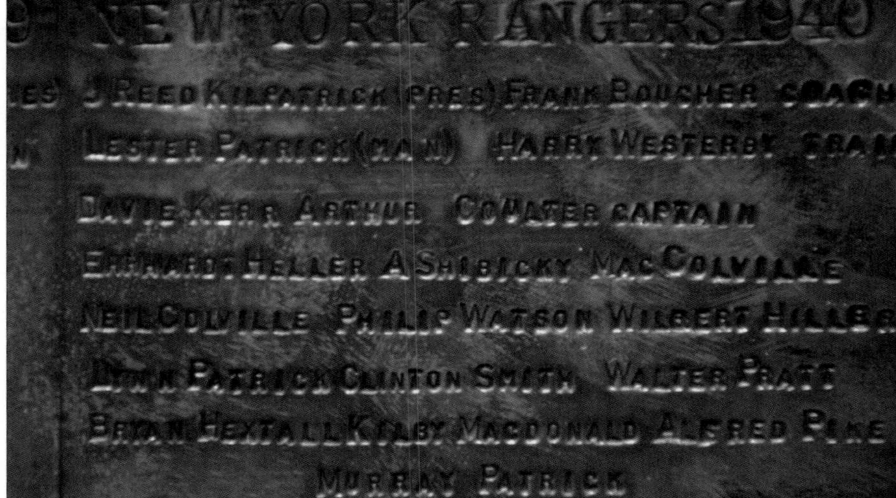

NEW YORK RANGERS 1940
REED KILPATRICK (PRES) FRANK BOUCHER
LESTER PATRICK (MAN) HARRY WESTERBY
DAVIE KERR ARTHUR COULTER CAPTAIN
HELLER A SHIBICKY MAC COLVILLE
NEIL COLVILLE PHILIP WATSON WILBERT HILLER
LYNN PATRICK CLINTON SMITH WALTER PRATT
BRYAN HEXTALL KILBY MACDONALD ALFRED PIKE
MURRAY PATRICK

Team engraving from the original band, later retired to the Hockey Hall of Fame

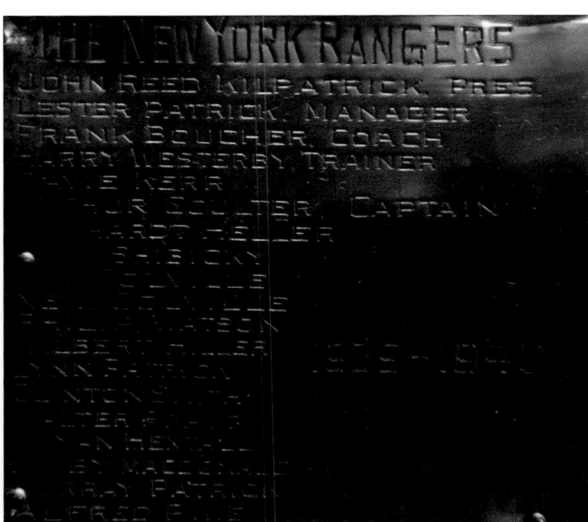

Team engraving from the Cup redesign which replaced the original band (above) but was itself replaced when the final and current Cup design was introduced in the late 1950s.

MUZZ PATRICK posed in a family picture after winning the Cup but he was more famous in hockey circles for a fight with Eddie Shore in the 1939 semis when he gave what all accounts describe as the worst drubbing Shore ever absorbed.

MATTHEW "MAC" COLVILLE, brother of Neil, joined the army in 1942 and played on the Allan Cup-winning Ottawa Commandos, one of the greatest amateur teams of all time.

CLINT SMITH once went 83 games without incurring a penalty. In 430 career games over ten seasons he received just nine minors.

KILBY MacDONALD won the Calder Trophy this year after scoring 15 goals, but after just five scores next year he was in the minors, then the army, before playing two final seasons with the Rangers at the end of the war (1943-45).

Goalie **DAVE KERR** played every minute this year for the Rangers, winning the Vezina Trophy and setting a record with three shutouts in the semi-finals vs. Boston.

FRANK BOUCHER was named new GM of the Rangers after Lester Patrick resigned. This was his first of eleven years as coach, though his only Stanley Cup as bench boss (he had won as a player on Broadway in 1928 and '33).

HARRY WESTERBY was short and stocky and had broken his nose countless times. He was famous among New York's hockey-loving children for dropping the team's broken sticks on a curb outside Madison Square Garden where youngsters looking for a souvenir would flock regularly.

Other players to appear for the Rangers this season: **CLIFF BARTON, JOHN POLICH, STAN SMITH**

The Rangers fill the Cup bowl with punch for their celebratory party.

1940 THE CHAMPIONS
1941 Boston Bruins

This Bruins team was virtually the same as the Cup-winning one from 1939. During the regular season, they established an NHL record by going 23 games without a loss (December 21-February 25). At the first game of the following season, all players were given special Stanley Cup coins to commemorate their victory. A few months later, Japan bombed Pearl Harbor, and within a year eight men from this Boston team were enlisted in the army, fighting far away from the roaring crowds of the NHL. Boston next won the Cup in 1970.

STANLEY CUP FINALS

Boston Bruins win best-of-seven Stanley Cup finals 4-0

*April 6, 1941	Detroit Red Wings 2 at Boston Bruins 3
*April 8, 1941	Detroit Red Wings 1 at Boston Bruins 2
**April 10, 1941	Boston Bruins 4 at Detroit Red Wings 2
**April 12, 1941	Boston Bruins 3 at Detroit Red Wings 1 {Bobby Bauer 8:43 2nd}

** played at Boston Garden* *** played at the Olympia, Detroit*

Members of the Bruins hold their prized treasure.

BOSTON	GP	G	A	P	Pim
Milt Schmidt	4	3	4	7	0
Eddie Wiseman	4	3	0	3	0
Roy Conacher	4	1	2	3	0
Woody Dumart	4	0	3	3	2
Pat McReavy	4	1	1	2	5
Flash Hollett	4	1	1	2	4
Terry Reardon	4	1	1	2	2
Bobby Bauer	4	1	1	2	0
Dit Clapper	4	0	2	2	2
Des Smith	4	0	2	2	2
Jack Crawford	4	0	2	2	0
Art Jackson	4	1	0	1	0
Herb Cain	4	0	1	1	0
Frank Brimsek	4	0	0	0	0
Mel Hill	4	0	0	0	0

In Goal	GP	W-L	Mins	GA	SO	Avg
Frank Brimsek	4	4-0	240	6	0	1.50

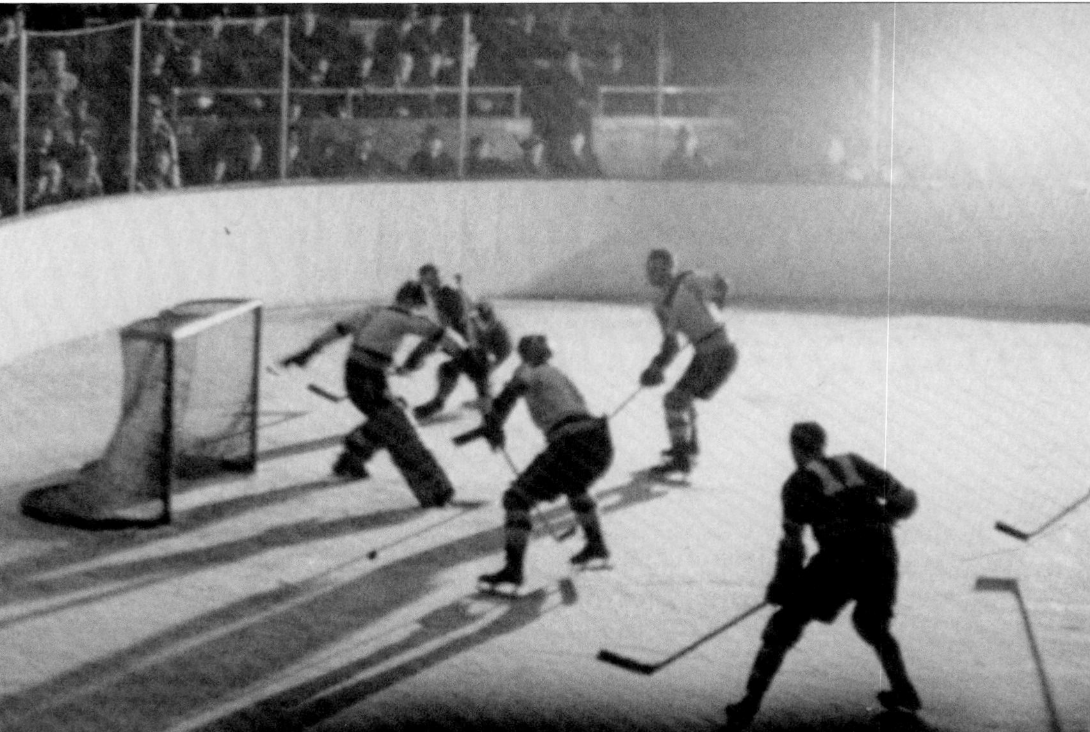

Action from the Boston Garden during the finals against Detroit. Frank Brimsek is in goal for the Bruins.

Team engraving from the shoulder of the original Cup

MILT SCHMIDT led all scorers with eleven points in the playoffs, though the Kraut Line was soon to be renamed the Kitchener Line (or, alternately, the Kitchener Kids) because of anti-German sentiments caused by WWII.

EDDIE WISEMAN led the playoffs with six goals. He had been acquired by the Bruins in the trade that sent Eddie Shore to the New York Americans, where the great defenceman played both in the NHL and the AHL team he recently purchased, the Springfield Indians.

ROY CONACHER was likely the most under-rated of the Conacher brothers, in large measure because of Lionel and Charlie's charisma and success. Roy, though, had twenty or more goals in eight of nine complete seasons he played in the league, retiring with 226 career goals in 1952.

WOODY DUMART and the entire Kraut Line played its last game during 1941-42 before going off to war. At the end of that game, members of the opposing Canadiens carried the three off the ice to wish them the best.

PAT McREAVY played only 55 NHL games but had a long and distinguished career in senior hockey in Owen Sound after the war.

Conn Smythe sold **FLASH HOLLETT** to Boston on January 15, 1936 for $15,000, a deal Smythe would later call the worst he ever made. Hollett scored the goal that eliminated the Leafs from the '39 playoffs and was, as his nickname suggested, the fastest player in the league.

TERRY REARDON finished with the Bruins and the NHL in 1947, but then acted as playing coach in Providence and later coached and managed the Baltimore Clippers in the AHL for some twenty years.

The venerable Boston Garden

BOBBY BAUER left for the army and didn't return to the NHL until 1946, one of the longest absences for enlisting players.

DIT CLAPPER won his third and final Cup in this the twilight of his great Bruins' career. The captain later took on managerial duties for the team and became the first and only player to be inducted into the Hockey Hall of Fame before retiring.

"Wes" on the Cup, **DES SMITH** was a steady and reliable defenceman who was unheralded though invaluable to the team's success.

JACK CRAWFORD played all his 13 years in Boston then stayed in the area to coach in the AHL. He later became the president of the Cape Cod Amateur Hockey League.

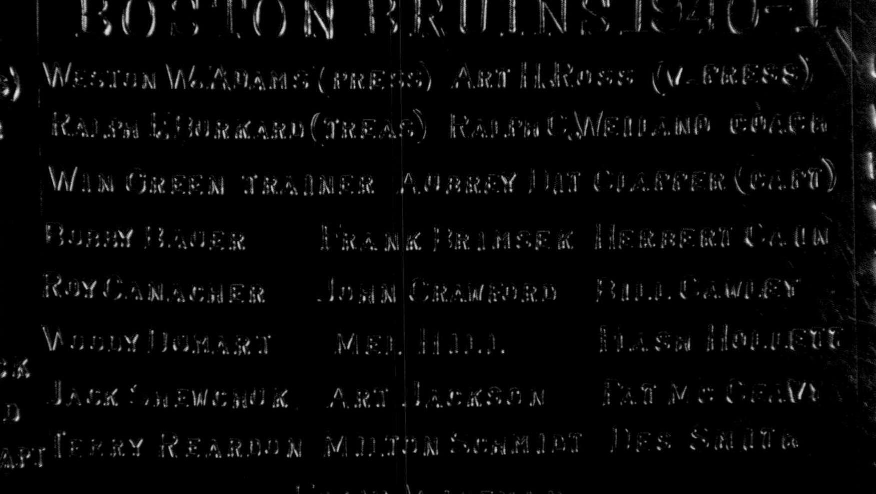

Team engraving from the Stanley Cup

Team engraving from the Cup redesign which replaced the original band but was itself replaced when the final and current Cup design was introduced in the late 1950s (above).

Not quite the measure of his Hall of Fame brother Harvey, **ART JACKSON** became coach of St. Catharines in OHA junior after the war, a job he quit to become personnel manager of Port Weller Dry Docks Ltd. in that city.

A rare 200-career-goal man, **HERB CAIN** scored the winner in game six of the semi-finals against Toronto to force a game seven which the Bruins won.

Quickly becoming one of the greatest of the greats, **FRANK BRIMSEK** had been the first goalie to win both the Vezina and Calder Trophies in the same year and was hailed as "Mister Zero," king of the shutout.

MEL HILL played on a line with Conacher and Cowley and scored the goal that eliminated the Leafs from the series, one he ranks right up there with his three OT winners in '39: "I came out of the corner and fired a hot shot past Turk Broda. We went on and rolled over Detroit in four straight games to win the Stanley Cup."

BILL COWLEY played only two playoff games because of a bad knee, though he won the Hart and Art Ross Trophies. His 62 points were well ahead of second-place finisher Bryan Hextall of the Rangers who had 44.

JACK SHEWCHUK'S is perhaps the most peculiar name in Cup-engraving history because his name was not on the original Cup but magically appeared when the Cup was re-modelled in 1957. He played just twenty games this year, which perhaps accounts for the initial omission.

Other players to appear for the Bruins this season: **GORD BRUCE, RED HAMILL**

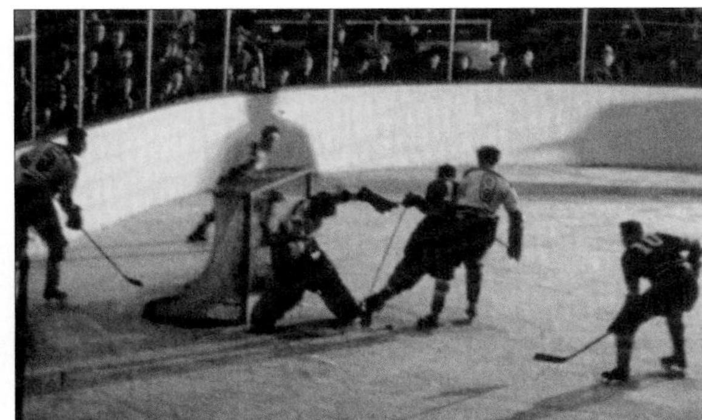

Action from the Stanley Cup finals in 1941 featuring Detroit playing in Boston.

1941 THE CHAMPIONS
1942 Toronto Maple Leafs

This Leafs team remains the only one to recover from being 3-0 down in the finals to win the Stanley Cup, accomplished under the coaching of Happy Day. Under coach Dick Irvin, the Leafs had gone to the finals seven times between 1932 and 1940, but won only once (1932). Day's system of defence, and his strategy after game three, proved the difference. He benched a number of regulars for game four and inserted rookies who responded to the pressure to win game after game, culminating with a 3-1 win on home ice to take the Cup in the most improbable manner. All players received gold coins which doubled as lifetime passes to Maple Leaf Gardens.

STANLEY CUP FINALS

Toronto Maple Leafs win best-of-seven Stanley Cup finals 4-3

*April 4, 1942 Detroit Red Wings 3 at Toronto Maple Leafs 2
*April 7, 1942 Detroit Red Wings 4 at Toronto Maple Leafs 2
**April 9, 1942 Toronto Maple Leafs 2 at Detroit Red Wings 5
**April 12, 1942 Toronto Maple Leafs 4 at Detroit Red Wings 3
*April 14, 1942 Detroit Red Wings 3 at Toronto Maple Leafs 9
**April 16, 1942 Toronto Maple Leafs 3 at Detroit Red Wings 0 [Broda]
*April 18, 1942 Detroit Red Wings 1 at Toronto Maple Leafs 3 {Pete Langelle 9:48 3rd}

** played at Maple Leaf Gardens, Toronto ** played at the Olympia, Detroit*

Toronto Maple Leafs, 1941-42

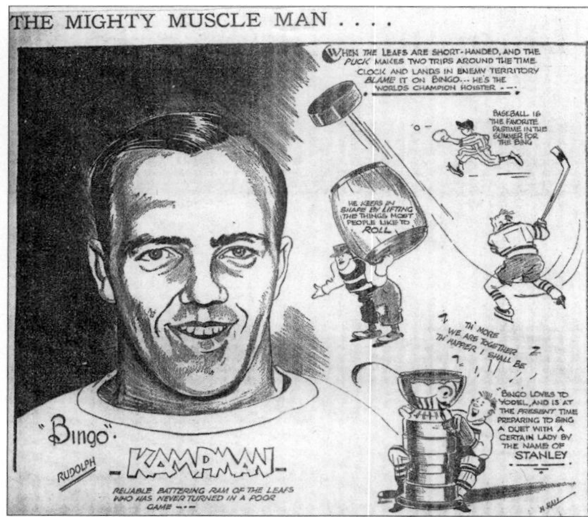

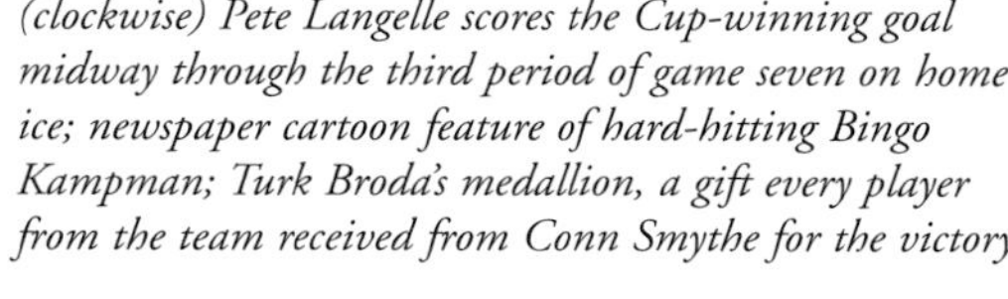

(clockwise) Pete Langelle scores the Cup-winning goal midway through the third period of game seven on home ice; newspaper cartoon feature of hard-hitting Bingo Kampman; Turk Broda's medallion, a gift every player from the team received from Conn Smythe for the victory.

Team engraving from the shoulder of the original Cup

TORONTO	GP	G	A	P	Pim
Billy Taylor	7	1	8	9	2
Sweeney Schriner	7	5	3	8	4
Don Metz	4	4	3	7	0
Syl Apps	7	3	4	7	2
Wally Stanowski	7	2	5	7	0
Lorne Carr	7	3	2	5	6
Nick Metz	7	2	3	5	4
Bob Goldham	7	2	2	4	22
John McCreedy	7	1	2	3	6
Bob Davidson	7	1	1	2	14
Pete Langelle	7	1	1	2	0
Bingo Kampman	7	0	2	2	8
Ernie Dickens	5	0	0	0	4
Turk Broda	7	0	0	0	0
Gord Drillon	3	0	0	0	0
Hank Goldup	3	0	0	0	0
Bucko McDonald	3	0	0	0	0
Gaye Stewart	3	0	0	0	0

In Goal	GP	W-L	Mins	GA	SO	Avg
Turk Broda	7	4-3	420	19	1	2.71

BILLY TAYLOR was later expelled from the league, along with Bruins teammate Don Gallinger, for gambling on NHL games with the mob in Detroit, a charge confirmed through wiretaps.

Born in the Soviet Union but raised in Calgary, **DAVE "SWEENEY" SCHRINER** tied game seven 1-1 with a power-play goal. He later scored the insurance goal to bring the Leafs this miracle Cup.

REG HAMILTON was defence partner and road roommate with Hap Day until Day retired. Every night he played, Hamilton earned his reputation for using his elbows and taking his man out of the play.

One of the keys to the comeback, **DON METZ** proved coach Day right for inserting him into the lineup for game four in place of Gord Drillon and sparking the win.

Captain **SYL APPS** led the playoffs with nine assists, won the Lady Byng for his sportsmanlike play, and soon joined Conn Smythe in his war efforts with the Sportsmen's Battalion.

WALLY "THE HAT" STANOWSKI had broken his ankle in his first NHL game but developed into a fine rushing defenceman. He, too, joined the army shortly after this victory.

Bought from the New York Americans, **LORNE CARR** was a two-time First All-Star Team right winger with the Leafs and their leading goal scorer in '42-'43 and '43-'44 with 27 and 36 goals, respectively.

Brother of Don, **NICK METZ** played on a line with Apps and Drillon, and this threesome was the team's best in igniting the historic comeback.

BOB GOLDHAM spent the next three years in the army after this victory, and upon being discharged resumed his career with Toronto, Chicago, and finally Detroit before retiring in 1956.

The career of **JOHNNY McCREEDY** was brief but his accomplishments many. Prior to his NHL term, McCreedy won a Memorial Cup, Allan Cup, and World Championship, a rare amateur triple.

A Toronto lad, "Rugged" **BOB DAVIDSON** was the premier checker in the league, assigned to shadow the opponent's best player every night.

Though Sweeney Schriner scored two goals in the final game, it was **PETE LANGELLE** who netted the Cup-winner midway through the third period of this incredible comeback.

RUDOLPH KAMPMAN got his nickname "Bingo" from the violent sounds that emanated from opponents after they had been hit by him. He won the Allan Cup with Sudbury in 1937 and again with the Ottawa Commandos in 1943, but he spent the last twenty years of his life in a nursing home.

ERNIE DICKENS didn't figure in the Leafs' long-term plans and was traded to Chicago in the blockbuster Max Bentley deal of 1947. He remained a Hawk for four years.

Team engraving from the Stanley Cup

Team engraving from the Cup redesign which replaced the original band but was itself replaced when the final and current Cup design was introduced in the late 1950s (above).

TURK BRODA'S name appears on this Cup twice, and perhaps rightly so. He was one of the great money goalies of all time (though the double engraving is likely simply an error).

GORD DRILLON and Bucko McDonald were benched for game four in favour of Don Metz and Hank Goldup, and they remained on the bench for the final four victories.

HANK GOLDUP had a career-high dozen goals this season, but just eight games into the next he was sent to the New York Rangers with Red Garrett for Babe Pratt, a key deal for the Leafs' '45 Cup win.

After retiring, **BUCKO McDONALD** served as a Liberal MP in the House of Commons as a representative for the riding of Parry Sound-Muskoka from 1949 to '57. He later coached in Parry Sound, where one of the youngsters on his team was Bobby Orr.

Rookie **GAYE STEWART** was one of the league's fastest skaters. He won the Calder Trophy despite his horrific stick-swinging duel with Jimmy Orlando of Detroit. He was brought up to replace Goldup for game five, a Toronto romp, and remained in the lineup for the rest of the series.

Fourteen-year-old **HUGH SMYTHE**, team mascot, attended Upper Canada College and later med school before becoming one of the team's physicians.

FRANK SELKE was named acting general manager when Conn Smythe went off to war as leader of the Sportsmen's Battery. Selke distinguished himself as a man able to run an NHL team on his own.

TIM DALY was called trainer, though to put him in the same context as current Leaf trainer Chris Broadhurst would be a grave insult to the latter! Daly was the man of funny words, the spirit-lifter, and, without doubt, the self-proclaimed laziest man ever in the Leafs' employ!

Prior to game four, coach **HAP DAY** read a letter to the team from a little girl who said she'd be ashamed to go to school the next day if the Leafs lost four in a row. If that wasn't motivation enough to win, he admonished, then he was helpless to do more for the players. They won.

Other players to appear for the Leafs this season: **JACK CHURCH**

1943 Detroit Red Wings

This Detroit victory was sweet revenge for Boston's sweep of the Wings two years previous. In the first round they made amends for their embarrassing loss to the Leafs the previous year (when they blew a 3-0 series lead) by eliminating Toronto in six close games. The Wings boarded a train right after the final game against the Bruins to return home, and en route Jack Adams presented the Cup to the players and the celebrating began. A small crowd of about fifty souls were at the station to greet the returning heroes the next morning.

STANLEY CUP FINALS

Detroit Red Wings win best-of-seven Stanley Cup finals 4-0

*April 1, 1943 Boston Bruins 2 at Detroit Red Wings 6
*April 4, 1943 Boston Bruins 3 at Detroit Red Wings 4
**April 7, 1943 Detroit Red Wings 4 at Boston Bruins 0 [Johnny Mowers]
**April 8, 1943 Detroit Red Wings 2 at Boston Bruins 0 {Joe Carveth 12:09 1st} [Johnny Mowers]

** played at the Olympia, Detroit ** played at Boston Garden*

Detroit Red Wings, 1942-43

DETROIT	GP	G	A	P	Pim
Sid Abel	4	1	5	6	2
Carl Liscombe	4	2	3	5	2
Don Grosso	4	3	0	3	4
Joe Carveth	4	3	0	3	2
Mud Bruneteau	3	3	0	3	0
Les Douglas	4	2	1	3	2
Eddie Wares	4	0	3	3	2
Jack Stewart	4	1	1	2	8
Jimmy Orlando	4	0	2	2	6
Syd Howe	3	1	0	1	0
Hal Jackson	4	0	1	1	4
Alex Motter	1	0	1	1	0
Adam Brown	4	0	0	0	2
Johnny Mowers	4	0	0	0	0
John Simon	3	0	0	0	0
Joe Fisher	1	0	0	0	0
Harry Watson	1	0	0	0	0

In Goal	GP	W-L	Mins	GA	SO	Avg
Johnny Mowers	4	4-0	240	5	2	1.25

Players, coaches, and staff celebrate Detroit's third Cup in eight years.

Team engraving from the shoulder of the original Cup

SID ABEL'S empty net goal March 28 vs. Toronto in the semis was the first ever in playoff competition. This was his finest playoff series. "I always wished that I had had more than one big Stanley Cup series," he said later.

As a rookie, **CARL LISCOMBE** had scored three goals in 1:52 back in '37-'38. Now he played on a line with Syd Howe and Mud Bruneteau and led the league in playoff points with 14.

DON GROSSO scored a hat trick in game three while playing with his left wrist in a cast, the result of an injury suffered in the semi-finals vs. Toronto.

JOE CARVETH had a rough start to his career, breaking his leg badly in both his first two seasons (1940-41 and '41-'42) before making an impact this year.

In his last year of an eleven-year career in the NHL, all with the Wings, **MUD BRUNETEAU** scored three goals in game one of the finals. His brother, Eddie, was with the Quebec Aces and played for Detroit the previous season and the following six, narrowly missing this Cup victory.

LES DOUGLAS played in Perth, Ontario for a number of years and saw action in only 52 Detroit games over four seasons before finishing his career in minor pro and senior hockey, winning the AHL scoring championship with the Cleveland Barons in 1949-50.

EDDIE WARES played on a line with Grosso and Abel and scored three goals in Detroit's six-game upset of the Cup-champion Leafs in the semi-finals.

JACK STEWART had originally been signed by Jack Adams in 1939 to replace Bucko McDonald who had been sold to Toronto.

JIMMY ORLANDO had been left badly dazed in the infamous stick-swinging incident with Gaye Stewart, perhaps the most violent episode in hockey's history.

On March 14, 1945, **SYD HOWE** passed Nels Stewart as the league's all-time points leader with 514 and retired the following year with 528.

HAL JACKSON had been acquired by Detroit in an Intra-League trade with Providence of the AHL. On December 15, 1940, he came to the Wings and off to the Reds went Cecil Dillon and Eddie Bush.

ALEX MOTTER'S career ostensibly ended this spring when he joined the army for two years. When he got out, he played in the AHL, but his last NHL game was the night of April 8, 1943, a Stanley Cup night to remember.

ADAM BROWN eliminated Toronto with an overtime goal at 9:21 in game six of the semi-finals, his only goal of these playoffs.

Team engraving from the replica Cup

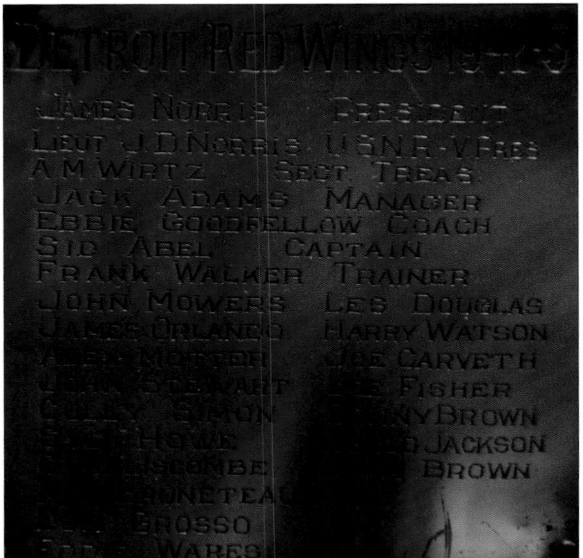

Team engraving from the Cup redesign which replaced the original band but was itself replaced when the final and current Cup design was introduced in the late 1950s.

JOHNNY MOWERS won the Vezina Trophy by a wide margin over Turk Broda (35 goals fewer allowed) and his six shutouts were more than the rest of the league combined (five)!

JOHN SIMON was nicknamed "Cully" as a diminutive for his middle name, Cullen.

JOE FISHER played only one regular season game and one playoff game this year, and immediately after victory he joined the army and never played in the NHL again, his last-ever NHL game the one that gave him his name on the Cup.

HARRY WATSON was acquired from the New York Americans and proved to be one of the reasons for victory. He went on to win four more Cups, with the Leafs, during the period 1947-51.

In his 13th and final NHL season, **EBBIE GOODFELLOW** played just eleven games. He also acted as coach Jack Adams' assistant, and when Adams was suspended during the playoffs after accosting an official, Goodfellow took over, unofficially, as playing coach, although he neither played in the playoffs nor was ever formally named Wings' coach!

CONNIE BROWN played just 23 regular season games and none in the playoffs in this his last year of NHL hockey.

FRANK "HONEY" WALKER started as trainer for the Detroit Olympics in the International League. Jack Adams brought him to the NHL where he retired in 1949. Walker also trained teams in baseball and football as well as some local-area boxers.

Prior to the start of the finals, **JACK ADAMS** boasted: "Just a year ago we were sitting on a three-game lead and counting our championship dollars. And what happened? Toronto beat us in four straight before we could blink an eye...This time we are going to win the finals with four games in a row."

Other players to appear for the Red Wings this season: **DICK BEHLING, JOHN HOLOTA, BILL JENNINGS, BILL QUACKENBUSH**

1943–1944 Montreal Canadiens

THE CHAMPIONS

The Canadiens lost only five games all season en route to their first Cup in 14 years and finished an incredible 25 points ahead of Detroit in the standings. Up 3-0 in the series but trailing in game four, the team received catcalls of "Fake! Fake!" from their fans who thought the team was tanking the game to play another for more gate receipts. They rallied, and became the first team to go through the playoffs undefeated. After the win, the team held a small luncheon rather than a large banquet, a more appropriate celebration during wartime.

STANLEY CUP FINALS

Montreal Canadiens win best-of-seven Stanley Cup finals 4-0

*April 4, 1944	Chicago Black Hawks 1 at Montreal Canadiens 5
**April 6, 1944	Montreal Canadiens 3 at Chicago Black Hawks 1
**April 9, 1944	Montreal Canadiens 3 at Chicago Black Hawks 2
*April 13, 1944	Chicago Black Hawks 4 at Montreal Canadiens 5 {(Toe Blake 9:12 OT)}

** played at the Forum, Montreal ** played at the Chicago Stadium*

Action from the Chicago-Montreal finals won by the Canadiens

MONTREAL	GP	G	A	P	Pim
Toe Blake	4	3	5	8	2
Maurice Richard	4	5	2	7	4
Elmer Lach	4	2	3	5	0
Phil Watson	4	2	1	3	6
Ray Getliffe	4	2	1	3	4
Butch Bouchard	4	0	3	3	0
Mike McMahon	4	1	0	1	12
Murph Chamberlain	4	1	0	1	2
Leo Lamoureux	4	0	1	1	2
Buddy O'Connor	3	0	1	1	2
Gerry Heffernan	2	0	1	1	0
Bob Fillion	2	0	0	0	2
Bill Durnan	4	0	0	0	0
Glen Harmon	4	0	0	0	0
Fern Majeau	1	0	0	0	0

In Goal	GP	W-L	Mins	GA	SO	Avg
Bill Durnan	4	4-0	249	8	0	1.93

(above and left) Action from the 1944 Stanley Cup finals featuring Bill Durnan in goal for Montreal fending off attacks from the Black Hawks.

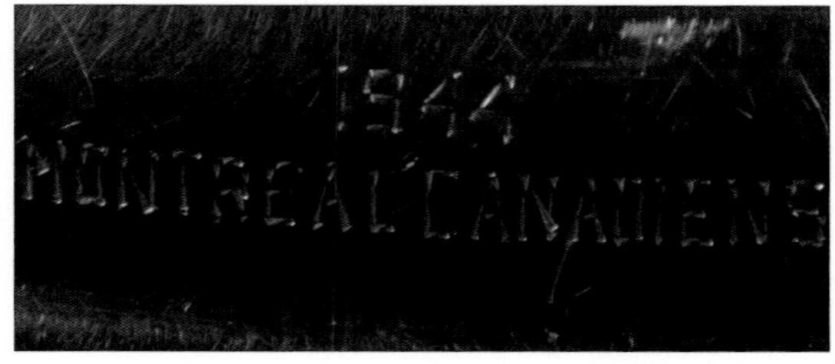

Team engraving from the shoulder of the Stanley Cup

TOE BLAKE did this year what Rocket Richard never did in 18 years with the Habs—win a scoring championship. Blake also led the playoffs with a record 18 points, including the Cup-winning goal in OT.

On March 23 in the semi-finals, **MAURICE RICHARD** scored all five goals of a 5-1 win over Toronto and was named all three stars. In game two of the finals, he again scored all Montreal goals, this time in a more modest 3-1 victory.

The great **ELMER LACH**-Richard-Blake trio placed 1-2-3 in scoring throughout the playoffs.

PHIL WATSON became Montreal property in a trade for Dutch Hiller and Charlie Sands when the Rangers discovered Watson couldn't travel across the border during the war.

RAY GETLIFFE had starred with Boston in the '39 Cup victory, but with two bad knees he was given up for dead by the Bruins. Nonetheless, he had five goals in nine playoff games this spring.

BUTCH BOUCHARD paired with Leo Lamoureux in a starring role on the blueline in the absence of the war-bound Ken Reardon.

In this his only full season in the NHL, **MIKE McMAHON** led the league in penalty minutes with 98.

MURPH CHAMBERLAIN was called a "hard rock" for good reason. He delivered punishing checks but could score as well, making him one of the game's best two-way players.

LEO LAMOUREUX soon turned to coaching, finishing with the Indianapolis Chiefs in the IHL when he died in 1961 at age 45 of acute hepatitis.

BUDDY O'CONNOR had centred a line on the Montreal Royals called the "Razzle Dazzle Line" with Pete Morin and Gerry Heffernan, and when he got to the Habs in 1941 he became known for his passing skills.

GERRY HEFFERNAN played just two years with the Habs though he had a long and distinguished career with the Quebec Royals in senior hockey.

The 22-year-old rookie **BOB FILLION** spent his entire career with the Habs, 327 games over seven seasons, before returning home to Quebec to return to private life.

The ambidextrous **BILL DURNAN** stopped Virgil Johnson of Chicago on a penalty shot in the Cup-deciding game.

GLEN HARMON came to Montreal in 1942 after having won the Memorial Cup the previous year with the Winnipeg Rangers. Neither big nor tough, he was nonetheless one of the more effective defencemen in the game.

Team engraving from the replica Cup

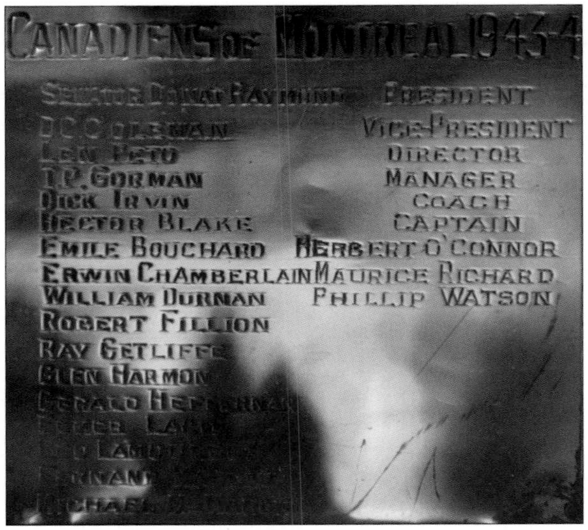

Team engraving from the Cup redesign which replaced the original band but was itself replaced when the final and current Cup design was introduced in the late 1950s.

FERN MAJEAU starred early in the season on a line with Buddy O'Connor and Gerry Heffernan.

A keen sportsman and businessman, team president **DONAT RAYMOND** was supremely well connected in the city and helped bring the Maroons into existence. He oversaw operations of the Windsor Hotel, was named a Senator in 1926, and raised cattle and bred race horses at Vercheres, Quebec. He was a three-time winner of the King's Plate with Irish Heat (1914), King Wave (1923), and Span (1930). Now, with the Maroons defunct, he was president of the Cup champion Club de Hockey.

Vice-president **D.C. COLEMAN** was the father of legendary sportswriter Jim and the president of CPR. He sat on the team's board of directors and had a seat directly behind the Canadiens players' bench.

LEN PETO, director of the Canadiens, was the vice-president and general manager of Canadian Car & Foundry Company Ltd., one of the larger builders of cars and planes in the country. He almost single-handedly formed the National Soccer League, the first of its kind in Canada, in appreciation for a sport he loved in his homeland as a child growing up in England.

TOMMY GORMAN quit the NHL two years later to manage the Ottawa Auditorium, bringing the Allan Cup back to the nation's capital in 1949.

DICK IRVIN was inducted into the Hockey Hall of Fame for his contribution to the game as a player, a career that ended in 1929 after he suffered a fractured skull from a hard check by Red Dutton.

Other players to appear for the Canadiens this season: **TOD CAMPEAU, BOBBY WALTON**

1944 — 1945 THE CHAMPIONS Toronto Maple Leafs

The Leafs blew a 3-0 lead in games, but unlike Detroit in 1942 the Blue and White won game seven to win the Cup. For game four, in Toronto, flags were flown at half mast to honour the death of Franklin Roosevelt. The Leafs scored a record-low nine goals in these finals as did the Wings, setting new standards for one team and both teams' scoring in the finals. The five shutouts combined also set a record, as did Frank McCool with his shutout minutes string in a finals series.

STANLEY CUP FINALS

Toronto Maple Leafs win best-of-seven Stanley Cup finals 4-3

*April 6, 1945	Toronto Maple Leafs 1 at Detroit Red Wings 0 (Sweeney Schriner 13:56 1st) [Frank McCool]
*April 8, 1945	Toronto Maple Leafs 2 at Detroit Red Wings 0 [Frank McCool]
**April 12, 1945	Detroit Red Wings 0 at Toronto Maple Leafs 1 (Gus Bodnar 3:02 3rd) [Frank McCool]
**April 14, 1945	Detroit Red Wings 5 at Toronto Maple Leafs 3
*April 19, 1945	Toronto Maple Leafs 0 at Detroit Red Wings 2 [Harry Lumley]
**April 21, 1945	Detroit Red Wings 1 at Toronto Maple Leafs 0 (Ed Bruneteau 14:16 OT) [Harry Lumley]
*April 22, 1945	Toronto Maple Leafs 2 at Detroit Red Wings 1 {Babe Pratt 12:14 3rd}

** played at the Olympia, Detroit   ** played at Maple Leaf Gardens, Toronto*

Toronto Maple Leafs, 1944-45

TORONTO	GP	G	A	P	Pim
Ted Kennedy	7	4	1	5	2
Mel Hill	7	1	2	3	4
Babe Pratt	7	1	1	2	4
Gus Bodnar	7	1	0	1	2
Elwyn Morris	7	1	0	1	2
Sweeney Schriner	7	1	0	1	2
Bob Davidson	7	0	1	1	0
Wally Stanowski	7	0	1	1	0
Nick Metz	3	0	1	1	0
Lorne Carr	7	0	0	0	5
Reg Hamilton	7	0	0	0	0
Art Jackson	7	0	0	0	0
Frank McCool	7	0	0	0	0
Don Metz	7	0	0	0	0

In Goal	GP	W-L	Mins	GA	SO	Avg
Frank McCool	7	4-3	434	9	3	1.24

A group of soldiers march in downtown Toronto in an effort to recruit volunteers to fight overseas. The Leafs' owner Conn Smythe did his part by establishing the Sportsmen's Battery into which NHL players could enlist. Many of his own team did just that, leaving the roster during the first half of the 1940s as thin as it ever was during Smythe's reign.

Ashtray given to Bob Davidson for the team's 1945 Stanley Cup victory.

Although his nickname is spelled "Teeter" on the Cup, **TED KENNEDY** was more frequently called "Teeder." He scored the game-winner in game one of the semis vs. Montreal with just 22 seconds left in the game to get the Leafs off on the right foot.

After 1939 when **MEL HILL** scored three OT goals to earn the nickname "Sudden Death," he never scored again in extra time.

BABE PRATT scored the Cup winner in what would prove to be his last full season in the league. "I saw I had to get it under him," he said of his shot off a Lumley rebound. And he did.

GUS BODNAR became a respected junior coach after playing, and was one of three bench bosses to guide the 1978 Canadian junior team, led by Wayne Gretzky, that won a bronze medal that year.

ROSS JOHNSTONE didn't appear in the playoffs, and by the fall, with the return of many war Leafs, couldn't find work in the NHL. He finished his career in the American league.

TOM "WINDY" O'NEILL was the team's jester and perhaps the finest pianist away from the rink among the NHL set.

PETE BACKOR didn't dress for the playoffs and this was his only year with the Leafs, but Backor had a long and distinguished career as a rushing and scoring defenceman in the AHL for many years, notably with the Leafs' farm team, in Pittsburgh.

Defence partner of Babe Pratt, **ELWYN "MOE" MORRIS** was a Grey Cup champion from the Toronto Argonauts and played with only one good eye after surgery to correct "cross-eyed" vision left him weak in one eye.

Veteran **SWEENEY SCHRINER** scored the only goal of game one of the finals and the next year, his last in the NHL, he scored his 200th career goal.

BOB DAVIDSON replaced Syl Apps as captain during the war years and his shadowing of Maurice Richard in the semis was key to the Leafs' victory. He retired after the next season.

Recently discharged from the army, **WALLY STANOWSKI** was key to Toronto's stifling "Happy Day defence."

NICK METZ and brother Don, from a farming family in Saskatchewan, both played their entire careers with the Leafs, careers interrupted when they joined Conn Smythe in the army. "They never had a bad game," the Hollerin' Major said of the pair.

A First Team All-Star in 1943 and '44, **LORNE CARR** led the team in scoring while playing with Schriner, his old linemate from the New York Americans.

As a teen, **REG HAMILTON** won a Memorial Cup with the Marlies. Their lineup in junior included Nick Metz, Pep Kelly, Bobby Bauer, and Johnny Acheson.

The younger brother of Busher, **ART JACKSON** began and ended his career in Toronto. He, Pep Kelly, and Nick Metz came to be known as the "War Babies" because they were all born 1914-15, during the height of World War I.

Team engraving from the Cup redesign which replaced the original band but was itself replaced when the final and current Cup design was introduced in the late 1950s.

FRANK McCOOL set finals records with three consecutive shutouts and a streak of 188:35 without allowing a goal. A former Calgary sportswriter, "Ulcers" won the Calder Trophy and filled the breach while Turk Broda was at war.

DON METZ was discharged from active duty in time for this year's playoffs. He had enlisted in the army in '42, becoming a second lieutenant, and later transferred to the RCAF as an L.A.C.

A university student in Toronto, **JACK McLEAN** played only home games for the team during the season and part of the playoffs.

After two years in the air force, **JOHNNY McCREEDY** rejoined the team in January after being discharged. He played only 64 games over two years, but won a Cup both seasons ('45 and '47)

KERRY DAY, coach Day's son, is on the Cup as mascot, a unique Toronto tradition (see also 1932, '42, and '67).

During the war, **J.P. BICKELL** played a key role in Lord Beaverbrook's Ministry of Aircraft Production.

Back in 1942, when Smythe was GM but not team owner, **ED BICKLE** had barred him from going into the dressing room to give the players a pep talk, early signs of an impending rift between the two.

BILL MacBRIEN was Gardens' president until Smythe took full control of the team.

The president of Noranda Mines and a great friend of Conn Smythe, **J.Y. MURDOCH** was called to the bar in 1913. A Toronto native, he was also vice-president and director of the Bank of Nova Scotia and had sat on the Board of Directors for CNR, 1936-39.

Friend and right-hand man to Conn Smythe for twenty years, **FRANK SELKE** and he had a falling out over Selke's acquiring Ted Kennedy without consultation (Smythe was in France). After the dismal 1945-46 season, Selke resigned and took over GM duties in Montreal.

CONN SMYTHE turned down offers to become NHL president so that he might instead focus on regaining control of the Gardens. During the finals, he camped out behind Lumley in Detroit's goal and screamed at him every chance he got!

In perhaps the most famous off-ice tactic in playoff history, **HAPPY DAY** roomed with the drinking, womanizing Babe Pratt all playoffs long to ensure that the Babe behaved and played to his full abilities. It worked.

In addition to being the Leafs' trainer from 1922-60, **TIM DALY** was trainer in the summer months in the International baseball league from 1911 to '48, notably with the New York Giants at the 1912 World Series.

ARCHIE CAMPBELL was a massage therapist, and anyone who had been treated by him swore he had hands of magic.

Other players to appear for the Leafs this season: **BILL EZINICKI**

1945 THE CHAMPIONS

1946 Montreal Canadiens

The Habs won the league title for the third straight year and went on to win the Cup as they had done in 1944. NHL President Dutton presented the Cup to the team on ice right after the victory, and early the following season Montreal mayor Camillien Houde presented each player with a gold ring bearing the crest of the city of Montreal.

STANLEY CUP FINALS

Montreal Canadiens win best-of-seven Stanley Cup finals 4-1

*March 30, 1946 Boston Bruins 3 at Montreal Canadiens 4 (Maurice Richard 9:08 OT)
*April 2, 1946 Boston Bruins 2 at Montreal Canadiens 3 (Jim Peters 16:55 OT)
**April 4, 1946 Montreal Canadiens 4 at Boston Bruins 2
**April 7, 1946 Montreal Canadiens 2 at Boston Bruins 3 (Terry Reardon 15:13 OT)
*April 9, 1946 Boston Bruins 3 at Montreal Canadiens 6 {Toe Blake 11:06 3rd}

** played at the Forum, Montreal ** played at Boston Garden*

Jubilant Canadiens celebrate Cup victory in their dressing room

MONTREAL	GP	G	A	P	Pim
Elmer Lach	5	3	4	7	0
Maurice Richard	5	3	2	5	0
Butch Bouchard	5	2	1	3	4
Murph Chamberlain	5	2	1	3	0
Dutch Hiller	5	2	1	3	0
Glen Harmon	5	1	2	3	0
Bob Fillion	5	2	0	2	2
Ken Mosdell	5	2	0	2	2
Toe Blake	5	1	0	1	5
Jim Peters	5	1	0	1	4
Frank Eddolls	4	0	1	1	0
Ken Reardon	5	0	0	0	4
Leo Lamoureux	5	0	0	0	2
Billy Reay	5	0	0	0	2
Bill Durnan	5	0	0	0	0
Buddy O'Connor	5	0	0	0	0
Gerry Plamondon	1	0	0	0	0

In Goal	GP	W-L	Mins	GA	SO	Avg
Bill Durnan	5	4-1	341	13	0	2.29

(above) The entire Canadiens team is welcomed to City Hall by Mayor Camillien Houde on November 20, 1946: (front row) Pierre Desmarais, Toe Blake, Mayor Houde, Dick Irvin, Murph Chamberlain, Glen Harmon—(middle row) Maurice Richard, Elmer Lach, Billy Reay, Leo Lamoureux, Ken Mosdell, Ken Reardon, Frank Eddolls, Jimmy Peters—(back row) Bill Durnan, Jean Barrette, Charles Mayer, Emile Bouchard, Hector Dubois, Bob Fillion, Ernie Cook, unknown police officer; (right) Fans rejoice their team's Cup victory (the trophy is in the background) the night of April 9, 1946.

ELMER LACH led the playoffs with 17 points and a record 12 goals. During his career he endured more than his share of serious injuries, notably a broken jaw (twice), a smashed cheekbone, and a fractured skull, not to mention dozens of cuts.

Although **MAURICE RICHARD** scored 50 goals in 50 games the previous year, the Habs lost to Toronto in the semi-finals. This year, with players—and top-flight goalies—back from the war, he had just 27, but the team won the Cup.

BUTCH BOUCHARD teamed with Ken Reardon to form the best defence tandem in the league and he was soon to become captain with the retirement of Toe Blake in 1948.

MURPH CHAMBERLAIN quit hockey in 1950 to pursue a career as a coach. "There's no future in it," he said of a job he would hold for some twenty years in various leagues from coast to coast.

DUTCH HILLER had played on the 1940 Rangers' Cup team, and in 1994, when the Blueshirts next won, he was given a ring for that victory, some 54 years after the fact.

The previous year, **GLEN HARMON** and his defence partner Frank Eddolls once went 34 games without being on ice for a goal against, remarkable testament to the duo's importance in this Cup win.

Left winger **BOBBY FILLION** had a career playoffs this season, scoring four goals in nine playoff games.

KEN MOSDELL interrupted his career to join the army (1942-44) and after playing most of this season with the Buffalo Bisons he joined the Canadiens for the final 13 games of the regular season and all of the playoffs, contributing four goals in the post-season.

TOE BLAKE finished third in scoring during the regular season and won the Lady Byng after accruing just one minor penalty all year. He injured his back in game one of the finals when he slid hard into the goalpost and played sparingly the rest of the way.

JIMMY PETERS served with the 3rd Canadian Heavy Recovery Unit that worked its way from Normandy into Belgium. He lost the tips of two fingers in a tank accident, but the injury was not serious enough to curtail his hockey career once the real fighting stopped.

Although a member of this team, **FRANK EDDOLLS** had a brief and inconspicuous career compared to the man Montreal traded to Toronto to get him—Ted Kennedy.

KEN REARDON was back with the team after serving overseas for most of three years during which time he also won the Allan Cup with the Ottawa Commandos in Canada before being awarded Field Marshal Montgomery's Certificate of Merit for his service in Europe.

LEO LAMOUREUX didn't score a goal in the playoffs, but as a defenceman he didn't have to. Realizing he wasn't long for the NHL, he became a coach soon after this win, a calling he practised until his untimely death in 1961.

BILLY REAY is one of a select group of players to win the Allan Cup, Memorial Cup, and Stanley Cup during his playing career—and all by the end of his first NHL season.

Team engraving from the replica Cup

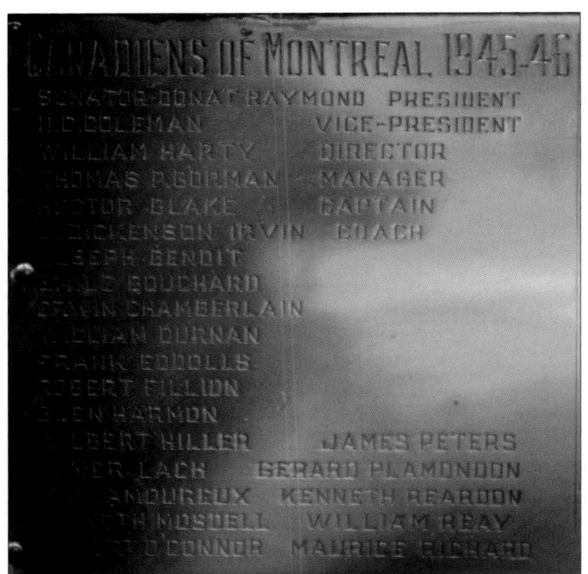

Team engraving from the Cup redesign which replaced the original band but was itself replaced when the final and current Cup design was introduced in the late 1950s.

His name misspelled "Durman" on the Cup, **BILL DURNAN** missed five weeks during the regular season with a broken hand yet still won his third straight Vezina Trophy. He quit the game in 1950 after suffering a nervous breakdown.

BUDDY O'CONNOR had a remarkable amateur career before finally breaking into the Canadiens' lineup, playing in five Allan Cups between 1935 and '41 with the Montreal Royals.

GERRY PLAMONDON was a lifelong fringe NHLer, playing five years in the big league but only for stints of 6, 3, 27, 37, and one game. He led the QSHL with 40 goals playing for the Valleyfield Braves and two years later scored 51 times for the Montreal Royals.

"We want to prove we are not just a wartime club," proud and defiant coach **DICK IRVIN** said after this victory.

Senator **DONAT RAYMOND** sent coach Dick Irvin a cheque for $1,000, so happy was he with the victory. He lived in the famous du Musee house in Montreal's famous Square Mile, the most prestigious area of the city and a home formerly owned by Sir Rodolphe Forget, a powerful, turn-of-the-century financier.

D'ALTON CORRY COLEMAN became the editor of the *Belleville Intelligencer* at the age of 19. He later worked for CPR, moving up to president. He was also a director with the Bank of Montreal and Odeon Theatres.

WILLIAM HARTY was a director with the Habs. His brother, Dr. J.J. (Jock) Harty, had played hockey with Queen's University on a famed team that played the first-ever international hockey series, against Yale (a 3-0 victory). Harty Arena in Kingston is named after Jock.

TOMMY GORMAN won his seventh Cup with his fourth franchise in a hockey career that knew little but success (Ottawa 1920, '21, and '23; Chicago '34; Maroons '35; Canadiens '44 and '46). As a promoter, he was responsible for bringing Phar Lap to Canada.

Other players to appear for Canadiens this season: **JOE BENOIT, VIC LYNN, MURDO MacKAY, MIKE McMAHON, LORRAIN THIBEAULT, MOE WHITE**

1946–1947 THE CHAMPIONS Toronto Maple Leafs

Incredibly, this was the first Toronto-Montreal finals. So nervous was Conn Smythe about overconfidence that he ordered the Cup to remain in Montreal. The next day at the Gardens, for photos and celebrations, the Cup was shipped up to Toronto. This was the youngest team in NHL history to win the Cup, and the lineup featured no fewer than six rookies of the 19 starters. Each player received a ring for the victory as well as a silver cigarette case and a blue and white cardigan.

STANLEY CUP FINALS

Toronto Maple Leafs win best-of-seven Stanley Cup finals 4-2

*April 8, 1947	Toronto Maple Leafs 0 at Montreal Canadiens 2 [Bill Durnan]
*April 10, 1947	Toronto Maple Leafs 4 at Montreal Canadiens 0 [Turk Broda]
**April 12, 1947	Montreal Canadiens 2 at Toronto Maple Leafs 4
**April 15, 1947	Montreal Canadiens 1 at Toronto Maple Leafs 2 (Syl Apps 16:36 OT)
*April 17, 1947	Toronto Maple Leafs 1 at Montreal Canadiens 3
**April 19, 1947	Montreal Canadiens 1 at Toronto Maple Leafs 2 {Ted Kennedy 14:39 3rd}

** played at the Forum, Montreal   ** played at Maple Leaf Gardens, Toronto*

The Cup-winning Leafs whoop it up at their celebration dinner

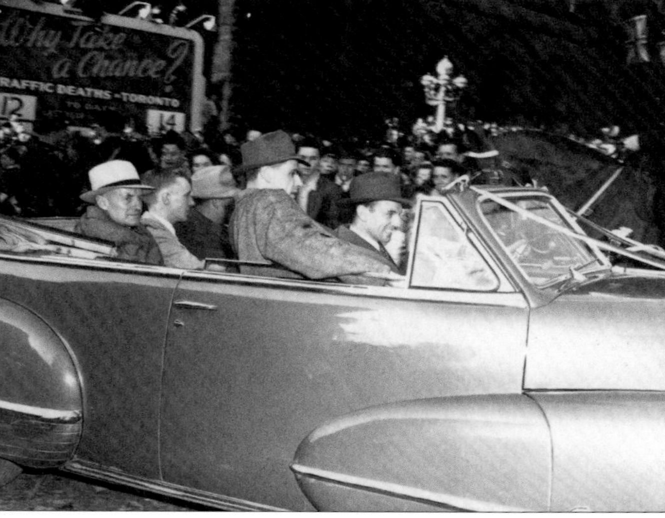

(clockwise) Action from the 1947 Cup finals at Maple Leaf Gardens; goalies Bill Durnan of Montreal (left) and Turk Broda congratulate each other after the deciding game; coach Hap Day (front seat, foreground) and Conn Smythe (white hat) partake in the victory celebrations in downtown Toronto.

TORONTO	GP	G	A	P	Pim
Ted Kennedy	6	3	2	5	2
Vic Lynn	6	3	1	4	12
Harry Watson	6	2	1	3	0
Gaye Stewart	6	1	2	3	6
Howie Meeker	6	0	3	3	6
Bud Poile	5	2	0	2	2
Gus Mortson	6	1	1	2	6
Syl Apps	6	1	1	2	0
Bill Barilko	6	0	2	2	6
Don Metz	6	0	2	2	4
Bill Ezinicki	6	0	0	0	16
Jim Thomson	6	0	0	0	12
Garth Boesch	6	0	0	0	6
Turk Broda	6	0	0	0	0
Joe Klukay	6	0	0	0	0
Wally Stanowski	5	0	0	0	0
Gus Bodnar	1	0	0	0	0
Nick Metz	1	0	0	0	0

In Goal	GP	W-L	Mins	GA	SO	Avg
Turk Broda	6	4-2	377	13	1	2.07

The controversial trade of Frank Eddolls to Montreal for **TED KENNEDY**, made by Frank Selke while Smythe was at war, proved genius as Teeder led the victory charge.

In game two, Maurice Richard hit **VIC LYNN** flush on the head with his stick, knocking him out and opening a cut above Lynn's left eye.

Although he played 14 games with the Leafs during the regular season, **SID SMITH** was in Pittsburgh the rest of the year and did not see action in the Stanley Cup playoffs.

After being acquired from Detroit for Billy Taylor, **HARRY WATSON** played on a line with Apps and Ezinicki and despite a bad knee helped the team to victory.

His first name misspelled "Gave" here, **GAYE STEWART** played with Bodnar and Poile and was considered the fastest skater in the league.

HOWIE MEEKER won the Calder Trophy over Gordie Howe and scored five goals in one game, though neither his career nor goal scoring would prove to be as enduring as Howe's.

Although his playing career was somewhat pedestrian, **BUD POILE** began his life as an executive in 1950 that continued well beyond his 1990 induction into the Hockey Hall of Fame as a Builder.

GUS MORTSON started a near riot in game three of the semi-finals in the Olympia when a fight with Gordie Howe spilled into the penalty box and stands and involved numerous fans.

SYL APPS placed fifth in the pole vault at the 1936 Summer Olympics and was signed by Conn Smythe after the owner saw young Apps play football and before he had ever seen young Sylvanus skate!

"BASHIN' BILL" BARILKO was playing hockey in Hollywood, for the PCHL Wolves, where he earned rave reviews and a callup to the Leafs for the last 18 games of the season and the playoffs.

Late in the regular season, **DON METZ** collided with Elmer Lach and broke his opponent's jaw. Lach's absence the rest of the season only enhanced Toronto's chances of victory.

BILL EZINICKI was assigned to shadow Maurice Richard and so frustrated the Montreal star in game two that Richard earned a game misconduct and one-game suspension for his violent retaliation.

JIM THOMSON, with partner Gus Mortson, formed the "Gold Dust Twins," the impenetrable defence combination on Toronto's blueline.

GARTH BOESCH was slow of foot but sure of defence, and as the only moustachioed player in the league he was hard to miss on the ice.

Upon his return to Canada from the war in January 1946, **TURK BRODA** promptly announced his retirement because he had lost five teeth in a game in England. He quickly changed his mind.

Although **JOE KLUKAY** was taken off the ice on a stretcher in game four after falling head first into the boards, he returned to play a solid series without missing a game.

Team engraving from the Cup redesign which replaced the original band but was itself replaced when the final and current Cup design was introduced in the late 1950s.

WALLY STANOWSKI missed the final game of the series and was replaced by Gus Bodnar, a call-up from Pittsburgh.

GUS BODNAR holds two terrific records. He scored a goal just 15 seconds into his first NHL game, and he recorded three assists in 21 seconds on Bill Mosienko's fastest-ever hat trick.

NICK METZ suffered separated ribs in game one of the finals and missed the rest of the finals.

BOB GOLDHAM broke his arm December 4 vs. Boston in a collision with Pat Egan and missed the rest of the season.

Although **ED BICKLE'S** name appears on this and subsequent Cups, it was not because of Conn Smythe's request. Bickle and Bill MacBrien had recently spear-headed an attempt to make Smythe league president so as to remove him from the Gardens and maintain control of the building themselves.

BILL MACBRIEN used to be closely associated with the CFL and gave the Selke family Grey Cup tickets each year.

J.P. BICKELL controlled McIntyre Mines. He was generous to Smythe with his money and was key to getting others to invest in the Leafs and the building of the Gardens.

J.Y. MURDOCH was director and president of numerous important businesses in the city, notably Standard Underground Cable Co. and Pamour Porcupine Mines.

A fiercely competitive man, **CONN SMYTHE** had survived a coup by some members of his Board of Directors of Maple Leaf Gardens to regain control of the club. During his war absence, the Gardens had been used for an increasing number of non-hockey events, producing vast revenues unseen during Smythe's pre-war regime but rankling the owner of hockey's church.

One of the most beloved of Leafs, coach **HAP DAY** was as fit and strong as most of his players. He walked quickly, led practises by example, and earned the respect of his team every day of his life.

A champion boxer in his less-portly youth, **TIM DALY**, the 'kinely ole trainer,' was barred from the fight game because authorities feared for his opponents' safety. Or, so he boasted.

CLIFFORD KEYLAND, the assistant trainer, wasn't with the team very long. When Frank Selke began a new farm team, the Cincinnati Mohawks, Keyland went to the States to work with that team.

The Leafs were the first team to put their team doctors on the Stanley Cup. A general surgeon, **DR. GALLOWAY** was affiliated with St. Joseph's Hospital.

DR. MACINTYRE'S medical practise emanated from his Runnymede Road home. It was as a neighbour to Smythe that the two men met and began a long professional relationship.

GEORGE "SQUIB" WALKER typified the Leaf organization under the aegis of Conn Smythe. The two had been friends since childhood, and when the owner needed a head scout, he called upon his hockey-smart bespectacled friend.

Other players to appear for the Leafs this season: **BOB DAWES, HARRY TAYLOR**

1947 1948 Toronto Maple Leafs

THE CHAMPIONS

This might have been the most dominant Leafs team of all time. They finished first overall during the regular schedule, and in the semi-finals lost only once to Boston before sweeping the Wings. The Leafs celebrated at a Detroit nightclub following the victory, and after arriving home the next day were paraded up Bay Street to City Hall.

STANLEY CUP FINALS

Toronto Maple Leafs win best-of-seven Stanley Cup finals 4-0

*April 7, 1948 Detroit Red Wings 3 at Toronto Maple Leafs 5
*April 10, 1948 Detroit Red Wings 2 at Toronto Maple Leafs 4
**April 11, 1948 Toronto Maple Leafs 2 at Detroit Red Wings 0 [Broda]
**April 14, 1948 Toronto Maple Leafs 7 at Detroit Red Wings 2 {Harry Watson 11:13 1st}

** played at Maple Leaf Gardens, Toronto ** played at the Olympia, Detroit*

(left to right) Conn Smythe, Syl Apps, and Hap Day celebrate.

TORONTO	GP	G	A	P	Pim
Harry Watson	4	5	1	6	4
Max Bentley	4	2	4	6	0
Syl Apps	4	2	2	4	0
Ted Kennedy	4	2	2	4	0
Les Costello	4	1	2	3	0
Vic Lynn	4	1	1	2	18
Bill Ezinicki	4	1	1	2	4
Joe Klukay	4	1	1	2	2
Gus Mortson	1	1	1	2	0
Howie Meeker	4	1	0	1	7
Garth Boesch	4	1	0	1	0
Jim Thomson	4	0	1	1	5
Phil Samis	3	0	1	1	2
Wally Stanowski	4	0	1	1	0
Bill Barilko	4	0	0	0	13
Nick Metz	4	0	0	0	2
Turk Broda	4	0	0	0	0

In Goal	GP	W-L	Mins	GA	SO	Avg
Turk Broda	4	4-0	240	7	1	1.75

(clockwise) Action from the finals series at Maple Leaf Gardens, featuring goalie Turk Broda; the Cup parade makes its way along Bay St. in downtown Toronto; Nick Metz, coach Hap Day, and Wally Stanowski hug the cherished mug.

After retiring in 1957, **HARRY WATSON** later became a coach, leading the Windsor Bulldogs to the 1963 Allan Cup.

After arriving from Chicago earlier in the year in a huge seven-player deal, **MAX BENTLEY** played without brother Doug for the first time (Doug never won a Cup in his career).

SYL APPS scored career goals number 199, 200, and 201 in his final regular season game and then a playoff goal in his final Cup game.

TED KENNEDY led the playoff scoring race with 14 points. He had been nicknamed Teeder by reporter Lloyd Johnson of the *Welland-Port Colborne Tribune*.

Soon after, **LES COSTELLO** quit the NHL, joined the priesthood, and helped establish the Flying Fathers, a group of hockey-playing priests who raised millions of dollars for charity.

VIC LYNN was with his fourth Original Six team and by 1954 became the only NHLer ever to play for all six during his career.

The best golfer in the NHL, **BILL EZINICKI** retired to swing his clubs professionally in the Boston area and earned more money as a golfer than he ever did playing hockey.

JOE KLUKAY was a right winger who shot left and was perhaps the best defensive forward of his day. Partnered with Nick Metz, they were the undisputed penalty-killing champs in the NHL.

GUS MORTSON suffered a broken leg in the first game of the finals when he and Jim Thomson teamed to crush Detroit's Jack Stewart.

He may have won the Calder Trophy over Gordie Howe the previous year, but in game two of the finals **HOWIE MEEKER** dropped the gloves and bravely fought old Elbows...and lost badly.

GARTH BOESCH had attended the training camp of the New York Americans but then enlisted in the war. Upon being discharged, he was signed by the Leafs.

JIM THOMSON'S favourite defensive trick was to put his stick between a forward's legs to slow him up and reign him in. It made up for his weak skating and allowed him to do what he did best—hit.

PHIL SAMIS played the year with Pittsburgh but Smythe called him up as playoff insurance. He appeared in five games, enough to get his name on the Cup.

A pipe smoker, **WALLY STANOWSKI** was Jim Thomson's frequent defence partner. Just 12 days after this victory, he was traded to the Rangers.

When **BILL BARILKO** first joined the Leafs he had sweater number 21. It wasn't until his final season that he wore the number 5 for which he became famous.

This proved to be **NICK METZ'S** last year of hockey. He returned to the family's wheat farm in Wilcox, Saskatchewan, and his brother joined him the next year.

As in the previous year, **SID SMITH** played most of the season in Pittsburgh, suiting up with the Leafs for 31 games.

Team engraving from the Cup redesign which replaced the original band but was itself replaced when the final and current Cup design was introduced in the late 1950s.

TURK BRODA won the Vezina and was named to the First All-Star Team, and at the end of game two got into a celebrated fight at centre ice with his Detroit counterpart Harry Lumley.

CONN SMYTHE was named Gardens president when Ed Bickle retired. "This is the greatest team we have ever had. They never failed me, and for the first time in my life I did not have to give a pep talk." Under his aegis, Maple Leaf Gardens was the centre of the hockey universe. Foster Hewitt's broadcasts emanated from the gondola, and every new innovation to hockey—from Plexiglas to game film to clocking player's ice time—began at MLG.

HAP DAY was a master strategist who, once his team had secured a playoff spot, rested his players, tried different line combinations, and worked on set plays in preparation for a run at the Cup.

BILL MacBRIEN had been part of the new-look Gardens during the war, booking all sorts of new shows and acts to the hockey temple in the absence of Conn Smythe, from swimming shows, to ice capades, to roller skating vanities.

GEORGE McCULLAGH was president and publisher of the *Globe and Mail.*

A prominent lawyer, **J.Y. MURDOCH** was partner in Holden, Murdoch, Walton, Finlay, and Robinson.

J.P. BICKELL happily sold his shares in the Gardens to Smythe after the war to ensure the GM could wrest control of the team and building from men who sought to isolate Smythe from the team's and building's operations.

ED BICKLE was a stockbroker by trade and a member of the Toronto Stock Exchange.

TIM DALY was, at one time, oilman for the Detroit Tigers and called the greatest thrill of his life being rub-down man for Ty Cobb.

Short and stocky, **ARCHIE CAMPBELL** also ran a local clinic. He was a therapist and masseur more than an equipment man.

DR. GALLOWAY'S son, Dave, once dated Vicky Smythe, Stafford's oldest daughter. Dave later became head of a computer company.

DR. MacINTYRE was, like Galloway, affiliated with St. Joe's Hospital. He was a smoker who always wore gloves when he had a cigarette in his hand, and over time the gloves became tar-stained.

Before the war, **ED FITKIN**, **GORD WALKER**, and **HAL WALKER** were considered the three kids on staff at the *Globe and Mail* sports desk. After a stint in the navy, Fitkin joined the Leafs as publicity director.

A part-time "bird dog," **SQUIB WALKER** scouted the city's and province's youth, looking for the next Apps or Davidson at the many small rinks, frozen ponds, and anonymous leagues.

KERRY DAY, son of Hap, was the Leafs' mascot and stick boy. He used to bring old equipment home from the Gardens and sell it to neighbourhood kids.

Other players to appear for the Leafs this season: **FLEMING MACKELL, JOHN McCORMACK, DON METZ, BUD POILE, TOD SLOAN, GAYE STEWART, CY THOMAS**

1948 THE CHAMPIONS
1949 Toronto Maple Leafs

This Leafs' team was the first NHL team to win three Cups in a row, and they did it after a sub-.500 season (22-25-13), only the second team after the 1938 Chicagos to accomplish such a dramatic turnaround from the regular season to the playoffs. In the finals, the Red Wings used oxygen tanks on their bench to try to recover their wind more quickly after being on the ice, but to no avail.

STANLEY CUP FINALS

Toronto Maple Leafs win best-of-seven Stanley Cup finals 4-0

*April 8, 1949	Toronto Maple Leafs 3 at Detroit Red Wings 2 (Joe Klukay 17:31 OT)
*April 10, 1949	Toronto Maple Leafs 3 at Detroit Red Wings 1
**April 13, 1949	Detroit Red Wings 1 at Toronto Maple Leafs 3
**April 16, 1949	Detroit Red Wings 1 at Toronto Maple Leafs 3 {Cal Gardner 19:45 2nd}

** played at the Olympia, Detroit ** played at Maple Leaf Gardens, Toronto*

Captain Ted Kennedy accepts the Cup on ice after victory

(clockwise) Goalie great Turk Broda takes a sip of champagne from the Cup; action is fierce around Broda in the Leafs' net during a game in Detroit; the Leafs' Bill Ezinicki (left) and Detroit's great left winger Ted Lindsay shakes hands after the final game.

TORONTO	GP	G	A	P	Pim
Sid Smith	4	3	1	4	0
Max Bentley	4	2	2	4	0
Jim Thomson	4	1	3	4	4
Ray Timgren	4	1	3	4	0
Ted Kennedy	4	1	2	3	2
Joe Klukay	4	1	2	3	2
Fleming Mackell	4	0	3	3	2
Bill Ezinicki	4	1	1	2	10
Cal Gardner	4	1	1	2	0
Gus Mortson	4	1	0	1	2
Bill Barilko	4	0	1	1	8
Garth Boesch	4	0	1	1	4
Harry Watson	4	0	1	1	2
Bill Juzda	4	0	0	0	4
Bob Dawes	4	0	0	0	2
Turk Broda	4	0	0	0	0
Vic Lynn	4	0	0	0	0

In Goal	GP	W-L	Mins	GA	SO	Avg
Turk Broda	4	4-0	258	5	0	1.16

Team engraving from the shoulder of the original Cup

After playing just one regular season game in his career, **SID SMITH** scored a record three power-play goals in game two and led Gordie Howe to ask after, "Who's Sid Smith?"

"Pound for pound," Conn Smythe said of **MAX BENTLEY**, "that's the best shot in hockey."

A clutch-and-grab, stay-at-home defenceman, **JIM THOMSON** had just 19 goals in 787 regular season games and two more in 63 playoff matches.

Left winger **RAY TIMGREN** scored only one goal all year (in 81 total games) and only 17 in 281 career games (regular season and playoffs).

TED KENNEDY assumed the captaincy this year after the retirement of Syl Apps.

JOE KLUKAY played but one game for the Leafs in the 1943 playoffs before enlisting in the army. It wasn't until 1946 that he was back in the NHL.

The son of **JACK MACKELL** who played on Ottawa's 1921 Stanley Cup team, Flem was equally small and fierce as his dad.

BILL EZINICKI'S name was on the original Cup but was omitted when the re-modelled version was created in 1957.

CAL GARDNER was acquired from the Rangers in a six-player deal that sent Stanowski to the Rangers. Although he scored the winning goal this year, his contributions were overshadowed by those of the more popular Bentley.

In eight of his 13 NHL seasons **GUS MORTSON** had more than 100 penalty minutes and four times he led the league in that department.

From the minute he stepped onto NHL ice, **BILL BARILKO** called himself "the Kid," in the third person, but his mates called him "Bashin' Bill" for his thunderous checks.

GARTH BOESCH retired a year later at 29 in order that he could return to the farm in Riceton, Saskatchewan and take over the family business after his father died.

HARRY WATSON was the last playing member of the New York Americans by the time he retired. In each of his first six NHL seasons, his goal production increased—10, 13, 14, 19, 21, to 26 this year.

BILL JUZDA turned down an offer to play in the CFL with the Winnipeg Blue Bombers because hockey paid better.

BOBBY DAWES had been a defenceman his whole career but coach Day used him to perfection as a fourth-line centre because of his defensive ability and excellent hands on the faceoff.

One of the game's greatest money goalies, **TURK BRODA** allowed just 15 goals in nine playoff games.

VIC LYNN got into a nasty stick-swinging fight with Red Hamill in February and was carried off the ice with a suspected fractured skull. He suffered a six-inch cut to his head and wore a helmet for a while, but he was in fine shape by the time the playoffs started.

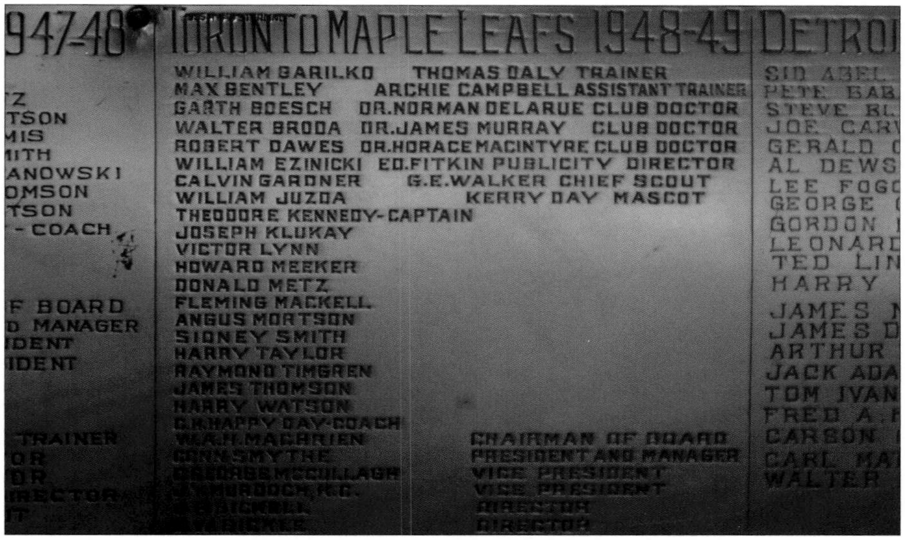

Team engraving from the Cup redesign which replaced the original band but was itself replaced when the final and current Cup design was introduced in the late 1950s.

TOD SLOAN played twice in the regular season but not at all for the Leafs in the playoffs.

HOWIE MEEKER later became a popular analyst on *Hockey Night in Canada*, espousing skills at the grass roots level.

DON METZ was the only Leafs to play for all five Cup teams of the 1940s in this his last season.

A two-time Memorial Cup winner in 1945 and '46, **HARRY TAYLOR** couldn't establish himself in the NHL.

HAP DAY won the Cup as a player and a coach, and also won a Memorial Cup. "It's defence that wins hockey games," he said, proud of his "Kitty Bar the Door" strategy that emphasized preventing goals over scoring them.

BILL MacBRIEN was still a director, but his attempted revolt to usurp Conn Smythe as team president failed and Smythe was in full command of Maple Leaf Gardens.

CONN SMYTHE expanded his empire to include stables for his racehorses and "C Smythe For Sand," a gravel company in the west end of the city that provided the raw material for many of the city's buildings.

A staunch Conservative, **GEORGE McCULLAGH** and Conn Smythe shared a love for horse racing that gave them plenty to talk about when they weren't on about politics.

J.Y. MURDOCH was another member of the board of directors of the Gardens.

J.P. BICKELL gave a speech the night of November 12, 1931, at the pre-game ceremonies the night the Gardens opened, testament to his importance in arranging the building's financing.

ED BICKLE was president of the Queen Elizabeth Hospital and the director of Manufacturers Life Insurance.

The master of the malaprop, trainer **TIM DALY** was beloved in the dressing room despite his penchant for cigars and reputation for not lifting so much as a single sock.

ARCHIE CAMPBELL was a victim of error. His name appears on the re-designed Stanley Cup but not the current Presentation Cup.

DR. NORMAN DELARUE, like Campbell, saw his name excised from the current Cup after it appeared on the initial redesign.

DR. JAMES MURRAY was a plastic surgeon. By and large, Smythe stayed away from orthopaedic surgeons because for every injury there was a specialist with greater understanding than any general practitioner.

DR. MacINTYRE loved junior hockey and frequently attended games as both physician and fan.

ED FITKIN'S name does not appear on the current Cup though it was on the original redesign at the time of victory.

"SQUIB" WALKER was a childhood friend of Conn Smythe and the first full-time scout for any of the NHL teams.

KERRY DAY was the son of Hap and this year's mascot and stick boy.

Other players to appear for the Leafs this season: **CHUCK BLAIR, AL BUCHANAN, RAY CERESINO, LES COSTELLO, RAY HANNIGAN, STAN KEMP, FRANK MATHERS, JOHN McCORMACK**

1949 THE CHAMPIONS

1950 Detroit Red Wings

"The moon shines tonight on pretty Red Wing," goes a line from Detroit's rally song, and how accurate a description this was of scheduling for this year's finals. Because the circus took over Madison Square Garden, the Wings were fortunate to play five of the seven finals games at home, including the last four in a row. After the final bell, the players threw their sticks into the crowd in celebration and during the Cup presentation the Rangers stayed on the ice!

STANLEY CUP FINALS

Detroit Red Wings win best-of-seven Stanley Cup finals 4-3

*April 11, 1950 New York Rangers 1 at Detroit Red Wings 4
**April 13, 1950 New York Rangers 3 Detroit Red Wings 1
**April 15, 1950 Detroit Red Wings 4 New York Rangers 0 [Harry Lumley]
*April 18, 1950 New York Rangers 4 at Detroit Red Wings 3 (Don Raleigh 8:34 OT)
*April 20, 1950 New York Rangers 2 at Detroit Red Wings 1 (Don Raleigh 1:38 OT)
*April 22, 1950 New York Rangers 4 at Detroit Red Wings 5+
*April 23, 1950 New York Rangers 3 at Detroit Red Wings 4 {(Pete Babando 28:31 OT)}

** played at the Olympia, Detroit*
*** played at Maple Leaf Gardens, Toronto because Madison Square Garden was previously booked for the circus*
+ although a Rangers home game, NHL rules did not permit a potential Stanley Cup deciding game to be played on neutral ice (i.e., Toronto), so all remaining games were played in Detroit

Game action from game two of the finals at Maple Leaf Gardens

(top left) Rangers goalie Charlie Rayner makes a save during game two action; (above) Detroit goalie Harry Lumley regains his balance as he watches play move up ice during game three.

Team engraving from the shoulder of the Stanley Cup

DETROIT	GP	G	A	P	Pim
Sid Abel	7	5	2	7	2
Ted Lindsay	6	4	2	6	6
Gerry Couture	7	4	2	6	0
George Gee	7	2	3	5	0
Pete Babando	5	2	2	4	2
Joe Carveth	7	1	3	4	4
Marty Pavelich	7	2	1	3	6
Jim McFadden	7	2	1	3	2
Jack Stewart	7	0	3	3	10
Al Dewsbury	5	0	3	3	8
Red Kelly	7	0	3	3	2
Jim Peters	5	0	2	2	0
Marcel Pronovost	6	0	1	1	4
Johnny Wilson	5	0	1	1	0
Leo Reise	7	0	0	0	8
Lee Fogolin	4	0	0	0	2
Harry Lumley	7	0	0	0	0
Steve Black	6	0	0	0	0
Max McNab	4	0	0	0	0
Clare Martin	3	0	0	0	0
Larry Wilson	2	0	0	0	0
Doug McKay	1	0	0	0	0

In Goal	GP	W-L	Mins	GA	SO	Avg
Harry Lumley	7	4-3	459	17	1	2.22

As a youngster, **SID ABEL** centred the Liniment Line; as a veteran, he now led the great Production Line featuring Gordie Howe and Ted Lindsay. He was interviewed live on the Hot Stove right after the victory.

After being presented the Cup, **TED LINDSAY** picked it up from the table and, for the first time, carried it around the ice for all to see. "I wanted them (the fans) to get a closer look, so I took it to the boards and very gradually I worked my way around the rink."

GERRY COUTURE scored four goals in nine minutes during a regular season game vs. Chicago on February 8 (a 9-2 win).

GEORGE GEE died tragically at age 50 while resting during the intermission of an oldtimers game between the Wings and a suburban junior team in Michigan.

Acquired in a trade at the start of the season, **PETE BABANDO** became the first player to win the Cup with a game seven, overtime goal.

The 31-year-old **JOE CARVETH** arrived in Detroit from Montreal in a trade for Calum McKay.

MARTY PAVELICH played all his NHL years with Detroit. He was a skilled and tenacious checker and was one of only four Wings (with Howe, Lindsay, and Kelly) to play on the team that won seven consecutive first place finishes.

JIM McFADDEN'S dramatic goal with just 4:03 left in game seven tied the score 4-4 and set the stage for Babando's overtime heroics.

On the bus trip back to Toledo where Detroit was staying, prior to game four, **JACK STEWART** promised to hammer his own players if they didn't get going. They got.

After his NHL days, **AL DEWSBURY** played on the Belleville McFarlands team that won gold at the World Championships in Prague in 1959.

A graduate of St. Mike's in Toronto, **RED KELLY** was a great rushing defenceman and this year won his first of eight Cups.

JIM PETERS was part of a huge trade with Boston prior to the start of the season that saw him come to Detroit with Babando, Clare Martin, and Lloyd Durham.

Although he did not play during the regular season, **MARCEL PRONOVOST** was called up from Omaha when Howe was injured in game one of the semis and Kelly shifted to forward.

JOHNNY WILSON and his brother, Larry, were both signed by Detroit at the same time and assigned to Windsor. Johnny was called up for one regular season game, and played eight more in the playoffs.

LEO REISE was only the second son of an NHL father to make the big show (the first was Ted Lindsay).

Considered the hardest checker in the game, **LEE FOGOLIN** moved to Chicago later in 1950 where he became team captain.

Despite missing seven regular season games because of injuries suffered while playing forward during a charity game, **"LUM"** (**HARRY LUMLEY**) saved the Wings with incredible goaltending.

Team engraving from the Cup redesign which replaced the original band but was itself replaced when the final and current Cup design was introduced in the late 1950s.

In the fall of 1950, **STEVE BLACK** was demoted to the Detroit farm team in Indianapolis. The move made him unhappy, and he demanded a trade.

MAX McNAB'S unspectacular playing career casts a dim light over his lengthy managerial career that has seen him manage Canadian teams in international play as well as Washington and New Jersey in the NHL.

In six NHL years, **CLARE MARTIN** managed to play for four Original Six teams, scoring a dozen goals in 237 career games.

Although he played only 152 NHL games, **LARRY WILSON** played pro in four decades and went on to coach the Red Wings for half a season in '76-'77.

Legend has it that frequent run-ins with **JACK ADAMS** prevented Doug McKay's name from appearing on the redesigned Cup!

GORDIE HOWE suffered a life-threatening injury in game one of the semis. When the Cup was presented to the Wings, the crowd took up a chant of "Gordie! Gordie!" until Howe came onto the ice. He returned the following year wearing a helmet.

"All they took (his players) was brandy-soaked sugar," GM **JACK ADAMS** said in response to Rangers' charges that the Wings had pumped up on Benzedrine for the finals.

Like Joe Stark with Chicago, **HARRY McQUESTON** was Detroit's spare goalie who never played a minute in the NHL! His name appeared on the initial re-design of the Cup but is not on the current Cup.

This was **"POP" JAMES NORRIS'S** last Cup with his son. In the summer of 1952, the financial and on-ice situations in Chicago were dire so Norris the elder despatched his son to the Hawks to revitalize the franchise. The plan worked, and may have saved the team and the NHL in the process.

In 1949, **JAMES NORRIS, JR.** became president of the International Boxing Club, a position he held until 1958.

"Every time I finish a deal," **ARTHUR WIRTZ** proclaimed, "I like to think I've made a new friend."

An injury prevented **TOMMY IVAN** from pursuing a pro career, but he remained in the game first as a scout for Detroit, then a coach at Omaha, and finally assuming the bench in Detroit where he formed the Production Line.

FRED HUBER assembled the Detroit media guides during the early years of their existence.

Known alternately as "Coop" or "old shovel shot," **CARSON COOPER** ended his playing days with the Wings and stayed on as head scout, discovering greats such as Red Kelly, Terry Sawchuk, Ted Lindsay, and Harry Lumley.

CARL MATTSON became Honey Walker's assistant in 1935 and when Walker retired in '47 he assumed head trainer duties.

WALTER HUMENIUK ("Gunzo") was a goalie on Windsor's junior B team when Tommy Ivan offered him a job in the Detroit organization as equipment manager. When Ivan left for Chicago in 1954, Humeniuk went with him.

Other players to appear for the Wings this season: **FRED GLOVER, GORD HAIDY, TERRY SAWCHUK, ENIO SCLISIZZI, GLEN SKOV**

1950–1951 Toronto Maple Leafs

THE CHAMPIONS

This has been the only finals series in which every game went into overtime, the Leafs emerging victorious four times to win their fourth Cup in five years. The hero of the hour was Bill Barilko, a defenceman known more for his heavy hits in his own end and not at all for his scoring prowess. Yet his diving lunge at the puck beat goalie Gerry McNeil in the Montreal net, and the heroic goal became the stuff of legend when Barilko was lost in a plane crash just a few weeks later, his last moment with the team a Cup-winning one.

STANLEY CUP FINALS

Toronto Maple Leafs win best-of-seven Stanley Cup finals 4-1

*April 11, 1951	Montreal Canadiens 2 at Toronto Maple Leafs 3 (Sid Smith 5:51 OT)
*April 14, 1951	Montreal Canadiens 3 at Toronto Maple Leafs 2 (Maurice Richard 2:55 OT)
**April 17, 1951	Toronto Maple Leafs 2 at Montreal Canadiens 1 (Ted Kennedy 4:47 OT)
**April 19, 1951	Toronto Maple Leafs 3 at Montreal Canadiens 2 (Harry Watson 5:15 OT)
*April 21, 1951	Montreal Canadiens 2 at Toronto Maple Leafs 3 {(Bill Barilko 2:53 OT)}

** played at Maple Leaf Gardens, Toronto   ** played at the Forum, Montreal*

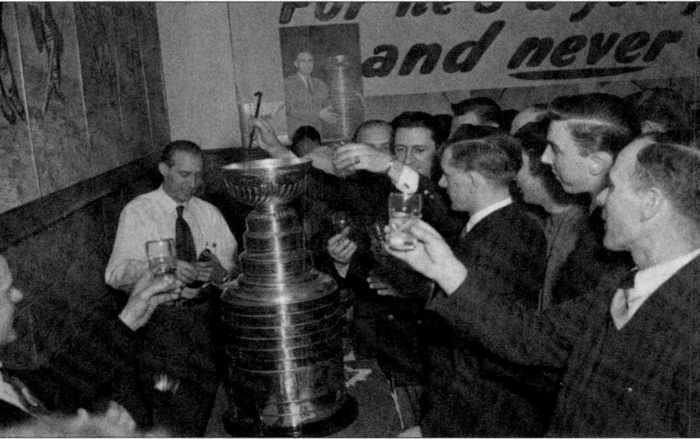

The Leafs celebrate victory in fine style.

(clockwise) Coach Joe Primeau is hoisted Cup-like by the players; Conn Smythe offers personal congratulations to the hero of the night, Bill Barilko; Barilko dives to swat the puck past Gerry McNeil of Montreal for the Cup-winning goal in overtime of game five.

TORONTO	GP	G	A	P	Pim
Tod Sloan	5	3	4	7	7
Sid Smith	5	5	1	6	0
Ted Kennedy	5	2	4	6	2
Max Bentley	5	0	4	4	2
Harry Watson	5	1	2	3	4
Howie Meeker	5	1	1	2	10
Bill Barilko	5	1	0	1	6
Gus Mortson	5	0	1	1	0
Fern Flaman	3	0	0	0	6
Jim Thomson	5	0	0	0	4
Bill Juzda	5	0	0	0	2
Fleming Mackell	5	0	0	0	2
Cal Gardner	5	0	0	0	0
Joe Klukay	5	0	0	0	0
Ray Timgren	5	0	0	0	0
Danny Lewicki	3	0	0	0	0
Al Rollins	3	0	0	0	0
Turk Broda	2	0	0	0	0

In Goal	GP	W-L	Mins	GA	SO	Avg
Al Rollins	3	3-0	193	5	0	1.55
Turk Broda	2	1-1	129	5	0	2.33

As much the hero as Barilko, **TOD SLOAN** tied game five with 32 seconds left in the third period with goalie Rollins on the bench for a sixth attacker.

Often called the team's Groucho Marx for his sense of humour, **SID SMITH** had a breakout year in 1950-51, scoring 30 goals, second-highest on the team to Tod Sloan's 31.

A crazed moment in the history of Cup engraving saw captain **TED KENNEDY'S** name badly mauled. He played on the number-one line with Sloan and Smith.

MAX BENTLEY, the Dipsy Doodle Dandy from Delisle, led the playoffs with eleven assists and 13 points.

Although he missed all of the semi-finals with an injury, **HARRY WATSON** was on the ice and made a key play leading up to Barilko's Cup-winning dive.

HOWIE MEEKER entered politics while still playing, winning a Liberal seat in Waterloo South (Toronto) in 1951 and '52.

The hero of the 1951 playoffs and subject of hockey's most famous photograph, **BARILKO** disappeared soon after this goal while on a fishing expedition in Ontario's remote North.

GUS MORTSON and defence partner Jim Thomson were not only close on the ice, they lived together in a Brunswick Avenue apartment.

A few days after this victory, **FERN FLAMAN** returned to work in Boston at his summer job—moving beer barrels.

JIM THOMSON was exiled to Chicago in 1957 for his part in trying to organize the NHL's first players' union.

After finishing his tour of duty of flying officer as a coastal command pilot, **BILL JUZDA** was traded to Toronto where he started in the minors but worked his way into the Leafs' lineup.

Midway during the following year, **FLEMING MACKELL** was traded to Boston.

CAL GARDNER later worked in radio in Toronto as colour man on Foster Hewitt's flagship station, CKFH, and his sons, Dave and Paul, both played in the NHL.

JOE KLUKAY was traded to Boston for Dave Creighton in 1952-53 but was back with the Blue and White for the last year and a half of his career before retiring in 1956 and becoming a tool and die maker in Michigan.

RAY TIMGREN later became a school principal with the North York Board of Education in Toronto.

DANNY LEWICKI was a 20-year-old rookie who became the first player in NHL history to win a Memorial Cup and Stanley Cup while still junior eligible.

In a year of transition, **AL ROLLINS** won the Vezina this year sharing the tending with Broda, but the next year he appeared in all 70 games for the Leafs.

"GOOSE" McCORMACK was traded at season's end after incurring the wrath of Smythe by getting married during the season.

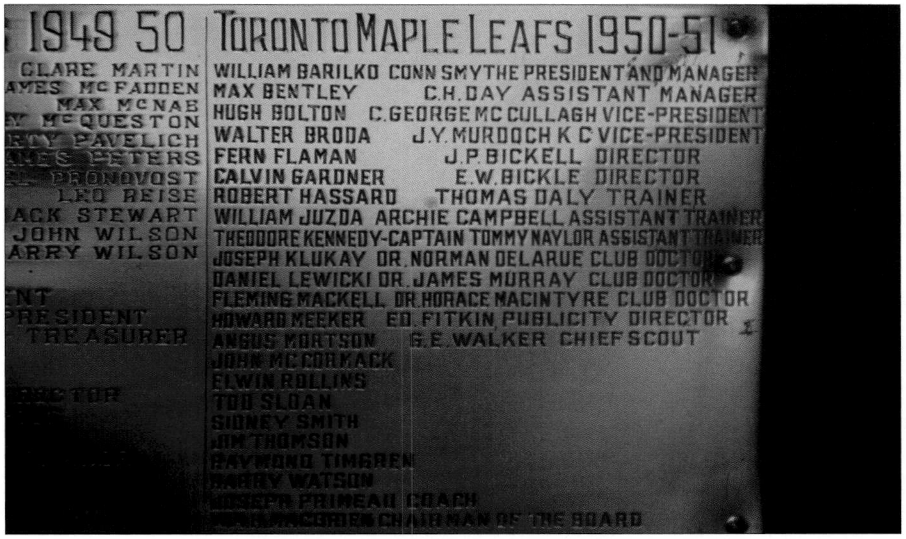

Team engraving from the Cup redesign which replaced the original band but was itself replaced when the final and current Cup design was introduced in the late 1950s.

This proved to be **TURK BRODA'S** last full year, though he played one more game with Toronto the next year before moving on to coaching in the Leafs' system.

With this Stanley Cup win, **JOE PRIMEAU** became the first man to coach Memorial, Allan, and Stanley Cup teams.

HUGH BOLTON played only 13 games and none in the playoffs. His career ended after he suffered an horrific broken leg in 1956.

Like Bolton, **BOB HASSARD** played just a handful of games (12), but as a centre he couldn't hope to play ahead of Kennedy, Sloan, Bentley, and Gardner.

BILL MacBRIEN and **J.Y. MURDOCH** were members of the team's board of directors.

Above all else, **CONN SMYTHE** valued loyalty as the greatest characteristic a man might possess, and his list of team captains, from Day to Apps to Kennedy, confirmed as much.

HAPPY DAY'S long tenure with the Leafs ended in 1957. He moved to St. Thomas, Ontario, and became successful as a maker of wood axe handles.

GEORGE McCULLAGH, publisher of the *Globe*, was also prominent in the city as a racehorse owner.

J.P. BICKELL died in the summer after a 30-year association with Conn Smythe. In recognition of Bickell's services to the club, Smythe introduced the Bickell Cup.

ED BICKLE was president of the Toronto Board of Trade. During World War I, he fought with the 15th Battalion, 1st Canadian Division, and was a Major with the 48th Highlanders.

Among the medicinal arsenal of trainer **TIM DALY** was the use of exactly one leech, which he would procure at a pharmacy and which usually lasted a long time.

THOMAS SUTTON NAYLER was in the Leafs' employ from 1927 to 1967. He is credited with helping Canada win the '72 Summit Series because of the portable skate sharpener he created which helped players overcome the awful conditions in Moscow.

DR. NORMAN DELARUE was the team's general surgeon and one of the few men Smythe trusted.

DR. JAMES MURRAY worked out of East General Hospital and later in life was stricken by Alzheimer's.

DR. MacINTYRE was also a golfing partner of Conn Smythe, though his skills in O.R. were greater than his abilities to read a green!

ED FITKIN later became assistant to the president in the WHA upon the league's establishment in 1972, though he suffered a debilitating stroke just a year later.

"SQUIB" WALKER had a dual role: he scouted and signed junior players in an official capacity for the Leafs. Unofficially, he sold insurance, usually to those same players just moments after getting their signature on a contract!

Other players to appear for the Leafs this season: **ANDY BARBE, GEORGE BLAIR, BOBBY COPP, PHIL MALONEY**

1951 1952 Detroit Red Wings

THE CHAMPIONS

This Wings team won eight playoff games in a row, the first to accomplish the double sweep. The city was overcome by a tide of octopi, a tradition of tossing that began the previous year in the playoffs when fish merchant Jerry Cusimano threw the fish onto the ice to indicate how the Wings had strangled the opposition (and also because an octopus had eight tentacles, the same number as wins needed for the Cup). After the win this year, the team and management went to the Book Cadillac Hotel on Washington Boulevard for a sumptuous party.

STANLEY CUP FINALS

Detroit Red Wings win best-of-seven Stanley Cup finals 4-0

*April 10, 1952 Detroit Red Wings 3 at Montreal Canadiens 1
*April 12, 1952 Detroit Red Wings 2 at Montreal Canadiens 1
**April 13, 1952 Montreal Canadiens 0 at Detroit Red Wings 3 [Terry Sawchuk]
**April 15, 1952 Montreal Canadiens 0 at Detroit Red Wings 3 {Metro Prystai 6:50 1st} [Terry Sawchuk]

** played at the Forum, Montreal ** played at the Olympia, Detroit*

Detroit Red Wings, 1951-52

DETROIT	GP	G	A	P	Pim
Ted Lindsay	4	3	0	3	4
Tony Leswick	4	2	1	3	14
Gordie Howe	4	2	1	3	2
Metro Prystai	4	2	1	3	0
Glen Skov	4	1	2	3	12
Marty Pavelich	4	1	2	3	2
Sid Abel	4	0	1	1	2
Alex Delvecchio	4	0	1	1	2
Johnny Wilson	4	0	1	1	0
Vic Stasiuk	3	0	1	1	0
Bob Goldham	4	0	0	0	4
Marcel Pronovost	4	0	0	0	2
Benny Woit	4	0	0	0	2
Terry Sawchuk	4	0	0	0	0
Red Kelly	3	0	0	0	0
Larry Zeidel	3	0	0	0	0
Leo Reise	2	0	0	0	0

In Goal	GP	W-L	Mins	GA	SO	Avg
Terry Sawchuk	4	4-0	240	2	2	0.50

Detroit goalie Terry Sawchuk makes one of several great saves in game three, earning his first shutout of the finals and third in seven games of the 1952 playoffs.

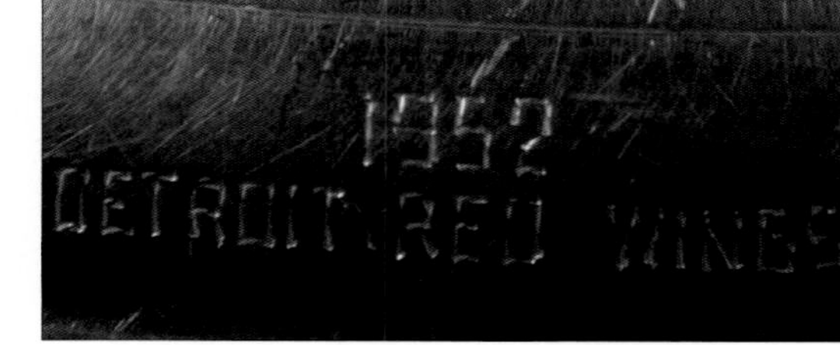

Team engraving from the shoulder of the Stanley Cup

TED LINDSAY scored a controversial empty net goal in game one that was first announced at 19:44 and then discovered to be 18:44, leaving Montreal coach Dick Irvin fuming that he had been forced to remove his goalie a minute earlier than necessary.

TONY LESWICK was one of the league's first trash talkers, drawing penalties but also attention.

"We were a unique bunch of guys. We bowled together, took our wives dancing together. We always knew we were going to win the whole thing because no one could outclass us in togetherness." **GORDIE HOWE**.

In the Cup-clinching game, **METRO PRYSTAI** was in on all three goals, scoring twice and assisting on Skov's goal.

GLEN SKOV'S brother, Art, was a referee. The playing Skov was also league Iron Man, playing every game for five straight years.

MARTY PAVELICH'S ability to anticipate the play came out of his keen ability to observe. "Hockey players are creatures of habit," he explained.

The next year **SID ABEL** became playing coach in Chicago and in 1957 he began an eleven-year term as Detroit's bench boss. He coached four All-Star games and later acted as GM for new franchises in St. Louis and Kansas City.

Alex "Belvecchio" (as his name appears on the Cup) was part of the checking line with Prystai and Wilson. "When our line got three goals that won the last game," **DELVECCHIO** enthused, "it was like an added feature."

After retiring, **JOHNNY WILSON** seemed to coach everywhere, from Princeton University to the Wings in the NHL.

Like many a Wing, **VIC STASIUK** never played a full season in Detroit, GM Adams preferring to bounce him between the big club and the minors year after harrowing year.

One of the great shot blockers of his time, **BOB GOLDHAM** credited Bucko McDonald with teaching him the tricks of the trade.

One of twelve children, **MARCEL PRONOVOST** became, not surprisingly, a team leader in Detroit. His tolerance of pain was legendary, for he played many a game with injuries that would have sidelined even the heartiest player.

BENNY WOIT packed a great deal of success into a compact career. In just five full NHL seasons, he won three Stanley Cups.

TERRY SAWCHUK ("Ukey") had 12 regular season shutouts this year and didn't allow a goal in the last two games of the finals. "He is their team," said a disconsolate Maurice Richard in defeat. Sawchuk set a record with four playoff shutouts.

Although **RED KELLY** would later play forward with Toronto, his 162 goals from defence was an all-time record when he retired.

LARRY ZEIDEL desperately wanted to leave the Quebec Aces to play out West, but after one year with Saskatoon he was lured to Detroit.

LEO REISE scored two overtime goals in the 1950 semi-finals against Toronto to help the Wings overcome the loss of Gordie Howe to injury.

Details from the stovepipe Cup showing both players and team

Although **TOMMY IVAN** has his name misspelled "Nivan," he was considered the best-dressed coach. "Even if I didn't have a dollar," he boasted, "I'd wear a good suit of clothes."

A career minor-league goalie who played not a minute in the NHL, **BILL TIBBS** makes the Cup here as the Red Wings' practise goalie.

ENIO SCLISIZZI travelled between the farm in Indianapolis and the Motor City more than any other player.

HUGH COFLIN played 31 games for Chicago in 1950-51 and then the rest of his career in the minors in Edmonton. His name appeared on the redesigned Cup of the day but not today's Cup when it was crafted in 1957.

One of many players to pursue a coaching career later, **FRED GLOVER** augmented his too brief skating career in the NHL with six years as a bench boss with the California Seals. He also played some 20 years in the AHL, mostly with Cleveland.

When he was a boy, **GLENN HALL** played forward and was team captain. One day, the goalie walked out, and Hall felt obligated to tend the twine. Thereafter, he never left the crease.

JAMES NORRIS died December 5, 1952 and brought about peals of sad tribute. Said Bill Tobin of Chicago: "The death of Jim Norris is a great loss not only to the Detroit Red Wings and the NHL but to hockey everywhere it is played. We in the NHL leaned on him heavily."

After his father's death, **JIM NORRIS, JR.** and **ARTHUR WIRTZ** sold their one-third interest in the club to their half-brother and half-sister, Bruce and Marguerite Norris, and they in turn bought the Black Hawks.

BRUCE NORRIS played hockey at Yale University until a serious knee injury ended a potential career. He continued to play, though, and in one Yale reunion game suffered a 100-stitch cut to his forehead.

"This is a team that shouldn't collapse," **JACK ADAMS** had earlier observed. "It is the youngest team in the league. Men like Ted Lindsay, Gordie Howe, Marty Pavelich, Lee Fogolin, Enio Sclisizzi, and Harry Lumley all appear to have ten years of NHL play ahead of them."

FRED HUBER stood 6'5" and was erudite and well spoken. He was Red Wings publicity director for many years.

Soon after this win, scout **CARSON COOPER** became lead bird dog for the New York Rangers, but even still he wore a Red Wing on his sleeve until the day he died.

Trainer **CARL MATTSON** was a super fixer-upper of charley-horses. He even had a reputation every now and then of circumventing the law by administering to a player a stitch or two in the absence of a doctor.

Before the war, **ROSS "LEFTY" WILSON** played ball briefly in the Red Sox organization. After, he became Detroit's trainer and practise goalie.

WALTER CROSSMAN watched the Olympia being built, day by day, as a curious child. He became a rink rat when the arena opened, and the Wings eventually offered him a job as a stick boy.

Other players to appear for the Wings this season: **BILL FOLK**, **LARRY WILSON**

1952 THE CHAMPIONS
1953 Montreal Canadiens

President Clarence Campbell presented the Cup on ice to captain Bouchard after the win, an the captain made a brief acceptance speech in both English and French. Earlier, Jim Hendy, owner of the Cleveland Barons of the AHL, had submitted a challenge to the eventual Cup winners, but it was dismissed on two grounds. One, the Barons had not yet won their own championship; two, a challenge must come from an equal challenger, and the AHL was agreed by all to be a lesser league than the NHL. As much a story this year as the finals was Boston's stunning upset of Detroit in a six-game semi-finals. The Montreal victory dinner was held at the Queen's Hotel (owned by Senator Raymond) and the MC was D.C. Coleman.

STANLEY CUP FINALS

Montreal Canadiens win best-of-seven Stanley Cup finals 4-1

*April 9, 1953	Boston Bruins 2 at Montreal Canadiens 4
*April 11, 1953	Boston Bruins 4 at Montreal Canadiens 1
**April 12, 1953	Montreal Canadiens 3 at Boston Bruins 0 [Gerry McNeil]
**April 14, 1953	Montreal Canadiens 7 at Boston Bruins 3
*April 16, 1953	Boston Bruins 0 at Montreal Canadiens 1 {(Elmer Lach 1:22 OT)} [Gerry McNeil]

** played at the Forum, Montreal ** played at Boston Garden*

Canadiens celebrate their 1953 Cup victory

(clockwise) Maurice Richard, Elmer Lach, coach Dick Irvin, and publicist Camil des Roches wish each other good cheer after the win; Lach holds the Cup-winning puck which he put into the Boston net in overtime; throngs of fans and media gather round the team as it receives the Cup during an on-ice presentation after Lach's deciding goal.

MONTREAL	GP	G	A	P	Pim
Maurice Richard	5	4	1	5	0
Ken Mosdell	5	2	2	4	4
Calum MacKay	5	1	2	3	6
Dickie Moore	5	2	0	2	9
Bert Olmstead	5	1	1	2	2
Floyd Curry	5	1	1	2	0
Elmer Lach	5	1	1	2	0
Doug Harvey	5	0	2	2	4
Dollard St. Laurent	5	0	2	2	2
Tom Johnson	5	1	0	1	4
Lorne Davis	5	1	0	1	2
Bernie Geoffrion	5	1	0	1	0
Paul Masnick	3	1	0	1	0
Eddie Mazur	5	0	1	1	11
Butch Bouchard	5	0	1	1	2
Billy Reay	4	0	0	0	0
Gerry McNeil	3	0	0	0	0
John McCormack	2	0	0	0	0
Jacques Plante	2	0	0	0	0
Paul Meger	1	0	0	0	0

In Goal	GP	W-L	Mins	GA	SO	Avg
Gerry McNeil	3	3-0	181	3	2	0.99
Jacques Plante	2	1-1	120	6	0	3.00

After the game, **MAURICE RICHARD** was so exhausted that he just sat in his stall in the dressing room and didn't move!

KEN MOSDELL missed much of the 1952 playoffs with a broken leg, but this year he played on a line with Davis and McKay and was outstanding. During the Cup presentation, he skated around the ice with his four-year-old daughter, Bonny.

BALDY MacKAY earned his stripes in the minors, but his first day in the NHL was an eye-opener. Coach Dick Irvin told him to lose 20 pounds off his 195-lbs. frame or else it was back to the minors. He lost the weight.

After a serious knee operation at the start of the year, **DICKIE MOORE** returned for the last 18 regular season games and played on a line with Reay and Geoffrion in the finals.

Few remember that **BERT OLMSTEAD** began his career with Chicago before coming to Montreal in a one-for-one trade for Leo Gravelle in 1950. He left before the team dinner in order to get back to the family farm in Saskatchewan to bring in the crop.

FLOYD CURRY had been a scorer in junior but the Habs needed a defensive-minded forward even more, so he developed into a player who could stop the other team's best players.

"I never saw it go in! I never saw it go in!" was all **ELMER LACH** could yell as teammates mobbed him after scoring the Cup-winner in overtime with a quick screen shot. In the celebrations that followed, Richard broke Lach's nose with his stick!

DOUG HARVEY had the exceptional and rare ability to speed up and slow down, almost imperceptibly, until too late, much to the frustration of his opponents.

DOLLARD ST. LAURENT was an identifiable name for any French-Canadian. The Dollard represented the Des Ormeaux who saved Montreal from the Iroquois in 1660; the St. Laurent for the St. Lawrence River.

TOM JOHNSON was a big, abrasive defenceman who got under the skin of his opponents. He and Calum MacKay were called "the Great Lovers" because they were both still single.

LORNE DAVIS had a peripatetic career as both player and coach, appearing only in the post-season this year and scoring a goal for good measure.

"BOOM BOOM" GEOFFRION played in every finals game of this decade for the Habs, an NHL record.

PAUL MASNICK played three games of the finals, scoring the middle goal of game three's 3-0 shutout victory.

EDDIE MAZUR played junior for Winnipeg, a Leafs' junior-sponsored team, but the Habs signed him to a contract with the Buffalo Bisons, a Montreal affiliate.

Captain **BUTCH BOUCHARD** had tremendous size and strength but never tried to intimidate opponents. He inherited the "C" in 1948 after Toe Blake retired.

At the end of his playing career, **BILLY REAY** went on to have a coaching career that endured 16 years and more than 1,100 games (though, amazingly, no Stanley Cups).

Details from the stovepipe Cup showing both players and team

GERRY McNEIL played much of the finals on a frozen ankle after stopping a sizzling Richard shot in practise. He got a diamond-encrusted Habs tie pin for the victory, which he turned into a ring and gave to his wife.

JOHN McCORMACK was sold by the Leafs to Montreal on September 23, 1951, in a straight cash transaction.

A rookie, **JACQUES PLANTE** showed all signs of greatness when he recorded a shutout in his first ever playoff game, a 3-0 win over Chicago in game six of the semi-finals. Coach Dick Irvin had benched Gerry McNeil when Montreal blew a 2-0 lead in games to fall behind 3-2 in the series.

PAUL MEGER suffered a career-ending fractured skull two years later and dropped the puck at the last game of the 1957 finals, at the Forum.

A call-up from the Quebec Aces for three games, **JEAN BELIVEAU, LE GROS BILL** scored a hat trick in his first game and five goals in all, though he wasn't eligible to skate in the playoffs and his name is not on Cup.

DICK GAMBLE played all regular season and most of the semi-finals, but not at all in the finals as coach Irvin shortened his bench.

At 6'4" 200 lbs., **"BUD" MacPHERSON** was the biggest defenceman in the league and a fine offensive talent as well.

DONAT RAYMOND was appointed to the Senate as a Liberal on December 20, 1926, though his position as president of the Canadiens had far more prestige in the eyes of most Montrealers.

DALTON "D.C." COLEMAN was director of the Canadian Arena Company, and the father of Jim, a prominent journalist.

NORTHEY had been a president of the MAAA during the days when snowshoeing was a respected sport in that club's itinerary. When the Stanley Cup became the exclusive domain of the professional NHL, he encouraged Sir Montagu Allan to donate a Cup bearing his name—Allan—for amateur champions of the country.

FRANK SELKE had played school hockey, though because he was always the smallest player he discovered his greatest ability was neutralizing the opponents' best player. He knew he would never go far as a player and managed his first team when he was just 13 years old.

This turned out to be **DICK IRVIN'S** fourth and final Stanley Cup. He holds two Cup records, one enviable, the other not. He coached more teams to the finals—16—than any other man, but his 12 Cup losses are also a record not likely to be broken.

Trainer **HECTOR DUBOIS** had been a steeplejack but he fell off a church spire, broke his back, and ended his career as a result.

Trainer **GASTON BETTEZ** has his name badly mauled as "Goston Bettes." He was an excellent skater for a roly-poly fellow and after retiring from the Habs became a very successful insurance broker.

Other players to appear for the Canadiens this season: **REG ABBOTT, DOUG ANDERSON, GERRY DESAULNIERS, IVAN IRWIN, ED LITZENBERGER, HAL MURPHY, ROLLIE ROUSSEAU, GAYE STEWART**

1953 THE CHAMPIONS

1954 Detroit Red Wings

For the first and only time, a woman, Marguerite Norris, was presented the Cup after Detroit's victory. The Habs, meanwhile, had skated off the ice immediately. "If I had shaken hands," coach Dick Irvin said, "I wouldn't have meant it." The victorious Wings held a celebration at the Sheraton-Cadillac Hotel in downtown Detroit at which time former Wings forward Gaye Stewart (now with the Habs) joined in the festivities.

STANLEY CUP FINALS

Detroit Red Wings win best-of-seven Stanley Cup finals 4-3

*April 4, 1954	Montreal Canadiens 1 at Detroit Red Wings 3
*April 6, 1954	Montreal Canadiens 3 at Detroit Red Wings 1
**April 8, 1954	Detroit Red Wings 5 at Montreal Canadiens 2
**April 10, 1954	Detroit Red Wings 2 at Montreal Canadiens 0 [Terry Sawchuk]
*April 11, 1954	Montreal Canadiens 1 at Detroit Red Wings 0 (Ken Mosdell 5:45 OT) [Gerry McNeil]
**April 13, 1954	Detroit Red Wings 1 at Montreal Canadiens 4
*April 16, 1954	Montreal Canadiens 1 at Detroit Red Wings 2 {(Tony Leswick 4:29 OT)}

** played at the Olympia, Detroit ** played at the Forum, Montreal*

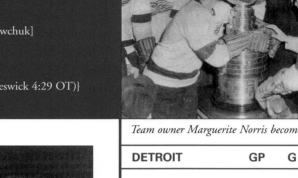

Team owner Marguerite Norris becomes the first woman to win the Cup.

(left) Ted Lindsay hugs the cherished trophy; (above) Gordie Howe (left) salutes Harry Lumley after Detroit eliminated the Leafs in the semi-finals.

DETROIT	GP	G	A	P	Pim
Alex Delvecchio	7	2	4	6	0
Red Kelly	7	3	1	4	0
Ted Lindsay	7	2	2	4	14
Metro Prystai	7	2	2	4	0
Gordie Howe	7	1	2	3	23
Johnny Wilson	7	2	0	2	0
Tony Leswick	7	1	1	2	8
Earl Reibel	4	1	1	2	0
Glen Skov	7	0	1	1	10
Marty Pavelich	7	0	1	1	4
Benny Woit	7	0	1	1	4
Bob Goldham	7	0	1	1	0
Marcel Pronovost	7	0	0	0	8
Bill Dineen	7	0	0	0	0
Terry Sawchuk	7	0	0	0	0
Jim Peters	6	0	0	0	0
Keith Allen	3	0	0	0	0
Gilles Dube	2	0	0	0	0

In Goal	GP	W-L	Mins	GA	SO	Avg
Terry Sawchuk	7	4-3	430	12	1	1.67

Team engraving from the bowl of the original Cup

With the retirement of Sid Abel, **ALEX DELVECCHIO** became the new centre for the Production Line, and his passing and smooth skating were perfect for Howe and Lindsay.

RED KELLY scored a critical game-winner in game four of the semi-finals vs. Toronto when his long shot late in the third period banked off Tim Horton and beat Harry Lumley.

Nicknamed "Ching" after the Hall of Famer of an earlier era, this **JOHNSON, EARL**, played one single, solitary game with the Wings to get his name on the Cup.

Terrible **TED LINDSAY** retired as the most penalized player in the game and the NHL's greatest left winger. He could hit, check, and score with equal ability, and his ferocious team leadership epitomized all that team captaincy stood for.

METRO PRYSTAI sometimes played on a checking line with Delvecchio and Johnny Wilson. Twice he was traded from Chicago to Detroit and once from Detroit to Chicago.

GORDIE HOWE led the league in scoring for the fourth straight year, and in game five of the semis scored nine seconds into the first period, an NHL record for the fastest goal from the start of a playoff game.

JOHNNY WILSON was one of only five Wings to play on all four Cup teams in the 1950s (Lindsay, Pavelich, Kelly, Pronovost) and later coached the team on three different occasions.

TONY LESWICK scored the Cup-winning goal in OT when his shot caromed off Doug Harvey's glove past Gerry McNeil.

Acquired at the start of the season, **EARL REIBEL** broke his cheekbone in a collision with Bert Olmstead in game four and missed the rest of the finals.

GLEN SKOV played on a line with Marty Pavelich and Tony Leswick. They were assigned the grand task of checking Montreal's top threesome of Beliveau-Moore-Geoffrion and did a masterful job.

Sometimes called "Madman," **MARTY PAVELICH** was a scorer in junior, but he became a checker when he moved up to Detroit and his game was forever defined as such.

BENNY WOIT played every game this season without scoring a single goal, regular season or playoffs (82 games).

Despite being the best shotblocker in the league, **BOB GOLDHAM** retired in 1956 with all his teeth intact.

MARCEL was one of three **PRONOVOST** children to make it to the big tent: Claude played briefly in the late 1950s and Jean played in the NHL over a span of three decades.

Patriarch of the **DINEEN** clan, **BILL** sired four sons who played pro—Gord, Kevin, and Peter made the NHL, while Shawn played in the AHL.

After one more year with Detroit, **TERRY SAWCHUK** was inexplicably traded to Boston while still very much at the height of his abilities.

In the dusk of his career, **JIM PETERS** was sent from Detroit to Chicago for nothing more than future considerations. He played senior hockey the following year.

Details from the stovepipe Cup showing both players and team

KEITH ALLEN'S name on this Cup is one of those unpredictable flukes of engraving history. He played just ten regular season games this year and made the Cup, but next year played 18 games and didn't! The difference might have been that he also played five times in this year's playoffs.

Two playoff games was the sum total of **GILLES DUBE'S** playing time in a Winged Wheel sweater, enough to get his name on the Cup.

ALGER ARBOUR, Hal Laycoe, and Russ Blinco were the only players to wear glasses during games. Arbour played 36 times in the regular season, but none in the playoffs.

DAVE GATHERUM played goal in three regular season games as an emergency call-up when Sawchuk was injured. Remarkably, he recorded a shutout in his first NHL game.

MARGUERITE NORRIS was the daughter of the recently deceased James Norris. At just 25 years of age, she became the first woman to have her name engraved on the Cup. Her entrance into NHL society was not without comment. Tom Fitzgerald had this to say in the *Boston Globe* of December 16, 1952: "Miss Norris is a 25-year-old brunette, and according to an admiring, if not overly elegant, description by one of her employees, is a 'real good looker and a regular.'"

Later in life, after three wives, **BRUCE A. NORRIS** went to work on a fourth. He became involved with Joyce Butler, who, though married with a child, made public her desire for a divorce to make way for a marriage with Norris. The "Butler Battle," as the press dubbed the story, created numerous lawsuits and counter-suits.

JACK ADAMS spent his whole executive life in Detroit, some 35 years and six Stanley Cups, before his death in 1962.

TOMMY IVAN'S tenure in Detroit ended this year, but what a remarkable time it was—six consecutive first place finishes in the regular season standings, and three Stanley Cups. He moved to Chicago to assume the role of GM and tackle new challenges.

JOHN MITCHELL was an assistant manager with the Hawks before joining the Red Wings for four years. He later took over the Johnstown Jets, and his daughter married Glen Sonmor, future NHL coach.

FRED HUBER stayed with the team until 1958 at which time he moved to Arizona to retire.

CARL MATTSON succeeded Honey Walker as trainer in 1949 after being his assistant for a number of years. Like Huber, he left in '58.

Detroit trainer **ROSS WILSON** played 16 minutes of a game on October 10, 1953, when starter Terry Sawchuk was injured. "Lefty" didn't allow a goal, though Montreal won the game 4-1. His name appeared on the original re-design of the Cup but is not on the current Cup.

Although his name is not on the '55 Cup, **WALTER CROSSMAN** earned a promotion from stick boy to assistant trainer. He remained with the club through the team's most recent Cup wins in 1997 and '98.

Other players to appear for the Red Wings this season: **MARCEL BONIN, JIM HAY, ED STANKIEWICZ, VIC STASIUK**

1954–1955 THE CHAMPIONS Detroit Red Wings

The Wings won the league championship for the seventh consecutive year and followed with a Cup win over Montreal that was played without Maurice Richard who had been suspended by Clarence Campbell for the balance of the season after the Rocket's assault on a linesman. The ensuing Richard Riot cost the Habs two points, the very margin of victory for first place and home ice advantage for Detroit, which won the Cup on home ice, in game seven. The Cup was again presented to Marguerite Norris, and the victory celebrations were again held at the Sheraton-Cadillac Hotel immediately after the game.

STANLEY CUP FINALS

Detroit Red Wings win best-of-seven Stanley Cup finals 4-3

*April 3, 1955 Montreal Canadiens 2 at Detroit Red Wings 4
*April 5, 1955 Montreal Canadiens 1 at Detroit Red Wings 7
**April 7, 1955 Detroit Red Wings 2 at Montreal Canadiens 4
**April 9, 1955 Detroit Red Wings 3 at Montreal Canadiens 5
*April 10, 1955 Montreal Canadiens 1 at Detroit Red Wings 5
**April 12, 1955 Detroit Red Wings 3 at Montreal Canadiens 6
*April 14, 1955 Montreal Canadiens 1 at Detroit Red Wings 3 {Gordie Howe 19:49 2nd}

** played at the Olympia, Detroit ** played at the Forum, Montreal*

GM Jack Adams admires the Cup after Detroit's victory.

DETROIT	GP	G	A	P	Pim
Gordie Howe	7	5	7	12	24
Ted Lindsay	7	5	6	11	6
Alex Delvecchio	7	6	4	10	0
Earl Reibel	7	2	5	7	2
Vic Stasiuk	7	3	3	6	2
Red Kelly	7	2	3	5	17
Marty Pavelich	7	1	2	3	12
Marcel Pronovost	7	1	2	3	2
Bob Goldham	7	0	2	2	2
Glen Skov	7	1	0	1	4
Jim Hay	5	1	0	1	0
Tony Leswick	7	0	1	1	10
Marcel Bonin	7	0	1	1	4
Benny Woit	7	0	0	0	4
Bill Dineen	7	0	0	0	2
Terry Sawchuk	7	0	0	0	0
Johnny Wilson	7	0	0	0	0

In Goal	GP	W-L	Mins	GA	SO	Avg
Terry Sawchuk	7	4-3	420	20	0	2.86

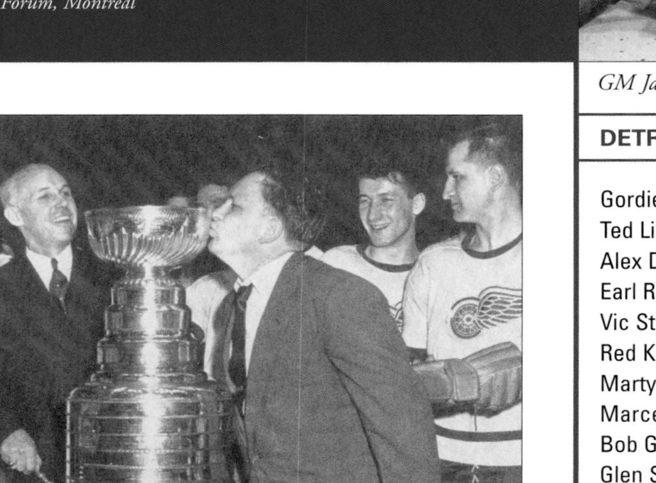

(left) Goalie Jacques Plante makes a save and watches the puck drop between his pads; (above) Detroit coach Jimmy Skinner kisses the Cup during the on-ice presentation and festivities.

Team engraving from the shoulder of the original Cup

Although **GORDIE HOWE** did not play his final NHL game until 1980, this proved to be, incredibly, his last Stanley Cup.

In a game on January 22 at Maple Leaf Gardens, **TED LINDSAY** came to Howe's defence when a skirmish developed with a fan. Terrible Ted clubbed the heckler with his stick and was suspended ten days for his bravery.

No player has skated for one team longer than "Fats," **ALEX DELVECCHIO**, who played for the Wings for 24 years. He later coached and managed the Wings during the dark days of the 1970s.

EARL REIBEL worked the Production Line with Howe and Abel, and this troika set a playoff record with a combined 51 points.

After a slow apprenticeship with Chicago and Detroit, **VIC STASIUK** blossomed in Boston with five consecutive 19+-goal seasons playing on the famous Uke Line.

RED KELLY duked it out with Butch Bouchard in game five, earning a major and misconduct, his first such penalties in eight years.

In addition to scouting for the Red Wings, **MARTY PAVELICH** teamed up with Gordie Howe and Ted Lindsay in a plastics venture business after retiring

Although his twenty years with Detroit were far from over, this was **MARCEL PRONOVOST'S** last Cup with the Wings. His final victory came with Toronto's Over-the-Hill Gang in 1967.

Post-NHL, **BOB GOLDHAM** played many oldtimers' games and became a popular TV analyst on *Hockey Night in Canada* for many years, providing astute observations of the nuances of the modern game.

The on-ice microphone to be used by Clarence Campbell to present the Stanley Cup broke, so players hoisted **GLEN SKOV** to a mic above the ice so he could free it and give it to Campbell.

"Red Eye" **JIM HAY** had turned more than a few heads at training camp in 1953. As a member of the farm team in Edmonton, he fought Ted Lindsay in an exhibition game, a melee that lasted six minutes on the ice and continued in the penalty box.

Referee Bill Chadwick called **TONY LESWICK** one of the original trash talkers and claimed the Red Wing made the most disparaging remarks about a player's family or personal history to gain a psychological edge.

MARCEL BONIN was usually addressed as "Hec" (his middle name) by his teammates, to differentiate him from the team's other Marcel, Pronovost. Bonin took pride in his body, sculpted by weightlifting and enhanced by his having wrestled a 600-lb. bear one time.

BENNY WOIT'S last NHL year was '56-'57 with Chicago but he played another decade of minor pro before turning to coaching and then moving to Thunder Bay, Ontario, to become a grain trimmer.

Details from the stovepipe Cup showing both players and team

After a solid rookie season in which the Wings won the Cup, **BILL DINEEN** was warmly welcomed by Jack Adams at this year's camp. The GM promised the player just reward for the fine first season and increased his salary from $6,000 to $6,500.

"Ukey was the greatest goalie who ever lived," claimed roommate Bob Goldham of **TERRY SAWCHUK**. Few would disagree, though the goalie was never called the nicest man alive. He drank too much, had spousal difficulties, and remained pained by injury most of his playing career.

JOHNNY WILSON was right in the middle of the NHL's Iron Man streak having played more than eight full seasons—580 consecutive games—until 1960, a league record until Andy Hebenton broke the mark.

JIMMY SKINNER replaced Tommy Ivan as coach and at the time was the only bench boss in the league who hadn't played in the NHL at one time.

LARY HILLMAN was an 18-year-old rookie starting a 19-year career, winning his first of four Cups spread over three teams (Toronto in '64 and '67 and Montreal in '69).

BRUCE NORRIS took control of the Wings in 1955, at 31 the NHL's youngest team president. He never won a Cup in that capacity, though he remained in charge of Detroit until 1982 when he sold the team, and insodoing severed a Norris connection to the Wings that began in 1933.

"I'm not predicting we'll win the Stanley Cup," **JACK ADAMS** said after his Wings swept the Leafs in four straight games in the semi-finals, "but it will take a super-human effort to keep us from winning."

Chief scout **JOHN MITCHELL** had been an NHL ref between 1932 and '37. He had coached in the AHL and had been a GM in the EAHL, and in 1962 he became assistant to Sid Abel with the Wings.

FRED HUBER, the team's publicity director was also a founding member of the IHL and was instrumental in the evolution of media as a tool to promote a team through public relations.

CARL MATTSON was the Red Wings' trainer.

Although he stuck to his trainer's duties this year, **ROSS WILSON** played twice more in goal—for the opponents, no less!—in years to come when injury forced a starting goalie to the dressing room.

GLENN HALL played two regular season games, not enough to get his name on the Cup. Although he would have a phenomenal year in '55-'56, playing in every game and recording a dozen shutouts, Jack Adams opted to trade him to allow Sawchuk to become the number one goaler in Detroit.

As a child, **MARGUERITE NORRIS** was the youngest and smallest of the Norris children. As a result, she was forced to play goal in the family's homemade rink at shinny time. As owner and president of the Wings, she spoiled the players, buying them presents on road trips and leaving the surprise packages on their seats for the train ride home.

Other players to appear for the Wings this season: **KEITH ALLEN, LORNE DAVIS, DON POILE, METRO PRYSTAI, ED ZENIUK**

1955 THE CHAMPIONS
1956 Montreal Canadiens

The Saturday after victory, Montreal mayor Jean Drapeau organized a Cup parade for the Habs, only the fifth of its kind since Montreal (1907), Ottawa (1923), and Toronto (1947 and 1948). It lasted nine hours and covered thirty miles and led coach Toe Blake to threaten Mayor Drapeau that they wouldn't win any more Cups in the furure if the parade would be such torture!

STANLEY CUP FINALS

Montreal Canadiens win best-of-seven Stanley Cup finals 4-1

*March 31, 1956	Detroit Red Wings 4 at Montreal Canadiens 6
*April 3, 1956	Detroit Red Wings 1 at Montreal Canadiens 5
**April 5, 1956	Montreal Canadiens 1 at Detroit Red Wings 3
**April 8, 1956	Montreal Canadiens 3 at Detroit Red Wings 0 [Jacques Plante]
*April 10, 1956	Detroit Red Wings 1 at Montreal Canadiens 3 {Maurice Richard 15:08 2nd}

** played at the Forum, Montreal ** played at the Olympia, Detroit*

Players from the Canadiens enjoy their Cup dinner.

(top) A float during the Cup parade wends its way along a street behind City Hall in Montreal; (left) goalie Jacques Plante fends off a Detroit attack during his shutout performance in game four in Detroit.

MONTREAL	GP	G	A	P	Pim
Jean Beliveau	5	7	3	10	8
Bert Olmstead	5	0	8	8	4
Bernie Geoffrion	5	3	3	6	2
Maurice Richard	5	2	2	4	12
Floyd Curry	5	1	3	4	4
Henri Richard	5	2	1	3	11
Claude Provost	5	1	2	3	2
Doug Harvey	5	0	3	3	6
Dickie Moore	5	0	3	3	6
Jackie LeClair	5	1	1	2	4
Don Marshall	5	1	0	1	0
Jean-Guy Talbot	4	0	1	1	2
Ken Mosdell	4	0	1	1	0
Tom Johnson	5	0	0	0	8
Bob Turner	5	0	0	0	4
Dollard St. Laurent	3	0	0	0	2
Jacques Plante	5	0	0	0	0
Butch Bouchard	1	0	0	0	0

In Goal	GP	W-L	Mins	GA	SO	Avg
Jacques Plante	5	4-1	300	9	1	1.80

On November 5, vs. Boston, the "Grand Jean" **BELIVEAU** scored three goals in 44 seconds. He led all players with 19 points in the playoffs en route to his first Stanley Cup. Not surprisingly, this was also the year he stood up and answered to the punishments of opponents who had tried to intimidate him. He had 143 penalty minutes, most in any season for him.

BERT OLMSTEAD led the league in assists in both the regular season (56, an NHL record) and playoffs (ten) playing on a line with Geoffrion and Beliveau.

"BOOM BOOM" GEOFFRION, thanks to his famous slapshot, won the scoring title in '54-'55 and a few years later became only the second man to score 50 goals in a season.

In the Cup-deciding game, **ROCKET RICHARD** and Beliveau scored on the same power play to stake the Habs to an early and insurmountable 2-0 lead.

Like Harvey Jackson, **FLOYD CURRY** quickly earned the nickname "Busher." He was scouted by Paul Hayes in Kirkland Lake and attended his first Montreal training camp at 15, though it would be a few years still before he broke into the NHL.

In his rookie season, the "Pocket Rocket" **HENRI RICHARD** was repeatedly challenged by opponents, and though his elder brother frequently helped out, Henri was a tough cookie in his own right.

CLAUDE PROVOST—"Prevost" here—won the Cup in his rookie season, thanks in large measure to his speed and terrific hustle.

In game two in Detroit, a fan taunted **DOUG HARVEY** mercilessly and later charged him with assault, claiming he had been hit by Harvey at one point.

"1956 was the best team I ever played on," **DICKIE MOORE** said later, "and beating Detroit, the team that had embarrassed us so often, was a big moment."

During the previous season, **JACKIE LeCLAIR** fell on the skate blade of the Leafs' Larry Cahan, severing two arteries in his throat, including the carotid, and came close to death. He was out a month, but made a full recovery.

DON MARSHALL had been a scorer in junior and the minors, but in his first shift with the Habs he broke his leg. When he returned, the team was going so well coach Blake used him as a penalty killer and he became the best in the league in that role.

In his first full season, **JEAN-GUY TALBOT** played on a star-studded defence, learning from the best and eventually replacing the greats for a new generation of Canadiens' blueliners.

KEN MOSDELL announced his retirement immediately after the win, though he later reneged and played with Chicago and parts of two more Cup-winning years with the Habs.

TOM JOHNSON came from an Icelandic-Canadian part of Manitoba, Baldur, a village of 500 people almost all of whom had emigrated from Iceland.

BOB TURNER played 478 regular season games and won five Cups partnered with the great Doug Harvey on defence. "I like the idea of winning the Stanley Cup in Montreal," he said later. "It was something I got used to."

Team engraving from the Stanley Cup

Team engraving from the shoulder of the Stanley Cup

One of ten children, **DOLLARD ST. LAURENT** learned to skate in Verdun, Quebec on a river that bears his name—the St. Lawrence. Every summer he returned to Verdun to run an insurance business with his brother.

This was **JACQUES PLANTE'S** first of five in a row—five Vezina Trophies, five Cups, five different spellings of his name on the trophy.

Captain **BUTCH BOUCHARD** accepted the Cup and skated gleefully around with it. After the victory, he returned to his other job, running his restaurant called "Chez Butch."

GASTON BETTEZ was used one time by coach Dick Irvin to get back at Detroit's Jack Adams who had called the Habs "hatchetmen." Irvin had the trainer dress up in woodsman's garb and come on the ice wielding a large axe during warmup.

TOE BLAKE, the first year coach, replaced Dick Irvin and was hired because he, more than any other, could handle the temperament of Maurice Richard. The players lifted him and sang "For He's A Jolly Good Fellow" after the victory.

The names that go on the Cup are sometimes different from the names the NHL includes in the team roster of Cup-winning teams. **CHARLIE HODGE** played the entire season with the Seattle Americans (WHL) but because he was more or less the team's backup goalie he has his name on the Cup.

When he was just 20, **FRANK SELKE** managed the Berlin Union Jacks, guiding them to the OHA semi-finals. He later took over the Toronto Marlies (in 1924) before joining forces with Conn Smythe and his newly-minted Maple Leafs.

DONAT RAYMOND'S brother, Adelard, was a much-decorated hero with the Royal Flying Corps in World War I and went on to establish the RCAF.

Canadiens vice president **D'ALTON COLEMAN** had a lifelong association with CPR that culminated with his being named president.

WILLIAM NORTHEY supervised and managed the construction of the Forum, in 1924, and later acted as treasurer for the Blue Bonnets racetrack.

KEN REARDON'S first job as Frank Selke's assistant had been as chief of staff of the Cincinnati Mohawks which won the U.S. amateur championships five years in a row.

HECTOR DUBOIS was the team's trainer.

Other players to appear for the Canadiens this season: **CONNIE BRODEN, WALLY CLUNE, JACQUES DESLAURIERS, DICK GAMBLE, BOB PERREAULT**

1956–1957 THE CHAMPIONS Montreal Canadiens

This playoff year featured brawls, upsets, and goals, all in quantity. The Bruins upset the Red Wings in one semi-finals, but although they had 17 points out of 28 from the Canadiens during the season it was the potent offense of Richard and Geoffrion that carried the day in the finals. The two Habs forwards accounted for eight of 15 goals the team scored in the five-game march to the Stanley Cup. Incredibly, this was the franchise's seventh Cup and each one had been won on home ice. A civic reception for the team was held at St. Helen's Island the day after the victory.

STANLEY CUP FINALS

Montreal Canadiens win best-of-seven Stanley Cup finals 4-1

*April 6, 1957 Boston Bruins 1 at Montreal Canadiens 5
*April 9, 1957 Boston Bruins 0 at Montreal Canadiens 1 (Jean Beliveau 2:27 2nd) [Jacques Plante]
**April 11, 1957 Montreal Canadiens 4 at Boston Bruins 2
**April 14, 1957 Montreal Canadiens 0 at Boston Bruins 2 [Don Simmons]
*April 16, 1957 Boston Bruins 1 at Montreal Canadiens 5 {Dickie Moore 0:14 2nd}

** played at the Forum, Montreal ** played at the Boston Garden*

The Habs receive the Cup on ice after their 1957 victory.

MONTREAL	GP	G	A	P	Pim
Bernie Geoffrion	5	4	2	6	2
Doug Harvey	5	0	5	5	6
Maurice Richard	5	4	0	4	2
Floyd Curry	5	2	2	4	0
Dickie Moore	5	1	3	4	2
Don Marshall	5	1	2	3	2
Jean Beliveau	5	1	1	2	6
Phil Goyette	5	1	1	2	2
Bert Olmstead	5	0	2	2	9
Henri Richard	5	0	2	2	8
Tom Johnson	5	0	2	2	2
Andre Pronovost	3	1	0	1	0
Dollard St. Laurent	5	0	1	1	9
Claude Provost	5	0	1	1	2
Connie Broden	4	0	1	1	0
Jean-Guy Talbot	5	0	0	0	6
Jacques Plante	5	0	0	0	0
Bob Turner	2	0	0	0	0

In Goal	GP	W-L	Mins	GA	SO	Avg
Jacques Plante	5	4-1	300	5	1	1.00

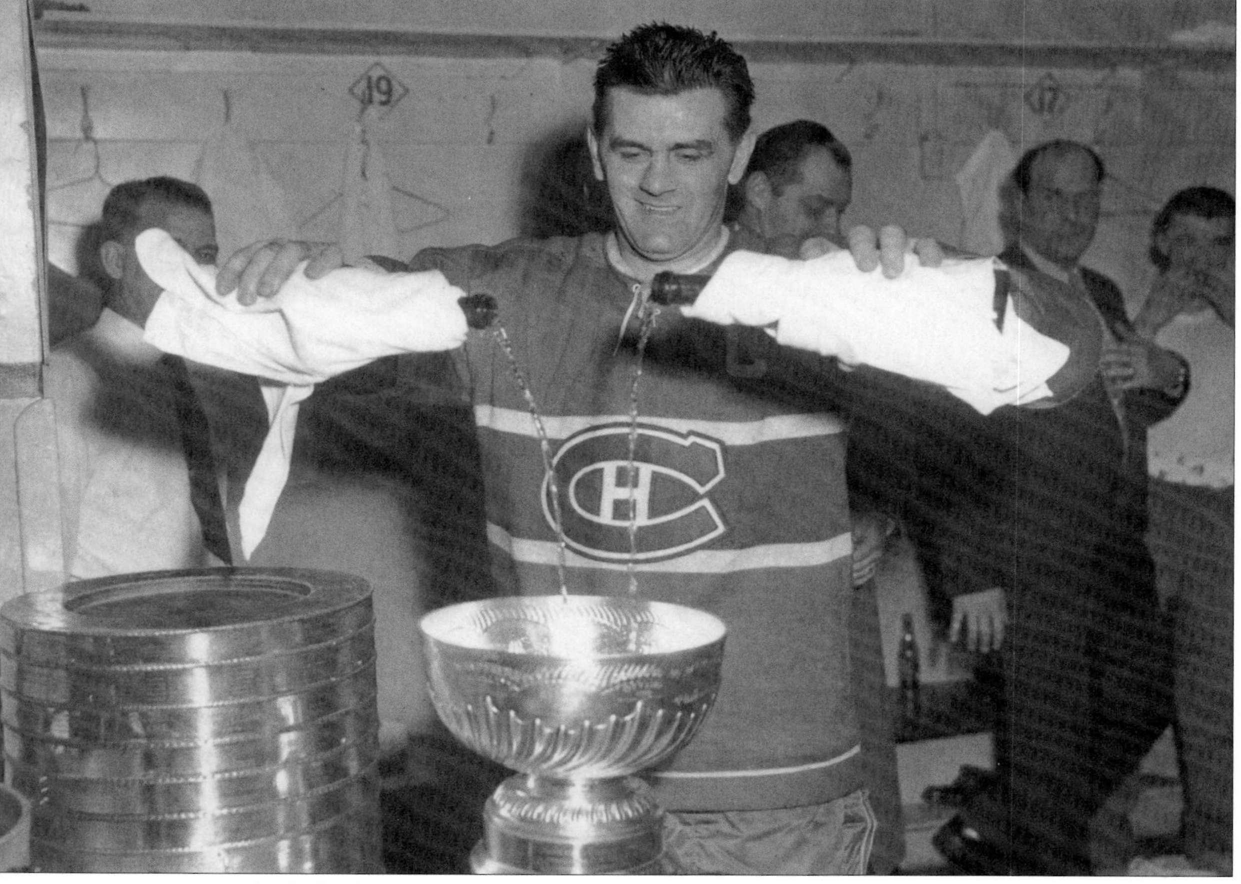

Maurice Richard takes the top half of the Cup away from the base and starts the champagne celebration in the dressing room after the Canadiens' win.

Although **BERNIE GEOFFRION** had been bothered by a bad elbow for much of the regular season, he regained his health in time for the playoffs and led all scorers with 18 points.

DOUG HARVEY was the Habs' representative of the controversial players' union that started in February 1957 but was quashed by the league owners in short order.

"You just can't compare him to ordinary mortals," spake Frank Selke on **ROCKET RICHARD**, who had had an operation to remove bone chips in his elbow earlier in the year before having another excellent season.

FLOYD CURRY Night at the Forum was held March 14 for the player who had appeared in 555 games for Montreal. He was showered with presents and thank-yous, notably in the form of a new car.

DICKIE MOORE suffered from a recurring shoulder dislocation problem that forced him to wear a special harness for the rest of his career.

DON MARSHALL'S versatility endeared him to coach Blake. Although he was listed as a centre, he frequently played the wing. "Every team must have a Marshall," Blake explained. "He could scale peaks on one set line, but we get more mileage out of him [moving him around]."

Ever the gentleman, **JEAN BELIVEAU** got into a rare scrap with one of the best, Lou Fontinato, in game one of the semi-finals vs. the Rangers.

A rookie call-up late in the season, **PHIL GOYETTE** earned increasing amounts of ice time as the playoffs continued.

OLMSTEAD couldn't skate," Jacques Plante explained of defenceman **BERT**. "And he isn't stylish. All he can do is win."

HENRI was the youngest of six Richard children born of a railroad carpenter. He was painfully shy growing up but was as much a Hall of Famer as his brother.

TOM JOHNSON was spotted by Frank Selke while playing for the Winnipeg Monarchs, a Leafs'-sponsored team, but Toronto wasn't interested in him and Selke signed him as a free agent for the Canadiens.

ANDRE PRONOVOST was the only new player added to the Canadiens from the previous Cup-winning season.

DOLLARD ST. LAURENT suffered an acute pinched nerve when he was 13 and had to give up skating for three years. At 16, he became stick and water boy for the Junior Canadiens and started skating with the team, working his leg back into shape and becoming an NHLer in the process.

CLAUDE PROVOST'S game changed forever at the 1961 All-Star Game when he sat beside Gordie Howe and noticed how short Howe's stick was. Provost cut his down accordingly and scored at about double his previous pace for the rest of his career.

CONNIE BRODEN retired after this season because he refused to play in the minors again (where he had played the entire regular season). He made a couple of brief and successful returns but retired for good in 1959.

Team engraving from the Stanley Cup

Team engraving from the replica Cup

Team engraving from the shoulder of the original Cup

JEAN-GUY TALBOT went the entire year without scoring a goal, but he was part of a defence corps that allowed the fewest goals in the league, culminating in the finals when the Bruins scored but six times in five games.

JACQUES PLANTE was just now starting to become famous for leaving the net to play the puck. "At one time," he explained, "I was playing with such a weak team that I had to leave my cage to keep control of the puck."

BOB TURNER played in six successive All-Star Games (1956-61) though he never made the end of the year First or Second All-Star team voted on by the league's coaches.

"I've got some great hockey players here. But unless we play as a team, it won't matter." Coach **TOE BLAKE'S** philosophy.

GERRY McNEIL quit after one final insult from former coach Dick Irvin, but former teammate and current coach Blake signed him to a full-salary contract as a backup who played only sparingly.

WILLIAM NORTHEY came from the old school and rued the transfer in social popularity from amateur to professional sports. Nonetheless, he embraced the NHL wholeheartedly for its qualities.

DONAT RAYMOND sat on many of the city's most important boards, including the Chamber of Commerce, Board of Trade, Reform Club, the Fire Insurance Company of Canada, and the Cercle Universitaire.

One of the game's hardest hitters, **KEN REARDON** was known for getting from A to B by the fastest possible route—a straight line—regardless of who or what stood in his way.

"Strong defence, good physical condition, and team work are the elements that make for a winning hockey team," **FRANK SELKE** offered. "I began to realize this when I was 14 and had a year of managing behind me."

HECTOR DUBOIS was the Canadiens' trainer.

Trainer **LARRY AUBUT** sold ads for the team programme in the summer. He had an office at the Forum, but during the season he was the Habs' equipment man.

Other players to appear for the Canadiens this season: **GENE ACHTYMICHUK, RALPH BACKSTROM, MURRAY BALFOUR, GLENN CRESSMAN, BRONCO HORVATH, AL JOHNSON, JACKIE LeCLAIR, BUD MacPHERSON, GUY ROUSSEAU, STAN SMRKE, JERRY WILSON**

1957 THE CHAMPIONS
1958 Montreal Canadiens

Montreal had all it could handle in the finals, a series whose turning point came in overtime of game five, with each team having won twice. An extra period goal from Maurice Richard proved the margin of victory, and Boston succumbed on home ice three nights later. Boston fans booed so vociferously during the Cup presentation to Montreal that the league's board of governors questioned whether to make the on-ice presentation of the Cup ever again.

STANLEY CUP FINALS

Montreal Canadiens win best-of-seven Stanley Cup finals 4-2

*April 8, 1958	Boston Bruins 1 at Montreal Canadiens 2
*April 10, 1958	Boston Bruins 5 at Montreal Canadiens 2
**April 13, 1958	Montreal Canadiens 3 at Boston Bruins 0 [Jacques Plante]
**April 15, 1958	Montreal Canadiens 1 at Boston Bruins 3
*April 17, 1958	Boston Bruins 2 at Montreal Canadiens 3 (Maurice Richard 5:45 OT)
**April 20, 1958	Montreal Canadiens 5 at Boston Bruins 3 {Bernie Geoffrion 19:26 2nd}

** played at the Forum, Montreal ** played at the Boston Garden*

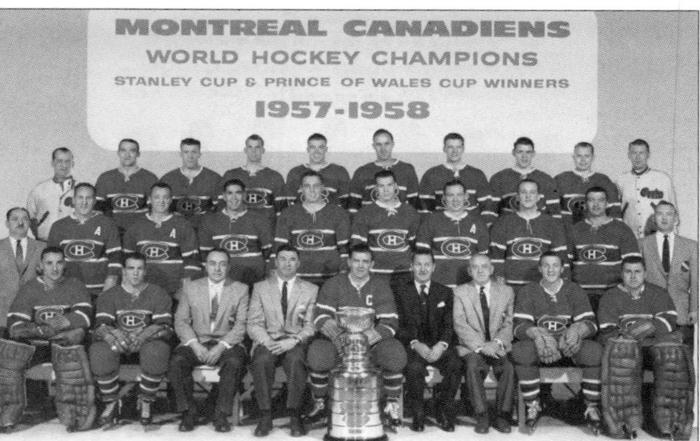

Montreal Canadiens, 1957-58

MONTREAL	GP	G	A	P	Pim
Bernie Geoffrion	6	5	3	8	0
Doug Harvey	6	2	5	7	8
Jean Beliveau	6	2	4	6	8
Dickie Moore	6	1	5	6	2
Maurice Richard	6	4	1	5	8
Henri Richard	6	1	2	3	9
Claude Provost	6	1	0	1	2
Marcel Bonin	5	0	1	1	10
Don Marshall	6	0	1	1	0
Bert Olmstead	5	0	1	1	0
Andre Pronovost	6	0	0	0	10
Dollard St. Laurent	4	0	0	0	8
Jean-Guy Talbot	6	0	0	0	6
Phil Goyette	6	0	0	0	2
Bob Turner	6	0	0	0	2
Ab McDonald	1	0	0	0	2
Jacques Plante	6	0	0	0	0
Floyd Curry	3	0	0	0	0
Al Langlois	3	0	0	0	0
Tom Johnson	2	0	0	0	0
Connie Broden	1	0	0	0	0

In Goal	GP	W-L	Mins	GA	SO	Avg
Jacques Plante	6	4-2	366	14	1	2.30

(left) Newspaper cartoon announces the Habs' third straight Cup victory; (top) Bert Olmstead's miniature Stanley Cup bowl.

Team engraving from the shoulder of the original Cup

That **"BOOM BOOM" GEOFFRION** was alive was a miracle in itself. After being hit by a stick early in the year, he required life-saving bowel surgery to repair a perforated intestine and missed most of the season.

DOUG HARVEY'S remarkable endurance was never more noticeable than game three of the finals when he played about 45 minutes. It was hockey's gain that he had rejected pro offers in both baseball and football during his youth.

JEAN BELIVEAU was completing the final year of his five-year, $100,000 contract. It was now up to GM Selke to work out another agreement with his star, with a nice raise, keeping him the highest paid player in the game.

Diggin' **DICKIE MOORE** won the Art Ross Trophy by four points over teammate Henri Richard, despite playing with a broken wrist that handicapped him for much of the year.

Like Moore and Geoffrion, **MAURICE RICHARD** missed much of the regular season, in his case because of a serious Achilles tendon injury. Yet he scored three goals in a 4-3 win over Detroit to eliminate the Wings in the semis, and four more goals in the finals.

In just his third year, **HENRI RICHARD** led the league in assists with 52 and finished second in points with 80, just four behind teammate Dickie Moore.

In game one of the finals, **CLAUDE PROVOST** was hit in the face by Leo Labine's stick, smashing his nose and loosening many front teeth.

MARCEL BONIN was acquired from Boston in the Intra-League Draft (via Springfield of the AHL) on June 4, 1957.

DON MARSHALL was later traded to the New York Rangers in a blockbuster deal that saw the Habs also give up on Jacques Plante and Phil Goyette.

BERT OLMSTEAD had knee problems which the Habs believed meant the end of his career. They let Toronto claim him in the Draft, and he won another Cup with the Leafs in '62 to prove the Habs wrong.

ANDRE PRONOVOST scored the back-breaking, overtime goal against Detroit in the semi-finals that gave the Habs an insurmountable 3-0 lead in the series.

DOLLARD ST. LAURENT wore a special face mask to protect a broken cheekbone, but he had to discard it when the league ruled it was potentially injurious to other players.

JEAN-GUY TALBOT broke his leg in February during practise when he collided with Claude Laforge, who himself was a callup to replace the injured Bert Olmstead. Talbot missed a month but was healthy for the playoffs.

Although **PHIL GOYETTE** was goalless in the finals, he scored four times in the semi-finals, including a hat trick in the opening game of that series.

BOB TURNER had 28 points in the regular season, almost triple the number of his next best season (ten points in '61-'62 with Chicago).

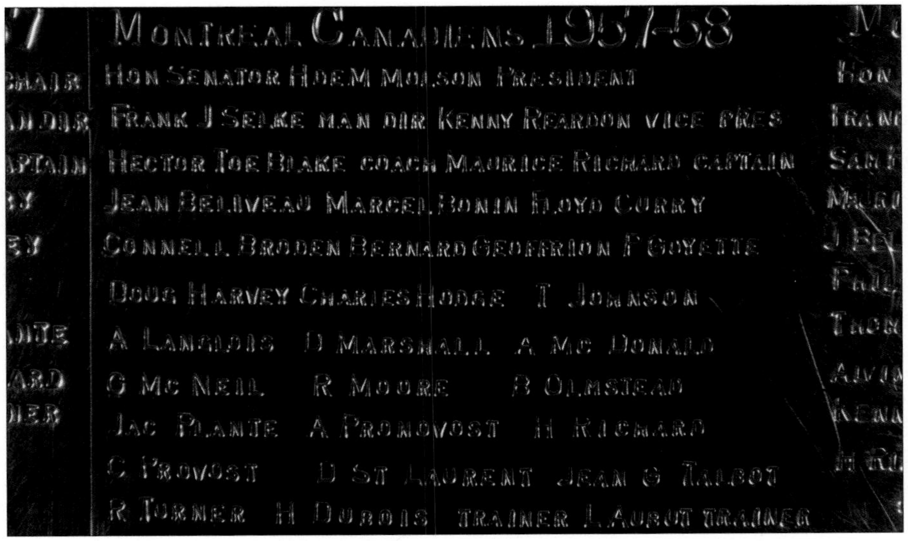

Team engraving from the Stanley Cup

AB McDONALD made two brief appearances in these playoffs—once in the semis, once in the finals—to start his career on a Cup-winning note.

JACQUES PLANTE was knocked unconscious in game three vs. Detroit when he was hit from behind by Bob Bailey while out of his crease to play the puck. He recovered, and Montreal went on to win the game, 2-1.

GERRY McNEIL spent the full year in Rochester, though technically he was the Habs' backup and as a result got his name on the Cup even though he didn't play a single minute for the team.

In his last season, **FLOYD CURRY** went out with a whimper, not a bang, playing only half a season and dressing only three times in the finals.

AL LANGLOIS played the final game of the regular season for the Canadiens, and seven more in the playoffs, to win a Cup in what started out as a minor pro season for the youngster.

TOM JOHNSON was a master of recovery. He would poke his stick at the puck, forcing the skater to the outside, then turn inside and go to the net before the puck carrier got there. He was never outsmarted on a play.

CONNIE BRODEN became the first player to win a gold medal at the World Championships (in 1958 with the Whitby Dunlops) and a Stanley Cup in the same year.

CHARLIE HODGE was recalled to spot Plante on occasion, but his 12 regular season appearances was not enough to get his name on the Cup.

MURRAY BALFOUR scored a goal in his first game after being called up during the season. He had played twice the previous year.

Coming out of retirement for two regular season games, **KEN MOSDELL** did not play enough to get his name on the Cup.

The Honourable **HARTLAND DE MONTARVILLE MOLSON** bought the team at the start of the season for $4 million from another Senator and friend, Donat Raymond.

Shortly after this victory, **FRANK SELKE** announced that a picture of Dick Irvin would hang in the Canadiens' dressing room, the first and only coach so honoured by the team.

In March 1973, **KEN REARDON** exchanged stick and puck for bait and tackle as he was named manager of the Atlantic Salmon Association (ASA).

BLAKE was brother and taskmaster both to the players. He ruled with "an iron fist in a velvet glove," as one account described, and extracted top performances from every skater.

DONAT RAYMOND'S name first appeared on the Cup in 1926 and this was his last appearance as the Molson family took over full operations of the team. Raymond died five years later of a heart attack at the Hotel Dieu Hospital in Montreal.

HECTOR DUBOIS remained the team's trainer.

LARRY AUBUT was nicknamed Red, and players pronounced his name "Awe-butt."

Other players to appear for the Canadiens this season: **GENE ACHTYMICHUK, JOHN AIKEN, RALPH BACKSTROM, JACK BOWNASS, LEN BRODERICK, BILLY CARTER, CLAUDE LAFORGE, STAN SMRKE**

1958–1959 THE CHAMPIONS Montreal Canadiens

Despite Toronto's miracle stretch run to qualify for the playoffs, the Leafs were no match for Montreal in the finals as the Habs became the first team to win four Cups in a row. They started the year by beating the All-Stars 6-3 in the annual game, only the third time the Cup champs had prevailed over the best of the rest. The Cup was carried onto the ice only briefly. It was given to the team more formally at a party at the Queen Elizabeth Hotel in Montreal immediately after the game where it was handed over to Jean Beliveau and Butch Bouchard.

STANLEY CUP FINALS

Montreal Canadiens win best-of-seven Stanley Cup finals 4-1

*April 9, 1959 Toronto Maple Leafs 3 at Montreal Canadiens 5
*April 11, 1959 Toronto Maple Leafs 1 at Montreal Canadiens 3
**April 14, 1959 Montreal Canadiens 2 at Toronto Maple Leafs 3 (Dick Duff 10:06 OT)
**April 16, 1959 Montreal Canadiens 3 at Toronto Maple Leafs 2
*April 18, 1959 Toronto Maple Leafs 3 at Montreal Canadiens 5 {Marcel Bonin 9:55 2nd}

** played at the Forum, Montreal ** played at Maple Leaf Gardens, Toronto*

Marcel Bonin (#18) and Bernie Geoffrion hold the Cup.

MONTREAL	GP	G	A	P	Pim
Ralph Backstrom	5	3	4	7	8
Bernie Geoffrion	5	3	4	7	6
Henri Richard	5	1	5	6	5
Doug Harvey	5	0	6	6	10
Marcel Bonin	5	3	2	5	2
Dickie Moore	5	2	3	5	8
Claude Provost	5	2	2	4	2
Tom Johnson	5	2	1	3	2
Ab McDonald	5	1	1	2	0
Phil Goyette	5	0	2	2	0
Andre Pronovost	5	1	0	1	0
Bob Turner	5	0	1	1	8
Jean-Guy Talbot	5	0	1	1	6
Don Marshall	5	0	1	1	0
Al Langlois	4	0	0	0	2
Maurice Richard	4	0	0	0	2
Jacques Plante	5	0	0	0	0
Bill Hicke	1	0	0	0	0

In Goal	GP	W-L	Mins	GA	SO	Avg
Jacques Plante	5	4-1	310	12	0	2.32

(above) Goalie Jacques Plante is at his brave best, covering the lower part of the net as players from both sides fight for puck possession; (right) Marcel Bonin and coach Toe Blake celebrate the team's fourth straight Cup after the game of April 18, 1959, at the Forum.

Montreal signed **RALPH BACKSTROM** on the recommendation of their minor league scout Sam Pollock, and Backstrom produced a Calder Trophy season.

In 1960-61, **BERNIE GEOFFRION** scored 50 goals in 64 games, the first player to hit 50 since Maurice Richard in 1944-45.

HENRI RICHARD was only six when his brother made the NHL, so he rarely saw Maurice play. When they became teammates, the Rocket credited his younger brother with keeping him in the game longer than he might otherwise have remained.

Goalie **CHARLIE HODGE** acted as backup to Plante which this season consisted of playing exactly two games.

IAN CUSHENAN was purchased by Chicago in the hopes he could replace Junior Langlois, but ultimately his defensive work proved not up to Montreal snuff and he was sold right back to the Hawks in the summer.

When Jean Beliveau went down with an injury, **KEN MOSDELL** came out of retirement for three games in the series against Chicago, enough to get his name on the Cup one last time.

DOUG HARVEY'S penchant for passing when most players would shoot was easily explained: "I would not get any bonus for scoring a certain number of goals during one season, so why not help those who were paid?"

MARCEL BONIN was the surprise hero of the playoffs who raised the level of his game under pressure and led the league with ten goals after scoring only 13 all season. But he had a secret weapon: he used Rocket Richard's gloves after Richard went down with an injury early in the post season. When Maurice returned to action, he had to use a new pair to ensure Bonin continued his scoring ways!

DICKIE MOORE produced the rare double of leading the league in scoring for both the regular season (96) and playoffs (17 points).

CLAUDE PROVOST scored the winning goals in games five and six of the semi-finals versus Chicago, including the series clincher at 18:32 of the third period, and in the finals he scored the second and third goals in Montreal's 3-1 win over Toronto in game two.

TOM JOHNSON won the Norris Trophy and was voted to the First All-Star Team on defence as well, usurping Harvey who had won the Norris each of the previous four years.

ALVIN (AB) McDONALD replaced Bert Olmstead full-time on left wing and made a solid contribution to the team.

The classic hockey-as-a-kid story holds true for **PHIL GOYETTE**. He and his brother, Ray, had a backyard rink in Lachine, Quebec thanks to their industrious father who froze their lawn morning and night all winter long.

Despite never scoring more than 16 goals in a season, **ANDRE PRONOVOST** later scored 50 with Muskegon in the IHL where he ended up after expansion.

BOB TURNER played for Montreal in 1961 when Chicago upset the five-time champs in the semi-finals. That summer, he was traded to the Hawks, and a year later his team again

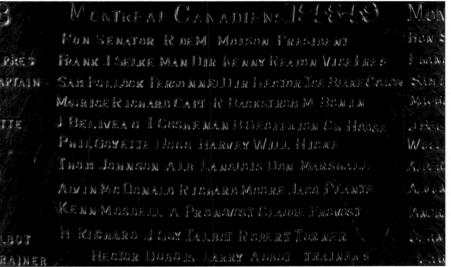

Team engraving from the Stanley Cup

Team engraving from the shoulder of the original Cup

defeated Montreal in the semi-finals of the 1962 playoffs.

JEAN-GUY TALBOT was quickly becoming an all-around defenceman. He could move the puck, play well behind his own blueline, and developed a sense for hard, timely bodychecks.

DON MARSHALL'S goal production plummeted this year to ten, down from 22 the previous season when he scored timely and important goals down the stretch run of the regular season.

AL LANGLOIS earned a spot on the team after a spot had been opened with the selling of St. Laurent to Chicago.

After breaking his ankle in Chicago in mid-January, **MAURICE RICHARD** missed the rest of the regular season and was a shadow of his former self in these playoffs.

JACQUES PLANTE'S hockey philosophy was honest and simple: "You never get tired of winning the Cup. Each time I would have paid money to win that Cup."

BILL HICKE made his NHL debut in game two of the finals, enough to get his name on the Cup.

After cracking two vertebrae in game three of the semi-finals against Chicago, **JEAN BELIVEAU** missed the finals altogether, though his absence seemed hardly to bother the team.

Coaches **TOE BLAKE** and Punch Imlach had a war of words all finals. Said Imlach: "We're going to beat them in six games. A good fighting club with balance will beat a club that has superstars on it every time." Replied Blake: "I guess everything is all settled then. I don't see any reason for playing the finals unless perhaps for the money."

Senator **MOLSON** played an important role in improving the league's owner-player relations and was key to securing the financing for the building of the first Hockey Hall of Fame in 1961.

It was under the direction of **FRANK SELKE** that the Forum's roof was raised and the seating capacity increased from 9,600 to 13,925 and the building upgraded to reflect more the on-ice success of the team.

KEN REARDON—his name misspelled "Readon"—had been a fighter and winner all his life. Orphaned at 14, he and his three siblings moved out to Winnipeg to live with their uncle. Ken rode a bike eight hours a day as a CNR telegraph messenger and played hockey at nights. After two years, he gave up the wheels and focused on hockey (as did his brother, Terry, who also made the NHL).

SAMUEL PATTERSON SMYTH POLLOCK would become general manager in Montreal in 1964 after 16 years in the organization. He became known for chewing on a handkerchief during tense times.

HECTOR DUBOIS and **LARRY AUBUT** were the trainers responsible for equipment and the well-being of the players, day in and day out.

Other players to appear for the Canadiens this season: **CLAUDE CYR, CLAUDE PRONOVOST**

1959–1960 THE CHAMPIONS Montreal Canadiens

Often called the best NHL team of all time, the Habs set two remarkable records this year: this was their fifth Cup in a row and their tenth successive appearance in the finals. Montreal Mayor Fournier held a reception at City Hall for the players and their wives when they returned to the city, though this was to be Montreal's last Cup for five years.

STANLEY CUP FINALS

Montreal Canadiens win best-of-seven Stanley Cup finals 4-0

*April 7, 1960 Toronto Maple Leafs 2 at Montreal Canadiens 4
*April 9, 1960 Toronto Maple Leafs 1 at Montreal Canadiens 2
**April 12, 1960 Montreal Canadiens 5 at Toronto Maple Leafs 2
**April 14, 1960 Montreal Canadiens 4 at Toronto Maple Leafs 0
{Jean Beliveau 8:16 1st} [Jacques Plante]

** played at the Forum, Montreal ** played at Maple Leaf Gardens, Toronto*

Players from Montreal and Toronto shake hands after the final game.

(clockwise) Montreal Mayor Jean Drapeau watches Maurice Richard do a radio interview on April 16, 1960; Richard accepts the Stanley Cup right after the game from NHL president Clarence Campbell; action from the Toronto-Montreal finals.

MONTREAL	GP	G	A	P	Pim
Henri Richard	4	3	5	8	9
Bernie Geoffrion	4	0	6	6	0
Dickie Moore	4	2	3	5	2
Jean Beliveau	4	4	0	4	4
Maurice Richard	4	1	2	3	2
Doug Harvey	4	2	0	2	6
Phil Goyette	4	2	0	2	2
Al Langlois	4	0	2	2	12
Marcel Bonin	4	0	2	2	6
Don Marshall	4	1	0	1	0
Jean-Guy Talbot	4	0	1	1	4
Bill Hicke	4	0	1	1	0
Andre Pronovost	4	0	1	1	0
Claude Provost	4	0	1	1	0
Ralph Backstrom	4	0	0	0	2
Tom Johnson	4	0	0	0	2
Jacques Plante	4	0	0	0	0
Bob Turner	4	0	0	0	0

In Goal	GP	W-L	Mins	GA	SO	Avg
Jacques Plante	4	4-0	240	5	1	1.25

"When I see my name on the Cup, I think of all the great players I had with me...That 1960 team was the best I ever played on." **HENRI RICHARD**.

BERNIE GEOFFRION set a record not likely to be broken: 53 consecutive games in the Stanley Cup finals, going from 1951 to 1960.

"If we had to sum up in a word what makes us go, I'd say 'pride,'" **DICKIE MOORE** said, reflecting on his team's unparalleled success.

Centre **JEAN BELIVEAU** was an uncharacteristic model of streaky this season. He went goalless in 12 of the first 16 games on the year, then was past 20 by Christmas and had fans thinking 50, and ended up with only 34, well below his league-leading total of 45 a year ago.

AB McDONALD was a spare part who didn't see much ice time on many nights. He was one of a few Montreal players of his era who was happy for a trade, to Chicago, where he could be given a chance to make a greater contribution.

After scoring in game three of the finals, **MAURICE RICHARD** pocketed the puck, a sign for all to see that this was his last year in the league. After the game, Leafs coach Punch Imlach came into the dressing room to congratulate the Rocket personally.

"When you win 4-0 in four games and after four Cup titles, you don't get too excited." **DOUG HARVEY**, adopting an attitude so different from Plante's of the previous spring.

PHIL GOYETTE played on a line with Pronovost and Provost for years. In the off season, he worked for a brokerage house and pursued that career full-time after retiring.

AL LANGLOIS was nicknamed Junior because his father had the same name. He had one regret from his Cup days with the Habs: "In all the times I was around the Stanley Cup during team celebrations," he said, "I never had my picture taken alone with the Stanley Cup."

MARCEL BONIN'S career came to an end in a game versus Detroit on February 9, 1962, when he suffered a serious back injury that eventually forced him to retire.

DON MARSHALL scored the opening goal of game three of the finals to get the team off on the right track en route to a 5-2 win and a commanding 3-0 lead in the series.

JEAN-GUY TALBOT scored a goal in game three of the semi-finals against Chicago, his first career playoff goal in 43 games.

BILL HICKE arrived in Montreal to praises of "the new Rocket" following a 41-goal year with Rochester and two, 50-goal seasons with Regina out West, but after scoring just three times in 43 games with the Habs, he struggled just to keep his job.

Unrelated to the three other NHL **PRONOVOSTS**—Claude, Jean, and Marcel—**ANDRE** was traded early the next season to Boston for Jean-Guy Gendron.

CLAUDE PROVOST scored an empty-netter in the last second of game two of the finals, but referee Powers ruled the red light flashed before the green and refused to count it.

Team engraving from the Stanley Cup

Team engraving from the shoulder of the original Cup

RALPH BACKSTROM played in three Memorial Cups under Sam Pollock and won the Calder Trophy in 1959-60. He injured his knee at the start of this year and suffered a bit of the sophomore jinx in a sub-par second NHL season.

When Frank Selke signed **TOM JOHNSON**, the joke was that the Manitoba native had never played in a covered arena and wouldn't last a minute in the NHL. Six Cups later, Johnson proved his critics wrong.

On November 1, 1959, hockey changed forever. That night, goalie **JACQUES PLANTE** was hit by a shot, and after leaving the ice for stitches returned wearing a facemask. Incredibly, in game four of the semi-finals, he was hit in the face by an Earl Balfour shot and, despite the mask, had to leave the game for repairs.

BOB TURNER later coached the Regina Pats to a Memorial Cup win in 1974. "That was definitely a greater thrill for me than winning the Stanley Cup," he confessed. "It meant a lot to me to coach young players to a championship."

"This is the greatest hockey team ever assembled," remarked **FRANK SELKE**, who retired to his 168-acre farm in Rigaud, Quebec, to raise Belted Galloway cattle and some 100 species of chickens.

J-C TREMBLAY was the lone rookie to crack the lineup and make an appearance with the team this season.

CHARLIE HODGE appeared in exactly one game all year, replacing the injured Jacques Plante who played the other 69 games and every playoff minute for the Canadiens.

SENATOR MOLSON served as president, then chairman of the Habs, from 1957 to '68 and was responsible for the upgrading and modernizing of the Forum in the 1960s.

Midway through the season, **KEN REARDON** was named vice-president of the team, just reward for a loyal relationship that dated back to 1940.

Technically, **SAM POLLOCK** was still not part of the Habs. He had coached the farm team in Rochester briefly and currently was general manager of the Hull-Ottawa Canadiens in junior hockey.

In 1972, four years after **TOE BLAKE** retired, the team held a special dinner for their coach, at which time they gave him a special trophy made putatively in part of silver from the original Stanley Cup.

Despite being "mere" trainers, **HECTOR DUBOIS** and **LARRY AUBUT** have their name on the Cup more than most players in the history of the game!

Other players to appear for the Canadiens this season: **REG FLEMING, CEC HOEKSTRA**

1960 THE CHAMPIONS
1961 Chicago Black Hawks

"The Black Hawks have come in four years from drinking beer in the cellar to drinking champagne in the penthouse," described one reporter of the team's ascent. For whatever reason, "Black Hawks" is in quotations marks, the only nickname on the Cup so represented. As important as the victory in the finals was Chicago's elimination of Montreal in the semi-finals, the first time the Habs had been beaten in the playoffs since 1955. The victory was sparked by Murray Balfour's goal in triple overtime of game three. The Hawks were snowed in in Detroit after clinching the Cup, so James Norris invited everyone to his hotel for a party, on condition that they bring the Cup! The Hawks were later given a downtown parade in Chicago, and each player received a Stanley Cup ring.

STANLEY CUP FINALS

Chicago Black Hawks win best-of-seven Stanley Cup finals 4-2

*April 6, 1961	Detroit Red Wings 2 at Chicago Black Hawks 3
**April 8, 1961	Chicago Black Hawks 1 at Detroit Red Wings 3
*April 10, 1961	Detroit Red Wings 1 at Chicago Black Hawks 3
**April 12, 1961	Chicago Black Hawks 1 at Detroit Red Wings 2
*April 14, 1961	Detroit Red Wings 3 at Chicago Black Hawks 6
**April 16, 1961	Chicago Black Hawks 5 at Detroit Red Wings 1 {Ab McDonald 18:49 2nd}

** played at the Chicago Stadium ** played the the Olympia, Detroit*

Players and wives pose for a portrait with Stanley at the team dinner.

(clockwise) Action from the 1961 Cup finals between Detroit and the Black Hawks at the Stadium in Chicago; Arthur Wirtz (left) and James D. Norris examine the names on the Cup; NHL president Clarence Campbell and James Norris look at a mini-Cup.

CHICAGO	GP	G	A	P	Pim
Pierre Pilote	6	2	6	8	2
Stan Mikita	6	3	4	7	2
Bobby Hull	6	2	5	7	2
Murray Balfour	5	3	3	6	4
Bill Hay	6	1	3	4	8
Ken Wharram	6	2	1	3	10
Ron Murphy	6	2	1	3	0
Eric Nesterenko	6	1	1	2	2
Ab McDonald	6	1	1	2	0
Jack Evans	6	1	0	1	10
Reggie Fleming	6	1	0	1	2
Tod Sloan	6	0	1	1	6
Elmer Vasko	6	0	1	1	6
Dollard St. Laurent	5	0	1	1	2
Ed Litzenberger	4	0	1	1	0
Al Arbour	3	0	0	0	2
Wayne Hicks	1	0	0	0	2
Earl Balfour	6	0	0	0	0
Glenn Hall	6	0	0	0	0
Wayne Hillman	1	0	0	0	0
Chico Maki	1	0	0	0	0

In Goal	GP	W-L	Mins	GA	SO	Avg
Glenn Hall	6	4-2	360	12	0	2.00

PIERRE PILOTE'S slash on Eddie Shack in a game March 11 vs. Toronto precipitated a bench-clearing brawl and a record 41 penalties.

The first Czech-born star in the NHL, **STAN MIKITA** invented the banana blade. After winning, he was joined in the Chicago dressing room by Gordie Howe for a glass of champagne.

"He puts the fear of God in you," affirmed Detroit goalie Hank Bassen of **BOBBY HULL'S** famous slapper.

MURRAY BALFOUR played on a line with Hull and Hay dubbed the Million Dollar Line. His goal in triple overtime of game three in the semis against Montreal turned the series around and was key to winning a matchup his team likened to the finals.

After graduating from the University of Colorado with a degree in geology, **"RED" HAY** abandoned academia for a career in hockey.

KEN WHARRAM played on the Skooter Line with Mikita and McDonald but was forced into retirement a number of years later at age 36 because of a heart condition.

RON MURPHY is given the name "Robert" on the Cup. His career was fraught with injury, notably to a shoulder that was in such a chronic state that he finally had to retire.

ERIC NESTERENKO had quit the Leafs to return to school, but when the Hawks offered him the chance to play weekend games only, he agreed and later played full-time during this Cup-winning season.

After winning the Cup with Montreal in 1960, **AB McDONALD** was part of a multi-player trade to Chicago and won again with the Hawks. "I felt better winning the Stanley Cup with Chicago as a first- or second-line player than I did winning it twice with Montreal and playing as a fourth-line player," he admitted.

Between 1948 and '58, **JACK EVANS** had been bounced up and down in the Rangers' system, but during that time he could boast to have played for every single coach the franchise had had except for Lester Patrick.

REG FLEMING is perhaps best remembered for two nasty stick-swinging incidents, one with Gilles Tremblay of Montreal that required 35 stitches to close Tremblay's head and another when he speared Eddie Shack of Toronto.

TOD SLOAN had won a Memorial Cup with St. Mike's and spent the next dozen years in the Leafs' system before Toronto sold him outright to Chicago in the summer of 1958 where he retired after this year's victory.

An awkward skater with size, **ELMER VASKO** instilled fear in opponents when he started a rush, thus earning the moniker "Moose."

A stay-at-home defenceman, **DOLLARD ST. LAURENT** won his fifth Cup in nine years.

In January 1960, **ED LITZENBERGER** was involved in a car accident that killed his wife and seriously injured himself. As Chicago captain, it was he who accepted the Cup from president Campbell after the victory.

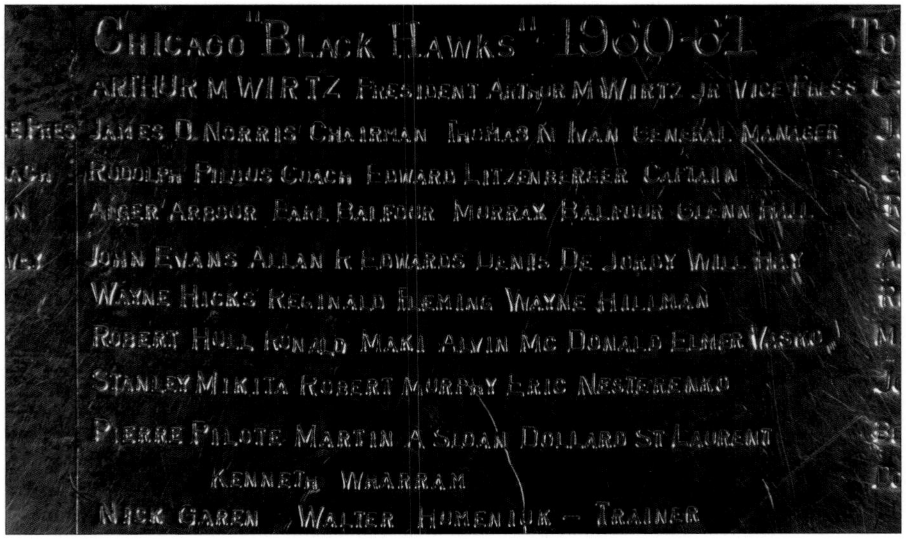

Team engraving from the Stanley Cup

AL ARBOUR was a bespectacled, rangy defenceman who was a bit awkward and rough around the edges but effective nonetheless.

The only American on the team, **WAYNE HICKS** had a son, Alex, who later played in the NHL as well. Junior assisted on Joe Mullen's 500th career goal in 1997.

EARL BALFOUR was in his last season, but after two more seasons in the minors he was reinstated as an amateur and played five more years of senior hockey in southern Ontario.

He was called Mr. Goalie for good reason, and his 501 consecutive games is a record that tenders will never, ever be broken. Incredibly, this was the only Cup in **GLENN HALL'S** illustrious 18-year career.

Introductions don't get any better than this. **WAYNE HILLMAN** made his NHL debut on April 16, 1961, the night the Hawks won the Cup, and got his name on the mug after just one night's play!

His real name was **RONALD** (aka "Chico") **MAKI**, and his brother was Wayne who got into a vicious stick fight with Ted Green in 1969 that almost cost Green his life.

"We can't skate with most teams," coach **RUDY PILOUS** admitted. "We got to knock them down."

ROY EDWARDS split the 1960-61 season between the Buffalo Bisons (AHL) and Sault Ste. Marie Thunderbirds (EPHL). He never played a single game for the Hawks before being selected by Pittsburgh in the Expansion Draft in 1967.

Why **DENIS DEJORDY'S** name is on the Cup is anyone's guess. Although he was Chicago property, he didn't play a single minute with the team all year, much like Joe Stark with the '34 Hawks whose name is also on the Cup.

The pinnacle of years of hard work and millions of dollars in losses, this Cup win was sweet justice for Arthur Wirtz and **JIM NORRIS** as they spent years investing in good players and developing a farm system.

ARTHUR WIRTZ was the father of Bill who became the club president in 1966.

"I'd much rather win the Stanley Cup than the Kentucky Derby," **JIM NORRIS** remarked. He was perhaps the only Original Six owner who didn't meddle in his team's hockey operations. He hired the right people, and let them do their jobs.

On the one hand, this was the culmination of seven years' work. On the other, **TOMMY IVAN** would be vilified a few years later for trading Phil Esposito, Ken Hodge, and Fred Stanfield to Boston.

Trainer **NICK GAREN** began life as Nick Garenovich but shortened his name for convenience. He later worked for the Rangers.

WALTER HUMENIUK, aka "Gunzo," became the team's practise goalie, the result of Glenn Hall almost never practising and ensuring his Iron Man streak continued. Humeniuk also owned a hockey equipment store that outfitted most of the U.S.-based teams in the '60s and '70s, and the trademark "Gunzo's" can be seen on hockey sticks of the day.

Other players to appear for Chicago this season: none

1961–1962 Toronto Maple Leafs

THE CHAMPIONS

A story of mythic proportions unfolded this summer when, after this Cup victory, the remains of Bill Barilko were discovered in Ontario's remote North. The Leafs hadn't won the Cup since 1951, the year Barilko disappeared, so the story was propagated that the team wouldn't, couldn't, win another until he was finally laid to rest. More directly, the team won because of Punch Imlach's style of play—nothing fancy; just determination, hard work, and pride. Each player received a special ring to commemorate the victory, consisting of a gold band with a white gold, raised maple leaf in the centre. It was during this year's semi-finals, in Chicago, that a Montreal fan tried to steal the Cup from its glass display case in the Chicago Stadium.

STANLEY CUP FINALS

Toronto Maple Leafs win best-of-seven Stanley Cup finals 4-2

*April 10, 1962	Chicago Black Hawks 1 at Toronto Maple Leafs 4
*April 12, 1962	Chicago Black Hawks 2 at Toronto Maple Leafs 3
**April 15, 1962	Toronto Maple Leafs 0 at Chicago Black Hawks 3 (Horvath 19:21 en) [Glenn Hall]
**April 17, 1962	Toronto Maple Leafs 1 at Chicago Black Hawks 4
*April 19, 1962	Chicago Black Hawks 4 at Toronto Maple Leafs 8
**April 22, 1962	Toronto Maple Leafs 2 at Chicago Black Hawks 1 {Dick Duff 14:14 3rd}

** played at Maple Leaf Gardens, Toronto   ** played at Chicago Stadium*

Players celebrate on ice after their six-game Cup win.

(above) Members of the Leafs make their way through an enormous parade crowd at City Hall in downtown Toronto; (left) action from the Chicago-Toronto finals of 1962.

TORONTO	GP	G	A	P	Pim
Frank Mahovlich	6	4	3	7	21
George Armstrong	6	3	4	7	0
Tim Horton	6	1	6	7	12
Dick Duff	6	1	4	5	16
Ron Stewart	6	0	5	5	2
Bob Pulford	6	3	0	3	14
Billy Harris	6	2	1	3	0
Dave Keon	6	2	1	3	0
Red Kelly	6	1	2	3	0
Bob Baun	6	0	3	3	15
Bob Nevin	6	1	1	2	4
Carl Brewer	6	0	1	1	18
Allan Stanley	6	0	1	1	2
Bert Olmstead	4	0	1	1	0
Eddie Shack	5	0	0	0	12
Ed Litzenberger	4	0	0	0	2
Johnny Bower	4	0	0	0	0
Don Simmons	3	0	0	0	0
Al Arbour	2	0	0	0	0

In Goal	GP	W-L	Mins	GA	SO	Avg
Johnny Bower	4	2-1	195	7	0	2.15
Don Simmons	3	2-1	165	8	0	2.91

Chicago owner Jim Norris had offered one million dollars for **FRANK MAHOVLICH** at the 1962 All-Star Game in Toronto, but the Leafs refused to become involved in the public relations stunt and held on to their star.

Captain **GEORGE ARMSTRONG** became the first leader to hand the Cup off to other teammates so they, too, could go for a victory lap with the cherished mug.

BILLY MacMILLAN had been invited to the Rangers' training camp after playing junior with the Lethbridge Native Sons, but when his father passed away he opted for an education at the University of Denver.

TIM HORTON assisted on the Cup-winning goal with a spectacular end-to-end rush before passing off to Duff alone in front of the Chicago goal. Horton led the team in playoff points this year with 16.

Despite missing more than a quarter of the season with a broken ankle, **RICHARD "DICK" DUFF** returned to form in time for the playoffs.

RON STEWART was one of the longest-serving Leafs of all time, a member of the team since 1952.

Though not a great scorer, **BOB PULFORD** was a great two-way player and penalty killer who could be counted on to score 20 goals a season.

BILLY HARRIS took his interest in photography into the dressing room after the victory, creating his own catalogue of images documenting the Leafs' Cup victory.

DAVE KEON had quite a year. He played in the All-Star Game, was named to the NHL's Second All-Star team, and won the Lady Byng Trophy.

RED KELLY played for the Leafs and later sat as an MP for York West in the House of Commons. He had to miss the celebrations to return to Ottawa but had the Cup for an afternoon at his house in the summer. "He [his new baby] did a full load in the Cup, so we all chuckle when they drink out of it now," he later told of his newborn.

BOB BAUN and Bobby Hull were famous for their on-ice matchups. "Our battles went back to when we were 12 or 13...He was always playing left wing and I was on the right defence," Baun recalled.

In game six, it was **BOB NEVIN'S** inspirational play that ignited the Leafs to victory. With the team down 1-0, he converted a Big M pass to tie the game and then drew a penalty that led to a Dick Duff goal that won the Cup in the third period.

CARL BREWER had paid his dues early in his career—fighting the league's toughest, getting fined and suspended—and developing a reputation that earned him respect enough not to have to fight at every provocation later in his career.

The first man to hug **ALLAN STANLEY** after the victory was his father who had come down from Timmins for the game and dashed out onto the ice after the final bell.

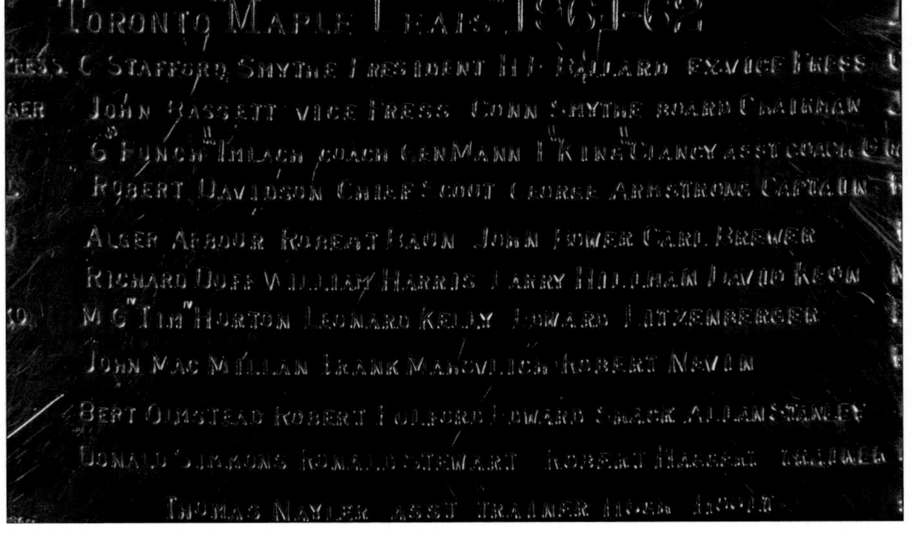

Team engraving from the Stanley Cup

BERT OLMSTEAD missed much of the playoffs with a broken shoulder but re-appeared in game three of the finals. He had been an assistant coach for Imlach briefly after the coach had claimed him at the Intra-League draft in 1958.

During the victory parade up Yonge St. in downtown Toronto, **EDDIE SHACK** stood in the back of a car and danced the latest sensation, the Twist.

LITZENBERGER was claimed on waivers by the Leafs from Detroit on December 29, 1961, but his best years (three, 30-goal seasons with Chicago) were now behind him.

The oldest player in the league, **JOHNNY BOWER** would remain so for another eight years before he hung up his pads for good.

Goalie **DON SIMMONS** replaced Bower in game four because of injury and played the rest of the series to win the Cup.

AL ARBOUR and Ed Litzenberger both achieved fame by winning the Cup with Chicago the previous year, then this year with the Leafs, two of only a dozen men to perform the double with different teams.

LARRY HILLMAN played for all Original Six teams except the Hawks and Rangers, winning Cups with Detroit, Toronto, and Montreal in a career that lasted 19 NHL years and another three in the WHA.

For his decades of service, **TOMMY NAYLER** was honoured this summer by the NHL and given a special plaque. In 1976, he was inducted into the Canadian Athletic Trainers' Association's Hall of Fame, in Winnipeg.

HUGH HOULT was the son of Jack Hoult and Miriam Smythe, sister of Hugh and daughter of Conn Smythe.

CONN SMYTHE'S plan was for his son, Stafford, to inherit the team and building, a plan that was scuppered by Stafford's misguided friendship with the manipulative Ballard.

Said Conn Smythe of **BALLARD**: "I would not give him a job at ten cents a week. His way of doing things is not mine."

JOHN BASSETT eventually sold his stock in the Leafs but his son a semi-successful run at the Gardens a number of years later as owner of the WHA Toros.

CONN SMYTHE had resigned as governor and put his son Stafford in his place. Conn was immediately named honourary governor, though he quickly severed contact with the team because of his dislike for Harold Ballard.

When he had been hired in 1958, coach **PUNCH IMLACH** vowed to leave his own mark on the team right from the get-go. "First, I'll run things my way, Mr. Smythe," he began. "If it doesn't work, we'll run it your way." It worked.

FRANCIS CLANCY inherited the name **KING** from his equally athletic father, though King the Younger more than lived up to the weight of the name during his Hall of Fame life in hockey.

BOB DAVIDSON was a lifelong Leaf who had been scouting almost since the day he retired in 1946. He became head scout in 1951 after the sudden death of Squib Walker.

Other players to appear for the Leafs this season: **ARNIE BROWN, BRIAN CONACHER, ALEX FAULKNER, LARRY KEENAN, LES KOZAK**

1962 THE CHAMPIONS 1963 Toronto Maple Leafs

For the first and only time since the NHL took control of the Cup in 1927, not a single playoff game went into overtime. The Leafs won the league title for the first time in fifteen years and then played almost unbeatable hockey in the playoffs. "We tried," said Detroit star Gordie Howe, shaking his head, "but it was like grumbling against thunder." The players' Cup rings of the year before were recalled and the Leafs installed a bigger diamond. The team's name on the Cup, however, was badly mangled, and history is left only with "Maple Leas."

STANLEY CUP FINALS

Toronto Maple Leafs win best-of-seven Stanley Cup finals 4-1

*April 9, 1963	Detroit Red Wings 2 at Toronto Maple Leafs 4
*April 11, 1963	Detroit Red Wings 2 at Toronto Maple Leafs 4
**April 14, 1963	Toronto Maple Leafs 2 at Detroit Red Wings 3
**April 16, 1963	Toronto Maple Leafs 4 at Detroit Red Wings 2
*April 18, 1963	Detroit Red Wings 1 at Toronto Maple Leafs 3 {Eddie Shack 13:28 3rd}

** played at Maple Leaf Gardens, Toronto* *** played at the Olympia, Detroit*

Toronto Maple Leafs, 1962-63

TORONTO	GP	G	A	P	Pim
Dave Keon	5	4	2	6	0
Red Kelly	5	2	2	4	2
Tim Horton	5	1	3	4	4
Allan Stanley	5	0	4	4	4
Bob Nevin	5	3	0	3	0
Dick Duff	5	2	1	3	2
Ed Litzenberger	5	1	2	3	4
George Armstrong	5	1	2	3	0
Bob Pulford	5	0	3	3	8
Ron Stewart	5	2	0	2	2
Eddie Shack	5	1	1	2	4
Bob Baun	5	0	1	1	6
Carl Brewer	5	0	1	1	4
Frank Mahovlich	4	0	1	1	4
Kent Douglas	5	0	1	1	2
Billy Harris	5	0	1	1	0
Johnny Bower	5	0	0	0	0
John MacMillan	1	0	0	0	0

In Goal	GP	W-L	Mins	GA	SO	Avg
Johnny Bower	5	4-1	300	10	0	2.00

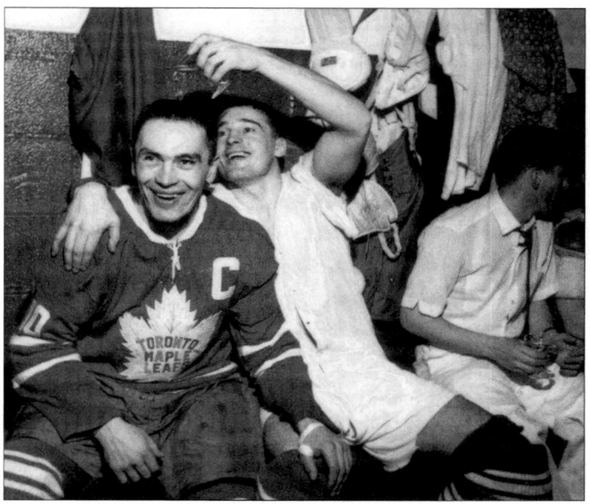

(clockwise) Dave Keon beats Terry Sawchuk with a shot while short-handed late in the first period of game five at Maple Leaf Gardens to give the Leafs an early 1-0 lead; a lighter given to the players to commemorate their victory; Frank Mahovlich douses captain George Armstrong in the dressing room after the final game.

DAVE KEON scored two goals in the Cup-deciding game, both short-handed to tie a league record. He also won the Lady Byng for the second straight year, accruing just two minor penalties in those two seasons.

RED KELLY could have been a Leaf from Day One of his career, but when Leafs super-scout Squib Walker took a look at Red at St. Mike's, he saw a player he didn't think would last 20 games.

Almost blind without his contact lenses, **TIM HORTON** made the Second All-Star team this season.

LARRY HILLMAN was Johnny Bower's dream—a solid, reliable, stay-at-home defenceman who had little interest in what happened north of his own blueline.

ALLAN STANLEY later opened the Beehive Resort on Sturgeon Lake, named in honour of the famous Corn Syrup Company that produced popular photos of hockey's stars during the 1940s and '50s.

Red Kelly gave **BOB NEVIN** much credit for their success with linemate Frank Mahovlich: "He's much more important to the team than people realize. Without him, Frank and I wouldn't get so many goals."

DICK DUFF set an NHL record by scoring two goals in the first 1:08 of game one, April 9, 1963 against the Wings, the fastest two goals from the start of a game.

ED LITZENBERGER is one of only two players to be traded during his rookie year and win the Calder Trophy, a feat he accomplished in 1954-55 when he started with Montreal but was sold to Chicago in December 1954.

Captain **GEORGE ARMSTRONG** took the Stanley Cup from the hands of NHL president Clarence Campbell after the final bell to begin the traditional skate around the rink.

After five part-time years of study at McMaster University, **BOB PULFORD** finally earned his B.A. this summer.

RON STEWART played the finals with cracked ribs but nonetheless scored four goals during these playoffs, two of which came in game two of the finals.

EDDIE SHACK had a knack for being in the right place at the right time. His Cup-winning goal in game five this year broke a 1-1 tie midway through the third period when a Kent Douglas shot hit him, then Doug Barkley, and trickled past a helpless Terry Sawchuk. Fortunately for Eddie, they all count.

Although **BOBBY BAUN** missed 22 games during the regular season with a knee injury, he had fully recovered for the playoffs when he continued to become one of the more determined shot-blockers in the league.

While Red Kelly's injury prevented him from partaking of the post-game celebrations, **CARL BREWER** suffered an even worse fate. With less than five minutes left in the final game, he broke his arm in a collision but watched the end of the game from the boards.

THE BIG M, FRANK MAHOVLICH, suffered from a knee injury that forced him to miss game two of the finals. Incredibly, he didn't score a single goal in the semi-finals or finals.

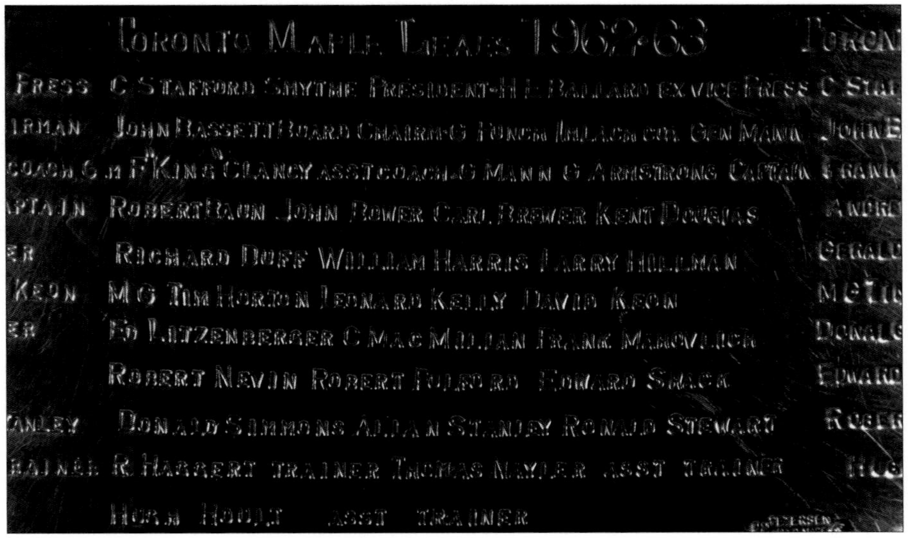

Team engraving from the Stanley Cup

Defenceman **KENT DOUGLAS** was the team's only rookie for the year. He won the Calder Trophy and Stanley Cup, a double that would not be accomplished again until the year 2000 with Scott Gomez in New Jersey.

BILLY HARRIS later coached in more places and at more levels than anyone before or since: Canadian, Swedish, and Italian national teams; Ontario junior; WHA; Canadian university.

PUNCH IMLACH liked to use Don Simmons in goal to get Johnny Bower going. When Bower complained of a sore leg, the coach would holler, "Where's Simmons?" to which Bower would hurriedly reply: "I'm okay! I'm okay!"

BILLY MacMILLAN played only a handful of games this year and went to Detroit early the following season after the Wings picked him up on waivers.

When the Leafs struggled early in the season, coach Imlach put part of the blame squarely on the pads of **JOHNNY BOWER**. He benched the number-one goalie and recalled **DON SIMMONS** from the minors, a move that motivated Bower to pick up his game.

BOBBY HAGGERT'S mother, Elsie, worked at the Gardens, serving sandwiches and drinks to both the media and visiting hockey executives in the Press Lounge.

TOMMY NAYLER was an inventor extraordinaire who didn't confine his scientific knowledge to hockey. Back in 1924 he had produced the first set of balanced golf clubs in Canada.

HUGH HOULT'S father, Jack, worked at Conn Smythe's gravel pits. After the war, Conn hired him to run the box office. Son Hugh was the stick boy for the team.

STAFFORD SMYTHE had been general manager of the Marlies when the team won back-to-back Memorial Cups in '55 and '56. He then became chairman of the Leafs' GM committee, dubbed the Silver Seven, that eventually hired Punch Imlach.

On August 15, 1972, **BALLARD** was convicted on 47 of 49 counts of fraud, though he spent only one year in jail, at Millhaven.

JOHN BASSETT was not only a member of the Leafs' Silver Seven GM committee of the late 1950's, he was also heavily involved in the *Toronto Telegram*, CFTO-TV, the Argonauts football club, and the federal PC party.

PUNCH IMLACH: "There is nothing unusual in our success. We work harder and practise longer than any of the other clubs."

KING CLANCY is the only man to play all six positions in one game, coach and referee an All-Star Game, coach an NHL team and referee in the NHL. Truly, he did it all.

Other players to appear for the Leafs this season: **AL ARBOUR, NORM ARMSTRONG, ANDRE CHAMPAGNE, BRUCE DRAPER, BRONCO HORVATH, JIM MIKOL, ROD SEILING**

1963 THE CHAMPIONS
1964 Toronto Maple Leafs

The finals was one of the closest in NHL history. Two games were won in overtime (one win each), while two others were won in the final seconds, Pulford winning game one for Toronto at 19:58, Delvecchio winning game three for the Red Wings at 19:43. Only the final game lacked the drama of the rest of the series. Last year, the team's name was misspelled on the Cup; this year's was worse—"Leaes." Toronto movie theatres showed games away from Toronto on a pay-per-view basis.

STANLEY CUP FINALS

Toronto Maple Leafs win best-of-seven Stanley Cup finals 4-3

*April 11, 1964	Detroit Red Wings 2 at Toronto Maple Leafs 3
*April 14, 1964	Detroit Red Wings 4 at Toronto Maple Leafs 3 (Larry Jeffrey 7:52 OT)
**April 16, 1964	Toronto Maple Leafs 3 at Detroit Red Wings 4
**April 18, 1964	Toronto Maple Leafs 4 at Detroit Red Wings 2
*April 21, 1964	Detroit Red Wings 2 at Toronto Maple Leafs 1
**April 23, 1964	Toronto Maple Leafs 4 at Detroit Red Wings 3 (Bob Baun 1:43 OT)
*April 25, 1964	Detroit Red Wings 0 at Toronto Maple Leafs 4 {Andy Bathgate 3:04 1st} [Johnny Bower]

** played at Maple Leaf Gardens, Toronto ** played at the Olympia, Detroit*

Toronto Maple Leafs, 1963-64

(clockwise) Johnny Bower makes a great save as two Wings go in unmolested on the Leafs' goalie; Leafs players visit City Hall to sign the official reception book and receive honours for their Cup win; goalie Terry Sawchuk makes the save as the Leafs' George Armstrong is held at bay by Larry Jeffrey.

TORONTO	GP	G	A	P	Pim
Frank Mahovlich	7	1	7	8	0
George Armstrong	7	4	3	7	10
Red Kelly	7	2	4	6	2
Don McKenney	5	1	5	6	0
Dave Keon	7	4	1	5	0
Andy Bathgate	7	3	2	5	12
Bob Pulford	7	3	2	5	10
Allan Stanley	7	1	3	4	12
Bob Baun	7	1	2	3	16
Ron Stewart	7	0	3	3	2
Billy Harris	7	1	1	2	4
Tim Horton	7	0	2	2	12
Gerry Ehman	7	1	0	1	2
Carl Brewer	5	0	1	1	10
Ed Litzenberger	1	0	0	0	10
Eddie Shack	7	0	0	0	4
Larry Hillman	6	0	0	0	2
Johnny Bower	7	0	0	0	0
Jim Pappin	7	0	0	0	0
Al Arbour	1	0	0	0	0

In Goal	GP	W-L	Mins	GA	SO	Avg
Johnny Bower	7	4-3	430	17	1	2.37

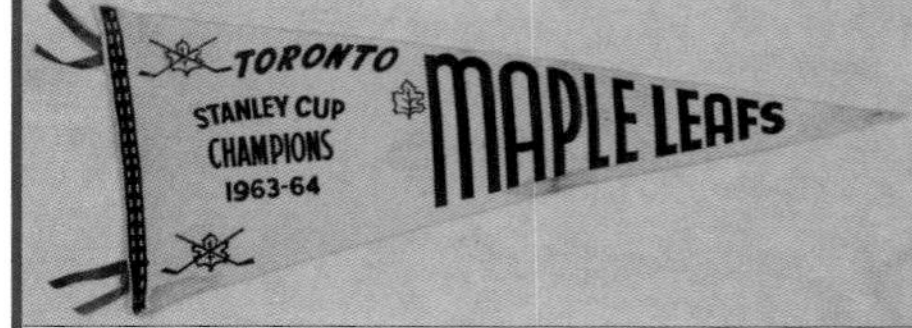

FRANK MAHOVLICH suffered bouts of depression throughout his tenure with the Leafs, the result of pressure put on him by coach Imlach. Punch would call him "Maholovich" in public, force him to practise longer than his mates, and push him to efforts the Big M wasn't capable of delivering.

His name misspelled "Armstrog," "Chief Shoot-the-Puck"—**GEORGE ARMSTRONG**—became Leafs captain in 1957 and wore the "C" for 12 years, longer than any other player in league history until Steve Yzerman came along.

After playing the final game with a bad leg injury, **RED KELLY** collapsed in the shower, was rushed to hospital, and missed the celebrations.

DON McKENNEY had six points in the finals even though he tore knee ligaments in game five and had to watch the Cup victory from the press box.

Conn Smythe went into the visitors' room at Maple Leaf Gardens exactly once. That moment came the night of October 31, 1979, **DAVE KEON'S** first time at MLG as a member of another team, Hartford.

ANDY BATHGATE was acquired in a huge deal during the season after leading the Rangers in scoring for the previous eight years.

No more dramatic goal has been scored in a non-Cup-winning game than **BOB PULFORD'S** score in game one of the finals, a short-handed, game-winning score at 19:58 of the third period.

ALLAN STANLEY had been the centre of the biggest deal ever between an NHL team (the Rangers) and a minor pro team (Providence of the AHL) when the Blueshirts acquired him for six players.

One of the most heroic moments in hockey came in game six of the finals. **BOBBY BAUN** blocked a shot by Alex Delvecchio and could not get up. He was removed on a stretcher with a cracked ankle, but returned later in the third period. In overtime, his fluttering shot beat goalie Terry Sawchuk, and the Leafs finished their series comeback with a game seven win.

RON STEWART was discovered by Squib Walker while playing juvenile in 1948 in Calgary.

After nine almost uninterrupted years as a Leaf, **BILLY HARRIS** found himself in the minors for part of the next season and on his way to Detroit the year after.

During a pre-season game versus the Quebec Aces on September 22 in Quebec City, **TIM HORTON** and Bob Pulford were charged with disturbing the peace after kicking over a number of garbage cans. They were fined $50.

Between 1955 and '67, **GERRY EHMAN** played just 132 NHL games. This year, he played just four games before the playoffs and scored one goal in nine post-season matches.

CARL BREWER enrolled at the University of Toronto a couple of years later when he quit the team after another, final row with Punch Imlach, though his career was not yet over.

Now an extra with the Leafs, **ED LITZENBERGER** spent most of the year in Rochester and played only one game in the playoffs after 19 during the regular season.

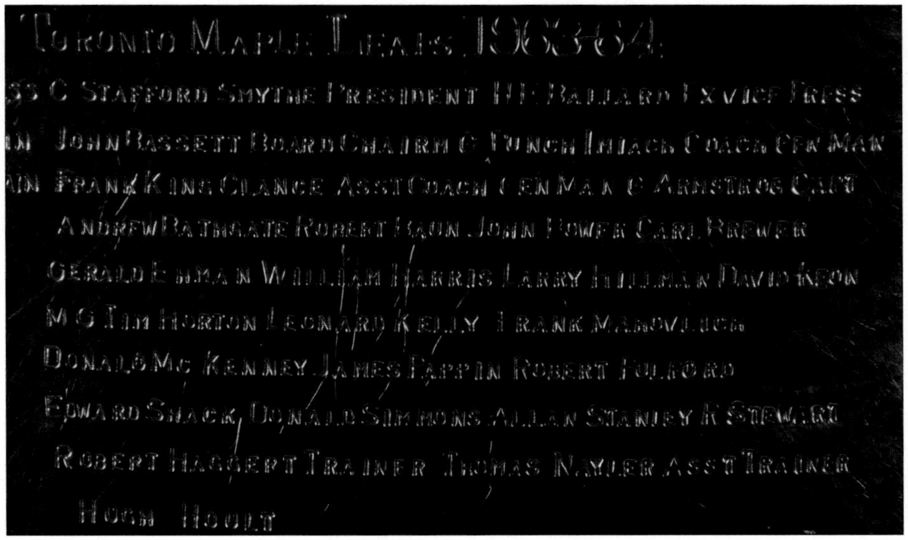

Team engraving from the Stanley Cup

EDDIE SHACK couldn't read or write, quit school at 13 after being transferred umpteen times for discipline problems, but was as financially savvy as any NHLer of his day.

LARRY HILLMAN was recalled from Rochester after John MacMillan was sold to Detroit. He remained the rest of the season and dressed for most of the playoffs for the Leafs.

Each training camp, **JOHNNY BOWER** was supposed to retire. Too old. Poor eyesight. Too slow. Each year he continued to guard the net with unparalleled ferocity. In the Leaf dressing room after the victory, Gordie Howe swapped sticks with Bower and toasted him a glass of champagne.

In each of his five seasons with the Leafs, **JIM PAPPIN** was bounced up and down from the NHL to the minors, resulting in a palpable hatred for coach Imlach that eventually led to the player's trade.

DON SIMMONS, for the second year in a row, had his name on the Cup even though he didn't tend the goal during the playoffs.

AL ARBOUR played just six regular season games but got his name on the Cup by dressing for game two of the finals, his only playoff appearance.

STAFFORD SMYTHE died October 13, 1971, of alcohol abuse and a broken heart, just days before he and Ballard were to stand trial on dozens of fraud charges. "He was persecuted to death by his enemies," father Conn had engraved on his son's headstone.

HAROLD BALLARD had been manager of the Marlies for a number of years.

JOHN BASSETT owned the *Toronto Telegram* and Baton Broadcasting (with partner John David Eaton) but after unsuccessful bids to buy all MLG stock from Ballard and Smythe, Bassett sold his shares in the team.

On off days, when the Wings were relaxing, coach **PUNCH IMLACH** put the Leafs through gruelling two-hour practises. Love him or hate him, his methods worked.

KING CLANCY was involved in the game from his first appearance in the NHL in 1921 until his death, in Toronto, on November 11, 1986.

BOBBY HAGGERT was soon to be fired by the Leafs for his role with Sports Representatives Ltd., a licensing outfit that competed directly with Maple Leaf Sports Productions, the official representatives of the Leafs players.

TOMMY NAYLER revolutionized skate sharpening. Previously, the stone used on the machine spun across the blade, creating grooves all along the blade. Nayler turned the stone on its side so it cut along with the blade, giving a much smoother cut.

HUGH HOULT was the son of Jack Hoult who was married to one of Conn Smythe's daughters. Hugh, therefore, was Conn's grandson and the team's stick boy this year.

Other players to appear for the Leafs this season: **ARNIE BROWN, KENT DOUGLAS, DICK DUFF, RON ELLIS, JOHN MacMILLAN, BOB NEVIN, PETE STEMKOWSKI**

1964 THE CHAMPIONS

1965 Montreal Canadiens

Some thirteen members of this team won the Stanley Cup for the first time, a sign of just how revamped the Montreal lineup had been from its glory days of the late 1950s to the start of a new, "quiet" dynasty of the '60s. The city held a parade for the players, its first in Montreal since 1956, and Mayor Drapeau held a reception for the team at the Mount Royal Chalet.

STANLEY CUP FINALS

Montreal Canadiens win best-of-seven Stanley Cup finals 4-3

*April 17, 1965 Chicago Black Hawks 2 at Montreal Canadiens 3
*April 20, 1965 Chicago Black Hawks 0 at Montreal Canadiens 2 [Gump Worsley]
**April 22, 1965 Montreal Canadiens 1 at Chicago Black Hawks 3
**April 25, 1965 Montreal Canadiens 1 at Chicago Black Hawks 5
*April 27, 1965 Chicago Black Hawks 0 at Montreal Canadiens 6 [Charlie Hodge]
**April 29, 1965 Montreal Canadiens 1 at Chicago Black Hawks 2
*May 1, 1965 Chicago Black Hawks 0 at Montreal Canadiens 4 {Jean Beliveau 0:14 1st} [Gump Worsley]

** played at the Forum, Montreal ** played at Chicago Stadium*

Team engraving from the shoulder of the Stanley Cup

(left) Jean Beliveau holds the Cup high for everyone in the Forum to admire; (above) the Canadiens attract thousands of their fans to a parade to City Hall after the win.

MONTREAL	GP	G	A	P	Pim
Jean Beliveau	7	5	5	10	18
Dick Duff	7	3	5	8	5
J.C. Tremblay	7	1	5	6	14
Bobby Rousseau	7	1	5	6	4
Henri Richard	7	3	0	3	20
John Ferguson	7	2	1	3	13
Ted Harris	7	0	3	3	34
Yvan Cournoyer	7	2	0	2	0
Ralph Backstrom	7	1	1	2	4
Claude Provost	7	0	2	2	12
Red Berenson	7	0	1	1	2
Noel Picard	3	0	1	1	0
Terry Harper	7	0	0	0	19
Jean-Guy Talbot	7	0	0	0	18
Jim Roberts	7	0	0	0	14
Claude Larose	7	0	0	0	4
Jean Gauthier	2	0	0	0	4
Dave Balon	5	0	0	0	0
Gump Worsley	4	0	0	0	0
Charlie Hodge	3	0	0	0	0

In Goal	GP	W-L	Mins	GA	SO	Avg
Gump Worsley	4	3-1	240	5	2	1.25
Charlie Hodge	3	1-2	180	7	1	2.33

JEAN BELIVEAU won the Conn Smythe Trophy, introduced this year to honour the best player of the playoffs and named after the great Leafs builder.

DICK DUFF was acquired during the season when Sam Pollock traded Bill Hicke and Jean-Guy Morissette to the Rangers for Duff and Dave McComb to replace Gilles Tremblay who had broken his ankle.

J.C.TREMBLAY complained that the maintenance workers at the Stadium in Chicago purposefully made the ice slow to hinder the faster Habs, an hypothesis supported by the fact that the home team won all seven games.

BOBBY ROUSSEAU was slated to play in the 1960 Olympics in place of Dave Keon, whom the Leafs refused to allow play because they wanted him for themselves.

HENRI RICHARD followed in the footsteps of Toe Blake and opened a bar in the city where the team ended up each year the Canadiens won the Cup.

In the first period of game five, **JOHN FERGUSON** beat up Eric Nesterenko with a flurry of punches that rendered "Nester" ineffective the rest of the series.

Quiet and under-rated and unnoticed by most fans, **TED HARRIS** was one of the more respected defencemen in the game.

YVAN COURNOYER was considered one of the first power-play specialists, utilizing his great speed and shot.

RALPH BACKSTROM played on a line with Ferguson and Larose and rode in the same parade car as Fergie, though some fans got the two players confused, much to Backstrom's delight.

CLAUDE PROVOST (aka "Joe") was given the assignment of shadowing Bobby Hull. "I've never been checked like that in my life," the Golden Jet said after the Montreal victory.

RED BERENSON wasn't long for this idyllic Montreal world. He played just three games and the playoffs this year and half the next year before the Canadiens traded him to the Rangers.

NOEL PICARD went to St. Louis in the 1967 Expansion Draft, but his career came to an end in November '71 after he destroyed his ankle horseback riding.

TERRY HARPER made the Canadiens on the strength of his defensive play and excelled in large measure because of his admiration for coach Toe Blake.

JEAN-GUY TALBOT played part of the season up on left wing. He responded with two goals in one game, the first and only time he ever accomplished this feat!

JIM ROBERTS became the team's number one penalty killer, so his three goals were not much of a concern for coach Toe Blake.

CLAUDE LAROSE was in his first full season with the team, and on February 2 he scored his 21st goal of the year and looked like a shoe-in for the Calder Trophy. But from that game through the entire rest of the season, Larose counted just one assist.

From 1960 to '67, **GAUTHIER** played mostly in the Montreal farm system (with the exception of '62-'63) and this year was no different. He was recalled as playoff insurance and played just two games of the finals.

Team engraving from the Stanley Cup

DAVE BALON was particularly tough on his skates, but just a few years later he quit the game because of prolonged bouts of weakness which were later diagnosed as multiple sclerosis.

JIM PETERS played just 13 games with the Habs, and a month after the season ended he was traded to the Rangers.

Why **ERNIE WAKELY'S** name is on this Cup is almost incomprehensible. As a member of the Montreal organization he played with Omaha in the CPHL and with Cleveland and Quebec in the AHL, but he was never near the Forum at any time during the season.

BRYAN WATSON'S first nickname was "Superpest" because of annoying methods he used when shadowing a player. By the time he retired, in 1979, he was the most penalized player in league history.

Although he had been tending the goal since 1952, this was **GUMP WORSLEY'S** first trip to the finals.

Although he had had his name on the Cup a few times, this was only the second year **CHARLIE HODGE** appeared in the playoffs at all (in 1964, the Habs, with Hodge in goal, lost to the Leafs in a seven-game semi-finals).

Trainer **ANDREW GALLEY** succeeded Gaston Bettez. He had been the longtime trainer for the Montreal Royals, going back to their days as Allan Cup winners in the 1940s.

LARRY AUBUT was the team's assistant trainer.

The Honourable **HARTLAND MOLSON** himself had been an athlete in his youth, playing in the 1926 Memorial Cup finals and later with the Dominion champion football team at Royal Military College.

The vice-president of Molson Breweries, **DAVID MOLSON** attended the University of Brussels before writing for the *Montreal Gazette* and later becoming president of the Canadian Arena Company that controlled the Habs.

Although he worked on a regular basis for S. Albert and Company, a fuel and oil distributing business in Montreal, **MAURICE RICHARD** still represented the Canadiens first and foremost.

This was **SAM POLLOCK'S** rookie season as general manager after years in the Montreal organization. He was replacing the retired Frank Selke who had been with the club since 1946 and had won six Stanley Cups.

Coach **TOE BLAKE'S** strategy was simple: take Bobby Hull out of the play. It worked, and, as a result, the Habs won.

JACQUES LAPERRIERE had played all season with Montreal, but in the final game of the semi-finals vs. Toronto he broke his ankle and missed the entire finals series.

GILLES TREMBLAY began the season with the Habs, but in a game on December 17, 1964, against the Leafs he collided with Ron Ellis, broke his leg, and missed the rest of the season.

Other players to appear for the Canadiens this season: **ANDRE BOUDRIAS, BILL HICKE, KEITH McCREARY, LEON ROCHEFORT**

1965–1966 Montreal Canadiens

THE CHAMPIONS

During the regular season, a group of University of Montreal students broke into the visitors' dressing room at the Forum and stole all the Detroit sweaters as a prank. They were caught and given stiff rebuke by a judge. In 1977, another group from the U of M tried to steal the Stanley Cup from its home at the Hockey Hall of Fame. Despite losing the first two games of the finals, at home, the Habs rallied to win four in a row and claim their second straight Stanley Cup, this time away from the Forum. The team's nickname is badly misspelled on the Cup!

STANLEY CUP FINALS

Montreal Canadiens win best-of-seven Stanley Cup finals 4-2

*April 24, 1966	Detroit Red Wings 3 at Montreal Canadiens 2
*April 26, 1966	Detroit Red Wings 5 at Montreal Canadiens 2
**April 28, 1966	Montreal Canadiens 4 at Detroit Red Wings 2
**May 1, 1966	Montreal Canadiens 2 at Detroit Red Wings 1
*May 3, 1966	Detroit Red Wings 1 at Montreal Canadiens 5
**May 5, 1966	Montreal Canadiens 3 at Detroit Red Wings 2 {(Henri Richard 2:20 OT)}

** played at the Forum, Montreal ** played at the Olympia, Detroit*

Captain Jean Beliveau and teammates celebrate victory on ice

MONTREAL CANADIENS 1965-66
HON. H. DE M. MOLSON CHAIRMAN J.D. MOLSON PRES.
S. POLLOCK GEN. MGR. H. TOE BLAKE COACH J. BELIVEAU CAPT.
R. BACKSTROM D. BALON Y. COURNOYER R. ROUSSEAU
RICHARD DUFF J. FERGUSON TERRANCE HARPER
EDWARD HARRIS CHARLES HODGE J. LAPERRIERE
CLAUDE LAROSE NOEL PRICE CLAUDE PROVOST
HENRI RICHARD JAMES ROBERTS LEON ROCHEFORT
JEAN GUY TALBOT GILLES TREMBLAY
JEAN CLAUDE TREMBLAY LORNE WORSLEY
ANDREW GALLEY TRAINER
LARRY AUBUT ASST. TRAINER

Team engraving from the replica Cup

Team engraving from the shoulder of the replica Cup

(left) Detroit goalie Roger Crozier did what very few players have done—he won the Conn Smythe Trophy despite playing for the losing side in the Cup finals. Nonetheless, the 24-year-old allowed just 18 goals in six games against a much more powerful Montreal team and was the main reason the series was as close as it was.

MONTREAL	GP	G	A	P	Pim
J.C. Tremblay	6	1	5	6	0
Jean Beliveau	6	3	2	5	0
Henri Richard	6	1	4	5	2
Dave Balon	6	2	2	4	16
Ralph Backstrom	6	2	2	4	2
Gilles Tremblay	6	2	2	4	0
Dick Duff	6	1	3	4	2
Yvan Cournoyer	6	2	1	3	0
Terry Harper	6	1	2	3	4
Bobby Rousseau	6	1	2	3	4
Leon Rochefort	4	1	1	2	4
Claude Provost	6	1	1	2	2
Jim Roberts	6	0	1	1	10
Jean-Guy Talbot	6	0	1	1	8
Noel Price	1	0	1	1	0
John Ferguson	6	0	0	0	8
Ted Harris	6	0	0	0	4
Gump Worsley	6	0	0	0	0
Claude Larose	2	0	0	0	0

In Goal	GP	W-L	Mins	GA	SO	Avg
Gump Worsley	6	4-2	362	14	0	2.32

J.C. TREMBLAY earned the facetious nickname "J.C. Superstar" because after the Conn Smythe was awarded to Crozier he smashed his fist against the dressing room wall, tossed towels, and threw a tantrum at not having won himself.

"Next year, I think we can do it," boasted **JEAN BELIVEAU** to Mayor Drapeau's pledge for a third Cup in a row to coincide with Canada's Centennial celebrations.

HENRI RICHARD'S winning goal in overtime created much controversy. Coming in on goal, he fell and slid into the net with the puck under him. Referee Frank Udvari wasted no time in counting the goal, though the Red Wings were incensed.

DAVE BALON played on a newly-formed line with Henri Richard and Leon Rochefort, though Toe Blake sent him to the minors for nine games to show his displeasure with what he thought was inconsistent play from Balon.

RALPH BACKSTROM scored the overtime goal to win game one of the semi-finals, 2-1 over Boston, his first shot on goal in the game and his first OT goal in eleven years with the Habs.

GILLES TREMBLAY played most of his career on left wing with Beliveau at centre and Bernie Geoffrion on the right side (and later Yvan Cournoyer, after Boom Boom was traded).

DICK DUFF'S trademark consistency, which he had established in Toronto, deserted him somewhat in Montreal. He scored 21 goals this year, dipped to 12 the next, and shot back to 25 the year after.

"It's a dream," **YVAN COURNOYER** said of the win. "You play in the street and you think, 'maybe one day I'll get there.'" And here he was!

TERRY HARPER remained with the Habs thanks to the shrewdness of Frank Selke. Back in 1963, Selke feared he'd lose Harper in the newly-created Amateur Draft, so he instructed the player's junior coach to play him at right wing. Harper, a natural defenceman, looked completely out of his element, so no other team took an interest in him. The next year, Selke moved him back to the blueline.

Although a classy and gentlemanly player, **BOBBY ROUSSEAU** was suspended for two games the following season for elbowing referee Art Skov.

LEON ROCHEFORT played in a Montreal system deep in talent between '63 and '67 and appeared with the Habs in just 40 regular season and 14 playoff games. He scored the second goal of the deciding game this year to give the Canadiens a 2-0 lead in the game.

CLAUDE PROVOST was one of few players to be part of two dynasties, the Habs of the '50s (five Cups) and the Habs of the '60s (four more). He is the man to have won the most Stanley Cups (nine) who is not in the Hockey Hall of Fame.

JIM ROBERTS'S moment of glory came in the series-clinching game of the semi-finals versus Toronto when he scored early in the third period to give the Habs a solid 3-1 lead in the game (they won 4-1).

Team engraving from the Stanley Cup

Entering the twilight of his career, **JEAN-GUY TALBOT** found renewed energy in his role as a penalty killer, becoming one of the league's best and earning extra ice time from coach Blake.

NOEL PRICE later helped the Nova Scotia Voyageurs win two AHL titles. "I always felt prouder of those championships than the Stanley Cup," he admitted, "because I contributed more to winning them."

JOHN FERGUSON was more active off ice than on. He and his uncle bred horses in British Columbia, and he operated a hockey school and worked for a women's clothing company, among many other endeavours. As a result, he set up John Ferguson Enterprises Limited to minimize his taxes and maximize his profits. Hockey was incidental—his joy, but not his livelihood.

TED HARRIS was one of the few men not only to endure an extended tenure with Eddie Shore's Springfield Indians (four years) but to have nothing but good things to say about the dictatorial coach, crediting Shore with making him an NHL-quality defenceman.

Delirious with delight, **GUMP WORSLEY** got on the train with his team for the return trip to Montreal saying only that, "I'm going to get drunk."

CLAUDE LAROSE rebounded from a disastrous last half of the previous season to score 15 goals, but a goalless playoffs spelled the beginning of the end for his first stint with the Habs.

CHARLIE HODGE shared the Vezina Trophy with Worsley. He had been in the Montreal system since 1955 and had won the Vezina on his own in 1964, in the final game of the season, allowing two fewer goals that night than Glenn Hall.

HARTLAND MOLSON was perhaps the most powerful and well-respected man in the city. He was president of Molson Industries Limited, a director of the Bank of Montreal and Sun Life Assurance Company, and a Senator in the House of Commons since 1955.

DAVID MOLSON attended each Montreal home game, sitting behind the players' bench with the watchful gaze of a man who controlled the destiny of every life in the building, from the players to the peanut sellers.

SAM POLLOCK made just one trade between the '65 Cup and this year's roster, acquiring Noel Price in a six-player deal of mostly spare parts on July 8, 1965.

TOE BLAKE came from a family of eleven children, four of whom died in infancy. He got his nickname because as a boy one of his sisters pronounced "Hector" like "Hectoe" and over the years the diminutive was shortened to just "Toe."

JACQUES LAPERRIERE won the Norris Trophy despite missing the last 13 games and all of the playoffs with a serious knee injury.

ANDREW GALLEY, trainer, also worked for years with the Montreal Royals baseball team.

LARRY AUBUT was assistant trainer to Galley with the Habs and with the Royals as well.

Other players to appear for the Canadiens this season: **RED BERENSON, JEAN GAUTHIER, DANNY GRANT, DON JOHNS**

1966–1967 THE CHAMPIONS Toronto Maple Leafs

This last, great Leafs team was nicknamed the Over-the-Hill Gang or Punch's Old Folks Home because the core of the team consisted of players near or over 40 years old. This was the last year of the Original Six, the last year the Leafs won the Cup, and the last year the NHL existed before Alan Eagleson brought the NHL Players' Association into the game as a negotiating and bargaining force that finally gave the players some clout come contract time. This was also the oldest team ever to win the Stanley Cup.

STANLEY CUP FINALS

Toronto Maple Leafs win best-of-seven Stanley Cup finals 4-2

*April 20, 1967	Toronto Maple Leafs 2 at Montreal Canadiens 6
*April 22, 1967	Toronto Maple Leafs 3 at Montreal Canadiens 0 [Johnny Bower]
**April 25, 1967	Montreal Canadiens 2 at Toronto Maple Leafs 3 (Bob Pulford 28:26 OT)
**April 27, 1967	Montreal Canadiens 6 at Toronto Maple Leafs 3
*April 29, 1967	Toronto Maple Leafs 4 at Montreal Canadiens 1
**May 2, 1967	Montreal Canadiens 1 at Toronto Maple Leafs 3 {Jim Pappin 19:24 2nd}

** played at the Forum, Montreal ** played at Maple Leaf Gardens, Toronto*

Players gather around captain George Armstrong who holds the Cup.

(clockwise) Players scuffle during a break in play of game four at Maple Leaf Gardens; Montreal's young star, Rogie Vachon, watches play unfold from his goal crease; the Leafs are feted at new City Hall following their victory in Canada's centennial year.

TORONTO	GP	G	A	P	Pim
Jim Pappin	6	4	4	8	6
Bob Pulford	6	1	6	7	0
Pete Stemkowski	6	2	4	6	4
Tim Horton	6	2	3	5	8
Mike Walton	6	2	1	3	0
Red Kelly	6	0	3	3	2
Brian Conacher	6	1	1	2	19
Ron Ellis	6	1	1	2	4
Larry Hillman	6	1	1	2	0
Dave Keon	6	1	1	2	0
Frank Mahovlich	6	0	2	2	8
George Armstrong	6	1	0	1	4
Marcel Pronovost	6	1	0	1	4
Allan Stanley	6	0	1	1	6
Bob Baun	5	0	0	0	2
Eddie Shack	4	0	0	0	8
Aut Erickson	1	0	0	0	2
Terry Sawchuk	4	0	0	0	0
Johnny Bower	3	0	0	0	0
Milan Marcetta		0	0	0	0

In Goal	GP	W-L	Mins	GA	SO	Avg
Johnny Bower	3	2-0	163	3	1	1.10
Terry Sawchuk	4	2-2	225	12	0	3.20

The "A" is missing from **"STAFFORD SMYTHE,"** one of the three owners of the team after his father relinquished control of the Leafs.

"Press" for **HAROLD BALLARD'S** title is used here as short for "President" for the man who convinced Stafford to sell him a third of Conn's shares in the team.

Chairman of the Board, **JOHN BASSETT**, disgusted by Harold Ballard, sold his share of the ownership pie a few years later shortly after Ballard was sent to jail after being convicted on dozens of charges of fraud.

The "G" stands for George, though everyone called him **PUNCH**. "I don't care how old a guy is," **IMLACH** barked in defence of his team. "If he produces, he plays for me."

KING CLANCY won his first Cup as a player with Ottawa in 1923 and this was his last, some 44 years later.

BOB DAVIDSON was a lifelong Leaf as a player, a captain, and a scout for more than 30 years. He got Dave Keon onto the Leafs' negotiation list through a complex deal with Springfield Indians owner Eddie Shore who promised to sponsor Keon's junior team in Noranda in exchange for a player—Ted Harris.

"Buiss" is a typo short form for "Business" much like "Press" for Ballard. **JOHN ANDERSON** was in charge of publicity for the team.

The longest-serving captain in Leaf history, **GEORGE ARMSTRONG** celebrated his fourth and last Cup.

Although his name is on this Cup, **BOBBY BAUN** did not attend the Cup parade out of pride. He saw little action in the finals—Imlach going with what he felt were more capable defencemen—and as a result Baun didn't feel that he had contributed enough to warrant the glory.

Everyone called him **"JOHNNY,"** but **BOWER** at 42 was the oldest goalie to win the Cup.

BRIAN was one in a long line of **CONACHERS**. His father, Charlie, won the sacred bowl as did uncles Lionel and Roy. Brian scored two goals in game six against Chicago in the semi-finals that allowed the Leafs to eliminate the Hawks.

A lifelong Leaf, **RON ELLIS** scored the all-important opening goal in the deciding game of the finals.

Acquired in a multi-player deal in May 1965, **AUT ERICKSON** played only once with the Leafs, the first game of the finals. He served a too-many-men penalty in the first period.

LARRY HILLMAN was claimed by the Leafs after being exposed by Boston at the 1960 Intra-League draft. He won another Cup two years later with Montreal.

His name was **MILES HORTON** but from a young age his mother called him **"TIM."** He served with the Leafs for 20 years and 1,185 games, both team records.

RED KELLY won his last of eight Cups (four each with Detroit and Toronto) and retired after this win to coach the expansion Los Angeles Kings.

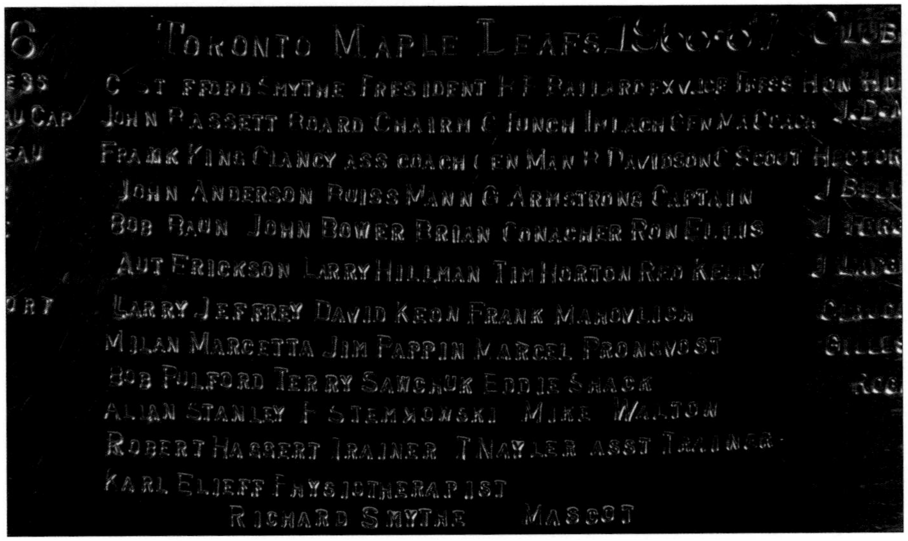

Team engraving from the Stanley Cup

LARRY JEFFREY played every game of the semi-finals then not a minute in the finals.

Future captain, **DAVE KEON** won the Conn Smythe trophy on the strength of his exceptional two-way play. If the Leafs are to win, fans used to write in placards, they have to turn the "Key-on."

FRANK MAHOVLICH suffered terribly under the rule of coach Imlach and had his worst scoring season in almost a decade. Late the following year he was traded to Detroit.

Like Erickson, **MILAN MARCETTA** appeared for the Leafs only in the playoffs, playing three games—April 11 and 13 vs. Chicago, and April 22 vs. Montreal.

One of Imlach's punching bags, **JIM PAPPIN** was a quality NHLer who played more in the minors than with the Leafs as an example of what power Imlach had over the players. This year, however, Pappin led the league in playoff points with 15.

MARCEL PRONOVOST arrived in Toronto with Aut Erickson but he had the Detroit Cup-winning pedigree of Red Kelly. He retired as a Leaf in December 1969.

BOB PULFORD played 14 years with the Leafs and was part of all four Toronto bowls in the 1960s. "When Imlach put out his old guys at the end to protect the lead, it was something I'll never forget," he said of the dramatic ending.

The 36-year old **TERRY SAWCHUK** combined with Bower to play with a pride that belied his age and bones. "Some nights you stop 'em, some nights you don't," he said philosophically of his net guardian duties.

"The Entertainer" was more than just a buffoon. Coming off a 26-goal season, **EDDIE SHACK** scored just eleven in '66-'67 and was a scratch in two of the six games in the finals.

"Snowshoes" **ALLAN STANLEY** played one more year after this, making it an even ten seasons with the Leafs after coming over from Boston in 1958.

PETE STEMKOWSKI was unlucky in that the "K" in his moniker was hacked into the Cup backwards.

Like Mahovlich, **MIKE WALTON** suffered under Imlach's tyrannical rule, though he did outlast him. He went on to Boston to win the Cup again in 1972.

BOB HAGGERT later became director of the Canadian Rhythmic Gymnastic Federation, in large part because of his daughter's international participation, at a time when the 'sport' was hoping to make its Olympic breakthrough.

TOMMY NAYLER had been with the Leafs since 1929. He pioneered many of the early improvements to equipment including the white protector for the back of skate blades, the ankle guard, and thumb protector on gloves.

A part-time employee for the Leafs with his own business in the city, **KARL ELIEFF** worked the players' muscles over whenever they had difficulties.

RICHARD SMYTHE was the grandson of Conn. His dad, Conn's son Hugh, had his name on the '42 Cup as the team's mascot.

Other players to appear for the Leafs this season: **JOHN BRENNEMAN, WAYNE CARLETON, KENT DOUGLAS, BRUCE GAMBLE, DICK GAMBLE, BRENT IMLACH, JIM McKENNY, DUANE RUPP, BRIT SELBY, AL SMITH, GARY SMITH**

1967–1968 Montreal Canadiens

The Habs had a week off between the semi-finals and the finals after eliminating Chicago in five games while watching the Blues defeat Minnesota in seven, hard-fought games. This was the only series (with the exception of the '51 finals) in which all games were decided by one goal and the first time since 1926 that a Stanley Cup game had been played in the West. The city of Montreal put on a parade for the players, stretching from the Forum to Lafontaine Park and finishing with a reception at Mount Royal. In the summer, the Cup was on display at the Quebec Pavilion at the "Man and His World" exhibition in Montreal.

STANLEY CUP FINALS

Montreal Canadiens win best-of-seven Stanley Cup finals 4-0

*May 5, 1968 Montreal Canadiens 3 at St. Louis Blues 2 (Jacques Lemaire 1:41 OT)
*May 7, 1968 Montreal Canadiens 1 at St. Louis Blues 0 [Gump Worsley]
**May 9, 1968 St. Louis Blues 3 at Montreal Canadiens 4 (Bobby Rousseau 1:13 OT)
**May 11, 1968 St. Louis Blues 2 at Montreal Canadiens 3 {J.C. Tremblay 11:40 3rd}

** played at the Arena, St. Louis ** played at the Forum, Montreal*

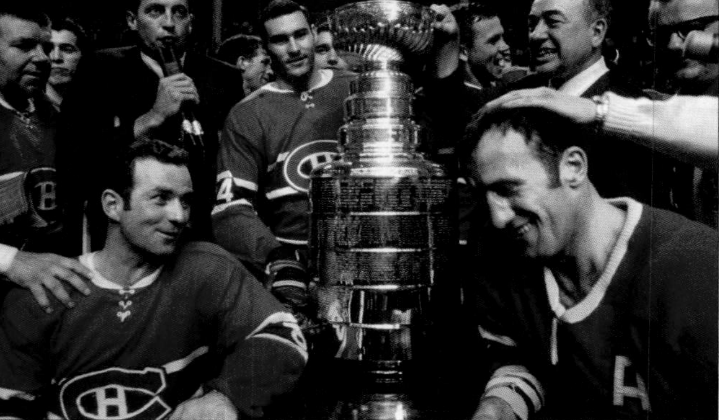

Players gather around coach Toe Blake and the Cup.

MONTREAL	GP	G	A	P	Pim
Yvan Cournoyer	4	2	2	4	2
Henri Richard	4	2	1	3	0
John Ferguson	4	0	3	3	4
Serge Savard	4	2	0	2	0
Jacques Lemaire	4	1	1	2	4
Dick Duff	4	1	1	2	2
Ralph Backstrom	4	1	1	2	0
J. C. Tremblay	4	1	1	2	0
Bobby Rousseau	4	1	0	1	6
Ted Harris	4	0	1	1	6
Claude Provost	4	0	1	1	2
Claude Larose	4	0	1	1	0
Jacques Laperriere	4	0	0	0	6
Terry Harper	4	0	0	0	4
Carol Vadnais	1	0	0	0	2
Danny Grant	4	0	0	0	0
Gump Worsley	4	0	0	0	0
Mickey Redmond	2	0	0	0	0
Jean Beliveau	1	0	0	0	0

In Goal	GP	W-L	Mins	GA	SO	Avg
Gump Worsley	4	4-0	243	7	1	1.73

(clockwise) Gump Worsley and Henri Richard share a car on the victory parade; players and wives hold the Cup at the team's victory dinner; the dinner featured speeches and dancing with the Cup prominently on display.

"The Roadrunner," **YVAN COURNOYER**, scored 63 goals in his last year of junior before embarking on a 16-year, ten Stanley Cup-career with the Habs.

Although not as celebrated a figure as his older brother, Maurice, **HENRI RICHARD** played more games, scored more points, and won more Cups than the Rocket.

One of hockey's first goons, **JOHN FERGUSON** nonetheless averaged nearly 20 goals a season in his eight NHL years.

Defenceman **SERGE SAVARD** was at the start of a tremendous career that would endure into the 1980s and inspire broadcaster Danny Gallivan to coin the term "Savardian spinarama."

In a career plagued by injuries and misfortune, **GILLES TREMBLAY** was encouraged by the Habs to give up his number 21 sweater and take Bernie Geoffrion's 5. Tremblay responded with, ironically, a 21-goal season.

ROGIE VACHON shared the Vezina Trophy this year with Gump Worsley. In 1977, Rogie was credited with the first goal scored by a goalie, but a day later video replay showed that Vic Venasky touched the puck before the Islanders shot the puck into their own net on a delayed penalty.

Rookie **JACQUES LEMAIRE** scored two overtime goals in these playoffs, a record for first year players that stands to this day.

DICK DUFF was playing with his third Original Six team (after Toronto and the Rangers). This was his fifth Cup of the 1960s in a year when he had, at age 32, his best offensive season in a decade.

RALPH BACKSTROM had been in the NHL since 1956, played in six All-Star Games, and recorded seven, 20-goal seasons during his career.

In addition to a 13-year career with the Canadiens, **J.C. TREMBLAY** played every season of the WHA's existence, 1972-1979.

BOBBY ROUSSEAU scored a goal on February 15, 1962, against the Leafs on a penalty shot. What made this unique was that he skated in over the blueline and took a slap shot to score!

TED HARRIS was victim to the exclusivity of the Original Six. He didn't skate on an NHL sheet of ice until 1963 when he was 27 years old, such was the depth of each team in the league.

Another unheralded player on an almost entirely French-Canadian roster, **CLAUDE PROVOST** played all of his 1,005 NHL games with the Habs.

CLAUDE LAROSE was traded in the off season to Minnesota where he was named team captain, but two years later he was re-acquired by the Habs for Bobby Rousseau.

JACQUES LAPERRIERE won the Norris Trophy in 1966, just prior to the arrival of Bobby Orr, though he wasn't an offensively explosive defenceman. Rather, he was rock solid on the blueline and an impenetrable force in his own end.

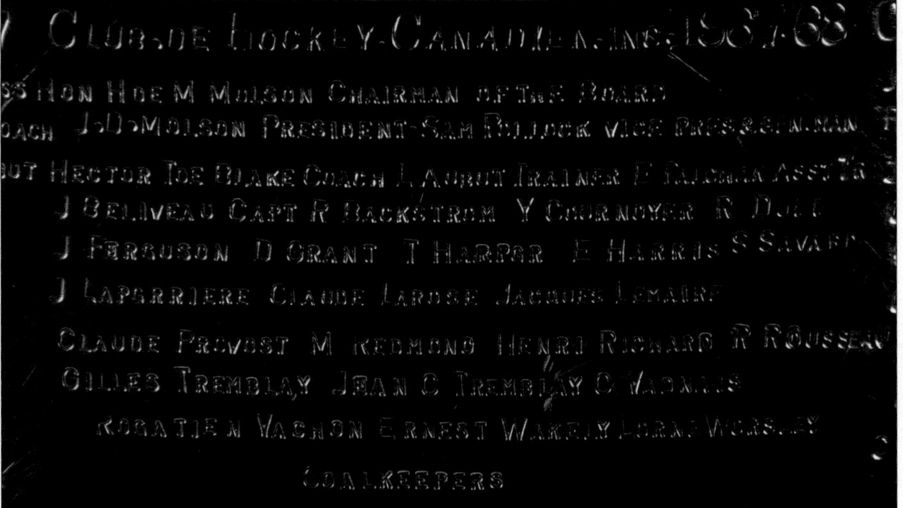

Team engraving from the Stanley Cup

Team engraving from the shoulder of the replica Cup

TERRY HARPER was in the middle of a bad luck streak which saw him score just once in over 200 games, but his was a remarkable life. When he was 12, he suffered burns to most of his body when a can of gasoline exploded as he burned a pile of garbage. He was in the hospital three months.

CAROL VADNAIS played defence as a junior before moving to forward with Montreal. His time with the Habs was short, though, and he was claimed by Oakland in the summer's Intra-League Draft.

Although he didn't play much, **DANNY GRANT** became the first player to win the Stanley Cup one year and then the Calder Trophy the year after.

In a remarkable career that lasted until he was 45 years old, the Gumper, **GUMP WORSLEY**, won four Cups in five years with the Habs in the 1960s.

A native of Kirkland Lake and graduate of the Peterborough Petes, the 21-year old **MICKEY REDMOND** was but a part-time rookie this season.

Team captain **JEAN BELIVEAU** missed almost all of the finals because of a painful bone chip in his ankle.

As in '64-'65, **ERNIE WAKELY** did not play a single minute with the team. In fact, his only NHL time to date had been a single game for the Canadiens back in the 1962-63 regular season.

In 1928, in his youth, **HARTLAND MOLSON** moved to Paris and worked for the Banque Adam. He played for the Paris Canadians hockey club and then the European Canadians team which played in a tournament in Davos and included teammate and future NHL president, Clarence Campbell.

Under the guidance of **DAVID MOLSON**, who rejected the proposal to build a new arena at the Place Des Arts in downtown Montreal, the Forum was completely renovated right after this Cup-winning season at a cost of $10 million.

SAM POLLOCK became GM of Montreal in 1964, winning the Cup his first year and now claiming his third world championship in four years.

TOE BLAKE had coached his last. "I've had enough," he confessed. "The pressure is too much." And he retired, nine Cups on his mantle in just 13 years of coaching.

LARRY AUBUT was the team's trainer.

Assistant trainer **EDDIE PALCHAK** was a distant relative of Mike Bossy. In the 1990s, he became a purchasing agent for the Canadiens.

Other players to appear for the Canadiens this season: **GARY MONAHAN, BRYAN WATSON**

1968 THE CHAMPIONS
1969 Montreal Canadiens

"They say that to be great, you must be hungry and humble," St. Louis coach Scotty Bowman commented. "The Montreal team is hungry, but not humble. They are haughty." Shortly, Bowman would leave his own haughty mark on this same Canadiens team after leaving the humble St. Louis organization for the Habs. For the second year in a row, the Canadiens won a finals against the expansion Blues, and again in a particularly close four-game sweep.

STANLEY CUP FINALS

Montreal Canadiens win best-of-seven Stanley Cup finals 4-0

*April 27, 1969 St. Louis Blues 1 at Montreal Canadiens 3
*April 29, 1969 St. Louis Blues 1 at Montreal Canadiens 3
**May 1, 1969 Montreal Canadiens 4 at St. Louis Blues 0 [Rogie Vachon]
**May 4, 1969 Montreal Canadiens 2 at St. Louis Blues 1 {John Ferguson 3:02 3rd}

** played at the Forum, Montreal ** played at the Arena, St. Louis*

Montreal Canadiens, 1968-69

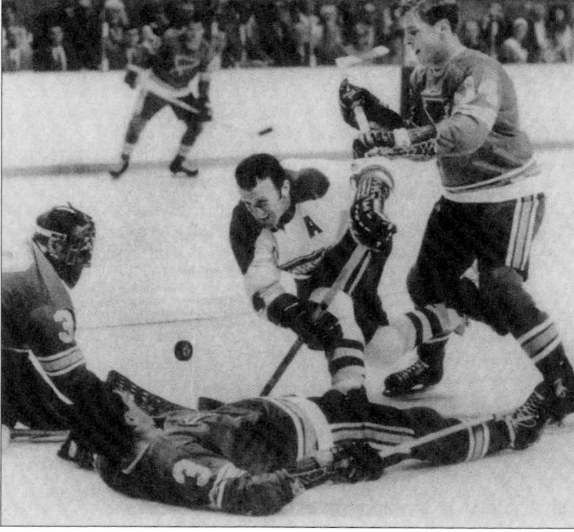

(clockwise) The victory parade makes its way through Montreal's downtown; game action from the St. Louis-Montreal finals; Jean Beliveau greets fans along the parade route.

MONTREAL	GP	G	A	P	Pim
Dick Duff	4	4	2	6	2
Jean Beliveau	4	0	5	5	4
Yvan Cournoyer	4	1	3	4	0
John Ferguson	4	2	0	2	20
Serge Savard	4	1	1	2	8
Ralph Backstrom	4	1	1	2	4
J. C. Tremblay	4	0	2	2	6
Ted Harris	4	1	0	1	6
Jacques Lemaire	4	1	0	1	4
Bobby Rousseau	4	1	0	1	2
Henri Richard	4	0	1	1	2
Mickey Redmond	4	0	1	1	0
Claude Provost	3	0	1	1	0
Jacques Laperriere	4	0	0	0	22
Terry Harper	4	0	0	0	4
Rogie Vachon	4	0	0	0	0
Christian Bordeleau	3	0	0	0	0

In Goal	GP	W-L	Mins	GA	SO	Avg
Rogie Vachon	4	4-0	240	3	1	0.75

This was **DICK DUFF'S** last full year in Montreal though he finished the playoffs with a career-high six goals. He was traded to Los Angeles midway through the next season after a conflict with management that was admittedly mostly his fault.

"In the playoffs," **JEAN BELIVEAU** said after the first two games of the series against Boston, "the Canadiens are lucky." They won both those games in overtime and went on to win the semi-finals, Beliveau scoring his one and only career OT goal in game six to eliminate the Bruins.

"When I see those eyes looking out from behind the mask," **YVAN COURNOYER** said of his adversary and long-time Habs goaler, Jacques Plante, "I want my shots to come from cannons."

"We're all in this thing to make money," **JOHN FERGUSON** said prior to the finals, "and when we've got a chance to do it, we're not going to blow it."

In 1984, **LARRY HILLMAN** was stricken with Guillian-Barre Syndrome that paralyzed him completely for a short period of time and forced him to learn how to walk again, which he did.

GILLES TREMBLAY played his last game on February 11, 1969, forced to retire because of severe allergy problems which caused acute asthma that almost killed him. No amount of testing or warm weather could cure him, and he never played again.

SERGE SAVARD didn't miss a game the entire year, and his outstanding play in the finals earned him this year's Conn Smythe Trophy honours.

Midway through 1970-71, **RALPH BACKSTROM** was involved in one of the more brilliant trades ever made as Sam Pollock sent him to Los Angeles to ensure the Kings improved and the Seals finished in last place. Montreal owned the Seals' first round draft choice, and Silent Sam wanted to ensure he'd be able to select the year's best prospect—Guy Lafleur.

J.C. TREMBLAY later played in the WHA, continuing his career even after the loss of a kidney because of a tumorous growth.

TED HARRIS played all of Montreal's 90 games this year, along with Cournoyer the only member of the Habs to do so.

JACQUES LEMAIRE won eight Cups in a dozen years, a record not likely to be equalled by a player.

Speedy forward **BOBBY ROUSSEAU**, played one more season before being traded to the North Stars and then Rangers at the end of his career.

The Pocket Rocket, **HENRI RICHARD**, was in his 13th season with the Habs. He was limited to just nine goals, however, his lowest total, after missing 16 games with an injury and being hampered much of the rest of the season.

MICKEY REDMOND became part of the showcase deal when Montreal acquired Frank Mahovlich in 1970-71 from Detroit. He went on to score 50 goals twice in a season with the Wings before a back injury ended his career prematurely.

Team engraving from the Stanley Cup

Team engraving from the shoulder of the Stanley Cup

There were only two players in NHL history to win the Cup in both their rookie season and final season: Cooney Weiland (with Boston in '29 and '39), and, this year, **CLAUDE PROVOST**.

This represented the first year since 1963 that **JACQUES LAPERRIERE** hadn't played the All-Star Game, though Stanley Cup honours more than made up for the showcase-game snub.

TERRY HARPER was later traded by Los Angeles to Detroit in a compensation case. He sued the league to stay in L.A. and lost.

Perhaps the greatest goalie of the modern era not in the Hockey Hall of Fame, **ROGIE VACHON** had a spectacular 7-1 record and 1.42 average in eight playoff games this year.

TONY ESPOSITO won the Cup this year and the Calder Trophy the year after. His first initial "A" refers to the more formal "Anthony." Ironically, Tony O's contribution to this team was minimal, but although he became one of the league's greatest post-expansion netminders, he never won another Cup.

Although **GUMP WORSLEY** played seven games in the playoffs, he played second fiddle to the younger Vachon in the finals and warmed the bench for the final four games of the season.

CHRISTIAN BORDELEAU is likely the only player to win a Stanley Cup (this year) before winning a Memorial Cup (which he accomplished with the Junior Canadiens in 1970).

Brothers **DAVID**, **PETER**, and **WILLIAM MOLSON** bought the team from their cousin, Hartland. David had been team president; Peter an insurance executive; and, William a seat-holder on the Montreal Stock Exchange.

SAM POLLOCK'S strategy was simple: "We're always trying to look ahead two or three years. If we see a player, even a star player, who is showing signs of losing his touch, we go after young people in the hope that when the star is finally through as a player, we'll have somebody ready and waiting to step in...Usually, the most we'll ever change in one year is one player, sometimes two."

The players gave coach **CLAUDE RUEL** a horse to celebrate the victory, a four-year-old named Mr. Paul.

LARRY AUBUT was the team's trainer.

Stocky and strong, **ED PALCHAK** was a quiet man who took care of the team's equipment.

Other players to appear for the Canadiens this season: **BOB BERRY, RON CARON, JUDE DROUIN, FRED GLOVER, LUCIEN GRENIER, GUY LAPOINTE, GARRY MONAHAN, ERNIE WAKELY**

1969–1970

THE CHAMPIONS

Boston Bruins

For the first time in Stanley Cup history, there were no Canadian teams in the playoffs competing for the hallowed bowl. The Bruins set a four-game finals record by scoring 20 goals this year, culminating with Bobby Orr's remarkable Mother's Day goal flying through the air. In the dressing room after victory there were as many fathers as players. The Bruins became the first team in NHL history to win the Cup without a captain. There were four "co-captains"—Johnny Bucyk, Ed Westfall, Phil Esposito, and the injured Ted Green—but it was Bucyk who accepted the Cup from president Clarence Campbell. Said Harry Sinden: "One day, a young fellow with exceptional talent and leadership might become the captain. I think he's wearing number four."

STANLEY CUP FINALS

Boston Bruins win best-of-seven Stanley Cup finals 4-0

*May 3, 1970 Boston Bruins 6 at St. Louis Blues 1
*May 5, 1970 Boston Bruins 6 at St. Louis Blues 2
**May 7, 1970 St. Louis Blues 1 at Boston Bruins 4
**May 10, 1970 St. Louis Blues 3 at Boston Bruins 4 {(Bobby Orr 0:40 OT)}

** played at the Arena, St. Louis ** played at Boston Garden*

Jim Lorentz, Ed Westfall, and John McKenzie cradle the Stanley Cup.

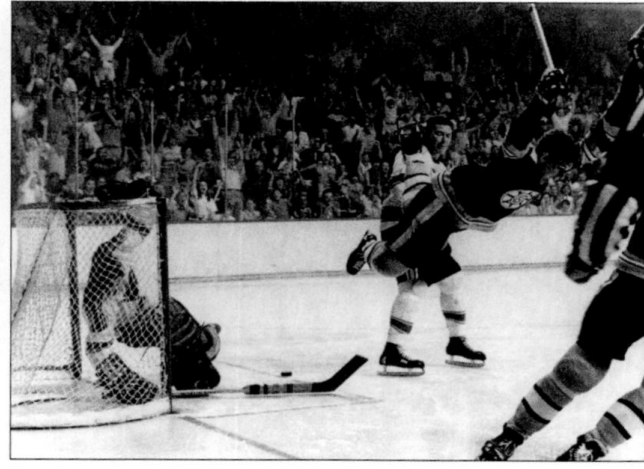

(clockwise) Johnny Bucyk takes the Cup for a lap around the ice to share the glory of the moment with fans in the Garden; Bobby Orr's flying goal won the Bruins this Cup forty seconds into overtime of game four; Orr and trainer Frosty Forristall have a Cup portrait taken for posterity.

BOSTON	GP	G	A	P	Pim
Phil Esposito	4	2	6	8	4
Johnny Bucyk	4	6	0	6	0
Derek Sanderson	4	3	3	6	8
John McKenzie	4	1	4	5	14
Bobby Orr	4	1	4	5	6
Fred Stanfield	4	1	3	4	4
Rick Smith	4	1	3	4	2
Ed Westfall	4	2	1	3	0
Ken Hodge	4	0	3	3	2
Wayne Cashman	4	2	0	2	8
Wayne Carleton	4	1	1	2	0
Don Awrey	4	0	1	1	12
Dallas Smith	4	0	1	1	6
Gary Doak	4	0	0	0	2
Gerry Cheevers	4	0	0	0	0
Jim Lorentz	4	0	0	0	0
Don Marcotte	4	0	0	0	0
Bill Lesuk	2	0	0	0	0
Bill Speer	1	0	0	0	0

In Goal	GP	W-L	Mins	GA	SO	Avg
Gerry Cheevers	4	4-0	241	7	0	1.74

PHIL ESPOSITO led the playoff scoring parade with a record 27 points, making good on his promise to win the Cup three years after arriving from Chicago.

JOHNNY BUCYK had been with the Bruins since 1957 and played on the Uke Line with Bronco Horvath and Vic Stasiuk.

DEREK SANDERSON'S dad spent $100 on a pair of skates for his son when the boy was 14 on condition that the father would get the "ring" when his son won the Cup.

ACE BAILEY was part of a rare and fortunate group of players to have been teammates of both Bobby Orr and Wayne Gretzky (with Edmonton, in the WHA, in 1978-79).

At the Bruins' civic parade following the victory, "Pie Face" **JOHNNY McKENZIE** poured a can of beer on Mayor Kevin White's head, to the delight of one and all.

BOBBY ORR won the Conn Smythe Trophy for his playoff heroics to go with the Art Ross, Norris, and Hart, a quadruple accomplishment no one will ever duplicate.

"We worked as one big family in Boston," **FRED STANFIELD** said, "and we worked for one common goal—the Stanley Cup."

RICK SMITH was in his first full season with the Bruins after splitting the previous year between the big club and the minors.

Nicknamed "18" for his sweater number, **ED WESTFALL** provided masterful checking of Bobby Hull.

KEN HODGE had been influenced in Chicago by Hull and Mikita to use a banana blade stick. When he got to Boston, he used a straighter blade and his scoring literally doubled.

"Every night we played, he did something either new or better than it had ever been done before and he left me amazed. Every night," **WAYNE CASHMAN** said of Bobby Orr.

WAYNE CARLETON—"Swoop" to his friends—came to Boston from Toronto where he had suffered under, but outlasted, coach Punch Imlach.

Known as "Elbows," **DON AWREY** played left defence with an abrasive style that suited the Bruins.

From 1961-67, **DALLAS SMITH** could not make the team. From '67 on, when the Bruins were becoming a powerhouse, he was one of the team's best players.

GARY DOAK was one of the few player changes over the coming summer as he was exposed in the Expansion Draft and scooped up by Vancouver.

He of the scarred mask, **GERRY CHEEVERS** set a new NHL record with ten consecutive playoff victories.

JIM LORENTZ, later the voice of the Buffalo Sabres, had his pro hockey beginnings with these Bruins. He was traded to St. Louis in the summer.

DON MARCOTTE was called up from the farm midway through the season to fill the role of penalty killer. "I didn't mind," he said. "I'm just happy to be in the NHL."

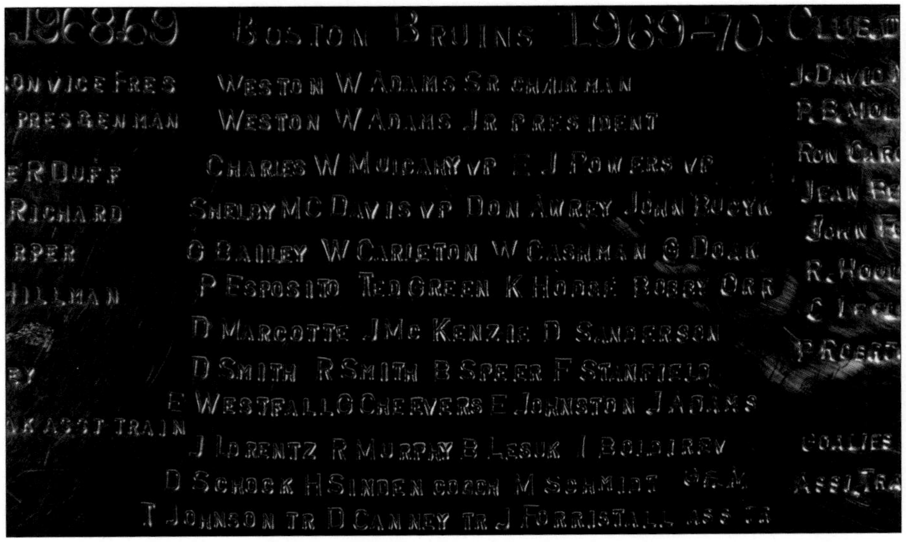

Team engraving from the Stanley Cup

After playing just three regular season and two playoff games this year, **BILL LESUK** had his name on the Cup.

BILL SPEER died in February 1989 at age 46 when his snowmobile sank in the Fenelon Falls, Ontario area.

Two days after the Cup parade, coach **HARRY SINDEN** followed through on his threat over a new contract with the Bruins. He resigned and turned to a business in prefabricated housing.

TED GREEN got involved in a vicious stick-swinging battle with Wayne Maki during which he suffered a fractured skull. He took a full year to recover.

ED JOHNSTON filled in for Cheevers late in the season when a shoulder injury shelved "Cheesie."

JOHN ADAMS was the team's third goalie, a minor leaguer who did not even make his NHL debut, with Boston, until the '72-'73 season.

RON MURPHY didn't see any playoff action and appeared in only 20 regular season games in his last of 18 NHL seasons.

Despite playing only two regular season games all year **BOLDIREV** had his name on the Cup. Don Awrey, who played 72 games with Montreal in '75-'76, is not on that year's Cup.

RON SCHOCK appeared only once in the playoffs. He was a utility forward who could play anywhere up front.

MILT SCHMIDT found himself at home late one night as Stanley Cup custodian after a party. Not knowing what else to do, he put it in an unused crib and little Lord Stanley had the quietest sleep of the year.

Although he was the team's general manager, **TOM JOHNSON** is misidentified as "tr" for trainer on the Cup! Johnson's own playing career had ended when Chico Maki's skate sliced through the back of his left leg.

Trainer **DAN CANNEY** came on board in the early 1960s. He was loyal to a fault and lived with Bobby Orr and other bachelors on the team for a short period.

In the 1977 quarter-finals, **FROSTY FORRISTALL** and Wayne Cashman cut the L.A. Forum's cable to the anthem singer's mike just before she was about to offer a copycat rendition of the Flyers' own "God Bless America" strategy as motivation for the hometown Kings.

WESTON ADAMS SR. had been chairman of the board until 1964 when the corporate structure of the team changed with Walter Brown's death. Adams became president of the Bruins and the team's representative for the league's Board of Governors.

WESTON ADAMS JR. played baseball and football but couldn't skate well enough to play hockey. He inherited the title of team president from his father, in 1969, at age 24.

CHARLES MULCAHY was vice president and general counsel for the Bruins.

EDDIE POWERS succeeded Walter Brown as president of the Boston Garden in September 1964 after Brown's sudden death.

Although written like "Shelby McDavis," **SHELBY M.C. DAVIS** was the team's vice-president.

Other players to appear for the Bruins this season: **NICK BEVERLEY, JIM HARRISON, FRANK SPRING, TOM WEBSTER, BARRY WILKINS**

1971 Montreal Canadiens

Without doubt, the turning point in these playoffs came early for Montreal. In the quarter-finals against Boston, the Bruins had won the first game 3-1 and were winning 5-1 midway through game two. Montreal scored six unanswered goals to tie the series and won game seven, in Boston, to advance. This series also introduced the league to the playoff heroics of goalie Ken Dryden who won the Conn Smythe Trophy *before* winning the Calder Trophy the next year.

STANLEY CUP FINALS

Montreal Canadiens win best-of-seven Stanley Cup finals 4-3

*May 4, 1971 Montreal Canadiens 1 at Chicago Black Hawks 2 (Jim Pappin 21:11 OT)
*May 6, 1971 Montreal Canadiens 3 at Chicago Black Hawks 5
**May 9, 1971 Chicago Black Hawks 2 at Montreal Canadiens 4
**May 11, 1971 Chicago Black Hawks 2 at Montreal Canadiens 5
*May 13, 1971 Montreal Canadiens 0 at Chicago Black Hawks 2 [Tony Esposito]
**May 16, 1971 Chicago Black Hawks 3 at Montreal Canadiens 4
*May 18, 1971 Montreal Canadiens 3 at Chicago Black Hawks 2 {Henri Richard 2:34 3rd}

** played at the Chicago Stadium ** played at the Forum, Montreal*

Hall of Famers Ken Dryden, Jean Beliveau, and Frank Mahovlich.

(clockwise) Bobby Orr is thwarted by goalie Ken Dryden; Jean Beliveau and Henri Richard hold the Cup while the bespectacled Ken Dryden holds the Conn Smythe Trophy; Gerry Cheevers manages to keep the puck out despite the traffic in front of his goal.

MONTREAL	GP	G	A	P	Pim
Frank Mahovlich	7	4	4	8	4
Pete Mahovlich	7	5	2	7	16
Yvan Cournoyer	7	4	2	6	6
Jacques Lemaire	7	3	1	4	11
Jean Beliveau	7	1	3	4	6
Henri Richard	7	2	1	3	2
Guy Lapointe	7	1	2	3	19
Rejean Houle	7	0	3	3	10
J.C. Tremblay	7	0	3	3	7
Jacques Laperriere	7	0	3	3	2
Terry Harper	7	0	2	2	10
John Ferguson	6	0	1	1	8
Marc Tardif	7	0	0	0	19
Phil Roberto	5	0	0	0	12
Leon Rochefort	6	0	0	0	6
Pierre Bouchard	3	0	0	0	2
Ken Dryden	7	0	0	0	0
Claude Larose	2	0	0	0	0
Bob Murdoch	2	0	0	0	0

In Goal	GP	W-L	Mins	GA	SO	Avg
Ken Dryden	7	4-3	441	18	0	2.45

FRANK MAHOVLICH provided a laugh at the civic reception when he made a point of showing Mayor Drapeau the white shoes of Henri Richard.

PETE MAHOVLICH had been a prospect Montreal had acquired from Detroit for whom the Little M played more in the minors than in the NHL.

LEFLEY lucked out with his name on the Cup. He played only once in the regular season and once in the playoffs, spending most of the year with the Voyageurs in the AHL.

Incredibly, **YVAN COURNOYER** was a plus player in the category every year he was in the league.

Despite his team successes, **JACQUES LEMAIRE** was never named to an All-Star team. He scored from centre ice on Tony Esposito in game seven to make the score 2-1 Chicago and begin a comeback 3-2 win for the Cup.

Many credit **JEAN BELIVEAU** with the tradition of the Stanley Cup victory lap, showing the Cup up close to fans in the rail seats. Truth be known, though, as early as 1934 Louis Trudel had performed a similar celebration with the Hawks.

Coach Al MacNeil benched **HENRI RICHARD** for a full game during the season, and the Pocket Rocket responded by criticizing the boss. "How can you hope to win with such an incompetent behind the bench?" he asked in frustration.

Rookie **GUY LAPOINTE** was fortunate to have J.C. Tremblay as a defence partner, the veteran a steadying influence for the newcomer trying to establish himself on a Cup-quality team.

Nicknamed "Peanuts," **REJEAN HOULE** shadowed Bobby Hull into the ice during the finals, one of the keys to victory.

JEAN-CLAUDE TREMBLAY was later invited to represent Canada at the 1972 Summit Series, an offer that was withdrawn by the NHL after Tremblay signed with the WHA.

JACQUES "LAPPY" LAPERRIERE became an Honoured Member of the Hockey Hall of Fame despite playing just 691 games, one of the lower totals for the modern era.

This proved to be **TERRY HARPER'S** final year in Montreal as he was unable to get along with incoming coach Scotty Bowman.

JOHN FERGUSON'S career ended moments after this final victory. He retired at age 32.

MARC TARDIF was the next great hero in Quebec, but he fled the Habs and signed a more lucrative contract in the WHA with the Los Angeles Sharks.

PHIL ROBERTO'S time in Montreal was brief and not necessarily satisfying: "When I made a mistake in Montreal, bang! I was on the bench. You don't learn much on the bench. You learn more in the minors," he opined.

LEON ROCHEFORT had been with Montreal briefly during the '65-'66 Cup season. Philadelphia claimed him in the '67 Expansion Draft, and he was sent to the Rangers two years later only to be sent to Los Angeles three days later. In 1970, the Canadiens re-acquired him.

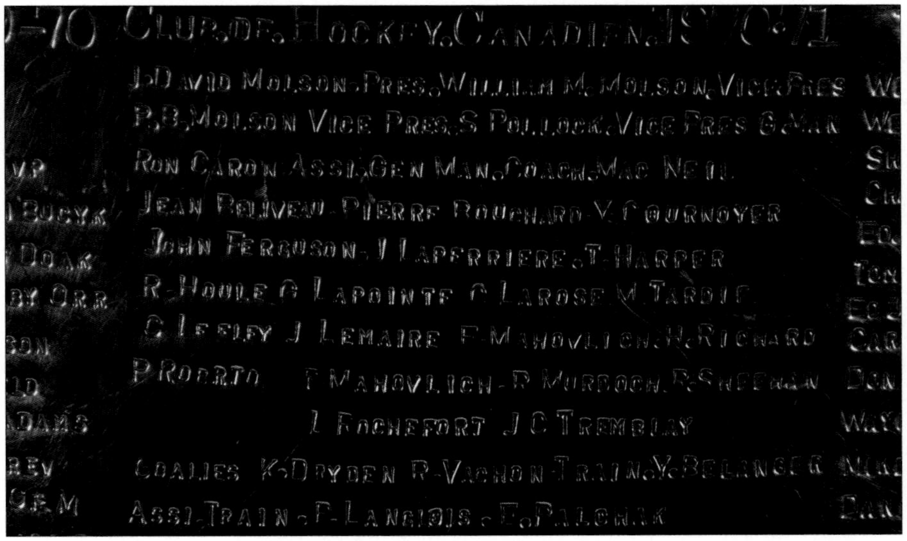

Team engraving from the Stanley Cup

PIERRE BOUCHARD quickly became known as the team's enforcer, a tag he disliked and tried to shake most of his career.

With just six games of regular-season play in the NHL under his belt, **KEN DRYDEN** won the Conn Smythe Trophy before he won the Calder Trophy in '71-'72.

After a two-year hiatus in Minnesota, **CLAUDE LAROSE** was back on terra firma in Montreal where he had played the first six years of his NHL career.

SERGE SAVARD played just 37 regular season games and missed all of the playoffs because of injury, so despite being a regular on the team he did not make the engraver's list this year.

BOBBY SHEEHAN played for seven teams in a career that spanned three decades, though those numbers deceive. His stats read 310 games played, a career greatly diminished by his "lifestyle." "They seemed to have something against single guys," Sheehan said of the Habs' philosophy after he was let go.

YVES BELANGER had been part of the concession department and decided to become a therapist.

Assistant trainer **PHIL LANGLOIS** was a teenaged stick boy who was taken on by Ed Palchak as a helper.

Trainer **ED PALCHAK** served in the same capacity in November 2003 for the historic outdoor game in Edmonton, featuring the alumni of the Oilers and Canadiens.

Coach **AL MacNEIL'S** feuds with some of his players were so volatile that he received death threats during the playoffs and had to move his family out of home as a precautionary measure.

ROGIE VACHON was once the goalie of the future in Montreal. But with the emergence of Dryden, he was dealt to Los Angeles.

BOB MURDOCH, by his own admission, played but a small role on this team. He dressed for only one regular season game and two more in the finals.

This was to be **DAVID MOLSON'S** last Cup as he would sell the team in December to the Bronfmans at $22 a share, less than the $30 a share the Leafs were going for. "I can't figure it," he said. "The Forum is as good as the Gardens or better."

BILL MOLSON was the only one of the family to continue to attend games after they had sold the club right at the end of the calendar year while Senator Raymond was on vacation.

PETER MOLSON had a certain power with the NHL's board of directors, yet his apparent love for the team and game—which he vowed he would make his life's work—seemed to vanish when he and brother Bill sold the team.

Perhaps **SAM POLLOCK'S** best trade (and there were many good ones) involved acquiring Pete Mahovlich and Bart Crashley from Detroit in 1969 for Garry Monahan and Doug Piper.

RON CARON acted as Pollock's right-hand man and travelled with the team exclusively because of Pollock's refusal to fly!

Other players to appear for the Canadiens this season: **RALPH BACKSTROM, GUY CHARRON, BILL COLLINS, FRAN HUCK, PHIL MYRE, LARRY PLEAU, MICKEY REDMOND**

1971 THE CHAMPIONS

1972 Boston Bruins

This was the first Boston-Rangers final since 1929 when the Bruins won their first Cup, and for the win this year the Bruins had their name butchered at the engraver's who used a Q instead of an O in the city name! After taking a 3-1 lead in games against the Rangers in the finals, Boston leader Phil Esposito remarked, "If those guys (the Rangers) think they're going to beat us three in a row, they're full of crap. And you can spell that K-R-A-P—that's Park spelled backward."

STANLEY CUP FINALS

Boston Bruins win best-of-seven Stanley Cup finals 4-2

*April 30, 1972	New York Rangers 5 at Boston Bruins 6
*May 2, 1972	New York Rangers 1 at Boston Bruins 2
**May 4, 1972	Boston Bruins 2 at New York Rangers 5
**May 7, 1972	Boston Bruins 3 at New York Rangers 2
*May 9, 1972	New York Rangers 3 at Boston Bruins 2
**May 11, 1972	Boston Bruins 3 at New York Rangers 0 {Bobby Orr 11:18 1st} [Gerry Cheevers]

** played at Boston Garden* *** played at Madison Square Garden, New York*

Don Awrey and Phil Esposito give Stanley a hug.

BOSTON	GP	G	A	P	Pim
Ken Hodge	6	5	3	8	19
Bobby Orr	6	4	4	8	17
Phil Esposito	6	0	8	8	14
Mike Walton	6	1	4	5	6
Wayne Cashman	6	3	1	4	15
Johnny Bucyk	6	1	2	3	2
Fred Stanfield	6	1	2	3	0
John McKenzie	6	0	2	2	25
Ed Westfall	6	0	2	2	10
Derek Sanderson	6	1	0	1	26
Ace Bailey	6	1	0	1	14
Don Marcotte	5	1	0	1	6
Don Awrey	6	0	1	1	21
Carol Vadnais	6	0	1	1	13
Dallas Smith	6	0	1	1	10
Ted Green	4	0	0	0	0
Gerry Cheevers	3	0	0	0	0
Ed Johnston	3	0	0	0	0

In Goal	GP	W-L	Mins	GA	SO	Avg
Ed Johnston	3	2-1	180	6	0	2.00
Gerry Cheevers	3	2-1	180	10	1	3.33

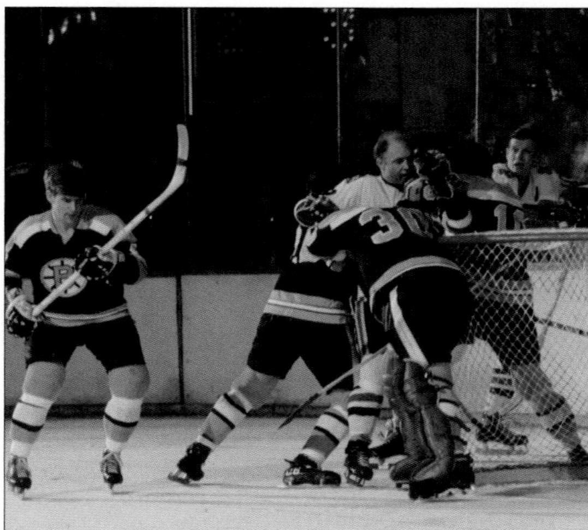

(clockwise) Fans in downtown Boston give the Bruins a massive reception following the win; Milt Schmidt (left) and Boston Mayor White share a laugh at the civic reception for the team; goalie Gerry Cheevers tries to keep his crease clear of players as Bobby Orr makes his way to the action.

Although **KEN HODGE** grew up in Canada, he was born in Birmingham, England and as such is the answer to the trivia question, "Who was the first non-Canadian-born 50-goal scorer in the NHL?"

BOBBY ORR led the playoffs with 19 assists and became the first player to win two Conn Smythe Trophies. He played on a wobbly knee, and off-season surgery cost him a chance to play in the September '72 Summit Series.

Although he was a star this year, **PHIL ESPOSITO** made even greater contributions to hockey at the Summit Series. He scored an incredible 76 goals with the Bruins this year to shatter the record that would stand until Wayne Gretzky broke it more than a decade later.

MIKE WALTON moved up to left wing on the top line when Ken Hodge was injured and turned in an excellent year with 28 goals. Shortly after the victory, he returned to Orillia, Ontario to run his sports camp/hockey school with friend, neighbour, and teammate Bobby Orr.

WAYNE CASHMAN was just starting to blossom this year. He was not coach Johnson's first choice to replace Ron Murphy on a line with Esposito and Hodge, but once "Cash" played port side with those two, the highest-scoring line in hockey was born (though he played right wing for a while when Hodge went down with a broken ankle).

JOHNNY BUCYK arrived in Boston when the Red Wings acquired Terry Sawchuk on June 10, 1957. Forty-seven years later, Bucyk is still with the team as president of the alumni association.

FRED STANFIELD had a career-high 79 points, many of which came on the league's best power-play. "We knew each time we stepped on the ice with it," he said of the man advantage, "we could score. It was awesome."

In a measure of sweet retribution, Mayor Kevin White doused **JOHN McKENZIE** with beer during the Cup parade to avenge a similar drenching at the hands of "Pie Face" in 1970.

ED WESTFALL'S success with Boston meant that when he became available in the Expansion Draft the Islanders pounced. He retired the year before the Isles won their first of four Cups.

DEREK SANDERSON, considered the best two-way player in the game, signed a million-dollar contract with the WHA in the summer and never had an impact on the game again. He drank and drugged his fortune away and returned to the NHL a pale shadow of his former, remarkable self.

GARNET "ACE" BAILEY had a huge impact on the outcome of the finals. In game one, the Bruins quickly built a 5-1 lead, but by the third period the score was tied 5-5. Coach Johnson benched Westfall and gave Bailey the extra ice time, and Ace responded by beating Brad Park one-on-one and firing the winning goal at 17:44 of the third.

DON MARCOTTE was always a fan favourite for his physical play and his honest effort every night. The previous year he had been given the team's "Seventh Player Award" as the Bruins' unsung hero.

From worst to first. **CAROL VADNAIS** started the season with California but was traded in February '72 to Boston with Don O'Donoghue for Reg Leach, Rick Smith, and Bob Stewart.

Team engraving from the Stanley Cup

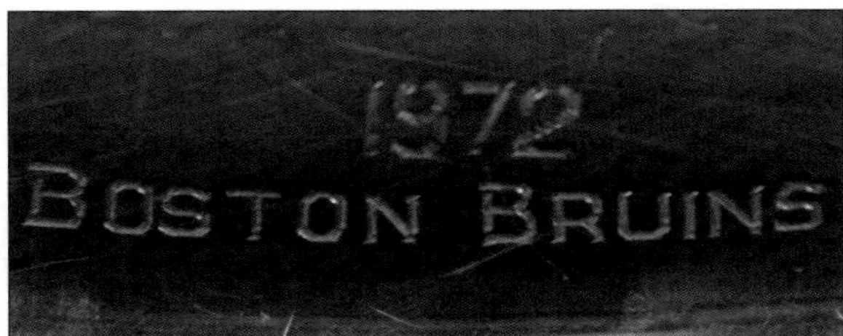

Team engraving from the shoulder of the replica Cup

DALLAS SMITH was capable offensively and one of the stronger players in the league, but it was his defensive partner, Bobby Orr, who deservedly got more of the credit for success.

Part of the history of Cup engravings are their inconsistencies. **DON AWREY** played the entire season with the '75-'76 Habs, but missed the playoffs because of injury and never got his name on the Cup. As a result, rules were formalized to ensure deserving players were honoured.

TED GREEN was one of five players general manager Schmidt let go to the WHA just a month after winning the Cup.

Like teammate Derek Sanderson, goalie **GERRY CHEEVERS** signed with the WHA in the summer. Unlike "Turk," "Cheesie"returned to the NHL and had an impact for a few years still.

DAN CANNEY was the kind of loyal and meticulous trainer who would make sure every sweater was hanging just right for the players in the dressing room. He later worked for a Boston area racetrack.

"FROSTY" FORRISTALL was in charge of drawing fresh "scars" on Gerry Cheevers' goalie mask periodically to show where the goalie would have been hit without the mask. Forristall later worked for the Toronto Blue Jays before succumbing to cancer in 1995.

ED JOHNSTON was later named to Team Canada for the Summit Series, and unknown to even the most astute trivia experts he was the backup goalie on the bench for all eight games.

WESTON ADAMS SR. was club president from 1936-51 and '64-'69. The native of Springfield, Massachusetts was inducted into the Hockey Hall of Fame this summer of '72 and died just a year later.

WESTON ADAMS JR.'S grandfather was the first team president in 1924 and he now represented the third generation of Adams associated with the club. "Never look back—always ahead," was his modus operandi.

SHELBY DAVIS was Boston's vice president.

CHARLES MULCAHY was vice president and general counsel for the Bruins.

EDWARD POWERS was the Bruins' vice president and treasurer.

Oddly, **MILT SCHMIDT'S** name wasn't on the 1970 Cup even though it was his remarkable trade with Chicago that brought the Cup to Boston. He had succeeded Lynn Patrick as coach in 1954, and stayed behind the bench until 1966 (with the exception of the '61-'62 season).

Other players to appear for the Bruins this season: **NICK BEVERLEY, IVAN BOLDIREV, CHRIS HAYES, RON JONES, REG LEACH, TERRY O'REILLY, GARRY PETERS, MATT RAVLICH, DOUG ROBERTS, BOB STEWART**

1972–1973 THE CHAMPIONS Montreal Canadiens

The Canadiens set a record with 33 goals in this finals series, and the teams combined to set another record for most goals in a finals game with the 8-7 score in game five. In the WHA's first year, Bobby Hull's Winnipeg Jets won the Avco Cup, emblematic of supremacy in that league. Afterward, the Golden Jet challenged the Canadiens to a one-game Stanley Cup showdown. The Habs quietly ignored the offer and celebrated their NHL victory.

STANLEY CUP FINALS

Montreal Canadiens win best-of-seven Stanley Cup finals 4-2

*April 29, 1973	Chicago Black Hawks 3 at Montreal Canadiens 8
*May 1, 1973	Chicago Black Hawks 1 at Montreal Canadiens 4
**May 3, 1973	Montreal Canadiens 4 at Chicago Black Hawks 7
**May 6, 1973	Montreal Canadiens 4 at Chicago Black Hawks 0 [Ken Dryden]
*May 8, 1973	Chicago Black Hawks 8 at Montreal Canadiens 7
**May 10, 1973	Montreal Canadiens 6 at Chicago Black Hawks 4 {Yvan Cournoyer 8:13 3rd}

** played at the Forum, Montreal ** played at the Chicago Stadium*

The Habs pour off the bench to celebrate their Cup win in 1973.

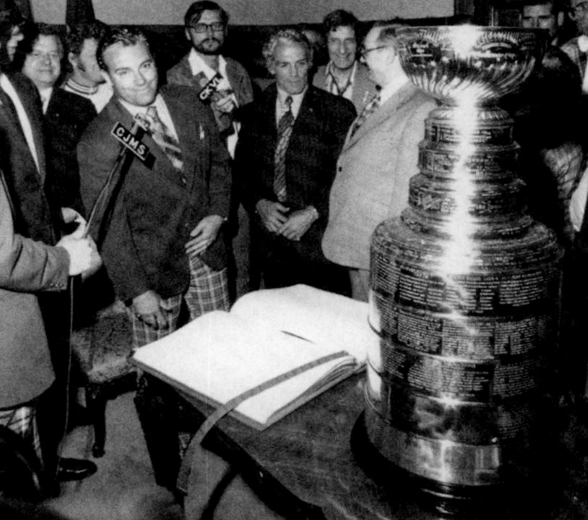

(clockwise) Enormous crowds gather downtown to cheer the Habs for their win; Henri Richard and admirers join in the victory party; coach Scotty Bowman (left) and Henri Richard attend the reception for the Canadiens at City Hall.

MONTREAL	GP	G	A	P	Pim
Yvan Cournoyer	6	6	6	12	0
Jacques Lemaire	6	3	9	12	0
Frank Mahovlich	6	5	6	11	0
Pete Mahovlich	6	3	5	8	12
Claude Larose	6	3	4	7	2
Marc Tardif	6	3	3	6	4
Chuck Lefley	6	3	3	6	2
Guy Lapointe	6	1	3	4	8
Henri Richard	6	2	1	3	0
Rejean Houle	6	1	2	3	0
Jacques Laperriere	2	1	1	2	0
Larry Robinson	6	0	2	2	2
Murray Wilson	6	0	2	2	2
Guy Lafleur	6	0	2	2	0
Serge Savard	6	1	0	1	6
Pierre Bouchard	6	1	0	1	4
Jim Roberts	6	0	0	0	6
Bob Murdoch	4	0	0	0	2
Ken Dryden	6	0	0	0	0

In Goal	GP	W-L	Mins	GA	SO	Avg
Ken Dryden	6	4-2	360	21	1	3.50

YVAN COURNOYER led the playoffs with 25 points, including a record 15 goals. He won the Conn Smythe Trophy and set a six-game finals record by scoring six goals.

JACQUES LEMAIRE and Cournoyer both had 12 points in the finals to tie Gordie Howe's record. Lemaire is also one of a small group to have scored two Stanley Cup-winning goals in his career.

FRANK MAHOVLICH scored his 500th career goal and 1,000th career point before capping the year with a Stanley Cup, the sixth and last of his Hall of Fame career.

PETE MAHOVLICH showed up at the victory party with three water pistols and proceeded to drench everyone in sight.

CLAUDE LAROSE broke his leg sliding into the goalpost in the second period of the final game of the playoffs. He demanded that the ambulance driver take him back to the Stadium so that he could celebrate with his mates and he later flew home on a stretcher with the team.

"Speed, as they say, kills," opined speedy left winger **MARC TARDIF**. "Speed will do it every time," he said of the Habs' greatest strength.

CHUCK LEFLEY came out of nowhere to score 21 goals in his first NHL season even though he had shown only moderate ability around the net in junior and minor pro.

GUY LAPOINTE was the up-and-coming star defenceman of the team. He had a great shot, good skating ability, and a knack for making hard, clean hits.

"I'm 37 and I've slowed some...However, one thing I'd like to do first is carry that Stanley Cup around the ice...I've seen others do it and it's just something I've always dreamed of doing," said **HENRI RICHARD**, who assumed the captaincy when Beliveau retired.

REJEAN HOULE played his entire NHL career with the Habs, but it was a career separated by three years with the Quebec Nordiques in the WHA, beginning this summer (1973-76).

JACQUES LAPERRIERE scored a career-high seven goals, led the league with a +78 despite missing 21 games during the season, and had just 34 penalty minutes as one of the toughest defencemen in the league.

The 1971 Amateur Draft year featured Lafleur and Dionne, and although eleven NHL teams had a chance to select **LARRY ROBINSON**, only Montreal saw the opportunity.

MURRAY WILSON scored the game-winning goal in game three against Buffalo in the quarter-finals to give the Habs an insurmountable 3-0 lead in games.

GUY LAFLEUR was the only son of a welder father who also had four daughters. Like Beliveau, "the Flower" played junior in Quebec City.

SERGE SAVARD was coming off the incredible Summit Series victory in September '72 and continued his strong play by recording a +70 in the plus/minus category.

Team engraving from the Stanley Cup

Team engraving from the shoulder of the Stanley Cup

PIERRE BOUCHARD was big and somewhat slow and awkward, his greatest asset being his size and physical presence.

JIM ROBERTS had been acquired the previous season and was re-joining coach Scotty Bowman for whom he had played in St. Louis since 1967. Their connection and respect continued after Roberts retired when Bowman hired him as an assistant in Buffalo.

"MUD" MURDOCH had a pedestrian playing career but went on to coach in the WHA and later in Europe.

Earlier in the season, while playing for Kansas City in the CHL, **MICHEL PLASSE** became the first pro goalie to score a goal when he shot the puck into the empty Oklahoma City net.

Rookie **STEVE SHUTT** had quite an adjustment to make. The previous year he led the OHL with 63 goals for the Marlies. This year in the NHL he struggled to score eight times. As a result, he was in the press box for all but one playoff game.

No greater shock came to the Cup champions than at season's end when goalie **KEN DRYDEN** announced his plans to leave the game for a year to finish his law degree.

Trainer **BOB WILLIAMS** was the first American-born member of the Habs' dressing room staff, though his stay with the team was brief.

ED PALCHAK was the team's longtime assistant trainer.

JACQUES COURTOIS was named president of the club in December 1971 as a result of the Bronfmans' purchase of the club from the Molson family.

Upon retiring in 1972, **JEAN BELIVEAU** was made a director of Carena Bancorp, the company that ran the team, and to extend the relationship the Jean Beliveau Foundation was set up to help minor hockey players.

Brothers **PETER** and **EDWARD BRONFMAN** were cousins of Edgar and Charles Bronfman, owners of distilleries, real estate, and myriad holdings that made the family among the world's wealthiest.

SAM POLLOCK'S judgement of skill always ranked first in the NHL, but even in his day he had a budget within which to work. This summer, those financial concerns forced him to refuse to renegotiate Ken Dryden's contract. Dryden sat out a year, the Habs lost the Cup, and a reconciliation resulted.

The son of a blacksmith who emigrated to Canada from Scotland, **SCOTTY BOWMAN** took 16 years of scouting and coaching in the amateur and pro ranks to get to Montreal and the Stanley Cup.

Other players to appear for the Canadiens this season: **CHUCK ARNASON, DAVE GARDNER, DALE HOGANSON, YVON LAMBERT, RANDY ROTA, WAYNE THOMAS**

1973–1974 THE CHAMPIONS Philadelphia Flyers

How did the Flyers pull this off? They had beaten the Bruins only once in their past 28 games, but managed to stifle Bobby Orr and Phil Esposito in the process. Coach Fred Shero's edict was a simple one: no one player (i.e., Orr) can beat an entire team. The "Broad Street Bullies" became the first expansion team to win the Cup, abetted by a live performance of "God Bless America" by Kate Smith prior to game six of the series. The Flyers were the youngest team to win the Cup.

STANLEY CUP FINALS

Philadelphia Flyers win best-of-seven Stanley Cup finals 4-2

*May 7, 1974 Philadelphia Flyers 2 at Boston Bruins 3
*May 9, 1974 Philadelphia Flyers 3 at Boston Bruins 2 (Bobby Clarke 12:01 OT)
**May 12, 1974 Boston Bruins 1 at Philadelphia Flyers 4
**May 14, 1974 Boston Bruins 2 at Philadelphia Flyers 4
*May 16, 1974 Philadelphia Flyers 1 at Boston Bruins 5
**May 19, 1974 Boston Bruins 0 at Philadelphia Flyers 1
{Rick MacLeish 14:48 1st} [Bernie Parent]

** played at Boston Garden **played at the Spectrum, Philadelphia*

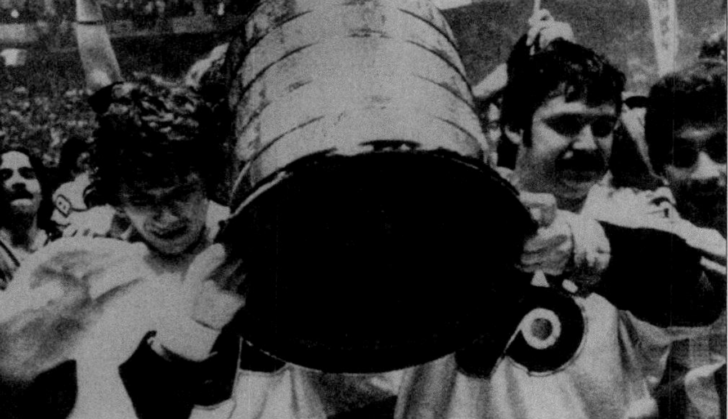

Bobby Clarke (left) and Bernie Parent carry the Stanley Cup.

PHILADELPHIA	GP	G	A	P	Pim
Bobby Clarke	6	3	3	6	14
Rick MacLeish	6	2	3	5	4
Andre Dupont	6	2	1	3	33
Dave Schultz	6	1	2	3	38
Don Saleski	6	0	3	3	6
Bill Flett	6	0	3	3	4
Orest Kindrachuk	6	2	0	2	11
Tom Bladon	6	1	1	2	21
Bill Barber	6	1	1	2	2
Terry Crisp	6	1	1	2	2
Ross Lonsberry	6	1	1	2	2
Joe Watson	6	0	2	2	16
Ed Van Impe	6	0	2	2	13
Bill Clement	3	1	0	1	2
Jim Watson	6	0	1	1	30
Simon Nolet	6	0	1	1	0
Bruce Cowick	6	0	0	0	7
Bernie Parent	6	0	0	0	0
Gary Dornhoefer	3	0	0	0	0

In Goal	GP	W-L	Mins	GA	SO	Avg
Bernie Parent	6	4-2	372	13	1	2.10

Philadelphia defenceman Ed Van Impe corrals Boston's Ken Hodge as Bernie Parent covers the puck during the 1974 Cup finals in Philadelphia.

BOBBY CLARKE was the faceoff king. He won most of the draws, and those he lost he'd poke his stick between the legs of the opposing centre to tie him up effectively.

Two years ago, **RICK MacLEISH** was playing for the Richmond Robins in Virginia. A year later, he scored 50 goals and 100 points with the Flyers, and this season he led the playoffs with 22 scoring points.

ANDRE DUPONT'S finest career moments came in game two of the finals when he scored the tying goal and set up Clarke for the OT winner.

BOB TAYLOR had been sentenced to thirty days in jail and fined $500 for assaulting a peace officer during a game the previous season when he helped teammate Don Saleski during a brawl with a fan who had pulled Saleski's hair.

DAVE "THE HAMMER" SCHULTZ was a true goon. He incurred a record 348 penalty minutes this year, yet impressively also scored 20 goals and assisted on Clarke's winner in game two.

DON SALESKI (a.k.a. Big Bird) epitomized the Flyers' team—a goon to outsiders, a forward motivated by team spirit within the dressing room and an inspiration to those around him.

BILL FLETT left the NHL to sign a lucrative contract with the New York Raiders of the WHA, but when the club failed to pay him he returned to the Flyers. He was frequently maligned in other cities for his long and scraggly beard.

Playing on a line with Saleski and Schultz, **OREST KINDRACHUK** saw more action along the boards as a mucker and grinder than in front of the net, where the scorers usually hang out.

TOM BLADON later had the best game for a defenceman in league history when, on the night of December 11, 1977, he had four goals and four assists in an 11-1 win over the Cleveland Barons.

The master diver, **BILL BARBER** was likely the first to draw penalties (Flyers' view) by faking being tripped (opponents' view). Either way, his style of play helped the Flyers win a Cup.

Despite the crazy celebrations as the clock ran down in the final game, **TERRY CRISP** had the presence of mind to scoop the game puck as a cherished memory of an historic victory.

While most players put their false teeth in a glass before skating out onto the ice, **ROSS LONSBERRY** removed his toupee before putting on his helmet (of course!) and playing.

JOE WATSON later became poster boy for touch-up on icings after he was checked into the boards chasing the puck, shattering his kneecap, and ending his career. Yet 30 years on, the NHL refuses to implement a rule that has been used internationally for decades.

A heavy hitter on the blueline, **ED VAN IMPE** was, improbably, runner-up to Bobby Orr in the Calder Trophy voting in 1967.

Team engraving from the replica Cup

Pained by a knee injury sustained during the semi-finals against the Rangers, **BILL CLEMENT** missed the first two games of the finals, but thanks to motivation by captain Clarke played the rest of the way in a limited, though effective, capacity.

Although Joe's brother, **JIM WATSON**, was also a defenceman with the team, the two rarely played together, though they grew up on the same farm in Smithers, B.C..

SIMON NOLET scored 13 goals in the first 17 games of the regular season playing on a line with Clarke, then missed six weeks with an eye injury before returning to help with the Stanley Cup drive.

BRUCE COWICK appeared only in the playoffs this year and was lost to Washington in the Expansion Draft during the summer.

Goalie **BERNIE PARENT** won the Conn Smythe and Vezina Trophies this year. Without him, there is no Cup in Philadelphia.

GARY DORNHOEFER suffered a shoulder injury in game three of the finals and was reduced to watching the victory from the anonymity of the press box.

BOB KELLY was called "Mad Dog" or "The Hound" by teammates for his reckless abandon and his ability to hit seemingly every player on the ice during his every shift.

BARRY ASHBEE suffered a career-ending injury during the Rangers series on April 28, 1974, when he was struck in the eye by a slapshot.

Coach **FRED SHERO** had appeared in two playoff games for the Rangers as a player when the team lost to Detroit in 1950. Prior to game six, he uttered the now famous line: "If we win tonight, we will walk together forever."

Trainer **FRANK LEWIS** had been a talented musician who jammed with the likes of Tommy Dorsey, Jack Teagarten, and Ted Lewis before hanging up his horn and entering hockey.

ED SNIDER was the man responsible for bringing hockey to Philadelphia back in 1967. Despite being chairman of the board, he had always considered himself more a fan than an owner.

"Imagine!" **JOE SCOTT** screamed. "Two million people turning out for a parade! It's unbelievable!"

EUGENE DIXON was well established in the city and sat on many important boards, notably the Church Farm School, Lafayette College, and Temple University.

KEITH ALLEN acted as general manager and head coach for the Seattle Totems for nine years before coaching the Flyers for the first two years of the team's existence. He moved into the GM's position in December '69.

MIKE NYKOLUK spent the better part of 16 years and 1,069 games in the AHL as a player before joining Fred Shero to help run practises as an assistant coach.

MARCEL PELLETIER had been called the "Vagabond Goalie" because he played for some 13 teams in a 20-year pro career. His only two NHL stints came 12 years apart, 1950-51 with Chicago, and then '62-'63 with the Rangers.

Other players to appear for the Flyers this season: **SERGE LAJEUNESSE, AL MacADAM**

1974–1975 THE CHAMPIONS Philadelphia Flyers

Entering this finals, the Sabres had been winless against the Flyers in the previous 13 meetings in a matchup that featured the beauty and speed of the French Connection Line in Buffalo (Gilbert Perreault, Rick Martin, and Rene Robert) against the fighting, brawling Broad Street Bullies. Unfortunately for hockey, the fighting won out for a second straight year. In game three, fog became so thick on Buffalo ice that the game was held up while players skated around with towels to clear the air. At another point, a bat appeared above the ice and Buffalo's Jim Lorentz killed it with a swat of his stick. This was the first time two expansion teams played in the finals. The Flyers' victory parade ended inside a packed JFK Stadium.

STANLEY CUP FINALS

Philadelphia Flyers win best-of-seven Stanley Cup finals 4-2

*May 15, 1975 Buffalo Sabres 1 at Philadelphia Flyers 4
*May 18, 1975 Buffalo Sabres 1 at Philadelphia Flyers 2
**May 20, 1975 Philadelphia Flyers 4 at Buffalo Sabres 5 (Rene Robert 18:29 OT)
**May 22, 1975 Philadelphia Flyers 2 at Buffalo Sabres 4
*May 25, 1975 Buffalo Sabres 1 at Philadelphia Flyers 5
**May 27, 1975 Philadelphia Flyers 2 at Buffalo Sabres 0
{Bob Kelly 0:11 3rd} [Bernie Parent]

** played at the Spectrum, Philadelphia   ** played at Memorial Auditorium, Buffalo*

The Flyers celebrate their second straight Cup.

(clockwise) For one of the few times in the series, Bernie Parent surrenders a Buffalo goal, at the fog-plagued Memorial Auditorium; Parent stands his ground as the Sabres' Jim Schoenfeld tries to get to the net; Parent displays the hardware from his spectacular season—the Conn Smythe Trophy, Stanley Cup, and Vezina Trophy.

PHILADELPHIA	GP	G	A	P	Pim
Bill Barber	6	2	4	6	0
Bobby Clarke	6	2	3	5	2
Reggie Leach	6	3	1	4	0
Bob Kelly	5	2	2	4	7
Rick MacLeish	6	1	3	4	2
Terry Crisp	4	0	4	4	0
Ross Lonsberry	6	2	1	3	2
Gary Dornhoefer	6	2	0	2	14
Dave Schultz	6	2	0	2	13
Don Saleski	6	1	1	2	8
Ed Van Impe	6	0	2	2	8
Ted Harris	6	0	2	2	2
Orest Kindrachuk	5	0	2	2	2
Larry Goodenough	2	0	2	2	2
Jim Watson	6	0	2	2	0
Andre Dupont	6	1	0	1	10
Bill Clement	5	1	0	1	2
Tom Bladon	4	0	1	1	8
Joe Watson	6	0	0	0	2
Bernie Parent	6	0	0	0	0

In Goal	GP	W-L	Mins	GA	SO	Avg
Bernie Parent	6	4-2	378	20	1	3.17

One of the more decorated Flyers in team history, **BILL BARBER** had his number 7 retired by the team and he became an inductee of the Hockey Hall of Fame.

Captain **BOBBY CLARKE** doted on his coach's methods. "Hockey has been revolutionized by Shero's system," he declared.

BOB TAYLOR returned to the Flyers after retiring and later still joined the team's broadcasting crew. More recently, he did TV for Tampa Bay this past, Cup-winning season.

REGGIE "THE RIFLE" LEACH was the team's scoring star. Part Ojibway, he was one of the few Natives to make the NHL.

BOB KELLY idolized Rocket Richard and Gordie Howe as a kid, but when he made it to the NHL he played more like John Ferguson and Eddie Shack.

"You never know when the guy is happy or sad," Dornhoefer said of **RICK MacLEISH**. "Rick just never changes his expression. To be quite honest, I've never seen him smile."

After retiring in 1977, **TERRY CRISP** stayed with the Flyers as Shero's assistant. During the previous year, he was sent to the farm team in Springfield to take over as coach.

A scorer with grit, **LONSBERRY** had seven 20-goal seasons during a 15-year career that took him to Boston, Los Angeles, and Pittsburgh.

"There was something missing for me when we won the Cup the second time," **DORNHOEFER** confessed. "I was so tired and worn out that I was happy the season was finally over."

DAVE SCHULTZ surpassed last year's record penalty season by amassing a staggering 472 penalty minutes this year.

DON SALESKI went from this Cup team to the lowly Colorado Rockies the next season. After a fight with coach Don Cherry, he found himself in the minors and then retired.

ED VAN IMPE used part of his Cup-winning paycheque to upgrade the kitchen of an old house he had been renovating and named it the "Lord Stanley Memorial Kitchen."

TED HARRIS had been talked out of retirement by Shero at the start of the year but followed through with his intentions at season's end to take on coaching duties with Minnesota.

A rare example of a player who began at a Canadian university (Saskatchewan), **"O" KINDRACHUK** was praised by coach Shero for being the league's best man in the corners.

LARRY GOODENOUGH was a late season call-up who got most of his ice time in practise and was on a plane to Thunder Bay while the Flyers were on their parade route. The chauffeur with the "Goodenough" nameplate drove an empty car, the player not feeling he had done enough to join in the celebrations.

JIM WATSON'S playing days went downhill quickly after he suffered three major injuries: he blocked a shot with his face, took a stick to the eye, and had spinal fusion surgery on his back, the cumulative effects of which ended his career.

Called "Moose" because he resembled Moose Vasko, **DUPONT** was called something else by Rangers farm system director Dennis Ball, the man who first brought him to the NHL: "He's like a great big St. Bernard dog," Ball said. "He's such a nice kid." Opponents begged to differ.

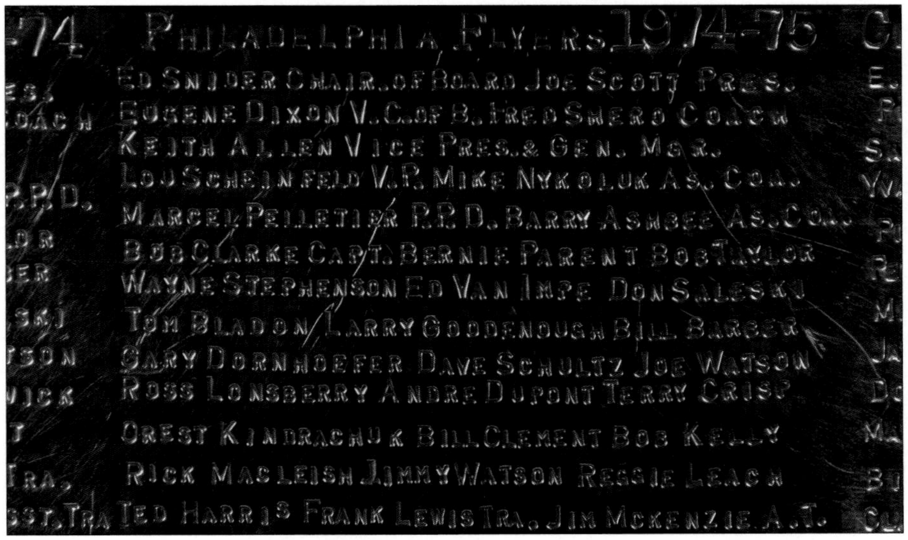

Team engraving from the Stanley Cup

BILL CLEMENT, never known as a scorer, provided the insurance goal in the 2-0 Cup-clinching game. Most nights he was regarded as one of the best penalty-killers in the game.

After playing eight full seasons in the NHL, **TOM BLADON** ended his career by playing briefly with three teams in '80-'81 before being sent to the minors for good.

WAYNE STEPHENSON became the number-one goalie the next year after Patent missed much of the year with a serious eye injury which eventually cost him his career.

JOE WATSON was the last man on the roster from the expansion team lineup in 1967, staying with the team until 1978 when he was sold outright to Colorado.

For the second straight year **BERNIE PARENT** won both the Vezina and Conn Smythe Trophies, testaments to his dominance and the importance of goaltending in the playoffs.

FRANK LEWIS began his career as a trainer with the old Philadelphia Ramblers. He moved on to the Jersey Devils, and then the Flyers, as an assistant, in '67.

JIM McKENZIE had worked for the Pittsburgh Penguins, and in baseball he worked in the Texas League before coming to assist Frank Lewis in 1972.

ED SNIDER graduated from the University of Maryland and was responsible for bringing hockey to Philadelphia in 1967.

JOE SCOTT remained active with charitable institutions for years, particularly for hospitals and Jewish organizations. A soccer stadium was erected in Hadera, Israel in his honour.

EUGENE DIXON chaired numerous boards for hospitals in the Philadelphia area and also acted as Director for the Atlantic City Racing Association.

FRED SHERO'S motto was simple: the refs can't call everything. Though he maintained he never sent a player out with verbal orders to start a fight, the records nonetheless show the Flyers fought their way to two Stanley Cups.

KEITH ALLEN won Cups with Detroit in 1954 and '55 after which he coached and managed in the WHL for a decade before joining the expansion Flyers in 1967.

The man who named the team's building The Spectrum, **LOU SCHEINFELD** quit his job as a newspaper reporter to become the Flyers' vice-president and the building's president.

MIKE NYKOLUK was the NHL's first full-time assistant coach. He played briefly with the Leafs in the 1950s, a team he would later coach in the '80s.

MARCEL PELLETIER started as coach of the Jersey Devils, the Flyers' farm team, and moved up to become the team's director of player personnel.

BARRY ASHBEE played the better part of ten years in the minors before the Flyers acquired his services and made him a mainstay on their blueline.

Other players to appear for the Flyers this season: **MIKE BOLAND, SERGE LAJEUNESSE, JACK McILHARGEY, RANDY OSBURN, BOB SIROIS**

1975

THE CHAMPIONS

1976 Montreal Canadiens

Montreal won the Cup right in Philadelphia and despite Kate Smith's singing of "God Bless America" which usually inspired the Flyers to victory. Back in Montreal with the Cup, the Habs made a series of pilgrimages, to Claude St. Jean's restaurant, to "Fridays," a favourite bar, to Toe Blake's Tavern, and finally to Henri Richard's bar. This was a critical Cup victory for hockey as skill handily defeated braun.

STANLEY CUP FINALS

Montreal Canadiens win best-of-seven Stanley Cup finals 4-0

*May 9, 1976	Philadelphia Flyers 3 at Montreal Canadiens 4
*May 11, 1976	Philadelphia Flyers 1 at Montreal Canadiens 2
**May 13, 1976	Montreal Canadiens 3 at Philadelphia Flyers 2
**May 16, 1976	Montreal Canadiens 5 at Philadelphia Flyers 3 {Guy Lafleur 14:18 3rd}

** played at the Forum, Montreal   ** played at the Spectrum, Philadelphia*

(left to right) Jim Roberts, Doug Jarvis, and Bob Gainey with the Cup.

MONTREAL	GP	G	A	P	Pim
Guy Lafleur	4	2	5	7	2
Steve Shutt	4	3	3	6	0
Pete Mahovlich	4	1	4	5	4
Pierre Bouchard	4	2	0	2	2
Jacques Lemaire	4	2	0	2	2
Larry Robinson	4	1	1	2	4
Yvan Cournoyer	4	1	1	2	0
Doug Risebrough	4	0	2	2	2
Guy Lapointe	4	1	0	1	8
Jim Roberts	4	1	0	1	0
Bob Gainey	4	0	1	1	12
Bill Nyrop	4	0	1	1	2
Murray Wilson	3	0	1	1	0
Mario Tremblay	2	0	0	0	7
Yvon Lambert	3	0	0	0	4
Serge Savard	4	0	0	0	2
Ken Dryden	4	0	0	0	0
Doug Jarvis	4	0	0	0	0
Rick Chartraw	2	0	0	0	0

In Goal	GP	W-L	Mins	GA	SO	Avg
Ken Dryden	4	4-0	240	9	0	2.25

Serge Savard (standing, left) and Yvan Cournoyer (standing, right) take in the cheers during the Cup parade of 1976.

GUY LAFLEUR won the Art Ross Trophy this year, the first non-Boston or Chicago player to win it in a dozen years.

As a junior, **STEVE SHUTT** played for the Toronto Marlies on a line with Billy Harris and Dave Gardner, the highest-scoring trio in the OHA.

The Little M, **PETE MAHOVLICH**, loved to party, and in these his halcyon days he could score 100 points and stay out on Crescent Street until no more drinks could be found.

The son of Habs great Butch **BOUCHARD**, **PIERRE** had all the sympathy in the world from his coach. "There's nothing tougher than for a son to come into a town where his father is a legend," Bowman observed.

One of the game's best two-way centres, **JACQUES LEMAIRE** had four hockey-playing brothers, none of whom made it to the NHL.

LARRY ROBINSON was an anchor on defence. "Big Bird" won the Conn Smythe Trophy for his formative presence on the blueline. "There's nothing he can't do," Boston coach Don Cherry conceded.

YVAN COURNOYER'S career was shortened by a persistent back injury, but although he failed to play 1,000 career games he was inducted into the Hockey Hall of Fame after retiring.

DOUG RISEBROUGH bettered John Ferguson's team penalty minutes record with 198 in his first season in only 64 games played. In the summer, he took power skating lessons to improve his leg strength, and a Stanley Cup was his due reward.

Robinson, Savard, and **GUY LAPOINTE** were at their collective peaks, known as the Big Three and regarded as the best defensive corps in the NHL.

In a weird quirk of consistency, **JIM ROBERTS** scored either 13 or 14 goals in all of his top six seasons in the NHL (he had 13 this year).

BOB GAINEY'S name is badly misspelled on this engraving. Soviet coach Viktor Tikhonov said of him: "He is technically the best player in the world today." While the "technically" purposefully allowed for players such as Bobby Orr and Guy Lafleur to squeeze ahead of Gainey, the point was made.

Although he was the starting quarterback for the 1969 state champion team in Minnesota, **BILL NYROP** enrolled in Business Administration at Notre Dame, played hockey, and was drafted by the Habs in 1972.

MURRAY WILSON won a Cup with the Habs in his rookie season (1972-73) and during his short career won four Cups in seven seasons. His car in the victory parade conked out at one point, but that didn't bother him—he hopped into a bar for a beer, and caught up to the others a little while later.

MARIO TREMBLAY worked his way into the Habs lineup as a defensive specialist, playing with Lambert and Risebrough, despite being a goal-scorer in junior.

From the get-go, **YVON LAMBERT** was touted as a French-Canadian version of John Ferguson, able to supply the Habs with the one ingredient they recently lacked—physical toughness.

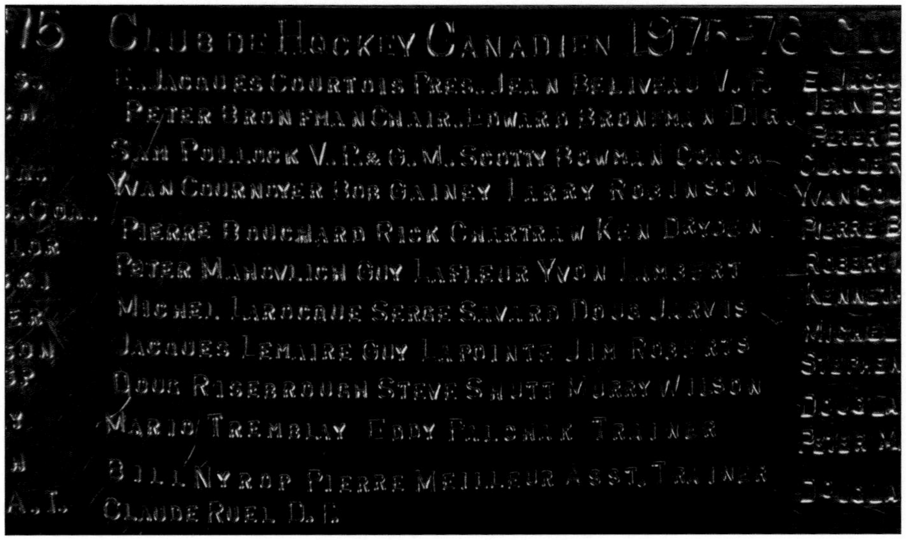

Team engraving from the Stanley Cup

"This is not only a victory for the Canadiens, it is a victory for hockey," **SERGE SAVARD** explained. "I hope that this era of intimidation and violence that is hurting our national sport is coming to an end."

KEN DRYDEN was in vintage form again this year with a 42-10-8 record in the regular season and just one loss in 13 playoff games en route to another Vezina Trophy and Stanley Cup.

DOUG JARVIS'S junior coach in Peterborough was Roger Neilson who extolled the virtues of the young centre's play at both ends of the ice.

Without doubt, **RICK CHARTRAW** was the finest NHLer ever born in Venezuela, a fact attributable to his father's job. Chartraw was a defenceman by training, but Bowman converted him effectively to forward for the playoffs.

Although he played seven full seasons with Montreal, **MICHEL LAROCQUE** was forever backup to Dryden and never played when the Cup was on the line.

EDDIE PALCHAK was the team's ever-present trainer.

"Boom Boom" **PIERRE MEILLEUR** was also a chauffeur for Serge Savard and later became a player agent for a short time.

CLAUDE RUEL'S playing career was cut short in 1958 when he lost an eye in an accident playing for the Junior Canadiens. He later coached the Habs before settling into a lengthy career as the director of player development.

JACQUES COURTOIS was a high-powered lawyer in Montreal who travelled with the team every playoffs. In the Montreal tradition, he sat behind the players' bench at home games.

PETER BRONFMAN and brother Edward later ran Brass Can, the holdings of the family. It was only then that they became immensely wealthy.

When **EDWARD BRONFMAN** sold the Habs for $18 million, he and Peter retained ownership of the Forum itself for many years after.

"I get a little upset with people when they tell me how lucky we are to have great players like Lafleur, Lapointe, Savard, Robinson...We scouted them, we assessed them. That's not luck. That's hard work." **SAM POLLOCK.**

Key to the victory was coach **SCOTTY BOWMAN'S** strategy for stopping Bobby Clarke. He rotated three centres, taking 25-second shifts against the Flyers' captain to wear him out.

JEAN BELIVEAU'S official title was "Vice President and Director of Corporate Relations." Unofficially, he was simply the god of Cups past to remind the current team what pride and tradition were all about.

Other players to appear for the Canadiens this season: **RON ANDRUFF, DON AWREY, GLENN GOLDUP, SEAN SHANAHAN, JOHN VAN BOXMEER**

1976 1977 Montreal Canadiens

THE CHAMPIONS

During the regular season the Habs had a record of 60-8-12, the best ever and a record for fewest losses that stands to this day. Although Detroit later won 62 games in an 82-game season in 1995-96, Montreal's 132 points this year was also still a record. In the playoffs, the Canadiens swept St. Louis in the quarter-finals, beat the Islanders in six games in the semi-finals, and then swept the Bruins to claim their second straight Cup.

STANLEY CUP FINALS

Montreal Canadiens win best-of-seven Stanley Cup finals 4-0

*May 7, 1977 Boston Bruins 3 at Montreal Canadiens 7
*May 10, 1977 Boston Bruins 0 at Montreal Canadiens 3 [Ken Dryden]
**May 12, 1977 Montreal Canadiens 4 at Boston Bruins 2
**May 14, 1977 Montreal Canadiens 2 at Boston Bruins 1 {(Jacques Lemaire 4:32 OT)}

** played at the Forum, Montreal ** played at Boston Garden*

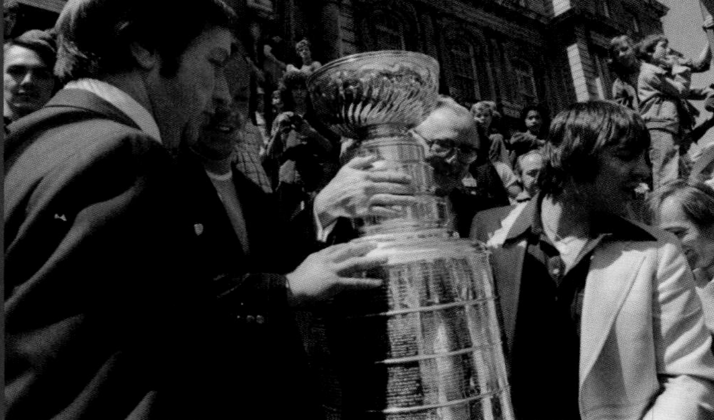

Yvan Cournoyer and Serge Savard take the Cup from City Hall.

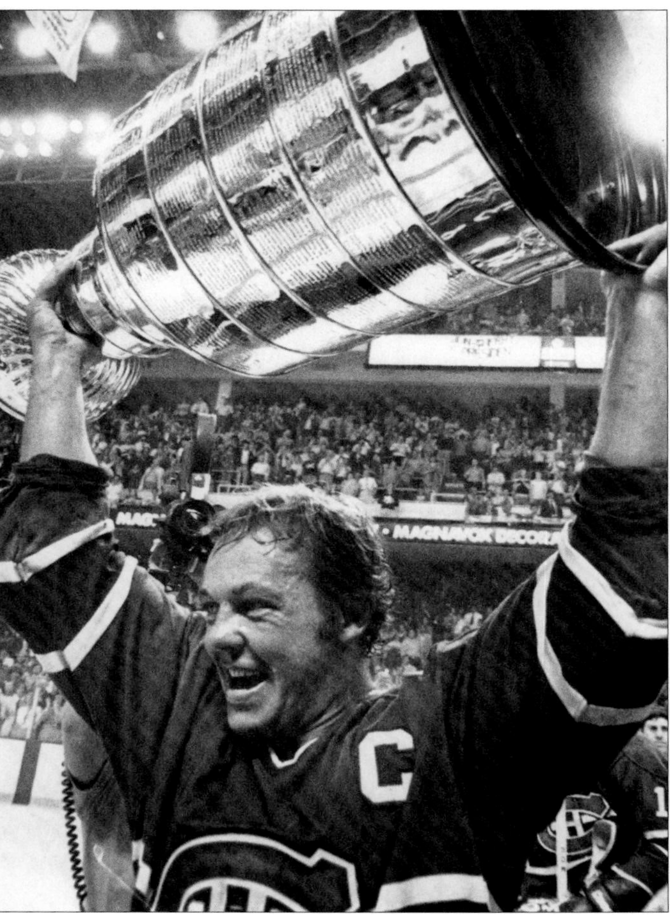

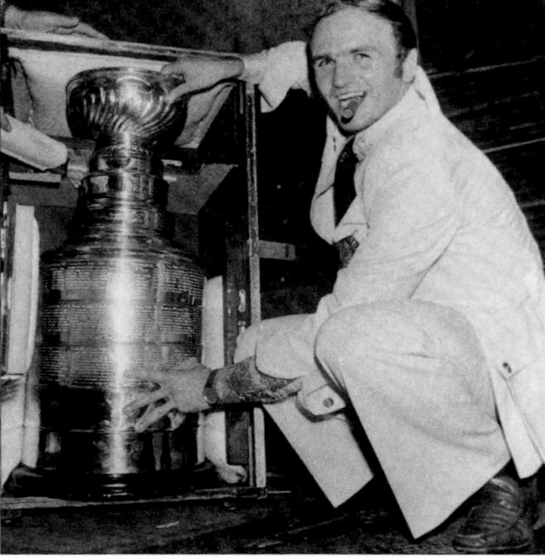

(clockwise) Captain Cournoyer holds high the great hockey prize; goalie Ken Dryden, in his trademark crouch, watches play closely in front of his crease; Jacques Lemaire chomps on the traditional, celebratory stogie while putting Stanley to bed in his traveling case.

MONTREAL	GP	G	A	P	Pim
Guy Lafleur	4	2	7	9	4
Jacques Lemaire	4	4	2	6	2
Steve Shutt	4	2	3	5	0
Yvon Lambert	4	2	2	4	6
Pete Mahovlich	4	1	3	4	4
Guy Lapointe	4	0	4	4	0
Doug Risebrough	2	2	1	3	2
Larry Robinson	4	0	3	3	6
Mario Tremblay	4	2	0	2	5
Serge Savard	4	0	2	2	0
Rick Chartraw	4	1	0	1	4
Pierre Bouchard	4	0	1	1	6
Murray Wilson	4	0	1	1	6
Doug Jarvis	4	0	1	1	0
Bob Gainey	4	0	0	0	12
Jim Roberts	4	0	0	0	4
Ken Dryden	4	0	0	0	0
Pierre Mondou	2	0	0	0	0
Bill Nyrop	1	0	0	0	0
Mike Polich	1	0	0	0	0

In Goal	GP	W-L	Mins	GA	SO	Avg
Ken Dryden	4	4-0	240	6	1	1.50

GUY LAFLEUR led the playoff scoring with 26 points and won the Conn Smythe Trophy. A consummate gentleman, he was generally first on the ice and last off at practise, so his development into the game's best right winger was by hard work.

The centre for Lafleur, **LEMAIRE** was the reason for Montreal's success. When he retired, so ended the Montreal dynasty.

In his fourth NHL season, **SHUTT** continued to improve his goal-scoring by fifteen a season, from 15 to 30 to 45 to 60 this year.

Although French-Canadian, **YVON LAMBERT** was acquired by the Habs in the Reverse Draft in 1971 when Detroit—who had drafted him in 1970—made him available.

The good times ended after this season as **MAHOVLICH** found himself traded to Pittsburgh by December '77, the victim of his own irresponsibility and silliness off-ice.

GUY LAPOINTE was one of the league's premier practical jokers. He began this season with Team Canada, winners of the '76 Canada Cup, taping Phil Esposito's lucky shower sandals together with rolls and rolls of tape.

Considered the club's tough guy, **DOUG RISEBROUGH** played on a Kid Line with Mario Tremblay and Yvon Lambert, a physical and aggressive threesome.

LARRY ROBINSON grew up in Marvelville, Ontario where he was a marvel...as a centreman. It wasn't until Junior B, in Brockville, that the defense-strapped team asked him to play on the blueline.

MARIO TREMBLAY got off to a rocky start with the Habs, sitting out 24 games this year as he learned the ropes in the NHL under the demanding, Cup-winning gaze of Scotty Bowman.

SERGE SAVARD joined Lapointe for the '76 Canada Cup, then played in the All-Star Game and had one of the best offensive seasons of his career.

Despite being a solid blueliner, **RICK CHARTRAW** was forever condemned to be the least-used defenseman on the Montreal roster. "I live in a fur-lined doghouse," he quipped. "I'm well treated, but they don't use me."

BOUCHARD was a defenceman who scored just 24 goals in 595 career games and only three more in 76 playoff games.

The older brother of soon-to-be-great Doug Wilson, **MURRAY** ("Murry" on the Cup) was a fluid skater whose career was cut short by a recurring back injury.

DOUG JARVIS was acquired from the Leafs for Greg Hubick before either had played a single NHL game. The red-head in Montreal stepped into the lineup and didn't miss a single game until his eleventh season, a record 964 games later.

The prototypical two-way forward, **BOB GAINEY** was so good at both ends of the ice it seemed ludicrous to call him "defensive" but equally insulting not to.

JIM ROBERTS was a utility forward who could kill penalties, check the other team's top forwards, score the occasional goal, and make the players around him raise their level of play.

Of the team's season, goalie **KEN DRYDEN** commented: "There were an inordinate number of games we won without even a reasonable amount of difficulty."

Team engraving from the Stanley Cup

PIERRE MONDOU played the year with Nova Scotia before being called up for the playoffs to make his NHL debut. Although he played only four games, they were the right ones and he got his name on the Cup.

NYROP was an American who loved the land, particularly the wide expanse of Montana. After next season he quietly retired, returning three years later with Minnesota for a single season.

REJEAN HOULE captained the Memorial Cup-winning Junior Canadiens in 1969, a team that included Gil Perreault, Rick Martin, Marc Tardif, Bobby Lalonde, and Jocelyn Guevrement.

Like the great Glenn Hall, goalie **MICHEL LAROCQUE** was famous for throwing up before every game, though unlike Hall he rarely played.

Known as "the Shadow," **MIKE POLICH** graduated from the University of Minnesota without being drafted. The Habs were the only NHLers to give him a chance.

COURNOYER replaced Henri Richard as captain and continued a long Montreal tradition which saw the captain retire with the team and go on to a place in the Hockey Hall of Fame.

JACQUES COURTOIS was a Montreal lawyer and president of the team.

People around the NHL viewed **SAM POLLOCK'S** reign in two ways: one, it was bad for the game because the outcome was known before the season started: two, it was hockey at its best and should be appreciated as such.

JEAN BELIVEAU'S was not a hands-on job with this Habs team, but his presence, and fingers-full of Cup rings, had only a positive impact on a team required to win.

"When you have an eighty-game schedule," **BOWMAN** explained, "you have to be able to utilize your full bench, and you can't afford to have even one selfish player on your team."

Despite being a wealthy owner, **PETER BRONFMAN** was always in awe of the players, even to the point of being shy about asking for a stick.

EDWARD BRONFMAN and brother, Peter, were cousins to the Seagram's Bronfmans, but not poor by any stretch. They later acquired Labatt's Brewery.

CLAUDE RUEL was a born scout, devoted to the development of young players through patience and calm guidance, not screaming and shouting.

FLOYD CURRY was assistant general manager to Sam Pollock, but a number of years later he took a step back and became the team's director of advertising sales.

One of **RON CARON'S** great finds as director of player development was goalie Michel Larocque, whom he touted when Bunny was just thirteen years old.

PIERRE MEILLEUR continued to act as the team's assistant trainer.

ED PALCHAK, forever in the team's employ, was the trainer again this Cup season.

Other players to appear for the Canadiens this season: **BRIAN ENGBLOM, JOHN VAN BOXMEER**

1977–1978 Montreal Canadiens

THE CHAMPIONS

Montreal had a tremendous team, obviously, but the psychological advantage the Canadiens possessed over the Bruins was remarkable. The first time the teams met in the playoffs came in 1929 when Boston swept the Canadiens three in a row in a best-of-five semi-finals. Montreal won in 1930 and '31 en route to back-to-back Cups, and in their next 18 meetings, stretching from 1943 to 1987, Montreal won each and every series, an unparalleled edge in NHL matchups. In 1978, Boston had, for all intents and purposes, lost the Cup even before the players stepped on the ice for game one of the finals.

STANLEY CUP FINALS

Montreal Canadiens win best-of-seven Stanley Cup finals 4-2

*May 13, 1978 Boston Bruins 1 at Montreal Canadiens 4
*May 16, 1978 Boston Bruins 2 at Montreal Canadiens 3 (Guy Lafleur 13:09 OT)
**May 18, 1978 Montreal Canadiens 0 at Boston Bruins 4 [Gerry Cheevers]
**May 21, 1978 Montreal Canadiens 3 at Boston Bruins 4 (Bobby Schmautz 6:22 OT)
*May 23, 1978 Boston Bruins 1 at Montreal Canadiens 4
**May 25, 1978 Montreal Canadiens 4 at Boston Bruins 1 {Mario Tremblay 9:20 1st}

** played at the Forum, Montreal ** played at Boston Garden*

Captain Yvan Cournoyer and teammates celebrate their victory.

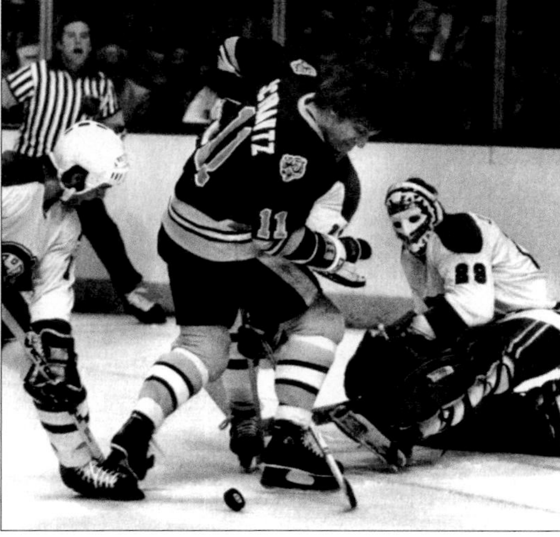

(clockwise) Henri Richard carries the Cup through the streets of Montreal; Boston's Bobby Schmautz tries to get control of the puck for a chance on goalie Ken Dryden; members of the Canadiens sign the official guest book at City Hall in Montreal.

Team engraving from the shoulder of the Stanley Cup

MONTREAL	GP	G	A	P	Pim
Larry Robinson	6	2	4	6	4
Guy Lafleur	6	3	2	5	8
Steve Shutt	6	3	1	4	2
Pierre Mondou	6	1	3	4	4
Mario Tremblay	3	2	1	3	14
Yvan Cournoyer	6	1	2	3	6
Jacques Lemaire	6	1	2	3	6
Yvon Lambert	6	1	2	3	2
Doug Jarvis	6	0	3	3	10
Serge Savard	6	0	3	3	4
Bob Gainey	6	1	1	2	10
Rejean Houle	6	1	1	2	4
Bill Nyrop	5	0	2	2	6
Guy Lapointe	6	0	2	2	5
Doug Risebrough	6	1	0	1	7
Pierre Larouche	2	1	0	1	0
Gilles Lupien	2	0	0	0	17
Pierre Bouchard	4	0	0	0	5
Ken Dryden	6	0	0	0	0
Rick Chartraw	3	0	0	0	0
Brian Engblom	1	0	0	0	0

In Goal	GP	W-L	Mins	GA	SO	Avg
Ken Dryden	6	4-2	379	13	0	2.06

"It was Larry Robinson who killed us," commented Boston's **DON MARCOTTE** on the performance of the Conn Smythe Trophy winner.

MURRAY WILSON suffered a lower back injury in November, underwent serious surgery, and missed the rest of the season.

GUY LAFLEUR led the league with 60 goals and 132 points. He was smack dab in the middle of his Hall of Fame career.

Earlier in **STEVE SHUTT'S** career, coach Bowman was so convinced the player was overweight from eating too much on road trips that he had assistant Claude Ruel follow him.

In this his first season, **MONDOU** scored 19 goals in the regular season and then had the game winner in game five of the finals.

Although **MARIO TREMBLAY** appeared in only five playoff games and scored two post-season goals, both came in the Cup-winning game.

COURNOYER scored five goals in one game during the '74-'75 season, versus Chicago. Amazingly, he didn't score his first goal of that night until 8:17 of the second period.

Though not a big man, **JACQUES LEMAIRE** entered the NHL with a reputation for a slapshot that rivalled Hull's and Mikita's.

Coach Bowman on **YVON LAMBERT**: "You need a guy who can plant himself in front of the goal and defy the other team to move him. He'll get the deflections and rebounds in there...Yvon's the key."

DOUG JARVIS was an outstanding defensive forward and faceoff specialist and was the most famous player to come out of Brantford until Wayne Gretzky.

SERGE SAVARD played centre until he was 15 years old, and in junior under coach Scotty Bowman he had plenty of time to learn the blueline game while continuing to be a scoring threat.

BOB GAINEY scored only once in the finals, but more important he helped limit the potent Boston offence to just 13 goals in six games.

Scouted by Gilles Laperriere, brother of Jacques, **REJEAN HOULE** managed to score 30 goals a year while never playing on the team's number-one line or the power play, and usually against the opponent's best players.

No greater irony in life can be gleaned than from the fate of **BILL NYROP**. A fitness freak who ate and drank properly and took superb care of his body, he was ravaged by cancer and died in 1995 at age 43.

GUY LAPOINTE suffered a frightening eye injury in December '77 after being hit by a deflected shot. He underwent delicate surgery and a long convalescence but made a full recovery.

DOUG RISEBROUGH represented one of five 1st-round draft selections Montreal owned in 1974.

In November '77, **PIERRE LAROUCHE** was traded from an unhappy situation in Pittsburgh to his beloved Habs.

CLUB DE HOCKEY CANADIEN 1977-78
E. JACQUES COURTOIS PRES. SAM POLLOCK V.P. & G.M.
JEAN BELIVEAU V.P. & D.C.R. SCOTT BOWMAN COACH
PETER BRONFMAN DIR. EDWARD BRONFMAN DIR.
A.G.M. AL MacNEIL D.P.D. ED PALCHAK H.T. P. MEILLEUR A.T.
CLAUDE RUEL D.P. FLOYD CURRY A.G.M. RON CARON A.G.M.
YVAN COURNOYER GUY LAFLEUR KENNETH DRYDEN
MICHEL LAROCQUE RICK CHARTRAW REJEAN HOULE
PIERRE LAROUCHE BRIAN ENGBLOM YVON LAMBERT
JACQUES LEMAIRE ROBERT GAINEY GUY LAPOINTE
DOUGLAS JARVIS GILLES LUPIEN PIERRE MONDOU
LARRY ROBINSON WILLIAM NYROP MURRAY WILSON
SERGE SAVARD STEPHEN SHUTT MARIO TREMBLAY
PIERRE BOUCHARD DOUGLAS RISEBROUGH

Team engraving from the Stanley Cup

GILLES LUPIEN was the former operator of a lumber supply company. At 6'6" he had the reputation as a thug, but in the dressing room it was his spirit that kept him on the team.

PIERRE BOUCHARD was involved in a controversy this summer when he was claimed on waivers by Washington. When the Caps tried to trade him back to Montreal for Rod Schutt (the player Washington really wanted) the league revoked the deal, saying Bouchard had to placed on waivers by the Caps. As a result, the Habs lost a player they never wanted to lose.

Unbeknownst to most fans, **MICHEL LAROCQUE** was the fourth goalie at Team Canada '72 training camp behind Dryden, Tony Esposito, and Ed Johnston. He was used exclusively in practise for training and preparations.

KEN DRYDEN'S fitful career was in full glory this year. He led the league with a 2.05 GAA and lost only seven games of 52 played.

Symbolic of his struggles for respect on ice by his coach, **RICK CHARTRAW** sued various media outlets (four newspapers and one radio station) and his landlord for malicious reports the landlord apparently made of him in an attempt to collect rent Chartraw allegedly was late in paying.

Montreal drafted **BRIAN ENGBLOM** in 1975, enticing him to leave the University of Wisconsin to pursue his NHL dream.

JACQUES COURTOIS was team president for les Canadiens.

Although **SAM POLLOCK** was a brilliant GM who owned 5% of the team, he was more than just a hockey guy. He collected Canadian painting and raised purebred Jersey cattle, and his true love was baseball, not the puck game.

As the team's vice president, **JEAN BELIVEAU** was, incredibly, pilloried by the press for his handling of the Bouchard deal.

One of **SCOTTY BOWMAN'S** legendary strategies for motivating his players was to ensure that, as a club, the players both respected him fearfully and loathed him passionately.

PETER and **EDWARD BRONFMAN** decided to sell the team to Molson Breweries on August 4, 1978, starting a 20-year reign for the beermakers that ended in the spring of 2001.

AL MacNEIL'S timing as a player in the 1960s could not have been worse. He left Toronto two years before the team became a dynasty, arrived in Montreal two years after the Canadiens had won five in a row, and arrived in Chicago a year after the Hawks had won the Cup!

ED PALCHAK and **PIERRE MEILLEUR** were the team's trainers in perpetuity.

The Habs were not just the best team in the league, they were also the deepest in talent, credit for which went largely to **CLAUDE RUEL** and his sharp scouting staff.

FLOYD CURRY was the team's assistant general manager this year, a lifetime Montrealer who held a variety of positions with the club, beginning as a player in 1947.

A former school teacher, **RON CARON** so impressed Pollock with his memory and knowledge of the game that he hired him as a scout and to oversee the entire Montreal developmental system.

Other players to appear for the Canadiens this season: **PAT HUGHES**, **PETE MAHOVLICH**, **MIKE POLICH**, **ROD SCHUTT**

1978 THE CHAMPIONS
1979 Montreal Canadiens

The Habs got into the finals by beating Boston in overtime in game seven of the semi-finals. They had tied the game on a Guy Lafleur goal with just 1:14 left the third period on the most infamous too-many-men penalty in NHL history, Don Cherry's team going down to a most humbling defeat on May 10, the same date that Bobby Orr had flown through the air to win the Cup for the Bruins in 1970. In the finals, the Rangers were no match for a Montreal team intent on winning its fourth successive Cup.

STANLEY CUP FINALS

Montreal Canadiens win best-of-seven Stanley Cup finals 4-1

*May 13, 1979 New York Rangers 4 at Montreal Canadiens 1
*May 15, 1979 New York Rangers 2 at Montreal Canadiens 6
**May 17, 1979 Montreal Canadiens 4 at New York Rangers 1
**May 19, 1979 Montreal Canadiens 4 at New York Rangers 3 (Serge Savard 7:25 OT)
*May 21, 1979 New York Rangers 1 at Montreal Canadiens 4
{Yvon Lambert 1:02 2nd}

** played at the Forum, Montreal ** played at Madison Square Garden, New York*

Captain Serge Savard takes a victory lap with the Cup.

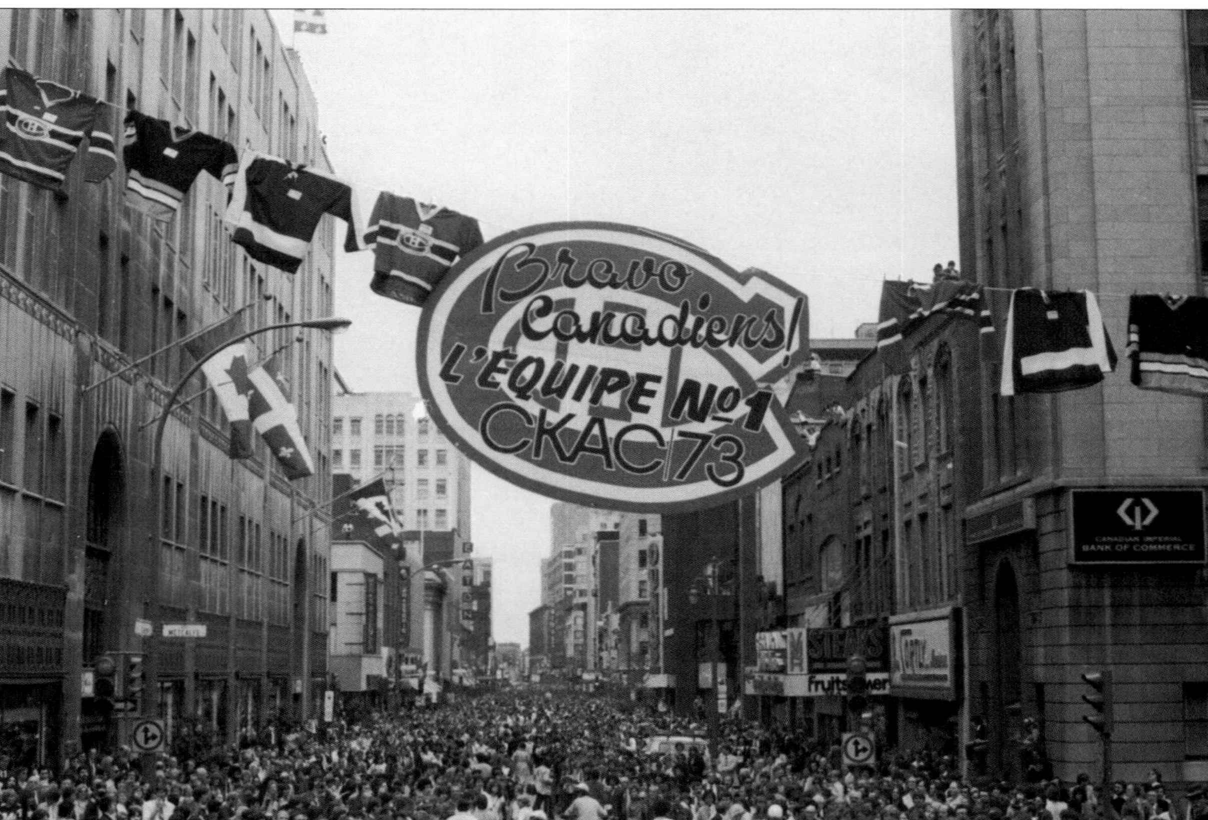

St. Catherine St. in downtown Montreal is a sea of fans and supporters for the Canadiens' parade.

MONTREAL	GP	G	A	P	Pim
Jacques Lemaire	5	4	3	7	2
Yvon Lambert	5	2	4	6	4
Steve Shutt	5	2	4	6	2
Bob Gainey	5	3	2	5	6
Rejean Houle	5	1	4	5	2
Guy Lafleur	5	2	1	3	0
Doug Risebrough	5	1	2	3	12
Serge Savard	5	1	2	3	2
Rick Chartraw	5	1	1	2	12
Mario Tremblay	5	1	1	2	4
Doug Jarvis	5	0	2	2	2
Mark Napier	5	1	0	1	2
Larry Robinson	5	0	1	1	0
Rod Langway	5	0	0	0	12
Pierre Mondou	5	0	0	0	2
Gilles Lupien	4	0	0	0	2
Ken Dryden	5	0	0	0	0
Brian Engblom	5	0	0	0	0
Michel Larocque	1	0	0	0	0
Pierre Larouche	1	0	0	0	0

In Goal	GP	W-L	Mins	GA	SO	Avg
Michel Larocque	1	0-0	20	0	0	0.00
Ken Dryden	5	4-1	287	11	0	2.30

Like teammate Dryden, **JACQUES LEMAIRE** sensed the end was nigh. He retired from the NHL to coach and play in Switzerland and returned to Canada to pursue a career behind NHL benches.

It was **YVON LAMBERT** who scored the overtime goal to eliminate Boston in the semi-finals.

STEVE SHUTT commenting on his game: "A lot of people don't notice me out there. I know that. But at the end of the game...I'll have a goal and two assists."

"Bob is the guts of the team," Dryden said in reference to **BOB GAINEY'S** tenacity of spirit and ability to motivate those around him to play smart, winning hockey.

As a rookie, **REJEAN HOULE** had been given a stall between Jean Beliveau and Henri Richard.

GUY LAFLEUR made Cup history this year, stealing the Cup from the trunk of Claude Mouton's car and taking it to a barbecue in Thurso, Quebec, where he put it on display on the front lawn.

DOUG "RISER" RISEBROUGH entered the league as an abrasive, nasty, hard-hitting rookie and never let up until the day he retired.

A true testament to **SERGE SAVARD'S** early reputation came at the 1967 Expansion Draft when Pollock left Carol Vadnais available so he could protect the emerging, speedy hulk.

Early the next season, **RICK CHARTRAW** finally got his wish—to leave Montreal. He was traded to Los Angeles and later played for the Rangers and Edmonton.

MARIO TREMBLAY came into his own this season, scoring a career-high 30 goals and establishing himself as a two-way player with the requisite playoff grit.

Four years in the league for **DOUG JARVIS**. Four Stanley Cups. "He's our good luck charm," Risebrough joked.

MARK NAPIER had jumped to the WHA from junior as an 18-year old baby, but when the Habs drafted him he hurried to the NHL and won a Cup in this his first season.

Despite a middling junior career and little NHL interest in **LARRY ROBINSON** at draft time, Claude Ruel felt confident in Big Bird's skating ability and selected him 20th overall in 1971.

"ROCKET" ROD LANGWAY was born in Taiwan and raised in Boston, but he made a name for himself in these finals by knocking Phil Esposito around and shutting down the Rangers' offense.

Although **PIERRE MONDOU** was just 24, this would be his last Cup. In 1985, he suffered an eye injury in a game against Hartford. He never regained full vision.

GILLES LUPIEN'S career was thoroughly pedestrian, taking him to many leagues and many more cities. After retiring, he became a player agent, claiming Felix Potvin as one of his more prominent clients.

Just 31, **KEN DRYDEN**, too, retired at season's end to pursue a career in law which, in truth he never did, moving on to writing *The Game*, a bestselling account of his years in hockey.

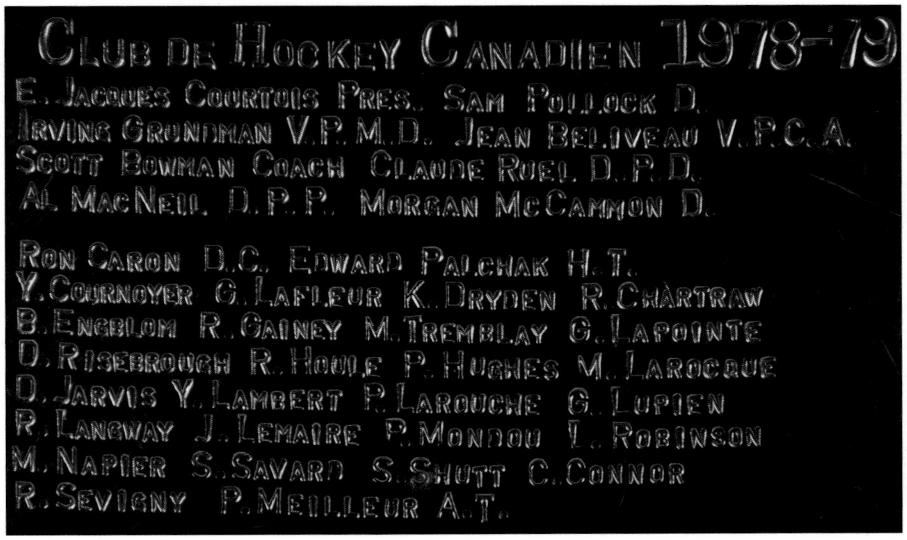

CLUB DE HOCKEY CANADIEN 1978-79
E. JACQUES COURTOIS PRES. SAM POLLOCK D.
IRVING GRUNDMAN V.P. M.D. JEAN BELIVEAU V.P.C.A.
SCOTT BOWMAN COACH CLAUDE RUEL D.P.D.
AL MACNEIL D.P.P. MORGAN McCAMMON D.
RON CARON D.C. EDWARD PALCHAK H.T.
Y.COURNOYER G.LAFLEUR K.DRYDEN R.CHARTRAW
B.ENGBLOM R.GAINEY M.TREMBLAY G.LAPOINTE
D.RISEBROUGH R.HOULE P.HUGHES M.LAROCQUE
D.JARVIS Y.LAMBERT P.LAROUCHE G.LUPIEN
R.LANGWAY J.LEMAIRE P.MONDOU L.ROBINSON
M.NAPIER S.SAVARD S.SHUTT C.CONNOR
R.SEVIGNY P.MEILLEUR A.T.

Team engraving from the Stanley Cup

BRIAN ENGBLOM was now an established defenceman on the team who had developed into an effective member of the blueline.

GUY LAPOINTE owned a 1938 Chevy, right out of Bonnie and Clyde, one of many vintage cars he drove around town for showy pleasure.

PAT HUGHES scored nine goals in half a season with the Habs and was traded to Pittsburgh in the summer in a deal that brought goalie Denis Herron to Montreal.

In perhaps the unluckiest moment of his career, goalie **LAROCQUE** was scheduled to start game two of the finals but during the warmup was injured by a Doug Risebrough shot. He was again forced to the sidelines to watch Dryden play.

PIERRE LAROUCHE scored 50 goals a season with two teams (Montreal and Pittsburgh) and came within two of a record third team when he scored 48 times for the Rangers in 1983-84.

SCOTTY BOWMAN craved Pollock's job with Montreal, but the Habs considered him a coach and passed him over as GM when Pollock resigned. Incensed, Bowman moved on.

YVAN COURNOYER retired just 15 games into the season but for sentimental reasons still had his name engraved on the Cup for a tenth time.

This was the year **CAM CONNOR** scored a fluke goal in double overtime against Toronto on his first shift of the night. It led Leafs goalie Mike Palmateer to quip, "That's one thing I can't do—stop a guy who doesn't know what he's doing."

RICHARD SEVIGNY represents another in a short list of examples of players whose name is on the Cup even though he never played a single minute with the Habs all year.

JACQUES COURTOIS won his fourth Cup as president of the Canadiens.

This proved to be **POLLOCK'S** last Stanley Cup with the team before he retired from hockey.

IRVING GRUNDMAN took over for Sam Pollock as GM at the start of the year but after this Cup win his tenure was a disaster. He was fired a year later.

JEAN BELIVEAU'S post-NHL life was busier than his playing days. He made countless personal appearances and acted as spokesman and ambassador for the Canadiens.

A dedicated Hab for life, **CLAUDE RUEL** (director of player development) returned behind the bench during 1979-80.

AL MACNEIL had coached the team to the '71 Cup before returning to minor pro hockey for six years. He later returned to the Habs as director of player personnel.

MORGAN McCAMMON became president of the team in 1977 when the Bronfmans sold the club to Molson Breweries.

The times were high and lively now, but four years later the Habs cleaned house, firing **RON CARON**, Grundman, and many others from management.

ED PALCHAK and **PIERRE MEILLEUR** worked the dressing room as trainers.

Other players to appear for the Canadiens this season: **DAVE LUMLEY, DAN NEWMAN**

1979 – 1980 THE CHAMPIONS New York Islanders

Closer and closer each year did the Islanders come to the Cup in the years leading up to this victory. They had been eliminated in the semis in 1978 by Toronto and the next year in the semis by the Rangers, but this year signalled the end of the Canadiens dynasty. The turning point came in the quarter-finals when the Islanders beat Boston twice in the Garden in overtime to take a 2-0 lead in that series en route to a five-game win. In the semis, they again opened on the road and again won both games, in Buffalo, including a double OT win in game two. And, in the finals, again on the road, they started the series with an OT win over the Flyers, thus becoming the first team to win the Cup while opening three successive series on the road.

STANLEY CUP FINALS

New York Islanders win best-of-seven Stanley Cup finals 4-2

*May 13, 1980	New York Islanders 4 at Philadelphia Flyers 3 (Denis Potvin 4:07 OT)
*May 15, 1980	New York Islanders 3 at Philadelphia Flyers 8
**May 17, 1980	Philadelphia Flyers 2 at New York Islanders 6
**May 19, 1980	Philadelphia Flyers 2 at New York Islanders 5
*May 22, 1980	New York Islanders 3 at Philadelphia Flyers 6
**May 24, 1980	Philadelphia Flyers 4 at New York Islanders 5 {(Bob Nystrom 7:11 OT)}

** played at the Spectrum, Philadelphia   ** played at Nassau Coliseum, Long Island*

Bryan Trottier whoops it up with the home crowd as victory nears.

NY ISLANDERS	GP	G	A	P	Pim
Mike Bossy	6	4	7	11	4
Denis Potvin	6	5	4	9	6
Bryan Trottier	6	4	4	8	0
Clark Gillies	6	2	6	8	13
Stefan Persson	6	3	4	7	10
Butch Goring	6	3	3	6	0
Bob Nystrom	6	3	1	4	30
Duane Sutter	6	1	3	4	28
Bob Bourne	6	0	4	4	2
John Tonelli	6	0	3	3	4
Lorne Henning	6	1	1	2	0
Garry Howatt	6	0	1	1	21
Gord Lane	6	0	0	0	28
Dave Langevin	6	0	0	0	9
Bob Lorimer	6	0	0	0	6
Ken Morrow	6	0	0	0	6
Wayne Merrick	6	0	0	0	0
Billy Smith	6	0	0	0	0
Chico Resch	1	0	0	0	0

In Goal	GP	W-L	Mins	GA	SO	Avg
Billy Smith	6	4-2	351	23	0	3.93
Chico Resch	1	0-0	20	2	0	6.00

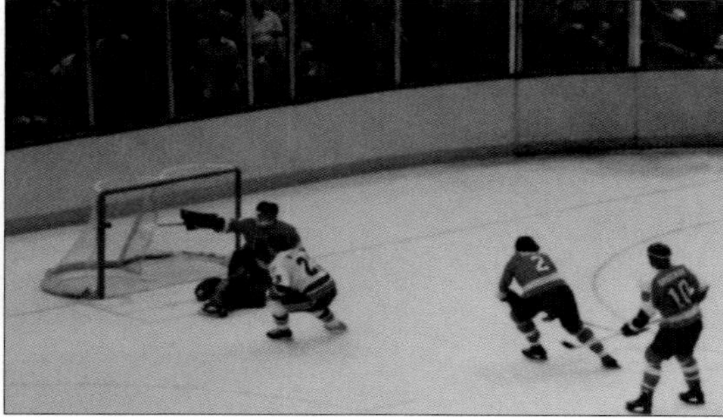

(left) Captain Denis Potvin hoists the Cup for the first time in Islanders' history; (above) Bob Nystrom scores the Cup-winning goal at 7:11 of overtime in game six at Nassau Coliseum.

Team engraving from the Replica Cup

MIKE BOSSY reached the 100 career goals mark faster than any player in NHL history, doing it in 125 games and besting Maurice Richard who had scored his first century in 134 games (and, yes, faster even than Gretzky).

Although **DENIS POTVIN** was drafted by the Islanders, Sam Pollock had done everything possible to bring him to Montreal.

BRYAN TROTTIER won the Conn Smythe, led the playoffs in scoring, and had two short-handed goals in one period on April 8. After the victory, he took the Cup home and slept with it, a dream date with a lady named Stanley.

Signed as a free agent, the 27-year old **ANDERS KALLUR** was playing in his rookie season after five years in the Swedish pro leagues.

One of the Islanders' worst draft choices, **ALEX McKENDRY** went 14th overall in 1976—ahead of Mike Liut, Brian Sutter, and Reed Larson—and played just 16 total games under Al Arbour.

Nicknamed "Jethro," **CLARK GILLIES** played his best hockey whenever the other team tried to rattle him, a tactic that only "woke him up," as it were. When he had the Cup for a day, Gillies took it home and fed his dog from the sacred bowl.

Drafted a remote 214th in 1974, **STEFAN PERSSON** stayed in Sweden for three years before joining the Islanders in '77. He and Kallur became the first Swedish-trained players to win the Cup.

His best years behind him, **GORING** was Bill Torrey's second choice as a late acquisition (after Darryl Sittler) to take some centre-ice heat off number-one man Bryan Trottier. It worked.

BOB NYSTROM'S overtime Cup-winning goal came at a casino man's dream time—7:11.

This was the first of six Stanley Cups for the **SUTTER** household, **DUANE** staying with the Islanders as an 18-year old after being drafted 17th overall the previous spring.

BOB BOURNE was drafted by Kansas City but traded to the Islanders before playing a game with the Scouts.

JOHN TONELLI left junior at age 18 to join Houston of the WHA. His linemates were Gordie and son Mark Howe. It was Tonelli's pass that set up Nystrom's winning goal.

LORNE HENNING tied an NHL record by scoring three short-handed goals during the playoffs.

GERRY HOWATT was a remarkable battler. He had had epilepsy since he was 14, but through careful administration of his medicine—Primidone—three times daily, he hadn't had a seizure since age 18.

So nervous was **GORD LANE** during this year's playoffs that whenever he so much as saw food before a game, he threw up. He lost fifteen pounds en route to this Cup win.

At the WHA Expansion Draft in 1979, it was, ironically, Edmonton that traded **LANGEVIN** to the Islanders. The New Yorkers, in turn, eventually beat the Oilers to win the Cup in '83.

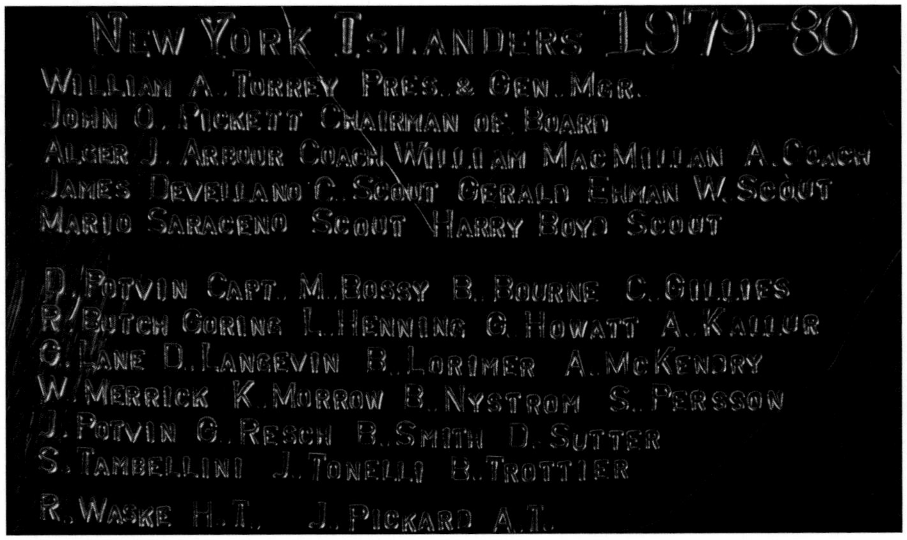

Team engraving from the current Stanley Cup

BOB LORIMER was a defensive defenceman who made a mark for himself as a hitter, not scorer. Coach Arbour had no qualms about using him in any situation.

KEN MORROW had arguably the best winning year a player could ever hope to have, playing on the USA's gold medal team at the 1980 Olympics, then joining the Islanders and winning the Cup just a few months later.

WAYNE MERRICK was acquired during 1977-78 because Bill Torrey felt the team needed a speedy centre. He was right.

Coach **AL ARBOUR**: "Every Canadian boy dreams about it from the first time he goes out to play shinny on a pond. He dreams about seeing his name on the Stanley Cup."

A utility forward used sparingly (and brother of superstar defenceman Denis), **JEAN POTVIN** doubled as a radio commentator for games he didn't play. In the finals, he didn't play at all, but he was on radio for the whole series!

There was a measure of bitterness in the victory for **CHICO RESCH** in that he felt he had never been given a chance at the number-one goaling job behind Billy Smith.

Near the start of the year **BILLY SMITH** became the first NHL goalie to be credited with scoring a goal after being the last man to touch the puck before the Colorado Rockies put it into their own empty net on a delayed penalty.

STEVE TAMBELLINI came of fine hockey stock. His father, Addie, was a member of the 1961 Trail Smoke Eaters team that won a gold medal for Canada at the World Championships in Switzerland.

RON WASKE developed personalized training programs for every player on the team, both for off season workouts and during the 80-game grind. The result was one of the best injury records in the league.

JIM PICARD first found employment in the NHL with the California Golden Seals when Bill Torrey was executive vice-president of the team.

After the dressing room celebrations and party, **BILL TORREY** took the Cup to his Long Island home where thousands of neighbouring fans came to partake in the revelry.

One of **JOHN PICKETT'S** first moves after buying the team was to secure a favourable 30-year lease at the Nassau County Coliseum on Long Island.

Assistant coach **BILLY MacMILLAN** left the Islanders after this victory to become head coach of the Colorado Rockies.

Starting his career as a coach in the Toronto Hockey League, **JIM DEVELLANO** worked his way up to Ontario scout for St. Louis for five years (1967-72) and joined the expansion Islanders in the summer of '72.

"TEX" EHMAN was a fringe player during a 428-game NHL career, but this translated into becoming a good scout once his playing days were done.

MARIO SARACENO was the team's Quebec scout. His brother, Henry, was credited with discovering Mike Bossy.

HARRY BOYD was the Islanders' Ontario scout.

Other players to appear for the Islanders this season: **RICHARD BRODEUR, BILLY HARRIS, MIKE HORDY, RANDY JOHNSTON, MIKE KASZYCKI, DAVE LEWIS, GARTH McGUIGAN, YVON VAUTOUR**

1980 THE CHAMPIONS

1981 New York Islanders

The Islanders, name badly misspelled on the Cup, set a five-game series record by scoring 26 goals. They opened their defence of the Cup by sweeping the Leafs in the preliminary round, outscoring Toronto 20-4. They then faced the up-and-coming Oilers, swinging the momentum in that matchup by winning game four in overtime and taking a 3-1 lead and winning in six games. They swept the Rangers in a subway series in the semi-finals, and the surprising North Stars, who had done well just to get to the finals, proved little match for the Isles in the ultimate round.

STANLEY CUP FINALS

New York Islanders win best-of-seven Stanley Cup finals 4-1

*May 12, 1981 Minnesota North Stars 3 at New York Islanders 6
*May 14, 1981 Minnesota North Stars 3 at New York Islanders 6
**May 17, 1981 New York Islanders 7 at Minnesota North Stars 5
**May 19, 1981 New York Islanders 2 at Minnesota North Stars 4
*May 21, 1981 Minnesota North Stars 1 at New York Islanders 5
{Wayne Merrick 5:37 1st}

** played at Nassau Coliseum, Long Island ** played at the Met Centre, Minnesota*

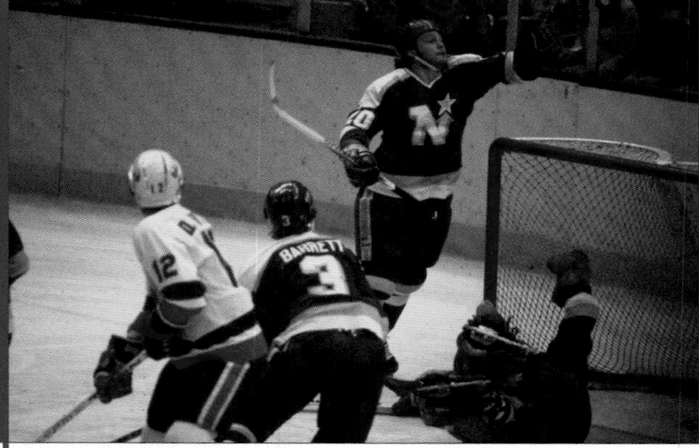

Minnesota goalie Gilles Meloche sprawls to make a save.

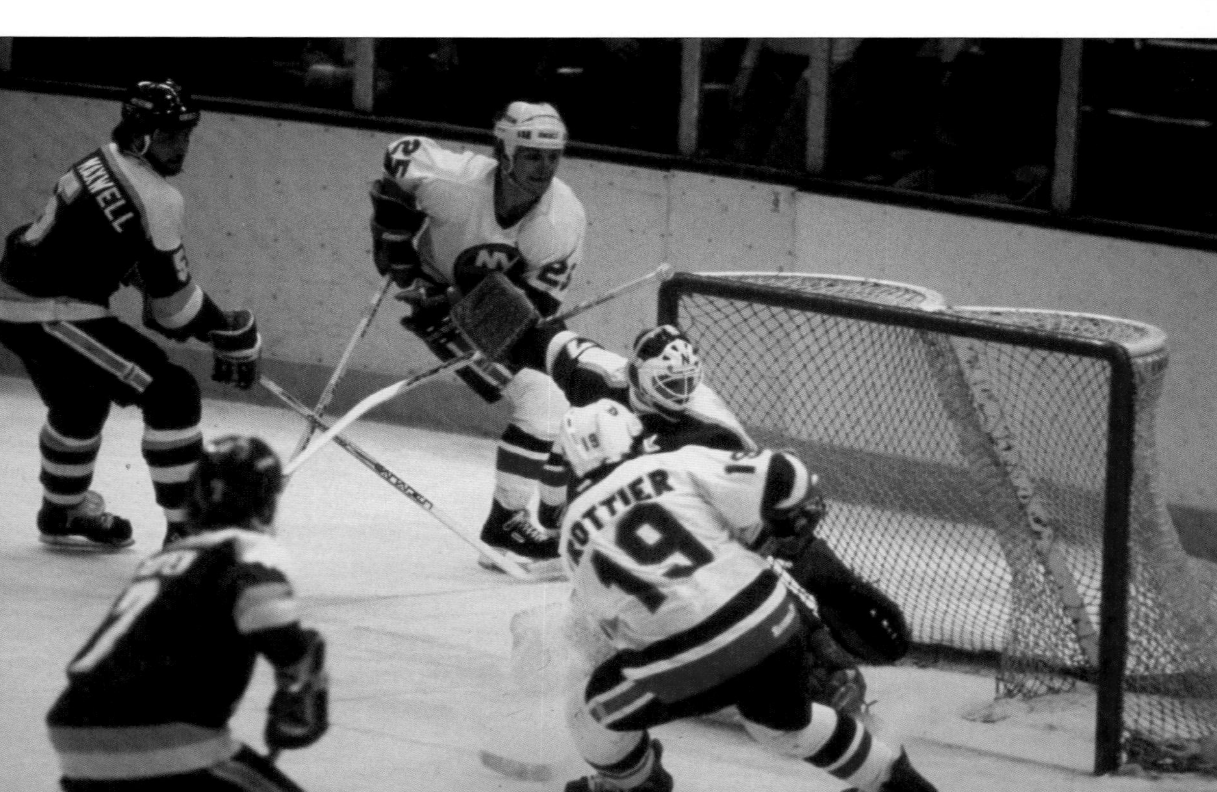

Bryan Trottier tips a perfect pass past goalie Gilles Meloche while teammate Clark Gillies looks on from behind the goal in game one of the 1981 finals.

NY ISLANDERS	GP	G	A	P	Pim
Mike Bossy	5	4	4	8	0
Wayne Merrick	5	3	5	8	0
Butch Goring	5	5	2	7	0
Bryan Trottier	5	2	5	7	14
Denis Potvin	5	2	4	6	8
John Tonelli	5	0	5	5	8
Bob Nystrom	5	2	2	4	10
Anders Kallur	5	2	2	4	4
Billy Carroll	5	1	3	4	0
Mike McEwen	5	2	1	3	2
Bob Bourne	5	1	2	3	12
Clark Gillies	5	0	3	3	8
Dave Langevin	5	0	2	2	10
Gord Lane	5	1	0	1	18
Ken Morrow	5	1	0	1	2
Duane Sutter	5	0	1	1	0
Bob Lorimer	5	0	0	0	9
Billy Smith	5	0	0	0	0

In Goal	GP	W-L	Mins	GA	SO	Avg
Billy Smith	5	4-1	300	16	0	3.20

It was quite a year for **MIKE BOSSY**. First, he scored 50 goals in 50 games, the first player to do so since Maurice Richard in 1944-45, and then he amassed 35 playoff points to lead the NHL in post-season scoring.

WAYNE MERRICK remained true to his small-town roots, returning to his farm outside Sarnia in the summers and studying at the University of Western Ontario.

BUTCH GORING won the Conn Smythe Trophy and scored the first two goals of the final game to send the team on its way to victory. He was a superb presence at both ends of the ice.

After retiring, **GERRY HOWATT** joined the Harvey Lakind firm of International Artists and Athletes Management as a hockey-specialist player agent.

BRYAN TROTTIER set a record by scoring a point in 18 straight games in this year's playoffs and 27 in a row going back to 1980.

DENIS POTVIN scored three power-play goals in one game against Edmonton this spring en route to a record 25 points by a defenceman in one playoffs.

Regarded as the hardest worker on the team and the best cornerman in the NHL, **JOHN TONELLI** also scored 35 goals during the regular season and emerged as the premier left winger in the game.

BOB NYSTROM'S middle name was Thore, but although he was born in Sweden he grew up first in Hamilton, Ontario and later British Columbia.

This was **ANDERS KALLUR'S** finest offensive season. He scored 36 goals on a team with two other Swedes (Nystrom and Persson) and two Americans (Morrow and Langevin).

BILLY CARROLL was a rookie call-up toward the end of the season, but he was so impressive he not only stuck around he became a leader during the playoffs.

MIKE McEWEN went from worst (Colorado) to first at the trade deadline, a wanted player because of his skating and his offensive production from the blueline.

During his career, **BOB BOURNE** uprooted his family from Long Island to Kelowna, B.C. where there existed a superb spina bifida clinic which could make life more comfortable for his afflicted son, Jeffrey.

CLARK GILLIES: "You've got to learn to hate losing before you learn to win."

Coach Al Arbour likened **DAVE LANGEVIN** to an old teammate from his own playing days, Bob Goldham, who didn't skate very well but made up as a shotblocker and hard, clean hitter.

Cut by the Fort Wayne Comets of the IHL in 1973 because he was a fighter and not much else, **GORD LANE** got his career back on track under the watchful eyes of Torrey and Arbour.

KEN MORROW was in his first full year with the team after graduating from Bowling Green University in 1979. His strength was defence, and at 6'4" he utilized his size and reach to take the man effectively.

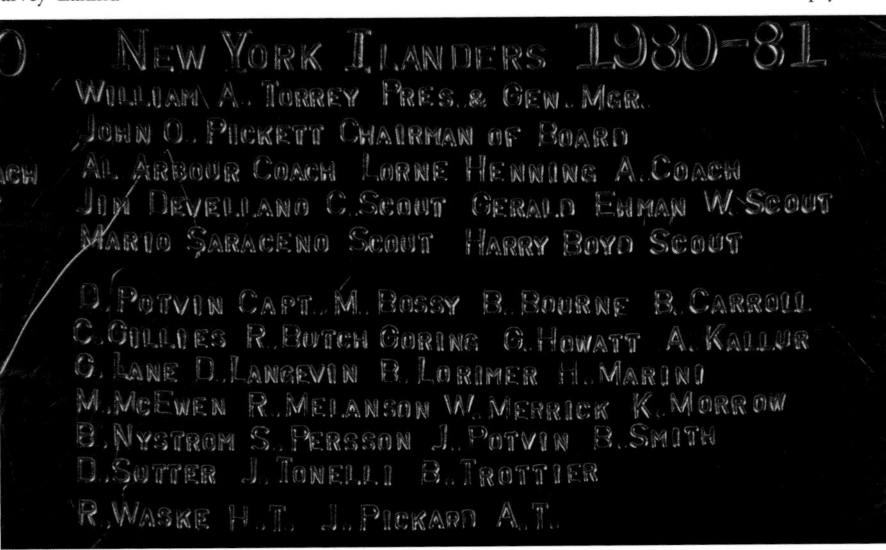

NEW YORK ISLANDERS 1980-81
WILLIAM A. TORREY PRES. & GEN. MGR.
JOHN O. PICKETT CHAIRMAN OF BOARD
AL ARBOUR COACH LORNE HENNING A. COACH
JIM DEVELLANO C. SCOUT GERALD EHMAN W. SCOUT
MARIO SARACENO SCOUT HARRY BOYD SCOUT
D. POTVIN CAPT. M. BOSSY B. BOURNE B. CARROLL
C. GILLIES R. BUTCH GORING G. HOWATT A. KALLUR
G. LANE D. LANGEVIN B. LORIMER H. MARINI
M. McEWEN R. MELANSON W. MERRICK K. MORROW
B. NYSTROM S. PERSSON J. POTVIN B. SMITH
D. SUTTER J. TONELLI B. TROTTIER
R. WASKE H.T. J. PICKARD A.T.

Team engraving from the current Stanley Cup

Nicknamed "Dog," **DUANE SUTTER** barked at opponents with a fury to win that was seldom seen in sport.

BOB LORIMER was one of the few players to be traded during the dynasty, going to Colorado with Dave Cameron for a 1st-round draft choice in 1983. The Islanders had good reason to want that selection, which proved to be 3rd overall. They selected Pat LaFontaine.

BILLY SMITH set season and career penalty minutes records for a goalie during his career, the result of his stick-swinging style of clearing his crease of incoming traffic.

AL ARBOUR: "We had...a nice blend of everything. If a team wanted to play us tough, we could be tough. If they wanted a finesse game, we'd give them finesse. We were very adjustable and we were always changing."

HECTOR MARINI played all the previous year on the farm in Indianapolis and was called up for 14 games and nine more in the playoffs this season to get his name on the Cup.

MELANSON was a 20-year old rookie, full of promise, and a perfect backup to Smith under whom he could apprentice.

STEFAN PERSSON missed the finals and the champagne-sipping with a broken jaw sustained in the Edmonton series when he was hit by a puck.

In a continuation from the previous year's arrangements, **JEAN POTVIN** dressed for only 18 regular season games and not at all in the playoffs, though he again did radio work in what was his final season of playing.

BILL TORREY attended St. Lawrence University for business and psychology, and it was his business acumen that helped get him a job in the NHL via p.r. work in the AHL and later with the Oakland Seals.

So impressed had **PICKETT** been in 1978 by Bill Torrey's vision for the team that he bought the Islanders and helped transform a floundering franchise into an NHL dynasty.

LORNE HENNING was an original Islander, the team's second selection in 1972, but in '80-'81 he played just nine games before retiring to become an assistant coach with the team.

JIM DEVELLANO became director of scouting but soon was named GM of the Indianapolis farm team and assistant GM of the Isles.

GERRY EHMAN and Al Arbour had both been bit players on Toronto's '63-'64 Cup team. Ehman finished his playing career from 1967 to '71 with the Oakland/California franchise and then joined St. Louis as a scout.

MARIO SARACENO scouted for the Islanders in Quebec, and **HARRY BOYD** was the team's Ontario scout.

A native of Canton, New York, **RON WASKE** graduated from St. Lawrence University with a degree in Physical Education. A player of some repute, he learned much about the hockey body through first-hand experience.

An original Islander from 1972, **JIM PICKARD** was responsible for everything in the dressing room, from sharpening skates to managing equipment to ordering and handling the players' sticks.

Other players to appear for the Islanders this season: **CHICO RESCH, BRENT SUTTER, STEVE TAMBELLINI**

1981–1982 New York Islanders

The Islanders' road to their third Cup in a row was made easier by Los Angeles's stunning upset of the Oilers in the first round of the playoffs, an upset that pivoted on the biggest blown lead in playoff history. With the series tied 1-1, the Oilers flew to a 5-0 lead in game three only to see the Kings rally for an improbable 6-5 win and then a 7-4 win in the fifth and deciding game. The Islanders recovered from near disaster in their first-round series against Pittsburgh, needing an heroic overtime goal from John Tonelli in the fifth game to eliminate the Pens. They beat the Rangers in six, swept the Nordiques, and then swept the Canucks who, like the North Stars the previous year, had accomplished their all just by reaching the finals.

STANLEY CUP FINALS

New York Islanders win best-of-seven Stanley Cup finals 4-0

*May 8, 1982	Vancouver Canucks 5 at New York Islanders 6 (Mike Bossy 19:58 OT)
*May 11, 1982	Vancouver Canucks 4 at New York Islanders 6
**May 13, 1982	New York Islanders 3 at Vancouver Canucks 0 [Billy Smith]
**May 16, 1982	New York Islanders 3 at Vancouver Canucks 1 {Mike Bossy 5:00 2nd}

** played at Nassau Coliseum, Long Island ** played at Pacific Coliseum, Vancouver*

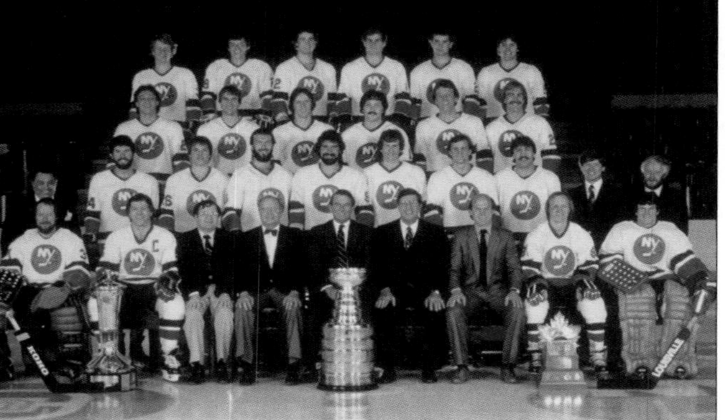

New York Islanders, 1981-82

NY ISLANDERS	GP	G	A	P	Pim
Denis Potvin	4	2	7	9	4
Mike Bossy	4	7	1	8	0
Bryan Trottier	4	1	6	7	10
Stefan Persson	4	0	5	5	4
Clark Gillies	4	2	1	3	8
Butch Goring	4	1	2	3	2
Bob Nystrom	4	2	0	2	21
Bob Bourne	4	1	1	2	17
Billy Carroll	4	1	1	2	2
John Tonelli	4	0	2	2	4
Brent Sutter	4	0	2	2	0
Duane Sutter	4	1	0	1	32
Tomas Jonsson	2	0	1	1	2
Wayne Merrick	4	0	1	1	0
Gord Lane	4	0	0	0	22
Dave Langevin	4	0	0	0	2
Anders Kallur	4	0	0	0	0
Ken Morrow	4	0	0	0	0
Billy Smith	4	0	0	0	0
Mike McEwen	2	0	0	0	0

In Goal	GP	W-L	Mins	GA	SO	Avg
Billy Smith	4	4-0	260	10	1	2.31

Vancouver goalie Richard Brodeur stops Butch Goring from in close during the 1982 finals on Long Island.

Talented and driven by success, **DENIS POTVIN** was the best of a post-Bobby Orr generation of rushing defencemen, though by no means equal to the great Number Four. Nonetheless, no one can take away his Stanley Cups. "That's what I treasure," he said of the famous bowl.

MIKE BOSSY won the Conn Smythe Trophy, setting a finals record for a four-game series by scoring seven goals. In all, he had 17 in the playoffs, and not a single penalty.

BRYAN TROTTIER led the playoffs with 29 points after recording his fifth straight 100-point season.

STEFAN PERSSON played in the '81 Canada Cup for Sweden at the start of the year and in these playoffs he recorded a career-high 14 assists despite missing six games of the post-season with a separated shoulder.

HECTOR MARINI'S career was rooted mostly in the minors, one that ended in late 1985 the result of a serious eye injury.

After two early playoff exits in the 1970s (thanks to the Leafs and Rangers), captain **CLARK GILLIES** turned in his "C" so the team could re-group and re-focus.

Named an assistant coach at the start of the season, **BUTCH GORING** was famous for wearing the same helmet he had worn since he was 12 years old.

BOB NYSTROM'S skating ability was his greatest liability early in his career, so he hired Laura Stamm, a figure skater, to help him improve his footwork. His four career overtime goals suggested it was time well spent.

BOB BOURNE was the team's player rep at NHLPA meetings, and he left Team Canada's training camp at the '81 Canada Cup because he didn't have a contract and wasn't confident in getting one under the current method of equal compensation that was in place at the time.

BILLY CARROLL was a high scorer in junior with the London Knights but when he got to the Islanders he discovered they wanted him as a checker, a role he filled to perfection.

In the first playoff series, a best-of-five against Pittsburgh, **JOHN TONELLI** emerged as the hero. The Penguins were leading 3-2 in the deciding game but Tonelli tied the score with just 2:21 left and added the game winner in overtime to send the Islanders on their way to another Cup.

The **SUTTER** family was the most amazing family in the history of sports. **BRENT** was one of six brothers to play in the NHL, amassing more than 5,000 games played as a group.

Perhaps part of **DUANE SUTTER'S** competitive spirit came from his childhood when all of the brothers walked to and from school every day together, always arriving home with at least one bloodied nose or shin among them!

In his rookie season, **TOMAS JONSSON** proved most effective during the division finals against the Rangers, getting extra ice time after countryman Persson missed the entire series with a separated shoulder.

NEW YORK ISLANDERS 1981-82
WILLIAM A. TORREY PRES. & GEN. MGR.
JOHN O. PICKETT JR. CHAIRMAN
JIM DEVELLANO A.G.M. & DIR. SCOUTING
AL ARBOUR COACH LORNE HENNING ASST. COACH
GERRY EHMAN HEAD SCOUT
D. POTVIN CAPT. M. BOSSY B. BOURNE B. CARROLL
G. GILBERT C. GILLIES R. BUTCH GORING T. JONSSON
A. KALLUR G. LANE D. LANGEVIN H. MARINI
M. McEWEN R. MELANSON W. MERRICK K. MORROW
B. NYSTROM S. PERSSON B. SMITH B. SUTTER
D. SUTTER J. TONELLI B. TROTTIER
R. WASKE H.T. J. PICKARD A.T.

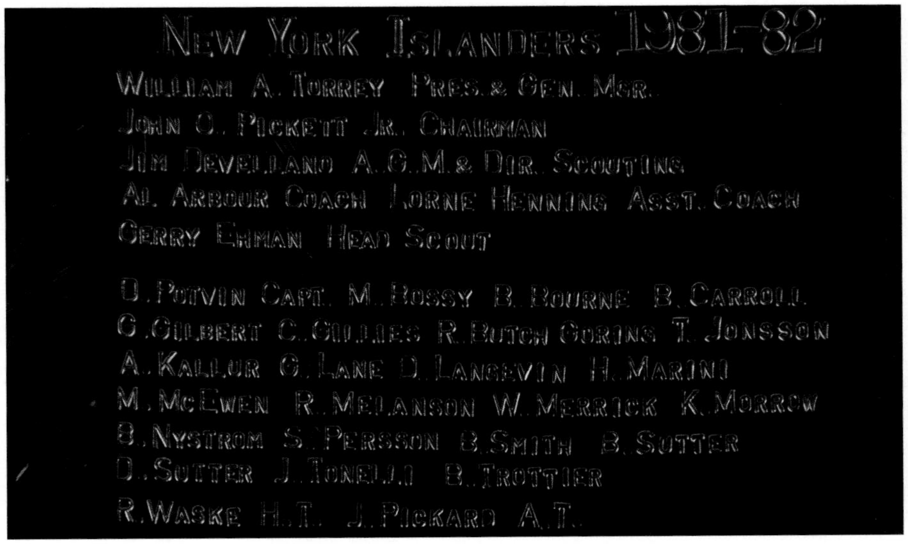

Team engraving from the current Stanley Cup

The third line of Tonelli-Nystrom-Merrick was likely the best in the league. It could check, hit, score, win games, do everything needed to win the Stanley Cup.

GORD LANE later became a playing assistant coach for the Islanders' farm team in Springfield, hoping to learn the puck game as coach and move into the NHL at some point.

DAVE LANGEVIN didn't jump into the NHL in 1974 the minute he was drafted. Instead, he finished his teaching degree at the University of Minnesota-Duluth before pursuing his pro dreams.

The team's second-leading goal scorer the previous season behind Bossy, **ANDERS KALLUR** slumped this season to just half the 36 goals of '80-'81, and adding just one more all playoffs.

After the victory, **KEN MORROW** drove home with the Cup one day only to be pulled over by the police. Speeding? Drunk driving? Nope. The officers saw the Cup in the back seat and just wanted to have a look.

Flaky and controversial, **BILLY SMITH** proved to be one of the most successful playoff goalies of all time with an incredible 88-36 record in the post-season.

MIKE McEWEN grew up in Toronto where he was scouted by the Pittsburgh Pirates and Houston Aeros as a pitching prospect, but when they heard he played hockey in the winter, the teams backed off.

After a strong training camp in September '81, **GREG GILBERT** went to the minors to do the opposite of what most coaches asked for of a demoted player. Coach Arbour told him to cut out the defensive work and start scoring goals!

Goalie **MELANSON** split the season almost evenly with Smith, but in the playoffs the more experienced Smith played all but 64 minutes.

RON WASKE started as an assistant with the Jacksonville Barons of the AHL before joining the Islanders in 1974. He also taught sports medicine at St. John's.

Assistant trainer **JIM PICKARD** was likeliest the best golfer on the team.

BILL TORREY'S code of managerial conduct was simple—keep your draft choices and build your team from there. The Isles' dynasty featured eight first-rounders and countless other lower selections who were scouted to perfection by Torrey's team of bird dogs.

Team chairman **JOHN PICKETT** had never tied on a pair of skates in his life. His closest brush with sports was as a pitcher in semi-pro baseball in Texas.

JIM DEVELLANO'S tremendous success and skill also spelled doom for his employment with the Islanders. This summer he accepted a job as general manager of Detroit.

AL ARBOUR kept a detailed scouting report of every player in the NHL and knew every weakness and tendency of every opponent—on ice and off.

As a lifetime Islander, **LORNE HENNING** had the respect of players and management alike, and many felt he was being groomed to succeed Arbour as coach.

GERRY EHMAN became director of player personnel in 1978 and many of the Islanders' top draft choices were made according to his recommendations.

Other players to appear for the Islanders this season: **NEIL HAWRYLIW**

1982 THE CHAMPIONS

1983 New York Islanders

The highest-scoring team in NHL history, Edmonton scored just six goals in the four games of the finals! Wayne Gretzky, who earlier had registered two, four-goal games in these playoffs, was held goalless thanks to great checking and Billy Smith's aggressive crease behaviour. This was a victory of sorts for both teams: the Islanders took home the Cup, and the Oilers learned what it took to win it.

STANLEY CUP FINALS

New York Islanders win best-of-seven Stanley Cup finals 4-0

*May 10, 1983 New York Islanders 2 at Edmonton Oilers 0 [Billy Smith]
*May 12, 1983 New York Islanders 6 at Edmonton Oilers 3
**May 14, 1983 Edmonton Oilers 1 at New York Islanders 5
**May 17, 1983 Edmonton Oilers 2 at New York Islanders 4 {Mike Bossy 12:39 1st}

** played at Northlands Coliseum, Edmonton ** played at Nassau Coliseum, Long Island*

Duane Sutter scores the winning goal in the series opener.

Islanders' defenceman Tomas Jonsson tries to cut off Wayne Gretzky, who is also being watched by goalie Billy Smith and Butch Goring (in front). It was in large part because of the Islanders' ability to hold Gretzky goalless in the finals that the New Yorkers won their fourth successive Cup.

NY ISLANDERS	GP	G	A	P	Pim
Duane Sutter	4	2	5	7	0
Brent Sutter	4	3	2	5	10
Ken Morrow	4	3	2	5	2
Bob Bourne	4	2	2	4	6
Mike Bossy	3	2	2	4	0
Bryan Trottier	4	1	3	4	4
Denis Potvin	4	0	3	3	4
Tomas Jonsson	4	1	1	2	8
Anders Kallur	4	1	1	2	4
Bob Nystrom	4	1	1	2	2
Stefan Persson	4	0	2	2	4
John Tonelli	4	1	0	1	0
Clark Gillies	4	0	1	1	6
Dave Langevin	4	0	1	1	0
Gord Lane	4	0	0	0	2
Billy Carroll	4	0	0	0	0
Butch Goring	4	0	0	0	0
Wayne Merrick	4	0	0	0	0
Billy Smith	4	0	0	0	0
Greg Gilbert	1	0	0	0	0

In Goal	GP	W-L	Mins	GA	SO	Avg
Billy Smith	4	4-0	240	6	1	1.50

Although he was a scorer in junior, **DUANE SUTTER** became known more as a checker and physical force once he got to the NHL, even though he led the team in points in this finals.

"Nothing was ever handed to us as a family, nothing," said "Pup" **BRENT SUTTER** of his childhood. "We grew up, seven boys in a two bedroom house that didn't have running water."

PAUL BOUTILIER was nicknamed "Tree Trunk" because of his huge thighs, muscles developed as a kid running with his father up and down the hills of Cape Breton.

A free agent signing after being drafted by Washington, **HALLIN** was among the second wave of Swedes to come to the NHL.

Although he was a reliable offensive player who had three 30- and three 20-goal seasons, it took **BOB BOURNE** 699 regular season games before he recorded his first hat trick!

KEN MORROW traipsed around Long Island with the Cup, taking it to many bars and restaurants so as many people as possible could have their picture taken with it.

Incredibly, **MIKE BOSSY** scored all four game-winning goals in the semi-finals against Boston and five overall in these playoffs, both NHL records.

A week after victory, **BRYAN TROTTIER** treated his teammates to an exhibition of his guitar-playing at the team party!

DENIS POTVIN made a pact with his ailing father—he would win the Cup if his dad fought through the suffering and treatments he was undergoing to be there for the victory. They both kept their ends of the bargain.

TOMAS JONSSON was the team's leading +/- man in the regular season at +40, and his 50 points helped make him a third-line version of Bryan Trottier, a two-way superstar.

ANDERS KALLUR saw his NHL stock plummet as his goal count stood at just six for the year. In the playoffs, though, he picked up his game and recorded 15 points in 20 games.

BOB NYSTROM was the kind of player no one noticed until he won a game for his team. "There are so many guys in the world with more talent than me. I think about those guys a lot," he said after victory.

STEFAN PERSSON was traded to Winnipeg near the end of the '85-'86 season but preferred retirement to reporting to the Jets, a decision that nullified the deal.

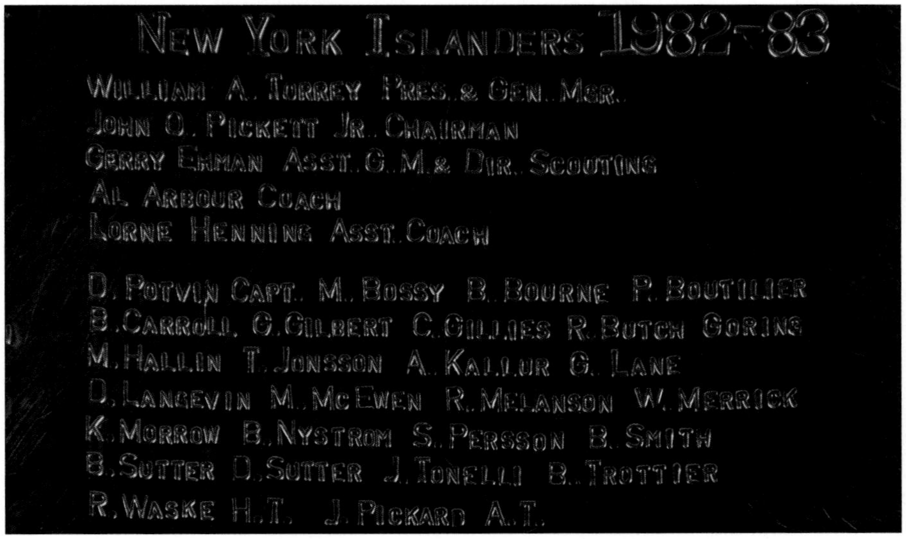

As a child, **JOHN TONELLI** and his brother created their own homemade Cup from an ashtray and a lamp which they competed for in their basement games of hockey.

As a teenager, **CLARK GILLIES** was a better baseball prospect than hockey. He could hit for power and had a good arm as a catcher, but scouts said he was too...timid!

By this point in the season, **DAVE LANGEVIN** had lost three of four ligaments in his right knee. Another injury to the pin a month earlier meant he didn't see playoff action until the finals.

GORD LANE shaved his trademark beard before game two of the finals. "I didn't play much in game one," he reasoned, "so I thought I would shave and Al Arbour wouldn't recognize me."

NEW YORK ISLANDERS 1982-83
WILLIAM A. TORREY PRES. & GEN. MGR.
JOHN O. PICKETT JR. CHAIRMAN
GERRY EHMAN ASST. G.M. & DIR. SCOUTING
AL ARBOUR COACH
LORNE HENNING ASST. COACH
D. POTVIN CAPT. M. BOSSY B. BOURNE P. BOUTILIER
B. CARROLL G. GILBERT C. GILLIES R. BUTCH GORING
M. HALLIN T. JONSSON A. KALLUR G. LANE
D. LANGEVIN M. McEWEN R. MELANSON W. MERRICK
K. MORROW B. NYSTROM S. PERSSON B. SMITH
B. SUTTER D. SUTTER J. TONELLI B. TROTTIER
R. WASKE H.T. J. PICKARD A.T.

Team engraving from the current Stanley Cup

BILLY CARROLL was key to the number one penalty-killing unit in the league that held Gretzky pointless in the first three games of the finals.

Nearing the end of his career, **BUTCH GORING** became more mindful of his coaching aspirations which were eventually to lead him back to the Island.

From Cup hero in 1981, **WAYNE MERRICK** had now been relegated to the press box for most of the playoffs. When he did dress, he saw limited action.

The downside to **MIKE McEWEN'S** offensive talent from the blueline was that defensively he was erratic and inconsistent, weaknesses that got him traded early the next season.

Emerging from the shadows of Billy Smith, goalie **ROLLIE MELANSON** played 44 games this year with a superb 24-12-5 record, but although he saw some action in the playoffs, he didn't play at all in the finals.

Slashing and hacking opponents from the safety of his crease, **BILLY SMITH** out-psyched the Oilers after spearing Glenn Anderson and Gretzky in short order, though he won the Conn Smythe Trophy on his goaltending merits.

GREG GILBERT spent half a season on the farm in Indianapolis but when he got the call to the big team he developed into one of the best scorers and checkers in the NHL.

Not long after this victory, **BILL TORREY** was both criticized and praised—criticized for keeping the team intact for so long and leaving no post-Cup legacy, praised for keeping together a team for so long and ensuring a great dynasty!

RON WASKE was an important part of the National Athletic Trainers' Association, a group which helped keep him at the forefront of medical advancement and injury treatment.

JIM PICKARD joined the Islanders in 1973 and was as popular in the dressing room as any of the players.

Owner **JOHN PICKETT** was a private man who got his greatest joy as owner by being a fan. "My reward," he said, "comes when we score an overtime goal to beat Pittsburgh in the fifth game of the series."

GERRY EHMAN rose to the position of assistant general manager and director of scouting because of his experience, dedication, and knowledge. He played with Al Arbour in Toronto; they worked together in St. Louis; and, in 1974, Arbour and Torrey brought him to Long Island.

Coach **AL ARBOUR** had been involved in a rare back-to-back wins during his playing days, winning the Cup with Chicago in 1961 and another team, the Leafs, the following year. When asked where he could fit another ring on his already busy hands, he deadpanned, "I'll find room. I've got ten fingers."

LORNE HENNING'S success as an assistant coach with the Isles led to numerous job offers to be head man elsewhere. He rejected Vancouver but took on the head coaching job in Minnesota.

Other players to appear for the Islanders this season: **KEVIN DEVINE, GORD DINEEN, DARCY REGIER**

1983 THE CHAMPIONS
1984 Edmonton Oilers

Edmonton, like the Islanders, had to lose in order to learn how to win, a process that ended the previous year with a sweep to these Islanders in the finals. The process was a never-ending series of inheritance, right from the days of the first dynasty, in Toronto, in the 1940s. The Oilers had to win just once on Long Island to start the 1984 finals series before returning home for three straight games in the days of the ill-fated 2-3-2 series format. Wild street celebrations in Edmonton turned ugly after Cup victory and police were called in to quell what nearly became a dangerous riot.

STANLEY CUP FINALS

Edmonton Oilers win best-of-seven Stanley Cup finals 4-1

*May 10, 1984 Edmonton Oilers 1 at New York Islanders 0 [Grant Fuhr]
*May 12, 1984 Edmonton Oilers 1 at New York Islanders 6
**May 15, 1984 New York Islanders 2 at Edmonton Oilers 7
**May 17, 1984 New York Islanders 2 at Edmonton Oilers 7
**May 19, 1984 New York Islanders 2 at Edmonton Oilers 5 {Ken Linseman 0:38 2nd}

** played at Nassau Coliseum, Long Island ** played at Northlands Coliseum, Edmonton*

The Oilers' bench erupts in joy as the team nears its first Stanley Cup.

EDMONTON	GP	G	A	P	Pim
Wayne Gretzky	5	4	3	7	4
Jari Kurri	5	1	5	6	2
Mark Messier	5	3	1	4	4
Kevin McClelland	5	2	2	4	16
Paul Coffey	5	2	2	4	0
Glenn Anderson	5	1	3	4	8
Willy Lindstrom	5	2	1	3	0
Dave Semenko	5	1	2	3	4
Charlie Huddy	5	0	3	3	4
Pat Hughes	5	0	3	3	4
Ken Linseman	5	1	1	2	26
Dave Lumley	5	1	1	2	17
Kevin Lowe	5	1	0	1	4
Randy Gregg	5	1	0	1	2
Pat Conacher	2	1	0	1	0
Lee Fogolin	5	0	1	1	6
Dave Hunter	3	0	1	1	6
Don Jackson	5	0	0	0	13
Jaroslav Pouzar	5	0	0	0	6
Grant Fuhr	3	0	0	0	0
Andy Moog	3	0	0	0	0

In Goal	GP	W-L	Mins	GA	SO	Avg
Andy Moog	3	2-0	128	4	0	1.88
Grant Fuhr	3	2-1	172	8	1	2.79

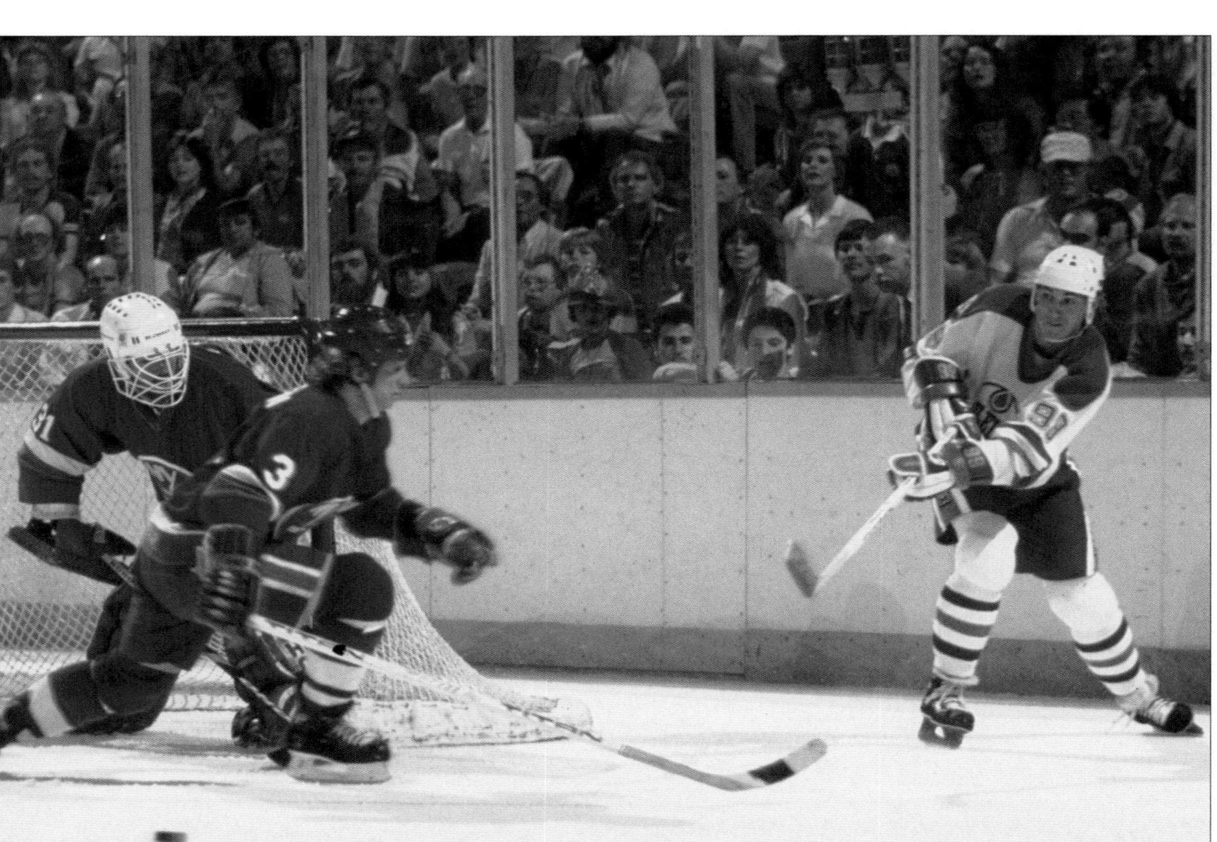

Wayne Gretzky feathers a pass past Tomas Jonsson and goalie Billy Smith into the slot for an Edmonton scoring chance.

WAYNE GRETZKY led the playoffs with 35 points after a season in which he scored a preposterous 205 points. "There's no feeling like lifting that Stanley Cup," he said later. "It's like your firstborn child."

Fresh off a 50-goal, 100-point season, **KURRI** became the first Finnish-trained player to have his name on the Stanley Cup.

MARK MESSIER was a leader on ice and off. He scored the critical go-ahead goal in game three that inspired his team to victory and won the Conn Smythe Trophy for his performance.

KEVIN McCLELLAND was a mid-season acquisition from Pittsburgh who proved to be a solid utility forward as someone who could fight when the occasion called for a little toughness.

A complex personality in the prime of a Hall of Fame career, **PAUL COFFEY** recorded an incredible 126 points on the year.

GLENN ANDERSON was called alternately "Mork" or "Space Cadet" by his teammates because they jokingly said that he came from another planet.

One minute **LINDSTROM** was playing for the Winnipeg Jets, the next he had been traded to the Oilers at the deadline in '83 and was playing alongside Wayne Gretzky. A year later he was dandling the Stanley Cup.

DAVE SEMENKO'S nickname in the dressing room was Sam or Semenk, though around the league he was called Cementhead for his agreed lack of talent and pugilistic skills in creating open ice for number 99.

CHARLIE HUDDY was never drafted after graduating from the Oshawa Generals, but his agent, Gus Badali, also represented Gretzky and arranged a tryout for Huddy with the Oil.

The previous year in the regular season **PAT HUGHES** set an incredible NHL record by scoring two short-handed goals just 25 seconds apart in a game vs. St. Louis.

LINSEMAN had been nicknamed "The Rat" by Philadelphia teammate Bobby Clarke in the 1970s, a name well deserved.

"I'm very lucky to be here," **LUMLEY** said in the dressing room. He had played college hockey at the University of New Hampshire. One Christmas, he was going to drive home to Toronto with friends, but his mother convinced him to save time and fly. His friends drove but were involved in a serious accident, one being killed, the two others badly burned.

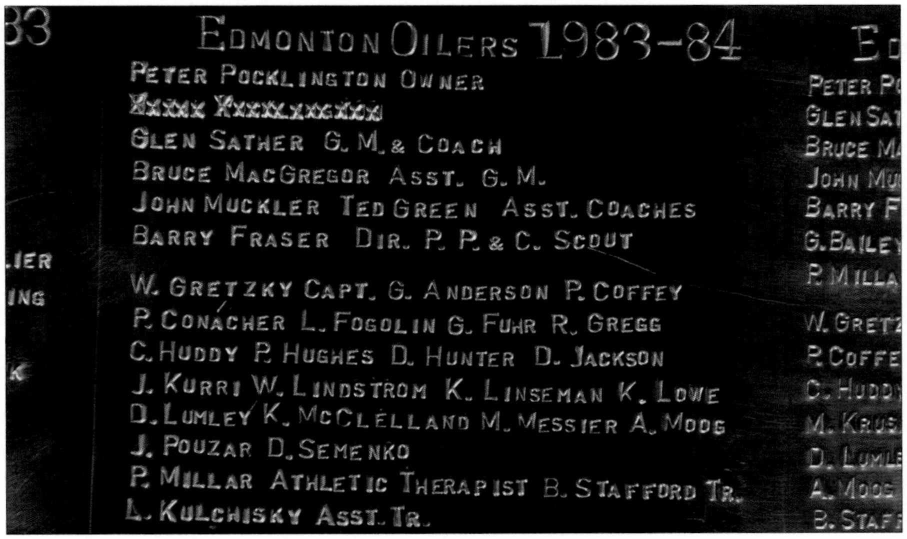

A native of Lachute, Quebec, **KEVIN LOWE** became the first English-speaking captain of the Quebec Remparts in junior and in 1979 was the Oilers' first-ever draft choice in the NHL.

The only medical doctor in the NHL, **RANDY GREGG** studied at the University of Alberta, played at the 1980 Olympics, coached and played for two years with the Kokudo Bunnies in Japan, became an orthopaedic surgeon, and then signed with the Oilers, in 1982.

His only season with the Oilers turned out to be **PAT CONACHER'S** most rewarding. He had been Rangers property since the 1979 draft but after being released in the summer of '83 didn't catch on with Edmonton until October and spent half a season in the minors.

Team engraving from the abandoned ring (see p. 10)

LEE FOGOLIN'S father, Lidio, won a Stanley Cup with Detroit in 1949-50, and Lee's accomplishments this season put them in the record book as the first father-son tandem to win Cups.

Perhaps the finest modern family besides the Sutters were the **HUNTERS**. Dale, Dave, and Mark were Petrolia's answer to Viking's idea of a hockey player—hard-nosed, competitive, successful. **DAVE** had a career-high 22 goals this year.

DON JACKSON was happy playing in Minnesota and working there in the summer as a real estate agent. He was upset at being traded to Edmonton, but with a slumping market put his business ambitions on hold and became a key fifth defenceman on the Oilers' blueline.

JAROSLAV POUZAR became only the third player after Connie Broden and Ken Morrow to win both a World Championship gold medal and the Stanley Cup.

Time and again his teammates would say what the stats didn't—that goalie **GRANT FUHR** was the Oilers' MVP.

ANDY MOOG appeared in seven playoff games and had a perfect 4-0 record. He proved himself to be almost the equal of Fuhr, but without being given the ice time he eventually decided a trade would be best.

XXXX refers to **BASIL POCKLINGTON**, Peter's father, who had nothing to do with the team, save the familial connection to the owner. Though the name was engraved on the Cup, the NHL decreed it should be X'd out because it had no merit being there! It does not appear at all on the Replica Cup.

PETE MILLAR was the Oilers' athletic therapist and **BARRIE STAFFORD** the trainer.

Trainer **LYLE KULCHISKY** was the man put in charge, late one debauched night, of taking the Cup to a garage to have the dents in the Cup repaired, a journey that didn't go all that well.

No sooner had **PETER POCKLINGTON'S** team won the Stanley Cup than his company, Fidelity Trust, vowed to sue him for the $10 million he had owed its shareholders for more than a year.

BRUCE MacGREGOR'S playing career was highlighted by the '64-'65 season in Detroit when he played on a line with the aged Ted Lindsay and scored 21 goals, almost double his previous best of eleven.

GLEN SATHER got his start in the NHL before finishing his playing career with the Oilers in the WHA, becoming playing coach late in the '76-'77 season.

Few remember that **JOHN MUCKLER** coached the Minnesota North Stars in 1968-69 to a pitiful 6-23-6 record during his brief stay behind the bench of the second-year expansion team.

BARRY FRASER was the team's chief scout. He began his career working for the Kitchener Rangers, and his first great success was drafting Larry Robinson for that team.

Other players to appear for the Oilers this season: **KEN BERRY, JOHN BLUM, RICK CHARTRAW, DEAN CLARK, RAY COTE, TOM GORENCE, STEVE GRAVES, MARC HABSCHEID, KARI JALONEN, REG KERR, LARRY MELNYK, JIM PLAYFAIR, TOM ROULSTON, GORD SHERVEN, TODD STRUEBY, RAIMO SUMMANEN**

1984–1985 Edmonton Oilers

THE CHAMPIONS

Typical of this consistent and dominating march to a second straight Cup was the Oilers' first-round encounter with Los Angeles. There would be no wild 10-8 shootouts, no blown leads, no upsets with this now experienced team. The Oil methodically won three in a row, two in overtime, and played poised hockey that marked the maturity of a true championship team. They cruised past their usual victims, the Winnipeg Jets, in four straight, then beat Chicago in six to qualify for the finals where the Flyers provided little resistance.

STANLEY CUP FINALS

Edmonton Oilers win best-of-seven Stanley Cup finals 4-1

*May 21, 1985 Edmonton Oilers 1 at Philadelphia Flyers 4
*May 23, 1985 Edmonton Oilers 3 at Philadelphia Flyers 1
**May 25, 1985 Philadelphia Flyers 3 at Edmonton Oilers 4
**May 28, 1985 Philadelphia Flyers 3 at Edmonton Oilers 5
**May 30, 1985 Philadelphia Flyers 3 at Edmonton Oilers 8 {Paul Coffey 17:57 1st}

** played at the Spectrum, Philadelphia ** played at Northlands Coliseum, Edmonton*

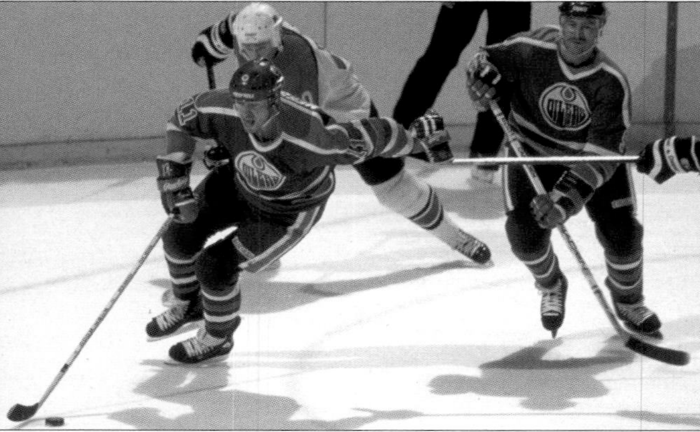

Game action from the 1985 Cup finals, in Philadelphia.

Edmonton's Mike Krushelnyski gets in behind Flyers' defenceman Mark Howe for an excellent chance on goalie Bob Froese.

EDMONTON	GP	G	A	P	Pim
Wayne Gretzky	5	7	4	11	0
Paul Coffey	5	3	8	11	6
Jari Kurri	5	1	6	7	0
Mark Messier	5	2	4	6	6
Charlie Huddy	5	1	5	6	6
Mike Krushelnyski	5	2	2	4	4
Willy Lindstrom	5	3	0	3	2
Glenn Anderson	5	1	1	2	12
Dave Hunter	5	1	0	1	25
Kevin McClelland	5	0	1	1	41
Randy Gregg	4	0	1	1	2
Don Jackson	5	0	0	0	35
Dave Semenko	4	0	0	0	14
Lee Fogolin	5	0	0	0	8
Kevin Lowe	5	0	0	0	4
Esa Tikkanen	3	0	0	0	4
Pat Hughes	4	0	0	0	2
Dave Lumley	1	0	0	0	2
Grant Fuhr	5	0	0	0	0
Mark Napier	5	0	0	0	0
Billy Carroll	2	0	0	0	0
Larry Melnyk	1	0	0	0	0
Jaroslav Pouzar	1	0	0	0	0

In Goal	GP	W-L	Mins	GA	SO	Avg
Grant Fuhr	5	4-1	300	13	0	2.60

WAYNE GRETZKY led the playoffs again with a record 47 points and won the Conn Smythe Trophy. He scored three goals in one period in the finals to tie a league record.

PAUL COFFEY set a myriad of records for defencemen in these playoffs: most goals, one playoff (12); most assists, one playoff (25); most points, one playoff (37); most assists, one game (5); most points, one game (6).

JARI KURRI set a record for most goals in one playoff year with 19, breaking by one Reggie Leach's mark. Kurri also had a record four hat tricks in the '85 playoffs.

MARK MESSIER'S great uncle, Howard Dea, was a member of the 1923 Edmonton Eskimos team that lost the Stanley Cup challenge that year to the Ottawa Senators.

HUDDY was an important part of the Oilers' increased commitment to defence and was one of the team's top +/- men every season.

MIKE KRUSHELNYSKI was acquired near the start of the season and landed a plum job as left winger to Gretzky and Kurri.

LINDSTROM was nicknamed "the Wisp" because of his slight build and great speed, but make no mistake—he was a complete player.

GLENN ANDERSON became known as "Kamikaze" because of his reckless abandon in driving to the net down the right side, his off wing.

DAVE HUNTER was an original NHL-Oilers forward, starting his career with the team in the WHA and staying with the team through the 1979 Expansion Draft.

KEVIN McCLELLAND set a Stanley Cup finals record with 29 penalty minutes in one game, including 25 in one period, during the game of May 30, 1985.

RANDY GREGG, the good doctor, was not above applying a few sutures to bleeding teammates when the team doctor or trainer was not near at hand.

DON JACKSON had been so upset by the trade that sent him from his native Minnesota to Edmonton that he quit for a couple of weeks at training camp in 1981.

DAVE SEMENKO never had a 200-penalty minute season in the NHL, his reputation keeping him out of as many fights as he got into.

LEE FOGOLIN was claimed by Edmonton from Buffalo at the 1979 Expansion Draft and stayed with the Oilers until 1987 when he went back to Buffalo.

KEVIN LOWE drew good-natured jeers and cheers from his teammates when he began to write a regular column in the *Edmonton Sun*, a behind-the-scenes look at the team.

After Gretzky was closely checked in game one, Sather took Krushelnyski off the top line and and used **TIKKANEN**, who had yet to play in the NHL!

Ironically, **PAT HUGHES'S** wife later ran a publishing house in Michigan and published a book on the Stanley Cup.

Team engraving from the current Stanley Cup

DAVE LUMLEY won a Cup with Edmonton the previous year, but Hartford claimed him in the Waiver Draft prior to the '84-'85 season. Halfway through the year, the Whalers put him on waivers only to have the Oilers re-claim him!

ANDY MOOG had been with the Oilers since 1980 and seemed certain to be the number-one man until Fuhr came along and rendered Moog's presence a moot point.

Amazingly, goalie **GRANT FUHR** faced penalty shots in consecutive games of the finals, games four and five, stopping both Ron Sutter and Dave Poulin.

"I appreciated that '85 Cup a lot more," said **NAPIER** comparing this win to his first Cup, with the Habs in 1979.

After three Cups with the Islanders, **BILLY CARROLL** was claimed on waivers by Edmonton and became the only player to win Cups with both 1980s dynasties.

LARRY MELNYK scored a goal in game two of the Conference finals, his first in 157 games over a five year period.

JAROSLAV POUZAR was acquired so that he could play left wing with Gretzky and Kurri, but when that didn't work out his solid two-way play stood him in good stead.

BARRY STAFFORD and **LYLE KULCHISKY** were the team's trainers.

PETER POCKLINGTON'S financial woes forced him to evermore desperate measures, including threats to move the team, to try to extract greater revenue from the City for money generated by the Coliseum.

SATHER attended university in the off season during his playing days to help prepare him for a career in coaching after he hung up his skates.

BRUCE MacGREGOR had a fine, 14-year career in the NHL as a player, finishing with the Oilers in the WHA.

JOHN MUCKLER made it as far as the EHL as a player before turning to coaching.

TED GREEN never returned to the NHL after winning the Cup with Boston in '72. Like many of the Oil staff, he joined the team via his WHA connections and credentials.

"ACE" BAILEY was no relation to the Leafs' Hall of Famer of the same surname and nickname. Like Ted Green, he won Cups with the Bruins in '70 and '72.

CHADWICK played every game in goal for the Leafs for two consecutive seasons (1956-58) during a brief career in the NHL in which he didn't play even one minute in the playoffs.

LORNE DAVIS finished his playing career way back in 1960 but was part of a scouting staff that had seemingly infinite NHL experience and knowledge.

MATTI VAISANEN coached Finland's national junior team and became a part-time Oilers' scout (on the recommendation of Barry Fraser).

PETE MILLAR was the Oilers' athletic therapist.

DR. GORDON CAMERON was the club physician.

Other players to appear for the Oilers this season: **MARCO BARON, RAY COTE, MARC HABSCHEID, TERRY MARTIN, DARYL REAUGH, GORD SHERVEN, STEVE SMITH, RAIMO SUMMANEN, MIKE ZANIER**

1985 THE CHAMPIONS 1986 Montreal Canadiens

The Habs caught a huge break when the Flames eliminated the Oilers thanks to an own goal by Edmonton's Steve Smith in game seven of the conference finals, thus paving the way for the underdog Habs to win the Cup. As in 1971, it was rookie goaltending that made the difference, this year's amazing performance coming from Patrick Roy. Celebrations in downtown Montreal turned ugly and nearly devolved into a full-scale riot. Eleven men were arrested and charged with looting.

STANLEY CUP FINALS

Montreal Canadiens win best-of-seven Stanley Cup finals 4-1

*May 16, 1986 Montreal Canadiens 2 at Calgary Flames 5
*May 18, 1986 Montreal Canadiens 3 at Calgary Flames 2 (Skrudland 0:09 OT)
**May 20, 1986 Calgary Flames 3 at Montreal Canadiens 5
**May 22, 1986 Calgary Flames 0 at Montreal Canadiens 1 [Patrick Roy]
*May 24, 1986 Montreal Canadiens 4 at Calgary Flames 3 {Bobby Smith 10:30 3rd}

** played at Olympic Saddledome, Calgary ** played at the Forum, Montreal*

David Maley (helmet) and Guy Carbonneau celebrate.

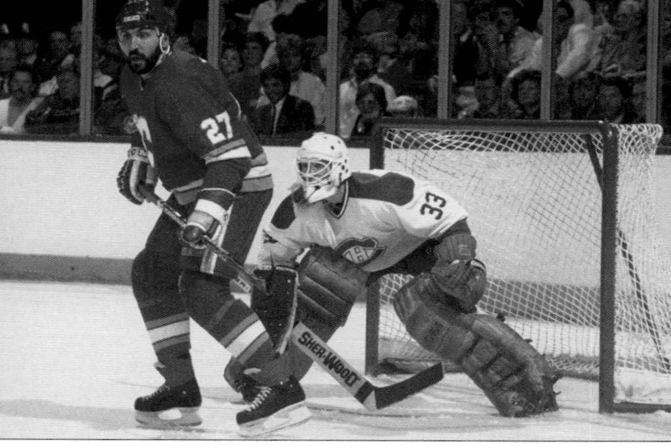

(clockwise) Calgary's John Tonelli tries to screen Patrick Roy; a relaxed Bob Gainey enjoys the spoils of victory during a city celebration with the Conn Smythe Trophy (won by Roy) and Stanley Cup on display; downtown Montreal is crammed with revelers during the Cup parade.

MONTREAL	GP	G	A	P	Pim
Mats Naslund	5	3	4	7	0
Bobby Smith	5	2	2	4	8
Chris Chelios	5	1	3	4	19
Gaston Gingras	4	2	1	3	0
Claude Lemieux	5	1	2	3	31
David Maley	5	1	2	3	2
Guy Carbonneau	5	0	3	3	23
Larry Robinson	5	0	3	3	15
Brian Skrudland	5	2	0	2	32
Mike McPhee	5	0	2	2	24
Mike Lalor	5	0	2	2	19
Bob Gainey	5	1	0	1	2
Rick Green	5	1	0	1	0
Kjell Dahlin	4	1	0	1	0
Ryan Walter	5	0	1	1	2
Chris Nilan	3	0	0	0	49
John Kordic	5	0	0	0	15
Craig Ludwig	5	0	0	0	14
Patrick Roy	5	0	0	0	0
Serge Boisvert	2	0	0	0	0
Stephane Richer	1	0	0	0	0
Steve Rooney	1	0	0	0	0

In Goal	GP	W-L	Mins	GA	SO	Avg
Patrick Roy	5	4-1	301	12	1	2.39

NASLUND was the first European to play for the Habs. He led the team in scoring in the regular season and playoffs.

BOBBY SMITH centred Mats Naslund and Kjell Dahlin to form the team's most potent line.

CHRIS CHELIOS later achieved another personal dream when he was made captain by his hometown Chicago Blackhawks.

After winning the Hobey Baker Award in 1984, **TOM KURVERS** joined the Habs for two years.

GINGRAS ranked his Calder Cup win the previous year as a more important moment, "because the Stanley Cup wouldn't have been possible without the Calder Cup."

CLAUDE LEMIEUX was called up late in the regular season only after Ryan Walter suffered a broken ankle.

The rookie **DAVID MALEY** played just three regular season games and seven more in the playoffs.

GUY CARBONNEAU later won another Cup with current teammate and future Dallas GM Bob Gainey.

Thanks to Steve Shutt, **ROBINSON** became interested in polo in the summers, joining the Montreal Polo Club and raising polo ponies.

BRIAN SKRUDLAND scored the fastest playoff overtime goal in NHL history, nine seconds into OT of game two of the finals.

MIKE McPHEE worked his way into the lineup by virtue of his size, scoring, and commitment to teamwork.

Rookie **MIKE LALOR** became one of a handful of undrafted players to win the Cup, signing as a free agent with the Habs.

Montreal's Cup was most rewarding for **GAINEY** who, after being named captain in 1981, was the old man on a rebuilding team.

Drafted 1st overall by the pitiful Washington Capitals in 1976, **RICK GREEN** was one of the league's best shot blockers.

The Montreal media used **KJELL DAHLIN'S** Swedish military training as an anti-aircraft gunner as metaphor for the player's scoring ability.

After suffering a broken ankle March 29, forward **RYAN WALTER** figured his season was done, but he managed to get in shape and play all five games of the finals.

Tough guy **CHRIS NILAN** amassed an incredible 141 penalty minutes in this year's 18-game-long playoffs.

JOHN KORDIC later died in Quebec City during a night of alcohol and drugs that ended in a fatal fight with police.

"When I found out Montreal took me [in the draft], I thought, 'Oh, great! I'll never make the team,'" **LUDWIG** said in 1980.

Upon learning that if he played 40 games of the regular season (to reach the 400-game career mark) **TREMBLAY** would collect $250,000 at age 55, **MARIO** came out of retirement.

By his own admission, **SVOBODA** contributed little to this Cup victory: "Almost anybody had more to do with it than I did. The skate sharpener. The guys who sweep the ice."

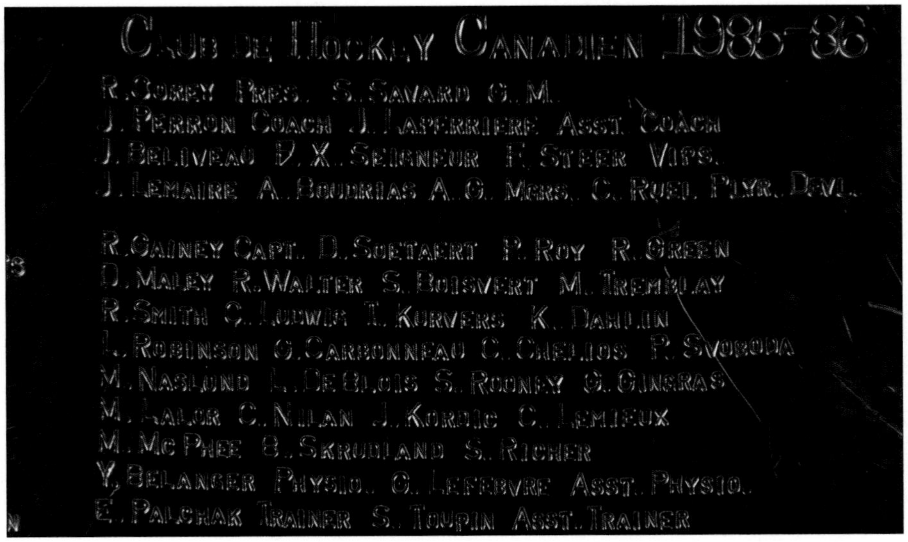

Team engraving from the current Stanley Cup

LUCIEN DEBLOIS became a free agent after the season because the team forgot to tender him a contract by July 1.

Physiotherapist **YVON BELANGER** was nicknamed "Speedy" because he walked so slowly.

Trainer **GAETAN LEFEBVRE'S** association with the Habs began in 1974 when the 15-year-old became the team's stick boy.

EDDIE PALCHAK was the team's ancient and loyal trainer.

SYLVAIN TOUPIN was the team's assistant trainer who was later fired by Pat Burns when he took over as coach.

SERGE BOISVERT was a rare example of a player going to Japan before making his NHL debut, in 1982, with Toronto.

SOETAERT and **PENNEY** were supposed to be the men in goal for the Habs this season, but Roy usurped the pair.

Rookie **PATRICK ROY** won the Conn Smythe. Without him, the Habs never would have won this Stanley Cup.

Sniper **STEPHANE RICHER** was outfitted in number 44 by the Habs in the hopes he'd become the next Jean Beliveau.

Coach Jean Perron dressed **ROONEY** for game five of the finals to ensure Rooney's name would appear on the Cup.

COREY'S appointment as team president in December 1982 had political overtones in that he had worked for O'Keefe Breweries, chief rivals to Molson and owners of the Habs.

SERGE SAVARD'S father, Laurent, was mayor of Landrienne, Quebec and imbued in his son an interest and ambition in politics that gave Serge his nickname—The Senator.

As Claude Ruel had done in 1968 and Al MacNeil in '70, **JEAN PERRON** won the Cup with Montreal as a rookie coach.

Back in 1979, **LAPERRIERE** had been front-runner to become new coach after the departure of Scotty Bowman, but he was told he'd have to drop his legal action against the team before being considered for the job, something he refused to do.

JEAN BELIVEAU, senior vice-president of corporate affairs, continued to represent not only the Canadiens but the NHL itself.

FRANCIS-XAVIER SEIGNEUR was the team's vice-president of marketing and worthy, in the club's eyes, of Cup engraving.

FRED STEER, the vice-president of finance and administration, was also fortunate enough to have his name on the Cup.

Coach the previous season, **JACQUES LEMAIRE** was back with the team in a reduced capacity as director of player personnel.

Director of scouting **ANDRE BOUDRIAS** had been a player in the Habs' organization during the 1960s.

CLAUDE RUEL had been in the Cleveland Indians baseball system until he lost an eye in an accident and turned his good eye to scouting.

Other players to appear for the Canadiens this season: **RANDY BUCYK, DOM CAMPEDELLI, KENT CARLSON, SHAYNE CORSON, SERGIO MOMESSO, STEVE PENNEY, ALFIE TURCOTTE**

1986 THE CHAMPIONS

1987 Edmonton Oilers

Although Philadelphia coach Mike Keenan brought the Stanley Cup into the dressing room before game six to motivate his Flyers to victory, the Oilers, at home for game seven, made sure he couldn't find the Cup to do the same before the last game of the year. This was the first game seven of the finals since Montreal beat Chicago in 1971. The Oilers cruised through their first three series, winning each in five games and not facing a stiff test until the Flyers in the finals.

STANLEY CUP FINALS

Edmonton Oilers win best-of-seven Stanley Cup finals 4-3

*May 17, 1987 Philadelphia Flyers 2 at Edmonton Oilers 4
*May 20, 1987 Philadelphia Flyers 2 at Edmonton Oilers 3 (Jari Kurri 6:50 OT)
**May 22, 1987 Edmonton Oilers 3 at Philadelphia Flyers 5
**May 24, 1987 Edmonton Oilers 4 at Philadelphia Flyers 1
*May 26, 1987 Philadelphia Flyers 4 at Edmonton Oilers 3
**May 28, 1987 Edmonton Oilers 2 at Philadelphia Flyers 3
*May 31, 1987 Philadelphia Flyers 1 at Edmonton Oilers 3 {Jari Kurri 14:59 2nd}

** played at Northlands Coliseum, Edmonton ** played at the Spectrum, Philadelphia*

Members of the Oilers take the Cup for a celebratory lap.

(clockwise) Edmonton's helmetless Esa Tikkanen tries to beat goalie Ron Hextall; Wayne Gretzky takes a taste of champagne from the Holy Grail of hockey; Glenn Anderson beats Hextall with a low shot, stick side, in game three.

EDMONTON	GP	G	A	P	Pim
Wayne Gretzky	7	2	9	11	2
Jari Kurri	7	5	4	9	4
Paul Coffey	7	2	4	6	14
Glenn Anderson	7	4	1	5	14
Mark Messier	7	2	3	5	10
Kevin Lowe	7	2	1	3	4
Randy Gregg	7	1	2	3	0
Mike Krushelnyski	7	1	1	2	6
Charlie Huddy	7	0	2	2	10
Craig MacTavish	7	0	2	2	6
Marty McSorley	7	1	0	1	10
Kevin McClelland	7	1	0	1	4
Dave Hunter	7	0	1	1	4
Jaroslav Pouzar	3	0	1	1	2
Kent Nilsson	7	0	1	1	0
Craig Muni	5	0	1	1	0
Esa Tikkanen	7	0	0	0	6
Steve Smith	3	0	0	0	6
Kelly Buchberger	3	0	0	0	5
Reijo Ruotsalainen	7	0	0	0	4
Grant Fuhr	7	0	0	0	0

In Goal	GP	W-L	Mins	GA	SO	Avg
Grant Fuhr	7	4-3	427	17	0	2.39

WAYNE GRETZKY led the playoffs with 34 points, including his 177th career playoff point to establish a new record.

On April 9, 1987, **JARI KURRI** tied a record by scoring three power-play goals in a game.

JEFF BEUKEBOOM played only half the regular season with the team, at 22 still a developing prospect.

Acquired at the trade deadline as a spare part, **MOE LEMAY** saw almost no playoff action.

Defenceman **PAUL COFFEY** missed part of the year with injuries and had just 67 points.

Later in his career, **GLENN ANDERSON** happily combined hockey with culture, playing in European leagues as well as touring with the Canadian National Team.

At the height of his powers, **"MOOSE" MESSIER** also owned "No. 11," a boutique clothing manufacturer.

After the Oilers were eliminated in the '86 playoffs, **KEVIN LOWE**, Gretzky, and Coffey flew directly to Phoenix to get away from it all and prepare mentally for this season.

GREGG had retired in 1986 to practise medicine, but Glen Sather lured him back.

MIKE KRUSHELNYSKI was drafted by Boston on the recommendation of Tom Johnson who liked his size and speed.

CHARLIE HUDDY had reported out of shape to the training camp in 1980 and spent most of the season in the minors.

The helmetless **CRAIG MACTAVISH** had spent a year in jail after being convicted of vehicular homicide, and the Oilers were the only team prepared to give him a second hockey life.

Inheritor to Dave Semenko's boxing gloves and pew in the penalty box, **MCSORLEY** was a protector of talent first and foremost.

One of the team's tough guys, **KEVIN MCCLELLAND** averaged more than 200 penalty minutes a year in his four seasons with the Oilers.

DAVE HUNTER had a reputation as a top checker, routinely shadowing the best the other team had to offer.

JAROSLAV POUZAR had spent all of '85-'86 and most of '86-'87 playing in Germany before rejoining the Oilers for the last dozen games of the regular season and into the playoffs.

KENT NILSSON was called by Gretzky the most skilled player he had ever seen. In the '87 playoffs, Nilsson shone on a line with Glenn Anderson and Mark Messier.

The Oilers took defenceman **CRAIG MUNI** from Toronto and his steady play gave him a series of Stanley Cups in Edmonton.

ESA TIKKANEN was often called "The Grate One" because he was the best, most annoying forward in the game.

Gretzky made his first handoff of the Cup to **STEVE SMITH**, a great gesture of support after the gaffe in '86.

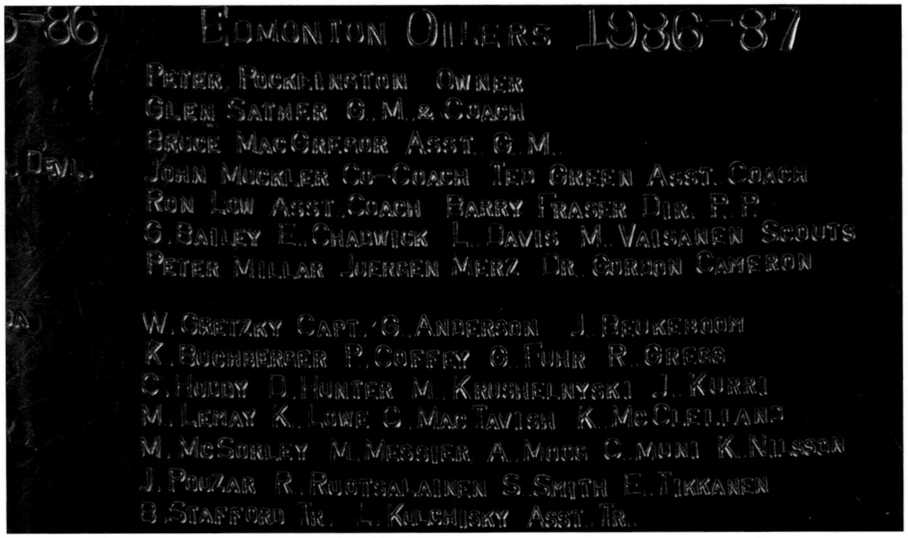

Team engraving from the current Stanley Cup

Goalie **ANDY MOOG'S** father, Don, was backup goalie at the 1955 World Championships when Canada won gold.

After spending the regular season with Nova Scotia in the AHL, **BUCHBERGER** played in three games of the finals.

REIJO RUOTSALAINEN bolted the Rangers the previous summer. The Oilers acquired him at the trade deadline.

Goalie **GRANT FUHR** was renowned for his playoff calm, often golfing the afternoon of a Cup game before turning in a brilliant performance in the evening.

PETER POCKLINGTON was once sued for $7 million by a psychic who testified that her advice to him led to the Oilers winning the Stanley Cup and that he had promised her a percentage of the millions of dollars earned from that win.

Coach **SATHER'S** earliest nickname was "Chick," one he acquired as a 15-year-old playing senior hockey for the Wainwright Commandos of the Battle River Hockey League.

A native Edmontonian, **BRUCE MACGREGOR** became the team's assistant director of marketing in 1976.

JOHN MUCKLER had been with the Oilers since 1981 and had been promised the head coaching job by Glen Sather since 1984. Yet in 1987, he was still Slats's assistant.

TED GREEN was a winner at every level, from a Memorial Cup to Cups in Boston as a player, Avco Cups in the WHA, and now another series of Cups as an assistant with the Oilers.

Sather saw in **RON LOW** something of himself—a journeyman player of limited talent who was articulate and a keen observer of the game.

Head scout **BARRY FRASER** was a much sought after GM by other clubs, but he rejected all offers and remained with the Oil until retiring to Mexico in 2000.

BAILEY had helped the Edmonton Oil Kings beat the Bruins' junior team, the Bobby Orr-led Oshawa Generals, in the 1966 Memorial Cup.

CHADWICK came to Edmonton with ten years of scouting behind him and the dual skill of being a goalie coach as well, his experience including the tutoring of a young Chico Resch.

LORNE DAVIS had played for four teams over a 95-game career that saw him win the Stanley Cup with the '53 Canadiens.

MATTI VAISANEN tipped Barry Fraser about the development of a 17-year-old named Jari Kurri when the Oilers, still in the WHA, came to Helsinki for a pre-season game.

PETER MILLAR was still with the team as athletic therapist.

JUERGEN MERZ was the Oilers' massage therapist.

DR. GORDON CAMERON was the Oilers' physician.

LYLE KULCHISKY assisted trainer Barrie Stafford in the dressing room.

BARRIE STAFFORD acted as Team Canada's trainer at three Canada Cups ('84, '87, and '91) and the 1996 World Cup and '94 World Championships.

Other players to appear for the Oilers this season: **LEE FOGOLIN, DANNY GARE, STEVE GRAVES, STU KULAK, NORMAND LACOMBE, DAVE LUMLEY, MIKE MOLLER, MARK NAPIER, DAVE SEMENKO, RAIMO SUMMANEN, WAYNE VAN DORP**

1987 THE CHAMPIONS 1988 Edmonton Oilers

The Oilers did what no other team has done before or since: they went undefeated at home all playoffs, reeling off eleven consecutive wins. Once the Cup was theirs, the players took the trophy to places it had never gone to before. It was scratched after falling from the stage at the Boom Boom Room in Edmonton, and after more, greater damage, it was taken, in the middle of the night, to Freedom Ford, a local garage station, where mechanic Al Braun tried to repair the extensive damage.

STANLEY CUP FINALS

Edmonton Oilers win best-of-seven Stanley Cup finals 4-0

*May 18, 1988	Boston Bruins 1 at Edmonton Oilers 2
*May 20, 1988	Boston Bruins 2 at Edmonton Oilers 4
**May 22, 1988	Edmonton Oilers 6 at Boston Bruins 3
**May 24, 1988	Edmonton Oilers 3 at Boston Bruins 3+
*May 26, 1988	Boston Bruins 3 at Edmonton Oilers 6 {Wayne Gretzky 9:44 2nd}

** played at Northlands Coliseum, Edmonton ** played at Boston Garden*
+ blackout at 16:37 of second period forced game's cancellation (statistics still count)

Gretzky and bride-to-be Janet Jones share a personal Cup moment.

(left) Teammates gather around Gretzky for the first of what would become a traditional on-ice team portrait with the Cup; (above) Gretzky eludes Boston defenceman Ray Bourque with a pass.

Team engraving from the shoulder of the Replica Cup

EDMONTON	GP	G	A	P	Pim
Wayne Gretzky	5	3	10	13	0
Esa Tikkanen	5	6	3	9	18
Glenn Anderson	5	3	3	6	4
Jari Kurri	5	1	4	5	4
Craig Simpson	5	3	1	4	10
Steve Smith	5	0	4	4	2
Kevin McClelland	5	1	2	3	26
Mike Krushelnyski	5	1	2	3	6
Mark Messier	5	1	2	3	4
Randy Gregg	5	0	3	3	4
Kevin Lowe	5	0	2	2	4
Craig Muni	5	0	2	2	0
Normand Lacombe	5	1	0	1	4
Keith Acton	5	1	0	1	0
Marty McSorley	5	0	0	0	4
Craig MacTavish	5	0	0	0	2
Geoff Courtnall	5	0	0	0	0
Grant Fuhr	5	0	0	0	0
Jeff Beukeboom	4	0	0	0	0
Charlie Huddy	1	0	0	0	0

In Goal	GP	W-L	Mins	GA	SO	Avg
Grant Fuhr	5	4-0	277	12	0	2.60

WAYNE GRETZKY again led the playoffs, with 43 points. After the final siren, he gathered his team at centre ice for an on-ice team portrait, a tradition each team since has emulated.

When he was three years old, **ESA TIKKANEN** was Helsinki's team mascot during league play. At 16, he played junior in Saskatchewan to learn the Canadian style of play.

GLENN ANDERSON'S Cup celebrations turned horribly wrong in the summer. He hosted a party at his house, but a good friend of his ended up dying in hospital as a result of nearly drowning in his swimming pool.

DAVE HANNAN was part of the Simpson-for-Coffey trade, a reliable two-way centre who could check, kill penalties, and chip in the odd goal.

"He's our Walter Alston," Gretzky said of **KURRI**, who had a reputation for signing one-year contracts, just as Alston had done through 20 years with the L.A. Dodgers.

CRAIG SIMPSON arrived early in the season in the Paul Coffey trade. He became the first player in league history to score 50 goals during a season in which he played for two teams.

STEVE SMITH led all Oilers defencemen with 55 points during the regular season.

KEVIN McCLELLAND became the team's career penalty minutes leader this season while also scoring the 50th goal of his career.

In this his last year in Edmonton, **KRUSHELNYSKI** became part of the historic trade of Gretzky to L.A. in the summer.

MARK MESSIER'S leadership was centred on one expression he'd repeat over and over: discipline over emotion. That's how he played when the Stanley Cup was on the line, and that's why he won six Cups during his career.

RANDY GREGG was a man of conviction, pride, and determination. He left the Oilers at the start of the year to play for the Canadian National Team and the Olympics, in Calgary, joining the Oilers afterward.

LOWE played the last two games of the finals with a cast on his wrist and two ribs broken. "Know what it takes to win the Stanley Cup?" Gretzky asked reporters rhetorically. "Guys like Kevin."

When Coffey was sent to Pittsburgh, **CRAIG MUNI** became the team's number-one defenceman. What he lacked in Coffey-like offense he made up for in Muni-like commitment to his own end of the ice.

Playing in his first full NHL season after being drafted by Buffalo in 1984, **LACOMBE** scored the game winner in game four of the Smythe Division semi-finals versus Winnipeg.

KEITH ACTON scored only twice in the playoffs, but both were game winners.

McSORLEY incurred a three-game suspension in the division finals after performing hari kari with his stick on an innocent Mike Bullard of Calgary.

"MacT," as his teammates called **CRAIG MacTAVISH**, played all 99 games for the team this year.

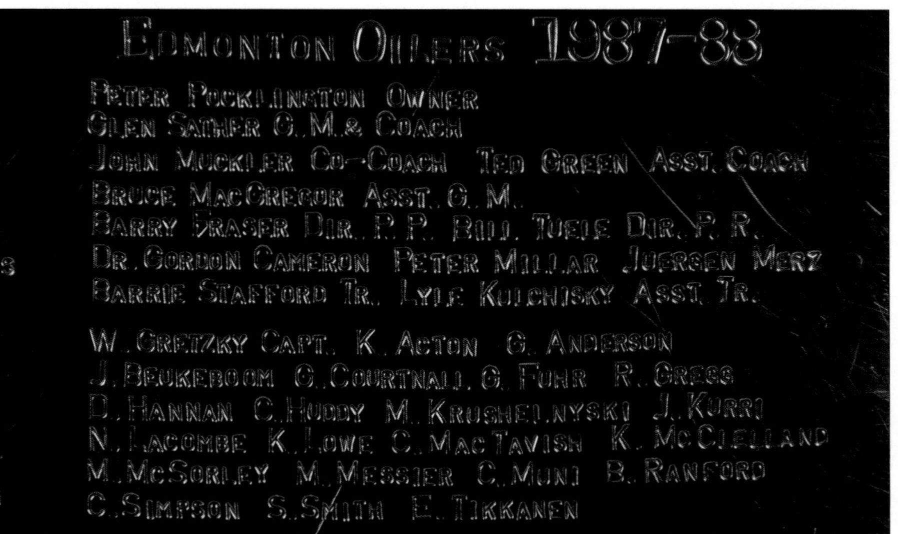

Team engraving from the current Stanley Cup

GEOFF COURTNALL came from Boston during the season, then played against his former mates in the finals.

Goalie **GRANT FUHR** played an astounding 75 games this year, winning a league-high 40 times. He became the first goalie to win 16 playoff games in one year.

Although goalie **BILL RANFORD** dressed for all 19 playoff games, he didn't play one minute behind Fuhr, though his patience would soon be rewarded.

Big **JEFF BEUKEBOOM** was a defensive specialist known for his thundering checks more than his goals.

CHARLIE HUDDY earned his way onto the team in 1982 through luck and hard work. The luck occurred because regulars Risto Siltanen and Gary Lariviere went down which injuries.

For years, **POCKLINGTON** denied that his business failures would ever lead to selling his greatest "asset," Wayne Gretzky. But just weeks after this fourth Cup in five years, that's exactly what "Peter Puck" did.

SATHER had drafted so brilliantly between 1979 and '83, but his selections from '83 to '90 were not as successful, leaving a huge void for the team as the 1980s dynasty players got older.

JOHN MUCKLER was never offered the chance to coach Team Canada internationally, so he petitioned USA Hockey for a job because of his dual citizenship. Nothing ever came of the public application.

TED GREEN'S miraculous recovery from his near-fatal stick-swinging duel with Wayne Maki in 1969 was later made into a book and then a screenplay.

BRUCE MacGREGOR played with three Edmonton-based teams before making his NHL debut in 1960-61: the Edmonton Maple Leaf Athletic Association, the Oil Kings, and then the Flyers.

BARRY FRASER became chief scout in the team's last WHA year, 1978-79, a culmination of experience that began with the Cleveland Crusaders in the league's first season (1972-73).

BILL TUELE was the director of public relations for the Oilers.

Prior to a game in January, **BARRIE STAFFORD** lost hold of a skate while sharpening it and suffered a gash along his wrist that required an emergency trip to the hospital. Just like a player, though, he was back at the rink by game time.

Assistant trainer **LYLE KULCHISKY** was the lucky one assigned the task of taking the Cup to Freedom Ford in the middle of the night for not so successful repairs!

DR. GORDON CAMERON was the Oilers' team physician.

PETER MILLAR worked in the dressing room as athletic trainer and therapist.

JUERGEN MERZ was the team's massage therapist.

Other players to appear for the Oilers this season: **KELLY BUCHBERGER, DAVE DONNELLY, STEVE DYKSTRA, JIM ENNIS, STEVE GRAVES, DAVE HUNTER, CHRIS JOSEPH, MARK LAMB, MOE LEMAY, MOE MANTHA, SCOTT METCALFE, JOHN MINER, TOM McMURCHY, SELMAR ODELEIN, DARYL REAUGH, WARREN SKORODENSKI, JOHN SKUDRA, JIM WIEMER**

1988–1989 Calgary Flames

THE CHAMPIONS

The Flames became the first team to defeat the Canadiens on Forum ice for the Cup (although in 1928, the Rangers defeated the other Montreal habitants of the Forum, the Maroons, at the Forum). Incredibly, the Flames did not win a single playoff series after this Cup victory until 2004, but 1989 was the culmination of years of careful planning, a defeat in the '86 finals, and the maturation of a group of players with a perfect blend of excellent goaltending, fast defence, balanced scoring, and solid checking on the forward lines.

STANLEY CUP FINALS

Calgary Flames win best-of-seven Stanley Cup finals 4-2

*May 14, 1989 Montreal Canadiens 2 at Calgary Flames 3
*May 17, 1989 Montreal Canadiens 4 at Calgary Flames 2
**May 19, 1989 Calgary Flames 3 at Montreal Canadiens 4 (Ryan Walter 38:08 OT)
**May 21, 1989 Calgary Flames 4 at Montreal Canadiens 2
*May 23, 1989 Montreal Canadiens 2 at Calgary Flames 3
**May 25, 1989 Calgary Flames 4 at Montreal Canadiens 2 {Doug Gilmour 11:02 3rd}

** played at Olympic Saddledome, Calgary ** played at the Forum, Montreal*

The Flames celebrate their first Cup win in franchise history.

Captain Lanny McDonald hoists the Cup in his final act as player as delirious teammates share in a dream that took every day of McDonald's career to realize.

CALGARY	GP	G	A	P	Pim
Al MacInnis	6	5	4	9	18
Joe Mullen	6	5	3	8	4
Joel Otto	6	2	6	8	2
Doug Gilmour	6	4	3	7	6
Colin Patterson	6	1	1	2	16
Theoren Fleury	6	1	1	2	2
Joe Nieuwendyk	6	1	1	2	2
Rob Ramage	6	0	2	2	10
Jim Peplinski	4	0	2	2	10
Jamie Macoun	6	0	2	2	8
Tim Hunter	4	0	2	2	6
Lanny McDonald	3	1	0	1	2
Mark Hunter	4	0	1	1	12
Dana Murzyn	6	0	1	1	8
Brad McCrimmon	6	0	1	1	6
Brian MacLellan	6	0	1	1	4
Hakan Loob	6	0	1	1	0
Ric Nattress	6	0	0	0	12
Gary Roberts	6	0	0	0	8
Mike Vernon	6	0	0	0	0
Jiri Hrdina	3	0	0	0	0

In Goal	GP	W-L	Mins	GA	SO	Avg
Mike Vernon	6	4-2	397	16	0	2.42

AL MacINNIS led the playoffs with 31 points, the first time a defenceman had done so since Bobby Orr tied Phil Esposito in 1972.

A child of Hell's Kitchen in New York City, **JOE MULLEN** possessed remarkable determination to make the NHL.

JOEL OTTO is one of only four palindromic players in the NHL (Jiri Latal, Gary Lupul, and Joffrey Lupul are the others).

Defenceman **GARY SUTER'S** Cup celebrations were done in a jacket and tie and a jaw wired shut after suffering a break in the first round of the playoffs.

Superstitious during the playoffs, **DOUG GILMOUR** had to shake Don Cherry's hand before each game of the finals.

Undrafted after graduating from Clarkson University, **COLIN PATTERSON** signed as a free agent on March 24, 1983.

THEO FLEURY was the smallest player in the league but also one of the toughest. "It's the greatest day of my life," he said.

A cousin of Jeff Beukeboom, **JOE NIEUWENDYK** followed his Calder Trophy season of 51 goals in '87-'88 with another 51 goals.

ROB RAMAGE represented the best and worst of trades: his acquisition the previous year was one of the key's to the team's win; the price paid included losing Brett Hull.

PEPLINSKI was the only player still on the team who had been with Calgary during the first year in the city, in 1980-81.

MACOUN was testament to perseverance, becoming one of the finest undrafted defencemen in the history of the modern game.

TIM HUNTER was the first Flames player to graduate from the team's minor hockey program to make the NHL.

LANNY McDONALD scored his 500th goal and 1,000th point during the season, and scored a goal in the final game after sitting out the previous three.

MARK HUNTER'S brothers, Dave and Dale, also played in the NHL. Mark missed ten playoff games with injury.

MURZYN came to Calgary early in 1988 in a five-player trade.

BRAD McCRIMMON was nicknamed "Sarge" in reference to his Sergeant Bilko haircut.

MacLELLAN'S fortune was Perry Berezan's bad luck, the former joining the Flames from Minnesota at the trade deadline.

HAKAN LOOB became the first Swede to score 50 goals in a season, a feat he accomplished on the final day of '87-'88 with just 3:05 left in the game.

RIC NATTRESS teamed with Macoun on defence to form the best tandem in the league, limited in talent offensively but impenetrable in their own end.

Goalie **RICK WAMSLEY** learned from the best, having Jacques Plante as his goalie coach during his early NHL years in St. Louis.

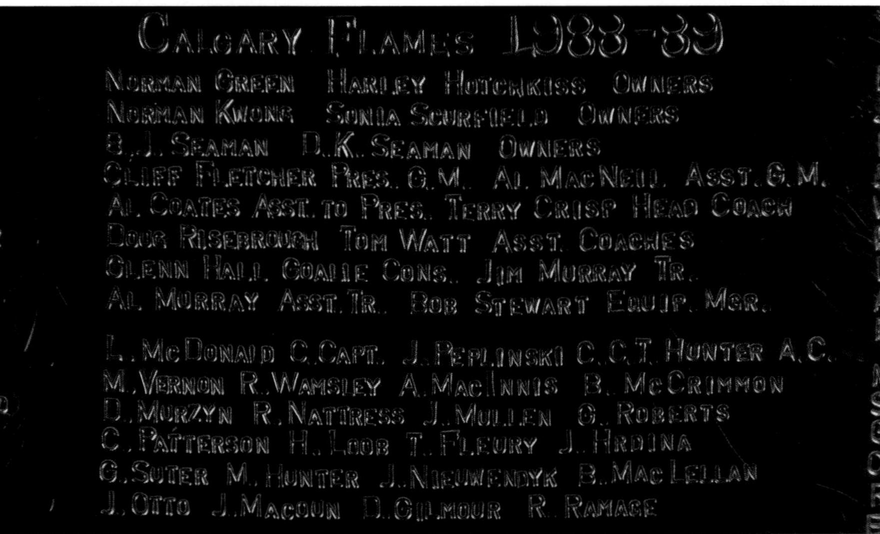

Team engraving from the current Stanley Cup

Forward **GARY ROBERTS** played minor hockey with Joe Nieuwendyk, and like his Flames teammate was also an outstanding lacrosse player who had won the Mann Cup.

Goalie **MIKE VERNON'S** glove save on a breakaway in overtime of game seven in round one against Vancouver was one of the great Stanley Cup moments of all time.

"GEORGE" HRDINA joined the Flames after playing for Czechoslovakia in the '88 Olympics.

Team owner **NORMAN GREEN** initiated the restoration and preservation of numerous historically important buildings in Calgary.

HARLEY HOTCHKISS had spent all his adult life in Calgary working in oil, gas, real estate, and agriculture.

One of the few men to win both the Stanley Cup and Grey Cup, **NORMAN KWONG** played 13 years in the CFL and is a member of the Canadian Football Hall of Fame.

SCURFIELD became only the second woman to have her name engraved on the Cup after Marguerite Norris in 1954.

BYRON SEAMAN was a geophysicist and later partnered with his brother in one of the largest oil companies in Canada.

"DOC" SEAMAN, Byron's brother, was an RCAF pilot in World War II for five years, touring England, Italy, and North Africa before embarking on a life in oil at home in Canada.

One of GM **CLIFF FLETCHER'S** smartest moves involved bringing in Bert Olmstead and Glenn Hall during the playoffs to talk to the players about what it takes to win the Cup.

MacNEIL began his career as a player, an eight-year NHLer, before turning to coaching.

As assistant to president Cliff Fletcher, **AL COATES** worked closely to build the team.

TERRY CRISP paid his dues before being hired as an NHL coach with the Flames in 1987. After the following season, he was fired.

One of the few players with Stanley Cup experience, **DOUG RISEBROUGH** had won four Cups in Montreal.

No greater example of **TOM WATT'S** abilities can be gleaned than his unprecedented nine Canadian university championships with the University of Toronto Blues.

"Mr. Goalie," **GLENN HALL**, joined the Flames as a goalie coach in 1983, and in his six years with the team the Flames' GAA went from 3.86 to 2.78.

Trainer **"BEARCAT" MURRAY** was a legend in Calgary, dating from his days with the Calgary Centennials in junior, to the day he joined the Flames in 1980.

The only trainer father-son combination in the NHL, **AL MURRAY** learned from his dad, Bearcat. He became assistant to dad in 1975 in the WHA and joined the Flames in 1987.

BOB STEWART joined the Atlanta Flames in 1973 as equipment man and was still going strong after 17 seasons.

Other players to appear for the Flames this season: **RICK CHERNOMAZ, SHANE CHURLA, BRIAN GLYNN, STU GRIMSON, STEVE GUENETTE, RICK LESSARD, SERGEI PRIAKIN, PAUL RANHEIM, DAVE REIERSON, KEN SABOURIN**

1989–1990 THE CHAMPIONS Edmonton Oilers

This was the only one of the Oilers' five Cup wins that wasn't won on home ice, but when the team got back to Alberta they had a right fine time of things, taking the Cup one night to Yannios Psalios' Greek Restaurant on White Avenue and then the Forum Motor Inn, two local strip joints in Edmonton. For the players and fans alike, the victory also had a special place in their hearts because in the post-Gretzky era, it was the least expected of their Cup wins.

STANLEY CUP FINALS

Edmonton Oilers win best-of-seven Stanley Cup finals 4-1

*May 15, 1990 Edmonton Oilers 3 at Boston Bruins 2 (Petr Klima 55:13 OT)
*May 18, 1990 Edmonton Oilers 7 at Boston Bruins 2
**May 20, 1990 Boston Bruins 2 at Edmonton Oilers 1
**May 22, 1990 Boston Bruins 1 at Edmonton Oilers 5
*May 24, 1990 Edmonton Oilers 4 at Boston Bruins 1 {Craig Simpson 9:31 2nd}

** played at Boston Garden ** played at Northlands Coliseum, Edmonton*

Petr Klima examines the names on the Cup after winning in 1990.

EDMONTON	GP	G	A	P	Pim
Craig Simpson	5	4	4	8	6
Jari Kurri	5	3	5	8	2
Glenn Anderson	5	4	3	7	6
Esa Tikkanen	5	3	2	5	10
Mark Messier	5	0	5	5	6
Joe Murphy	5	2	2	4	4
Steve Smith	5	1	2	3	13
Mark Lamb	5	0	3	3	2
Adam Graves	5	2	0	2	0
Craig MacTavish	5	0	2	2	2
Reijo Ruotsalainen	5	0	2	2	2
Petr Klima	5	1	0	1	0
Martin Gelinas	5	0	1	1	2
Randy Gregg	5	0	1	1	0
Charlie Huddy	5	0	0	0	4
Kelly Buchberger	5	0	0	0	2
Craig Muni	5	0	0	0	2
Kevin Lowe	5	0	0	0	0
Bill Ranford	5	0	0	0	0

In Goal	GP	W-L	Mins	GA	SO	Avg
Bill Ranford	5	4-1	355	8	0	1.35

Captain Mark Messier raises the Cup to celebrate Edmonton's fifth—and least likeliest—Cup since 1984. He is flanked by longtime teammates Kevin Lowe (left) and Jari Kurri (right).

SIMPSON led the league in this year's playoffs with 16 goals.

After a decade in Edmonton, **JARI KURRI** left the team this summer to play in Italy.

"The bigger the game, the better he plays," Sather said of **GLENN ANDERSON**, the left shooting right winger.

BEUKEBOOM and **STEVE SMITH** operated a hockey school in Edmonton called Twin Towers (for obvious reasons).

TIKKANEN was nicknamed "Tikki Talky" because of his incomprehensible annunciation in either Finnish or English.

From bar to strip joint to city street, **MARK MESSIER** made sure everyone in Edmonton had a chance to see the Cup.

MURPHY was a member of the Oilers' Kid Line with Adam Graves and Martin Gelinas.

SMITH later played for the arch-enemy Calgary Flames at the end of his career.

LAMB was a team roper at the rodeo in the off-season, an activity that prepared him for a career in the NHL when it didn't threaten it.

In 1988, **ADAM GRAVES** won gold with Team Canada at the World Junior Championships.

CRAIG MACTAVISH was the last helmetless NHLer but played as phyically intensely as any player in the game.

REIJO RUOTSALAINEN started this year with New Jersey before coming to the Oilers on March 6, 1990.

PETR KLIMA was stoned on a penalty shot by Boston goalie Reggie Lemelin in game two of the finals.

The 19-year-old **MARTIN GELINAS** was the centrepiece of the trade that sent Wayne Gretzky to Los Angeles.

RANDY GREGG captained the Canadian Olympic team in 1980 and won gold in 1981 at the World Student Games.

Like many an Oiler in the 1980s, **HUDDY** ended up playing in L.A. in the early '90s, a repercussion of the Gretzky trade.

KELLY BUCHBERGER missed all of the previous year's playoffs because of injury, but this year he was back and healthy.

Unwanted by the Leafs, the Oilers signed **CRAIG MUNI** as a free agent and he won three Cups in the next four years.

KEVIN LOWE is the current GM of the Oilers and is married to former Canadian Olympic skier Karen Percy.

SMITH made the NHL's All Rookie team for his regular season play, but in the playoffs he dressed for only three games.

Although **DAVE BROWN** played the full season, coach John Muckler had him in the press box for all but three playoff games.

ELDON "POKEY" REDDICK shared his one career shutout with Daniel Berthiaume and thus doesn't officially have one to his credit!

BILL RANFORD won the Conn Smythe this year.

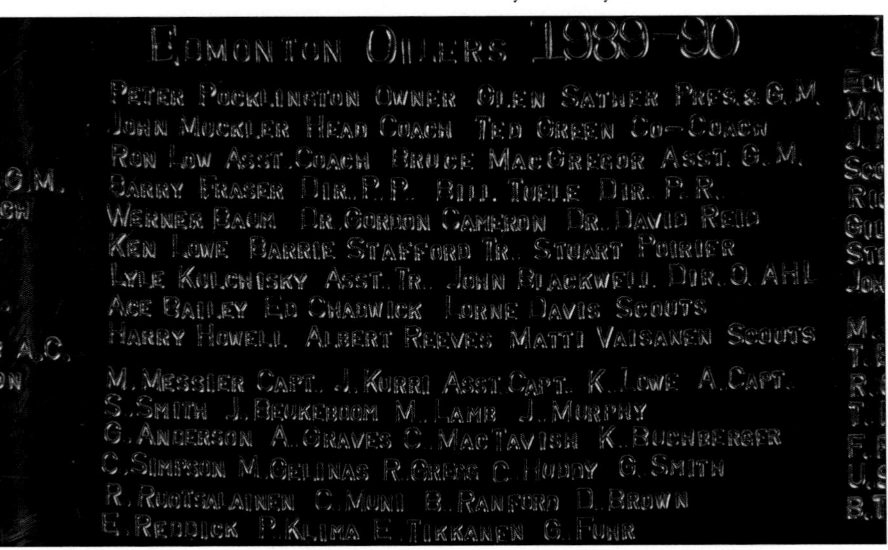

Team engraving from the current Stanley Cup

GRANT FUHR was suspended by NHL president John Ziegler for one full season after admitting to cocaine use.

Most people felt **PETER POCKLINGTON** ripped the heart out of the team by trading Gretzky to Los Angeles.

Sather traded **JIMMY CARSON** to Detroit in a seven-player deal that saw the Oilers acquire Klima, Murphy, and Graves.

This was **JOHN MUCKLER'S** first season as head coach. The year could not have ended more perfectly.

TED GREEN was given the title of "co-coach" this year while Muckler was called simply "coach."

A retired goalie, **RON LOW** now taught the art of puck-stopping to the Oilers' crease guardians.

MACGREGOR'S son tried to follow in his father's footsteps but he never made it to the NHL. Instead, Brad joined the Oilers' front office in the business operations department.

BARRY FRASER came of old hockey stock. His uncle was "Scotty" Bowman who had won the Stanley Cup with the Detroit Red Wings in 1936 and '37.

BILL TUELE was in charge of public relations for the Oilers.

WERNER BAUM was Edmonton's vice-president of finance.

DR. GORDON CAMERON and **DR. DAVID REID** were club physicians.

Trainer **KEN LOWE** was the older brother of defenceman Kevin. This was his first season with the Oilers after seven years in the CFL.

Trainer **BARRIE STAFFORD** also wrote a column for *The Hockey News* which detailed the aspects of his work with the team.

STUART POIRIER was massage therapist for the aching players.

"SPARKY" KULCHISKY had a quieter time with the Cup this year as it was returned to the Hockey Hall of Fame undamaged!

JOHN BLACKWELL was the director of operations for the farm team, the Cape Breton Oilers.

Through his Boston connections, scout **ACE BAILEY**, arranged a private team party in Beantown at the Blackstone restaurant.

ED CHADWICK might have had a longer NHL career had he not played for the Leafs at a time the team had Johnny Bower.

A former player, **LORNE DAVIS** was a scout for the team. He had won a Cup with Montreal in 1952-53.

HARRY HOWELL played more games than any other man in NHL history without winning a Cup—1,411—yet in his first year as a scout he got his name on the cherished trophy!

ALBERT REEVES and **MATTI VAISANEN** were scouts for the team.

Other players to appear for the Oilers this season: **BRUCE BELL, JIMMY CARSON, PETER ERIKSSON, RANDY EXELBY, MIKE GREENLAY, CHRIS JOSEPH, NORMAND LACOMBE, TOM LEHMANN, FRANCOIS LEROUX, NORM MACIVER, KEVIN McCLELLAND, VLADIMIR RUZICKA, ANATOLI SEMENOV, TREVOR SIM, MIKE WARE**

1990–1991 Pittsburgh Penguins

This was the first Cup for a team that had been around since 1967 and had been on the brink of bankruptcy many times since. Of course, the fortunes of the club changed in 1984 when the Penguins drafted Mario Lemieux first overall. The 8-0 game to clinch the Cup was the widest margin of defeat for a Cup-deciding game in the NHL history of Lord Stanley's bowl.

STANLEY CUP FINALS

Pittsburgh Penguins win best-of-seven Stanley Cup finals 4-2

*May 15, 1991 Minnesota North Stars 5 at Pittsburgh Penguins 4
*May 17, 1991 Minnesota North Stars 1 at Pittsburgh Penguins 4
**May 19, 1991 Pittsburgh Penguins 1 at Minnesota North Stars 3
**May 21, 1991 Pittsburgh Penguins 5 at Minnesota North Stars 3
*May 23, 1991 Minnesota North Stars 4 at Pittsburgh Penguins 6
**May 25, 1991 Pittsburgh Penguins 8 at Minnesota North Stars 0
{Ulf Samuelsson 2:00 1st} [Tom Barrasso]

** played at Civic Arena, Pittsburgh ** played at Met Centre, Minnesota*

The exultant Penguins gather on ice for their Cup-winners' portrait.

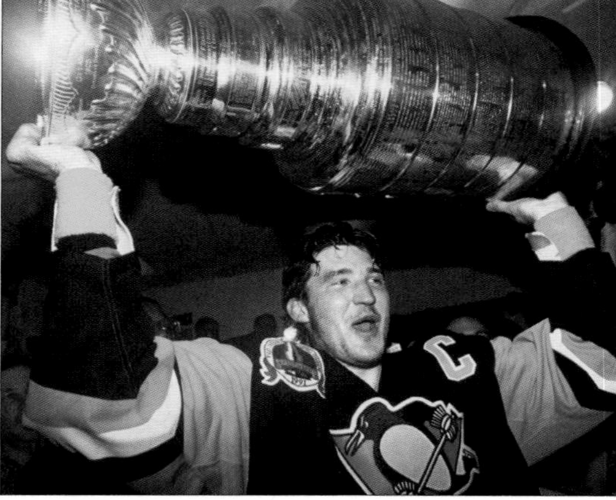

(clockwise) North Stars' goalie Brian Hayward thwarts one Pittsburgh attack; the amazing Mario Lemieux lifts high that which is the dream of every NHLer; Brian Bellows tries to come out front while being watched closely by goalie Tom Barrasso.

Team engraving from the Replica Cup

PITTSBURGH	GP	G	A	P	Pim
Mario Lemieux	5	5	7	12	6
Larry Murphy	6	1	9	10	6
Joe Mullen	6	3	5	8	0
Kevin Stevens	6	4	3	7	27
Ron Francis	6	3	3	6	6
Jaromir Jagr	6	0	5	5	0
Phil Bourque	6	2	2	4	4
Ulf Samuelsson	6	2	1	3	12
Bob Errey	6	2	1	3	8
Mark Recchi	6	2	1	3	8
Bryan Trottier	6	1	2	3	14
Peter Taglianetti	5	0	3	3	8
Scott Young	1	1	1	2	0
Paul Coffey	5	0	2	2	0
Troy Loney	6	1	0	1	26
Jim Paek	5	1	0	1	2
Gord Roberts	6	0	0	0	23
Randy Gilhen	5	0	0	0	12
Paul Stanton	6	0	0	0	8
Tom Barrasso	6	0	0	0	0
Jiri Hrdina	2	0	0	0	0
Frank Pietrangelo	1	0	0	0	0

In Goal	GP	W-L	Mins	GA	SO	Avg
Tom Barrasso	6	3-2	319	13	1	2.45
Frank Pietrangelo	1	1-0	40	3	0	4.50

MARIO LEMIEUX missed the first 50 games of the year with back problems. He needed the trainer to tie his skate laces, but he led all scorers with 44 points in the post-season.

LARRY MURPHY set two records for defencemen in the finals, one for most points in a finals series (nine) and one for most points in a finals game (four assists, in game five).

JOE MULLEN later played for USA in a qualifying tournament in late 1998 to ensure the country was not relegated to B pool for the 1999 World Championships.

KEVIN STEVENS led all scorers with 17 playoff goals. His dad, Arthur Stevens, had been a baseball player in the Cincinnati Reds organization.

FRANCIS was in his tenth season with Hartford when the Whalers traded their leading scorer to Pittsburgh near the deadline.

Rookie **JAROMIR JAGR** would later inherit the mantle of Mario's hero status in Pittsburgh.

When he had the Cup in the summer, **PHIL BOURQUE** heard a rattle from within and decided to dismantle the Cup to get to the source.

ULF SAMUELSSON arrived in Pittsburgh during the season by trade.

BOB ERREY'S short-handed goal to open the scoring in game two of the finals got the Pens off to a great start that led to victory and tied the series 1-1.

MARK RECCHI'S 40 goals and 113 total points led the team, and his 34 playoff points were second only to Lemieux.

A veteran captain from a dynasty a decade earlier, **BRYAN TROTTIER** summoned desire from within to make a valuable contribution to the victory.

During this season, **TAGLIANETTI** returned home to Framingham, Massachusetts to have his number 18 retired by the Framingham South Flyers where he played minor hockey.

SCOTT YOUNG won this Cup at age 23, but his best days were still to come with Quebec and then Colorado.

PAUL COFFEY felt some measure of vindication for demanding a trade out of Edmonton in 1987 as he led this Penguins team from the blueline and won his fourth Cup.

TROY LONEY missed the first 28 games of the season after serious off-season knee surgery but made a full recovery.

JIM PAEK was born in Seoul, Korea but raised in Toronto. He once played for and coached a Korean-Canadian team that played in Korea.

A part-time Penguin and enforcer, the 6'4" 237-lbs. **JAY CAUFIELD** played just 23 regular season games.

GRANT JENNINGS was a late addition to the team, coming to the Pens in the Francis trade and adding size and toughness to the Pittsburgh blueline.

BARRY PEDERSON underwent surgery a few years earlier to remove a tumor the size of a golf ball from under his right arm.

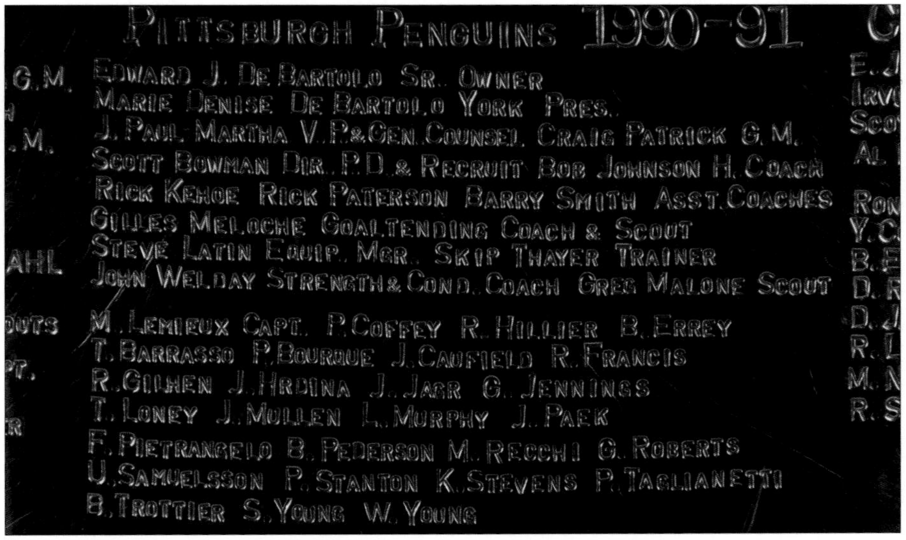

Team engraving from the current Stanley Cup

Goalie **WENDELL YOUNG** suffered a dislocated right shoulder in a game February 26 and missed the rest of the season.

HILLIER missed 34 games this season with a broken foot before recovering and joining the team for the stretch run.

GORD ROBERTS first appeared in the Stanley Cup finals a decade earlier, with Minnesota in 1981.

RANDY GILHEN was in a stretch in his career when he played for six teams in as many years.

Rookie defenceman **PAUL STANTON** graduated from the University of Wisconsin, then spent a year in the IHL before making the Pens at training camp in 1990.

TOM BARRASSO went on to become the winningest American-born goalie in NHL history.

JIRI HRDINA also won a Stanley Cup in 1989 and had played at two Olympics, two Canada Cups, and six World Championships.

In his first playoffs, goalie **FRANK PIETRANGELO** set a team record with a shutout sequence that lasted 112:19.

Owner **DeBARTOLO** had been awarded the Order of Merit by the government of Italy and the Ellis Island Medal of Honour.

Team president **MARIE DeBARTOLO** also owned the San Francisco 49ers football team.

MARTHA began his association with the DeBartolo family and the Penguins in 1978 when he was named team vice-president.

CRAIG PATRICK'S bloodlines went back to grandfather Lester with New York's 1928 Cup victory.

BOWMAN'S name is on this Cup as the team's Director of Player Development and Recruitment, a job he held for two years.

"It's a great day for hockey," was coach **BOB JOHNSON'S** diurnal mantra.

RICK KEHOE played in the NHL for 14 years. After retiring, he stayed with the team as an assistant coach.

RICK PATERSON'S name is in the Chicago record books for scoring two short-handed goals in just 2:30.

One of the first proponents of the trap, assistant coach **BARRY SMITH** had learned his strategy while coaching in Sweden.

A goalie turned scout, **GILLES MELOCHE** didn't appear in a playoff game until his tenth year in the league.

STEVE LATIN bolted the Detroit Red Wings dressing room in 1988 after being their equipment manager for six years.

CHARLES "SKIP" THAYER was the Penguins' trainer.

WELDAY apprenticed at Penn State University, first as an assistant strength coach for athletes, then as a teacher's assistant.

GREG MALONE was an ex-NHLer who had played in Pittsburgh. In 1989, he was named the team's head scout.

Other players to appear for the Penguins this season: **BRAD AITKEN, ROB BROWN, JOHN CULLEN, CHRIS DAHLQUIST, JEFF DANIELS, GORD DINEEN, JIM JOHNSON, JIM KYTE, JAMIE LEACH, KEN PRIESTLAY, TONY TANTI, ZARLEY ZALAPSKI**

1992 Pittsburgh Penguins

With this year's inscription, a new ring was started on the Cup with a record 52 names under this Pens' entry. At one point during the playoffs, they tied an NHL record by winning eleven straight games. The season almost didn't finish because of a players' strike that began on April 1. As soon as the players walked, two men from Lethbridge Community College in Alberta contacted Stanley Cup trustee Brian O'Neill about a challenge series for the Cup. James Hogaboam and Scott Greer, broadcasting students, formed the Lethbridge Kodiaks and hoped to play a team from Toronto radio station CFNY for the Stanley Cup, but O'Neill, of course, nixed the plan.

STANLEY CUP FINALS

Pittsburgh Penguins win best-of-seven Stanley Cup finals 4-0

*May 26, 1992	Chicago Blackhawks 4 at Pittsburgh Penguins 5
*May 28, 1992	Chicago Blackhawks 1 at Pittsburgh Penguins 3
**May 30, 1992	Pittsburgh Penguins 1 at Chicago Blackhawks 0 [Tom Barrasso]
**June 1, 1992	Pittsburgh Penguins 6 at Chicago Blackhawks 5 {Ron Francis 7:59 3rd}

** played at Civic Arena, Pittsburgh ** played at Chicago Stadium*

Defenceman Larry Murphy celebrates his first Stanley Cup.

(above) Rick Tocchet tries to beat Chicago goalie Ed Belfour with a deke.

PITTSBURGH	GP	G	A	P	Pim
Mario Lemieux	4	5	3	8	0
Rick Tocchet	4	2	6	8	2
Kevin Stevens	4	2	3	5	0
Larry Murphy	4	1	2	3	2
Ron Francis	4	1	2	3	0
Jim Paek	4	0	3	3	2
Jaromir Jagr	4	2	0	2	2
Shawn McEachern	4	0	2	2	0
Phil Bourque	4	1	0	1	0
Bob Errey	3	1	0	1	0
Paul Stanton	4	0	1	1	20
Kjell Samuelsson	4	0	1	1	2
Troy Loney	4	0	1	1	0
Gord Roberts	4	0	0	0	8
Ulf Samuelsson	4	0	0	0	2
Bryan Trottier	4	0	0	0	2
Tom Barrasso	4	0	0	0	0
Jock Callender	4	0	0	0	0
Jiri Hrdina	3	0	0	0	0
Dave Michayluk	1	0	0	0	0

In Goal	GP	W-L	Mins	GA	SO	Avg
Tom Barrasso	4	4-0	240	10	1	2.50

Team engraving from the shoulder of the Replica Cup

Captain **MARIO LEMIEUX** became the first player since Bernie Parent in 1974 and '75 to win consecutive Conn Smythes.

TOCCHET missed seven playoff games with a shoulder injury.

KEVIN STEVENS became the first player ever to score 50 goals, 100 points, and 200 penalty minutes in the same season.

In '81-'82, **MULLEN** was the first to score 20 goals in both the NHL and minor pro in the same season.

Durable and reliable, **MURPHY** had 77 points during the regular season and now had more than 700 career points.

FRANCIS scored 20 goals for the eleventh straight year and led the playoffs with 19 assists.

PAEK led all rookies with 40 points and was named the Pens' rookie of the year.

JAGR scored a playoff goal on a penalty shot against John Vanbiesbrouck of the Rangers.

McEACHERN had played for Team USA at the '92 Olympics before joining the team.

Undrafted, **PHIL BOURQUE** signed with Pittsburgh in 1983.

Drafted by the Pens from Peterborough, **BOB ERREY** played all of his 518 NHL games to date with Pittsburgh.

In only his second full NHL season, **PAUL STANTON** had two Cups to his credit.

ULF SAMUELSSON was acquired from Philadelphia in a blockbuster deal on February 19, 1992.

A reliable left-winger, **TROY LONEY** was on ice for only two goals in the last two series of the playoffs.

GORD ROBERTS was the younger brother by 15 years of NHLer Doug Roberts.

In his final full year, **BRYAN TROTTIER** was celebrating his sixth Cup, four with the Islanders, two now with Pittsburgh.

Goalie **TOM BARRASSO** won 25 games this season and tied a record with eleven straight playoff victories.

JOCK CALLANDER was the IHL's all-time career leader in goals and games played. He was recalled to Pittsburgh only for the playoffs.

This was **JIRI HRDINA'S** third Cup in four years and his last season in the NHL.

DAVE MICHAYLUK played just 14 NHL games from 1981-83, then spent the next nine full seasons in the minors.

Goalie **KEN WREGGET** was relegated to the backup role behind Barrasso after coming over from the Flyers.

On December 3, 1991, **JAY CAUFIELD** had been suspended ten games for coming off the bench to join in an altercation.

A fringe NHLer, **JAMIE LEACH** was assigned to Muskegon of the IHL after 38 games.

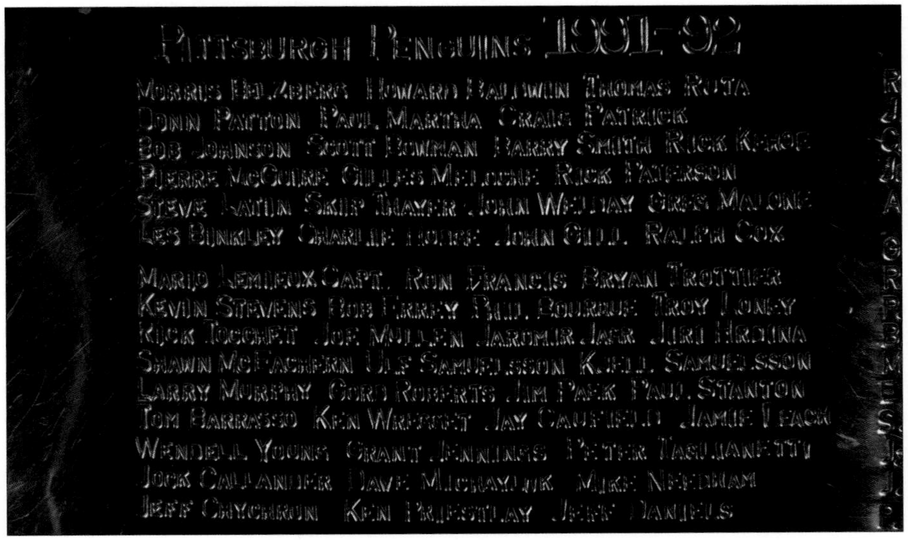

Team engraving from the current Stanley Cup

Two of **GRANT JENNINGS'S** four goals this year were short-handed, but as the playoffs went on his playing time decreased.

PETER TAGLIANETTI played 44 games in the regular season before an injury sidelined him for the rest of the year.

The 22-year-old **MIKE NEEDHAM** played all year with Muskegon but was recalled during the playoffs.

JEFF CHYCHRUN was acquired mid-season from Los Angeles in the deal that sent Paul Coffey to the Kings.

Although he played 50 regular season games with Pittsburgh, **KEN PRIESTLAY** was demoted on March 10.

JEFF DANIELS played only the first two games of the year with Pittsburgh, then was sent to Muskegon.

A native of Calgary, owner **MORRIS BELZBERG** opened the first Budget Rent-A-Car in Canada, in 1962.

HOWARD BALDWIN began his involvement in hockey back in 1973 as the founder of the New England Whalers of the WHA.

An alternate governor of the NHL, **THOMAS RUTA** received degrees from both Fordham and Pace Universities.

DONN PATTON worked in the Flyers' organization from 1981 to '88 before joining Baldwin's team in 1991.

PAUL MARTHA played in the NFL from '64 to 1970, while attending law school at Duquesne.

A fringe player in the NHL, **CRAIG PATRICK** played on the '76 Canada Cup team for the USA.

BOB JOHNSON passed away in October 1991, but his name nonetheless went on the Cup.

SCOTTY BOWMAN became coach after incumbent Bob Johnson became seriously ill.

Asistant coach **BARRY SMITH** was brought to Pittsburgh by Scotty Bowman, whom he knew from their days in Buffalo.

RICK KEHOE had nine 25+-goal seasons in his decade in Pittsburgh and is second all-time in games played with 722.

PIERRE McGUIRE, GILLES MELOCHE, RICK PATERSON, GREG MALONE, RALPH COX, JOHN GILL and **CHARLIE HODGE** were all part of the team's scouting staff.

Equipment manager **STEVE LATIN** had been in the NHL 21 years and had been manager for USA at the '91 Canada Cup.

A member of the first Penguins team in 1967-68, **BINKLEY** returned in 1976 and joined the front office in '89.

A native of Toronto, Ohio, **JOHN WELDAY** had been the team's strength and conditioning coach since 1988.

SKIP THAYER was the team's trainer.

Goalie **FRANK PIETRANGELO** had been in the Penguins organization since they drafted him 64th overall in 1983.

Other players to appear for the Penguins this season: **PAUL COFFEY, GORD DINEEN, GLEN MULVENNA, TODD NELSON, MARK RECCHI**

1992 THE CHAMPIONS

1993 Montreal Canadiens

The Habs set a record with ten straight overtime wins this playoffs and tied another record with eleven wins in a row at one point (set by Pittsburgh the previous year). To celebrate the Cup centennial, each player was allowed to take the Cup home for a day. Since then, it's become a tradition. The aftermath of the victory, however, was not something the city of Montreal had much to cheer about. As in 1986, riots ruined the celebrations and forced the city to shorten the parade route and cancel the team's open party. Some $10 million in damages were committed.

STANLEY CUP FINALS

Montreal Canadiens win best-of-seven Stanley Cup finals 4-1

*June 1, 1993 Los Angeles Kings 4 at Montreal Canadiens 1
*June 3, 1993 Los Angeles Kings 2 at Montreal Canadiens 3 (Eric Desjardins 0:51 OT)
**June 5, 1993 Montreal Canadiens 4 at Los Angeles Kings 3 (John LeClair 0:34 OT)
**June 7, 1993 Montreal Canadiens 3 at Los Angeles Kings 2 (John LeClair 14:37 OT)
*June 9, 1993 Los Angeles Kings 1 at Montreal Canadiens 4 {Kirk Muller 3:51 2nd}

** played at the Forum, Montreal ** played at the Great Western Forum, Los Angeles*

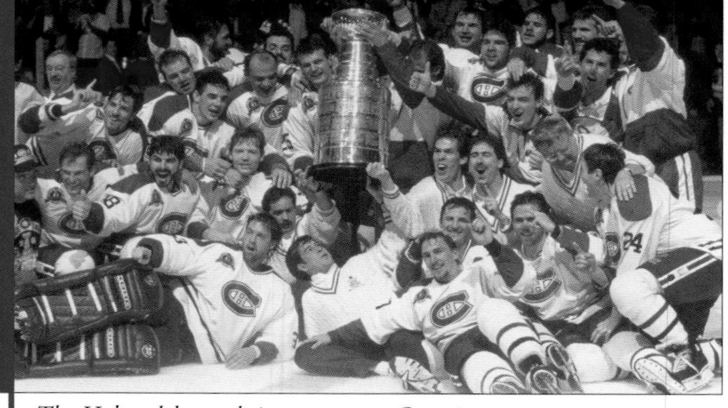

The Habs celebrate their most recent Cup victory.

(clockwise) Montreal's John LeClair leaps behind Darryl Sydor at the Los Angeles blueline; chanteuse Celine Dion poses for a Cup picture with Patrick Roy; Stephan Lebeau is stopped by Kings' goalie Kelly Hrudey from in close.

MONTREAL	GP	G	A	P	Pim
Eric Desjardins	5	3	1	4	6
Kirk Muller	5	2	2	4	6
John LeClair	5	2	2	4	0
Vincent Damphousse	5	1	3	4	8
Stephan Lebeau	5	1	2	3	4
Mike Keane	4	0	3	3	2
Paul DiPietro	5	2	0	2	0
Mathieu Schneider	5	1	1	2	8
Ed Ronan	5	1	1	2	6
Brian Bellows	5	1	1	2	4
Gilbert Dionne	5	1	1	2	4
Lyle Odelein	5	0	2	2	6
Benoit Brunet	5	0	1	1	2
Gary Leeman	5	0	1	1	2
Guy Carbonneau	5	0	1	1	0
Kevin Haller	3	0	1	1	0
Patrice Brisebois	5	0	0	0	8
J.J. Daigneault	5	0	0	0	6
Patrick Roy	5	0	0	0	0
Donald Dufresne	1	0	0	0	0
Sean Hill	1	0	0	0	0
Denis Savard	1	0	0	0	0

In Goal	GP	W-L	Mins	GA	SO	Avg
Patrick Roy	5	4-1	315	11	0	2.10

ERIC DESJARDINS became the first defenceman in Cup finals history to score a hat trick, scoring all three Montreal goals (including the winner in OT) on June 3, 1993.

"CAPTAIN KIRK" MULLER took the Cup to hometown Kingston for a day of celebrations on the Cup's 100th birthday.

JESSE BELANGER played just 19 regular season games and nine more in the playoffs.

ROB RAMAGE went to Montreal from Tampa Bay at the trade deadline. Just weeks later, he held the Cup above his head.

JOHN LeCLAIR became the first player since 1950 to score back-to-back overtime goals. In the summer, he took the Cup to Vermont for a day.

DAMPHOUSSE was given number 25 when he joined the team because the Habs felt he played like another 25—Jacques Lemaire.

STEPHAN LEBEAU and his younger brother, Patrick, played with the Habs together briefly in 1990-91.

After playing for Canada at the 1987 World Junior Championships, **MIKE KEANE** had a tattoo put on his left breast of Garfield, the comic cat, holding a Canadian flag.

PAUL DiPIETRO started the season battling mono and wondering if he'd ever play with the team full-time. But by the playoffs he had become a scoring hero, recording eight goals in 15 games.

Although **MATHIEU SCHNEIDER'S** abilities as a player were never in question, his reputation drove him from the city.

ED RONAN was drafted by Montreal in 1987 prior to a four-year career at Boston University.

When **BRIAN BELLOWS** arrived in Montreal the previous summer, he boldly promised the media a 30-goal season and went out and delivered 40 goals.

As a kid, **GILBERT DIONNE** played hockey on the streets of Drummondville, Quebec like every other boy. But, he wore a Kings sweater in honour of his much older brother, future Hall of Famer, Marcel.

The team's designated fighter, **LYLE ODELEIN** led the Habs with 205 penalty minutes.

BENOIT BRUNET had played his entire career in Montreal, dating back to his first NHL game on February 2, 1989.

GARY LEEMAN scored 51 goals with Toronto in '89-'90, but just three years later he arrived in Montreal a bit player with few goals left in his stick.

Along with Roy, **CARBONNEAU** was the only Habs on this team to have won the club's other most improbable Cup, in 1986.

KEVIN HALLER was a defensive defenceman, though in '92-'93 he had a career-high eleven goals and 25 points.

PATRICE BRISEBOIS was in his first full season with the Habs, though in later years the savage Montreal media would call him "Breeze-by" when he had a bad game.

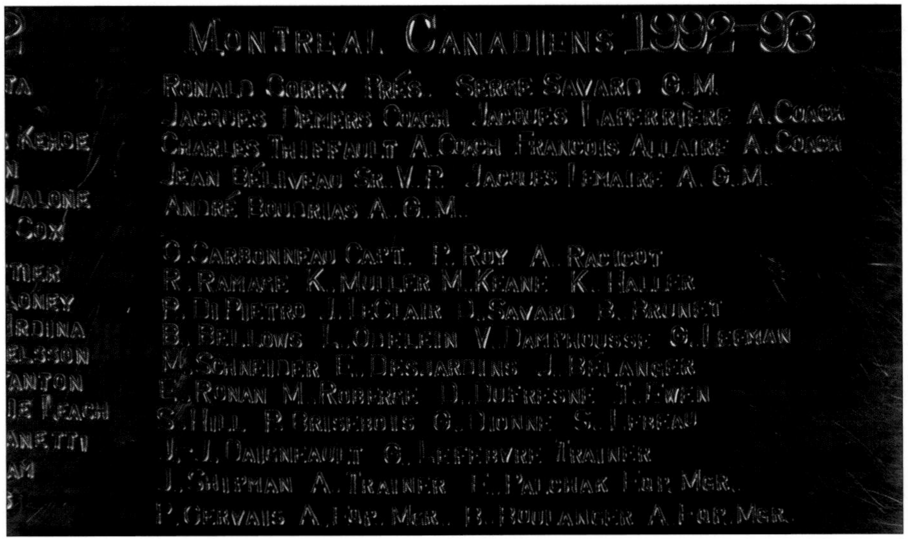

Team engraving from the current Stanley Cup

Goalie **ANDRE RACICOT** had the ignominious nickname of "Red Light" appended to his surname.

J.J. DAIGNEAULT etched his name inside the Cup this summer after taking it apart.

PATRICK ROY won the Conn Smythe, becoming only the second goalie after Bernie Parent to have won it twice.

Coach Jacques Demers dressed **DONALD DUFRESNE** for the final game of the playoffs to ensure his name got on the Cup.

Like Jesse Belanger, **SEAN HILL** had no sooner won the Cup than he was claimed in the Expansion Draft.

Captain Guy Carbonneau handed the Cup first to **DENIS SAVARD** who was dressed in jacket and tie because he was in the press box for the clinching game.

Undrafted when he graduated from the Quebec junior league in 1984, **MARIO ROBERGE** played in a variety of small leagues until the Habs signed him in 1988.

A tough hombre on ice, **TODD EWEN** later wrote and illustrated a children's book called *A Frog Named Hop*.

GAETAN LEFEBVRE advised all players in the organization specifically about diet.

JOHN SHIPMAN was sometimes used as a practise goalie. He later worked for Jacques Demers in Tampa Bay.

The ageing **EDDIE PALCHAK** was still around packing the team equipment for this surprise Cup team.

PIERRE GERVAIS got the phone call of his life when Wayne Gretzky invited him to be a trainer for Team Canada at the 2002 Olympics.

BOBBY BOULANGER was the man to whom credit goes for espying Marty McSorley's illegal stick during this year's finals.

COREY sat directly behind the Habs' bench at every home game, his gaze full of expectation.

SERGE SAVARD was fired in October '95 after the team missed the playoffs in '94-'95 and started the new season with an 0-4-0 record.

At the end of the series, Wayne Gretzky gave **JACQUES DEMERS** his stick as a congratulatory souvenir.

JACQUES LAPERRIERE'S own playing career had ended early because of injuries.

Assistant coach **THIFFAULT** joined the Habs in 1990, a year after working as an assistant coach for Italy's National team.

FRANCOIS ALLAIRE was a student of goaltending who coached Roy to his butterfly style of play.

The great **JEAN BELIVEAU** was a fixture with the Habs, as proud and reliable as the very "C H" itself.

LEMAIRE'S successful tenure as coach encouraged New Jersey to lure him from Montreal to become head coach.

ANDRE BOUDRIAS joined the Montreal organization in 1983 as an assistant coach for the farm team in Nova Scotia.

Other players to appear for the Canadiens this season: **PATRICK CARNBACK, FREDERIC CHABOT, ERIC CHARRON, PATRIK KJELLBERG, BRIAN SKRUDLAND, TURNER STEVENSON**

1993–1994 New York Rangers

The drought was over for Rangers' fans who were seeing the Cup for the first time since 1940, the city's last triumph. The team featured no fewer than seven former Cup-winning members of the Edmonton Oilers. This year also marked the modern era of the Cup itself as the sacred bowl was taken on a tour of the city day and night in a manner it had never experienced before. The Cup appeared on the David Letterman Show; it was used as a trough by Kentucky Derby winner Go For Gin; it went to Yankee Stadium, fell out of the back of a car, and saw umpteen bars and restaurants. The Rangers returned the Cup to the Hockey Hall of Fame in four pieces that needed 36 hours of welding to repair.

STANLEY CUP FINALS

New York Rangers win best-of-seven Stanley Cup finals 4-3

*May 31, 1994 Vancouver Canucks 3 at New York Rangers 2 (Greg Adams 19:26 OT)
*June 2, 1994 Vancouver Canucks 1 at New York Rangers 3
**June 4, 1994 New York Rangers 5 at Vancouver Canucks 1
**June 7, 1994 New York Rangers 4 at Vancouver Canucks 2
*June 9, 1994 Vancouver Canucks 6 at New York Rangers 3
**June 11, 1994 New York Rangers 1 at Vancouver Canucks 4
*June 14, 1994 Vancouver Canucks 2 at New York Rangers 3 {Mark Messier 13:29 2nd}

** played at Madison Square Garden, New York ** played at Pacific Coliseum, Vancouver*

Broadway celebrates its first Cup since 1940.

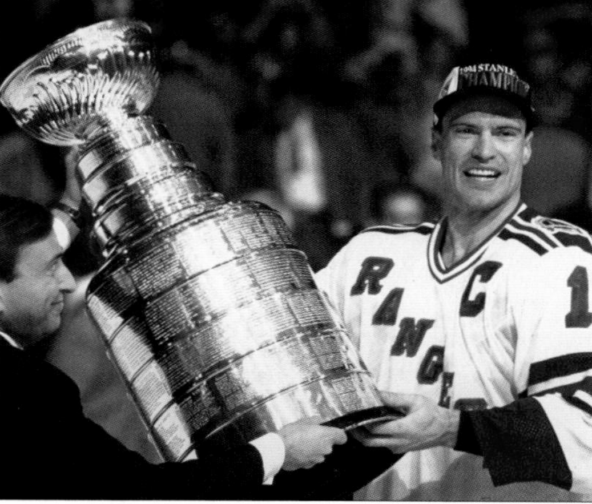

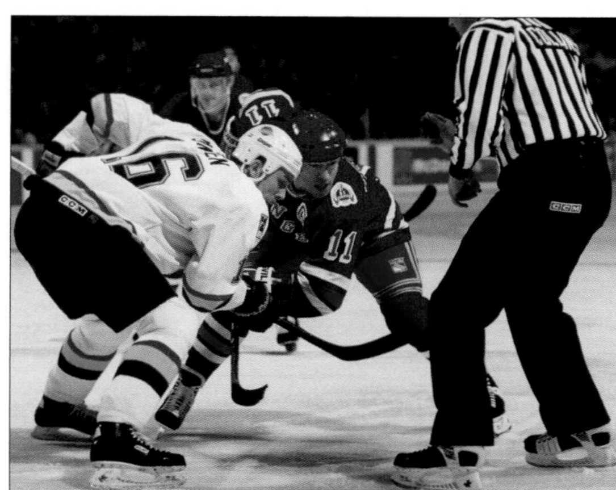

(clockwise) Vancouver's Murray Craven watches Esa Tikkanen as play moves up ice; the Rangers rejoice while the Canucks sag at the final horn of game seven; captain Mark Messier becomes a hero with his leadership; Trevor Linden and Messier square off in the faceoff circle.

NY RANGERS	GP	G	A	P	Pim
Brian Leetch	7	5	6	11	4
Alexei Kovalev	7	4	3	7	2
Mark Messier	7	2	5	7	17
Sergei Zubov	6	1	5	6	0
Steve Larmer	7	4	0	4	2
Adam Graves	7	1	3	4	4
Glenn Anderson	7	2	1	3	4
Doug Lidster	7	2	0	2	10
Jeff Beukeboom	7	0	2	2	25
Sergei Nemchinov	7	0	2	2	2
Esa Tikkanen	7	0	1	1	12
Craig MacTavish	7	0	1	1	6
Stephane Matteau	7	0	1	1	6
Greg Gilbert	7	0	1	1	2
Brian Noonan	7	0	1	1	0
Jay Wells	7	0	0	0	8
Kevin Lowe	6	0	0	0	6
Joey Kocur	6	0	0	0	2
Mike Richter	7	0	0	0	0
Alexander Karpovtsev	2	0	0	0	0
Nick Kypreos	1	0	0	0	0

In Goal	GP	W-L	Mins	GA	SO	Avg
Mike Richter	7	4-3	439	19	0	2.60

LEETCH took the Cup to the Columbian Presbyterian Hospital for a visit to heart transplant patient Brian Buluver.

MIKE HUDSON carried a family's sorrow in his heart. In 1990, his older brother, Chris, died in a boating mishap.

ALEXEI KOVALEV had the makings of a 40-goal scorer but, in fact, scored 23 times in this his sophomore season.

"We know we have to win it. We can win it. And we are going to win it." **MARK MESSIER** said, guaranteeing victory prior to game six of the Conference finals against New Jersey.

SERGEI ZUBOV took the Cup to the Restaurant National, a nightclub in Brighton Beach.

STEVE LARMER had played eleven consecutive full seasons in his 13-year Hawks career.

Late in '93-'94, it was a Messier pass that set up **GRAVES'S** 50th goal of the season, the first ex-Oiler to hit the 50 mark.

ANDERSON'S fortune was Mike Gartner's misfortune, for the two swapped teams (Toronto and the Rangers) at the trading deadline.

DOUG LIDSTER'S reputation as a weak defensive player held true even on this Cup team as he posted a Rangers-worst -12 during the regular season.

BEUKEBOOM was one of an incredible seven former Oilers who were collected by the Rangers for another run at the Cup.

A roommate of Tretiak during his Red Army days, **SERGEI NEMCHINOV** was the lowest Rangers draft choice ever to make the team (244th overall in 1990).

At 14, **TIKKANEN** was a better prospect than Jari Kurri, and by 19 he had mastered the NHL game by playing junior in Regina.

MacTAVISH played just 12 regular season games and the playoffs before signing with Philadelphia in the off-season.

STEPHANE MATTEAU scored two double overtime goals in these playoffs, only the fourth player in NHL history to do so (Mel Hill, Maurice Richard, Petr Klima).

Left winger **GREG GILBERT** last won the Cup with the Islanders eleven years previous.

BRIAN NOONAN and Nick Kypreos took the Cup on MTV Prime Time Beach House where it was filled with raw clams and oysters.

JAY WELLS'S disciplined toughness was a contributing factor in the victory.

By playing in his 192nd career playoff game this year, **LOWE** moved into fourth place all-time in this category.

Goalie **GLENN HEALY** was one of the few players to appear for the Islanders and Rangers in consecutive seasons.

Even though he played fewer games required for engraving rights, **MIKE HARTMAN** still has his name on the Cup thanks to the efforts of Mike Gartner who fought to have the rule waived in Hartman's and Olczyk's case.

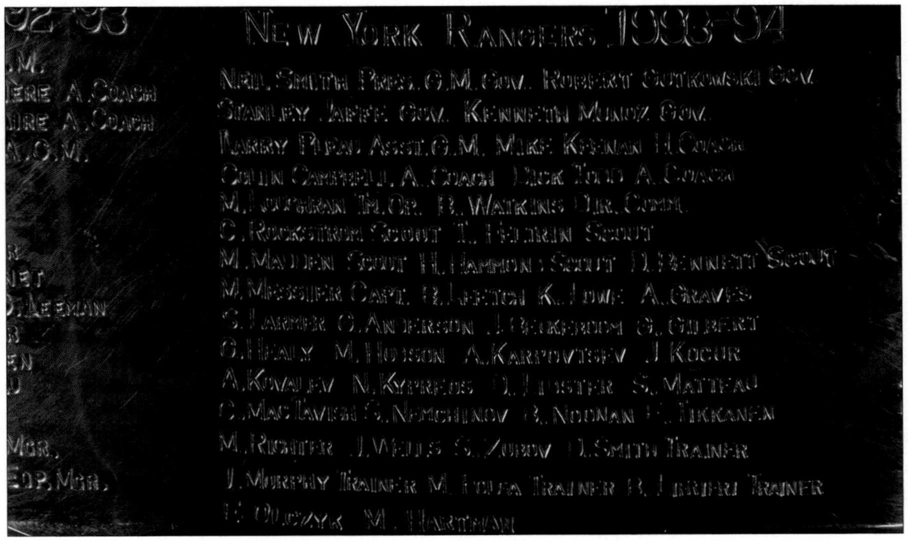

Team engraving from the current Stanley Cup

JOEY KOCUR took the Cup back to a rec team in Detroit that he had played with during the players' strike of 1992.

Goalie **MIKE RICHTER** stopped Pavel Bure on a penalty shot in game four of the finals.

ALEXANDER KARPOVTSEV made the leap from the Soviet league successfully in this his NHL rookie season.

NICK KYPREOS took the Cup dancing at the China Club and on to Yankee Stadium on June 21, 1994.

ED OLCZYK is best known for a trip to Belmont race track where he fed Kentucky Derby winner Go For Gin out of the Cup.

FOLGA was a rare breed among the dressing room staff, an equipment manager who was also a certified athletic trainer.

"God only knows whose lips have been on that thing," **BRUCE "THE MASSEUSE" LIFRIERI** joked.

Medical trainer **DAVE SMITH** had played and coached in Europe before joining the Blueshirts in 1984.

JOE MURPHY had been playing rec hockey in a men's league when then Rangers' trainer Nick Garen asked Murphy to come to MSG to help out. That had been 16 years ago.

In 1991, **SMITH** had become the first hockey player to be inducted into the Western Michigan University Hall of Fame.

LARRY PLEAU'S career began at the 1968 Olympics when he played for the U.S.

MIKE KEENAN was the toast of the town for bringing the Cup to Manhattan, but just weeks later he was vilified for leaving to coach St. Louis.

"When you win the Stanley Cup, you feel cleansed—that it was all worth it." **COLIN CAMPBELL**.

Assistant **DICK TODD** coached Canada to gold at the 1991 World Junior Championships.

MATTHEW LOUGHRAN was the manager for team operations.

BARRY WATKINS was the director of communications.

The Rangers' European scout, **CHRISTER ROCKSTROM**, started with the Detroit Red Wings in 1984 as their scout.

TONY FELTRIN was a fringe NHLer in the 1980s whose career ended after a serious eye injury in an AHL game.

MARTIN MADDEN had been in hockey administration for a quarter of a century, starting as a scout for the Flyers ('69-'75).

HERB HAMMOND scouted U.S. colleges and high schools.

DARWIN BENNETT joined the Rangers in 1993 after spending the previous eight years with the Nordiques.

KENNETH MUNOZ was vice president and general counsel.

STANLEY JAFFE was the team's governor and **ROBERT GUTKOWSKI** was its alternate governor.

Other players to appear for the Rangers this season: **PETER ANDERSSON, MIKE GARTNER, JIM HILLER, DAN LACROIX, TODD MARCHANT, JOBY MESSIER, MATTIAS NORSTROM, JAMES PATRICK, DARREN TURCOTTE**

1994–1995 THE CHAMPIONS New Jersey Devils

The dispute between the NHL and the players led to a lockout which reduced the season to a mere 48 games, the same number that was last played in the 1941-42 season when the Leafs won the Cup. In '94-'95, it was New Jersey that capitalized on the short season. Despite having a mediocre "regular season" with a record of 22-18-8, the Devils took their game to another level in the playoffs, losing just four games en route to the first Cup victory in franchise history. The closest they came to danger this post-season was in the conference finals when they were tied 2-2 in games with Philadelphia, but a 3-2 win in game five and a 4-2 win in game six eliminated the Flyers and took the Devils to the finals where they swept the emerging Detroit Red Wings.

STANLEY CUP FINALS

New Jersey Devils win best-of-seven Stanley Cup finals 4-0

*June 17, 1995 New Jersey Devils 2 at Detroit Red Wings 1
*June 20, 1995 New Jersey Devils 4 at Detroit Red Wings 2
**June 22, 1995 Detroit Red Wings 2 at New Jersey Devils 5
**June 24, 1995 Detroit Red Wings 2 at New Jersey Devils 5 {Neal Broten 7:56 2nd}

** played at Joe Louis Arena, Detroit ** played at Meadowlands Arena, New Jersey*

The Devils go from Mickey Mouse to penthouse with this Cup victory.

Devils' star defenceman Scott Niedermayer kisses the finest object a hockey player can kiss—the Stanley Cup.

NEW JERSEY	GP	G	A	P	Pim
Neal Broten	4	3	3	6	4
John MacLean	4	1	4	5	0
Stephane Richer	4	2	2	4	0
Scott Niedermayer	4	1	3	4	0
Bill Guerin	4	0	4	4	12
Shawn Chambers	4	2	1	3	0
Bruce Driver	4	1	2	3	0
Claude Lemieux	4	2	0	2	4
Bobby Holik	4	1	1	2	8
Sergei Brylin	3	1	1	2	4
Jim Dowd	1	1	1	2	2
Scott Stevens	4	0	2	2	4
Tommy Albelin	4	0	2	2	2
Tom Chorske	3	0	2	2	0
Randy McKay	4	1	0	1	0
Bob Carpenter	4	0	1	1	2
Brian Rolston	2	0	1	1	0
Ken Daneyko	4	0	0	0	6
Valeri Zelepukin	3	0	0	0	4
Martin Brodeur	4	0	0	0	0
Mike Peluso	4	0	0	0	0

In Goal	GP	W-L	Mins	GA	SO	Avg
Martin Brodeur	4	4-0	206	7	0	1.75

TOMMY ALBELIN had been a member of the team since being traded from Quebec in 1988.

MARTIN BRODEUR'S father, Denis, won a bronze medal as the goalie on the Canadian team that played in the 1956 Olympics.

BROTEN was acquired from Dallas midway through the season, just in time to score the Cup-winning goal for Jersey.

After just 26 career NHL games, **SERGEI BRYLIN'S** name went on the Cup. He had played the previous three seasons with Red Army.

The first American to score 50 goals in a season, a decade earlier, **BOBBY CARPENTER** crowned his career with this victory.

From the dregs of Tampa Bay to champagne-sipping in New Jersey, all in the space of a few weeks for **SHAWN CHAMBERS**.

TOM CHORSKE played in Italy for part of the lockout, then returned to help the Devils beat all comers.

DANTON COLE came to New Jersey in the same deal that had Chambers come from Tampa Bay.

A lifelong Devil, **KEN DANEYKO** spent a dozen years with the team and reaped rewards only loyalty could offer.

He didn't play in the finals, but his 17 regular season games and three playoff games was enough for **KEVIN DEAN** to be on the Cup.

Another New Jersey draft choice to make the team, **JIM DOWD** saw action only in game two of the finals, and he had a goal and assist in that 4-2 win.

DRIVER entered the NHL the same year as Daneyko, 1983-84.

Drafted 5th overall in 1989, **BILL GUERIN** had three assists in the Cup-clinching game.

Hulking **BOBBY HOLIK** centred the team's "Crash Line" featuring Mike Peluso and Randy McKay.

CLAUDE LEMIEUX scored the winner in game one and won the Conn Smythe Trophy.

Despite missing all of '91-'92 with an injury, **JOHN MACLEAN** was otherwise an Iron Man, missing just 22 games in the previous seven seasons.

CHRIS MCALPINE appeared in just 24 regular season games, then not a minute in the playoffs.

RANDY MCKAY had 12 points in the '95 playoffs (including eight goals), remarkable totals given that in the regular season he had only five goals and the same number of points.

SCOTT NIEDERMAYER made good on his 3rd overall draft selection in '91 by providing solid defence and contributing to the team's scoring.

MIKE PELUSO saw his role reduced come playoff time. He took the Cup for a ride in his pick-up truck in the summertime.

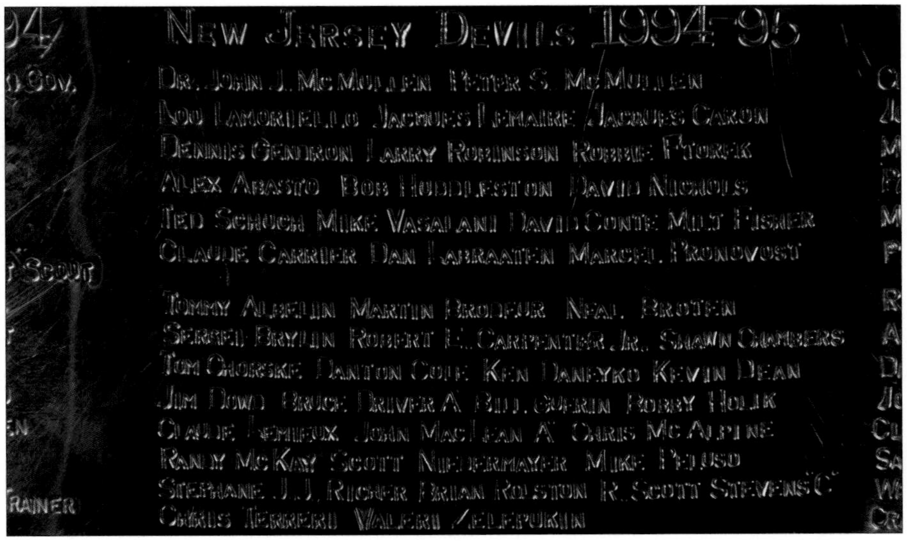

Team engraving from the current Stanley Cup

The "J.J." differentiates this **STEPHANE RICHER** from Stephane J.G. Richer of the Florida Panthers.

BRIAN ROLSTON'S contributions were subtle yet effective as coach Lemaire gave him spot duty in the early rounds and sat him for the finals.

Captain **SCOTT STEVENS'S** arrival in Jersey in 1991 as compensation for losing Brendan Shanahan paid high dividends.

Goaler **CHRIS TERRERI** hosted an oceanside golf benefit at a Rhode Island country club at which he landed in a heli-copter, Cup in hand!

A native of Voskresensk, Soviet Union, **VALERI ZELEPUKIN** travelled farthest to get to the Stanley Cup, having played for many years with Khimik and Red Army.

Owner and chairman **DR. JOHN MCMULLEN** was the first of 43 names on the 1994-95 Cup.

Son of Dr. John, **PETER MCMULLEN** was the vice-president of operations and human resources for the team.

LOU LAMORIELLO coached Providence College for 15 years until being named president and GM of the Devils in 1987.

LEMAIRE became one of a few men to win a Cup as both player and coach. He took the Cup on his boat during the summer.

JACQUES CARON was the team's goaltending coach.

"RED" GENDRON, the video doctor, took the Cup to his mother-in-law's house in Berlin, New Hampshire.

ROBBIE FTOREK'S name graces the Cup here because he was coach of the team's minor league affiliate in Albany.

ALEX ABASTO was the team's assistant equipment manager.

BOB HUDDELSTON was Jersey's all-important massage therapist. He had been in broadcasting for twenty years.

Medical trainer **TED SCHUCH** joined the Devils in 1988.

A strength and conditioning coach, **VASALANI** had learned his trade with the Washington Capitals.

An assistant coach to Jacques Lemaire, **ROBINSON** formed a perfect tandem with his former teammate from the Habs.

CONTE, director of scouting, played overseas for five years. Notable teammates included Jari Kurri and Kari Eloranta.

MILT FISHER was a member of New Jersey's extensive scouting staff that built the team in which 17 players on this roster were draft choices.

A European scout living in Sweden, **DAN LABRAATEN** played pro for more than 20 years.

Scout **CLAUDE CARRIER** lived in Quebec and his duties included U.S. Colleges and Eastern Canada.

MARCEL PRONOVOST'S name first appeared on the Cup in 1950 and again in 2000, a fifty-year span that is the longest in Cup history.

Other players to appear for the Devils this season: **DAVID EMMA, BEN HANKINSON, JAROSLAV MODRY, ALEX SEMAK, REID SIMPSON, JASON SMITH**

1995 THE CHAMPIONS
1996 Colorado Avalanche

Quebec City's loss was Denver, Colorado's gain. In the ever-changing financial picture that has been the NHL, Quebec found it could no longer compete in the hockey marketplace. There was no money for a new arena, and the "small market" realities meant that the Nordiques weren't long for the league. In the summer of '95, the team moved to Denver, to the same arena the old Rockies had played in 15 years ago, and a new franchise was born. But, the team was pretty much the same that the Nordiques had said goodbye to, and after the victory there was talk about holding an Avalanche parade in Quebec City, though nothing ever came of it.

STANLEY CUP FINALS

Colorado Avalanche win best-of-seven Stanley Cup finals 4-0

*June 4, 1996 Florida Panthers 1 at Colorado Avalanche 3
*June 6, 1996 Florida Panthers 1 at Colorado Avalanche 8
**June 8, 1996 Colorado Avalanche 3 at Florida Panthers 2
**June 10, 1996 Colorado Avalanche 1 at Florida Panthers 0 {Uwe Krupp 44:31 OT} [Patrick Roy]

** played at McNichols Sports Arena, Denver ** played at Miami Arena, Miami*

Colorado's Mike Ricci whoops it up in the dressing room.

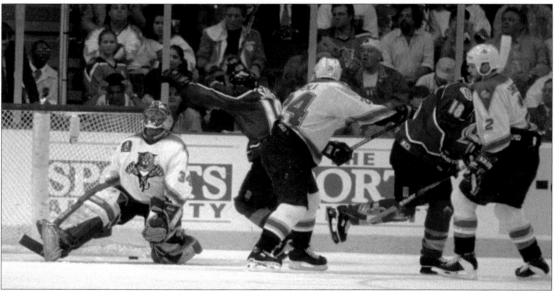

COLORADO	GP	G	A	P	Pim
Peter Forsberg	4	3	2	5	0
Joe Sakic	4	1	4	5	2
Adam Deadmarsh	4	0	4	4	4
Uwe Krupp	4	2	1	3	2
Rene Corbet	4	2	1	3	0
Valeri Kamensky	4	1	2	3	8
Jon Klemm	4	2	0	2	0
Mike Keane	4	1	1	2	0
Scott Young	4	1	1	2	0
Sandis Ozolinsh	4	0	2	2	4
Alexei Gusarov	4	0	2	2	2
Mike Ricci	4	1	0	1	6
Claude Lemieux	2	1	0	1	4
Adam Foote	4	0	1	1	4
Curtis Leschyshyn	4	0	1	1	4
Sylvain Lefebvre	4	0	1	1	2
Warren Rychel	3	0	0	0	19
Patrick Roy	4	0	0	0	0
Stephane Yelle	4	0	0	0	0
Dave Hannan	3	0	0	0	0

In Goal	GP	W-L	Mins	GA	SO	Avg
Patrick Roy	4	4-0	284	4	1	0.85

(top) Uwe Krupp beats Florida goalie John Vanbiesbrouck with a shot from the point in triple overtime of game four to give the Avalanche the Stanley Cup; (left) the Avs' Stephane Yelle (left) meets "Rudy," actor Daniel Ruettiger of the inspirational movie who was part of Colorado's ring ceremony on October 6, 1996.

PETER FORSBERG has the distinction of being the first-ever player to take the Cup to Europe, to his home town of Ornskoldsvik, Sweden.

Captain **SAKIC** led the playoffs with 34 points, including an incredible six game-winning goals, and won the Conn Smythe.

DEADMARSH was only the latest in a long line of players to have his name misspelled on the Cup—Deadmarch. But unlike the others, he demanded the error be fixed—and it was!

UWE KRUPP developed an interest in dogsled racing and celebrated his Cup win with huskies Castro, China, and Drago.

RENE CORBET was recalled from Cornwall of the AHL in December '95 and stayed the year, scoring two goals in the finals.

VALERI KAMENSKY was a native of Voskresensk, home of Igor Larionov, Viktor Kozlov, and Valeri Zelepukin, Cup winners all who learned the game at the local Khimik Arena.

JON KLEMM took the Cup back to Cranbrook, British Columbia to the arena where he played his minor hockey.

MIKE KEANE was traded to the Avs from Montreal where he had inherited the vaunted captaincy after Kirk Muller had been traded.

SCOTT YOUNG was a native of Shrewsbury, Massachusetts and took the Cup home where he was given a special welcome.

SANDIS OZOLINSH came to the Avs in a big trade at the start of the season with Owen Nolan going to San Jose in return.

In 1990, **ALEXEI GUSAROV** was the youngest player to be released by Red Army and the first to be released through Mosprosport, the official Soviet negotiating committee.

MIKE RICCI owned a cottage near Wilberforce where he hosted a party. Among the guests were Cheryl and Ken Riley, a couple who had tried unsuccessfully to have children. Cheryl kissed the Cup, and, like a miracle, became pregnant! They named their son Stanley, and gave him a middle initial of "C" for Cup.

CLAUDE LEMIEUX became the first player in 35 years to win consecutive Cups with different teams, having won the previous spring with New Jersey.

From the Soo to the Avs to the World Cup and Olympics, **ADAM FOOTE** was one of the outstanding defencemen in his own end of the ice.

CURTIS LESCHYSHYN spent his day with the Cup in Saskatoon, Saskatchewan.

SYLVAIN LEFEBVRE took the Cup to his lakefront cottage in Baldwin Mills, Quebec, where he had his daughter baptized in it.

At age 10, young **WARREN RYCHEL** was harvesting wheat at the Staplefox farm near Strathroy, Ontario, when he became submerged in a deep pile of grain being poured through a funnel. Pat Stapleton and friends heard the cries for help and pulled Rychel to safety.

Goalie **PARTICK ROY** hosted a charity golf tournament with the Cup in Lake Tahoe, Nevada.

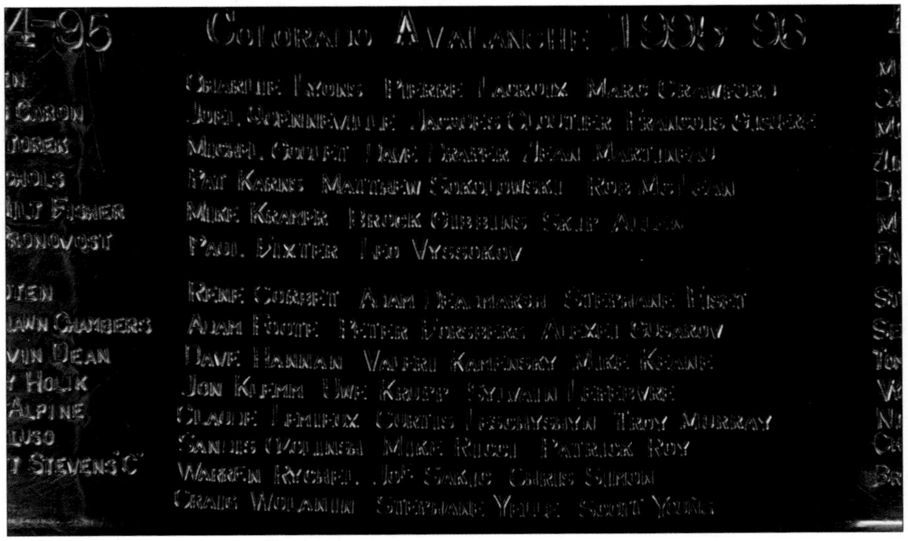

Team engraving from the current Stanley Cup

TROY MURRAY retired at season's end after 15 years in the NHL and fresh off his first career Cup.

YELLE hosted a party in his hometown of Bourget, Quebec, population 949, one of the smallest places the Cup had ever been.

CRAIG WOLANIN took the Cup to his mom's house back home in Michigan.

STEPHANE FISET might have been the Avs goalie of the future, but that title turned to "backup" the day Patrick Roy arrived.

DAVE HANNAN was one of those paradoxical Cup-winning players—a fourth-liner who was invaluable to a team but one always on the move.

CHARLIE LYONS was the president of Ascent Sports, owners of the team.

CHRIS SIMON took the Cup to Ontario's North. He went fishing with it with his brother, dad, and grandfather.

PIERRE LACROIX had been a player agent for 21 years prior to being hired by the then Quebec Nordiques in 1994.

CRAWFORD played in the NHL for six years (1981-87). At 35, he was the third-youngest coach since 1924 to win the Cup.

JOEL QUENNEVILLE'S experience in Colorado went back to his playing days with the Rockies who played in the same building two decades previous.

JACQUES CLOUTIER had been the team's goalie coach but assumed the more complete duties of assistant coach when Jacques Martin left the team to become bench boss in Ottawa.

GIGUERE was named assistant GM in 1993 because of his combined experience in business and his knowledge of the NHL.

MICHEL GOULET was a lifelong Nordiques and the team's director of player personnel. He had never won a Cup as a player.

Chief scout **DRAPER** arrived in Colorado with years of experience, as both the director of scouting for the CAHA and as a GM in the OHL, going back to 1976.

JEAN MARTINEAU was the team's director of media relations and team services.

PAT KARNS worked his way up to become head trainer to start this season in Denver.

MATTHEW SOKOLOWSKI was a kinesiologist for the Avs.

ROB McLEAN worked the dressing room as equipment manager.

MIKE KRAMER and **BROCK GIBBONS** were the team's assistant equipment managers.

SKIP ALLEN was the Avs' strength and conditioning coach.

Video coach **PAUL FIXTER** prepared tape of NHL games to study teams around the league.

LEO VYSSOKOV was the team's massage therapist.

Other players to appear for the Avalanche this season: **PAUL BROUSSEAU, ANDREI KOVALENKO, CLAUDE LAPOINTE, JANNE LAUKKANEN, JOSEF MARHA, AARON MILLER, ANDERS MYRVOLD, OWEN NOLAN, MARTIN RUCINSKY, JOHN SLANEY, JOCELYN THIBAULT, LANDON WILSON**

1996–1997 Detroit Red Wings

THE CHAMPIONS

The city had waited 42 years to see the Cup again after having last won it in 1955. The lost time was made up with tremendous celebrations, starting right after the game when the players took the Cup to Big Daddy's in West Bloomfield for an all-night party. All happiness, however, was destroyed just a few nights later when a limousine carrying Viacheslav Fetisov, Vladimir Konstantinov, and masseuse Sergei Mnatsakanov crashed into a tree, the result of the chauffeur's intoxication. Fetisov recovered, but Konstantinov has been wheelchair-bound ever since.

STANLEY CUP FINALS

Detroit Red Wings win best-of-seven Stanley Cup finals 4-0

*May 31, 1997 Detroit Red Wings 4 at Philadelphia Flyers 2
*June 3, 1997 Detroit Red Wings 4 at Philadelphia Flyers 2
**June 5, 1997 Philadelphia Flyers 1 at Detroit Red Wings 6
**June 7, 1997 Philadelphia Flyers 1 at Detroit Red Wings 2
{Darren McCarty 13:02 2nd}

** played at CoreStates Center, Philadelphia ** played at Joe Louis Arena, Detroit*

The Cup makes its first appearance in Red Square, Moscow.

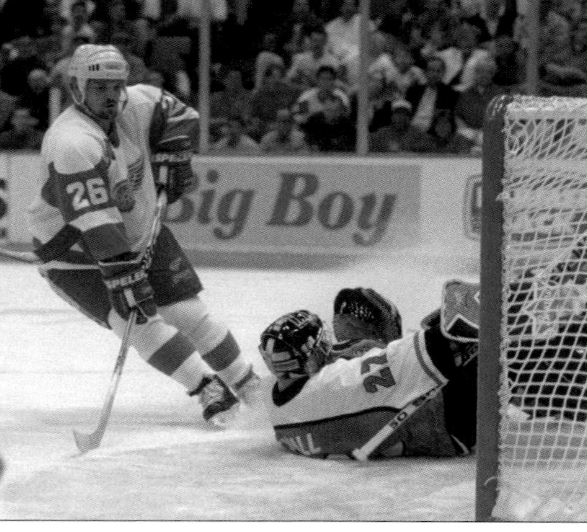

(clockwise) Slava Fetisov takes a sip of champers from the Cup in the dressing room after the clinching game; Joey Kocur has a great chance on Flyers' goalie Ron Hextall; forward Martin Lapointe takes the Cup to a summer camp for kids with cancer, outside Montreal, where he and the Cup were welcomed as heroes.

DETROIT	GP	G	A	P	Pim
Sergei Fedorov	4	3	3	6	2
Brendan Shanahan	4	3	1	4	0
Steve Yzerman	4	3	1	4	0
Martin Lapointe	4	2	1	3	6
Kirk Maltby	4	2	1	3	2
Darren McCarty	4	1	2	3	4
Larry Murphy	4	0	3	3	0
Joey Kocur	4	1	1	2	2
Viacheslav Fetisov	4	0	2	2	10
Vyacheslav Kozlov	4	0	2	2	0
Nicklas Lidstrom	4	1	0	1	0
Tomas Sandstrom	4	0	1	1	4
Doug Brown	4	0	1	1	2
Kris Draper	4	0	1	1	2
Igor Larionov	4	0	0	0	4
Vladimir Konstantinov	4	0	0	0	2
Bob Rouse	4	0	0	0	0
Mike Vernon	4	0	0	0	0
Aaron Ward	4	0	0	0	0

In Goal	GP	W-L	Mins	GA	SO	Avg
Mike Vernon	4	4-0	240	6	0	1.50

While Fetisov, Larionov, and Kozlov took the Cup home, **SERGEI FEDOROV** refused to join his comrades for the trip.

SHANAHAN took the Cup on a tour through Mimico. Later, in a quieter moment, he took the Cup to his father's grave.

Captain **STEVE YZERMAN** took the Cup to Birch Run, Michigan, a small town where an NHL-sponsored rink had opened.

HOLMSTROM played only in game one of the playoffs after splitting the regular season between Detroit and Adirondack.

At 21, **DANDENAULT** was the youngest player on the team. He was relegated to the press box for the playoffs.

HODSON was the team's third goalie who appeared in only six regular season games.

MARTIN LAPOINTE took the Cup to his hockey school in Montreal to the delight of the awestruck kids.

In his first full season, **KIRK MALTBY** scored just three goals in 66 regular season games but five more in only 20 playoff games.

DARREN McCARTY took the Cup to a tomato farm in Leamington, Ontario.

MURPHY hosted a badminton tournament in his backyard in Peterborough. The winners had their picture taken with the Cup; the losers with a toilet seat. Sadly, he wound up in the toilet seat picture!

KOCUR had been lured out of retirement by the Wings in December 1996 and celebrated by taking the Cup fishing.

Steve Yzerman hoisted the Cup first, and then sought out Russian veteran **SLAVA FETISOV** for the first handoff.

VYACHESLAV KOZLOV scored the game winner in game two of the Conference semi-finals versus Anaheim on the power-play in triple overtime.

NICKLAS LIDSTROM was third in league scoring for defencemen during the regular season.

TOMAS SANDSTROM joined the Wings in a mid-season trade from Pittsburgh, but at the end of the year he signed as a free agent with Anaheim.

DOUG BROWN took the Cup to his father-in-law's home. Wellington Mara owned the New York Giants and had a large house in Rye, New York.

It was the vicious hit **KRIS DRAPER** absorbed from Claude Lemieux the previous playoffs that helped the team win the Cup.

The great **IGOR LARIONOV** took the Cup to the Hungry Duck, a Canadian-owned bar in Moscow.

KONSTANTINOV was lucky to be alive after the crash. He spent the next year trying to regain use of his muscles.

PUSHOR was in his first full season with the team, though coach Bowman used the rookie only five times in the playoffs.

Despite being the number-one man all year, goalie **CHRIS OSGOOD** appeared in only two playoff games.

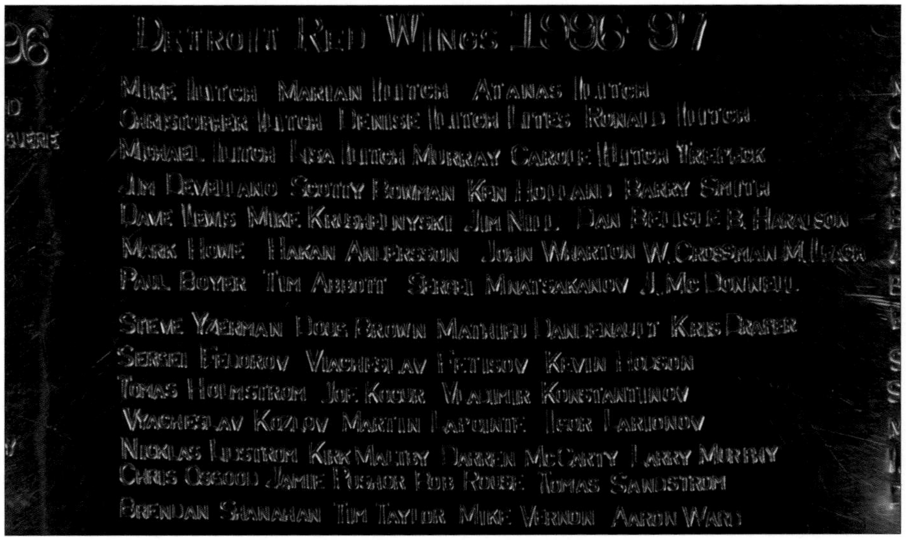

Team engraving from the current Stanley Cup

BOB ROUSE won his first Cup in this his 14th NHL season. He had signed with the Wings as a free agent in 1994.

VERNON was backup to Osgood during the regular season, but the veteran was the number-one man for the playoffs.

WARD took the Cup to the Children's Cancer Hospital in Ann Arbour, Michigan in the summer for his day with the silver bowl.

MIKE ILITCH, **MARIAN ILITCH**, **ATANAS ILITCH**, **CHRISTOPHER ILITCH**, **DENISE ILITCH LITES**, **RONALD ILITCH**, **MICHAEL ILITCH**, **LISA ILITCH**, and **MURRAY CAROLE ILITCH TREPECK** are all listed on this Cup as co-owners of the team.

After 15 years with the Wings, **DEVELLANO** finally won the Cup again as he had with the dynastic Islanders from 1980-83.

During the on-ice celebrations, coach **SCOTTY BOWMAN** went to the dressing room, donned his skates, and returned to the ice to take Stanley for a stroll!

Future GM **KEN HOLLAND** took the Cup to Vernon, British Columbia to be with his parents.

SMITH came to Detroit at the insistence of Scotty Bowman after the two had been part of the Penguins' Cups in 1991 and '92.

LEWIS had been a member of the New York Islanders in 1980 but he was traded just before the first Cup. As a result, he had to wait another 17 seasons to get his name on the Cup!

After retiring as a player, **KRUSHELNYSKI** pursued a career in coaching which led him right back to another Cup.

JIM NILL, director of player development, took the Cup to a local arena in Hanna, Alberta, to celebrate.

DAN BELISLE began with the Wings as an assistant coach and became a scout for the team in 1986.

BRUCE HARALSON was the team's Western scout.

MARK HOWE'S main function was to teach the team's young defencemen, most recently Jamie Pushor, Anders Eriksson, and Jan Golubovsky.

HAKAN ANDERSSON was the team's director of European scouting.

Trainer **JOHN WHARTON** served as head trainer for Team Russia's entry in the 1996 World Cup.

WALLY CROSSMAN had worked with the club since the old Detroit Olympia opened. The 87-year old had been in the dressing room for half a century.

MARK LEACH was the Detroit scout for US colleges.

PAUL BOYER had been a student equipment manager for Lake Superior in 1992 before moving to the NHL.

Assistant equipment manager **TIM ABBOTT** apprenticed with Adirondack for four years.

SERGEI MNATSAKANOV had been the masseur and trainer for Moscow Dynamo before heading to America.

JOE McDONNELL was Detroit's scout for Eastern Canada.

Other players to appear for the Red Wings this season: **ANDERS ERIKSSON**, **BOB ERREY**, **STU GRIMSON**, **MIKE KNUBLE**, **GREG JOHNSON**, **MARK MAJOR**, **MIKE RAMSEY**

1997 THE CHAMPIONS

1998 Detroit Red Wings

This was a tribute victory for the team, honouring the value Vladimir Konstantinov had had to the team prior to his accident. Upon receiving the Cup, captain Steve Yzerman turned around and gave the wheelchair-bound spiritual leader the Cup while teammates took him around the ice in celebration.

STANLEY CUP FINALS

Detroit Red Wings win best-of-seven Stanley Cup finals 4-0

*June 9, 1998	Washington Capitals 1 at Detroit Red Wings 2
*June 11, 1998	Washington Capitals 4 at Detroit Red Wings 5 (Kris Draper 15:24 OT)
**June 13, 1998	Detroit Red Wings 2 at Washington Capitals 1
**June 16, 1998	Detroit Red Wings 4 at Washington Capitals 1 {Martin Lapointe 2:26 2nd}

** played at Joe Louis Arena, Detroit ** played at MCI Center, Washington*

Russian-born teammates surround Vladimir Konstantinov.

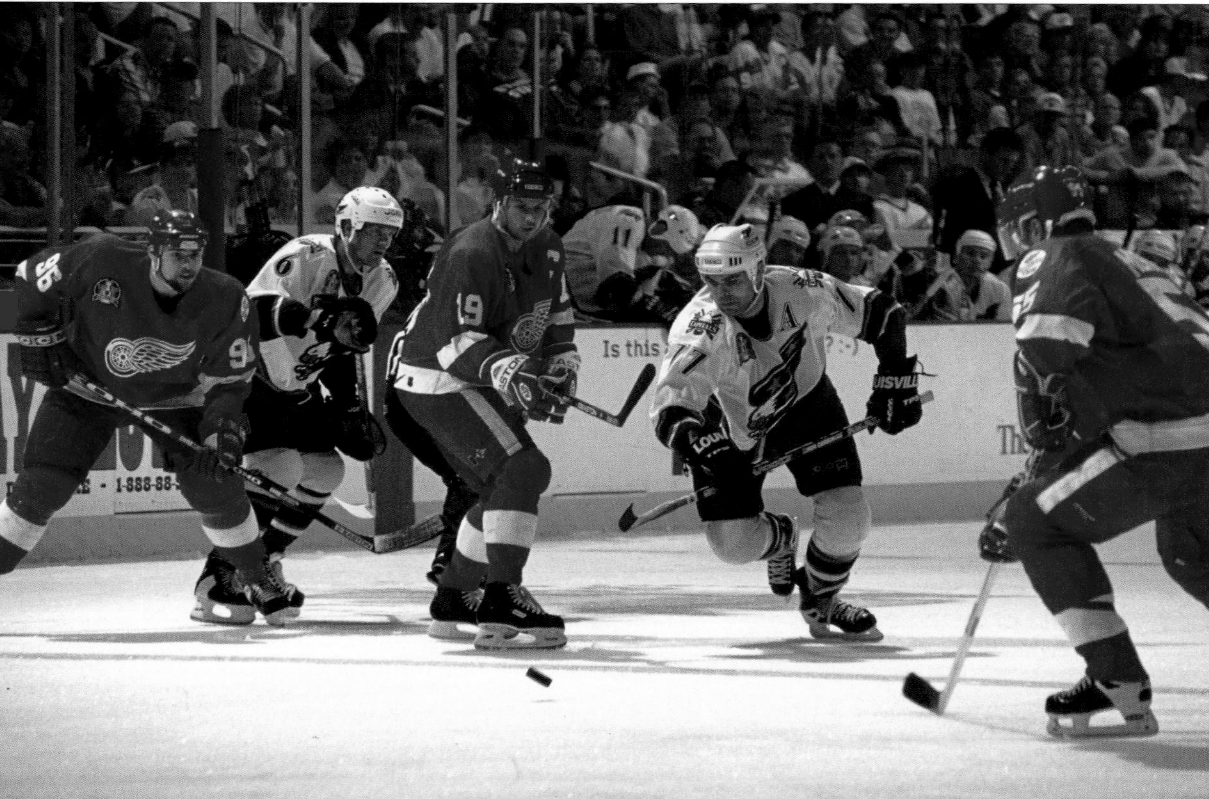

Washington's Adam Oates tries to control the puck while dealing with three Wings—Tomas Holmstrom, captain Steve Yzerman, and defenceman Larry Murphy.

DETROIT	GP	G	A	P	Pim
Doug Brown	4	3	2	5	0
Tomas Holmstrom	4	1	4	5	2
Steve Yzerman	4	2	2	4	2
Martin Lapointe	4	2	1	3	6
Sergei Fedorov	4	1	2	3	0
Viacheslav Fetisov	4	0	3	3	2
Nicklas Lidstrom	4	1	1	2	2
Larry Murphy	4	1	1	2	0
Igor Larionov	4	0	2	2	4
Darren McCarty	4	0	2	2	2
Joey Kocur	4	1	0	1	4
Kris Draper	4	1	0	1	2
Anders Eriksson	4	0	1	1	4
Bob Rouse	4	0	1	1	2
Vyacheslav Kozlov	4	0	1	1	0
Brendan Shanahan	4	0	1	1	0
Kirk Maltby	4	0	0	0	6
Jamie Macoun	4	0	0	0	0
Chris Osgood	4	0	0	0	0

In Goal	GP	W-L	Mins	GA	SO	Avg
Chris Osgood	4	4-0	254	7	0	1.65

DOUG BROWN scored the tieing goal in game two of the finals with just 4:14 left, a game the Wings won in OT.

TOMAS HOLMSTROM took the Cup to his home in Sweden during the summer, taking it to a restaurant.

YZERMAN has been captain of a team (the Wings) longer than any player in NHL history, wearing the "C" since 1986.

MARTIN LAPOINTE took the Cup to his cottage outside Montreal for a party and then on to a kids hockey school.

AARON WARD took the Cup to Mott's Children's Hospital in Ann Arbour, Michigan.

DANDENAULT played much of the regular season but just three times in the playoffs.

SERGEI FEDOROV had a Cup party at his house in honour of his second victory in as many years.

FETISOV'S final year as a player ended with this Cup victory. He became assistant coach with New Jersey and won again in 2000.

NICKLAS LIDSTROM took the Cup to a restaurant and had a low-key party for family and friends.

LARRY MURPHY took the Cup to his wife's farm and fed her horses carrots out of the Cup!

Legendary **IGOR LARIONOV** was the "L" in the famed KLM Line (with Krutov and Makarov) of the Soviet Union.

McCARTY took the Cup to Big Boy Restaurant in Detroit, then to Little Daddy's, an eatery he owned with Bob Probert.

JOEY KOCUR had a career-high four goals in these playoffs, almost equalling his regular season total of six.

KRIS DRAPER took the Cup to Originals, a bar on Bayview Ave. in Toronto, and let his cousins eat Cheerios out of it!

ANDERS ERIKSSON had the Cup in Sweden. He had a small house party, then took the Cup to an arena and hosted a hockey game, the Cup going to the winning team.

BRENT GILCHRIST signed as a free agent in the summer of 1997. After this Cup win, he was claimed by Tampa Bay in the Waiver Draft but then re-acquired by the Wings.

With Mike Vernon out of the Detroit picture, goalie **JAMIE HODSON** moved in as Osgood's backup, much as Osgood had done the previous year with the veteran Vernon.

MIKE KNUBLE and **WARD** took the Cup out to midfield during halftime of a Michigan Wolverines football game.

At 34, **BOB ROUSE** was let go by the Wings after the season.

KOZLOV contributed to the win with a team record-tying four game-winning goals in the playoffs, most dramatically in the Conference finals versus Dallas in games one and four.

BRENDAN SHANAHAN played for Team Canada during the mid-season break at the Olympic Winter Games in Nagano.

KIRK MALTBY rented a hall and hosted a private party in Cambridge, Ontario.

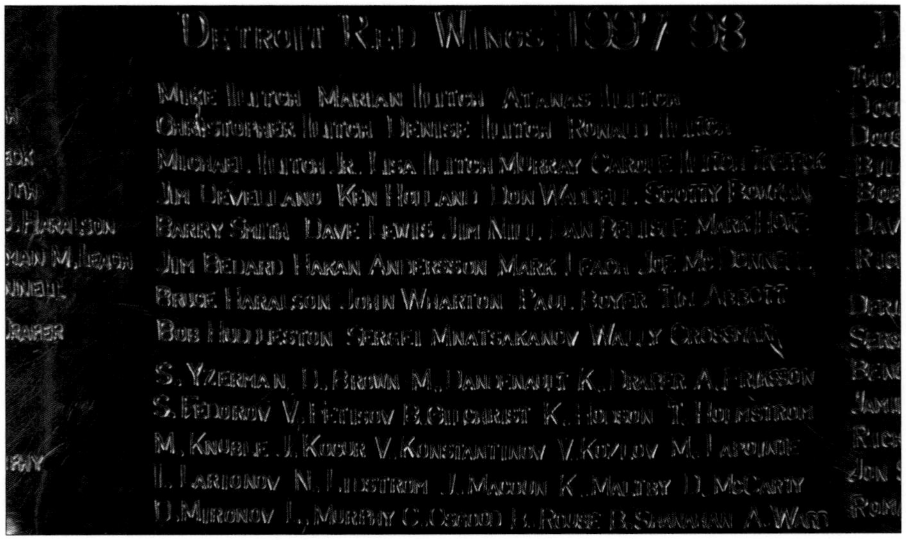

Detroit Red Wings 1997-98

Mike Ilitch Marian Ilitch Atanas Ilitch
Christopher Ilitch Denise Ilitch Ronald Ilitch
Michael Ilitch Jr. Lisa Ilitch Murray Carole Ilitch Trepeck
Jim Devellano Ken Holland Don Waddell Scotty Bowman
Barry Smith Dave Lewis Jim Nill Dan Belisle Mark Howe
Jim Bedard Hakan Andersson Mark Leach Joe McDonnell
Bruce Haralson John Wharton Paul Boyer Tim Abbott
Bob Huddleston Sergei Mnatsakanov Wally Crossman
S. Yzerman D. Brown M. Dandenault K. Draper A. Eriksson
S. Fedorov V. Fetisov B. Gilchrist K. Hodson T. Holmstrom
M. Knuble J. Kocur V. Konstantinov V. Kozlov M. Lapointe
I. Larionov N. Lidstrom J. Macoun K. Maltby D. McCarty
D. Mironov L. Murphy C. Osgood B. Rouse B. Shanahan A. Ward

Team engraving from the current Stanley Cup

JAMIE MACOUN arranged for a helicopter to fly over his house at night and shine a giant spotlight on the Cup displayed in an otherwise dark backyard.

A dog lover, **CHRIS OSGOOD** took the Cup golfing and then on the town to bars and restaurants in and around Detroit.

VLADIMIR KONSTANTINOV did not play for the Wings this year, but he was an emotional and spiritual part of the team.

MIKE ILITCH, MARIAN ILITCH, ATANAS ILITCH, CHRISTOPHER ILITCH, DENISE ILITCH, RONALD ILITCH, MIKE ILITCH JR., LISA ILITCH MURRAY, CAROLE ILITCH TREPECK. During their time with the Cup, co-owners Mike and Marian Ilitch took it to a drug awareness function in Lansing, Michigan.

A little-known fact that became a point of controversy for **JIM DEVELLANO** was his investment in the Toronto Maple Leafs, a deal he had arranged back in the 1970s.

KEN HOLLAND shaped this Cup team through drafts in the 1980s and trades in the '90s.

DON WADDELL was assistant general manager for the Wings.

After winning the Cup in 1973, coach **SCOTTY BOWMAN** named his new son Stanley Glenn, Stanley for the Cup, Glenn for Hall (the goalie he admired the most).

BARRY SMITH took the Cup to his cottage south of Buffalo where he had a private party at a neighbourhood restaurant.

Assistant coach **DAVE LEWIS** leased a Viper and drove around his Northville, Michigan home with the Cup in the back seat.

JIM NILL became Detroit's director of player development in 1994.

DAN BELISLE played four games in the NHL, but his greater career was as a coach.

Although he never won the Cup as a player, **MARK HOWE** joined father Gordie as an engraved member of Cup history thanks to his role as scout for his alma mater.

Goalie coach **JIM BEDARD** took the Cup down to the very base of Niagara Falls.

HAKAN ANDERSSON, MARK LEACH, JOE McDONNELL, and **BRUCE HARALSON** were part of the team's scouting department.

Trainer **JOHN WHARTON** produced a CD, the profits from which went to the families of Konstantinov and Mnatsakanov.

PAUL BOYER began his NHL career as an assistant equipment manager for New Jersey in 1993-94.

Assistant equipment manager **TIM ABBOTT** had been with the Wings for six years.

BOB HUDDLESTON was a newly-arrived masseur with the team.

SERGEI MNATSAKANOV no longer worked with the team because of his crippling accident.

WALLY CROSSMAN was the octogenarian who opened the Wings players' bench leading to the ice.

Other players to appear for the Red Wings this season: **JAN GOLUBOVSKY, DARRYL LAPLANTE, NORM MARACLE, DMITRI MIRONOV, JAMIE PUSHOR**

1998–1999 Dallas Stars

For the second time in three years, a team that relocated won the Cup. The Stars had been the Minnesota North Stars until 1993 when they ditched the "North" to head south to football country in Texas. Theirs was a controversial victory because of the NHL's crease rule. All season, officials had been disallowing goals if any offensive player's skate (or even a part of one) was in the crease. Yet when Brett Hull pushed a rebound past Dominik Hasek midway through the third overtime period of game six, the Stars jumped over the boards and the gates opened to allow a flood of cameramen, reporters, and fans onto the ice, even though a simple replay showed the goal should not have counted. The Stars had a parade in downtown Dallas after the win.

STANLEY CUP FINALS

Dallas Stars win best-of-seven Stanley Cup finals 4-2

*June 8, 1999	Buffalo Sabres 3 at Dallas Stars 2 (Jason Woolley 15:30 OT)
*June 10, 1999	Buffalo Sabres 2 at Dallas Stars 4
**June 12, 1999	Dallas Stars 2 at Buffalo Sabres 1
**June 15, 1999	Dallas Stars 1 at Buffalo Sabres 2
*June 17, 1999	Buffalo Sabres 0 at Dallas Stars 2 [Ed Belfour]
**June 19, 1999	Dallas Stars 2 at Buffalo Sabres 1 {Brett Hull 54:51 OT}

** played at Reunion Arena, Dallas ** played at Marine Midland Arena, Buffalo*

Jamie Langenbrunner takes Stanley for a relaxing time in a raft.

Buffalo goalie Dominik Hasek holds his ground on this rush, though he was on the losing end of this six-game series.

DALLAS	GP	G	A	P	Pim
Mike Modano	6	0	7	7	8
Jere Lehtinen	6	2	3	5	0
Brett Hull	5	3	0	3	0
Joe Nieuwendyk	6	2	1	3	9
Jamie Langenbrunner	6	1	2	3	4
Sergei Zubov	6	0	3	3	2
Derian Hatcher	6	1	1	2	10
Craig Ludwig	6	1	1	2	10
Richard Matvichuk	6	0	2	2	6
Dave Reid	6	0	2	2	2
Darryl Sydor	6	1	0	1	8
Pat Verbeek	6	1	0	1	4
Brian Skrudland	6	0	1	1	8
Shawn Chambers	6	0	1	1	2
Tony Hrkac	3	0	1	1	2
Mike Keane	6	0	1	1	0
Benoit Hogue	2	0	0	0	2
Ed Belfour	6	0	0	0	0
Guy Carbonneau	6	0	0	0	0
Blake Sloan	6	0	0	0	0
Jon Sim	2	0	0	0	0

In Goal	GP	W-L	Mins	GA	SO	Avg
Ed Belfour	6	4-2	429	9	1	1.26

"It was the most emotionally and physically draining experience I've ever had," **MIKE MODANO** said of the playoffs.

JERE LEHTINEN took the Cup to his cottage on an island off the coast of Finland where he hosted a sauna party.

HULL scored the Cup-winning goal with his skate in the crease. "I can't say the Cup changed my life," he said casually.

JOE NIEUWENDYK scored six of Dallas's 16 game-winning goals and won the Conn Smythe for his playoff heroics.

JAMIE LANGENBRUNNER took the Cup in a boat, exercising the necessary precautions by having a life-jacket around the sacred silverware!

ZUBOV perhaps holds the record for having the largest animal in the Cup, a giant lobster whose claws extended well beyond the bowl.

DERIAN HATCHER was the first American-born captain of a Stanley Cup team.

LUDWIG took the Cup home, to Elk River, Minnesota, during the 4th of July celebrations.

MATVICHUK took the Cup home to Fort Saskatchewan, Alberta, but informally he took the Cup all over Dallas during the summer.

DAVE REID took the Cup to Toronto on one day and on to Peterborough for a second day.

DARRYL SYDOR hooked up with Doug Lidster for Cup fun, then took it on to Kamloops and then to a nearby remote island.

A churchgoer, **PAT VERBEEK** had the Cup blessed at a mass in Dallas after the victory.

BRIAN SKRUDLAND suffered a chest contusion and torn rib cartilage in February, returning only when the playoffs started.

SHAWN CHAMBERS began his career with the North Stars in Minnesota and returned to the team in 1997.

TONY HRKAC had been the property of three teams before the Stars re-acquired him in the summer of '98.

MIKE KEANE won the Cup with his third different team.

GRANT MARSHALL took the Cup to North Rustico, Prince Edward Island, the Cup's first trip to that province.

DEREK PLANTE was acquired by the Stars late in the season as playoff insurance and proved an invaluable addition.

BRENT SEVERYN made sure every person in Vegreville, Alberta had a chance to see the Cup.

ROMAN TUREK was the first Czech to take the Cup home. A crowd of more than 10,000 greeted him in Ceska Budejovice.

BENOIT HOGUE took the Cup to Montreal, to where his dad worked at a railway yard.

ED BELFOUR took the Cup home to Carmen, Manitoba, to his alma mater at North Dakota, and to a party in Chicago.

Checking forward **GUY CARBONNEAU** took the Cup to his father's gravesite for a private moment.

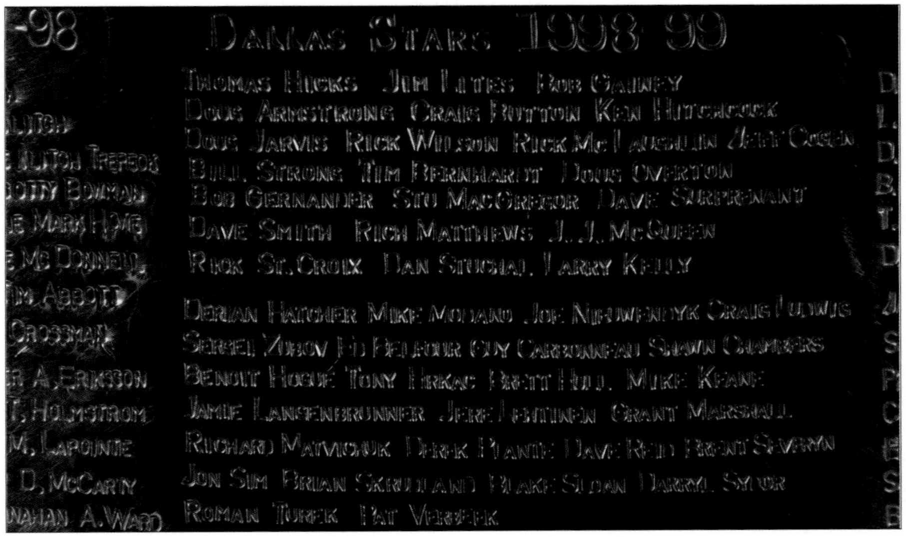

Team engraving from the current Stanley Cup

Rookie **BLAKE SLOAN** started the year in the IHL but finished the year holding the Stanley Cup.

New Glasgow, Nova Scotia declared his triumphal return **JON SIM** Day, the first native to bring the Cup to this small town.

THOMAS HICKS, owner of the Stars and chairman of the board, bought the team in 1995.

Team president **JIM LITES** performed double duty as president also of the Texas Rangers.

BOB GAINEY was one of many members of the 1970s Canadiens dynasty to go on to a successful career in management.

Assistant general manager **DOUG ARMSTRONG** handled the day-to-day operations of the hockey team.

CRAIG BUTTON, the director of scouting for 12 years, took the Cup to a Montreal bar.

KEN HITCHCOCK achieved greatness as a coach with Kamloops before Bob Gainey signed him for the Stars.

DOUG JARVIS became an assistant coach immediately after retiring, joining Minnesota in 1988.

Assistant coach **RICK WILSON** took the Cup to Bemidji State University.

RICK McLAUGHLIN was the team's vice president and chief financial officer.

JEFF COGEN was in charge of marketing and promotion.

BILL STRONG was the Stars' vice president of marketing and broadcasting.

Former goalie **TIM BERNHARDT** had been a scout for the NHL's Central Bureau before joining the Stars in 1992.

DOUG OVERTON was the team's director of pro scouting and was responsible for all players in North America.

BOB GERNANDER was an international scout who scoured the world over for undiscovered, young talent.

STU MacGREGOR left the Kamloops Blazers after 16 years to join the Stars as a scout at the start of this Cup-winning year.

DAVE SURPRENANT was vice-president of the Professional Hockey Athletic Training Society (PHATS).

DAVE SMITH and **RICK MATTHEWS** were the team's equipment managers.

Strength coach **J.J. McQUEEN** took the Cup up to Algonquin Park for a cottage party during the summer.

RICK ST. CROIX had been a backup goalie with Philadelphia and Toronto, never coming close to the Cup as a player.

DAN STUCHAL worked in the Stars' administrative offices.

LARRY KELLY was the director of public relations for the Stars.

Other players to appear for the Stars this season: **PETR BUZEK, JASON BOTTERILL, KELLY FAIRCHILD, MANNY FERNANDEZ, AARON GAVEY, SERGEY GUSEV, DAN KECZMER, DOUG LIDSTER, BRAD LUKOWICH, JAMIE WRIGHT**

1999–2000 New Jersey Devils

Nine players from '95 were on this year's winning team, the first time ever the final two games of the Cup finals both went into at least double overtime. The Devils lost at home in game five when they had a chance to win the Cup, but came right back and won game six on the road. In the Conference finals they overcame a 3-1 deficit in games against the Flyers to win three in a row and build momentum for the finals.

STANLEY CUP FINALS

New Jersey Devils win best-of-seven Stanley Cup finals 4-2

*May 30, 2000 Dallas Stars 3 at New Jersey Devils 7
*June 1, 2000 Dallas Stars 2 at New Jersey Devils 1
**June 3, 2000 New Jersey Devils 2 at Dallas Stars 1
**June 5, 2000 New Jersey Devils 3 at Dallas Stars 1
*June 8, 2000 Dallas Stars 1 at New Jersey Devils 0 (Mike Modano 46:21 OT) [Belfour]
**June 10, 2000 New Jersey Devils 2 at Dallas Stars 1 {Jason Arnott 28:20 OT}

** played at Continental Airlines Arena, New Jersey ** played at Reunion Arena, Dallas*

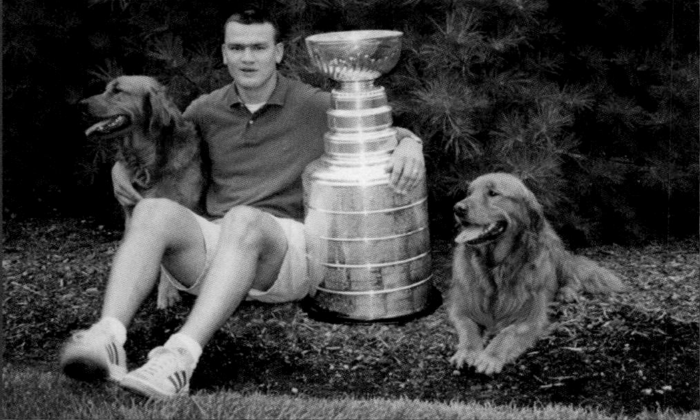

Bobby Holik enjoys the Cup at home with two of his best friends.

(top) Jason Arnott and friends go for a swim in Wasaga Beach, being sure to keep the Cup dry; (left) goalie Martin Brodeur is given plenty of protection in front of his own goal. The team surrendered just nine goals in this six-game series en route to Cup victory.

NEW JERSEY	GP	G	A	P	Pim
Jason Arnott	6	4	3	7	2
Petr Sykora	6	3	2	5	4
Patrik Elias	6	0	5	5	0
Brian Rafalski	6	1	3	4	4
Sergei Brylin	6	2	1	3	0
Scott Stevens	6	1	2	3	2
Ken Daneyko	6	1	1	2	4
John Madden	6	1	1	2	0
Alexander Mogilny	6	1	1	2	0
Jay Pandolfo	6	0	2	2	0
Scott Niedermayer	6	1	0	1	2
Bobby Holik	6	0	1	1	4
Claude Lemieux	6	0	1	1	4
Vladimir Malakhov	6	0	1	1	4
Colin White	6	0	1	1	4
Randy McKay	6	0	1	1	2
Sergei Nemchinov	6	0	1	1	2
Scott Gomez	6	0	1	1	0
Martin Brodeur	6	0	0	0	2

In Goal	GP	W-L	Mins	GA	SO	Avg
Martin Brodeur	6	4-2	434	9	0	1.24

The Wasaga Beach Minor Hockey Association retired **ARNOTT'S** number 9 during a summer day of Cup festivities.

BRAD BOMBARDIR played less than half a season (32 games) and not at all in the finals yet still got his name on the Cup.

For the second time, goalie **MARTIN BRODEUR** took the Cup to Mauriac St. in Montreal and hosted a street hockey game.

BRULE played the year in Albany and only once in the playoffs.

BRYLIN had a career-high in goals, assists, and points this year.

As he had done in '95, **KEN DANEYKO** took the Cup to Mezzanotte, his restaurant in Caldwell, New Jersey.

PATRIK ELIAS took the Cup home to the Czech Republic.

Alaska native **SCOTT GOMEZ** led rookies in scoring for both the regular season and playoffs.

BOBBY HOLIK, the master checker, used his size to upset opponents and keep them off balance.

STEVE KELLY was called up to the Devils after Albany had been eliminated from the playoffs.

CLAUDE LEMIEUX won his fourth Cup with his third team, a modern-day record and testament to his playoff worth.

JOHN MADDEN took the Cup to his mother's wedding.

VLADIMIR MALAKHOV was acquired from Montreal during the season.

Right winger **RANDY McKAY** had 16 regular season goals but not one in the playoffs.

ALEXANDER MOGILNY was acquired at the deadline from Vancouver, but he produced only four goals in the playoffs.

After scoring twice in the first round, **SERGEI NEMCHINOV** had just three points in the last three series of the Cup run.

A lifelong member of the Devils, **SCOTT NIEDERMAYER** led the defence in the playoffs with five goals.

Fighter **KRZYSZTOF OLIWA** did not play a single playoff minute for the team after playing all the regular season.

JAY PANDOLFO rang the closing bell to the New York Stock Exchange the day the Cup was there.

Undrafted, **BRIAN RAFALSKI** pursued a career in Europe before the Devils signed him as a free agent on June 18, 1999.

SUTTON was the first player to be acquired by New Jersey on three separate occasions. He spent most of the year in Albany.

Defenceman **SCOTT STEVENS** took both the Cup and Conn Smythe Trophy to a community centre in Peterborough.

After being injured early in the final game, **PETR SYKORA** was carried off on a stretcher. After the victory, coach Robinson put Sykora's sweater on to include him in the celebrations.

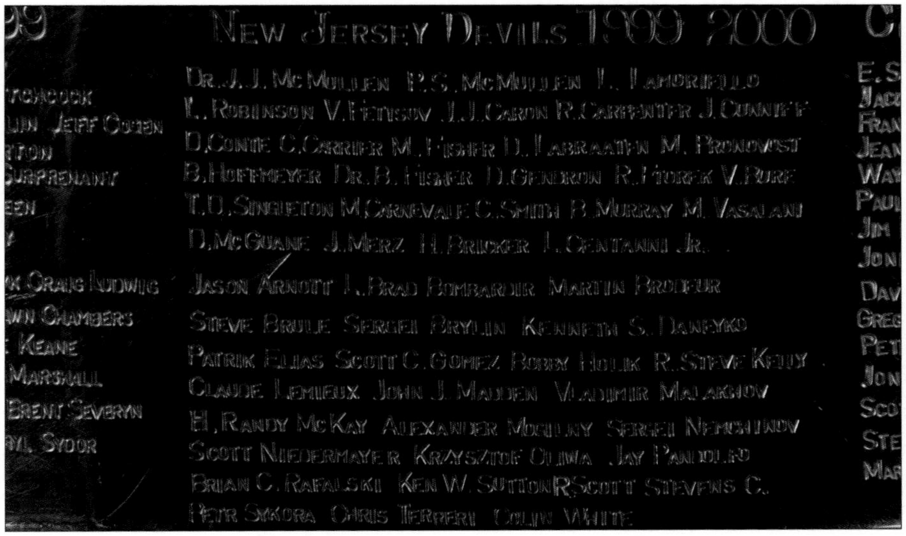

Team engraving from the current Stanley Cup

The team's backup goalie, **TERRERI** didn't play at all in the playoffs and saw action in only a dozen regular season games.

COLIN WHITE scored the only goal in a 1-0 win over Toronto in game two of their second-round matchup.

Owner **DR. JOHN McMULLEN** earned a Doctorate from the Swiss Federal Institute of Technology in Zurich.

PETER McMULLEN was the executive vice president and the son of team owner, John.

GM **LOU LAMORIELLO** was a man who put together a Stanley Cup lineup while maintaining a tight budget.

When head coach Robbie Ftorek was fired late in the season, **LARRY ROBINSON** directed the team to another Cup.

In his first year of retirement, **SLAVA FETISOV** took an assistant coach's job with his former team, and won another Cup.

JACQUES CARON had been with the Devils for eight years, primarily as a coach for goalies.

BOBBY CARPENTER became associate coach with the Devils after Ftorek was fired.

JOHN CUNIFF got his name on the Cup as head coach of the farm team in Albany.

DAVID CONTE, CLAUDE CARRIER, MILT FISHER, DAN LABRAATEN, MARCEL PRONOVOST, and **BOB HOFFMEYER** were all scouts for the Devils.

DR. BARRY FISHER got his name on the Cup by virtue of being the team orthopedist.

DENNIS GENDRON was the team's special assignment scout.

ROBBIE FTOREK is the only coach ever fired during the season to have his name on the Cup.

Fitness consultant **VLADIMIR BURE** was the father of Pavel and Valeri, though both children refuse to speak to their father who, they felt, pushed them too hard during their childhood.

TARAN SINGLETON was the video coordinator for the Stars.

MARIE CARNEVALE was an executive assistant.

CALLIE SMITH, a scouting staff assistant, became the most recent woman to have her name on the Cup.

BILL MURRAY graduated from the University of Texas-El Paso and joined the Devils in 1996.

MIKE VASALANI was the coordinator of all exercise programs.

A rookie to the team, **DANA McGUANE** apprenticed as equipment manager for the farm team's Albany River Rats.

A native of Berlin, Germany, massage therapist **JUERGEN MERZ** had a private practise in Vail, Colorado.

HARRY BRICKER and **LOU CENTANNI, JR.** were the team's assistant equipment managers.

Other players to appear for the Devils this season: **ERIC BERTRAND, WILLIE MITCHELL, BRENDAN MORRISON, LYLE ODELEIN, DENIS PEDERSON, DERON QUINT, BRIAN ROLSTON**

2000–2001 Colorado Avalanche

THE CHAMPIONS

The team's theme was "16W" for the 16 wins needed to claim the Stanley Cup, but as much as that was every player's commitment to getting the Cup in Ray Bourque's hands. A longtime star in Boston, Bourque had never taken the Bruins to victory, but this year, surrounded by a Hall of Fame cast, he was able to hoist the Cup for a first time. This was the first finals to go to a game seven since the Rangers and Vancouver in 1994.

STANLEY CUP FINALS

Colorado Avalanche win best-of-seven Stanley Cup finals 4-3

*May 26, 2001	New Jersey Devils 0 at Colorado Avalanche 5 [Roy]
*May 29, 2001	New Jersey Devils 2 at Colorado Avalanche 1
**May 31, 2001	Colorado Avalanche 3 at New Jersey Devils 1
**June 2, 2001	Colorado Avalanche 2 at New Jersey Devils 3
*June 4, 2001	New Jersey Devils 4 at Colorado Avalanche 1
**June 7, 2001	Colorado Avalanche 4 at New Jersey Devils 0 [Roy]
*June 9, 2001	New Jersey Devils 1 at Colorado Avalanche 3 {Alex Tanguay 4:57 2nd}

** played at Pepsi Center, Colorado ** played at Continental Airlines Arena, New Jersey*

The Avs have their team portrait taken with the Cup.

(clockwise) Ray Bourque (left) and Patrick Roy lift the Cup together; the four natives of Simcoe, Ontario, to have won the Cup celebrate together—(left to right) Rick Wamsley, Red Kelly, Rob Blake, and Chico Maki; Blake (right) and the Devils' Scott Gomez fight for position during the finals.

COLORADO	GP	G	A	P	Pim
Joe Sakic	7	4	5	9	2
Alex Tanguay	7	4	3	7	4
Rob Blake	7	2	3	5	4
Chris Drury	7	3	1	4	0
Adam Foote	7	1	3	4	16
Dan Hinote	7	1	3	4	11
Ville Nieminen	7	1	2	3	6
Martin Skoula	7	1	2	3	6
Milan Hejduk	7	0	3	3	0
Ray Bourque	7	1	1	2	2
Steve Reinprecht	7	1	1	2	0
Chris Dingman	7	0	2	2	10
Dave Reid	7	0	2	2	2
Eric Messier	7	0	1	1	6
Shjon Podein	7	0	1	1	6
Greg De Vries	7	0	0	0	6
Stephane Yelle	7	0	0	0	4
Jon Klemm	7	0	0	0	2
Patrick Roy	7	0	0	0	0

In Goal	GP	W-L	Mins	GA	SO	Avg
Patrick Roy	7	4-3	419	11	2	1.58

JOE SAKIC accepted the Cup from NHL Commissioner Gary Bettman and then swung it over to Ray Bourque.

MILAN HEJDUK had a career year with 41 goals in the regular season. In the playoffs, he led all scorers with 16 assists.

ALEX TANGUAY scored the first two goals of the final game, including the Cup winner, to lead the team to the Stanley Cup.

ROB BLAKE had been acquired near the trading deadline from Los Angeles, a move that put the Avs in the winner's circle.

CHRIS DRURY took the Cup to Yale/New Haven Children's Hospital in his home state of Connecticut.

"It's everything I thought it would be," **RAY BOURQUE** said after lifting the Cup.

NIEMINEN'S father played against young Ville until alcohol got the better of him. "I think he was there," he said after the victory.

In the summer, **ADAM FOOTE** had a pool party in Toronto for hundreds of friends.

DAN HINOTE had been drafted by the Avs out of the United States Military Academy at West Point where he was on the road to his dream of becoming an FBI agent.

SHJON PODEIN'S day with the Cup took place in Rochester, New York, his hometown.

Second-year NHLer **MARTIN SKOULA** took the Cup back to Litomerice in the Czech Republic.

Playing in his first full season, **STEVE REINPRECHT** started the year with Los Angeles but was traded to the Avs.

Drafted in 1982 by Boston, **DAVE REID** has signed as a free agent four times during his career.

Undrafted, **ERIC MESSIER** ended up playing roller hockey for the Montreal Roadrunners before being signed by Colorado.

CHRIS DINGMAN was traded to Carolina on draft day and had only a few days to celebrate the Cup win with his teammates.

JON KLEMM signed with the Quebec Nordiques as a free agent after being passed over in the draft.

Although he was drafted by New Jersey in 1992, **STEPHANE YELLE** was traded to Colorado at the '94 Entry Draft.

GREG DE VRIES had been coached by his dad and other men whom he remembered after the Cup victory.

Never drafted, **BRYAN MUIR** had been signed as a free agent by Edmonton in 1996.

Rookie **SCOTT PARKER** strapped the Cup to the back of his motorcycle and went for a spin in the summer.

Goalie **PATRICK ROY** became the first player to win the Conn Smythe Trophy three times.

Centre **PETER FORSBERG** missed much of the playoffs after having his spleen removed.

Team engraving from the current Stanley Cup

Backup **DAVID AEBISCHER** had been the first Swiss goalie ever drafted, but he took a back seat to Roy in the playoffs.

Although **NOLAN PRATT** did not play a game in the finals, he appeared 46 times in the regular season.

STANLEY KROENKE bought the Avs, the NBA's Denver Nuggets, and the Pepsi Center for $450 million in the summer of 2000.

Avs GM **PIERRE LACROIX** had been rumoured to be leaving hockey to become business manager for his friend Celine Dion.

PAUL FIXTER was Colorado's video coach.

FRANCOIS GIGUERE was the team's goalie coach for Patrick Roy.

BRIAN MacDONALD became assistant general manager in 2000 after eight years with the team as a scout.

Hall of Famer **MICHEL GOULET** was the team's director of player personnel.

The vice president of communications and team services, **JEAN MARTINEAU** started with the team back in Quebec in 1986.

PAT KARNS earned his master's degree in phys ed from the University of Northern Colorado in 1987.

Kinesiologist **MATTHEW SOKOLOWSKI** was born in Poland and raised in New Brunswick.

MARK MILLER and **WAYNE FLEMMING** managed all equipment for the team.

DAVE RANDOLPH was the team's assistant equipment manager.

PAUL GOLDBERG was the team's strength and conditioning coach.

Massage therapist **GREGORIO PRADERA** was born in Mexico City and grew up in Spain. He was a professional jai-alai player for close to 20 years.

BRAD SMITH was a nine-year veteran of the NHL before becoming a member of the Avs' scouting department.

JIM HAMMETT, **GARTH JOY**, **STEVE LYONS**, and **JONI LEHTO** were all members of the Colorado scouting staff.

ORVAL TESSIER was now a scout, but he had also been an NHLer and minor pro star in the 1950s and '60s.

CHARLOTTE GRAHAME was the wife of Ron Grahame and mother of John Grahame. Yet it was Charlotte who got her name on the Cup first because she worked in the Avs' front office!

One day in 1988, **BOB HARTLEY** quit his day job to pursue his dream of coaching in the NHL.

Hall of Famer **BRYAN TROTTIER** joined the Avs as an assistant coach in 1998.

JACQUES CLOUTIER had been with the team as assistant coach since January '96.

Other players to appear for the Avs this season: **RICK BERRY, ROB SHEARER, JOEL PRPIC, YURI BABENKO, BRAD LARSEN, ADAM DEADMARSH, AARON MILLER, ALEXEI GUSAROV**

2001–2002 Detroit Red Wings

THE CHAMPIONS

Despite having a record of 2-4 in overtime games in the 2002 playoffs, the Wings won when they had to and for the third time in six years claimed the Cup. After beating Vancouver in six games and St. Louis in five, the Wings faced Colorado, one of the great rivalries of the present game, and it was a seven-game battle...until game seven. The Avalanche went up 3-2 in games from an overtime goal, but the Wings came back with consecutive shutouts from Domink Hasek, 2-0 in game six and then a stunning 7-0 whitewash of Patrick Roy and the Avs in the climactic game. In the finals, the Wings defeated a Carolina team that won the first game (in OT). Detroit won four straight after that opening loss to win the Cup in impressive fashion.

STANLEY CUP FINALS

Detroit Red Wings win best-of-seven Stanley Cup finals 4-1

*June 4, 2002	Carolina Hurricanes 3 at Detroit Red Wings 2 (Ron Francis 0:58 OT)
*June 6, 2002	Carolina Hurricanes 1 at Detroit Red Wings 3
**June 8, 2002	Detroit Red Wings 3 at Carolina Hurricanes 2 (Igor Larionov 54:47 OT)
**June 10, 2002	Detroit Red Wings 3 at Carolina Hurricanes 0 [Hasek]
*June 13, 2002	Carolina Hurricanes 1 at Detroit Red Wings 3 {Brendan Shanahan 14:04 2nd}

** played at Joe Louis Arena, Detroit ** played at Entertainment and Sports Arena, Raleigh*

Goalie Dominik Hasek rejoices in his first Cup victory.

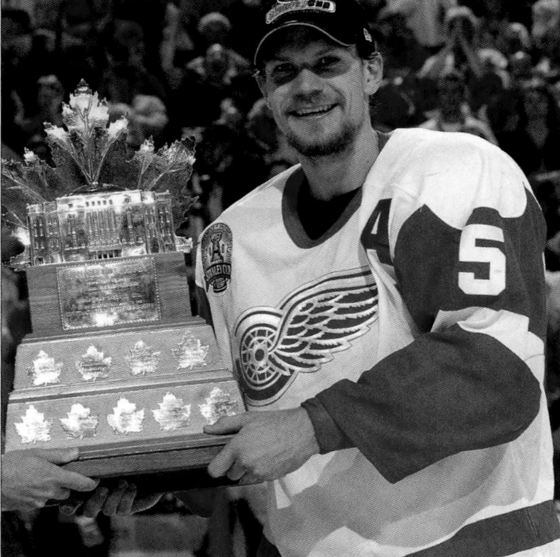

(clockwise) Carolina goalie Arturs Irbe is screened in front by Detroit's Brendan Shanahan; defenceman Nicklas Lidstrom became the first player from outside North America to win the Conn Smythe Trophy; Pavel Datsyuk takes the Cup to Yekaterinburg in Siberia at the very border of Asia and Europe in the Ural mountains.

DETROIT	GP	G	A	P	Pim
Sergei Fedorov	5	1	4	5	6
Igor Larionov	5	3	1	4	4
Steve Yzerman	5	0	4	4	0
Brendan Shanahan	5	3	0	3	6
Brett Hulll	5	2	1	3	2
Nicklas Lidstrom	5	1	2	3	2
Chris Chelios	5	0	3	3	4
Kirk Maltby	5	2	0	2	4
Kris Draper	5	1	1	2	4
Tomas Holmstrom	5	1	1	2	0
Frerik Olausson	5	0	2	2	2
Steve Duchesne	5	0	1	1	8
Boyd Devereaux	5	0	1	1	4
Luc Robitaille	5	0	1	1	4
Jiri Fischer	4	0	1	1	4
Darren McCarty	5	0	1	1	2
Mathieu Dandenault	5	0	0	0	2
Jiri Slegr	1	0	0	0	2
Pavel Datsyuk	5	0	0	0	0
Dominik Hasek	5	0	0	0	0

In Goal	GP	W-L	Mins	GA	SO	Avg
Dominik Hasek	5	4-1	355	7	1	1.18

STEVE YZERMAN gave one of the most heroic performances in Stanley Cup history this playoffs, skating on a knee so bad each shift offered excruciating pain when he went to the bench.

BRENDAN SHANAHAN and teammate Yzerman were the only two players this season to capture an historic double—gold at the Olympics in February, and Stanley Cup silver in June.

SERGEI FEDOROV won a bronze medal with Russia at the Olympics in Salt Lake City to go with his Stanley Cup.

BRETT HULL won a silver medal at the Olympics with USA to go with his second Stanley Cup.

NICKLAS LIDSTROM became the first European player to be given the Conn Smythe Trophy for playoff excellence.

CHRIS CHELIOS won his only other Cup 16 years previous, in 1986, a record.

TOMAS HOLMSTROM was drafted a lowly 257th overall by the Wings in 1994.

IGOR LARIONOV had no trouble getting excited about Detroit's home games, especially the frequent occasions when his daughters sang the national anthems!

After 15 seasons and 1,205 games, left winger **LUC ROBITAILLE** finally had his name on the Stanley Cup.

DARREN McCARTY scored a hat trick in Detroit's 5-3 win over Colorado in game one of the Western Conference finals.

Rookie **PAVEL DATSYUK** took the Cup back to his hometown of Sverdlovsk, Russia.

JIRI FISCHER was another great European draft choice of the Wings to have an impact with Detroit.

KIRK MALTBY and Draper, Draper and Maltby. Any time the other team's best players were on the ice, so was this pair.

Defenceman **FREDRIK OLAUSSON** signed as a free agent with Detroit after two years in Anaheim.

The 24-year-old **BOYD DEVEREAUX** played guitar with Kid Rock at a Cup party at the Beach Grill in St. Clair Shores.

STEVE DUCHESNE capped a 16-year career that extended beyond 1,100 regular-season games by winning his first Cup.

One of the league's premier checkers, **KRIS DRAPER** took the Cup for a visit to the Children's Hospital of Michigan.

MATHIEU DANDENAULT finished his seventh year with the team by winning his third Stanley Cup.

JIRI SLEGR came to the Wings from the non-playoff Atlanta Thrashers in a serendipitous mid-season trade.

The final years of **UWE KRUPP'S** career were fraught with pain and ill health, but he made it onto the Cup one last time.

Rookie **JASON WILLIAMS** was undrafted and unwanted until the Wings signed him to a contract in the fall of 2000.

Team engraving from the replica Cup

DOMINIK HASEK was only the second goalie to boast a Cup championship and an Olympic gold medal (Martin Brodeur, just months earlier, being the first).

As backup goalie to Dominik Hasek, **MANNY LEGACE** played for just eleven minutes of the 2002 playoffs.

MIKE ILITCH, MARIAN ILITCH, CHRISTOPHER ILITCH, DENISE ILITCH, RONALD ILITCH, MIKE ILITCH JR., LISA ILITCH MURRAY, ATANAS ILITCH, and **CAROLE ILITCH** are all on the Cup again as co-owners of the team.

JIM DEVELLANO now had 12 championship rings: six for the Stanley Cup, three for the Calder Cup (AHL), two Adams Cups (CHL), and one Riley Cup (ECHL).

GM **KEN HOLLAND** acquired goalie Dominik Hasek from Buffalo and signed Luc Robitaille and Brett Hull to make this a Cup-quality team.

As assistant general manager, **JIM NILL** was responsible for amateur scouting and overseeing the team's minor-league affiliate.

SCOTTY BOWMAN declared soon after the win that this season, in which he won his tenth Cup, was his last.

DAVE LEWIS had been an assistant coach for the Wings for some 15 years. He was named head coach to replace Bowman.

BARRY SMITH coached Norway at the World Championships in 1985 and '86.

As goalie coach, **JIM BEDARD** worked with both the NHL and AHL goalies in the Detroit system.

JOEY KOCUR was a video coach for two years before becoming an assistant in 2001.

JOHN WHARTON had been the team's head trainer for eleven seasons.

PIET VAN ZANT became the team's head trainer in the summer after three years as an assistant.

PAUL BOYER began his dressing room career as trainer at Lake Superior State University after earning a B.Sc. there.

PAUL MacDONALD was the team's vice president of finance.

NANCY BEARD was secretary to the team's executive.

Scout **DAN BELISLE** was a head coach with the Washington Capitals for just over a year before moving into scouting.

MARK HOWE made his own name in the NHL as a player and now as a pro scout.

BOB McCAMMON'S life in hockey began in 1960 as a player, but the team's pro scout was celebrating his first Stanley Cup.

HAKAN ANDERSSON, the team's director of European scouting, was considered the best in the business.

BRUCE HARALSON, MARK LEACH, JOE McDONNELL, and **GLENN MERKOSKY** were all members of the Red Wings' amateur scouting staff, focusing on players in the Canadian junior system and the U.S. college ranks.

Other players to appear for the Red Wings this season: **SEAN AVERY, MAXIM KUZNETSOV, JESSE WALLIN, LADISLAV KOHN, BRENT GILCHRIST, YURI BUTSAYEV**

2002–2003 THE CHAMPIONS

New Jersey Devils

The Devils won their third Stanley Cup since 1995 by playing good hockey throughout the playoffs and dominating, exceptional hockey at critical moments along the way. They reached their zenith in game seven of the finals against the upstart Mighty Ducks, a team that had no business being there and yet a team that was as resilient as it was surprising. In the final game, the Devils' defence and the goaltending of Martin Brodeur won the day. The team celebrated in the arena restaurant after the fans had left the building, and in the days after, the Cup appeared on the David Letterman Show, the New York Stock Exchange, at Yankee Stadium, and at numerous other places in the vicinity.

STANLEY CUP FINALS

New Jersey Devils win best-of-seven Stanley Cup finals 4-3

*May 27, 2003	Mighty Ducks of Anaheim 0 at New Jersey Devils 3 [Brodeur]
*May 29, 2003	Mighty Ducks of Anaheim 0 at New Jersey Devils 3 [Brodeur]
**May 31, 2003	New Jersey Devils 2 at Mighty Ducks of Anaheim 3 (Ruslan Salei 6:59 OT)
**June 2, 2003	New Jersey Devils 0 at Mighty Ducks of Anaheim 1 (Steve Thomas 0:39 OT) [Giguere]
*June 5, 2003	Mighty Ducks of Anaheim 3 at New Jersey Devils 6
**June 7, 2003	New Jersey Devils 2 at Mighty Ducks of Anaheim 5
*June 9, 2003	Mighty Ducks of Anaheim 0 at New Jersey Devils 3 [Brodeur] {Mike Rupp 2:22 2nd}

** played at Continental Airlines Arena, New Jersey ** played at Arrowhead Pond, Anaheim*

Scott Stevens heads off the ice with the precious silverware.

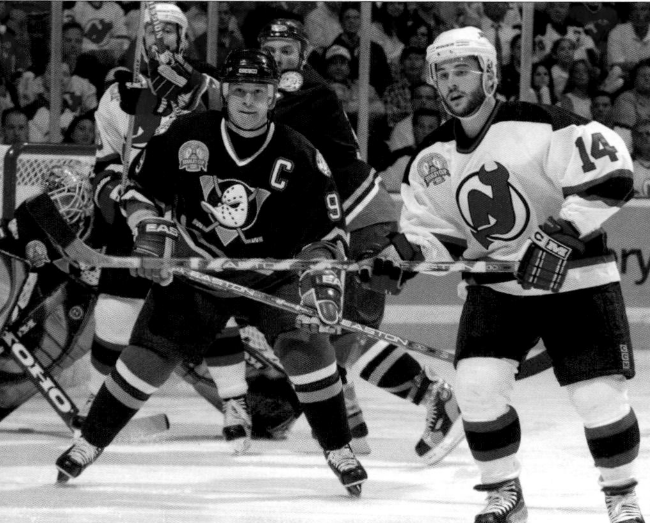

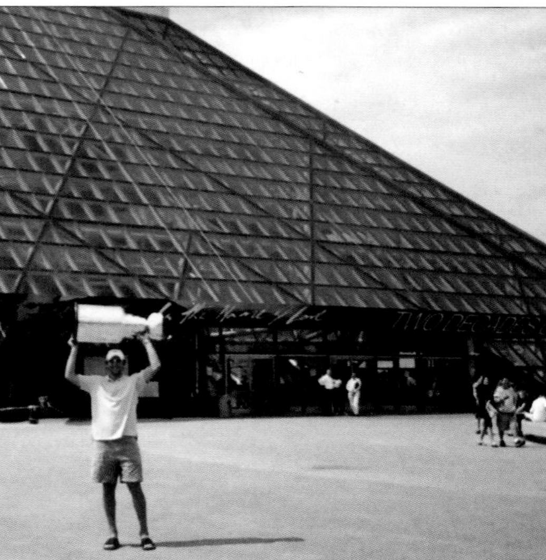

(clockwise) Anaheim's Paul Kariya and the Devils' Brian Gionta watch as play unfolds inside the Ducks' blueline; Mike Rupp takes the Cup to the Rock 'n' Roll Hall of Fame in Cleveland, Ohio; New Jersey's John Madden moves the puck up ice.

NEW JERSEY	GP	G	A	P	Pim
Patrick Elias	7	3	4	7	4
Brian Gionta	7	1	5	6	2
Jeff Friesen	7	5	0	5	0
Scott Gomez	7	2	3	5	0
Scott Niedermayer	7	0	5	5	4
Mike Rupp	4	1	3	4	0
Jamie Langenbrunner	7	2	1	3	6
Grant Marshall	7	2	1	3	4
Jay Pandolfo	7	2	1	3	0
Brian Rafalski	7	0	3	3	2
Colin White	7	0	2	2	4
Sergei Brylin	7	0	2	2	2
Scott Stevens	7	0	2	2	2
Oleg Tverdovsky	6	0	2	2	0
Pascal Rheaume	7	1	0	1	2
Turner Stevenson	3	0	1	1	10
Martin Brodeur	7	0	1	1	0
John Madden	7	0	1	1	0
Jim McKenzie	3	0	0	0	4
Tommy Albelin	7	0	0	0	0
Jiri Bicek	4	0	0	0	0
Ken Daneyko	1	0	0	0	0

In Goal	GP	W-L	Mins	GA	SO	Avg
Martin Brodeur	7	4-3	416	12	3	1.73
Corey Schwab	1	0-0	11	0	0	0.00

Minnesota native **JAMIE LANGENBRUNNER** led the playoffs with eleven goals.

SCOTT NIEDERMAYER'S mother publicly announced her wish that her other son, Rob, who played for the Ducks, win the Cup, Scott already having won it previously with the Devils.

JOHN MADDEN took the Cup to his hockey home in East Hampton, Connecticut.

JEFF FRIESEN took the Cup home to Loon Lake, Saskatchewan.

PATRIK ELIAS took the Cup to Trebic, the place of his birth.

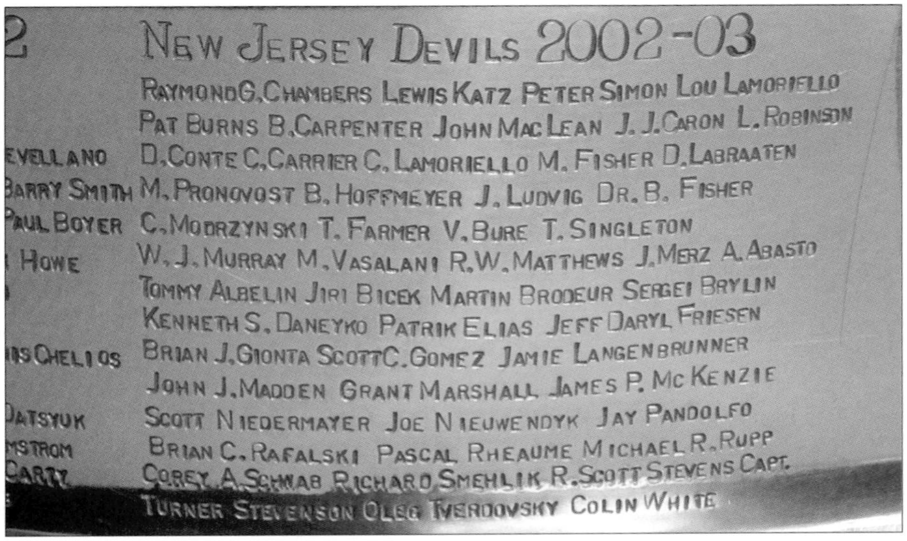

JAY PANDOLFO wanted a quiet time with the Cup in Boston, but by evening's end he wound up with rock group Aerosmith.

SCOTT GOMEZ celebrated his Cup victory on ice with friend Whoopi Goldberg.

After graduating from the University of Wisconsin with a degree in economics, **BRIAN RAFALSKI** went to Finland to play for three seasons.

JOE NIEUWENDYK took the Cup to a friend with whom he played at Cornell but who had since become paralyzed.

SCOTT STEVENS became the all-time leader in games played among defenceman this season.

BRIAN GIONTA had the Cup for a day in his hometown of Greece...New York.

GRANT MARSHALL took the Cup to Philthy McNasty's Bar & Grill, a popular hangout in Mississauga, Ontario.

COLIN WHITE took the Cup where it had been three years earlier, to his hometown of New Glasgow, Nova Scotia.

Rookie **MIKE RUPP** played just a few games all season, but his tip-in in the second period of game seven was the game-winning, Cup-winning score!

PASCAL RHEAUME was lucky enough to be traded mid-season from Atlanta, a non-playoff team, to the Cup champs.

OLEG TVERDOVSKY and teammate **SERGEI BRYLIN** took the Cup to Moscow.

TURNER STEVENSON made everyone in Prince George, British Columbia happy when he came home with the Cup.

TOMMY ALBELIN took the Cup to his daughter's school and then his son's school in a great display of "show 'n' tell."

RICHARD SMEHLIK took the Cup home to Ostrava, Czech Republic where a thousand fans lined up to see it.

JIRI BICEK played in 44 regular season games, earning the right to have his name on the Cup and a day with the trophy.

KEN DANEYKO was in and out of the lineup, but coach Burns made sure number 5 was in for the Cup-clinching game.

Like Tommy Albelin, **JIM McKENZIE** stopped kids in their tracks when he brought the Cup to his kids' school.

Team engraving from the replica Cup

Backup goalie **COREY SCHWAB** played just eleven games during the season and only 28 minutes in the playoffs.

Goalie sensation **MARTIN BRODEUR** won 16 games this playoffs, a record seven of which came by shutout.

RAYMOND CHAMBERS was co-owner of the New Jersey Devils.

LEWIS KATZ was the principal owner of the team.

PETER SIMON was chairman of the New Jersey Devils.

LOU LAMORIELLO been New Jersey's GM for the past 17 years and three Stanley Cups.

Coach **PAT BURNS** took the Cup home to Magog, Quebec, in the Eastern Townships to celebrate his first Cup win.

Assistant coach **BOBBY CARPENTER** retired in 1999. In four seasons behind the bench since, he had won two Cups.

JOHN MacLEAN played 15 years with the Devils, winning the Cup in 1995. After retiring in 2002, he joined the team as an assistant coach.

Goalie coach **JACQUES CARON** went to a friend's house for a low-key Cup party.

This season, **LARRY ROBINSON** was designated as a special assignment coach and now had been associated with all three Devils' Cup wins.

DAVID CONTE was the Devils' director of scouting.

CLAUDE CARRIER, assistant director of scouting, had been with the Devils for 20 years.

CHRIS LAMORIELLO, MILT FISHER, DAN LABRAATEN, BOB HOFFMEYER, and **JAN LUDVIG** were all members of the team's scouting staff.

Scout **MARCEL PRONOVOST** had been in hockey his whole life and an integral part of all three Devils' victories.

DR. BARRY FISHER was the team physician.

CHRIS MODRZYNSKI was the team's executive vice president.

TERRY FARMER, the vice president of ticket operations for the team, was the most recent in a growing list of women whose name graces the Cup.

Fitness consultant **VLADIMIR BURE** won medals in swimming at the 1968 and 1972 Olympics.

JUERGEN MERZ was Devils' massage therapist.

BILL MURRAY was the medical trainer.

MIKE VASALANI was strength and conditioning coach.

Equipment manager **RICH MATTHEWS** earned a degree in exercise science from Arizona State University.

TARAN SINGLETON worked with the team as video coordinator.

ALEX ABASTO was an assistant equipment manager.

Other players to appear for the Devils this season: **CHRISTIAN BERGLUND, STEPHEN GUOLLA, MIKE DANTON, CHRIS DARBY, RAYMOND GIROUX, ANDREI ZYUZIN**

2003 – 2004 THE CHAMPIONS Tampa Bay Lightning

It was a battle between two teams that no one expected to get as far as they did, a battle that came down to one game and one goal and home-ice advantage for the Lightning. Ruslan Fedotenko was the hero in the final game, scoring both goals in a 2-1 win for Tampa Bay. The Lightning became the first team from Florida to win the Cup, thanks in large part to their power play and their extraordinary record when scoring the first goal in these playoffs (14-2). Amazingly, a team no one expected to win it all eliminated the Islanders (4-1), Montreal (4-0), and Philadelphia (4-3) to make it to the finals.

STANLEY CUP FINALS

Tampa Bay wins Stanley Cup best-of-seven Stanley Cup finals 4-3

*May 25 Calgary Flames 4 at Tampa Bay Lightning 1
*May 27 Calgary Flames 1 at Tampa Bay Lightning 4
**May 29 Tampa Bay Lightning 0 at Calgary Flames 3 [Kiprusoff]
**May 31 Tampa Bay Lightning 1 at Calgary Flames 0 [Khabibulin]
*June 3 Calgary Flames 3 at Tampa Bay Lightning 2
**June 5 Tampa Bay Lightning 3 at Calgary Flames 2
*June 7 Calgary Flames 1 at Tampa Bay Lightning 2 {Ruslan Fedotenko 14:38 2nd}

*played at St. Pete Times Forum, Tampa Bay ** played at Pengrowth Saddledome, Calgary

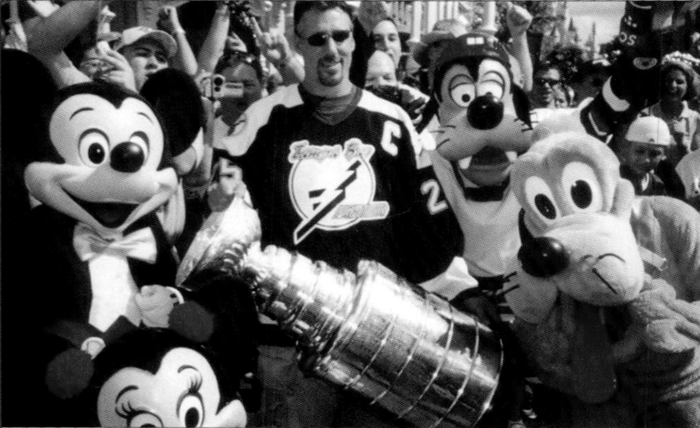

Dave Andreychuk takes the Cup to Walt DisneyWorld.

(above) Tampa's Vincent Lecavalier goes one-on-one with goalie Miikka Kiprusoff and is foiled in this attempt; (left) a duel between captains as Dave Andreychuk (left) and Jarome Iginla of Calgary fight for position.

TAMPA BAY	GP	G	A	P	Pim
Brad Richards	7	4	4	8	2
Martin St. Louis	7	4	2	6	2
Ruslan Fedotenko	6	3	1	4	4
Dave Andreychuk	7	0	4	4	4
Dan Boyle	7	1	2	3	4
Vincent Lecavalier	7	0	3	3	9
Fredrik Modin	7	1	1	2	4
Cory Stillman	6	0	2	2	7
Jassen Cullimore	7	0	2	2	4
Chris Dingman	7	0	1	1	24
Tim Taylor	7	0	1	1	2
Martin Cibak	4	0	1	1	0
Andre Roy	5	0	0	0	21
Cory Sarich	7	0	0	0	14
Pavel Kubina	6	0	0	0	12
Dimitry Afanasenkov	7	0	0	0	4
Brad Lukowich	4	0	0	0	4
Nolan Pratt	7	0	0	0	2
Nikolai Khabibulin	7	0	0	0	0
Darryl Sydor	7	0	0	0	0
Ben Clymer	4	0	0	0	0

In Goal	GP	W-L	Mins	GA	SO	Avg
Nikolai Khabibulin	7	4-3	456	14	1	1.84

His might be one of the greatest playoffs ever. **BRAD RICHARDS** scored a record seven game-winning goals, and in the playoffs the team was 9-0 when he scored a goal.

The amazing **MARTIN ST. LOUIS**, just 5'8", won the Hart and Art Ross Trophies as well this season.

RUSLAN FEDOTENKO scored two of his three goals in these finals when it mattered most—game seven of the Stanley Cup finals. He took the Cup to Kiev in the summer.

DAVE ANDREYCHUK won his first Cup at the end of this his 22nd season and having played more than 1,700 NHL games.

DAN BOYLE came from Florida in 2002 for nothing more than a draft choice.

Formerly the youngest captain in league history, **VINCENT LECAVALIER** established a presence on offense while adding muscle and grit to the lineup.

FREDRIK MODIN scored his only goal of the finals in game five when he tied the score 2-2 early in the third period.

CORY STILLMAN worked out in the off season with future Hall of Famer Scott Stevens at their cottages on Lake Catchacoma, near Peterborough, Ontario.

A hulking defenceman, **JASSEN CULLIMORE** has been with the Lightning since the '97-'98 season.

Ironically, left winger **CHRIS DINGMAN** was originally a Calgary draft choice a decade ago.

Forward **TIM TAYLOR** did not miss a game—regular season or playoffs—for the Lightning this season, 105 in all.

MARTIN CIBAK took the Cup from Pavel Kubina and drove it to Liptovsky Mikulas, Slovakia, his hometown.

Tough guy **ANDRE ROY** has his name on the Cup where thousands of NHLers before him never made it as far.

Defenceman **CORY SARICH** has been a member of the Lightning for five seasons.

PAVEL KUBINA took the Cup to Janovice, Czech Republic, a small town of 1,700 where he grew up.

DIMITRY AFANASENKOV took the Cup home to Arkhangelsk, Russia, where he took it to the mayor's office.

BRAD LUKOWICH won his first Cup with Dallas in 1998-1999 on a more defensive-minded team.

NOLAN PRATT was a big defensive defenceman who didn't get superstar accolades for his outstanding play.

NIKOLAI KHABIBULIN made the biggest save of the playoffs in the dying minutes of game seven, going post-to-post to rob defenceman Jordan Leopold.

DARRYL SYDOR came to Tampa in the off-season, bringing with him his experience of a Dallas Cup win in 1999.

Winger **BEN CLYMER** played most of the regular season with the team but just five times in the playoffs.

Tampa Bay's on-ice team portrait—the engraving for this year will be made sometime in November 2004.

SHANE WILLIS played only 12 time sin the regular season and not at all in the playoffs.

STAN NECKAR didn't play at all in the regular season but appeared twice in the playoffs.

ERIC PERRIN played 12 times in the playoffs, but not at all in the finals.

DARREN RUMBLE appeared five times in the regular season as a callup and not at all in the playoffs for the Lightning.

Backup goalie **JOHN GRAHAME** had a fine 18-9-1 record and 2.06 GAA in the regular season but filled in for Nikolai Khabibulin for only 33 minutes in the playoffs.

Some critics said that **JOHN TORTORELLA** did everything wrong in handling his players, but there's no better way to make players happy than to win the Cup.

CRAIG RAMSAY was a mainstay on the Buffalo blueline in the 1970s, but he never won a Cup until this hot night in Florida.

BILL BARBER, director of player personnel, displayed the Cup in Callander, Ontario, on Lake Nipissing.

JAY FEASTER worked for four years as assistant GM of the Lightning before becoming the head man in the summer of 2002.

Head pro scout **RICK PATERSON** took the Cup home to Kingston where he celebrated with hundreds of well wishers.

Assistant coach **JEFF REESE** was a former goalie who still holds the NHL record with three assists in a single game.

Owner **WILLIAM DAVIDSON** is a native of Detroit and bought the NBA's Pistons in 1974.

TOM WILSON became the team's CEO when Palace Sports & Entertainment took control of the Lightning in 1999.

President **RON CAMPBELL** is responsible for the daily operations of the building and team.

ERIC LAWSON was the team's strength and conditioning coach, and **TOM MULLIGAN** and **ADAM RAMBO** were Tampa Bay's trainers during their Cup season.

JAKE GOERTZEN became the team's head of scouting in 2000, though he goes back to day one of the franchise.

DR. IRA GUTTENTAG has been the team's medical director since 2002.

MIKE GRIEBEL was the team's massage therapist and **RAY THILL** and **DANA HEINZE** were equipment managers.

JIM PICKARD, who has his name on the Cup from his days as equipment manager for the Islanders during their dynastic 1980s, is an assistant to Thill in Tampa.

DANA HEINZE is the team's other assistant equipment manager.

A Winnipegger, **NIGEL KIRWAN** has worked with the Lightning for 12 years, a Tampa Bay original.

Other players to appear for Tampa Bay this season: **ALEXANDER SVITOV**

Stanley Cup Heroes

Although the Stanley Cup playoffs now last about two months, there are only two league trophies associated with them: the Stanley Cup itself and the Conn Smythe trophy, awarded to the best performer in the playoffs. What if there were two other trophies, one for the player who scores the Cup-winning goal and one for the player who has the most points in the playoffs? Named here for Bobby Orr, the legendary defenceman who scored arguably the most spectacular Cup-winning goal, in 1970, and for Gordie Howe, who played 32 years of professional hockey and led the NHL playoffs in scoring six times, this list shows that the winners of these two new trophies would almost never be the Conn Smythe winner. In other words, the Orr and Howe Trophies would highlight other heroes from the Stanley Cup who could be commemorated without merely duplicating the Conn Smythe winner.

Year	Stanley Cup	Conn Smythe	Orr Trophy	Howe Trophy
1918	Arenas		Corb Denneny	Alf Skinner
1919	no winner		none	Newsy Lalonde
1920	Ottawa		Jack Darragh	Frank Nighbor*
1921	Ottawa		Jack Darragh	Cy Denneny
1922	St. Pats		Babe Dye	Babe Dye
1923	Ottawa		Punch Broadbent	Punch Broadbent
1924	Canadiens		Howie Morenz	Howie Morenz
1925	Victoria		Cecil Hart	Howie Morenz
1926	Maroons		Nels Stewart	Nels Stewart
1927	Ottawa		Cy Denneny	Harry Oliver*
1928	Rangers		Frank Boucher	Frank Boucher
1929	Boston		Bill Carson	Andy Blair* Butch Keeling*
1930	Canadiens		Howie Morenz	Marty Barry*
1931	Canadiens		Johnny Gagnon	Cooney Weiland
1932	Toronto		Ace Bailey	Frank Boucher
1933	Rangers		Bill Cook	Cecil Dillon
1934	Chicago		Mush March	Larry Aurie
1935	Maroons		Baldy Northcott	Baldy Northcott*
1936	Detroit		Pete Kelly	Buzz Boll
1937	Detroit		Marty Barry	Marty Barry
1938	Chicago		Carl Voss	Johnny Gottselig
1939	Boston		Roy Conacher	Bill Cowley
1940	Rangers		Bryan Hextall	Phil Watson*
1941	Boston		Bobby Bauer	Milt Schmidt
1942	Toronto		Pete Langelle	Don Grosso
1943	Detroit		Joe Carveth	Carl Liscombe
1944	Canadiens		Toe Blake	Toe Blake
1945	Toronto		Babe Pratt	Joe Carveth
1946	Canadiens		Toe Blake	Elmer Lach
1947	Toronto		Ted Kennedy	Maurice Richard
1948	Toronto		Harry Watson	Ted Kennedy
1949	Toronto		Cal Gardner	Gordie Howe
1950	Detroit		Pete Babando	Pentti Lund
1951	Toronto		Bill Barilko	Maurice Richard*
1952	Detroit		Metro Prystai	Ted Lindsay*
1953	Canadiens		Elmer Lach	Ed Sandford
1954	Detroit		Tony Leswick	Dickie Moore
1955	Detroit		Gordie Howe	Gordie Howe
1956	Canadiens		Maurice Richard	Jean Beliveau
1957	Canadiens		Dickie Moore	Bernie Geoffrion
1958	Canadiens		Bernie Geoffrion	Fleming Mackell
1959	Canadiens		Marcel Bonin	Dickie Moore
1960	Canadiens		Jean Beliveau	Henri Richard*
1961	Chicago		Ab McDonald	Gordie Howe*
1962	Toronto		Dick Duff	Stan Mikita
1963	Toronto		Eddie Shack	Gordie Howe*
1964	Toronto		Andy Bathgate	Gordie Howe
1965	Canadiens		Jean Beliveau	Bobby Hull
1966	Canadiens	Roger Crozier	Henri Richard	Norm Ullman
1967	Toronto	Dave Keon	Jim Pappin	Jim Pappin
1968	Canadiens	Glenn Hall	J.C. Tremblay	Bill Goldsworthy
1969	Canadiens	Serge Savard	John Ferguson	Phil Esposito
1970	Boston	Bobby Orr	Bobby Orr	Phil Esposito
1971	Canadiens	Ken Dryden	Henri Richard	Frank Mahovlich
1972	Boston	Bobby Orr	Bobby Orr	Phil Esposito*
1973	Canadiens	Yvan Cournoyer	Yvan Cournoyer	Yvan Cournoyer
1974	Philadelphia	Bernie Parent	Rick MacLeish	Rick MacLeish
1975	Philadelphia	Bernie Parent	Bob Kelly	Rick MacLeish
1976	Canadiens	Reggie Leach	Guy Lafleur	Reggie Leach
1977	Canadiens	Guy Lafleur	Jacques Lemaire	Guy Lafleur
1978	Canadiens	Larry Robinson	Mario Tremblay	Guy Lafleur*
1979	Canadiens	Bob Gainey	Jacques Lemaire	Jacques Lemaire*
1980	Islanders	Bryan Trottier	Bob Nystrom	Bryan Trottier
1981	Islanders	Butch Goring	Wayne Merrick	Mike Bossy
1982	Islanders	Mike Bossy	Mike Bossy	Bryan Trottier
1983	Islanders	Billy Smith	Mike Bossy	Wayne Gretzky
1984	Edmonton	Mark Messier	Ken Linseman	Wayne Gretzky
1985	Edmonton	Wayne Gretzky	Paul Coffey	Wayne Gretzky
1986	Canadiens	Patrick Roy	Bobby Smith	Doug Gilmour*
1987	Edmonton	Ron Hextall	Jari Kurri	Wayne Gretzky
1988	Edmonton	Wayne Gretzky	Wayne Gretzky	Wayne Gretzky
1989	Calgary	Al MacInnis	Doug Gilmour	Al MacInnis
1990	Edmonton	Bill Ranford	Craig Simpson	Craig Simpson*
1991	Pittsburgh	Mario Lemieux	Ulf Samuelsson	Mario Lemieux
1992	Pittsburgh	Mario Lemieux	Ron Francis	Mario Lemieux
1993	Canadiens	Patrick Roy	Kirk Muller	Wayne Gretzky
1994	Rangers	Brian Leetch	Mark Messier	Brian Leetch
1995	New Jersey	Claude Lemieux	Sergei Brylin	Sergei Fedorov
1996	Colorado	Joe Sakic	Uwe Krupp	Joe Sakic
1997	Detroit	Mike Vernon	Darren McCarty	Eric Lindros
1998	Detroit	Steve Yzerman	Martin Lapointe	Steve Yzerman
1999	Dallas	Joe Nieuwendyk	Brett Hull	Peter Forsberg
2000	New Jersey	Scott Stevens	Jason Arnott	Brett Hull
2001	Colorado	Patrick Roy	Alex Tanguay	Joe Sakic
2002	Detroit	Nicklas Lidstrom	Brendan Shanahan	Peter Forsberg
2003	New Jersey	J-S Giguere	Mike Rupp	J. Langenbrunner
2004	Tampa Bay	Brad Richards	Ruslan Fedotenko	Brad Richards

* tied with others, but would win based on greater number of goals scored

the names

All names as they appear on the Stanley Cup and its various parts

This alphabetical list shows all the names stamped on the Stanley Cup. The person's name as he is most commonly called appears in the first column, followed by the exact spelling of how the name appears on the Cup, followed by any other information about the person that is engraved (scout, doctor, vice-president, etc.) followed by a reference to which Cup the name appears in that form.

THE STANLEY CUP

- **ib** inside original bowl
- **or** original base
- **sp** stovepipe (1930-31 to 1944-45)
- **re** redesign (1945-46 to 1955-56)
- **ret** retired band (1928-29 to 1939-40)
- **ab** abandoned band (1978-79 to 1990-91)
- **rep** replica Stanley Cup
- **sc** Presentation Stanley Cup

TEAM ABBREVIATIONS

- **AAA** Montreal AAA
- **BB** Boston Bruins
- **CAL** Calgary Flames
- **CHI** Chicago Black Hawks
- **COL** Colorado Avalanche
- **DAL** Dallas Stars
- **DET** Detroit Red Wings
- **EDM** Edmonton Oilers
- **KEN** Kenora Thistles
- **MC** Montreal Canadiens
- **MM** Montreal Maroons
- **MW** Montreal Wanderers
- **NJ** New Jersey Devils
- **NYR** New York Rangers
- **NYI** New York Islanders
- **OTT** Ottawa Senators
- **PHI** Philadelphia Flyers
- **PIT** Pittsburgh Penguins
- **TA** Toronto Arenas
- **TSP** Toronto St. Pats
- **TML** Toronto Maple Leafs
- **VIC** Victoria Cougars
- **VM** Vancouver Millionaires

NOTE: An underlined letter means it has an imperfection of some sort on the Cup. A slash (/) indicates a line break on the Cup.

NAME	YEAR TEAM	EXACT CUP SPELLING
Abasto, Alex	1994-95 NJ	ALEX ABASTO (rep)
	1994-95 NJ	ALEX ABASTO (sc)
	2002-03 NJ	A. ABASTO (rep)
	2002-03 NJ	A. ABASTO (sc)
Abbott, Tim	1996-97 DET	TIM ABBOTT (rep)
	1996-97 DET	TIM ABBOTT (sc)
	1997-98 DET	TIM ABBOTT (rep)
	1997-98 DET	TIM ABBOTT (sc)
Abel, Clarence "Taffy"	1927-28 NYR	C. ABEL (sp)
	1927-28 NYR	C ABEL (ret)
	1933-34 CHI	CLARENCE ABEL (sp)
	1933-34 CHI	TAFFY ABEL (ret)
	1933-34 CHI	TAFFY ABEL (sc)
Abel, Sid	1942-43 DET	SID ABEL CAPTAIN (sp)
	1942-43 DET	SID ABEL CAPTAIN (rep)
	1942-43 DET	SID ABEL CAPTAIN (sc)
	1949-50 DET	SID ABEL CAPTAIN (re)
	1949-50 DET	SID ABEL CAPTAIN (rep)
	1949-50 DET	SID ABEL CAPTAIN (sc)
	1951-52 DET	SID ABEL — CAPTAIN (re)
	1951-52 DET	SID ABEL CAPTAIN (rep)
	1951-52 DET	SID ABEL CAPTAIN (sc)
Acton, Keith	1987-88 EDM	K. ACTON (ab)
	1987-88 EDM	K. ACTON (rep)
	1987-88 EDM	K. ACTON (sc)
Adams, Charles	1928-29 BB	CHARLES F. ADAMS PRES. (or)
	1928-29 BB	CHARLES F. ADAMS PRES. (rep)
	1928-29 BB	CHARLES F. ADAMS PRES (sc)
Adams, Jack	1935-36 DET	JACK ADAMS MANAGER (sp)
	1935-36 DET	JACK ADAMS MAN CUACH (ret)
	1936-37 DET	JACK ADAMS MANAGER (sp)
	1936-37 DET	JACK ADAMS (MAN COACH) (ret)
	1942-43 DET	JACK ADAMS MANAGER (sp)
	1942-43 DET	JACK ADAMS MANAGER (rep)
	1942-43 DET	JACK ADAMS MANAGER (sc)
	1949-50 DET	JACK ADAMS MANAGER (re)
	1949-50 DET	JACK ADAMS MANAGER (rep)
	1949-50 DET	JACK ADAMS MANAGER (sc)
	1951-52 DET	JACK ADAMS - GENERAL MANAGER (re)
	1951-52 DET	JACK ADAMS GEN. MANAGER (rep)
	1951-52 DET	JACK ADAMS GEN MANAGER (sc)
	1953-54 DET	JACK ADAMS, GENERAL MANAGER (re)
	1953-54 DET	JACK ADAMS GEN. MANAGER (rep)
	1953-54 DET	JACK ADAMS GEN MANAGER (sc)
	1954-55 DET	JACK ADAMS, GENERAL MANAGER (re)
	1954-55 DET	JACK ADAMS GEN. MANAGER (rep)
	1954-55 DET	JACK ADAMS GEN MANAGER (sc)
Adams, John	1926-27 OTT	JOHN J. ADAMS (or)
	1926-27 OTT	JOHN J. ADAMS (rep)
	1926-27 OTT	JOHN J. ADAMS (sc)
Adams, John	1969-70 BB	J. ADAMS (rep)
	1969-70 BB	J ADAMS (sc)
Adams, Weston	1938-39 BB	WESTON W. ADAMS / PRESIDENT (sp)
	1938-39 BB	WESTON W ADAMS PRESIDENT (ret)
	1940-41 BB	WESTON W. ADAMS, PRESIDENT (sp)
	1940-41 BB	WESTON W. ADAMS PRES. (rep)
	1940-41 BB	WESTON W. ADAMS (PRESS) (sc)
	1969-70 BB	WESTON W. ADAMS SR. CHAIRMAN (rep)
	1969-70 BB	WESTON W ADAMS SR CHAIRMAN (sc)
	1971-72 BB	WESTON W. ADAMS CHAIRMAN OF BOARD (rep)
	1971-72 BB	WESTON W. ADAMS CHAIRMAN OF BOARD (sc)
Adams, Weston Jr.	1969-70 BB	WESTON W. ADAMS JR. PRESIDENT (rep)
	1969-70 BB	WESTON W ADAMS JR PRESIDENT (sc)
	1971-72 BB	WESTON W. ADAMS JR. PRESIDENT (rep)
	1971-72 BB	WESTON W. ADAMS JR. PRESIDENT (sc)
Aebischer, David	2000-01 COL	DAVID AEBISCHER (rep)
	2000-01 COL	DAVID AEBISCHER (sc)
Ahearn, Frank	1926-27 OTT	T.F. AHEARN PRESIDENT (or)
	1926-27 OTT	T.F. AHEARN PRESIDENT (rep)
	1926-27 OTT	T.F. AHEARN PRESIDENT (sc)
Ahern, Bob	1907 MW	BOB. AHERN. (ib)
	1907 MW	BOB AHERN (rep)
	1907 MW	BOB AHERN (sc)
Aitkenhead, Andy	1932-33 NYR	ANDREW AITKENHEAD (sp)
	1932-33 NYR	ANDREW AITKENHEAD (ret)
Aird, Sir John	1931-32 TML	SIR JOHN AIRD (sp)
Albelin, Tommy	1994-95 NJ	TOMMY ALBELIN (rep)
	1994-95 NJ	TOMMY ALBELIN (sc)
	2002-03 NJ	TOMMY ALBELIN (rep)
	2002-03 NJ	TOMMY ALBELIN (sc)
Allaire, Francois	1992-93 MC	FRANCOIS ALLAIRE A. COACH (rep)
	1992-93 MC	FRANCOIS ALLAIRE A. COACH (sc)
Allen, Keith	1953-54 DET	KEITH ALLEN (re)
	1953-54 DET	KEITH ALLEN (rep)
	1953-54 DET	KEITH ALLEN (sc)
	1973-74 PHI	KEITH ALLEN VICE PRES. & GEN. MGR. (rep)
	1973-74 PHI	KEITH ALLEN VICE PRES. & GEN. MGR. (sc)
	1974-75 PHI	KEITH ALLEN VICE PRES. & GEN. MGR. (rep)
	1974-75 PHI	KEITH ALLEN VICE PRES. & GEN. MGR. (sc)
Allen, Skip	1995-96 COL	SKIP ALLEN (rep)
	1995-96 COL	SKIP ALLEN (sc)
Anderson, Glenn	1983-84 EDM	G. ANDERSON (ab)
	1983-84 EDM	G. ANDERSON (rep)
	1983-84 EDM	G. ANDERSON (sc)
	1984-85 EDM	G. ANDERSON (ab)
	1984-85 EDM	G. ANDERSON (rep)
	1984-85 EDM	G. ANDERSON (sc)

Name	Season	Team	Engraving
	1986-87	EDM	G. ANDERSON (ab)
	1986-87	EDM	G. ANDERSON (rep)
	1986-87	EDM	G. ANDERSON (sc)
	1987-88	EDM	G. ANDERSON (ab)
	1987-88	EDM	G. ANDERSON (rep)
	1987-88	EDM	G. ANDERSON (sc)
	1989-90	EDM	G. ANDERSON (ab)
	1989-90	EDM	G. ANDERSON (rep)
	1989-90	EDM	G. ANDERSON (sc)
	1993-94	NYR	G. ANDERSON (rep)
	1993-94	NYR	G. ANDERSON (sc)
Anderson,	1924-25	VIC	J. ANDERSON. (or)
Jocko	1924-25	VIC	J. ANDERSON (rep)
	1924-25	VIC	J. ANDERSON. (sc)
Anderson,	1966-67	TML	JOHN ANDERSEN BUSINESS MGR. (rep)
John	1966-67	TML	JOHN ANDERSON BUISS MANN (sc)
Andersson,	1996-97	DET	HAKAN ANDERSSON (rep)
Hakan	1996-97	DET	HAKAN ANDERSSON (sc)
	1997-98	DET	HAKAN ANDERSSON (rep)
	1997-98	DET	HAKAN ANDERSSON (sc)
	2001-02	DET	HAKAN ANDERSSON (rep)
	2001-02	DET	HAKAN ANDERSSON (sc)
Apps, Syl	1941-42	TML	SYL APPS. CAPT. (sp)
	1941-42	TML	SYL APPS CAPT. (rep)
	1941-42	TML	SYL APPS (CAPT) (sc)
	1946-47	TML	SYLVANUS APPS CAPTAIN (re)
	1946-47	TML	SYL APPS CAPTAIN (rep)
	1946-47	TML	SYL APPS CAPTAIN (sc)
	1947-48	TML	SYLVANUS APPS — CAPTAIN (re)
	1947-48	TML	SYL APPS CAPT. (rep)
	1947-48	TML	SYL APPS CAPT (sc)
Arbour, Al	1953-54	DET	ALGER ARBOUR (re)
	1953-54	DET	ALGER ARBOUR (rep)
	1953-54	DET	ALGER ARBOUR (sc)
	1960-61	CHI	AL ARBOUR (rep)
	1960-61	CHI	ALGER ARBOUR (sc)
	1961-62	TML	ALGER ARBOUR (rep)
	1961-62	TML	ALGER ARBOUR (sc)
	1979-80	NYI	ALGER J. ARBOUR COACH (ab)
	1979-80	NYI	ALGER J. ARBOUR COACH (rep)
	1979-80	NYI	ALGER J. ARBOUR COACH (sc)
	1980-81	NYI	AL ARBOUR COACH (ab)
	1980-81	NYI	AL ARBOUR COACH (rep)
	1980-81	NYI	AL ARBOUR COACH (sc)
	1981-82	NYI	AL ARBOUR COACH (ab)
	1981-82	NYI	AL ARBOUR COACH (rep)
	1981-82	NYI	AL ARBOUR COACH (sc)
	1982-83	NYI	AL ARBOUR COACH (ab)
	1982-83	NYI	AL ARBOUR COACH (rep)
	1982-83	NYI	AL ARBOUR COACH (sc)
Armstrong,	1998-99	DAL	DOUG ARMSTRONG (rep)
Doug	1998-99	DAL	DOUG ARMSTRONG (sc)
Armstrong,	1961-62	TML	GEORGE ARMSTRONG CAPTAIN (rep)
George	1961-62	TML	GEORGE ARMSTRONG CAPTAIN (sc)
	1962-63	TML	G. ARMSTRONG CAPTAIN (rep)
	1962-63	TML	G ARMSTRONG CAPTAIN (sc)
	1963-64	TML	G. ARMSTRONG CAPT. (rep)
	1963-64	TML	G ARMSTROG CAPT (sc)
	1966-67	TML	G. ARMSTRONG CAPTAIN (rep)
	1966-67	TML	G ARMSTRONG CAPTAIN (sc)
Arnold,	1925-26	MM	T. ARNOLD. (Vice-Pres.) (or)
Thomas	1925-26	MM	T. ARNOLD (VICE-PRES) (rep)
	1925-26	MM	T. ARNOLD. (Vice-Pres) (sc)
	1934-35	MM	THOMAS ARNOLD (sp)
	1934-35	MM	THOMAS ARNOLD (ret)
Arnott,	1999-00	NJ	JASON ARNOTT (rep)
Jason	1999-00	NJ	JASON ARNOTT (sc)
Ashbee,	1973-74	PHI	BARRY ASHBEE (rep)
Barry	1973-74	PHI	BARRY ASHBEE (sc)
	1974-75	PHI	BARRY ASHBEE ASST. COACH (rep)
	1974-75	PHI	BARRY ASHBEE AS. COA. (sc)
Asmundson,	1932-33	NYR	OSCAR ASMUNDSON (sp)
Ossie	1932-33	NYR	OSCAR ASMUNDSON (ret)
Aubut,	1956-57	MC	LARRY AUBUT TRAINERS* (rep)
Larry	1956-57	MC	LARRY AUBUT TRAINER'S* (sc)
			* refers also to Hector Dubois
	1957-58	MC	L. AUBUT TRAINER (rep)
	1957-58	MC	L AUBUT TRAINER (sc)
	1958-59	MC	LARRY AUBUT TRAINERS* (rep)
	1958-59	MC	LARRY AUBUT TRAINERS* (sc)
			* refers also to Hector Dubois
	1959-60	MC	LARRY AUBUT TRAINER (rep)
	1959-60	MC	LARRY AUBUT TRAINER (sc)
	1964-65	MC	LARRY AUBUT ASST. TRAINER (rep)
	1964-65	MC	LARRY AUBUT ASST TRAINER (sc)
	1965-66	MC	LARRY AUBUT ASST. TRAINER (rep)
	1965-66	MC	LARRY AUBUT ASST TRAINER (sc)
	1967-68	MC	L. AUBUT TR. (rep)
	1967-68	MC	L•AUBUT TRAINER• (sc)
	1968-69	MC	L. AUBUT TRAINER (rep)
	1968-69	MC	L AUBUT TRAINER (sc)
Aurie, Larry	1935-36	DET	LARRY AURIE R.WING (sp)
	1935-36	DET	LARRY AURIE (ret)
	1936-37	DET	LARRY AURIE R.WING (sp)
	1936-37	DET	LARRY AURIE (ret)
Awrey, Don	1969-70	BB	DON AWREY (rep)
	1969-70	BB	DON AWREY (sc)
	1971-72	BB	DON AWREY (rep)
	1971-72	BB	DON AWREY (sc)

Name	Season	Team	Engraving
Babando,	1949-50	DET	PETE BABANDO (re)
Pete	1949-50	DET	PETE BABANDO (rep)
	1949-50	DET	PETE BABANDO (sc)
Backor,	1944-45	TML	PETE BACKOR (sp)
Pete	1944-45	TML	PETE BACKOR (rep)
	1944-45	TML	PETE BACKOR (sc)
Backstrom,	1958-59	MC	R. BACKSTROM (rep)
Ralph	1958-59	MC	R BACKSTROM (sc)
	1959-60	MC	RALPH BACKSTROM (rep)
	1959-60	MC	RALPH BACKSTROM (sc)
	1964-65	MC	RALPH BACKSTROM (rep)
	1964-65	MC	RALPH BACKSTROM (sc)
	1965-66	MC	R. BACKSTROM (rep)
	1965-66	MC	R BACKSTROM (sc)
	1967-68	MC	R. BACKSTROM (rep)
	1967-68	MC	R•BACKSTROM (sc)
	1968-69	MC	R. BACKSTROM (rep)
	1968-69	MC	R BACKSTROM (sc)
Bailey,	1969-70	BB	G. BAILEY (rep)
Garnet "Ace"	1969-70	BB	G BAILEY (sc)
	1971-72	BB	GARNET BAILEY (rep)
	1971-72	BB	GARNET BAILEY (sc)
	1984-85	EDM	G. BAILEY (ab)
	1984-85	EDM	G. BAILEY (rep)
	1984-85	EDM	G. BAILEY (sc)
	1986-87	EDM	G. BAILEY (ab)
	1986-87	EDM	G. BAILEY (rep)
	1986-87	EDM	G. BAILEY (sc)
	1989-90	EDM	ACE BAILEY (ab)
	1989-90	EDM	ACE BAILEY (rep)
	1989-90	EDM	ACE BAILEY (sc)
Bailey,	1931-32	TML	I. BAILEY (sp)
Irvine "Ace"	1931-32	TML	A BAILEY (ret)
Baldwin,	1991-92	PIT	HOWARD BALDWIN (rep)
Howard	1991-92	PIT	HOWARD BALDWIN (sc)
Balfour,	1960-61	CHI	EARL BALFOUR (rep)
Earl	1960-61	CHI	EARL BALFOUR (sc)
Balfour,	1960-61	CHI	MURRAY BALFOUR (rep)
Murray	1960-61	CHI	MURRAY BALFOUR (sc)
Ballard,	1961-62	TML	H.E. BALLARD EX.V.P. (rep)
Harold	1961-62	TML	H E BALLARD EX-VICE PRESS (sc)
	1962-63	TML	H.E. BALLARD EX.V.P. (rep)
	1962-63	TML	H E BALLARD EX VICE PRESS (sc)
	1963-64	TML	H.E. BALLARD EX. VICE PRES. (rep)
	1963-64	TML	H E BALLARD EX VICE PRESS (sc)
	1966-67	TML	H.E. BALLARD EXEC.V.P. (rep)
	1966-67	TML	H E BALLARD EX VICE PRESS (sc)
Balon, Dave	1964-65	MC	DAVID BALON (rep)
	1964-65	MC	DAVID BALON (sc)
	1965-66	MC	D. BALON (rep)
	1965-66	MC	D BALON (sc)
Barber, Bill	1973-74	PHI	BILL BARBER (rep)
	1973-74	PHI	BILL BARBER (sc)
	1974-75	PHI	BILL BARBER (rep)
	1974-75	PHI	BILL BARBER (sc)
Barilko, Bill	1946-47	TML	WILLIAM BARILKO (re)
	1946-47	TML	WILLIAM BARILKO (rep)
	1946-47	TML	WILLIAM BARILKO (sc)
	1947-48	TML	WILLIAM BARILKO (re)
	1947-48	TML	BILL BARILKO (rep)
	1947-48	TML	BILL BARILKO (sc)
	1948-49	TML	WILLIAM BARILKO (re)
	1948-49	TML	BILL BARILKO (rep)
	1948-49	TML	BILL BARILKO (sc)
	1950-51	TML	WILLIAM BARILKO (re)
	1950-51	TML	BILL BARILKO (rep)
	1950-51	TML	BILL BARILKO (sc)
Barrasso,	1990-91	PIT	T. BARRASSO (ab)
Tom	1990-91	PIT	T. BARRASSO (rep)
	1990-91	PIT	T. BARRASSO (sc)
	1991-92	PIT	TOM BARRASSO (rep)
	1991-92	PIT	TOM BARRASSO (sc)
Barry, Marty	1935-36	DET	MARTIN BARRY — CENTER (sp)
	1935-36	DET	MARTIN BARRY (ret)
	1936-37	DET	MARTIN BARRY CENTER (sp)
	1936-37	DET	MARTIN BARRY (ret)
Bassett,	1961-62	TML	JOHN BASSETT VICE PRES. (rep)
John	1961-62	TML	JOHN BASSETT VICE PRESS (sc)
	1962-63	TML	JOHN BASSETT CHAIRMAN OF BOARD (rep)
	1962-63	TML	JOHN BASSETT BOARD CHAIRM (sc)
	1963-64	TML	JOHN BASSETT CHAIRMAN OF BOARD (rep)
	1963-64	TML	JOHN BASSETT BOARD CHAIRM (sc)

Name	Season	Team	Engraving
	1966-67	TML	JOHN BASSETT CHAIRMAN (rep)
	1966-67	TML	JOHN BASSETT BOARD CHAIRM (sc)
Bathgate, Andy	1963-64	TML	ANDREW BATHGATE (rep)
	1963-64	TML	ANDREW BATHGATE (sc)
Bauer, Bobby	1938-39	BB	R. BAUER (sp)
	1938-39	BB	R BAUER (ret)
	1940-41	BB	ROBERT BAUER. (sp)
	1940-41	BB	BOBBY BAUER (rep)
	1940-41	BB	BOBBY BAUER (sc)
Baum, Werner	1989-90	EDM	WERNER BAUM (ab)
	1989-90	EDM	WERNER BAUM (rep)
	1989-90	EDM	WERNER BAUM (sc)
Baun, Bobby	1961-62	TML	ROBERT BAUN (rep)
	1961-62	TML	ROBERT BAUN (sc)
	1962-63	TML	ROBERT BAUN (rep)
	1962-63	TML	ROBERT BAUN (sc)
	1963-64	TML	ROBERT BAUN (rep)
	1963-64	TML	ROBERT BAUN (sc)
	1966-67	TML	BOB BAUN (rep)
	1966-67	TML	BOB BAUN (sc)
Beard, Nancy	2001-02	DET	NANCY BEARD (rep)
	2001-02	DET	NANCY BEARD (sc)
Bedard, Jim	1997-98	DET	JIM BEDARD (rep)
	1997-98	DET	JIM BEDARD (sc)
	2001-02	DET	JIM BEDARD (rep
	2001-02	DET	JIM BEDARD (sc)
Belanger, Jesse	1992-93	MC	J. BELANGER (rep)
	1992-93	MC	J. BÉLANGER (sc)
Belanger, Yves	1970-71	MC	TRAINER Y. BELANGER (rep)
	1970-71	MC	TRAIN. Y. BELANGER (sc)
	1985-86	MC	Y. BÉLANGER PHYSIO. (ab)
	1985-86	MC	Y. BÉLANGER PHYSIO. (rep)
	1985-86	MC	Y. BELANGER PHYSIO. (sc)
Belfour, Ed	1998-99	DAL	ED BELFOUR (rep)
	1998-99	DAL	ED BELFOUR (sc)
Belisle, Dan	1996-97	DET	DAN BELISLE (rep)
	1996-97	DET	DAN BELISLE (sc)
	1997-98	DET	DAN BELISLE (rep)
	1997-98	DET	DAN BELISLE (sc)
	2001-02	DET	DAN BELISLE (rep)
	2001-02	DET	DAN BELISLE (sc)
Beliveau, Jean	1955-56	MC	J. BELIVEAU (re)
	1955-56	MC	J. BELIVEAU (rep)
	1955-56	MC	J BELIVEAU (sc)
	1956-57	MC	JEAN BELIVEAU (rep)
	1956-57	MC	JEAN BELIVEAU (sc)
	1957-58	MC	JEAN BELIVEAU (rep)
	1957-58	MC	JEAN BELIVEAU (sc)
	1958-59	MC	J. BELIVEAU (rep)
	1958-59	MC	J BELIVEAU (sc)
	1959-60	MC	J. BELIVEAU (rep)
	1959-60	MC	J BELIVEAU (sc)
	1964-65	MC	JEAN BELIVEAU CAPTAIN (rep)
	1964-65	MC	IEAN BELIVEAU CAPTAIN (sc)
	1965-66	MC	J. BELIVEAU CAPT. (rep)
	1965-66	MC	J BELIVEAU CAP (sc)
	1967-68	MC	J. BELIVEAU CAPT. (rep)
	1967-68	MC	J BELIVEAU CAPT (sc)
	1968-69	MC	J. BELIVEAU CAPT. (rep)
	1968-69	MC	J BELIVEAU CAPT (sc)
	1970-71	MC	JEAN BELIVEAU (rep)
	1970-71	MC	JEAN BELIVEAU. (sc)
	1972-73	MC	JEAN BELIVEAU V.P. (rep)
	1972-73	MC	JEAN BELIVEAU•V.P. (sc)
	1975-76	MC	JEAN BELIVEAU V.P. (rep)
	1975-76	MC	JEAN BELIVEAU V.P. (sc)
	1976-77	MC	JEAN BELIVEAU V.P. & D.C.R. (rep)
	1976-77	MC	JEAN BELIVEAU V.P. & D.C.R. (sc)
	1977-78	MC	JEAN BELIVEAU V.P. & D.C.R. (rep)
	1977-78	MC	JEAN BELIVEAU V.P. & D.C.R (sc)
	1978-79	MC	JEAN BELIVEAU V.P.C.A. (ab)
	1978-79	MC	JEAN BELIVEAU V.P.C.A. (rep)
	1978-79	MC	JEAN BELIVEAU V.P.C.A. (sc)
	1985-86	MC	J. BÉLIVEAU (ab)
	1985-86	MC	J. BÉLIVEAU (rep)
	1985-86	MC	J. BELIVEAU (sc)
	1992-93	MC	JEAN BELIVEAU SR.V.P. (rep)
	1992-93	MC	JEAN BÉLIVEAU SR.V.P. (sc)
Bell, Billy	1923-24	MC	B. BELL (or)
	1923-24	MC	B. BELL (rep)
	1923-24	MC	B. BELL (sc)
Bellows, Brian	1992-93	MC	B. BELLOWS (rep)
	1992-93	MC	B. BELLOWS (sc)
Belzberg, Morris	1991-92	PIT	MORRIS BELZBERG (rep)
	1991-92	PIT	MORRIS BELZBERG (sc)
Benedict, Clint	1925-26	MM	C. BENEDICT. (or)
	1925-26	MM	C. BENEDICT (rep)
	1925-26	MM	C. BENEDICT (sc)
Bennett, Darwin	1993-94	NYR	D. BENNETT SCOUT (rep)
	1993-94	NYR	D. BENNETT SCOUT (sc)
Benoit, Joe	1945-46	MC	JOSEPH BENOIT (re)
	1945-46	MC	JOE BENOIT (rep)
	1945-46	MC	J. BENOIT (sc)
Bentley, Max	1947-48	TML	MAX BENTLEY (re)
	1947-48	TML	MAX BENTLEY (rep)
	1947-48	TML	MAX BENTLEY (sc)
	1948-49	TML	MAX BENTLEY (re)
	1948-49	TML	MAX BENTLEY (rep)
	1948-49	TML	MAX BENTLEY (sc)
	1950-51	TML	MAX BENTLEY (re)
	1950-51	TML	MAX BENTLEY (rep)
	1950-51	TML	MAX BENTLEY (sc)
Berenson, Gordon "Red"	1964-65	MC	GORDON BERENSON (rep)
	1964-65	MC	GORDON BERENSON (sc)
Bernhardt, Tim	1998-99	DAL	TIM BERNHARDT (rep)
	1998-99	DAL	TIM BERNHARDT (sc)
Bettez, Gaston	1952-53	MC	GOSTON BETTES — TRAINER (re)
	1952-53	MC	G. BETTES TR. (rep)
	1952-53	MC	G BETTES (TR) (sc)
	1955-56	MC	G. BETTEZ (re)
	1955-56	MC	G. BETTEX (rep)
	1955-56	MC	G BETTEX (sc)
Beukeboom, Jeff	1986-87	EDM	J. BEUKEBOOM (ab)
	1986-87	EDM	J. BEUKEBOOM (rep)
	1986-87	EDM	J. BEUKEBOOM (sc)
	1987-88	EDM	J. BEUKEBOOM (ab)
	1987-88	EDM	J. BEUKEBOOM (rep)
	1987-88	EDM	J. BEUKEBOOM (sc)
	1989-90	EDM	J. BEUKEBOOM (ab)
	1989-90	EDM	J. BEUKEBOOM (rep)
	1989-90	EDM	J. BEUKEBOOM (sc)
	1993-94	NYR	J. BEUKEBOOM (rep)
	1993-94	NYR	J. BEUKEBOOM (sc)
Bicek, Jiri	2002-03	NJ	JIRI BICEK (rep)
	2002-03	NJ	JIRI BICEK (sc)
Bickell, Jack	1931-32	TML	J.P.BICKELL, PRESIDENT. (sp)
	1931-32	TML	J P BICKELL (PRES) (ret)
	1944-45	TML	J.P.BICKELL CHAIRMAN OF THE BOARD (sp)
	1944-45	TML	J.P. BICKELL CHAIRMAN (rep)
	1944-45	TML	J.P. BICKELL CHAIRMAN (sc)
	1946-47	TML	J.P.BICKELL CHAIRMAN OF THE BOARD (re)
	1946-47	TML	J.P. BICKELL CHAIRMAN (rep)
	1946-47	TML	J.P. BICKELL CHAIRMAN (sc)
	1947-48	TML	J.P.BICKELL—DIRECTOR (re)
	1947-48	TML	J.P. BICKELL DIRECTOR (rep)
	1947-48	TML	J.P. BICKELL DIRECTOR (sc)
	1948-49	TML	J.P.BICKELL DIRECTOR (re)
	1948-49	TML	J.P. BICKELL DIRECTOR (rep)
	1948-49	TML	J R BICKELL DIRECTOR (sc)
	1950-51	TML	J.P.BICKELL DIRECTOR (re)
	1950-51	TML	J. BICKELL DIRECTOR (rep)
	1950-51	TML	J BICKELL DIRECTOR (sc)
Bickle, Ed	1931-32	TML	E.W.BICKLE, VICE-PRES. (sp)
	1931-32	TML	E W BICKLE (V PRES) (ret)
	1941-42	TML	E.W.BICKLE. VICE-PRES. (sp)
	1941-42	TML	E.W. BICKLE VICE PRES. (rep)
	1941-42	TML	E.W. BICKLE (VICE PRESS) (sc)
	1944-45	TML	E.W.BICKLE PRESIDENT (sp)
	1944-45	TML	E.W. BICKLE PRESIDENT (rep)
	1944-45	TML	E.W. BICKLE PRESIDENT (sc)
	1946-47	TML	E.W.BICKLE PRESIDENT (re)
	1946-47	TML	E.W. BICKLE PRES. (rep)
	1946-47	TML	E.W. BICKLE (PRES) (sc)
	1947-48	TML	E.W.BICKLE— DIRECTOR (re)
	1947-48	TML	E.W. BICKLE DIR. (rep)
	1947-48	TML	E.W. BICKLE (DER) (sc)
	1948-49	TML	E.W.BICKLE DIRECTOR (re)
	1948-49	TML	E.W. BICKLE DIR. (rep)
	1948-49	TML	E W BICKLE (DIR) (sc)
	1950-51	TML	E.W.BICKLE DIRECTOR (re)
	1950-51	TML	E.W. BICKLE DIRECTOR (rep)
	1950-51	TML	E W BICKLE DIRECTOR (sc)
Binkley, Les	1991-92	PIT	LES BINKLEY (rep)
	1991-92	PIT	LES BINKLEY (sc)
Birks, J.E.	1931-32	TML	MR.J.E.BIRKS (eb)
Blachford, Cecil	1907	MW	C. BLACHFORD. (ib)
	1907	MW	C. BLACHFORD (rep)
	1907	MW	C. BLACHFORD (sc)
Black, Steve	1949-50	DET	STEVE BLACK (re)
	1949-50	DET	STEVE BLACK (rep)
	1949-50	DET	STEVE BLACK (sc)
Blackwell, John	1989-90	EDM	JOHN BLACKWELL DIR.O.AHL (ab)
	1989-90	EDM	JOHN BLACKWELL DIR.O.AHL (rep)
	1989-90	EDM	JOHN BLACKWELL DIR.O.AHL (sc)
Bladon, Tom	1973-74	PHI	TOM BLADON (rep)
	1973-74	PHI	TOM BLADON (sc)
	1974-75	PHI	TOM BLADON (rep)
	1974-75	PHI	TOM BLADON (sc)
Blair, Andy	1931-32	TML	A. BLAIR (sp)
	1931-32	TML	A BLAIR (ret)

Name	Season / Team	Engraving
Blake,	1934-35 MM	H. BLAKE (sp)
Hector	1934-35 MM	H BLAKE (ret)
"Toe"	1943-44 MC	HECTOR BLAKE CAPTAIN (sp)
	1943-44 MC	HECTOR TOE BLAKE CAPTAIN (rep)
	1943-44 MC	HECTOR BLAKE CAPTAIN (sc)
	1945-46 MC	HECTOR BLAKE CAPTAIN (re)
	1945-46 MC	HECTOR TOE BLAKE CAPT. (rep)
	1945-46 MC	HECTOR BLAKE (CAPT) (sc)
	1955-56 MC	HECTOR TOE BLAKE, COACH (re)
	1955-56 MC	HECTOR "TOE" BLAKE COACH (rep)
	1955-56 MC	HECTOR TOE BLAKE COACH (sc)
	1956-57 MC	HECTOR TOE BLAKE COACH (rep)
	1956-57 MC	HECTOR TOE BLAKE COACH (sc)
	1957-58 MC	HECTOR TOE BLAKE COACH (rep)
	1957-58 MC	HECTOR TOE BLAKE COACH (sc)
	1958-59 MC	HECTOR TOE BLAKE COACH (rep)
	1958-59 MC	HECTOR TOE BLAKE COACH (sc)
	1959-60 MC	H. TOE BLAKE COACH (rep)
	1959-60 MC	H TOE BLAKE COACH (sc)
	1964-65 MC	HECTOR TOE BLAKE COACH (rep)
	1964-65 MC	HECTOR TOE BLAKE COACH (sc)
	1965-66 MC	H TOE BLAKE COACH (rep)
	1965-66 MC	H TOE BLAKE COACH (sc)
	1967-68 MC	HECTOR TOE BLAKE COACH (rep)
	1967-68 MC	HECTOR TOE BLAKE COACH (sc)
Blake, Rob	2000-01 COL	ROB BLAKE (rep)
	2000-01 COL	ROB BLAKE (sc)
Blinco, Russ	1934-35 MM	R. BLINCO (sp)
	1934-35 MM	R BLINCO (ret)
Bodnar, Gus	1944-45 TML	GUS BODNAR (sp)
	1944-45 TML	GUS BODNAR (rep)
	1944-45 TML	GUS BODNAR (sc)
	1946-47 TML	AUGUST BODNAR (re)
	1946-47 TML	GUS BODNAR (rep)
	1946-47 TML	GUS BOONAR (sc)
Boesch,	1946-47 TML	GARTH BOESCH (re)
Garth	1946-47 TML	GARTH BOESCH (rep)
	1946-47 TML	GARTH BOESCH (sc)
	1947-48 TML	GARTH BOESCH (re)
	1947-48 TML	GARTH BOESCH (rep)
	1947-48 TML	GARTH BOESCH (sc)
	1948-49 TML	GARTH BOESCH (re)
	1948-49 TML	GARTH BOESCH (rep)
	1948-49 TML	GARTH BOESCH (sc)
Boisvert,	1985-86 MC	S. BOISVERT (ab)
Serge	1985-86 MC	S. BOISVERT (rep)
	1985-86 MC	S. BOISVERT (sc)
Boldirev,	1969-70 BB	I BOLDIREV (rep)
Ivan	1969-70 BB	I BOLDIREV (sc)
Bolton,	1950-51 TML	HUGH BOLTON (re)
Hugh	1950-51 TML	HUGH BOLTON (rep)
	1950-51 TML	HUGH BOLTON (sc)
Bombardir,	1999-00 NJ	L. BRAD BOMBARDIR (rep)
Brad	1999-00 NJ	L. BRAD BOMBARDIR (sc)
Bonin,	1954-55 DET	MARCEL BONIN (re)
Marcel	1954-55 DET	MARCEL BONIN (rep)
	1954-55 DET	MARCEL BONIN (sc)
	1957-58 MC	MARCEL BONIN (rep)
	1957-58 MC	MARCEL BONIN (sc)
	1958-59 MC	M. BONIN (rep)
	1958-59 MC	M BONIN (sc)
	1959-60 MC	M. BONIN (rep)
	1959-60 MC	M BONIN (sc)
Boon,	1907 MW	DICK. BOON. (ib)
Dickie	1907 MW	DICK BOON (rep)
	1907 MW	DICK BOON (sc)
Bordeleau,	1968-69 MC	C. BORDELEAU (rep)
Christian	1968-69 MC	C BORDELEAU (sc)
Bossy, Mike	1979-80 NYI	M. BOSSY (ab)
	1979-80 NYI	M. BOSSY (rep)
	1979-80 NYI	M. BOSSY (sc)
	1980-81 NYI	M. BOSSY (ab)
	1980-81 NYI	M. BOSSY (rep)
	1980-81 NYI	M. BOSSY (sc)
	1981-82 NYI	M. BOSSY (ab)
	1981-82 NYI	M. BOSSY (rep)
	1981-82 NYI	M. BOSSY (sc)
	1982-83 NYI	M. BOSSY (ab)
	1982-83 NYI	M. BOSSY (rep)
	1982-83 NYI	M. BOSSY (sc)
Bouchard,	1943-44 MC	EMILE BOUCHARD (sp)
Emile	1943-44 MC	EMILE BOUCHARD (rep)
"Butch"	1943-44 MC	EMILE BOUCHARD (sc)
	1945-46 MC	EMILE BOUCHARD (re)
	1945-46 MC	EMILE BOUCHARD (rep)
	1945-46 MC	EMILE BOUCHARD (sc)
	1952-53 MC	EMILE BOUCHARD-CAPTAIN (re)
	1952-53 MC	EMILE BOUCHARD CAPT. (rep)
	1952-53 MC	EMILE BOUCHARD CAPT (sc)
	1955-56 MC	"BUTCH" BOUCHARD, CAPTAIN (re)
	1955-56 MC	BUTCH BOUCHARD CAPTAIN (rep)
	1955-56 MC	BUTCH BOUCHARD CAPTAIN (sc)
Bouchard,	1970-71 MC	PIERRE BOUCHARD (rep)
Pierre	1970-71 MC	PIERRE BOUCHARD. (sc)
	1972-73 MC	PIERRE BOUCHARD (rep)
	1972-73 MC	PIERRE BOUCHARD (sc)
	1975-76 MC	PIERRE BOUCHARD (rep)
	1975-76 MC	PIERRE BOUCHARD (sc)
	1976-77 MC	PIERRE BOUCHARD (rep)
	1976-77 MC	PIERRE BOUCHARD (sc)
	1977-78 MC	PIERRE BOUCHARD (rep)
	1977-78 MC	PIERRE BOUCHARD (sc)
Boucher,	1923-24 MC	B. BOUCHER (or)
Billy	1923-24 MC	B. BOUCHER (rep)
	1923-24 MC	B. BOUCHER (sc)
Boucher,	1923-24 MC	BOBBY BOUCHER (or)
Bobby	1923-24 MC	BOBBY BOCHER (rep)
	1923-24 MC	BOBBY BOCHER (sc)
Boucher,	1927-28 NYR	FRANK BOUCHER (sp)
Frank	1927-28 NYR	FRANK BOUCHER (ret)
	1932-33 NYR	FRANK BOUCHER (sp)
	1932-33 NYR	FRANK BOUCHER (ret)
	1939-40 NYR	FRANK BOUCHER. COACH (sp)
	1939-40 NYR	FRANK BOUCHER COACH (ret)
Boucher,	1926-27 OTT	GEO. BOUCHER CAPT (or)
George	1926-27 OTT	GEO BOUCHER CAPT (rep)
	1926-27 OTT	GEO BOUCHER CAPT (sc)
Boudrias,	1985-86 MC	A. BOUDRIAS A.G.MGRS.* (ab)
Andre	1985-86 MC	A. BOUDRIAS A.G.MGRS.* (rep)
	1985-86 MC	A. BOUDRIAS A.G.MGRS.* (sc)
		* refers also to Jacques Lemaire
	1992-93 MC	ANDRE BOUDRIAS A.G.M. (rep)
	1992-93 MC	ANDRÉ BOUDRIAS A.G.M. (sc)
Boulanger,	1992-93 MC	B. BOULANGER A. EQP. MGR. (rep)
Robert	1992-93 MC	B. BOULANGER A. EQP. MGR. (sc)
Bourgeault,	1927-28 NYR	L. BOURGAULT (sp)
Leo	1927-28 NYR	L BOURGAULT (ret)
Bourne,	1979-80 NYI	B. BOURNE (ab)
Bob	1979-80 NYI	B. BOURNE (rep)
	1979-80 NYI	B. BOURNE (sc)
	1980-81 NYI	B. BOURNE (ab)
	1980-81 NYI	B. BOURNE (rep)
	1980-81 NYI	B. BOURNE (sc)
	1981-82 NYI	B. BOURNE (ab)
	1981-82 NYI	B. BOURNE (rep)
	1981-82 NYI	B. BOURNE (sc)
	1982-83 NYI	B. BOURNE (ab)
	1982-83 NYI	B. BOURNE (rep)
	1982-83 NYI	B. BOURNE (sc)
Bourque,	1990-91 PIT	P. BOURQUE (ab)
Phil	1990-91 PIT	P. BOURQUE (rep)
	1990-91 PIT	P. BOURQUE (sc)
	1991-92 PIT	PHIL BOURQUE (rep)
	1991-92 PIT	PHIL BOURQUE (sc)
Bourque,	2000-01 COL	RAYMOND BOURQUE (rep)
Ray	2000-01 COL	RAYMOND BOURQUE (sc)
Boutilier,	1982-83 NYI	P. BOUTILIER (ab)
Paul	1982-83 NYI	P. BOUTILIER (rep)
	1982-83 NYI	P. BOUTILIER (sc)
Bower,	1961-62 TML	JOHN BOWER (rep)
Johnny	1961-62 TML	JOHN BOWER (sc)
	1962-63 TML	JOHN BOWER (rep)
	1962-63 TML	JOHN BOWER (sc)
	1963-64 TML	JOHN BOWER (rep)
	1963-64 TML	JOHN BOWER (sc)
	1966-67 TML	JOHN BOWER (rep)
	1966-67 TML	JOHN BOWER (sc)
Bowman,	1935-36 DET	RALPH BOWMAN L.DEFENSE (sp)
Ralph	1935-36 DET	RALPH BOWMAN (ret)
"Scotty"	1936-37 DET	RALPH BOWMAN L.DEFENSE (sp)
	1936-37 DET	RALPH BOWMAN (ret)
Bowman,	1972-73 MC	SCOTTY BOWMAN COACH (rep)
William	1972-73 MC	SCOTTY BOWMAN. COACH (sc)
"Scotty"	1975-76 MC	SCOTTY BOWMAN COACH (rep)
	1975-76 MC	SCOTTY BOWMAN COACH (sc)
	1976-77 MC	SCOTTY BOWMAN COACH (rep)
	1976-77 MC	SCOTTY BOWMAN COACH (sc)
	1977-78 MC	SCOTT BOWMAN COACH (rep)
	1977-78 MC	SCOTT BOWMAN COACH (sc)
	1978-79 MC	SCOTT BOWMAN COACH (ab)
	1978-79 MC	SCOTT BOWMAN COACH (rep)
	1978-79 MC	SCOTT BOWMAN COACH (sc)
	1990-91 PIT	SCOTT BOWMAN DIR.P.D. & RECRUIT (ab)
	1990-91 PIT	SCOTT BOWMAN DIR.P.D. & RECRUIT (rep)
	1990-91 PIT	SCOTT BOWMAN DIR.P.D. & RECRUIT (sc)
	1991-92 PIT	SCOTTY BOWMAN (rep)
	1991-92 PIT	SCOTTY BOWMAN (sc)
	1996-97 DET	SCOTTY BOWMAN (rep)
	1996-97 DET	SCOTTY BOWMAN (sc)
	1997-98 DET	SCOTTY BOWMAN (rep)
	1997-98 DET	SCOTTY BOWMAN (sc)
	2001-02 DET	SCOTTY BOWMAN (rep)
	2001-02 DET	SCOTTY BOWMAN (sc)

Name	Season/Team	Inscription
Boyd, Bill	1927-28 NYR	W. BOYD (sp)
	1927-28 NYR	W BOYD (ret)
Boyer, Paul	1996-97 DET	PAUL BOYER (rep)
	1996-97 DET	PAUL BOYER (sc)
	1997-98 DET	PAUL BOYER (rep)
	1997-98 DET	PAUL BOYER (sc)
	2001-02 DET	PAUL BOYER (rep)
	2001-02 DET	PAUL BOYER (sc)
Boyd, Harry	1979-80 NYI	HARRY BOYD SCOUT (ab)
	1979-80 NYI	HARRY BOYD SCOUT (rep)
	1979-80 NYI	HARRY BOYD SCOUT (sc)
	1980-81 NYI	HARRY BOYD SCOUT (ab)
	1980-81 NYI	HARRY BOYD SCOUT (rep)
	1980-81 NYI	HARRY BOYD SCOUT (sc)
Brennan, Doug	1932-33 NYR	DOUGLAS BRENNAN (sp)
	1932-33 NYR	DOUGLAS BRENNAN (ret)
Brewer, Carl	1961-62 TML	CARL BREWER (rep)
	1961-62 TML	CARL BREWER (sc)
	1962-63 TML	CARL BREWER (rep)
	1962-63 TML	CARL BREWER (sc)
	1963-64 TML	CARL BREWER (rep)
	1963-64 TML	CARL BREWER (sc)
Bricker, Harry	1999-00 NJ	H. BRICKER (rep)
	1999-00 NJ	H. BRICKER (sc)
Brimsek, Frank	1938-39 BB	F. BRIMSEK (sp)
	1938-39 BB	F BRIMSEK (ret)
	1940-41 BB	FRANK BRIMSEK (sp)
	1940-41 BB	FRANK BRIMSEK (rep)
	1940-41 BB	FRANK BRIMSEK (sc)
Brisebois, Patrice	1992-93 MC	P. BRISEBOIS (rep)
	1992-93 MC	P. BRISEBOIS (sc)
Broadbent, Harry		H. BROABENT. (ib)
		H. BROADBENT (rep) (etched upside down—doesn't refer specifically to any year)
	1925-26 MM	H.L. BROADBENT. (or)
	1925-26 MM	H.L. BROADBENT (rep)
	1925-26 MM	H.L. BROADBENT. (sc)
Broda, Walter "Turk"	1941-42 TML	WALTER BRODA (sp)
	1941-42 TML	WALTER BRODA (rep)
	1941-42 TML	TURK BRODA (sc)
	1946-47 TML	WALTER BRODA (re)
	1946-47 TML	WALTER BRODA (rep)
	1946-47 TML	WALTER BRODA (sc)
	1947-48 TML	WALTER BRODA (re)
	1947-48 TML	WALTER BRODA (rep)
	1947-48 TML	WALTER BRODA (sc)
	1948-49 TML	WALTER BRODA (re)
	1948-49 TML	WALTER BRODA (rep)
	1948-49 TML	WALTER BRODA (sc)
	1950-51 TML	WALTER BRODA (re)
	1950-51 TML	WALTER BRODA (rep)
	1950-51 TML	WALTER BRODA (sc)
Broden, Connie	1956-57 MC	CONNIE BRODEN (rep)
	1956-57 MC	CONNELL BRODEN (sc)
	1957-58 MC	CONNIE BRODEN (rep)
	1957-58 MC	CONNELL BRODEN (sc)
Brodeur, Martin	1994-95 NJ	MARTIN BRODEUR (rep)
	1994-95 NJ	MARTIN BRODEUR (sc)
	1999-00 NJ	MARTIN BRODEUR (rep)
	1999-00 NJ	MARTIN BRODEUR (sc)
	2002-03 NJ	MARTIN BRODEUR (rep)
	2002-03 NJ	MARTIN BRODEUR (sc)
Bronfman, Edward	1972-73 MC	EDWARD BRONFMAN EX.DIR. (rep)
	1972-73 MC	EDWARD BRONFMAN.EX.DIR• (sc)
	1975-76 MC	EDWARD BRONFMAN DIR. (rep)
	1975-76 MC	EDWARD BRONFMAN DIR. (sc)
	1976-77 MC	EDWARD BRONFMAN DIR. (rep)
	1976-77 MC	EDWARD BRONFMAN DIR. (sc)
	1977-78 MC	EDWARD BRONFMAN DIR. (rep)
	1977-78 MC	EDWARD BRONFMAN DIR. (sc)
Bronfman, Peter	1972-73 MC	PETER BRONFMAN CHAIRMAN (rep)
	1972-73 MC	PETER BRONFMAN.CHAIR. (sc)
	1975-76 MC	PETER BRONFMAN CHAIRMAN (rep)
	1975-76 MC	PETER BRONFMAN CHAIR. (sc)
	1976-77 MC	PETER BRONFMAN DIR. (rep)
	1976-77 MC	PETER BRONFMAN DIR. (sc)
	1977-78 MC	PETER BRONFMAN DIR. (rep)
	1977-78 MC	PETER BRONFMAN DIR. (sc)
Broten, Neal	1994-95 NJ	NEAL BROTEN (rep)
	1994-95 NJ	NEAL BROTEN (sc)
Brown, Adam	1942-43 DET	ADAM BROWN (sp)
	1942-43 DET	ADAM BROWN (rep)
	1942-43 DET	ADAM BROWN (sc)
Brown, Connie	1942-43 DET	CONNY BROWN (sp)
	1942-43 DET	CONNIE BROWN (rep)
	1942-43 DET	CONNIE BROWN (sc)
Brown, Dave	1989-90 EDM	D. BROWN (ab)
	1989-90 EDM	D. BROWN (rep)
	1989-90 EDM	D. BROWN (sc)
Brown, Doug	1996-97 DET	DOUG BROWN (rep)
	1996-97 DET	DOUG BROWN (sc)
	1997-98 DET	D. BROWN (rep)
	1997-98 DET	D. BROWN (sc)
Brule, Steve	1999-00 NJ	STEVE BRULE (rep)
	1999-00 NJ	STEVE BRULE (sc)
Brunet, Benoit	1992-93 MC	B. BRUNET (rep)
	1992-93 MC	B. BRUNET (sc)
Bruneteau, Mud	1935-36 DET	MUD BRUNETEAU R.WING (sp)
	1935-36 DET	MUD BRUNETEAU (ret)
	1936-37 DET	MUD BRUNETEAU—R.WING (sp)
	1936-37 DET	MUD BRUNETEAU (ret)
	1942-43 DET	MUD BRUNETEAU (sp)
	1942-43 DET	MUD BRUNETEAU (rep)
	1942-43 DET	MUD BRUNETEAU (sc)
Brylin, Sergei	1994-95 NJ	SERGEI BRYLIN (rep)
	1994-95 NJ	SERGEI BRYLIN (sc)
	1999-00 NJ	SERGEI BRYLIN (rep)
	1999-00 NJ	SERGEI BRYLIN (sc)
	2002-03 NJ	SERGEI BRYLIN (rep)
	2002-03 NJ	SERGEI BRYLIN (sc)
Buchberger, Kelly	1986-87 EDM	K. BUCHBERGER (ab)
	1986-87 EDM	K. BUCHBERGER (rep)
	1986-87 EDM	K. BUCHBERGER (sc)
	1989-90 EDM	K. BUCHBERGER (ab)
	1989-90 EDM	K. BUCHBERGER (rep)
	1989-90 EDM	K. BUCHBERGER (sc)
Bucyk, Johnny	1969-70 BB	JOHN BUCYK (rep)
	1969-70 BB	JOHN BUCYK (sc)
	1971-72 BB	JOHN BUCYK (rep)
	1971-72 BB	JOHN BUCYK (sc)
Bure, Vladimir	1999-00 NJ	V. BURE (rep)
	1999-00 NJ	V. BURE (sc)
	2002-03 NJ	V. BURE (rep)
	2002-03 NJ	V. BURE (sc)
Burkard, Ralph	1938-39 BB	RALPH F. BURKARD/TREASURER (sp)
	1938-39 BB	RALPH BURKARD (TREAS) (ret)
	1940-41 BB	RALPH F. BURKARD, TREASURER. (sp)
	1940-41 BB	RALPH F. BURKARD TREAS. (rep)
	1940-41 BB	RALPH F. BURKARD (TREAS) (sc)
Burke, Marty	1929-30 MC	MARTY BURKE. (sp)
	1929-30 MC	MARTY BURKE (ret)
	1930-31 MC	MARTIN BURKE (sp)
	1930-31 MC	MARTIN BURKE (ret)
Burns, Pat	2002-03 NJ	PAT BURNS (rep)
	2002-03 NJ	PAT BURNS (sc)
Button, Craig	1998-99 DAL	CRAIG BUTTON (rep)
	1998-99 DAL	CRAIG BUTTON (sc)
Cain, Herb	1934-35 MM	H. CAIN (sp)
	1934-35 MM	H CAIN (ret)
	1940-41 BB	HERBERT CAIN (sp)
	1940-41 BB	HERBERT CAIN (rep)
	1940-41 BB	HERBERT CAIN (sc)
Callander, Jock	1991-92 PIT	JOCK CALLANDER (rep)
	1991-92 PIT	JOCK CALLANDER (sc)
Callighen, Francis "Patsy"	1927-28 NYR	F. CALLIGHEN (sp)
	1927-28 NYR	F CALLIHIN (ret)
Cameron, Billy	1923-24 MC	B. CAMERON (or)
	1923-24 MC	B. CAMERON (rep)
	1923-24 MC	B. CAMERON (sc)
Cameron, Dr. Gordon	1984-85 EDM	DR. G. CAMERON TEAM PHY. (ab)
	1984-85 EDM	DR.G.CAMERON TEAM PHY. (rep)
	1984-85 EDM	DR.G.CAMERON TEAM PHY. (sc)
	1986-87 EDM	DR. GORDON CAMERON (ab)
	1986-87 EDM	DR. GORDON CAMERON (rep)
	1986-87 EDM	DR. GORDON CAMERON (sc)
	1987-88 EDM	DR. GORDON CAMERON (ab)
	1987-88 EDM	DR. GORDON CAMERON (rep)
	1987-88 EDM	DR. GORDON CAMERON (sc)
	1989-90 EDM	DR. GORDON CAMERON (ab)
	1989-90 EDM	DR. GORDON CAMERON (rep)
	1989-90 EDM	DR. GORDON CAMERON (sc)
Campbell, Archie	1944-45 TML	ARCHIE CAMPBELL, ASSISTANT TRAINER (sp)
	1944-45 TML	ARC CAMPBELL ASST. TRAINER (rep)
	1944-45 TML	ARC CAMPBELL (ASS TRAIN) (sc)
	1947-48 TML	ARCHIE CAMPBELL — ASSISTANT TRAINER (re)
	1947-48 TML	A. CAMPBELL ASST. TR. (rep)
	1947-48 TML	A. CAMPBELL (ASS• TR) (sc)
	1948-49 TML	ARCHIE CAMPBELL ASSISTANT TRAINER (re)
	1950-51 TML	ARCHIE CAMPBELL ASSISTANT TRAINER (re)
	1950-51 TML	A. CAMPBELL ASST. TR. (rep)
	1950-51 TML	A CAMPBELL (ASS TR) (sc)
Campbell, Colin	1993-94 NYR	COLIN CAMPBELL A.COACH (rep)
	1993-94 NYR	COLIN CAMPBELL A.COACH (sc)

Name	Season	Inscription
Canney, Dan	1969-70 BB	D. CANNEY TR. (rep)
	1969-70 BB	D CANNEY TR (sc)
	1971-72 BB	DAN CANNEY TRAINER (rep)
	1971-72 BB	DAN CANNEY TRAINER (sc)
Carbonneau, Guy	1985-86 MC	G. CARBONNEAU (ab)
	1985-86 MC	G. CARBONNEAU (rep)
	1985-86 MC	G. CARBONNEAU (sc)
	1992-93 MC	G. CARBONNEAU CAPT. (rep)
	1992-93 MC	G. CARBONNEAU CAPT. (sc)
	1998-99 DAL	GUY CARBONNEAU (rep)
	1998-99 DAL	GUY CARBONNEAU (sc)
Carey, Win	1927-28 NYR	W.F.CAREY, (DIR.) (sp)
	1927-28 NYR	W F CAREY (DIR) (ret)
Carleton, Wayne	1969-70 BB	W. CARLETON (rep)
	1969-70 BB	W CARLETON (sc)
Carnevale, Marie	1999-00 NJ	M. CARNEVALE (rep)
	1999-00 NJ	M. CARNEVALE (sc)
Caron, Jacques	1994-95 NJ	JACQUES CARON (rep)
	1994-95 NJ	JACQUES CARON (sc)
Caron, Jacques	1999-00 NJ	J.J. CARON (rep)
	1999-00 NJ	J.J. CARON (sc)
	2002-03 NJ	J.J. CARON (rep)
	2002-03 NJ	J.J. CARON (sc)
Caron, Ron	1970-71 MC	RON CARON ASST.GEN.MGR. (rep)
	1970-71 MC	RON CARON ASSI.GEN.MAN. (sc)
	1976-77 MC	RON CARON A.G.M (rep)
	1976-77 MC	RON CARON A.G.M. (sc)
	1977-78 MC	RON CARON A.G.M. (rep)
	1977-78 MC	RON CARON A.G.M. (sc)
	1978-79 MC	RON CARON D.C. (ab)
	1978-79 MC	RON CARON D.C. (rep)
	1978-79 MC	RON CARON D.C. (sc)
Carpenter, Bob	1994-95 NJ	ROBERT E. CARPENTER JR. (rep)
	1994-95 NJ	ROBERT E. CARPENTER JR. (sc)
	1999-00 NJ	R. CARPENTER (rep)
	1999-00 NJ	R. CARPENTER (sc)
	2002-03 NJ	B. CARPENTER (rep)
	2002-03 NJ	B. CARPENTER (sc)
Carr, Lorne	1941-42 TML	LORNE CARR (sp)
	1941-42 TML	LORNE CARR (rep)
	1941-42 TML	LORNE CARR (sc)
	1944-45 TML	LORNE CARR (sp)
	1944-45 TML	LORNE CARR (rep)
	1944-45 TML	LORNE CARR (sc)
Carrier, Claude	1994-95 NJ	CLAUDE CARRIER (rep)
	1994-95 NJ	CLAUDE CARRIER (sc)
	1999-00 NJ	C. CARRIER (rep)
	1999-00 NJ	C. CARRIER (sc)
	2002-03 NJ	C. CARRIER (rep)
	2002-03 NJ	C. CARRIER (sc)
Carroll, Billy	1980-81 NYI	B. CARROLL (ab)
	1980-81 NYI	B. CARROLL (rep)
	1980-81 NYI	B. CARROLL (sc)
	1981-82 NYI	B. CARROLL (ab)
	1981-82 NYI	B. CARROLL (rep)
	1981-82 NYI	B. CARROLL (sc)
	1982-83 NYI	B. CARROLL (ab)
	1982-83 NYI	B. CARROLL (rep)
	1982-83 NYI	B. CARROLL (sc)
	1984-85 EDM	B. CARROLL (ab)
	1984-85 EDM	B. CARROLL (rep)
	1984-85 EDM	B. CARROLL (sc)
Carson, Bill "Doc"	1928-29 BB	"DOC" CARSON (or)
	1928-29 BB	DOC CARSON (rep)
	1928-29 BB	DOC CARSON (sc)
	1928-29 BB	B CARSON (ret)
Carson, Frank	1925-26 MM	R.F. CARSON. (or)
	1925-26 MM	R.F. CARSON (rep)
	1925-26 MM	R.F. CARSON. (sc)
Carson, Gerry	1929-30 MC	GERALD CARSON. (sp)
	1929-30 MC	GERALD CARSON (ret)
Carveth, Joe	1942-43 DET	JOE CARVETH (sp)
	1942-43 DET	JOE CARVETH (rep)
	1942-43 DET	JOE CARVETH (sc)
	1949-50 DET	JOE CARVETH (re)
	1949-50 DET	JOE CARVETH (rep)
	1949-50 DET	JOE CARVETH (sc)
Cashman, Wayne	1969-70 BB	W. CASHMAN (rep)
	1969-70 BB	W CASHMAN (sc)
	1971-72 BB	WAYNE CASHMAN (rep)
	1971-72 BB	WAYNE CASHMAN (sc)
Cattarinich, Joe	1923-24 MC	JOS. CATTARINICH (or)
	1923-24 MC	JOS. CATTARINIGH (rep)
	1923-24 MC	JOS. CATTARINICH (sc)
	1929-30 MC	JOS CATTARINICH. VICE-PRES. (sp)
	1929-30 MC	JOS CATTARINICH (V PRES) (ret)
	1930-31 MC	JOS. CATTARINICH, VICE-PRESIDENT (sp)
	1930-31 MC	JOS CATTARINICH (V PRESS) (ret)
Caufield, Jay	1990-91 PIT	J. CAUFIELD (ab)
	1990-91 PIT	J. CAUFIELD (rep)
	1990-91 PIT	J. CAUFIELD (sc)
	1991-92 PIT	JAY CAUFIELD (rep)
	1991-92 PIT	JAY CAUFIELD (sc)
Cayford, Art	1925-26 MM	A.F. CAYFORD. / (Sec-Treas) (or)
	1925-26 MM	A.F. CAYFORD / (SEC-TREAS) (rep)
	1925-26 MM	A.F. CAYFORD / (Sec-Treas) (sc)
Centanni, Lou Jr.	1999-00 NJ	L. CENTANNI JR. (rep)
	1999-00 NJ	L. CENTANNI JR. (sc)
Chabot, Lorne	1927-28 NYR	L. CHABOT (sp)
	1927-28 NYR	L. CHABOT (ret)
	1931-32 TML	L. CHABOT (sp)
	1931-32 TML	L CHABUT (ret)
Chadwick, Ed	1984-85 EDM	E. CHADWICK (ab)
	1984-85 EDM	E. CHADWICK (rep)
	1984-85 EDM	E. CHADWICK (sc)
	1986-87 EDM	E. CHADWICK (ab)
	1986-87 EDM	E. CHADWICK (rep)
	1986-87 EDM	E. CHADWICK (sc)
	1989-90 EDM	ED CHADWICK (ab)
	1989-90 EDM	ED CHADWICK (rep)
	1989-90 EDM	ED CHADWICK (sc)
Chamberlain, Murph	1943-44 MC	ERWIN CHAMBERLAIN (sp)
	1943-44 MC	MURPH CHAMBERLAIN (rep)
	1943-44 MC	ERVIN CHAMBERLAIN (sc)
	1945-46 MC	ERWIN CHAMBERLAIN (re)
	1945-46 MC	MURPH CHAMBERLAIN (rep)
	1945-46 MC	ERWIN CHAMBERLAIN (sc)
Chambers, Raymond	2002-03 NJ	RAYMOND G. CHAMBERS (rep)
	2002-03 NJ	RAYMOND G. CHAMBERS (sc)
Chambers, Shawn	1994-95 NJ	SHAWN CHAMBERS (rep)
	1994-95 NJ	SHAWN CHAMBERS (sc)
	1998-99 DAL	SHAWN CHAMBERS (rep)
	1998-99 DAL	SHAWN CHAMBERS (sc)
Chartraw, Rick	1975-76 MC	RICK CHARTRAW (rep)
	1975-76 MC	RICK CHARTRAW (sc)
	1976-77 MC	RICK CHARTRAW (rep)
	1976-77 MC	RICK CHARTRAW (sc)
	1977-78 MC	RICK CHARTRAW (rep)
	1977-78 MC	RICK CHARTRAW (sc)
	1978-79 MC	R. CHARTRAW (ab)
	1978-79 MC	R. CHARTRAW (rep)
	1978-79 MC	R. CHARTRAW (sc)
Cheevers, Gerry	1969-70 BB	G. CHEEVERS (rep)
	1969-70 BB	G CHEEVERS (sc)
	1971-72 BB	GERRY CHEEVERS (rep)
	1971-72 BB	GERRY CHEEVERS (sc)
Chelios, Chris	1985-86 MC	C. CHELIOS (ab)
	1985-86 MC	C. CHELIOS (rep)
	1985-86 MC	C. CHELIOS (sc)
	2001-02 DET	CHRIS CHELIOS (rep)
	2001-02 DET	CHRIS CHELIOS (sc)
Chipchase, ——	1907 MW	M^{r}. CHIPCHASE (ib)
	1907 MW	Mr CHIPCHASE (rep)
	1907 MW	M^{r}. CHIPCHASE (sc)
Chorske, Tom	1994-95 NJ	TOM CHORSKE (rep)
	1994-95 NJ	TOM CHORSKE (sc)
Chychrun, Jeff	1991-92 PIT	JEFF CHYCHRUN (rep)
	1991-92 PIT	JEFF CHYCHRUN (sc)
Clancy, Frank "King"	1926-27 OTT	FRANK M. CLANCY (or)
	1926-27 OTT	FRANK M. CLANCY (rep)
	1926-27 OTT	FRANK M. CLANCY (sc)
	1931-32 TML	F. CLANCY (sp)
	1931-32 TML	F CLANCY (ret)
	1961-62 TML	F. KING CLANCY ASST. COACH (rep)
	1961-62 TML	F "KING" CLANCY ASST COACH GM (sc)
	1962-63 TML	F. KING CLANCY ASST. COACH G. MANN (rep)
	1962-63 TML	F "KING" CLANCY ASST COACH• G MANN (sc)
	1963-64 TML	FRANK KING CLANCY ASST. COACH GEN.MGR. (rep)
	1963-64 TML	FRANK KING CLANCE ASST COACH GEN MAN (sc)
	1966-67 TML	F. KING CLANCY ASST.GEN.MGR.—COACH (sc)
	1966-67 TML	FRANK KING CLANCY ASS COACH GEN MAN (sc)
Clapper, Aubrey "Dit"	1928-29 BB	"DIT" CLAPPER (sp)
	1928-29 BB	D CLAPPER (ret)
	1938-39 BB	A. CLAPPER (sp)
	1938-39 BB	A CLAPPER (ret)
	1940-41 BB	AUBREY "DIT" CLAPPER CAPTAIN (sp)
	1940-41 BB	AUBREY DIT CLAPPER CAPT. (rep)
	1940-41 BB	AUBREY DIT CLAPPER (CAPT) (sc)
Clarke, Bobby	1973-74 PHI	BOB CLARKE CAPT. (rep)
	1973-74 PHI	BOB CLARKE CAPT. (sc)
	1974-75 PHI	BOB CLARKE CAPT. (rep)
	1974-75 PHI	BOB CLARKE CAPT. (sc)

Name	Season / Team	Inscription
Cleghorn, Odie	1923-24 MC	O. CLEGHORN (or)
	1923-24 MC	O. CLEGHORN (rep)
	1923-24 MC	O. CLEGHORN (sc)
Cleghorn, Sprague	1923-24 MC	S. CLEGHORN (or)
	1923-24 MC	S. CLEGHORN (rep)
	1923-24 MC	S. CLEGHORN (sc)
Clement, Bill	1973-74 PHI	BILL CLEMENT (rep)
	1973-74 PHI	BILL CLEMENT (sc)
	1974-75 PHI	BILL CLEMENT (rep)
	1974-75 PHI	BILL CLEMENT (sc)
Cloutier, Jacques	1995-96 COL	JACQUES CLOUTIER (rep)
	1995-96 COL	JACQUES CLOUTIER (sc)
	2000-01 COL	JACQUES CLOUTIER (rep)
	2000-01 COL	JACQUES CLOUTIER (sc)
Coates, Al	1988-89 CAL	AL COATES ASST. TO PRES. (ab)
	1988-89 CAL	AL COATES ASST. TO PRES. (rep)
	1988-89 CAL	AL COATES ASST. TO PRES. (sc)
Coffey, Paul	1983-84 EDM	P. COFFEY (ab)
	1983-84 EDM	P. COFFEY (rep)
	1983-84 EDM	P. COFFEY (sc)
	1984-85 EDM	P. COFFEY (ab)
	1984-85 EDM	P. COFFEY (rep)
	1984-85 EDM	P. COFFEY (sc)
	1986-87 EDM	P. COFFEY (ab)
	1986-87 EDM	P. COFFEY (rep)
	1986-87 EDM	P. COFFEY (sc)
	1990-91 PIT	P. COFFEY (ab)
	1990-91 PIT	P. COFFEY (rep)
	1990-91 PIT	P. COFFEY (sc)
Coflin, Hugh	1951-52 DET	HUGH COFLIN (re)
	1951-52 DET	HUGH COFLIN (sc)
Cogen, Jeff	1998-99 DAL	JEFF COGEN (rep)
	1998-99 DAL	JEFF COGEN (sc)
Cole, Danton	1994-95 NJ	DANTON COLE (rep)
	1994-95 NJ	DANTON COLE (sc)
Coleman, D.C.	1943-44 MC	D.C. COLEMAN VICE-PRESIDENT (sp)
	1943-44 MC	D.C. COLEMAN V.PRES. (rep)
	1943-44 MC	D.C. COLEMAN (V PRESS) (sc)
	1945-46 MC	D.C. COLEMAN VICE-PRESIDENT (re)
	1945-46 MC	D.C. COLEMAN V.PRES. (rep)
	1945-46 MC	D.C. COLEMAN (V PRES) (sc)
	1952-53 MC	D.C. COLEMAN - VICE PRESIDENT (re)
	1952-53 MC	D.C. COLEMAN V.PRES. (rep)
	1952-53 MC	D C COLEMAN (V PRES) (sc)
	1955-56 MC	D.C. COLEMAN (re)
	1955-56 MC	D.C. COLEMAN. V.PRES. (rep)
	1955-56 MC	D C COLEMAN V PRES (sc)
Colville, Mac	1939-40 NYR	MAC COLVILLE (sp)
	1939-40 NYR	MAC COLVILLE (ret)
Colville, Neil	1939-40 NYR	NEIL COLVILLE (sp)
	1939-40 NYR	NEIL COLVILLE (ret)
Conacher, Brian	1966-67 TML	BRIAN CONACHER (rep)
	1966-67 TML	BRIAN CONACHER (sc)
Conacher, Charlie	1931-32 TML	C. CONACHER (sp)
	1931-32 TML	C CONACHER (ret)
Conacher, Lionel	1933-34 CHI	LIONAL CONACHER (sp)
	1933-34 CHI	T CONACHER (ret)
	1934-35 MM	L. CONACHER (sp)
	1934-35 MM	L CONACHER (ret)
Conacher, Pat	1983-84 EDM	P. CONACHER (ab)
	1983-84 EDM	P. CONACHER (rep)
	1983-84 EDM	P. CONACHER (sc)
Conacher, Roy	1938-39 BB	R. CONACHER (sp)
	1938-39 BB	R CONACHER (ret)
	1940-41 BB	ROY CONACHER (sp)
	1940-41 BB	ROY CONACHER (rep)
	1940-41 BB	ROY CONACHER (sc)
Connell, Alec	1926-27 OTT	ALEX CONNELL (or)
	1926-27 OTT	ALEX CONNELL (rep)
	1926-27 OTT	ALEX CONNELL (sc)
	1934-35 MM	A. CONNELL (sp)
	1934-35 MM	A CONNELL (ret)
Connor, Cam	1978-79 MC	C. CONNOR (ab)
	1978-79 MC	C. CONNOR (rep)
	1978-79 MC	C. CONNOR (sc)
Conte, David	1994-95 NJ	DAVID CONTE (rep)
	1994-95 NJ	DAVID CONTE (sc)
	1999-00 NJ	D. CONTE (rep)
	1999-00 NJ	D. CONTE (sc)
	2002-03 NJ	D. CONTE (rep)
	2002-03 NJ	D. CONTE (sc)
Cook, Bill	1927-28 NYR	W. COOK, (CAPT.) (sp)
	1927-28 NYR	W COOK (CAPT) (ret)
	1932-33 NYR	W COOK, CAPT. (sp)
	1932-33 NYR	W COOK (CAPT) (ret)
Cook, Bun	1927-28 NYR	F. COOK (sp)
	1927-28 NYR	F COOK (ret)
	1932-33 NYR	F COOK (sp)
	1932-33 NYR	F COOK (ret)
Cook, Ernie	1943-44 MC	ERNIE COOK / TRAINER (rep)
	1943-44 MC	ERNIE COOK / TRAINER (sc)
Cook, Lloyd	1914-15 VM	Lloyd Cook (ib)
	1914-15 VM	Lloyd Cook (rep)
	1914-15 VM	Lloyd Cook (sc)
Cook, Tom	1933-34 CHI	THOMAS COOK (sp)
	1933-34 CHI	TOMMY COOK (ret)
Cooper, Carson	1949-50 DET	CARSON COOPER HEAD SCOUT (re)
	1949-50 DET	CARSON COOPER HEAD SCOUT (rep)
	1949-50 DET	CARSON COOPER HEAD SCOUT (sc)
	1951-52 DET	CARSON COOPER — CHIEF SCOUT (re)
	1951-52 DET	CARSON COOPER CHIEF SCOUT (rep)
	1951-52 DET	CARSON COOPER CHIEF SCOUT (sc)
Corbet, Rene	1995-96 COL	RENE CORBET (rep)
	1995-96 COL	RENE CORBET (sc)
Corey, Ronald	1985-86 MC	R. COREY PRÉS. (ab)
	1985-86 MC	R. COREY PRES. (rep)
	1985-86 MC	R. COREY PRES. (sc)
	1992-93 MC	RONALD COREY PRES. (rep)
	1992-93 MC	RONALD COREY PRES. (sc)
Corrigan, J.A.	1929-30 MC	*PHYSICIAN* / DR J.A. CORRIGAN (sp)
	1929-30 MC	J A CORRIAN (PHYSS) (ret)
	1930-31 MC	*PHYSICIAN* DR. J.A. CORRIGAN (sp)
	1930-31 MC	J A CORRIGAN (PHYSS) (ret)
Costello, Les	1947-48 TML	LESTER COSTELLO (re)
	1947-48 TML	LES COSTELLO (rep)
	1947-48 TML	LES COSTELLO (sc)
Cotton, Harold "Baldy"	1931-32 TML	H. COTTON (sp)
	1931-32 TML	H COTTON (ret)
Cottrelle, George	1931-32 TML	G.R. COTTRELLE, VICE-PRES. (sp)
	1931-32 TML	G R COTTRELLE (V PRES) (ret)
	1941-42 TML	G.R. COTTRELLE PRESIDENT (sp)
	1941-42 TML	G.R. COTTRELLE PRES. (rep)
	1941-42 TML	G.R. COTTRELLE (PRESS) (sc)
Coulter, Art	1933-34 CHI	ARTHUR COULTER (sp)
	1933-34 CHI	ART COULTER (ret)
	1939-40 NYR	ARTHUR COULTER. CAPTAIN (sp)
	1939-40 NYR	ARTHUR COULTER CAPTAIN (ret)
Cournoyer, Yvan	1964-65 MC	YVAN COUNRNOYER (rep)
	1964-65 MC	YVAN COURNOYER (sc)
	1965-66 MC	Y. COURNOYER (rep)
	1965-66 MC	Y COURNOYER (sc)
	1967-68 MC	Y. COURNOYER (rep)
	1967-68 MC	Y COURNOYER (sc)
	1968-69 MC	Y. COURNOYER (rep)
	1968-69 MC	Y COURNOYER (sc)
	1970-71 MC	Y. COURNOYER (rep)
	1970-71 MC	Y. COURNOYER (sc)
	1972-73 MC	YVAN COURNOYER (rep)
	1972-73 MC	YVAN COURNOYER (sc)
	1975-76 MC	YVAN COURNOYER (rep)
	1975-76 MC	YVAN COURNOYER (sc)
	1976-77 MC	YVAN COURNOYER (rep)
	1976-77 MC	YVAN COURNOYER (sc)
	1977-78 MC	YVAN COURNOYER (rep)
	1977-78 MC	YVAN COURNOYER (sc)
	1978-79 MC	Y. COURNOYER (ab)
	1978-79 MC	Y. COURNOYER (rep)
	1978-79 MC	Y. COURNOYER (sc)
Courtnall, Geoff	1987-88 EDM	G. COURTNALL (ab)
	1987-88 EDM	G. COURTNALL (rep)
	1987-88 EDM	G. COURTNALL (sc)
Courtois, Jacques	1972-73 MC	JACQUES COURTOIS PRES. (rep)
	1972-73 MC	JACQUES COURTOIS.PRES. (sc)
	1975-76 MC	E. JACQUES COURTOIS PRES. (rep)
	1975-76 MC	E. JACQUES COURTOIS PRES. (sc)
	1976-77 MC	E. JACQUES COURTOIS PRES. (rep)
	1976-77 MC	E. JACQUES COURTOIS PRES. (sc)
	1977-78 MC	E. JACQUES COURTOIS PRES. (rep)
	1977-78 MC	E. JACQUES COURTOIS PRES. (sc)
	1978-79 MC	E. JACQUES COUROIS PRES. (ab)
	1978-79 MC	E. JACQUES COURTOIS PRES. (rep)
	1978-79 MC	E. JACQUES COURTOIS PRES. (sc)
Coutu, Billy	1923-24 MC	B. COUTU (or)
	1923-24 MC	B. COUTU (rep)
	1923-24 MC	B. COUTU (sc)
Couture, Gerry	1949-50 DET	GERALD COUTURE (re)
	1949-50 DET	G. COUTURE (rep)
	1949-50 DET	G COUTURE (sc)
Couture, Rosie	1933-34 CHI	ROSARIO COUTURE (sp)
	1933-34 CHI	ROSARIO COUTURE (ret)
Cowick, Bruce	1973-74 PHI	BRUCE COWICK (rep)
	1973-74 PHI	BRUCE COWICK (sc)
Cowley, Bill	1938-39 BB	W. COWLEY (sp)
	1938-39 BB	W COWLEY (ret)
	1940-41 BB	WM. COWLEY (ob)
	1940-41 BB	BILL COWLEY (rep)

Name	Season / Team	Engraving
	1940-41 BB	BILL CAWLEY (sc)
Cox, Ralph	1991-92 PIT	RALPH COX (rep)
	1991-92 PIT	RALPH COX (sc)
Crawford,	1938-39 BB	J. CRAWFORD (sp)
Jack	1938-39 BB	J CRAWFORD (ret)
	1940-41 BB	JOHN CRAWFORD. (sp)
	1940-41 BB	JOHN CRAWFORD (rep)
	1940-41 BB	JOHN CRAWFORD (sc)
Crawford,	1995-96 COL	MARC CRAWFORD (rep)
Marc	1995-96 COL	MARC CRAWFORD (sc)
Crisp, Terry	1973-74 PHI	TERRY CRISP (rep)
	1973-74 PHI	TERRY CRISP (sc)
	1974-75 PHI	TERRY CRISP (rep)
	1974-75 PHI	TERRY CRISP (sc)
	1988-89 CAL	TERRY CRISP HEAD COACH (ab)
	1988-89 CAL	TERRY CRISP HEAD COACH (rep)
	1988-89 CAL	TERRY CRISP HEAD COACH (sc)
Crossman	1951-52 DET	WALTER CROSSMAN—ASS'T. TRAINER (re)
Wally	1951-52 DET	WALTER CROSSMAN ASST. TR. (rep)
	1951-52 DET	WALTER CROSSMAN (ASS'T TR) (sc)
	1953-54 DET	WALTER CROSSMAN, STICK BOY (eb)
	1953-54 DET	W. CROSSMAN (rep)
	1953-54 DET	W CROSSMAN ST BOY (sc)
	1996-97 DET	W. CROSSMAN (rep)
	1996-97 DET	W. CROSSMAN (sc)
	1997-98 DET	WALLY CROSSMAN (rep)
	1997-98 DET	WALLY CROSSMAN (sc)
Cunniff,	1999-00 NJ	J. CUNNIFF (rep)
John	1999-00 NJ	J. CUNNIFF (sc)
Curry, Floyd	1952-53 MC	FLOYD CURRY (re)
	1952-53 MC	FLOYD CURRY (rep)
	1952-53 MC	FLOYD CURRY (sc)
	1955-56 MC	F. CURRY (re)
	1955-56 MC	F. CURRY (rep)
	1955-56 MC	F CURRY (sc)
	1956-57 MC	FLOYD CURRY (rep)
	1956-57 MC	FLOYD CURRY (sc)
	1957-58 MC	FLOYD CURRY (rep)
	1957-58 MC	FLOYD CURRY (sc)
	1976-77 MC	FLOYD CURRY A.G.M (rep)
	1976-77 MC	FLOYD CURRY A.G.M. (sc)
	1977-78 MC	FLOYD CURRY A.G.M. (rep)
	1977-78 MC	FLOYD CURRY A.G.M. (sc)
Cushenan,	1958-59 MC	I. CUSHENAN (rep)
Ian	1958-59 MC	I CUSHENAN (sc)
Cushing,	1925-26 MM	G. CUSHING. (Vice-Pres.) (or)
Gordon	1925-26 MM	G. CUSHING (VICE-PRES) (rep)
	1925-26 MM	G. CUSHING. (Vice-Pres) (sc)

Name	Season / Team	Engraving
Dahlin,	1985-86 MC	K. DAHLIN (ab)
Kjell	1985-86 MC	K. DAHLIN (rep)
	1985-86 MC	K. DAHLIN (sc)
Dahlstrom,	1937-38 CHI	CULLY DAHLSTROM (sp)
Cully	1937-38 CHI	CULLY DAHLSTROM (ret)
Daigneault,	1992-93 MC	J.-J. DAIGNEAULT (rep)
J.J.	1992-93 MC	J.-J. DAIGNEAULT (sc)
Daly, Tim	1931-32 TML	*TRAINER* T. DALY (sp)
	1931-32 TML	TIM DALY TRAINER (ret)
	1941-42 TML	TIM DALY. TRAINER (sp)
	1941-42 TML	TIM DALY TRAINER (rep)
	1941-42 TML	TIM DALY TRAINER (sc)
	1944-45 TML	TIM DALY TRAINER (sp)
	1944-45 TML	TIM DALY TRAINER (rep)
	1944-45 TML	TIM DALY TRAINER (sc)
	1946-47 TML	THOMAS DALY TRAINER (re)
	1946-47 TML	TIM DALY TRAINER (rep)
	1946-47 TML	TIM DALY TRAINER (sc)
	1947-48 TML	THOMAS DALY—TRAINER (re)
	1947-48 TML	THOMAS DALY TRAINER (rep)
	1947-48 TML	THOMAS DALY TRAINER (sc)
	1948-49 TML	THOMAS DALY TRAINER (re)
	1948-49 TML	TIM DALY TRAINER (rep)
	1948-49 TML	TIM DALY TRAINER (sc)
	1950-51 TML	THOMAS DALY TRAINER (re)
	1950-51 TML	THOMAS DALY TRAINER (rep)
	1950-51 TML	THOMAS DALY TRAINER (sc)
Damphousse,		
Vincent	1992-93 MC	V. DAMPHOUSSE (rep)
	1992-93 MC	V. DAMPHOUSSE (sc)
Dandenault,	1996-97 DET	MATHIEU DANDENAULT (rep)
Mathieu	1996-97 DET	MATHIEU DANDENAULT (sc)
	1997-98 DET	M. DANDENAULT (rep)
	1997-98 DET	M. DANDENAULT (sc)
	2001-02 DET	MATHIEU DANDENAULT (rep)
	2001-02 DET	MATHIEU DANDENAULT (sc)
Dandurand,	1923-24 MC	LÉO DANDURAND (or)
Leo	1923-24 MC	LÉO DANDURAND (rep)
	1923-24 MC	LÉO DANDURAND (sc)
	1929-30 MC	LEO DANDURAND. SEC-TREAS. (sp)
	1929-30 MC	LEO DANDURAND (SEC TREAS) (ret)
	1930-31 MC	LEO DANDURAND, SECRETARY (sp)
	1930-31 MC	LEO DANDURAND SECRETARY (ret)
Daneyko,	1994-95 NJ	KEN DANEYKO (rep)
Ken	1994-95 NJ	KEN DANEYKO (sc)
	1999-00 NJ	KENNETH S. DANEYKO (rep)
	1999-00 NJ	KENNETH S. DANEYKO (sc)
	2002-03 NJ	KENNETH S. DANEYKO (rep)
	2002-03 NJ	KENNETH S. DANEYKO (sc)
Daniels,	1991-92 PIT	JEFF DANIELS (rep)
Jeff	1991-92 PIT	JEFF DANIELS (sc)
Darragh,		
Harry	1931-32 TML	DARRAGH (sp)
Datsyuk,	2001-02 DET	PAVEL DATSYUK (rep)
Pavel	2001-02 DET	PAVEL DATSYUK (sc)
David, Louis	1923-24 MC	L HON. L.A. DAVID (or)
Athanase	1923-24 MC	L HON. L.A. DAVID (rep)
	1923-24 MC	L. HON. L.A. DAVID (sc)
	1929-30 MC	HON.L.A.DAVID.PRES. (sp)
	1929-30 MC	HON L A DAVID (PRES) (ret)
	1930-31 MC	HON.L.A.DAVID, C.R. PRESIDENT (sp)
	1930-31 MC	HON L A DAVID C R (PRESS) (ret)
Davidson,	1941-42 TML	BOB DAVIDSON (sp)
Bob	1941-42 TML	BOB DAVIDSON (rep)
	1941-42 TML	BOB DAVIDSON (sc)
	1944-45 TML	BOB DAVIDSON CAPTAIN (sp)
	1944-45 TML	BOB DAVIDSON CAPT. (rep)
	1944-45 TML	BOB DAVIDSON (CAPT) (sc)
	1961-62 TML	ROBERT DAVIDSON CHEIF SCOUT (rep)
	1961-62 TML	ROBERT DAVIDSON CHEIF SCOUT (sc)
	1966-67 TML	B. DAVIDSON C. SCOUT (rep)
	1966-67 TML	B DAVIDSON SCOUT (sc)
Davis,	1952-53 MC	LORNE DAVIS (re)
Lorne	1952-53 MC	LORNE DAVIS (rep)
	1952-53 MC	LORNE DAVIS (sc)
	1984-85 EDM	L. DAVIS (ab)
	1984-85 EDM	L. DAVIS (rep)
	1984-85 EDM	L. DAVIS (sc)
	1986-87 EDM	L. DAVIS (ab)
	1986-87 EDM	L. DAVIS (rep)
	1986-87 EDM	L. DAVIS (sc)
	1989-90 EDM	LORNE DAVIS SCOUTS* (ab)
	1989-90 EDM	LORNE DAVIS SCOUTS* (rep)
	1989-90 EDM	LORNE DAVIS SCOUTS* (sc)
		* refers also to Garnet "Ace" Bailey and Ed Chadwick
Dawes,	1948-49 TML	ROBERT DAWES (re)
Bobby	1948-49 TML	BOB DAWES (rep)
	1948-49 TML	BOB DAWES (sc)
Dawes,	1934-35 MM	K. T. DAWES (eb)
Kenneth	1934-35 MM	KT DAWES (ret)
Day,	1931-32 TML	C. DAY (sp)
Clarence	1931-32 TML	H DAY (ret)
"Happy"	1941-42 TML	HAP DAY. COACH (sp)
	1941-42 TML	HAP DAY COACH (rep)
	1941-42 TML	HAP DAY COACH (sc)
	1944-45 TML	HAPPY DAY COACH (sp)
	1944-45 TML	HAPPY DAY COACH (rep)
	1944-45 TML	HAPPY DAY COACH (sc)
	1946-47 TML	C. H. DAY COACH (re)
	1946-47 TML	C.H. DAY COACH (rep)
	1946-47 TML	C.H. DAY COACH (sc)
	1947-48 TML	HAPPY DAY — COACH (re)
	1947-48 TML	HAP DAY COACH (rep)
	1947-48 TML	HAP DAY COACH (sc)
	1948-49 TML	C.H. HAPPY DAY—COACH (re)
	1948-49 TML	HAPPY DAY COACH (rep)
	1948-49 TML	HAPPY DAY COACH (sc)
	1950-51 TML	C.H. DAY ASSISTANT MANAGER (re)
	1950-51 TML	C.H. DAY ASST. MANAGER (rep)
	1950-51 TML	C H DAY ASS'T MANAGER (sc)
Day, Kerry	1944-45 TML	KERRY DAY MASCOT (sp)
	1944-45 TML	KERRY DAY MASCOT (rep)
	1944-45 TML	KERRY DAY MASCOT (sc)
	1947-48 TML	KERRY DAY —MASCOT (re)
	1947-48 TML	KERRY DAY MASCOT (rep)
	1947-48 TML	KERRY DAY. MASCOT (sc)
	1948-49 TML	KERRY DAY MASCOT (re)
	1948-49 TML	KERRY DAY MASCOT (rep)
	1948-49 TML	KERRY DAY MASCOT (sc)
Deadmarsh,	1995-96 COL	ADAM DEADMARSH (rep)
Adam	1995-96 COL	ADAM DEADMARSH (sc)
Dean, Kevin	1994-95 NJ	KEVIN DEAN (rep)
	1994-95 NJ	KEVIN DEAN (sc)
DeBartolo,	1990-91 PIT	EDWARD J. DEBARTOLO SR. OWNER (ab)
Ed	1990-91 PIT	EDWARD J. DEBARTOLO SR. OWNER (rep)
	1990-91 PIT	EDWARD J. DEBARTOLO SR. OWNER (sc)
DeBartolo,	1990-91 PIT	MARIE DENISE DE BARTOLO
Marie		YORK PRES. (rep)
	1990-91 PIT	MARIE DENISE DE BARTOLO
		YORK PRES. (sc)
		* see also Marie DeBartolo York
DeBlois,	1985-86 MC	L. DEBLOIS (ab)
Lucien	1985-86 MC	L. DEBLOIS (rep)
	1985-86 MC	L. DEBLOIS (sc)

Name	Season	Engraving
DeJordy, Denis	1960-61 CHI	DENIS DE JORDY (rep)
	1960-61 CHI	DENIS DE JORDY (sc)
Delarue, Dr. Norman	1948-49 TML	DR. NORMAN DELARUE CLUB DOCTOR (re)
	1950-51 TML	DR. NORMAN DELARUE CLUB DOCTOR (re)
Delvecchio, Alex	1951-52 DET	ALEX DELVECCHIO (re)
	1951-52 DET	ALEX DELVECCHIO (rep)
	1951-52 DET	ALEX DELVECCHIO (sc)
	1953-54 DET	ALEX DELVECCHIO (re)
	1953-54 DET	ALEX DELVECCHIO (rep)
	1953-54 DET	ALEX BELVECCHIO (sc)
	1954-55 DET	ALEX DELVECCHIO (re)
	1954-55 DET	ALEX DELVECCHIO (rep)
	1954-55 DET	ALEX DELVECCHIO (sc)
Demers, Jacques	1992-93 MC	JACQUES DEMERS COACH (rep)
	1992-93 MC	JACQUES DEMERS COACH (sc)
Denneny, Cy	1926-27 OTT	CY DENNENY (or)
	1926-27 OTT	CY DENNENY (rep)
	1926-27 OTT	CY DENNENY (sc)
	1928-29 BB	"CY" DENNENY (or)
	1928-29 BB	"CY" DENNENY (rep)
	1928-29 BB	"CY" DENNENY (sc)
	(I) 1928-29 BB	CY DENNENNY (COACH) (ret)
	(II) 1928-29 BB	C DENNENY (ret)
Desjardins, Eric	1992-93 MC	E. DESJARDINS (rep)
	1992-93 MC	E. DESJARDINS (sc)
Devellano, Jim	1979-80 NYI	JAMES DEVELLANO C. SCOUT (ab)
	1979-80 NYI	JAMES DEVELLANO C. SCOUT (rep)
	1979-80 NYI	JAMES DEVELLANO C. SCOUT (sc)
	1980-81 NYI	JIM DEVELLANO C. SCOUT (ab)
	1980-81 NYI	JIM DEVELLANO C. SCOUT (rep)
	1980-81 NYI	JIM DEVELLANO C. SCOUT (sc)
	1981-82 NYI	JIM DEVELLANO A.G.M. & DIR. SCOUTING (ab)
	1981-82 NYI	JIM DEVELLANO A.G.M. & DIR. SCOUTING (rep)
	1981-82 NYI	JIM DEVELLANO A.G.M. & DIR. SCOUTING (sc)
	1996-97 DET	JIM DEVELLANO (rep)
	1996-97 DET	JIM DEVELLANO (sc)
	1997-98 DET	JIM DEVELLANO (rep)
	1997-98 DET	JIM DEVELLANO (sc)
	2001-02 DET	JIM DEVELLANO (rep)
	2001-02 DET	JIM DEVELLANO (sc)
Devereaux, Boyd	2001-02 DET	BOYD DEVEREAUX (rep)
	2001-02 DET	BOYD DEVEREAUX (sc)
De Vries, Greg	2000-01 COL	GREG DE VRIES (rep)
	2000-01 COL	GREG DE VRIES (sc)
Dewsbury, Al	1949-50 DET	AL DEWSBURY (re)
	1949-50 DET	AL DEWSBURY (rep)
	1949-50 DET	AL DEWSBURY (sc)
Dickens, Ernie	1941-42 TML	ERNIE DICKENS (sp)
	1941-42 TML	ERNIE DICKENS (rep)
	1941-42 TML	ERNIE DICKENS (sc)
Dillon, Cecil	1932-33 NYR	CECIL DILLON (sp)
	1932-33 NYR	CECIL DILLON (ret)
Dineen, Bill	1953-54 DET	WILLIAM DINEEN (re)
	1953-54 DET	WILLIAM DINEEN (rep)
	1953-54 DET	WILLIAM DINEEN (sc)
	1954-55 DET	WILLIAM DINEEN (re)
	1954-55 DET	WILLIAM DINEEN (rep)
	1954-55 DET	WILLIAM DINEEN (sc)
Dingman, Chris	2000-01 COL	CHRIS DINGMAN (rep)
	2000-01 COL	CHRIS DINGMAN (sc)
Dinsmore, Chuck	1925-26 MM	C.A. DINSMORE. (or)
	1925-26 MM	C.A. DINSMORE (rep)
	1925-26 MM	C.A. DINSMORE. (sc)
Dionne, Gilbert	1992-93 MC	G. DIONNE (rep)
	1992-93 MC	G. DIONNE (sc)
DiPietro, Paul	1992-93 MC	P. DIPIETRO (rep)
	1992-93 MC	P. DIPIETRO (sc)
Dixon, Eugene	1973-74 PHI	F. EUGENE DIXON JR. V. OF B. (rep)
	1973-74 PHI	F.EUGENE DIXON JR.V.C.OF B. (sc)
	1974-75 PHI	EUGENE DIXON V.C. OF B. (rep)
	1974-75 PHI	EUGENE DIXON V.C. OF B. (sc)
Doak, Gary	1969-70 BB	G. DOAK (rep)
	1969-70 BB	G DOAK (sc)
Donnelly, Thorne	1937-38 CHI	THORNE DONNELLEY/SECT + TREAS (sp)
	1937-38 CHI	THORNE DONNELLEY (SECT TREAS) (ret)
Dornhoefer, Gary	1973-74 PHI	GARY DORNHOEFER (rep)
	1973-74 PHI	GARY DORNHOEFER (sc)
	1974-75 PHI	GARY DORNHOEFER (rep)
	1974-75 PHI	GARY DORNHOEFER (sc)
Dorval, Napoleon	1923-24 MC	NAP. DORVAL (or)
	1923-24 MC	NAP DORVAL (rep)
	1923-24 MC	NAP DORVAL (sc)
Douglas, Kent	1962-63 TML	KENT DOUGLAS (rep)
	1962-63 TML	KENT DOUGLAS (sc)
Douglas, Les	1942-43 DET	LES DOUGLAS (sp)
	1942-43 DET	LES DOUGLAS (rep)
	1942-43 DET	LES DOUGLAS (sc)
Dowd, Jim	1994-95 NJ	JIM DOWD (rep)
	1994-95 NJ	JIM DOWD (sc)
Draper, Dave	1995-96 COL	DAVE DRAPER (rep)
	1995-96 COL	DAVE DRAPER (sc)
Draper, Kris	1996-97 DET	KRIS DRAPER (rep)
	1996-97 DET	KRIS DRAPER (sc)
	1997-98 DET	K. DRAPER (rep)
	1997-98 DET	K. DRAPER (sc)
	2001-02 DET	KRIS DRAPER (rep)
	2001-02 DET	KRIS DRAPER (sc)
Drillon, Gord	1941-42 TML	GORDON DRILLON (sp)
	1941-42 TML	GORDON DRILLON (rep)
	1941-42 TML	GORDON DRILLON (sc)
Driver, Bruce	1994-95 NJ	BRUCE DRIVER "A" (rep)
	1994-95 NJ	BRUCE DRIVER "A" (sc)
Drury, Chris	2000-01 COL	CHRIS DRURY (rep)
	2000-01 COL	CHRIS DRURY (sc)
Dryden, Ken	1970-71 MC	GOALIES K. DRYDEN* (rep)
	1970-71 MC	GOALIES K. DRYDEN* (sc)
		* refers also to Rogie Vachon
	1972-73 MC	KEN DRYDEN (rep)
	1972-73 MC	KEN DRYDEN (sc)
	1975-76 MC	KEN DRYDEN (rep)
	1975-76 MC	KEN DRYDEN (sc)
	1976-77 MC	KENNETH DRYDEN (rep)
	1976-77 MC	KENNETH DRYDEN (sc)
	1977-78 MC	KENNETH DRYDEN (rep)
	1977-78 MC	KENNETH DRYDEN (sc)
	1978-79 MC	K. DRYDEN (ab)
	1978-79 MC	K. DRYDEN (rep)
	1978-79 MC	K. DRYDEN (sc)
Dube, Gilles	1953-54 DET	GILLES DUBE (re)
	1953-54 DET	GILLES DUBE (rep)
	1953-54 DET	GILLES DUBE (sc)
Dubois, Hector	1952-53 MC	HECTOR DUBOIS-TRAINER (re)
	1952-53 MC	H. DUBOIS TR. (rep)
	1952-53 MC	H DUEBOIS (TR) (sc)
	1955-56 MC	H. DUBOIS (re)
	1955-56 MC	H. DUBOIS (rep)
	1955-56 MC	H DUBOIS (sc)
	1956-57 MC	HECTOR DUBOIS (rep)
	1956-57 MC	HECTOR DUBOIS (sc)
	1957-58 MC	H. DUBOIS TRAINER (rep)
	1957-58 MC	H DUBOIS TRAINER (sc)
	1958-59 MC	HECTOR DUBOIS (rep)
	1958-59 MC	HECTOR DUBOIS (sc)
	1959-60 MC	HECTOR DUBOIS TRAINER (rep)
	1959-60 MC	HECTOR DUBOIS TRAINER (sc)
Duchesne, Steve	2001-02 DET	STEVE DUCHESNE (rep)
	2001-02 DET	STEVE DUCHESNE (sc)
Duff, Dick	1961-62 TML	RICHARD DUFF (rep)
	1961-62 TML	RICHARD DUFF (sc)
	1962-63 TML	RICHARD DUFF (rep)
	1962-63 TML	RICHARD DUFF (sc)
	1964-65 MC	RICHARD DUFF (rep)
	1964-65 MC	RICHARD DUFF (sc)
	1965-66 MC	RICHARD DUFF (rep)
	1965-66 MC	RICHARD DUFF (sc)
	1967-68 MC	R. DUFF (rep)
	1967-68 MC	R DUFF (sc)
	1968-69 MC	R. DUFF (rep)
	1968-69 MC	R DUFF (sc)
Dufour, Ed	1923-24 MC	TRAINER/ED.DUFOUR (or)
	1923-24 MC	TRAINER/ED DUFOUR (rep)
	1923-24 MC	TRAINER/ED.DUFOUR (sc)
	1929-30 MC	ED DUFOUR. (sp)
	1929-30 MC	ED DUFOUR (ret)
	1930-31 MC	ED DUFOUR (sp)
	1930-31 MC	ED DUFOUR TRAINER (ret)
Dufresne, Donald	1992-93 MC	D. DUFRESNE (rep)
	1992-93 MC	D. DUFRESNE (sc)
Dugal, Jules	1930-31 MC	*BUSINESS MANAGER* JULES DUGAL (sp)
	1930-31 MC	JULES DUGAL MANN (ret)
Dumart, Woody	1938-39 BB	W. DUMART (sp)
	1938-39 BB	W DUMART (ret)
	1940-41 BB	WOODROW DUMART. (sp)
	1940-41 BB	WOODY DUMART (rep)
	1940-41 BB	WOODY DUMART (sc)
Dupont, Andre	1973-74 PHI	ANDRE DUPONT (rep)
	1973-74 PHI	ANDRE DUPONT (sc)
	1974-75 PHI	ANDRE DUPONT (rep)
	1974-75 PHI	ANDRE DUPONT (sc)
Durnan, Bill	1943-44 MC	WILLIAM DURNAN (sp)
	1943-44 MC	BILL DURNAN (rep)
	1943-44 MC	BILL DURMAN (sc)
	1945-46 MC	WILLIAM DURNAN (re)

Name	Season	Engraving
	1945-46 MC	BILL DURNAN (rep)
	1945-46 MC	BILL DURNAN (sc)
Eddolls, Frank	1945-46 MC	FRANK EDDOLLS (re)
	1945-46 MC	FRANK EDDOLLS (rep)
	1945-46 MC	FRANK EDDOLLS (sc)
Edwards, Allan	1960-61 CHI	ALLAN R. EDWARDS (rep)
	1960-61 CHI	ALLAN R EDWARDS (sc)
Ehman, Gerry	1963-64 TML	GERALD EHMAN (rep)
	1963-64 TML	GERALD EHMAN (sc)
	1979-80 NYI	GERALD EHMAN W. SCOUT (ab)
	1979-80 NYI	GERALD EHMAN W. SCOUT (rep)
	1979-80 NYI	GERALD EHMAN W. SCOUT (sc)
	1980-81 NYI	GERALD EHMAN W. SCOUT (ab)
	1980-81 NYI	GERALD EHMAN W. SCOUT (rep)
	1980-81 NYI	GERALD EHMAN W. SCOUT (sc)
	1981-82 NYI	GERRY EHMAN HEAD SCOUT (ab)
	1981-82 NYI	GERRY EHMAN HEAD SCOUT (rep)
	1981-82 NYI	GERRY EHMAN HEAD SCOUT (sc)
	1982-83 NYI	GERRY EHMAN ASST. G.M. & DIR. SCOUTING (ab)
	1982-83 NYI	GERRY EHMAN ASST. G.M. & DIR. SCOUTING (rep)
	1982-83 NYI	GERRY EHMAN ASST. G.M. & DIR. SCOUTING (sc)
Elias, Patrik	1999-00 NJ	PATRIK ELIAS (rep)
	1999-00 NJ	PATRIK ELIAS (sc)
	2002-03 NJ	PATRIK ELIAS (rep)
	2002-03 NJ	PATRIK ELIAS (sc)
Elieff, Karl	1966-67 TML	KARL ELIEFF PHYSIOTHERAPIST (rep)
	1966-67 TML	KARL ELIEFF PHYSIOTHERAPIST (sc)
Elliot, H.J.	1923-24 MC	H.J. ELLIOT C.R. (or)
	1923-24 MC	H.J. ELLIOT C.R. (rep)
	1923-24 MC	H.J. ELLIOT. C.R. (sc)
Ellis, Ron	1966-67 TML	RON ELLIS (rep)
	1966-67 TML	RON ELLIS (sc)
Ellsworth, Albert	1931-32 TML	MR. A. I. ELLSWORTH (sp)
Elmer, Wally	1924-25 VIC	W. ELMER. (or)
	1924-25 VIC	W. ELMER (rep)
	1924-25 VIC	W. ELMER. (sc)
Engblom, Brian	1977-78 MC	BRIAN ENGBLOM (rep)
	1977-78 MC	BRIAN ENGBLOM (sc)
	1978-79 MC	B. ENGBLOM (ab)
	1978-79 MC	B. ENGBLOM (rep)
	1978-79 MC	B. ENGBLOM (sc)
Erickson, Aut	1966-67 TML	AUT ERICKSON (rep)
	1966-67 TML	AUT ERICKSON (sc)
Eriksson, Anders	1997-98 DET	A. ERIKSSON (rep)
	1997-98 DET	A. ERIKSSON (sc)
Errey, Bob	1990-91 PIT	B. ERREY (ab)
	1990-91 PIT	B. ERREY (rep)
	1990-91 PIT	B. ERREY (sc)
	1991-92 PIT	BOB ERREY (rep)
	1991-92 PIT	BOB ERREY (sc)
Esposito, Phil	1969-70 BB	P. ESPOSITO (rep)
	1969-70 BB	P ESPOSITO (sc)
	1971-72 BB	PHIL ESPOSITO (rep)
	1971-72 BB	PHIL ESPOSITO (sc)
Esposito, Tony	1968-69 MC	P. FSPOSITO (rep)
	1968-69 MC	GOALIES A ESPOSITO* (sc)
		* refers also to Rogie Vachon and Gump Worsley
Evans, Jack	1960-61 CHI	JOHN EVANS (rep)
	1960-61 CHI	JOHN EVANS (sc)
Evans, Stewart	1934-35 MM	S. EVANS (sp)
	1934-35 MM	S EVANS (ret)
Ewen, Todd	1992-93 MC	T. EWEN (rep)
	1992-93 MC	T. EWEN (sc)
Ezinicki, Bill	1946-47 TML	WILLIAM EZINICKI (re)
	1946-47 TML	WILLIAM EZINICKI (rep)
	1946-47 TML	WILLIAM EZINICKI (sc)
	1947-48 TML	WILLIAM EZINICKI (re)
	1947-48 TML	BILL EZINICKI (rep)
	1947-48 TML	BILL EZINICKI (sc)
	1948-49 TML	WILLIAM EZINICKI (re)
Farmer, Terry	2002-03 NJ	T. FARMER (rep)
	2002-03 NJ	T. FARMER (sc)
Fedorov, Sergei	1996-97 DET	SERGEI FEDOROV (rep)
	1996-97 DET	SERGEI FEDOROV (sc)
	1997-98 DET	S. FEDOROV (rep)
	1997-98 DET	S. FEDOROV (sc)
	2001-02 DET	SERGEI FEDOROV (rep)
	2001-02 DET	SERGEI FEDOROV (sc)
Feltrin, Tony	1993-94 NYR	T. FELTRIN SCOUT (rep)
	1993-94 NYR	T. FELTRIN SCOUT (sc)
Ferguson, John	1964-65 MC	JOHN FERGUSON (rep)
	1964-65 MC	JOHN FERGUSON (sc)
	1965-66 MC	J. FERGUSON (rep)
	1965-66 MC	J FERGUSON (sc)
	1967-68 MC	J. FERGUSON (rep)
	1967-68 MC	J FERGUSON (sc)
	1968-69 MC	J. FERGUSON (rep)
	1968-69 MC	J FERGUSON (sc)
	1970-71 MC	JOHN FERGUSON (rep)
	1970-71 MC	JOHN FERGUSON. (sc)
Fetisov, Viacheslav	1996-97 DET	VIACHESLAV FETISOV (rep)
	1996-97 DET	VIACHESLAV FETISOV (sc)
	1997-98 DET	V. FETISOV (rep)
	1997-98 DET	V. FETISOV (sc)
	1999-00 NJ	V. FETISOV (rep)
	1999-00 NJ	V. FETISOV (sc)
Fillion, Bob	1943-44 MC	ROBERT FILLION (sp)
	1943-44 MC	BOB FILLION (rep)
	1943-44 MC	BOB FILLION (sc)
	1945-46 MC	ROBERT FILLION. (re)
	1945-46 MC	ROBERT FILLION (rep)
	1945-46 MC	ROBERT FILLION (sc)
Finnigan, Frank	1926-27 OTT	FRANK FINNIGAN (or)
	1926-27 OTT	FRANK FINNIGAN (rep)
	1926-27 OTT	FRANK FINNIGAN (sc)
	1931-32 TML	FINNIGAN (sp)
Fischer, Jiri	2001-02 DET	JIRI FISCHER (rep)
	2001-02 DET	JIRI FISCHER (sc)
Fiset, Stephane	1995-96 COL	STEPHANE FISET (rep)
	1995-96 COL	STEPHANE FISET (sc)
Fisher, Dr. Barry	1999-00 NJ	DR. B. FISHER (rep)
	1999-00 NJ	DR. B. FISHER (sc)
	2002-03 NJ	DR. B. FISHER (rep)
	2002-03 NJ	DR. B. FISHER (sc)
Fisher, Joe	1942-43 DET	JOE FISHER (sp)
	1942-43 DET	JOE FISHER (rep)
	1942-43 DET	JOE FISHER (sc)
Fisher, Milt	1994-95 NJ	MILT FISHER (rep)
	1994-95 NJ	MILT FISHER (sc)
	1999-00 NJ	M. FISHER (rep)
	1999-00 NJ	M. FISHER (sc)
	2002-03 NJ	M. FISHER (rep)
	2002-03 NJ	M. FISHER (sc)
Fitkin, Ed	1947-48 TML	ED FITKIN — PUBLICITY DIRECTOR (re)
	1947-48 TML	E.D. FITKIN PUB. DIR. (rep)
	1947-48 TML	E.D. FITKIN (PUB• DIR) (sc)
	1948-49 TML	ED. FITKIN PUBLICITY DIRECTOR (re)
	1950-51 TML	ED. FITKIN, PUBLICITY DIRECTOR (re)
	1950-51 TML	E.D. FITKIN PUB. DIRECTOR (rep)
	1950-51 TML	ED FITKIN PUB DERECTOR (sc)
Fixter, Paul	1995-96 COL	PAUL FIXTER (rep)
	1995-96 COL	PAUL FIXTER (sc)
	2000-01 COL	PAUL FIXTER (rep)
	2000-01 COL	PAUL FIXTER (sc)
Flaman, Fern	1950-51 TML	FERN FLAMAN (re)
	1950-51 TML	FERN FLAMAN (rep)
	1950-51 TML	FERN FLAMAN (sc)
Fleming, Reg	1960-61 CHI	REGINALD FLEMING (rep)
	1960-61 CHI	REGINALD FLEMING (sc)
Flemming, Wayne	2000-01 COL	WAYNE FLEMMING (rep)
	2000-01 COL	WAYNE FLEMMING (sc)
Fletcher, Cliff	1988-89 CAL	CLIFF FLETCHER PRES.G.M. (ab)
	1988-89 CAL	CLIFF FLETCHER PRES.G.M. (rep)
	1988-89 CAL	CLIFF FLETCHER PRES.G.M. (sc)
Flett, Bill	1973-74 PHI	BILL FLETT (rep)
	1973-74 PHI	BILL FLETT (sc)
Fleury, Theo	1988-89 CAL	T. FLEURY (ab)
	1988-89 CAL	T. FLEURY (rep)
	1988-89 CAL	T. FLEURY (sc)
Fogolin, Lee	1949-50 DET	LEE FOGOLIN (re)
	1949-50 DET	LEE FOGOLIN (rep)
	1949-50 DET	LEE FOGOLIN (sc)
Fogolin, Lee Jr.	1983-84 EDM	L. FOGOLIN (ab)
	1983-84 EDM	L. FOGOLIN (rep)
	1983-84 EDM	L. FOGOLIN (sc)
	1984-85 EDM	L. FOGOLIN (ab)
	1984-85 EDM	L. FOGOLIN (rep)
	1984-85 EDM	L. FOGOLIN (sc)
Folga, Mike	1993-94 NYR	M. FOLGA TRAINER (rep)
	1993-94 NYR	M. FOLGA TRAINER (sc)
Foote, Adam	1995-96 COL	ADAM FOOTE (rep)
	1995-96 COL	ADAM FOOTE (sc)
	2000-01 COL	ADAM FOOTE (rep)
	2000-01 COL	ADAM FOOTE (sc)
Forristall, John	1969-70 BB	J. FORRISTALL ASST.TR. (rep)
	1969-70 BB	J FORRISTALL ASS TR (sc)
	1971-72 BB	JOHN FORRISTALL ASST. TRAINER (rep)
	1971-72 BB	JOHN FORRISTALL ASS. TRA. (sc)
Forsberg, Peter	1995-96 COL	PETER FORSBERG (rep)
	1995-96 COL	PETER FORSBERG (sc)
	2000-01 COL	PETER FORSBERG (rep)

Name	Season	Engraving
	2000-01 COL	PETER FORSBERG (sc)
Foyston,	1924-25 VIC	F. FOYSTON. (or)
Frank	1924-25 VIC	F. FOYSTON (rep)
	1924-25 VIC	F. FOYSTON. (sc)
Francis, Ron	1990-91 PIT	R. FRANCIS (ab)
	1990-91 PIT	R. FRANCIS (rep)
	1990-91 PIT	R. FRANCIS (sc)
	1991-92 PIT	RON FRANCIS (rep)
	1991-92 PIT	RON FRANCIS (sc)
Franks, Jim	1936-37 DET	JAMES FRANKS GOAL (sp)
	1936-37 DET	JAMES FRANKS (ret)
Fraser,	1983-84 EDM	BARRY FRASER DIR. P.P. & C. SCOUT (ab)
Barry	1983-84 EDM	BARRY FRASER DIR. P.P. & C. SCOUT (rep)
	1983-84 EDM	BARRY FRASER DIR. P.P. & C. SCOUT (sc)
	1984-85 EDM	BARRY FRASER DIR. P.P. & CHIEF SCOUT (ab)
	1984-85 EDM	BARRY FRASER DIR. P.P & CHIEF SCOUT (rep)
	1984-85 EDM	BARRY FRASER DIR. P.P. & CHIEF SCOUT (sc)
	1986-87 EDM	BARRY FRASER DIR. P.P. (ab)
	1986-87 EDM	BARRY FRASER DIR. P.P. (rep)
	1986-87 EDM	BARRY FRASER DIR. P.P. (sc)
	1987-88 EDM	BARRY FRASER DIR. P.P. (ab)
	1987-88 EDM	BARRY FRASER DIR. P.P. (rep)
	1987-88 EDM	BARRY FRASER DIR. P.P. (sc)
	1989-90 EDM	BARRY FRASER DIR. P.P. (ab)
	1989-90 EDM	BARRY FRASER DIR. P.P. (rep)
	1989-90 EDM	BARRY FRASER DIR. P.P. (sc)
Fraser,	1924-25 VIC	G. FRASER. (or)
Gordon	1924-25 VIC	G. FRASER (rep)
	1924-25 VIC	G. FRASER. (sc)
Fredrickson,	1924-25 VIC	F. FREDRICKSON. (or)
Frank	1924-25 VIC	F. FREDRICKSON (rep)
	1924-25 VIC	F. FREDRICKSON. (sc)
	1928-29 BB	F FREDRICKSON (ret)
Friesen, Jeff	2002-03 NJ	JEFF DARYL FRIESEN (rep)
	2002-03 NJ	JEFF DARYL FRIESEN (sc)
Froelich, Ed	1933-34 CHI	EDWARD FROELICH *Trainer* (sp)
	1933-34 CHI	E FROELICH (TRAIN) (ret)
	1937-38 CHI	EDWARD FROELICH TRAINER (sp)
Frost, Harry	1938-39 BB	H. FROST (sp)
	1938-39 BB	H FROST (ret)
Ftorek,	1994-95 NJ	ROBBIE FTOREK (rep)
Robbie	1994-95 NJ	ROBBIE FTOREK (sc)
	1999-00 NJ	R. FTOREK (rep)
	1999-00 NJ	R. FTOREK (sc)
Fuhr, Grant	1983-84 EDM	G. FUHR (ab)
	1983-84 EDM	G. FUHR (rep)
	1983-84 EDM	G. FUHR (sc)
	1984-85 EDM	G. FUHR (ab)
	1984-85 EDM	G. FUHR (rep)
	1984-85 EDM	G. FUHR (sc)
	1986-87 EDM	G. FUHR (ab)
	1986-87 EDM	G. FUHR (rep)
	1986-87 EDM	G. FUHR (sc)
	1987-88 EDM	G. FUHR (ab)
	1987-88 EDM	G. FUHR (rep)
	1987-88 EDM	G. FUHR (sc)
	1989-90 EDM	G. FUHR (ab)
	1989-90 EDM	G. FUHR (rep)
	1989-90 EDM	G. FUHR (sc)
Gagnon,	1930-31 MC	JOHNNY GAGNON (sp)
Johnny	1930-31 MC	JOHNNY GAGNON (ret)
Gainey, Bob	1975-76 MC	BOB GAINEY (rep)
	1975-76 MC	BOB GAINEY (sc)
	1976-77 MC	ROBERT GAINEY (rep)
	1976-77 MC	ROBERT GAINY (sc)
	1977-78 MC	ROBERT GAINEY (rep)
	1977-78 MC	ROBERT GAINEY (sc)
	1978-79 MC	R. GAINEY (ab)
	1978-79 MC	R. GAINEY (rep)
	1978-79 MC	R. GAINEY (sc)
	1985-86 MC	R. GAINEY CAPT. (ab)
	1985-86 MC	R. GAINEY CAPT. (rep)
	1985-86 MC	R. GAINEY CAPT. (sc)
	1998-99 DAL	BOB GAINEY (rep)
	1998-99 DAL	BOB GAINEY (sc)
Gainor,	1928-29 BB	"DUTCH" GAINOR (or)
Norm	1928-29 BB	"DUTCH" GAINOR (rep)
"Dutch"	1928-29 BB	"DUTCH" GAINOR (sc)
	1928-29 BB	D GAINOR (ret)
	1934-35 MM	N. GAINOR (sp)
	1934-35 MM	N GAINOR (ret)
Galbraith,	1928-29 BB	PERCY GALBRAITH (or)
Percy	1928-29 BB	PERCEY GALBRAITH (rep)
	1928-29 BB	PERCEY GALBRAITH (sc)
	1928-29 BB	P GALBRAITH (ret)
Gallagher,	1936-37 DET	JOHN GALLAGHER DEFENSE (sp)
John	1936-37 DET	JOHN GALLAGHER (ret)
Galley,	1964-65 MC	ANDREW GALLEY TRAINER (rep)
Andrew	1964-65 MC	ANDREW GALLEY TRAINER (sc)
	1965-66 MC	ANDREW GALLEY TRAINER (rep)
	1965-66 MC	ANDREW GALLEY TRAINER (sc)
Galloway,	1946-47 TML	DR. R.J. GALLOWAY CLUB DOCTOR (re)
Dr. Robert	1946-47 TML	P.J. GALLOWAY (rep)
	1946-47 TML	R.J. GALLOWAY (sc)
	1947-48 TML	DR. R.J. GALLOWAY—CLUB DOCTOR (re)
	1947-48 TML	P.J. GALLOWAY (rep)
	1947-48 TML	P.J. GALLOWAY (sc)
Gamble,	1952-53 MC	DICK GAMBLE (re)
Dick	1952-53 MC	DICK GAMBLE (rep)
	1952-53 MC	DICK GAMBLE (sc)
Gardiner,	1933-34 CHI	CHARLES GARDINER *Captain* (sp)
Chuck	1933-34 CHI	CHARLES GARDINER (CAPT) (ret)
Gardner,	1948-49 TML	CALVIN GARDNER (re)
Cal	1948-49 TML	CAL GARDNER (rep)
	1948-49 TML	CAL GARDNER (sc)
	1950-51 TML	CAL GARDNER (rep)
	1950-51 TML	CAL GARDNER (sc)
Garen, Nick	1960-61 CHI	NICK GAREN . (rep)
	1960-61 CHI	NICK GAREN. (sc)
Gatherum,	1953-54 DET	DAVID GATHERUM (re)
Dave	1953-54 DET	DAVID GATHERUM (rep)
	1953-54 DET	DAVID GATHERUM (sc)
Gauthier,	1964-65 MC	JEAN GAUTHIER (rep)
Jean	1964-65 MC	JEAN GAUTHIER (sc)
Gee, George	1949-50 DET	GEORGE GEE (re)
	1949-50 DET	GEORGE GEE (rep)
	1949-50 DET	GEORGE GEE (sc)
Gelinas,	1989-90 EDM	M. GELINAS (ab)
Martin	1989-90 EDM	M. GELINAS (rep)
	1989-90 EDM	M. GELINAS (sc)
Gendron,	1994-95 NJ	DENIS GENDRON (rep)
Denis	1994-95 NJ	DENIS GENDRON (sc)
	1999-00 NJ	D. GENDRON (rep)
	1999-00 NJ	D. GENDRON (sc)
Geoffrion,	1952-53 MC	BERNARD GEOFFRION (re)
Bernie	1952-53 MC	B. GEOFFRION (rep)
	1952-53 MC	B GEOFFRION (sc)
	1955-56 MC	B. GEOFFRION (re)
	1955-56 MC	B. GEOFFRION (rep)
	1955-56 MC	B GEOFFRION (sc)
	1956-57 MC	BERNARD GEOFFRION (rep)
	1956-57 MC	BERNARD GEOFFRION (sc)
	1957-58 MC	BERNARD GEOFFRION (rep)
	1957-58 MC	BERNARD GEOFFRION (sc)
	1958-59 MC	B. GEOFFRION (rep)
	1958-59 MC	B GEOFFRION (sc)
	1959-60 MC	B. GEOFFRION (rep)
	1959-60 MC	B GEOFFRION (sc)
Gerard,	1925-26 MM	E. GERARD. (Mgr.) (or)
Eddie	1925-26 MM	F. GERAD. (Mgr) (rep)
	1925-26 MM	F. GERAD. (Mgr) (sc)
Gernander,	1998-99 DAL	BOB GERNANDER (rep)
Bob	1998-99 DAL	BOB GERNANDER (sc)
Gervais,	1992-93 MC	P. GERVAIS A.EQP.MGR. (rep)
Pierre	1992-93 MC	P. GERVAIS A.EQP.MGR. (sc)
Getliffe,	1938-39 BB	R. GETLIFFE (sp)
Ray	1938-39 BB	R SETLIFFE (ret)
	1943-44 MC	RAY GETLIFFE (sp)
	1943-44 MC	RAY GETLIFFE (rep)
	1943-44 MC	RAY GETLIFFE (sc)
Gibbins,	1995-96 COL	BROCK GIBBINS (rep)
Brock	1995-96 COL	BROCK GIBBINS (sc)
Giffels,	1935-36 DET	L.J. GIFFELS—BUSINESS MANAGER (eb)
Louis	1935-36 DET	L C GIFFELS BUIS (ret)
Giguere,	1995-96 COL	FRANCOIS GIGUERE (rep)
Francois	1995-96 COL	FRANCOIS GIGUERE (sc)
	2000-01 COL	FRANCOIS GIGUERE (rep)
	2000-01 COL	FRANCOIS GIGUERE (sc)
Gilbert,	1981-82 NYI	G. GILBERT (ab)
Greg	1981-82 NYI	G. GILBERT (rep)
	1981-82 NYI	G. GILBERT (sc)
	1982-83 NYI	G. GILBERT (ab)
	1982-83 NYI	G. GILBERT (rep)
	1982-83 NYI	G. GILBERT (sc)
	1993-94 NYR	G. GILBERT (rep)
	1993-94 NYR	G. GILBERT (sc)
Gilchrist,	1997-98 DET	B. GILCHRIST (rep)
Brent	1997-98 DET	B. GILCHRIST (sc)
Gilhen,	1990-91 PIT	R. GILHEN (ab)
Randy	1990-91 PIT	R. GILHEN (rep)
	1990-91 PIT	R. GILHEN (sc)
Gill, Dave	1926-27 OTT	D.N. GILL MANAGER (or)
	1926-27 OTT	D.N. GILL MANAGER (rep)
	1926-27 OTT	D.N. GILL MANAGER (sc)
Gill, John	1991-92 PIT	JOHN GILL (rep)

Name	Season	Team	Engraving
	1991-92	PIT	JOHN GILL (sc)
Gillies, Clark	1979-80	NYI	C. GILLIES (ab)
	1979-80	NYI	C. GILLIES (rep)
	1979-80	NYI	C. GILLIES (sc)
	1980-81	NYI	C. GILLIES (ab)
	1980-81	NYI	C. GILLIES (rep)
	1980-81	NYI	C. GILLIES (sc)
	1981-82	NYI	C. GILLIES (ab)
	1981-82	NYI	C. GILLIES (rep)
	1981-82	NYI	C. GILLIES (sc)
	1982-83	NYI	C. GILLIES (ab)
	1982-83	NYI	C. GILLIES (rep)
	1982-83	NYI	C. GILLIES (sc)
Gilmour, Doug	1988-89	CAL	D. GILMOUR (ab)
	1988-89	CAL	D. GILMOUR (rep)
	1988-89	CAL	D. GILMOUR (sc)
Gingras, Gaston	1985-86	MC	G. GINGRAS (ab)
	1985-86	MC	G. GINGRAS (rep)
	1985-86	MC	G. GINGRAS (sc)
Gionta, Brian	2002-03	NJ	BRIAN J. GIONTA (rep)
	2002-03	NJ	BRIAN J. GIONTA (sc)
Glass, "Pud"	1907	MW	PUD. GLASS. (ib)
	1907	MW	PUD GLASS (rep)
	1907	MW	PUD GLASS (sc)
Gleeson, Ed	1926-27	OTT	E.P. GLEESON TRAINER (or)
	1926-27	OTT	E.P. GLEESON TRAINER (rep)
	1926-27	OTT	E.P. GLEESON TRAINER (sc)
Glover, Fred	1951-52	DET	FRED GLOVER (re)
	1951-52	DET	FRED GLOVER (rep)
	1951-52	DET	FRED GLOVER (sc)
Goldberg, Paul	2000-01	COL	PAUL GOLDBERG (rep)
	2000-01	COL	PAUL GOLDBERG (sc)
Goldham, Bob	1941-42	TML	BOB GOLDHAM (sp)
	1941-42	TML	BOB GOLDHAM (rep)
	1941-42	TML	BOB GOLDHAN (sc)
	1946-47	TML	ROBERT GOLDHAM (re)
	1946-47	TML	BOB GOLDHAM (rep)
	1946-47	TML	BOB GOLDHAM (sc)
	1951-52	DET	BOB GOLDHAM (re)
	1951-52	DET	BOB GOLDHAM (rep)
	1951-52	DET	BOB GOLDHAM (sc)
	1953-54	DET	ROBERT GOLDHAM (re)
	1953-54	DET	ROBERT GOLDHAM (rep)
	1953-54	DET	ROBERT GOLDHAM (sc)
	1954-55	DET	ROBERT GOLDHAM (re)
	1954-55	DET	BOB GOLDHAM (rep)
	1954-55	DET	BOB GOLDHAM (sc)
Goldsworthy, Leroy	1933-34	CHI	LEROY GOLDSWORTHY (sp)
	1933-34	CHI	LEROY GOLDSWORTHY (ret)
Goldup, Hank	1941-42	TML	HANK GOLDUP (sp)
	1941-42	TML	HANK GOLDUP (rep)
	1941-42	TML	HANK GOLDUP (sc)
Gomez, Scott	1999-00	NJ	SCOTT C. GOMEZ (rep)
	1999-00	NJ	SCOTT C. GOMEZ (sc)
	2002-03	NJ	SCOTT C. GOMEZ (rep)
	2002-03	NJ	SCOTT C. GOMEZ (sc)
Goodenough, Larry	1974-75	PHI	LARRY GOODENOUGH (rep)
	1974-75	PHI	LARRY GOODENOUGH (sc)
Gooderham, George	1931-32	TML	MR. GEO. H. GOODERHAM (sp)
Goodfellow, Ebbie	1935-36	DET	EBBIE GOODFELLOW—R. DEFENSE (sp)
	1935-36	DET	EBBIE GOODFELLOW (ret)
	1936-37	DET	EBBIE GOODFELLOW—R. DEFENSE (sp)
	1936-37	DET	EBBIE GOODFELLOW (ret)
	1942-43	DET	EBBIE GOODFELLOW COACH (sp)
	1942-43	DET	EBBIE GOODFELLOW COACH (rep)
	1942-43	DET	EBBIE GOODFELLOW COACH (sc)
Goodman, Paul	1937-38	CHI	PAUL GOODMAN (sp)
Goring, Robert "Butch"	1979-80	NYI	R. BUTCH GORING (ab)
	1979-80	NYI	R. BUTCH GORING (rep)
	1979-80	NYI	R. BUTCH GORING (sc)
	1980-81	NYI	R. BUTCH GORING (ab)
	1980-81	NYI	R. BUTCH GORING (rep)
	1980-81	NYI	R. BUTCH GORING (sc)
	1981-82	NYI	R. BUTCH GORING (ab)
	1981-82	NYI	R. BUTCH GORING (rep)
	1981-82	NYI	R. BUTCH GORING (sc)
	1982-83	NYI	R. BUTCH GORING (ab)
	1982-83	NYI	R. BUTCH GORING (rep)
	1982-83	NYI	R. BUTCH GORING (sc)
Gorman, Ed	1926-27	OTT	ED F. GORMAN (or)
	1926-27	OTT	E.D.F. GORMAN (rep)
	1926-27	OTT	ED. F. GORMAN (sc)
Gorman, Tommy	1933-34	CHI	THOMAS P. GORMAN *MANAGER* (sp)
	1933-34	CHI	T P GORMAN (MAN) (ret)
	1934-35	MM	T.P. GORMAN/ VICE-PRESIDENT AND MANAGER (sp)
	1934-35	MM	T P GORMAN (V PRES) MAN (ret)
	1943-44	MC	T.P. GORMAN MANAGER (sp)
	1943-44	MC	T.P. GORMAN MANAGER (rep)
	1943-44	MC	T.P. CORMAN MANAGER (sc)
	1945-46	MC	THOMAS P. GORMAN MANAGER (re)
	1945-46	MC	THOMAS P. GORMAN MGR. (rep)
	1945-46	MC	THOMAS P. GORMAN (MAN) (sc)
Gottselig, Johnny	1933-34	CHI	JOHN GOTTSELIG (sp)
	1933-34	CHI	JOHN GOTTSELIG (ret)
	1937-38	CHI	JOHNNY GOTTSELIG (sp)
	1937-38	CHI	JOHNNY GOTTSELIG (ret)
Goulet, Michel	1995-96	COL	MICHEL GOULET (rep)
	1995-96	COL	MICHEL GOULET (sc)
	2000-01	COL	MICHEL GOULET (rep)
	2000-01	COL	MICHEL GOULET (sc)
Goyette, Phil	1956-57	MC	PHIL GOYETTE (rep)
	1956-57	MC	PHIL GOYETTE (sc)
	1957-58	MC	P. GOYETTE (rep)
	1957-58	MC	P GOYETTE (sc)
	1958-59	MC	PHIL GOYETTE (rep)
	1958-59	MC	PHIL GOYETTE (sc)
	1959-60	MC	PHIL GOYETTE (rep)
	1959-60	MC	PHIL GOYETTE (sc)
Gracie, Bob	1931-32	TML	GRACIE (sp)
	1934-35	MM	R.J. GRACIE (sp)
	1934-35	MM	R J GRACIE (ret)
Grahame, Charlotte	2000-01	COL	CHARLOTTE GRAHAME (rep)
	2000-01	COL	CHARLOTTE GRAHAME (sc)
Grant, Danny	1967-68	MC	D. GRANT (rep)
	1967-68	MC	D GRANT (sc)
Graves, Adam	1989-90	EDM	A. GRAVES (ab)
	1989-90	EDM	A. GRAVES (rep)
	1989-90	EDM	A. GRAVES (sc)
	1993-94	NYR	A. GRAVES (rep)
	1993-94	NYR	A. GRAVES (sc)
Gray, Alex	1927-28	NYR	A GRAY (ret)
Gray, Sir Henry	1929-30	MC	SIR HENRY GRAY. (sp)
	1929-30	MC	SIR HENRY GRAY (ret)
	1930-31	MC	SIR HENRY GRAY (sp)
	1930-31	MC	SIR HENRY GRAY (ret)
Green, Norman	1988-89	CAL	NORMAN GREEN (ab)
	1988-89	CAL	NORMAN GREEN (rep)
	1988-89	CAL	NORMAN GREEN (sc)
Green, Red	1928-29	BB	R GREEN (ret)
Green, Rick	1985-86	MC	R. GREEN (ab)
	1985-86	MC	R. GREEN (rep)
	1985-86	MC	R. GREEN (sc)
Green, Ted	1969-70	BB	TED GREEN (rep)
	1969-70	BB	TED GREEN (sc)
	1971-72	BB	TED GREEN (rep)
	1971-72	BB	TED GREEN (sc)
	1983-84	EDM	TED GREEN ASST. COACHES* (ab)
	1983-84	EDM	TED GREEN ASST. COACHES* (rep)
	1983-84	EDM	TED GREEN ASST. COACHES* (sc)
			* refers also to John Muckler
	1984-85	EDM	TED GREEN COACHES* (ab)
	1984-85	EDM	TED GREEN COACHES* (rep)
	1984-85	EDM	TED GREEN COACHES* (sc)
			* refers also to John Muckler
	1986-87	EDM	TED GREEN ASST. COACH (ab)
	1986-87	EDM	TED GREEN ASST. COACH (rep)
	1986-87	EDM	TED GREEN ASST. COACH (sc)
	1987-88	EDM	TED GREEN ASST. COACH (ab)
	1987-88	EDM	TED GREEN ASST. COACH (rep)
	1987-88	EDM	TED GREEN ASST. COACH (sc)
	1989-90	EDM	TED GREEN CO-COACH (ab)
	1989-90	EDM	TED GREEN CO-COACH (rep)
	1989-90	EDM	TED GREEN CO-COACH (sc)
Green, Win	1928-29	BB	"WIN" GREEN TRAINER (or)
	1928-29	BB	"WIN" GREEN TRAINER (rep)
	1928-29	BB	"WIN" GREEN TRAINER (sc)
	1928-29	BB	WIN GREEN/TRAINER (ret)
	1940-41	BB	WIN. GREEN., TRAINER. (sp)
	1940-41	BB	WIN GREEN TRAINER (rep)
	1940-41	BB	WIN GREEN TRAINER (sc)
Gregg, Randy	1983-84	EDM	R. GREGG (ab)
	1983-84	EDM	R. GREGG (rep)
	1983-84	EDM	R. GREGG (sc)
	1984-85	EDM	R. GREGG (ab)
	1984-85	EDM	R. GREGG (rep)
	1984-85	EDM	R. GREGG (sc)
	1986-87	EDM	R. GREGG (ab)
	1986-87	EDM	R. GREGG (rep)
	1986-87	EDM	R. GREGG (sc)
	1987-88	EDM	R. GREGG (ab)
	1987-88	EDM	R. GREGG (rep)
	1987-88	EDM	R. GREGG (sc)
	1989-90	EDM	R. GREGG (ab)
	1989-90	EDM	R. GREGG (rep)
	1989-90	EDM	R. GREGG (sc)
Gretzky, Wayne	1983-84	EDM	W. GRETZKY CAPT. (ab)
	1983-84	EDM	W. GRETZKY CAPT. (rep)

Name	Season/Team	Inscription
	1983-84 EDM	W. GRETZKY CAPT. (sc)
	1984-85 EDM	W. GRETZKY CAPT. (ab)
	1984-85 EDM	W. GRETZKY CAPT. (rep)
	1984-85 EDM	W. GRETZKY CAPT. (sc)
	1986-87 EDM	W. GRETZKY CAPT. (ab)
	1986-87 EDM	W. GRETZKY CAPT. (rep)
	1986-87 EDM	W. GRETZKY CAPT. (sc)
	1987-88 EDM	W. GRETZKY CAPT. (ab)
	1987-88 EDM	W. GRETZKY CAPT. (rep)
	1987-88 EDM	W. GRETZKY CAPT. (sc)
Griffis, Si	1914-15 VM	SI GRIFFIS (ib)
	1914-15 VM	SI GRIFFIS (rep)
	1914-15 VM	SI GRIFFIS (sc)
Grosso, Don	1942-43 DET	DON GROSSO (sp)
	1942-43 DET	DON GROSSO (rep)
	1942-43 DET	DON GROSSO (sc)
Grundman, Irv	1978-79 MC	IRVING GRUNDMAN V.P.M.D. (ab)
	1978-79 MC	IRVING GRUNDMAN V.P.M.D. (rep)
	1978-79 MC	IRVING GRUNDMAN V.P.M.D. (sc)
Guerin, Bill	1994-95 NJ	BILL GUERIN (rep)
	1994-95 NJ	BILL GUERIN (sc)
Guile, George	1907 MW	GEO. GUILE. (ib)
	1907 MW	GEO GUILE (rep)
	1907 MW	GEO GUILE (sc)
Gusarov, Alexei	1995-96 COL	ALEXEI GUSAROV (rep)
	1995-96 COL	ALEXEI GUSAROV (sc)
Gutkowski, Robert	1993-94 NYR	ROBERT GUTKOWSKI GOV. (rep)
	1993-94 NYR	ROBERT GUTKOWSKI GOV. (sc)
Haggert, Bob	1961-62 TML	ROBERT HAGGERT TRAINER (rep)
	1961-62 TML	ROBERT HAGGERT TRAINER (sc)
	1962-63 TML	R. HAGGERT TRAINER (rep)
	1962-63 TML	R HAGGERT TRAINER (sc)
	1963-64 TML	ROBERT HAGGERT TRAINER (rep)
	1963-64 TML	ROBERT HAGGERT TRAINER (sc)
	1966-67 TML	ROBERT HAGGERT TRAINER (rep)
	1966-67 TML	ROBERT HAGGERT TRAINER (sc)
Hainsworth, George	1929-30 MC	GEO. HAINSWORTH. (sp)
	1929-30 MC	GEO HAINSWORTH (ret)
	1930-31 MC	GEO HAINSWORTH (sp)
	1930-31 MC	GEO HAINSWORTH (ret)
Halderson, Harold "Slim"	1924-25 VIC	H. HALDERSON. (or)
	1924-25 VIC	H. HALDERSON (rep)
	1924-25 VIC	H. HALDERSON. (sc)
Hall, Glenn	1951-52 DET	GLEN HALL (re)
	1951-52 DET	GLIN HALL (rep)
	1951-52 DET	GLIN HALL (sc)
	1960-61 CHI	GLENN HALL (rep)
	1960-61 CHI	GLENN HALL (sc)
	1988-89 CAL	GLENN HALL GOALIE CONS. (ab)
	1988-89 CAL	GLENN HALL GOALIE CONS. (rep)
	1988-89 CAL	GLENN HALL GOALIE CONS. (sc)
Haller, Kevin	1992-93 MC	K. HALLER (rep)
	1992-93 MC	K. HALLER (sc)
Halliday, Milt	1926-27 OTT	MILTON HALLIDAY (or)
	1926-27 OTT	MILTON HALLIDAY (rep)
	1926-27 OTT	MILTON HALLIDAY (sc)
Hallin, Mats	1982-83 NYI	M. HALLIN (ab)
	1982-83 NYI	M. HALLIN (rep)
	1982-83 NYI	M. HALLIN (sc)
Hamill, Red	1938-39 BB	R. HAMILL (sp)
	1938-39 BB	R HAMILL (ret)
Hamilton, Reg	1941-42 TML	REG HAMILTON (sp)
	1941-42 TML	REG HAMILTON (rep)
	1941-42 TML	REG HAMILTON (sc)
	1944-45 TML	REG HAMILTON (sp)
	1944-45 TML	REG HAMILTON (rep)
	1944-45 TML	REG HAMILTON (sc)
Hammett, Jim	2000-01 COL	JIM HAMMETT (rep)
	2000-01 COL	JIM HAMMETT (sc)
Hammond, Herb	1993-94 NYR	H. HAMMOND SCOUT (rep)
	1993-94 NYR	H. HAMMOND SCOUT (sc)
Hammond, John	1927-28 NYR	J.S. HAMMOND, (PRES.) (sp)
	1927-28 NYR	J S HAMMOND (PRES) (ret)
Hannan, Dave	1987-88 EDM	D. HANNAN (ab)
	1987-88 EDM	D. HANNAN (rep)
	1987-88 EDM	D. HANNAN (sc)
	1995-96 COL	DAVE HANNAN (rep)
	1995-96 COL	DAVE HANNAN (sc)
Haralson, Bruce	1996-97 DET	B. HARALSON (rep)
	1996-97 DET	B. HARALSON (sc)
	1997-98 DET	BRUCE HARALSON (rep)
	1997-98 DET	BRUCE HARALSON (sc)
	2001-02 DET	BRUCE HARALSON (rep)
	2001-02 DET	BRUCE HARALSON (sc)
Harmon, Glen	1943-44 MC	GLEN HARMON (sp)
	1943-44 MC	GLEN HARMON (rep)
	1943-44 MC	GLEN HARMON (sc)
	1945-46 MC	GLEN HARMON (re)
	1945-46 MC	GLEN HARMON (rep)
	1945-46 MC	GLEN HARMON (sc)
Harper, Terry	1964-65 MC	TERRANCE HARPER (rep)
	1964-65 MC	TERRANCE HARPER (sc)
	1965-66 MC	TERRANCE HARPER (rep)
	1965-66 MC	TERRANCE HARPER (sc)
	1967-68 MC	T. HARPER (rep)
	1967-68 MC	T HARPER (sc)
	1968-69 MC	T. HARPER (rep)
	1968-69 MC	T HARPER (sc)
	1970-71 MC	T. HARPER (rep)
	1970-71 MC	T. HARPER (sc)
Harris, Billy	1961-62 TML	WILLIAM HARRIS (rep)
	1961-62 TML	WILLIAM HARRIS (sc)
	1962-63 TML	WILLIAM HARRIS (rep)
	1962-63 TML	WILLIAM HARRIS (sc)
	1963-64 TML	WILLIAM HARRIS (rep)
	1963-64 TML	WILLIAM HARRIS (sc)
Harris, Ted	1964-65 MC	EDWARD HARRIS (rep)
	1964-65 MC	EDWARD HARRIS (sc)
	1965-66 MC	EDWARD HARRIS (rep)
	1965-66 MC	EDWARD HARRIS (sc)
	1967-68 MC	E. HARRIS (rep)
	1967-68 MC	E HARRIS (sc)
	1968-69 MC	T. HARRIS (rep)
	1968-69 MC	E HARRIS (sc)
	1974-75 PHI	TED HARRIS (rep)
	1974-75 PHI	TED HARRIS (sc)
Hart, Cecil	1923-24 MC	CECIL M. HART (or)
	1923-24 MC	CECIL M. HART (rep)
	1923-24 MC	CECIL M. HART (sc)
	1929-30 MC	CECIL. M. HART. MANAGER. (sp)
	1929-30 MC	CECIL M HART MANAGER (ret)
	1930-31 MC	CECIL M. HART, *MANAGER* (sp)
	1930-31 MC	CECIL M HART MANAGER (ret)
Hart, Wilfred "Gizzy"	1924-25 VIC	H. HART. (or)
	1924-25 VIC	H. HART (rep)
	1924-25 VIC	H. HART. (sc)
Hartley, Bob	2000-01 COL	BOB HARTLEY (rep)
	2000-01 COL	BOB HARTLEY (sc)
Hartman, Mike	1993-94 NYR	M. HARTMAN (rep)
	1993-94 NYR	M. HARTMAN (sc)
Harty, William	1945-46 MC	WILLIAM HARTY DIRECTOR (re)
	1945-46 MC	WILLIAM HARTY DIR. (rep)
	1945-46 MC	WILLIAM HARTY (DIR) (sc)
Harvey, Doug	1952-53 MC	DOUG HARVEY (re)
	1952-53 MC	DOUG HARVEY (rep)
	1952-53 MC	DOUG HARVEY (sc)
	1955-56 MC	D. HARVEY (re)
	1955-56 MC	D. HARVEY (rep)
	1955-56 MC	D HARVEY (sc)
	1956-57 MC	DOUG HARVEY (rep)
	1956-57 MC	DOUG HARVEY (sc)
	1957-58 MC	DOUG HARVEY (rep)
	1957-58 MC	DOUG HARVEY (sc)
	1958-59 MC	DOUG HARVEY (rep)
	1958-59 MC	DOUG HARVEY (sc)
	1959-60 MC	D. HARVEY (rep)
	1959-60 MC	D HARVEY (sc)
Hasek, Dominik	2001-02 DET	DOMINIK HASEK (rep)
	2001-02 DET	DOMINIK HASEK (sc)
Hassard, Bob	1950-51 TML	ROBERT HASSARD (re)
	1950-51 TML	BOB HASSARD (rep)
	1950-51 TML	BOB HASSARD (sc)
Hatcher, Derian	1998-99 DAL	DERIAN HATCHER (rep)
	1998-99 DAL	DERIAN HATCHER (sc)
Hay, Bill	1960-61 CHI	BILL HAY (rep)
	1960-61 CHI	WILL HAY (sc)
Hay, Jim	1954-55 DET	JAMES HAY (re)
	1954-55 DET	JAMES HAY (rep)
	1954-55 DET	JAMES HAY (sc)
Healy, Glenn	1993-94 NYR	G. HEALY (rep)
	1993-94 NYR	G. HEALY (sc)
Heffernan, Gerry	1943-44 MC	GERALD HEFFERNAN (sp)
	1943-44 MC	JERRY HEFFERNAN (rep)
	1943-44 MC	JERRY HEFFERMAN (sc)
Hejduk, Milan	2000-01 COL	MILAN HEJDUK (rep)
	2000-01 COL	MILAN HEJDUK (sc)
Heller, Ehrhardt "Ott"	1932-33 NYR	EHRHARDT HELLER (sp)
	1932-33 NYR	EHRHARDT HELLER (ret)
	1939-40 NYR	EHRHARDT HELLER (sp)
	1939-40 NYR	EHRHARDT HELLER (ret)
Henning, Lorne	1979-80 NYI	L. HENNING (ab)
	1979-80 NYI	L. HENNING (rep)
	1979-80 NYI	L. HENNING (sc)
	1980-81 NYI	LORNE HENNING A. COACH (ab)
	1980-81 NYI	LORNE HENNING A. COACH (rep)
	1980-81 NYI	LORNE HENNING A. COACH (sc)
	1981-82 NYI	LORNE HENNING ASST. COACH (ab)

Name	Season	Engraving
	1981-82 NYI	LORNE HENNING ASST. COACH (rep)
	1981-82 NYI	LORNE HENNING ASST. COACH (sc)
	1982-83 NYI	LORNE HENNING ASST. COACH (ab)
	1982-83 NYI	LORNE HENNING ASST. COACH (rep)
	1982-83 NYI	LORNE HENNING ASST. COACH (sc)
Hern, Riley	1907 MW	RIELY HERN. (ib)
	1907 MW	RIELY HERN (rep)
	1907 MW	RIELY HERN (sc)
Hextall,	1939-40 NYR	BRYAN HEXTALL (sp)
Bryan	1939-40 NYR	BRYAN HEXTALL (ret)
Hicke, Bill	1958-59 MC	BILL HICKE (rep)
	1958-59 MC	WILL HICKE (sc)
	1959-60 MC	BILL HICKE (rep)
	1959-60 MC	WILL HICKE (sc)
Hicks,	1998-99 DAL	THOMAS HICKS (rep)
Thomas	1998-99 DAL	THOMAS HICKS (sc)
Hicks,	1960-61 CHI	WAYNE HICKS (rep)
Wayne	1960-61 CHI	WAYNE HICKS (sc)
Hill, Mel	1938-39 BB	M. HILL (sp)
	1938-39 BB	M HILL (ret)
	1940-41 BB	MEL. HILL (sp)
	1940-41 BB	MEL HILL (rep)
	1940-41 BB	MEL HILL (sc)
	1944-45 TML	MEL HILL (sp)
	1944-45 TML	MEL HILL (rep)
	1944-45 TML	MEL HILL (sc)
Hill, Sean	1992-93 MC	S. HILL (rep)
	1992-93 MC	S. HILL (sc)
Hiller,	1939-40 NYR	WILBERT HILLER (sp)
Wilbert	1939-40 NYR	WILBERT HILLER (ret)
"Dutch"	1945-46 MC	WILBERT HILLER (re)
	1945-46 MC	DUTCH HILLER (rep)
	1945-46 MC	DUTCH HILLER (sc)
Hillier,	1990-91 PIT	R. HILLIER (ab)
Randy	1990-91 PIT	R. HILLIER (rep)
	1990-91 PIT	R. HILLIER (sc)
Hillman,	1954-55 DET	LARRY HILLMAN (re)
Larry	1954-55 DET	LARRY HILLMAN (rep)
	1954-55 DET	LARRY HILLMAN (sc)
	1961-62 TML	LARRY HILLMAN (rep)
	1961-62 TML	LARRY HILLMAN (sc)
	1962-63 TML	LARRY HILLMAN (rep)
	1962-63 TML	LARRY HILLMAN (sc)
	1963-64 TML	LARRY HILLMAN (rep)
	1963-64 TML	LARRY HILLMAN (sc)
	1966-67 TML	LARRY HILLMAN (rep)
	1966-67 TML	LARRY HILLMAN (sc)
	1968-69 MC	L. HILLMAN (rep)
	1968-69 MC	L HILLMAN (sc)
Hillman,	1960-61 CHI	WAYNE HILLMAN (rep)
Wayne	1960-61 CHI	WAYNE HILLMAN (sc)
Hinote, Dan	2000-01 COL	DAN HINOTE (rep)
	2000-01 COL	DAN HINOTE (sc)
Hitchcock,	1998-99 DAL	KEN HITCHCOCK (rep)
Ken	1998-99 DAL	KEN HITCHCOCK (sc)
Hitchman,	1928-29 BB	LIONEL HITCHMAN CAPT (or)
Lionel	1928-29 BB	LIONEL HITCHMAN CAPT (rep)
	1928-29 BB	LIONEL HITCHMAN CAPT (sc)
	1928-29 BB	L HITCHMAN (ret)
Hodge,	1955-56 MC	C. HODGE (re)
Charlie	1955-56 MC	C. HODGE (rep)
	1955-56 MC	C HODGE (sc)
	1957-58 MC	CHARLES HODGE (rep)
	1957-58 MC	CHARLES HODGE (sc)
	1958-59 MC	C. HODGE (rep)
	1958-59 MC	CH HODGE (sc)
	1959-60 MC	CHARLIE HODGE (rep)
	1959-60 MC	CHARLES HODGE (sc)
	1964-65 MC	CHARLES HODGE (rep)
	1964-65 MC	CHARLES HODGE (sc)
	1965-66 MC	CHARLES HODGE (rep)
	1965-66 MC	CHARLES HODGE (sc)
	1991-92 PIT	CHARLIE HODGE (rep)
	1991-92 PIT	CHARLIE HODGE (sc)
Hodge, Ken	1969-70 BB	K. HODGE (rep)
	1969-70 BB	K HODGE (sc)
	1971-72 BB	KEN HODGE (rep)
	1971-72 BB	KEN HODGE (sc)
Hodge, Tom	1907 MW	TOM. HODGE. (ib)
	1907 MW	TOM HODGE (rep)
	1907 MW	TOM HODGE (sc)
Hodson,	1996-97 DET	KEVIN HODSON (rep)
Kevin	1996-97 DET	KEVIN HODSON (sc)
	1997-98 DET	K. HODSON (rep)
	1997-98 DET	K. HODSON (sc)
Hoffmeyer,	1999-00 NJ	B. HOFFMEYER (rep)
Bob	1999-00 NJ	B. HOFFMEYER (sc)
	2002-03 NJ	B. HOFFMEYER (rep)
	2002-03 NJ	B. HOFFMEYER (sc)
Hogue,	1998-99 DAL	BENOIT HOGUE (rep)
Benoit	1998-99 DAL	BENOIT HOGUE (sc)
Holik,	1994-95 NJ	BOBBY HOLIK (rep)
Bobby	1994-95 NJ	BOBBY HOLIK (sc)
	1999-00 NJ	BOBBY HOLIK (rep)
	1999-00 NJ	BOBBY HOLIK (sc)
Holland,	1996-97 DET	KEN HOLLAND (rep)
Ken	1996-97 DET	KEN HOLLAND (sc)
	1997-98 DET	KEN HOLLAND (rep)
	1997-98 DET	KEN HOLLAND (sc)
	2001-02 DET	KEN HOLLAND (rep)
	2001-02 DET	KEN HOLLAND (sc)
Hollett,	1938-39 BB	W. HOLLETT (sp)
Flash	1938-39 BB	W HOLLETT (ret)
	1940-41 BB	WM. HOLLETT (sp)
	1940-41 BB	FLASH HOLLETT (rep)
	1940-41 BB	FLASH HOLLETT (sc)
Holmes,	1924-25 VIC	H. HOLMES. (or)
Harry	1924-25 VIC	H. HOLMES (rep)
	1924-25 VIC	H. HOLMES (sc)
Holmstrom,	1996-97 DET	TOMAS HOLMSTROM (rep)
Tomas	1996-97 DET	TOMAS HOLMSTROM (sc)
	1997-98 DET	T. HOLMSTROM (rep)
	1997-98 DET	T. HOLMSTROM (sc)
	2001-02 DET	TOMAS HOLMSTROM (rep)
	2001-02 DET	TOMAS HOLMSTROM (sc)
Holota,	1942-43 DET	JOHNNY HOLOTA (rep)
Johnny	1942-43 DET	JOHNNY HOLOTA (sc)
Holway,	1925-26 MM	A.R. HOLWAY. (or)
Albert	1925-26 MM	A.R. HOLWAY (rep)
"Toots"	1925-26 MM	A.R. HOLWAY (sc)
Horner,		
Reginald	1931-32 TML	R. HORNER (sp)
"Red"	1931-32 TML	R HORNER (ret)
Horton,	1961-62 TML	M.G. TIM HORTON (rep)
Miles	1961-62 TML	M G "TIM" HORTON (sc)
"Tim"	1962-63 TML	M.G. TIM HORTON (rep)
	1962-63 TML	M G TIM HORTON (sc)
	1963-64 TML	M.G. TIM HORTON (rep)
	1963-64 TML	M G TIM HORTON (sc)
	1966-67 TML	TIM HORTON (rep)
	1966-67 TML	TIM HORTON (sc)
Hotchkiss,	1988-89 CAL	HARLEY HOTCHKISS OWNERS* (ab)
Harley	1988-89 CAL	HARLEY HOTCHKISS OWNERS* (rep)
	1988-89 CAL	HARLEY HOTCHKISS OWNERS* (sc)
		* refers also to Norman Green
Houle,	1970-71 MC	R. HOULE (rep)
Rejean	1970-71 MC	R. HOULE. (sc)
	1972-73 MC	REJEAN HOULE (rep)
	1972-73 MC	REJEAN HOULE (sc)
	1976-77 MC	REJEAN HOULE (rep)
	1976-77 MC	REJEAN HOULE (sc)
	1977-78 MC	REJEAN HOULE (rep)
	1977-78 MC	REJEAN HOULE (sc)
	1978-79 MC	R. HOULE (ab)
	1978-79 MC	R. HOULE (rep)
	1978-79 MC	R. HOULE (sc)
Hoult,	1961-62 TML	HUGH HOULT (rep)
Hugh	1961-62 TML	HUGH HOULT (sc)
	1962-63 TML	HUGH HOULT ASST. TRAINER (rep)
	1962-63 TML	HUGH HOULT ASST TRAINER (sc)
	1963-64 TML	HUGH HOULT (rep)
	1963-64 TML	HUGH HOULT (sc)
Howatt,	1979-80 NYI	G. HOWATT (ab)
Garry	1979-80 NYI	G. HOWATT (rep)
	1979-80 NYI	G. HOWATT (sc)
	1980-81 NYI	G. HOWATT (ab)
	1980-81 NYI	G. HOWATT (rep)
	1980-81 NYI	G. HOWATT (sc)
Howe,	1949-50 DET	GORDON HOWE (re)
Gordie	1949-50 DET	GORDON HOWE (rep)
	1949-50 DET	GORDON HOWE (sc)
	1951-52 DET	GORDON HOWE (re)
	1951-52 DET	GORDON HOWE (rep)
	1951-52 DET	GORDON HOWE (sc)
	1953-54 DET	GORDON HOWE (re)
	1953-54 DET	GORDON HOWE (rep)
	1953-54 DET	GORDON HOWE (sc)
	1954-55 DET	GORDON HOWE (re)
	1954-55 DET	GORDON HOWE (rep)
	1954-55 DET	GORDON HOWE (sc)
Howe, Mark	1996-97 DET	MARK HOWE (rep)
	1996-97 DET	MARK HOWE (sc)
	1997-98 DET	MARK HOWE (rep)
	1997-98 DET	MARK HOWE (sc)
	2001-02 DET	MARK HOWE (rep)
	2001-02 DET	MARK HOWE (sc)
Howe, Syd	1935-36 DET	SID HOWE — L.WING (sp)
	1935-36 DET	SID HOWE (ret)
	1936-37 DET	SID HOWE L.WING (sp)
	1936-37 DET	SID HOWE (ret)
	1942-43 DET	SYD HOWE (sp)

Name	Season	Team	Engraving
	1942-43	DET	SYD HOWE (rep)
	1942-43	DET	SYD HOWE (sc)
Howell, Harry	1989-90	EDM	HARRY HOWELL (ab)
	1989-90	EDM	HARRY HOWELL (rep)
	1989-90	EDM	HARRY HOWELL (sc)
Hoyt, Richard	1927-28	NYR	R.F. HOYT, (DIR.) (sp)
	1927-28	NYR	R F HOYT (DIR) (ret)
Hrdina, Jiri	1988-89	CAL	J. HRDINA (ab)
	1988-89	CAL	J. HRDINA (rep)
	1988-89	CAL	J. HRDINA (sc)
	1990-91	PIT	J. HRDINA (ab)
	1990-91	PIT	J. HRDINA (rep)
	1990-91	PIT	J. HRDINA (sc)
	1991-92	PIT	JIRI HRDINA (rep)
	1991-92	PIT	JIRI HRDINA (sc)
Hrkac, Tony	1998-99	DAL	TONY HRKAC (rep)
	1998-99	DAL	TONY HRKAC (sc)
Huber, Fred	1949-50	DET	FRED A. HUBER JR. PUB. DIRECTOR. (re)
	1949-50	DET	FRED A. HUBER JR. PUB. DIRECT (rep)
	1949-50	DET	FRED A HUBER JR (PUB DIRECT) (sc)
	1951-52	DET	FRED HUBER—PUBLIC RELATIONS (re)
	1951-52	DET	FRED HUBER PUB. RELATIONS (rep)
	1951-52	DET	FRED HUBER PUB RELATIONS (sc)
	1953-54	DET	FRED A. HUBER, JR., PUBLIC RELATIONS (re)
	1953-54	DET	FRED A. HUBER JR. P.R. (rep)
	1953-54	DET	FRED A HUBER JR (PUB REL) (sc)
	1954-55	DET	FRED A. HUBER, JR., PUBLIC RELATIONS (re)
	1954-55	DET	FRED A. HUBER JR. P.R. (rep)
	1954-55	DET	FRED A HUBER JR (PUB REL) (sc)
Huddleston, Bob	1994-95	NJ	BOB HUDDLESTON (rep)
	1994-95	NJ	BOB HUDDLESTON (sc)
	1997-98	DET	BOB HUDDLESTON (rep)
	1997-98	DET	BOB HUDDLESTON (sc)
Huddy, Charlie	1983-84	EDM	C. HUDDY (ab)
	1983-84	EDM	C. HUDDY (rep)
	1983-84	EDM	C. HUDDY (sc)
	1984-85	EDM	C. HUDDY (ab)
	1984-85	EDM	C. HUDDY (rep)
	1984-85	EDM	C. HUDDY (sc)
	1986-87	EDM	C. HUDDY (ab)
	1986-87	EDM	C. HUDDY (rep)
	1986-87	EDM	C. HUDDY (sc)
	1987-88	EDM	C. HUDDY (ab)
	1987-88	EDM	C. HUDDY (rep)
	1987-88	EDM	C. HUDDY (sc)
	1989-90	EDM	C. HUDDY (ab)
	1989-90	EDM	C. HUDDY (rep)
	1989-90	EDM	C. HUDDY (sc)
Hudson, Mike	1993-94	NYR	M. HUDSON (rep)
	1993-94	NYR	M. HUDSON (sc)
Hughes, Don	1926-27	OTT	DON HUGHES ASS'T TRAINER (or)
	1926-27	OTT	DON HUGHES ASST TRAINER (rep)
	1926-27	OTT	DON HUGHES ASST TRAINER (sc)
Hughes, Pat	1978-79	MC	P. HUGHES (ab)
	1978-79	MC	P. HUGHES (rep)
	1978-79	MC	P. HUGHES (sc)
	1983-84	EDM	P. HUGHES (ab)
	1983-84	EDM	P. HUGHES (rep)
	1983-84	EDM	P. HUGHES (sc)
	1984-85	EDM	P. HUGHES (ab)
	1984-85	EDM	P. HUGHES (rep)
	1984-85	EDM	P. HUGHES (sc)
Hull, Bobby	1960-61	CHI	ROBERT HULL (rep)
	1960-61	CHI	ROBERT HULL (sc)
Hull, Brett	1998-99	DAL	BRETT HULL (rep)
	1998-99	DAL	BRETT HULL (sc)
	2001-02	DET	BRETT HULL (rep)
	2001-02	DET	BRETT HULL (sc)
Humeniuk, Walter	1949-50	DET	WALTER HUMENIUK. ASST. TRAINER (re)
	1949-50	DET	W. HUMENIUK ASST. TRAINER (rep)
	1949-50	DET	W HUMENIUK ASS'T TRAIN (sc)
	1960-61	CHI	WALTER HUMENIUK — TRAINER (rep)
	1960-61	CHI	WALTER HUMENIUK — TRAINER (sc)
Hunter, Dave	1983-84	EDM	D. HUNTER (ab)
	1983-84	EDM	D. HUNTER (rep)
	1983-84	EDM	D. HUNTER (sc)
	1984-85	EDM	D. HUNTER (ab)
	1984-85	EDM	D. HUNTER (rep)
	1984-85	EDM	D. HUNTER (sc)
	1986-87	EDM	D. HUNTER (ab)
	1986-87	EDM	D. HUNTER (rep)
	1986-87	EDM	D. HUNTER (sc)
Hunter, Mark	1988-89	CAL	M. HUNTER (ab)
	1988-89	CAL	M. HUNTER (rep)
	1988-89	CAL	M. HUNTER (sc)
Hunter, Tim	1988-89	CAL	T. HUNTER ASST.C. (ab)
	1988-89	CAL	T. HUNTER ASST.C. (rep)
	1988-89	CAL	T. HUNTER A.C. (sc)

Name	Season	Team	Engraving
Ilitch, Atanas	1996-97	DET	ATANAS ILITCH (rep)
	1996-97	DET	ATANAS ILITCH (sc)
	1997-98	DET	ATANAS ILITCH (rep)
	1997-98	DET	ATANAS ILITCH (sc)
	2001-02	DET	ATANAS ILITCH (rep)
	2001-02	DET	ATANAS ILITCH (sc)
Ilitch, Carole	2001-02	DET	CAROLE ILITCH (rep)
	2001-02	DET	CAROLE ILITCH (sc)
			* see also Carol Ilitch Trepeck
Ilitch, Christopher	1996-97	DET	CHRISTOPHER ILITCH (rep)
	1996-97	DET	CHRISTOPHER ILITCH (sc)
	1997-98	DET	CHRISTOPHER ILITCH (rep)
	1997-98	DET	CHRISTOPHER ILITCH (sc)
	2001-02	DET	CHRISTOPHER ILITCH (rep)
	2001-02	DET	CHRISTOPHER ILITCH (sc)
Ilitch, Denise	1997-98	DET	DENISE ILITCH (rep)
	1997-98	DET	DENISE ILITCH (sc)
	2001-02	DET	DENISE ILITCH (rep)
	2001-02	DET	DENISE ILITCH (sc)
			* see also Denise Ilitch Lites
Ilitch, Marian	1996-97	DET	MARIAN ILITCH (rep)
	1996-97	DET	MARIAN ILITCH (sc)
	1997-98	DET	MARIAN ILITCH (rep)
	1997-98	DET	MARIAN ILITCH (sc)
	2001-02	DET	MARIAN ILITCH (rep)
	2001-02	DET	MARIAN ILITCH (sc)
Ilitch, Mike	1996-97	DET	MIKE ILITCH (rep)
	1996-97	DET	MIKE ILITCH (sc)
	1997-98	DET	MIKE ILITCH (rep)
	1997-98	DET	MIKE ILITCH (sc)
	2001-02	DET	MICHAEL ILITCH (rep)
	2001-02	DET	MICHAEL ILITCH (sc)
Ilitch, Mike Jr.	1996-97	DET	MICHAEL ILITCH (rep)
	1996-97	DET	MICHAEL ILITCH (sc)
	1997-98	DET	MICHAEL ILITCH JR. (rep)
	1997-98	DET	MICHAEL ILITCH JR. (sc)
	2001-02	DET	MICHAEL ILITCH JR. (rep)
	2001-02	DET	MICHAEL ILITCH JR. (sc)
Ilitch, Ronald	1996-97	DET	RONALD ILITCH (rep)
	1996-97	DET	RONALD ILITCH (sc)
	1997-98	DET	RONALD ILITCH (rep)
	1997-98	DET	RONALD ILITCH (sc)
	2001-02	DET	RONALD ILITCH (rep)
	2001-02	DET	RONALD ILITCH (sc)
Imlach, George "Punch"	1961-62	TML	G. PUNCH IMLACH COACH GEN.MGR. (rep)
	1961-62	TML	G "PUNCH" IMLACH COACH GEN MANN (sc)
	1962-63	TML	G. PUNCH IMLACH COACH GEN.MGR. (rep)
	1962-63	TML	G PUNCH IMLACH COA GEN MANN (sc)
	1963-64	TML	G. PUNCH IMLACH COACH G.M. (rep)
	1963-64	TML	G PUNCH IMIACH COACH GEN MAN (sc)
	1966-67	TML	G. PUNCH IMLACH GEN.MGR. COACH (rep)
	1966-67	TML	G PUNCH IMLACH GEN MA COACH (sc)
Irvin, Dick	1931-32	TML	DICK IRVIN, / *COACH* (sp)
	1931-32	TML	DICK IRVIN COACH (ret)
	1943-44	MC	DICK IRVIN COACH (ob)
	1943-44	MC	DICK IRVIN COACH (rep)
	1943-44	MC	DICK IRVIN COACH (sc)
	1945-46	MC	J. DICKENSON IRVIN COACH (re)
	1945-46	MC	DICK IRVIN COACH (rep)
	1945-46	MC	DICK IRVIN COACH (sc)
	1952-53	MC	DICK IRVIN-COACH (re)
	1952-53	MC	DICK IRVIN COACH (rep)
	1952-53	MC	DICK IRVIN COACH (sc)
Ivan, Tommy	1949-50	DET	TOM IVAN COACH (re)
	1949-50	DET	TOM IVAN COACH (rep)
	1949-50	DET	TOM IVAN COACH (sc)
	1951-52	DET	TOM IVAN—COACH (re)
	1951-52	DET	TOM IVAN COACH (rep)
	1951-52	DET	TOM IVAN COACH (sc)
	1953-54	DET	THOMAS N. IVAN, COACH (re)
	1953-54	DET	THOMAS IVAN COACH (rep)
	1953-54	DET	THOMAS NIVAN COACH (sc)
	1960-61	CHI	THOMAS N. IVAN GEN.MGR. (rep)
	1960-61	CHI	THOMAS N IVAN GENERAL MANAGER (sc)
Jackson, Art	1940-41	BB	ART. JACKSON (sp)
	1940-41	BB	ART JACKSON (rep)
	1940-41	BB	ART JACKSON (sc)
	1944-45	TML	ART JACKSON (sp)
	1944-45	TML	ART JACKSON (rep)
	1944-45	TML	ART JACKSON (sc)
Jackson, Don	1983-84	EDM	D. JACKSON (ab)
	1983-84	EDM	D. JACKSON (rep)
	1983-84	EDM	D. JACKSON (sc)
	1984-85	EDM	D. JACKSON (ab)
	1984-85	EDM	D. JACKSON (rep)
	1984-85	EDM	D. JACKSON (sc)

Name	Season/Team	Engraving
Jackson, Harold	1942-43 DET	HAROLD JACKSON (sp)
	1942-43 DET	HAROLD JACKSON (rep)
	1942-43 DET	HAROLD JACKSON (sc)
Jackson, Harvey	1931-32 TML	H. JACKSON (sp)
	1931-32 TML	H JACKSON (ret)
Jaffe, Stanley	1993-94 NYR	STANLEY JAFFE GOV. (rep)
	1993-94 NYR	STANLEY JAFFE GOV. (sc)
Jagr, Jaromir	1990-91 PIT	J. JAGR (ab)
	1990-91 PIT	J. JAGR (rep)
	1990-91 PIT	J. JAGR (sc)
	1991-92 PIT	JAROMIR JAGR (rep)
	1991-92 PIT	JAROMIR JAGR (sc)
Jarvis, Doug	1975-76 MC	DOUG JARVIS (rep)
	1975-76 MC	DOUG JARVIS (sc)
	1976-77 MC	DOUGLAS JARVIS (rep)
	1976-77 MC	DOUGLAS JARVIS (sc)
	1977-78 MC	DOUGLAS JARVIS (rep)
	1977-78 MC	DOUGLAS JARVIS (sc)
	1978-79 MC	D. JARVIS (ab)
	1978-79 MC	D. JARVIS (rep)
	1978-79 MC	D. JARVIS (sc)
	1998-99 DAL	DOUG JARVIS (rep)
	1998-99 DAL	DOUG JARVIS (sc)
Jeffrey, Larry	1966-67 TML	LARRY JEFFREY (rep)
	1966-67 TML	LARRY JEFFREY (sc)
Jenkins, Roger	1933-34 CHI	ROGER JENKINS (sp)
	1933-34 CHI	ROGER JENKINS (ret)
	1937-38 CHI	ROGER JENKINS (sp)
	1937-38 CHI	ROGER JENKINS (ret)
Jennings, Grant	1990-91 PIT	G. JENNINGS (ab)
	1990-91 PIT	G. JENNINGS (rep)
	1990-91 PIT	G. JENNINGS (sc)
	1991-92 PIT	GRANT JENNINGS (rep)
	1991-92 PIT	GRANT JENNINGS (sc)
Jennings, William	1907 MW	WILLIAM JENNINGS. (ib)
	1907 MW	WILLIAM JENNINGS (rep)
	1907 MW	WILLIAM JENNINGS (sc)
Johnson, Bob	1990-91 PIT	BOB JOHNSON H. COACH (ab)
	1990-91 PIT	BOB JOHNSON H. COACH (rep)
	1990-91 PIT	BOB JOHNSON H. COACH (sc)
	1991-92 PIT	BOB JOHNSON (rep)
	1991-92 PIT	BOB JOHNSON (sc)
Johnson, Earl	1953-54 DET	EARL JOHNSON (re)
Johnson, Ivan "Ching"	1927-28 NYR	I. JOHNSON (sp)
	1927-28 NYR	I JOHNSON (ret)
	1932-33 NYR	I JOHNSON (sp)
	1932-33 NYR	I JOHNSON (ret)
Johnson, Tom	1952-53 MC	TOM JOHNSON (re)
	1952-53 MC	TOM JOHNSON (rep)
	1952-53 MC	TOM JOHNSON (sc)
	1955-56 MC	T. JOHNSON (re)
	1955-56 MC	T. JOHNSON (rep)
	1955-56 MC	T JOHNSON (sc)
	1956-57 MC	T. JOHNSON (rep)
	1956-57 MC	T JOHNSON (sc)
	1957-58 MC	T. JOHNSON (rep)
	1957-58 MC	T JOHNSON (sc)
	1958-59 MC	TOM JOHNSON (rep)
	1958-59 MC	THOM JOHNSON (sc)
	1959-60 MC	TOM JOHNSON (rep)
	1959-60 MC	THOM JOHNSON (sc)
	1969-70 BB	T. JOHNSON TR. (rep)
	1969-70 BB	T JOHNSON TR (sc)
	1971-72 BB	TOM JOHNSON COACH (rep)
	1971-72 BB	TOM JOHNSON COACH (sc)
Johnson, Virgil	1937-38 CHI	VIRGIL JOHNSON (sp)
Johnston, Ed	1969-70 BB	E. JOHNSTON (rep)
	1969-70 BB	E JOHNSTON (sc)
	1971-72 BB	ED JOHNSTON (rep)
	1971-72 BB	ED JOHNSTON (sc)
Johnston, Ernie	1907 MW	ERNIE JOHNSTON. (ib)
	1907 MW	ERNIE JOHNSTON (rep)
	1907 MW	ERNIE JOHNSTON (sc)
Johnstone, Ross	1944-45 TML	ROSS JOHNSTONE (sp)
	1944-45 TML	ROSS JOHNSTONE (rep)
	1944-45 TML	ROSS JOHNSTONE (sc)
Joliat, Aurel	1923-24 MC	A. JOLIAT (or)
	1923-24 MC	A. JOLIAT (rep)
	1923-24 MC	A. JOLIAT (sc)
	1929-30 MC	AUREL JOLIAT. (sp)
	1929-30 MC	AUREL JOLIAT (ret)
	1930-31 MC	AUREL JOLIAT (sp)
	1930-31 MC	AUREL JOLIAT (ret)
Jonsson, Tomas	1981-82 NYI	T. JONSSON (ab)
	1981-82 NYI	T. JONSSON (rep)
	1981-82 NYI	T. JONSSON (sc)
	1982-83 NYI	T. JONSSON (ab)
	1982-83 NYI	T. JONSSON (rep)
	1982-83 NYI	T. JONSSON (sc)
Joy, Garth	2000-01 COL	GARTH JOY (rep)
	2000-01 COL	GARTH JOY (sc)
Juge, Amedee Monet	1929-30 MC	AMADEE MONET JUGE. (sp)
	1929-30 MC	AMEDEE MONET JUGE (ret)
	1930-31 MC	AMEDEE MONET JUGE. (sp)
	1930-31 MC	AMEDEE MONET JUGE (ret)
Juzda, Bill	1948-49 TML	WILLIAM JUZDA (re)
	1948-49 TML	WILLIAM JUZDA (rep)
	1948-49 TML	WILLIAM JUZOA (sc)
	1950-51 TML	WILLIAM JUZDA (re)
	1950-51 TML	BILL JUZDA (rep)
	1950-51 TML	BILL JUZDA (sc)
Kallur, Anders	1979-80 NYI	A. KALLUR (ab)
	1979-80 NYI	A. KALLUR (rep)
	1979-80 NYI	A. KALLUR (sc)
	1980-81 NYI	A. KALLUR (ab)
	1980-81 NYI	A. KALLUR (rep)
	1980-81 NYI	A. KALLUR (sc)
	1981-82 NYI	A. KALLUR (ab)
	1981-82 NYI	A. KALLUR (rep)
	1981-82 NYI	A. KALLUR (sc)
	1982-83 NYI	A. KALLUR (ab)
	1982-83 NYI	A. KALLUR (rep)
	1982-83 NYI	A. KALLUR (sc)
Kamensky, Valeri	1995-96 COL	VALERI KAMENSKY (rep)
	1995-96 COL	VALERI KAMENSKY (sc)
Kampman, Rudolph "Bingo"	1941-42 TML	BINGO KAMPMAN (sp)
	1941-42 TML	BINGO KAMPMAN (rep)
	1941-42 TML	BINGO KAMPMAN (sc)
Karakas, Mike	1937-38 CHI	MIKE KARAKAS (sp)
	1937-38 CHI	MIKE KARAKAS (ret)
Karns, Pat	1995-96 COL	PAT KARNS (rep)
	1995-96 COL	PAT KARNS (sc)
	2000-01 COL	PAT KARNS (rep)
	2000-01 COL	PAT KARNS (sc)
Karpovtsev, Alexander	1993-94 NYR	A. KARPOVTSEV (rep)
	1993-94 NYR	A. KARPOVTSEV (sc)
Katz, Lewis	2002-03 NJ	LEWIS KATZ (rep)
	2002-03 NJ	LEWIS KATZ (sc)
Keane, Mike	1992-93 MC	M. KEANE (rep)
	1992-93 MC	M. KEANE (sc)
	1995-96 COL	MIKE KEANE (rep)
	1995-96 COL	MIKE KEANE (sc)
	1998-99 DAL	MIKE KEANE (rep)
	1998-99 DAL	MIKE KEANE (sc)
Keeling, Melville "Butch"	1932-33 NYR	M S KEELING (sp)
	1932-33 NYR	M S KEELING (ret)
Keenan, Mike	1993-94 NYR	MIKE KEENAN H. COACH (rep)
	1993-94 NYR	MIKE KEENAN H. COACH (sc)
Kehoe, Rick	1990-91 PIT	RICK KEHOE (ab)
	1990-91 PIT	RICK KEHOE (rep)
	1990-91 PIT	RICK KEHOE (sc)
	1991-92 PIT	RICK KEHOE (rep)
	1991-92 PIT	RICK KEHOE (sc)
Kelly, Bob	1973-74 PHI	BOB KELLY (rep)
	1973-74 PHI	BOB KELLY (sc)
	1974-75 PHI	BOB KELLY (rep)
	1974-75 PHI	BOB KELLY (sc)
Kelly, Larry	1998-99 DAL	LARRY KELLY (rep)
	1998-99 DAL	LARRY KELLY (sc)
Kelly, Leonard "Red"	1949-50 DET	LEONARD KELLY (re)
	1949-50 DET	RED KELLY (rep)
	1949-50 DET	RED KELLY (sc)
	1951-52 DET	LEONARD KELLY (re)
	1951-52 DET	RED KELLY (rep)
	1951-52 DET	RED KELLY (sc)
	1953-54 DET	LEONARD KELLY (re)
	1953-54 DET	LEONARD KELLY (rep)
	1953-54 DET	LEONARD KELLY (sc)
	1954-55 DET	LEONARD KELLY (re)
	1954-55 DET	LEONARD KELLY (rep)
	1954-55 DET	LEONARD KELLY (sc)
	1961-62 TML	LEONARD KELLY (rep)
	1961-62 TML	LEONARD KELLY (sc)
	1962-63 TML	LEONARD KELLY (rep)
	1962-63 TML	LEONARD KELLY (sc)
	1963-64 TML	LEONARD KELLY (rep)
	1963-64 TML	LEONARD KELLY (sc)
	1966-67 TML	RED KELLY (rep)
	1966-67 TML	RED KELLY (sc)
Kelly, Pete	1935-36 DET	PETE KELLY R.WING (sp)
	1935-36 DET	PETE KELLY (ret)
	1936-37 DET	PETE KELLY R.WING (sp)
Kelly, Steve	1999-00 NJ	R. STEVE KELLY (rep)
	1999-00 NJ	R. STEVE KELLY (sc)

Name	Season / Team	Engraving
Kendall, Bill	1933-34 CHI	WILLIAM KENDALL (sp)
	1933-34 CHI	WILLIAM KENDALL (ret)
Kennedy, Rod	1907 MW	R. KENNEDY (ib)
	1907 MW	R. KENNEDY (rep)
	1907 MW	R. KENNEDY (sc)
Kennedy, Ted	1944-45 TML	TEETER KENNEDY (sp)
	1944-45 TML	TED KENNEDY (rep)
	1944-45 TML	TED KENNEDY (sc)
	1946-47 TML	THEODORE KENNEDY (re)
	1946-47 TML	TED KENNEDY (rep)
	1946-47 TML	TED KENNEDY (sc)
	1947-48 TML	THEODORE KENNEDY (re)
	1947-48 TML	TED KENNEDY (rep)
	1947-48 TML	TED KENNEDY (sc)
	1948-49 TML	THEODORE KENNEDY—CAPTAIN (re)
	1948-49 TML	TED KENNEDY CAPTAIN (rep)
	1948-49 TML	TED KENNEDY CAPTAIN (sc)
	1950-51 TML	THEODORE KENNEDY—CAPTAIN (re)
	1950-51 TML	TED KENNEDY (rep)
	1950-51 TML	TED KENNEDYY (sc)
Keon, Dave	1961-62 TML	DAVID KEON (rep)
	1961-62 TML	DAVID KEON (sc)
	1962-63 TML	DAVID KEON (rep)
	1962-63 TML	DAVID KEON (sc)
	1963-64 TML	DAVID KEON (rep)
	1963-64 TML	DAVID KEON (sc)
	1966-67 TML	DAVID KEON (rep)
	1966-67 TML	DAVID KEON (sc)
Kerr, Dave	1939-40 NYR	DAVIE KERR (sp)
	1939-40 NYR	DAVIE KERR (ret)
Keyland, Clifford	1946-47 TML	CLIFFORD KEYLAND ASS'T. TRAINER (re)
	1946-47 TML	CLIFFORD KEYLAND ASST. TRAINER (rep)
	1946-47 TML	CLIFFORD KEYLAND (ASS TRAIN) (sc)
Kilpatrick, John Reed	1939-40 NYR	JOHN REED KILPATRICK. PRES. (sp)
	1939-40 NYR	J REED KILPATRICK (PRES) (ret)
Kilrea, Hec	1926-27 OTT	HECTOR KILREA (or)
	1926-27 OTT	HECTOR KILREA (rep)
	1926-27 OTT	HECTOR KILREA (sc)
	1935-36 DET	HEC KILREA—GENERAL UTILITY (sp)
	1935-36 DET	HEC KILREA (ret)
	1936-37 DET	HEC KILREA—GENERAL UTILITY (sp)
Kilrea, Wally	1935-36 DET	WALTER KILREA CENTER (sp)
	1935-36 DET	WALTER KILREA (ret)
	1936-37 DET	WALTER KILREA CENTER (sp)
	1936-37 DET	WALTER KILREA (ret)
Kindrachuk, Orest	1973-74 PHI	OREST KINDRACHUK (rep)
	1973-74 PHI	OREST KINDRACHUK (sc)
	1974-75 PHI	OREST KINDRACHUK (rep)
	1974-75 PHI	OREST KINDRACHUK (sc)
Klein, Lloyd	1928-29 BB	L KLEIN (ret)
Klemm, Jon	1995-96 COL	JON KLEMM (rep)
	1995-96 COL	JON KLEMM (sc)
	2000-01 COL	JON KLEMM (rep)
	2000-01 COL	JON KLEMM (sc)
Klima, Petr	1989-90 EDM	P. KLIMA (ab)
	1989-90 EDM	P. KLIMA (rep)
	1989-90 EDM	P. KLIMA (sc)
Klukay, Joe	1946-47 TML	JOSEPH KLUKAY (re)
	1947-48 TML	JOSEPH KLUKAY (re)
	1947-48 TML	JOE KLUKAY (rep)
	1947-48 TML	JOE KLUKAY (sc)
	1948-49 TML	JOSEPH KLUKAY (re)
	1948-49 TML	JOE KLUKAY (rep)
	1948-49 TML	JOE KLUKAY (sc)
	1950-51 TML	JOSEPH KLUKAY (re)
	1950-51 TML	JOE KLUKAY (rep)
	1950-51 TML	JOE KLUKAY (sc)
Knuble, Mike	1997-98 DET	M. KNUBLE (rep)
	1997-98 DET	M. KNUBLE (sc)
Kocur, Joey	1993-94 NYR	J. KOCUR (rep)
	1993-94 NYR	J. KOCUR (sc)
	1996-97 DET	JOE KOCUR (rep)
	1996-97 DET	JOE KOCUR (sc)
	1997-98 DET	J. KOCUR (rep)
	1997-98 DET	J. KOCUR (sc)
	2001-02 DET	JOE KOCUR (rep)
	2001-02 DET	JOE KOCUR (sc)
Konstantinov, Vladimir	1996-97 DET	VLADIMIR KONSTANTINOV (rep)
	1996-97 DET	VLADIMIR KONSTANTINOV (sc)
	1997-98 DET	V. KONSTANTINOV (rep)
	1997-98 DET	V. KONSTANTINOV (sc)
Kordic, John	1985-86 MC	J. KORDIC (ab)
	1985-86 MC	J. KORDIC (rep)
	1985-86 MC	J. KORDIC (sc)
Kovalev, Alexei	1993-94 NYR	A. KOVALEV (rep)
	1993-94 NYR	A. KOVALEV (sc)
Kozlov, Vyacheslav	1996-97 DET	VYACHESLAV KOZLOV (rep)
	1996-97 DET	VYACHESLAV KOZLOV (sc)
	1997-98 DET	V. KOZLOV (rep)
	1997-98 DET	V. KOZLOV (sc)
Kramer, Mike	1995-96 COL	MIKE KRAMER (rep)
	1995-96 COL	MIKE KRAMER (sc)
Kroenke, Stanley	2000-01 COL	E. STANLEY KROENKE (rep)
	2000-01 COL	E. STANLEY KROENKE (sc)
Krupp, Uwe	1995-96 COL	UWE KRUPP (rep)
	1995-96 COL	UWE KRUPP (sc)
Krushelnyski, Mike	1984-85 EDM	M. KRUSHELNYSKI (ab)
	1984-85 EDM	M. KRUSHELNYSKI (rep)
	1984-85 EDM	M. KRUSHELNYSKI (sc)
	1986-87 EDM	M. KRUSHELNYSKI (ab)
	1986-87 EDM	M. KRUSHELNYSKI (rep)
	1986-87 EDM	M. KRUSHELNYSKI (sc)
	1987-88 EDM	M. KRUSHELNYSKI (ab)
	1987-88 EDM	M. KRUSHELNYSKI (rep)
	1987-88 EDM	M. KRUSHELNYSKI (sc)
	1996-97 DET	MIKE KRUSHELNYSKI (rep)
	1996-97 DET	MIKE KRUSHELNYSKI (sc)
Kulchisky, Lyle	1983-84 EDM	L. KULCHISKY ASST. TR. (ab)
	1983-84 EDM	L. KULCHISKY ASST. TR. (rep)
	1983-84 EDM	L. KULCHISKY ASST. TR. (sc)
	1984-85 EDM	L. KULCHISKY ASST. TR. (ab)
	1984-85 EDM	L. KULCHISKY ASST. TR. (rep)
	1984-85 EDM	L. KULCHISKY ASST. TR. (sc)
	1986-87 EDM	L. KULCHISKY ASST. TR. (ab)
	1986-87 EDM	L. KULCHISKY ASST. TR. (rep)
	1986-87 EDM	L. KULCHISKY ASST. TR. (sc)
	1987-88 EDM	LYLE KULCHISKY ASST. TR. (ab)
	1987-88 EDM	LYLE KULCHISKY ASST. TR. (rep)
	1987-88 EDM	LYLE KULCHISKY AAT. TR. (sc)
	1989-90 EDM	LYLE KULCHISKY ASST. TR. (ab)
	1989-90 EDM	LYLE KULCHISKY ASST. TR. (rep)
	1989-90 EDM	LYLE KULCHISKY ASST. TR. (sc)
Kurri, Jari	1983-84 EDM	J. KURRI (ab)
	1983-84 EDM	J. KURRI (rep)
	1983-84 EDM	J. KURRI (sc)
	1984-85 EDM	J. KURRI (ab)
	1984-85 EDM	J. KURRI (rep)
	1984-85 EDM	J. KURRI (sc)
	1986-87 EDM	J. KURRI (ab)
	1986-87 EDM	J. KURRI (rep)
	1986-87 EDM	J. KURRI (sc)
	1987-88 EDM	J. KURRI (ab)
	1987-88 EDM	J. KURRI (rep)
	1987-88 EDM	J. KURRI (sc)
	1989-90 EDM	J. KURRI ASST. CAPT. (ab)
	1989-90 EDM	J. KURRI ASST. CAPT. (rep)
	1989-90 EDM	J. KURRI ASST. CAPT. (sc)
Kurvers, Tom	1985-86 MC	T. KURVERS (ab)
	1985-86 MC	T. KURVERS (rep)
	1985-86 MC	T. KURVERS (sc)
Kwong, Norman	1988-89 CAL	NORMAN KWONG (ab)
	1988-89 CAL	NORMAN KWONG (rep)
	1988-89 CAL	NORMAN KWONG (sc)
Kypreos, Nick	1993-94 NYR	N. KYPREOS (rep)
	1993-94 NYR	N. KYPREOS (sc)
Labraaten, Dan	1994-95 NJ	DAN LABRAATEN (rep)
	1994-95 NJ	DAN LABRAATEN (sc)
	1999-00 NJ	D. LABRAATEN (rep)
	1999-00 NJ	D. LABRAATEN (sc)
	2002-03 NJ	D. LABRAATEN (rep)
	2002-03 NJ	D. LABRAATEN (sc)
Lach, Elmer	1943-44 MC	ELMER LACH (sp)
	1943-44 MC	ELMER LACH (rep)
	1943-44 MC	ELMER LACH (sc)
	1945-46 MC	ELMER LACH (re)
	1945-46 MC	ELMER LACH (rep)
	1945-46 MC	ELMER LACH (sc)
	1952-53 MC	ELMER LACH (re)
	1952-53 MC	ELMER LACH (rep)
	1952-53 MC	ELMER LACH (sc)
Lacombe, Normand	1987-88 EDM	N. LACOMBE (ab)
	1987-88 EDM	N. LACOMBE (rep)
	1987-88 EDM	N. LACOMBE (sc)
Lacroix, Pierre	1995-96 COL	PIERRE LACROIX (rep)
	1995-96 COL	PIERRE LACROIX (sc)
	2000-01 COL	PIERRE LACROIX (rep)
	2000-01 COL	PIERRE LACROIX (sc)
Lafleur, Guy	1972-73 MC	GUY LAFLEUR (rep)
	1972-73 MC	GUY LAFLEUR (sc)
	1975-76 MC	GUY LAFLEUR (rep)
	1975-76 MC	GUY LAFLEUR (sc)
	1976-77 MC	GUY LAFLEUR (rep)
	1976-77 MC	GUY LAFLEUR (sc)
	1977-78 MC	GUY LAFLEUR (rep)
	1977-78 MC	GUY LAFLEUR (sc)
	1978-79 MC	G. LAFLEUR (ab)
	1978-79 MC	G. LAFLEUR (rep)
	1978-79 MC	G. LAFLEUR (sc)

Name	Season/Team	Engraving
Laidlaw, Bob	1931-32 TML	MR. R.A. LAIDLAW (sp)
Lalor, Mike	1985-86 MC	M. LALOR (ab)
	1985-86 MC	M. LALOR (rep)
	1985-86 MC	M. LALOR (sc)
Lamb, Mark	1989-90 EDM	M. LAMB (ab)
	1989-90 EDM	M. LAMB (rep)
	1989-90 EDM	M. LAMB (sc)
Lambert, Yvon	1975-76 MC	YVON LAMBERT (rep)
	1975-76 MC	YVON LAMBERT (sc)
	1976-77 MC	YVON LAMBERT (rep)
	1976-77 MC	YVON LAMBERT (sc)
	1977-78 MC	YVON LAMBERT (rep)
	1977-78 MC	YVON LAMBERT (sc)
	1978-79 MC	Y. LAMBERT (rep)
	1978-79 MC	Y. LAMBERT (sc)
Lamoriello, Chris	2002-03 NJ	C. LAMORIELLO (rep)
	2002-03 NJ	C. LAMORIELLO (sc)
Lamoriello, Lou	1994-95 NJ	LOU LAMORIELLO (rep)
	1994-95 NJ	LOU LAMORIELLO (sc)
	1999-00 NJ	L. LAMORIELLO (rep)
	1999-00 NJ	L. LAMORIELLO (sc)
	2002-03 NJ	LOU LAMORIELLO (rep)
	2002-03 NJ	LOU LAMORIELLO (sc)
Lamoureux, Leo	1943-44 MC	LEO LAMOUREUX (sp)
	1943-44 MC	LEO LAMOUREUX (rep)
	1943-44 MC	LEO LAMOUREUZ (sc)
	1945-46 MC	LEO. LAMOUREUX (re)
	1945-46 MC	LEO LAMOUREUX (rep)
	1945-46 MC	LEO LAMOUREUX (sc)
Lane, Gord	1979-80 NYI	G. LANE (ab)
	1979-80 NYI	G. LANE (rep)
	1979-80 NYI	G. LANE (sc)
	1980-81 NYI	G. LANE (ab)
	1980-81 NYI	G. LANE (rep)
	1980-81 NYI	G. LANE (sc)
	1981-82 NYI	G. LANE (ab)
	1981-82 NYI	G. LANE (rep)
	1981-82 NYI	G. LANE (sc)
	1982-83 NYI	G. LANE (ab)
	1982-83 NYI	G. LANE (rep)
	1982-83 NYI	G. LANE (sc)
Lane, Myles	1928-29 BB	MYLES LANE (or)
	1928-29 BB	"MYLES" LANE (rep)
	1928-29 BB	"MYLES" LANE (sc)
	1928-29 BB	G O M LANE (ret)
Langelle, Pete	1941-42 TML	PETE LANGELLE (sp)
	1941-42 TML	PETE LANGELLE (rep)
	1941-42 TML	PETE LANGELLE (sc)
Langenbrunner, Jamie	1998-99 DAL	JAMIE LANGENBRUNNER (rep)
	1998-99 DAL	JAMIE LANGENBRUNNER (sc)
	2002-03 NJ	JAMIE LANGENBRUNNER (rep)
	2002-03 NJ	JAMIE LANGENBRUNNER (sc)
Langevin, Dave	1979-80 NYI	D. LANGEVIN (ab)
	1979-80 NYI	D. LANGEVIN (rep)
	1979-80 NYI	D. LANGEVIN (sc)
	1980-81 NYI	D. LANGEVIN (ab)
	1980-81 NYI	D. LANGEVIN (rep)
	1980-81 NYI	D. LANGEVIN (sc)
	1981-82 NYI	D. LANGEVIN (ab)
	1981-82 NYI	D. LANGEVIN (rep)
	1981-82 NYI	D. LANGEVIN (sc)
	1982-83 NYI	D. LANGEVIN (ab)
	1982-83 NYI	D. LANGEVIN (rep)
	1982-83 NYI	D. LANGEVIN (sc)
Langlois, Al	1957-58 MC	A. LANGLOIS (rep)
	1957-58 MC	A LANGLOIS (sc)
	1958-59 MC	ALBERT LANGLOIS (rep)
	1958-59 MC	ALB LANGLOIS (sc)
	1959-60 MC	ALBERT LANGLOIS (rep)
	1959-60 MC	ALBERT LANGLOIS (sc)
Langlois, Phil	1970-71 MC	ASST. TRAINER P. LANGLOIS (rep)
	1970-71 MC	ASSI. TRAIN. P. LANGLOIS. (sc)
Langway, Rod	1978-79 MC	R. LANGWAY (ab)
	1978-79 MC	R. LANGWAY (rep)
	1978-79 MC	R. LANGWAY (sc)
Laperriere, Jacques	1964-65 MC	JACQUES LAPERRIERE (rep)
	1964-65 MC	JACQUES LAPERRIERE (sc)
	1965-66 MC	J. LAPERRIERE (rep)
	1965-66 MC	J LAPERRIERE (sc)
	1967-68 MC	J. LAPERRIERE (rep)
	1967-68 MC	J LAPGRRIERE (sc)
	1968-69 MC	J. LAPERRIERE (rep)
	1968-69 MC	J LAPERRIERE (sc)
	1970-71 MC	J. LAPERRIERE (rep)
	1970-71 MC	J LAPERRIERE. (sc)
	1972-73 MC	JACQUES LAPERRIÈRE (rep)
	1972-73 MC	JACQUES LAPPERRIERE (sc)
	1985-86 MC	J. LAPERRIÈRE ASST. COACH (ab)
	1985-86 MC	J. LAPERRÌERE ASST. COACH (rep)
	1985-86 MC	J. LAPERRIERE ASST. COACH (sc)
	1992-93 MC	JACQUES LAPERRIERE A. COACH (rep)
	1992-93 MC	JACQUES LAPERRIÈRE A. COACH (sc)
Lapointe, Guy	1970-71 MC	G. LAPOINTE (rep)
	1970-71 MC	G. LAPOINTE. (sc)
	1972-73 MC	GUY LAPOINTE (rep)
	1972-73 MC	GUY LAPOINTE (sc)
	1975-76 MC	GUY LAPOINTE (rep)
	1975-76 MC	GUY LAPOINTE (sc)
	1976-77 MC	GUY LAPOINTE (rep)
	1976-77 MC	GUY LAPOINTE (sc)
	1977-78 MC	GUY LAPOINTE (rep)
	1977-78 MC	GUY LAPOINTE (sc)
	1978-79 MC	G. LAPOINTE (ab)
	1978-79 MC	G. LAPOINTE (rep)
	1978-79 MC	G. LAPOINTE (sc)
Lapointe, Martin	1996-97 DET	MARTIN LAPOINTE (rep)
	1996-97 DET	MARTIN LAPOINTE (sc)
	1997-98 DET	M. LAPOINTE (rep)
	1997-98 DET	M. LAPOINTE (sc)
Larionov, Igor	1996-97 DET	IGOR LARIONOV (rep)
	1996-97 DET	IGOR LARIONOV (sc)
	1997-98 DET	I. LARIONOV (rep)
	1997-98 DET	I. LARIONOV (sc)
	2001-02 DET	IGOR LARIONOV (rep)
	2001-02 DET	IGOR LARIONOV (sc)
Larmer, Steve	1993-94 NYR	S. LARMER (rep)
	1993-94 NYR	S. LARMER (sc)
Larochelle, Wildor	1929-30 MC	WILDOR LAROCHELLE (sp)
	1929-30 MC	WILDOR LAROCHELLE (ret)
	1930-31 MC	WILDOR LAROCHELLE (sp)
	1930-31 MC	WILDOR LAROCHELLE (ret)
Larocque, Michel	1975-76 MC	MICHEL LAROCQUE (rep)
	1975-76 MC	MICHEL LAROCQUE (sc)
	1976-77 MC	MICHEL LAROCQUE (rep)
	1976-77 MC	MICHEL LAROCQUE (sc)
	1977-78 MC	MICHEL LAROCQUE (rep)
	1977-78 MC	MICHEL LAROCQUE (sc)
	1978-79 MC	M. LAROCQUE (ab)
	1978-79 MC	M. LAROCQUE (rep)
	1978-79 MC	M. LAROCQUE (sc)
Larose, Claude	1964-65 MC	CLAUDE LAROSE (rep)
	1964-65 MC	CLAUDE LAROSE (sc)
	1965-66 MC	CLAUDE LAROSE (rep)
	1965-66 MC	CLAUDE LAROSE (sc)
	1967-68 MC	CLAUDE LAROSE (rep)
	1967-68 MC	CLAUDE LAROSE (sc)
	1970-71 MC	C. LAROSE (rep)
	1970-71 MC	C. LAROSE. (sc)
	1972-73 MC	CLAUDE LAROSE (rep)
	1972-73 MC	CLAUDE LAROSE (sc)
Larouche, Pierre	1977-78 MC	PIERRE LAROUCHE (rep)
	1977-78 MC	PIERRE LAROUCHE (sc)
	1978-79 MC	P. LAROUCHE (rep)
	1978-79 MC	P. LAROUCHE (sc)
Latin, Steve	1990-91 PIT	STEVE LATIN EQUIP. MGR. (ab)
	1990-91 PIT	STEVE LATIN EQUIP. MGR. (rep)
	1990-91 PIT	STEVE LATIN EQUIP. MGR. (sc)
	1991-92 PIT	STEVE LATIN (rep)
	1991-92 PIT	STEVE LATIN (sc)
Leach, Jamie	1991-92 PIT	JAMIE LEACH (rep)
	1991-92 PIT	JAMIE LEACH (sc)
Leach, Mark	1996-97 DET	M. LEACH (rep)
	1996-97 DET	M. LEACH (sc)
	1997-98 DET	MARK LEACH (rep)
	1997-98 DET	MARK LEACH (sc)
	2001-02 DET	MARK LEACH (rep)
	2001-02 DET	MARK LEACH (sc)
Leach, Reg	1974-75 PHI	REGGIE LEACH (rep)
	1974-75 PHI	REGGIE LEACH (sc)
Lebeau, Stephan	1992-93 MC	S. LEBEAU (rep)
	1992-93 MC	S. LEBEAU (sc)
LeClair, Jack	1955-56 MC	J. LECLAIR (eb)
	1955-56 MC	J. LECLAIR (rep)
	1955-56 MC	J LECLAIR (sc)
LeClair, John	1992-93 MC	J. LECLAIR (rep)
	1992-93 MC	J. LECLAIR (sc)
Leduc, Albert	1929-30 MC	ALBERT LEDUC. (sp)
	1929-30 MC	ALBERT LEDUC (ret)
	1930-31 MC	ALBERT LEDUC (sp)
	1930-31 MC	ALBERT LEDUC (ret)
Leeman, Gary	1992-93 MC	G. LEEMAN (rep)
	1992-93 MC	G. LEEMAN (sc)
Leetch, Brian	1993-94 NYR	B. LEETCH (rep)
	1993-94 NYR	B. LEETCH (sc)
Lefebvre, Gaetan	1985-86 MC	G. LEFEBVRE ASST. PHYSIO. (ab)
	1985-86 MC	G. LEFEBVRE ASST. PHYSIO. (rep)
	1985-86 MC	G. LEFEBVRE ASST. PHYSIO. (sc)
	1992-93 MC	G. LEFEBVRE TRAINER (rep)
	1992-93 MC	G. LEFEBVRE TRAINER (sc)
Lefebvre, Sylvain	1995-96 COL	SYLVAIN LEFEBVRE (rep)
	1995-96 COL	SYLVAIN LEFEBVRE (sc)

Player	Season/Team	Engraving
Lefley,	1970-71 MC	C. LEFLEY (rep)
Chuck	1970-71 MC	C. LEFLEY. (sc)
	1972-73 MC	CHUCK LEFLEY (rep)
	1972-73 MC	CHUCK LEFLEY (sc)
Legace,	2001-02 DET	MANNY LEGACE (rep)
Manny	2001-02 DET	MANNY LEGACE (sc)
Lehman,	1914-15 VM	HUGH LEHMAN (ib)
Hugh	1914-15 VM	HUGH LEHMAN (rep)
	1914-15 VM	HUGH LEHMAN (sc)
Lehtinen,	1998-99 DAL	JERE LEHTINEN (rep)
Jere	1998-99 DAL	JERE LEHTINEN (sc)
Lehto, Joni	2000-01 COL	JONI LEHTO (rep)
	2000-01 COL	JONI LEHTO (sc)
Lemaire,	1967-68 MC	JACQUES LEMAIRE (rep)
Jacques	1967-68 MC	JACQUES LEMAIRE (sc)
	1968-69 MC	J. LEMAIRE (rep)
	1968-69 MC	J LEMAIRE (sc)
	1970-71 MC	J. LEMAIRE (rep)
	1970-71 MC	J. LEMAIRE. (sc)
	1972-73 MC	JACQUES LEMAIRE (rep)
	1972-73 MC	JACQUES LEMAIRE (sc)
	1975-76 MC	JACQUES LEMAIRE (rep)
	1975-76 MC	JACQUES LEMAIRE (sc)
	1976-77 MC	JACQUES LEMAIRE (rep)
	1976-77 MC	JACQUES LEMAIRE (sc)
	1977-78 MC	JACQUES LEMAIRE (rep)
	1977-78 MC	JACQUES LEMAIRE (sc)
	1978-79 MC	J. LEMAIRE (ab)
	1978-79 MC	J. LEMAIRE (rep)
	1978-79 MC	J. LEMAIRE (sc)
	1985-86 MC	J. LEMAIRE (ab)
	1985-86 MC	J. LEMAIRE (rep)
	1985-86 MC	J. LEMAIRE (sc)
	1992-93 MC	JACQUES LEMAIRE A.G.M. (rep)
	1992-93 MC	JACQUES LEMAIRE A.G.M. (sc)
	1994-95 NJ	JACQUES LEMAIRE (rep)
	1994-95 NJ	JACQUES LEMAIRE (sc)
Lemay, Moe	1986-87 EDM	M. LEMAY (ab)
	1986-87 EDM	M. LEMAY (rep)
	1986-87 EDM	M. LEMAY (sc)
Lemieux,	1985-86 MC	C. LEMIEUX (ab)
Claude	1985-86 MC	C. LEMIEUX (rep)
	1985-86 MC	C. LEMIEUX (sc)
	1994-95 NJ	CLAUDE LEMIEUX (rep)
	1994-95 NJ	CLAUDE LEMIEUX (sc)
	1995-96 COL	CLAUDE LEMIEUX (rep)
	1995-96 COL	CLAUDE LEMIEUX (sc)
	1999-00 NJ	CLAUDE LEMIEUX (rep)
	1999-00 NJ	CLAUDE LEMIEUX (sc)
Lemieux,	1990-91 PIT	M. LEMIEUX CAPT. (ab)
Mario	1990-91 PIT	M. LEMIEUX CAPT. (rep)
	1990-91 PIT	M. LEMIEUX CAPT. (sc)
	1991-92 PIT	MARIO LEMIEUX CAPT. (rep)
	1991-92 PIT	MARIO LEMIEUX CAPT. (sc)
Lepine,	1929-30 MC	ALFRED PIT LEPINE. (sp)
Alfred	1929-30 MC	ALFRED PIT LEPINE (ret)
"Pit"	1930-31 MC	ALFRED LEPINE (sp)
	1930-31 MC	ALFRED LEPINE (ret)
Leschyshyn,	1995-96 COL	CURTIS LESCHYSHYN (rep)
Curtis	1995-96 COL	CURTIS LESCHYSHYN (sc)
Lesieur, Art	1930-31 MC	ARTHUR LESIEUR (sp)
	1930-31 MC	ARTHUR LESEUR (ret)
Lesuk, Bill	1969-70 BB	B. LESUK (rep)
	1969-70 BB	B LESUK (sc)
Leswick,	1933-34 CHI	JACK LESWICK (sp)
Jack	1933-34 CHI	JACK LESWICK (ret)
Leswick,	1951-52 DET	TONY LESWICK (re)
Tony	1951-52 DET	TONY LESWICK (rep)
	1951-52 DET	TONY LESWICH (sc)
	1953-54 DET	TONY LESWICK (re)
	1953-54 DET	TONY LESWICK (rep)
	1953-54 DET	TONY LESWICH (sc)
	1954-55 DET	TONY LESWICK (re)
	1954-55 DET	TONI LESWICK (rep)
	1954-55 DET	TONI LESWICK (sc)
Letourneau,	1923-24 MC	H.A. LETOURNEAU (or)
H.A.	1923-24 MC	H.A. LETOURNEAU (rep)
	1923-24 MC	H.A. LETOURNEAU (sc)
	1929-30 MC	H.A. LETOURNEAU. DIRECTORS. * (sp)
		* refers also to Amadee Monet Juge
	1929-30 MC	H A LETOVRNEAU DIRECTORS (ret)
Levinsky,	1931-32 TML	A. LEVINSKY (sp)
Alex	1931-32 TML	A LEVINSKY (ret)
	1937-38 CHI	ALEX LEVINSKY (sp)
	1937-38 CHI	ALEX LEVINSKY (ret)
Lewicki,	1950-51 TML	DANIEL LEWICKI (re)
Dan	1950-51 TML	DANIEL LEWICKI (rep)
	1950-51 TML	DANIEL LEWISKI (sc)
Lewis, Dave	1996-97 DET	DAVE LEWIS (rep)
	1996-97 DET	DAVE LEWIS (sc)
	1997-98 DET	DAVE LEWIS (rep)
	1997-98 DET	DAVE LEWIS (sc)
	2001-02 DET	DAVE LEWIS (rep)
	2001-02 DET	DAVE LEWIS (sc)
Lewis,	1973-74 PHI	FRANK LEWIS TRAINER (rep)
Frank	1973-74 PHI	FRANK LEWIS TRA. (sc)
	1974-75 PHI	FRANK LEWIS TR. (rep)
	1974-75 PHI	FRANK LEWIS TRA. (sc)
Lewis,	1935-36 DET	HERB LEWIS— L. WING (sp)
Herbie	1935-36 DET	HERB LEWIS (ret)
	1936-37 DET	HERB LEWIS L.WING (sp)
	1936-37 DET	HERB LEWIS (ret)
Lidster,	1993-94 NYR	D. LIDSTER (rep)
Doug	1993-94 NYR	D. LIDSTER (sc)
Lidstrom,	1996-97 DET	NICKLAS LIDSTROM (rep)
Nicklas	1996-97 DET	NICKLAS LIDSTROM (sc)
	1997-98 DET	N. LIDSTROM (rep)
	1997-98 DET	N. LIDSTROM (sc)
	2001-02 DET	NICKLAS LIDSTROM (rep)
	2001-02 DET	NICKLAS LIDSTROM (sc)
Lifrieri,	1993-94 NYR	B. LIFRIERI TRAINER (rep)
Bruce	1993-94 NYR	B. LIFRIERI TRAINER (sc)
Lindsay,	1949-50 DET	TED LINDSAY (re)
Ted	1949-50 DET	TED LINDSAY (rep)
	1949-50 DET	TED LINDSEY (sc)
	1951-52 DET	TED LINDSAY (re)
	1951-52 DET	TED LINDSAY (rep)
	1951-52 DET	TED LINDSAY (sc)
	1953-54 DET	TED LINDSAY (CAPT.) (re)
	1953-54 DET	TED LINDSAY CAPT. (rep)
	1953-54 DET	TED LINDSAY CAPT (sc)
	1954-55 DET	TED LINDSAY (CAPT.) (re)
	1954-55 DET	TED LINDSAY CAPT. (rep)
	1954-55 DET	TED LINDSAY CAPT (sc)
Lindstrom,	1983-84 EDM	W. LINDSTROM (ab)
Willy	1983-84 EDM	W. LINDSTROM (rep)
	1983-84 EDM	W. LINDSTROM (sc)
	1984-85 EDM	W. LINDSTROM (ab)
	1984-85 EDM	W. LINDSTROM (rep)
	1984-85 EDM	W. LINDSTROM (sc)
Linseman,	1983-84 EDM	K. LINSEMAN (ab)
Ken	1983-84 EDM	K. LINSEMAN (rep)
	1983-84 EDM	K. LINSEMAN (sc)
Liscombe,	1942-43 DET	CARL LISCOMBE (sp)
Carl	1942-43 DET	CARL LISCOMBE (rep)
	1942-43 DET	CARL LISCOMBE (sc)
Lites,		
Denise Ilitch	1996-97 DET	DENISE ILITCH LITES (rep)
	1996-97 DET	DENISE ILITCH LITES (sc)
Lites, Jim	1998-99 DAL	JIM LITES (rep)
	1998-99 DAL	JIM LITES (sc)
Litzenberger,	1960-61 CHI	EDWARD LITZENBERGER CAPTAIN (rep)
Ed	1960-61 CHI	EDWARD LITZENBERGER CAPTAIN (sc)
	1961-62 TML	EDWARD LITZENBERGER (rep)
	1961-62 TML	EDWARD LITZENBERGER (sc)
	1962-63 TML	ED LITZENBERGER (rep)
	1962-63 TML	ED LITZENBERGER (sc)
Loney, Troy	1990-91 PIT	T. LONEY (ab)
	1990-91 PIT	T. LONEY (rep)
	1990-91 PIT	T. LONEY (sc)
	1991-92 PIT	TROY LONEY (rep)
	1991-92 PIT	TROY LONEY (sc)
Lonsberry,	1973-74 PHI	ROSS LONSBERRY (rep)
Ross	1973-74 PHI	ROSS LONSBERRY (sc)
	1974-75 PHI	ROSS LONSBERRY (rep)
	1974-75 PHI	ROSS LONSBERRY (sc)
Loob,	1988-89 CAL	H. LOOB (ab)
Hakan	1988-89 CAL	H. LOOB (rep)
	1988-89 CAL	H. LOOB (sc)
Lorentz, Jim	1969-70 BB	J. LORENTZ (rep)
	1969-70 BB	J LORENTZ (sc)
Lorimer,	1979-80 NYI	B. LORIMER (ab)
Bob	1979-80 NYI	B. LORIMER (rep)
	1979-80 NYI	B. LORIMER (sc)
	1980-81 NYI	B. LORMIER (ab)
	1980-81 NYI	B. LORIMER (rep)
	1980-81 NYI	B. LORIMER (sc)
Loughlin,	1924-25 VIC	C. LOUGHLIN. (CAPT.) (or)
Clem	1924-25 VIC	C. LOUGHLIN (CAPT) (rep)
	1924-25 VIC	C. LOUGHLIN. (CAPT) (sc)
Loughran,	1993-94 NYR	M. LOUGHRAN TM. OP. (rep)
Matthew	1993-94 NYR	M. LOUGHRAN TM. OP. (sc)
Low, Ron	1986-87 EDM	RON LOW ASST. COACH (ab)
	1986-87 EDM	RON LOW ASST. COACH (rep)
	1986-87 EDM	RON LOW ASST. COACH (sc)
	1989-90 EDM	RON LOW ASST. COACH (ab)
	1989-90 EDM	RON LOW ASST. COACH (rep)
	1989-90 EDM	RON LOW ASST. COACH (sc)
Lowe, Ken	1989-90 EDM	KEN LOWE (ab)
	1989-90 EDM	KEN LOWE (rep)

Name	Year / Team	Inscription
	1989-90 EDM	KEN LOWE (sc)
Lowe, Kevin	1983-84 EDM	K. LOWE (ab)
	1983-84 EDM	K. LOWE (rep)
	1983-84 EDM	K. LOWE (sc)
	1984-85 EDM	K. LOWE (ab)
	1984-85 EDM	K. LOWE (rep)
	1984-85 EDM	K. LOWE (sc)
	1986-87 EDM	K. LOWE (ab)
	1986-87 EDM	K. LOWE (rep)
	1986-87 EDM	K. LOWE (sc)
	1987-88 EDM	K. LOWE (ab)
	1987-88 EDM	K. LOWE (rep)
	1987-88 EDM	K. LOWE (sc)
	1989-90 EDM	K. LOWE A. CAPT. (ab)
	1989-90 EDM	K. LOWE A. CAPT. (rep)
	1989-90 EDM	K. LOWE A. CAPT. (sc)
	1993-94 NYR	K. LOWE (rep)
	1993-94 NYR	K. LOWE (sc)
Ludvig, Jan	2002-03 NJ	J. LUDVIG (rep)
	2002-03 NJ	J. LUDVIG (sc)
Ludwig, Craig	1985-86 MC	C. LUDWIG (ab)
	1985-86 MC	C. LUDWIG (rep)
	1985-86 MC	C. LUDWIG (sc)
	1998-99 DAL	CRAIG LUDWIG (rep)
	1998-99 DAL	CRAIG LUDWIG (sc)
Lumley, Dave	1983-84 EDM	D. LUMLEY (ab)
	1983-84 EDM	D. LUMLEY (rep)
	1983-84 EDM	D. LUMLEY (sc)
	1984-85 EDM	D. LUMLEY (ab)
	1984-85 EDM	D. LUMLEY (rep)
	1984-85 EDM	D. LUMLEY (sc)
Lumley, Harry	1949-50 DET	HARRY LUMLEY (re)
	1949-50 DET	HARRY LUMLEY (rep)
	1949-50 DET	HARRY LUMLEY (sc)
Lupien, Gilles	1977-78 MC	GILLES LUPIEN (rep)
	1977-78 MC	GILLES LUPIEN (sc)
	1978-79 MC	G. LUPIEN (rep)
	1978-79 MC	G. LUPIEN (sc)
Lynn, Vic	1946-47 TML	VICTOR LYNN (re)
	1946-47 TML	VICTOR LYNN (rep)
	1946-47 TML	VICTOR LYNN (sc)
	1947-48 TML	VICTOR LYNN (re)
	1947-48 TML	VICTOR LYNN (rep)
	1947-48 TML	VICTOR LYNN (sc)
	1948-49 TML	VICTOR LYNN (re)
	1948-49 TML	VICTOR LYNN (rep)
	1948-49 TML	VICTOR LYNN (sc)
Lyons, Charlie	1995-96 COL	CHARLIE LYONS (rep)
	1995-96 COL	CHARLIE LYONS (sc)
Lyons, Steve	2000-01 COL	STEVE LYONS (rep)
	2000-01 COL	STEVE LYONS (sc)
MacBrien, Bill	1931-32 TML	MR. W.A.H. MACBRIEN (sp)
	1941-42 TML	W.A.H. MACBRIEN. VICE-PRES. (sp)
	1941-42 TML	W.A.H. MCBRIEN V. PRES. (rep)
	1941-42 TML	W.A.H. MCBRIEN (V PRESS) (sc)
	1944-45 TML	W.A.H. MACBRIEN VICE-PRESIDENT (sp)
	1944-45 TML	WA.H. MACBRIEN V. PRES. (rep)
	1944-45 TML	WA H MACBRIEN (V PRES) (sc)
	1946-47 TML	W.A.H. MACBRIEN VICE-PRESIDENT (re)
	1946-47 TML	W.A.H. MACBRIEN VICE PRES. (rep)
	1946-47 TML	W.A.H. MACBRIEN (VICE PRES) (sc)
	1947-48 TML	W.A.H. MAC BRIEN — CHAIRMAN OF BOARD (re)
	1947-48 TML	W.A.H. MACBRIEN CHAIRMAN (rep)
	1947-48 TML	W.A.H. MACBRIEN CHAIRMAN (sc)
	1948-49 TML	W.A.H. MACBRIEN—CHAIRMAN OF BOARD (re)
	1948-49 TML	W.A.H. MACBRIEN CHAIRMAN (rep)
	1948-49 TML	W A H MACBRIAN CHAIRMAN (sc)
	1950-51 TML	W.A.H. MACBRIEN CHAIRMAN OF THE BOARD (re)
	1950-51 TML	W.A.H. MACBRIEN CHAIRMAN (rep)
	1950-51 TML	W A H McBRIEN CHAIRMAN (sc)
MacDonald, Brian	2000-01 COL	BRIAN MACDONALD (rep)
	2000-01 COL	BRIAN MACDONALD (sc)
MacDonald, Kilby	1939-40 NYR	KILBY MACDONALD (sp)
	1939-40 NYR	KILBY MACDONALD (ret)
MacDonald, Paul	2001-02 DET	PAUL MACDONALD (rep)
	2001-02 DET	PAUL MACDONALD (sc)
MacDougall, Robert	1934-35 MM	R.E. MACDOUGALL (sp)
	1934-35 MM	RE MAC DOUGALL (ret)
MacDowell, Major W.	1926-27 OTT	MAJOR T.W. MACDOWELL V.C. VICE PRES. (or)
	1926-27 OTT	MAJOR T.W. MACDOWELL V.C. VICE PRES (rep)
	1926-27 OTT	MAJOR T.W. MACDOWELL VC. VICE PRES. (sc)
MacGregor, Bruce	1983-84 EDM	BRUCE MACGREGOR ASST. G.M. (ab)
	1983-84 EDM	BRUCE MACGREGOR ASST. G.M. (rep)
	1983-84 EDM	BRUCE MACGREGOR ASST.G.M. (sc)
	1984-85 EDM	BRUCE MACGREGOR ASST. G.M. (ab)
	1984-85 EDM	BRUCE MACGREGOR ASST.G.M. (rep)
	1984-85 EDM	BRUCE MACGREGOR ASST.G.M. (sc)
	1986-87 EDM	BRUCE MACGREGOR ASST. G.M. (ab)
	1986-87 EDM	BRUCE MACGREGOR ASST.G.M. (rep)
	1986-87 EDM	BRUCE MACGREGOR ASST.G.M. (sc)
	1987-88 EDM	BRUCE MACGREGOR ASST. G.M. (ab)
	1987-88 EDM	BRUCE MACGREGOR ASST.G.M. (rep)
	1987-88 EDM	BRUCE MACGREGOR ASST.G.M. (sc)
	1989-90 EDM	BRUCE MACGREGOR ASST. G.M. (ab)
	1989-90 EDM	BRUCE MACGREGOR ASST.G.M. (rep)
	1989-90 EDM	BRUCE MACGREGOR ASST.G.M. (sc)
MacGregor, Stu	1998-99 DAL	STU MACGREGOR (rep)
	1998-99 DAL	STU MACGREGOR (sc)
MacInnis, Al	1988-89 CAL	A. MACINNIS (ab)
	1988-89 CAL	A. MACINNIS (rep)
	1988-89 CAL	A. MACINNIS (sc)
MacIntyre, Horace	1946-47 TML	DR. HORACE MACINTYRE CLUB DOCTOR (re)
	1946-47 TML	HORACE MACINTYRE CLUB DOCTORS* (rep)
	1946-47 TML	HORACE MACINTYRE CLUB DOCTORS* (sc) * refers also to Dr. Galloway
	1947-48 TML	DR. HORACE MACINTYRE—CLUB DOCTOR (re)
	1947-48 TML	H. MAC INTYRE CLUB DOCTORS* (rep)
	1947-48 TML	H. MACINTYRE CLUP DOCTOR'S* (sc) * refers also to Dr. Galloway
	1948-49 TML	DR. HORACE MACINTYRE CLUB DOCTOR (re)
	1950-51 TML	DR. HORACE MACINTYRE CLUB DOCTOR (re)
MacKay, Calum	1952-53 MC	CALUM MACKAY (re)
	1952-53 MC	CALUM MCKAY (rep)
	1952-53 MC	CALUK MACKAY (sc)
MacKay, Mickey	1914-15 VM	MICKEY McKAY (ib)
	1914-15 VM	MICKEY M[c]KAY (rep)
	1914-15 VM	MICKEY McKAY (sc)
	1928-29 BB	"MICKEY" MACKAY (or)
	1928-29 BB	"MICKEY" MACKAY (rep)
	1928-29 BB	"MICKEY" MACKAY (sc)
	1928-29 BB	M MAC KAY (ret)
Mackell, Fleming	1948-49 TML	FLEMING MACKELL (re)
	1948-49 TML	FLEMING MACKELL (rep)
	1948-49 TML	FLEMING MACKELL (sc)
	1950-51 TML	FLEMING MACKELL (re)
	1950-51 TML	FLEMING MACKELL (rep)
	1950-51 TML	FLEMING MACKELL (sc)
MacKenzie, Bill	1934-35 MM	W. MCKENZIE (sp)
	1934-35 MM	W MCKENZIE (ret)
	1937-38 CHI	BILL MAC KENZIE (sp)
	1937-38 CHI	BILL MCKENZIE (ret)
Mackie, Howie	1936-37 DET	HOWARD MACKIE R.WING (sp)
MacLean, John	1994-95 NJ	JOHN MACLEAN "A" (rep)
	1994-95 NJ	JOHN MACLEAN "A" (sc)
	2002-03 NJ	JOHN MACLEAN (rep)
	2002-03 NJ	JOHN MACLEAN (sc)
MacLeish, Rick	1973-74 PHI	RICK MACLEISH (rep)
	1973-74 PHI	RICK MACLEISH (sc)
	1974-75 PHI	RICK MACLEISH (rep)
	1974-75 PHI	RICK MACLEISH (sc)
MacLellan, Brian	1988-89 CAL	B. MACLELLAN (ab)
	1988-89 CAL	B. MACLELLAN (rep)
	1988-89 CAL	B. MACLELLAN (sc)
MacMillan, Billy	1979-80 NYI	WILLIAM MACMILLAN A. COACH (ab)
	1979-80 NYI	WILLIAM MACMILLAN A. COACH (rep)
	1979-80 NYI	WILLIAM MACMILLAN A. COACH (sc)
MacMillan, John	1961-62 TML	JOHN MACMILLAN (rep)
	1961-62 TML	JOHN MACMILLAN (sc)
	1962-63 TML	C. MACMILLAN (rep)
	1962-63 TML	C MACMILLAN (sc)
MacNeil, Al	1970-71 MC	AL MACNEIL COACH (rep)
	1970-71 MC	COACH. MAC NEIL (sc)
	1977-78 MC	AL MACNEIL D.P.D. (rep)
	1977-78 MC	AL MACNEIL D.P.D. (sc)
	1978-79 MC	AL MACNEIL D.P.P. (ab)
	1978-79 MC	AL MACNEIL D.P.P. (rep)
	1978-79 MC	AL MACNEIL D.P.P. (sc)
	1988-89 CAL	AL MACNEIL ASST. G.M. (ab)
	1988-89 CAL	AL MACNEIL ASST. G.M. (rep)
	1988-89 CAL	L MACNEIL ASST. G.M. (sc)
Macoun, Jamie	1988-89 CAL	J. MACOUN (ab)
	1988-89 CAL	J. MACOUN (rep)
	1988-89 CAL	J. MACOUN (sc)
	1997-98 DET	J. MACOUN (rep)
	1997-98 DET	J. MACOUN (sc)
MacPherson, Bud	1952-53 MC	JIM MACPHERSON (re)
	1952-53 MC	JIM MACPHERSON (rep)
	1952-53 MC	JIM MACPHERSON (sc)

Name	Season	Team	Engraving
MacTavish,	1986-87	EDM	C. MACTAVISH (ab)
Craig	1986-87	EDM	C. MACTAVISH (rep)
	1986-87	EDM	C. MAC TAVISH (sc)
	1987-88	EDM	C. MAC TAVISH (ab)
	1987-88	EDM	C. MACTAVISH (rep)
	1987-88	EDM	C. MACTAVISH (sc)
	1989-90	EDM	C. MACTAVISH (ab)
	1989-90	EDM	C. MACTAVISH (rep)
	1989-90	EDM	C. MACTAVISH (sc)
	1993-94	NYR	C. MACTAVISH (rep)
	1993-94	NYR	C. MACTAVISH (sc)
Madden,	1999-00	NJ	JOHN J. MADDEN (rep)
John	1999-00	NJ	JOHN J. MADDEN (sc)
	2002-03	NJ	JOHN J. MADDEN (rep)
	2002-03	NJ	JOHN J. MADDEN (sc)
Madden,	1993-94	NYR	M. MADDEN SCOUT (rep)
Martin	1993-94	NYR	M. MADDEN SCOUT (sc)
Mahovlich,	1961-62	TML	FRANK MAHOVLICH (rep)
Frank	1961-62	TML	FRANK MAHOVLICH (sc)
	1962-63	TML	FRANK MAHOVLICH (rep)
	1962-63	TML	FRANK MAHOVLICH (sc)
	1963-64	TML	FRANK MAHOVLICH (rep)
	1963-64	TML	FRANK MAHOVLICH (sc)
	1966-67	TML	FRANK MAHOVLICH (rep)
	1966-67	TML	FRANK MAHOVLICH (sc)
	1970-71	MC	F. MAHOVLICH (rep)
	1970-71	MC	F. MAHOVLICH. (sc)
	1972-73	MC	FRANK MAHOVLICH (rep)
	1972-73	MC	FRANK MAHOVLICH (sc)
Mahovlich,	1970-71	MC	P. MAHOVLICH (rep)
Pete	1970-71	MC	P. MAHOVLICH. (sc)
	1972-73	MC	PETER MAHOVLICH (rep)
	1972-73	MC	PETER MAHOVLICH (sc)
	1975-76	MC	PETER MAHOVLICH (rep)
	1975-76	MC	PETER MAHOVLICH (sc)
	1976-77	MC	PETER MAHOVLICH (rep)
	1976-77	MC	PETER MAHOVLICH (sc)
Majeau,	1943-44	MC	FERNAND MAJEAU (ob)
Fern	1943-44	MC	FERNAND MAJEAU (rep)
	1943-44	MC	FERNAND MAJEAU (sc)
Maki, Ronald	1960-61	CHI	RONALD MAKI (rep)
"Chico"	1960-61	CHI	RONALD MAKI (sc)
Malakhov,	1999-00	NJ	VLADIMIR MALAKHOV (rep)
Vladimir	1999-00	NJ	VLADIMIR MALAKHOV (sc)
Maley,	1985-86	MC	D. MALEY (ab)
David	1985-86	MC	D. MALEY (rep)
	1985-86	MC	D. MALEY (sc)
Malone,	1990-91	PIT	GREG MALONE SCOUT (ab)
Greg	1990-91	PIT	GREG MALONE SCOUT (rep)
	1990-91	PIT	GREG MALONE SCOUT (sc)
	1991-92	PIT	GREG MALONE (rep)
	1991-92	PIT	GREG MALONE (sc)
Maltby,	1996-97	DET	KIRK MALTBY (rep)
Kirk	1996-97	DET	KIRK MALTBY (sc)
	1997-98	DET	K. MALTBY (rep)
	1997-98	DET	K. MALTBY (sc)
	2001-02	DET	KIRK MALTBY (rep)
	2001-02	DET	KIRK MALTBY (sc)
Mantha,	1929-30	MC	GEO MANTHA. (sp)
Georges	1929-30	MC	GEO MANTHA (ret)
	1930-31	MC	GEO. MANTHA (sp)
	1930-31	MC	GEO MANTHA (ret)
Mantha,	1923-24	MC	S. MANTHA (or)
Sylvio	1923-24	MC	S. MANTHA (rep)
	1923-24	MC	S. MANTHA (sc)
	1929-30	MC	SYLVIO MANTHA. (sp)
	1929-30	MC	SYLVIO MANTHA (ret)
	1930-31	MC	SYLVIO MANTHA (sp)
	1930-31	MC	SYLVIO MANTHA (ret)
Marcetta,	1966-67	TML	MILAN MARCETTA (rep)
Milan	1966-67	TML	MILAN MARCETTA (sc)
March,	1933-34	CHI	HAROLD MARCH (sp)
Harold	1933-34	CHI	HAROLD MARCH (ret)
"Mush"	1937-38	CHI	HAROLD MARCH (sp)
	1937-38	CHI	HAROLD MARCH (ret)
Marcotte,	1969-70	BB	D. MARCOTTE (rep)
Don	1969-70	BB	D. MARCOTTE (sc)
	1971-72	BB	DON MARCOTTE (rep)
	1971-72	BB	DON MARCOTTE (sc)
Marini,	1980-81	NYI	H. MARINI (ab)
Hector	1980-81	NYI	H. MARINI (rep)
	1980-81	NYI	H. MARINI (sc)
	1981-82	NYI	H. MARINI (ab)
	1981-82	NYI	H. MARINI (rep)
	1981-82	NYI	H. MARINI (sc)
Marker, Gus	1934-35	MM	A. MARKER (sp)
	1934-35	MM	A MARKER (ret)
Marshall,	1955-56	MC	D. MARSHALL (re)
Don	1955-56	MC	D. MARSHALL (rep)
	1955-56	MC	D. MARSHALL (sc)
	1956-57	MC	D. MARSHALL (rep)
	1956-57	MC	D. MARSHALL (sc)
	1957-58	MC	D. MARSHALL (rep)
	1957-58	MC	D MARSHALL (sc)
	1958-59	MC	DON MARSHALL (rep)
	1958-59	MC	DON MARSHALL (sc)
	1959-60	MC	DON MARSHALL (rep)
	1959-60	MC	DON MARSHALL (sc)
Marshall,	1998-99	DAL	GRANT MARSHALL (rep)
Grant	1998-99	DAL	GRANT MARSHALL (sc)
	2002-03	NJ	GRANT MARSHALL (rep)
	2002-03	NJ	GRANT MARSHALL (sc)
Marshall,	1907	MW	JACK MARSHALL. (ib)
Jack	1907	MW	JACK MARSHALL (rep)
	1907	MW	JACK MARSHALL (sc)
Martha,	1990-91	PIT	J. PAUL MARTHA V.P. & GEN. COUNSEL (ab)
Paul	1990-91	PIT	J. PAUL MARTHA V.P. & GEN. COUNSEL (rep)
	1990-91	PIT	J. PAUL MARTHA V.P. & GEN. COUNSEL (sc)
	1991-92	PIT	PAUL MARTHA (rep)
	1991-92	PIT	PAUL MARTHA (sc)
Martin,	1949-50	DET	CLARE MARTIN (re)
Clare	1949-50	DET	CLARE MARTIN (rep)
	1949-50	DET	CLARE MARTIN (sc)
Martineau,	1995-96	COL	JEAN MARTINEAU (rep)
Jean	1995-96	COL	JEAN MARTINEAU (sc)
	2000-01	COL	JEAN MARTINEAU (rep)
	2000-01	COL	JEAN MARTINEAU (sc)
Masnick,	1952-53	MC	PAUL MASNICK (re)
Paul	1952-53	MC	PAUL MASNICK (rep)
	1952-53	DET	PAUL MASNICK (sc)
Matteau,	1993-94	NYR	S. MATTEAU (rep)
Stephane	1993-94	NYR	S. MATTEAU (sc)
Matthews,	1998-99	DAL	RICH MATTHEWS (rep)
Rich	1998-99	DAL	RICH MATTHEWS (sc)
	2002-03	NJ	R.W. MATTHEWS (rep)
	2002-03	NJ	R.W. MATTHEWS (sc)
Mattson,	1949-50	DET	CARL MATTSON TRAINER (re)
Carl	1949-50	DET	C. MATTSON TRAINER (rep)
	1949-50	DET	C MATTSON TRAINER (sc)
	1951-52	DET	CARL MATTSON—TRAINER (re)
	1951-52	DET	CARL MATTSON TRAINER (rep)
	1951-52	DET	CARL MATTSON TRAINER (sc)
	1953-54	DET	CARL MATTSON, TRAINER (re)
	1953-54	DET	CARL MATTSON TRAINER (rep)
	1953-54	DET	CARL MATTSON TRAIN (sc)
	1954-55	DET	CARL MATTSON, TRAINER (re)
	1954-55	DET	CARL MATTSON TRAINER (rep)
	1954-55	DET	CARL MATTSON TRAINER (sc)
Matvichuk,	1998-99	DAL	RICHARD MATVICHUK (rep)
Richard	1998-99	DAL	RICHARD MATVICHUK (sc)
Mazur,	1952-53	MC	EDDIE MAZUR (re)
Eddie	1952-53	MC	EDDIE MAZURE (rep)
	1952-53	MC	EDDIE MAZUR (sc)
McAlpine,	1994-95	NJ	CHRIS MCALPINE (rep)
Chris	1994-95	NJ	CHRIS MCALPINE (sc)
McCaffrey,	1929-30	MC	ALBERT MACCAFFREY (sp)
Bert	1929-30	MC	ALBERT MAC CAFFREY (ret)
McCammon,			
Bob	2001-02	DET	BOB MCCAMMON (rep)
	2001-02	DET	BOB MCCAMMON (sc)
McCammon,			
Morgan	1978-79	MC	MORGAN MCCAMMON D. (ab)
	1978-79	MC	MORGAN MCCAMMON D. (rep)
	1978-79	MC	MORGAN MCCAMMON D. (sc)
McCarthy,			
Leighton	1931-32	TML	MR. LEIGHTON MCCARTHY (sp)
McCarty,	1996-97	DET	DARREN MCCARTY (rep)
Darren	1996-97	DET	DARREN MCCARTY (sc)
	1997-98	DET	D. MCCARTY (rep)
	1997-98	DET	D. MCCARTY (sc)
	2001-02	DET	DARREN MCCARTY (rep)
	2001-02	DET	DARREN MCCARTY (sc)
McClelland,	1983-84	EDM	K. MCCLELLAND (ab)
Kevin	1983-84	EDM	K. McCLELLAND (rep)
	1983-84	EDM	K. McCLELLAND (sc)
	1984-85	EDM	K. MCCLELLAND (ab)
	1984-85	EDM	K. McCLELLAND (rep)
	1984-85	EDM	K. McCLELLAND (sc)
	1986-87	EDM	K. MCCLELLAND (ab)
	1986-87	EDM	K. Mc CLELLAND (rep)
	1986-87	EDM	K. McCLELLAND (sc)
	1987-88	EDM	K. MCCLELLAND (ab)
	1987-88	EDM	K. MCCLELLAND (rep)
	1987-88	EDM	K. MCCLELLAND (sc)
McCool,	1944-45	TML	FRANK M[C]COOL (sp)
Frank	1944-45	TML	FRANK MCCOOL (rep)
	1944-45	TML	FRANK MCCOOL (sc)
McCormack,	1950-51	TML	JOHN MCCORMACK (re)
John	1950-51	TML	JOHN MCCORMACK (rep)

Name	Season/Team	Engraving
	1950-51 TML	JOHN MCCORMACK (sc)
	1952-53 MC	JOHN MCCORMACK (eb)
	1952-53 MC	JOHN MCCORMACK (rep)
	1952-53 MC	JOHN MCCORMACK (sc)
McCreedy,	1941-42 TML	JOHNNY McCREEDY (sp)
John	1941-42 TML	JOHNNY MCCREEDY (rep)
	1941-42 TML	JOHNNY MCCREEDY (sc)
	1944-45 TML	JOHNNY McCREEDY (sp)
	1944-45 TML	JOHNNY MCCREEDY (rep)
	1944-45 TML	JOHNNY MCCREEDY (sc)
McCrimmon,		
Brad	1988-89 CAL	B. MCCRIMMON (ab)
	1988-89 CAL	B. MCCRIMMON (rep)
	1988-89 CAL	B. MCCRIMMON (sc)
McCullagh,	1947-48 TML	C. GEORGE McCULLAGH—VICE-PRESIDENT (re)
George	1947-48 TML	C.G. MCCULLACH V. PRES, (rep)
	1947-48 TML	C.G. MCCULLACH (V PRES) (sc)
	1948-49 TML	C. GEORGE MCCULLAGH VICE PRESIDENT (re)
	1948-49 TML	C.G. MCCULLACH V. PRES. (rep)
	1948-49 TML	C G MCCULLACH (V PRES) (sc)
	1950-51 TML	C. GEORGE MCCULLAGH VICE-PRESIDENT (re)
	1950-51 TML	C.G. MCCULLACH V.PRES. (rep)
	1950-51 TML	C G MCCULLACH (V PRES) (sc)
McDavis,	1969-70 BB	SHELBY MCDAVIS V.P. (rep)
Shelby	1969-70 BB	SHELBY MC DAVIS VP (sc)
	1971-72 BB	SHELBY DAVIS VICE PRESIDENT (rep)
	1971-72 BB	SHELBY DAVIS VICE PRESIDENT (sc)
McDonald,	1957-58 MC	A. MC DONALD (rep)
Ab	1957-58 MC	A MCDONALD (sc)
	1958-59 MC	AB MC DONALD (rep)
	1958-59 MC	ALVIN MCDONALD (sc)
	1959-60 MC	AB MCDONALD (rep)
	1959-60 MC	ALVIN MCDONALD (sc)
	1960-61 CHI	AB MCDONALD (rep)
	1960-61 CHI	ALVIN MC DONALD (sc)
McDonald,	1935-36 DET	BUCKO McDONALD L.DEFENSE (sp)
Bucko	1935-36 DET	BUCKO McDONALD (ret)
	1936-37 DET	BUCKO McDONALD R.DEFENSE (sp)
	1936-37 DET	BUCKO MCDONALD (ret)
	1941-42 TML	BUCKO McDONALD (sp)
	1941-42 TML	BUCKO MCDONALD (rep)
	1941-42 TML	BUCKO MCDONALD (sc)
McDonald,	1988-89 CAL	L. MCDONALD C.CAPT. (ab)
Lanny	1988-89 CAL	L. MCDONALD C.CAPT. (rep)
	1988-89 CAL	L. MCDONALD C.CAPT. (sc)
McDonnell,	1996-97 DET	J. MCDONNELL (rep)
Joe	1996-97 DET	J. MCDONNELL (sc)
	1997-98 DET	JOE MCDONNELL (rep)
	1997-98 DET	JOE MCDONNELL (sc)
	2001-02 DET	JOE MCDONNELL (rep)
	2001-02 DET	JOE MCDONNELL (sc)
McEachern,	1991-92 PIT	SHAWN MC EACHERN (rep)
Shawn	1991-92 PIT	SHAWN MC EACHERN (sc)
McEwen,	1980-81 NYI	M. MCEWEN (ab)
Mike	1980-81 NYI	M. MCEWEN (rep)
	1980-81 NYI	M. MCEWEN (sc)
	1981-82 NYI	M. MCEWEN (ab)
	1981-82 NYI	M. MCEWEN (rep)
	1981-82 NYI	M. MCEWEN (sc)
	1982-83 NYI	M. MCEWEN (ab)
	1982-83 NYI	M. McEWEN (rep)
	1982-83 NYI	M. MCEWEN (sc)
McFadden,	1949-50 DET	JAMES McFADDEN (re)
Jim	1949-50 DET	JAMES MCFADDEN (rep)
	1949-50 DET	JAMES MCFADDEN (sc)
McFadyen,	1933-34 CHI	DONALD McFADYEN (sp)
Don	1933-34 CHI	DONALD Mc FADYEN (ret)
McGee,	1931-32 TML	HARRY McGEE, *VICE-PRES.* (sp)
Harry	1931-32 TML	HARRY MCGEE (V PRES) (ret)
McGuane,	1999-00 NJ	D. MCGUANE (rep)
Dana	1999-00 NJ	D. MCGUANE (sc)
McGuire,	1991-92 PIT	PIERRE MCGUIRE (rep)
Pierre	1991-92 PIT	PIERRE MCGUIRE (sc)
McKay,	1994-95 NJ	RANDY MCKAY (rep)
Randy	1994-95 NJ	RANDY MCKAY (sc)
	1999-00 NJ	H. RANDY MCKAY (rep)
	1999-00 NJ	H. RANDY MCKAY (sc)
McKendry,	1979-80 NYI	A. MCKENDRY (ab)
Alex	1979-80 NYI	A. MCKENDRY (rep)
	1979-80 NYI	A. MCKENDRY (sc)
McKenna,	1929-30 MC	JIM McKENNA. (sp)
Jim	1929-30 MC	JIM MC KENNA TRAINER (ret)
	1930-31 MC	JIM McKENNA (sp)
	1930-31 MC	JIM MCKENNA ** (ret)
		** refers to name and title above
		ED DUFOUR TRAINER
McKenney,	1963-64 TML	DONALD MCKENNEY (rep)
Don	1963-64 TML	DONALO MC KENNEY (sc)
McKenzie,	1973-74 PHI	JIM MCKENZIE ASST. TRAINER (rep)
Jim	1973-74 PHI	JIM McKENZIE ASST.TRA (sc)
	1974-75 PHI	JIM MCKENZIE ASST.TR. (rep)
	1974-75 PHI	JIM MCKENZIE A.T. (sc)
McKenzie,	2002-03 NJ	JAMES P. MCKENZIE (rep)
Jim	2002-03 NJ	JAMES P. MCKENZIE (sc)
McKenzie,	1969-70 BB	J. MCKENZIE (rep)
John	1969-70 BB	JMC KENZIE (sc)
	1971-72 BB	JOHN MCKENZIE (rep)
	1971-72 BB	JOHN MCKENZIE (sc)
McKerrow,	1907 MW	C. McKERROW (ib)
Clarence	1907 MW	C. McKERROW (rep)
	1907 MW	C. McKERROW (sc)
McLaughlin,	1933-34 CHI	FREDERIC MCLAUGHLIN/PRESIDENT (sp)
Frederic	1933-34 CHI	FREDERIC Mc LAUGHLIN (PRES) (ret)
	1937-38 CHI	FREDERIC McLAUGHLIN/PRESIDENT (sp)
McLaughlin,	1998-99 DAL	RICK MCLAUGHLIN (rep)
Rick	1998-99 DAL	RICK MCLAUGHLIN (sc)
McLean,	1944-45 TML	JACK McLEAN (sp)
Jack	1944-45 TML	JACK MCLEAN (rep)
	1944-45 TML	JACK MCLEAN (sc)
McLean,	1995-96 COL	ROB MCLEAN (rep)
Rob	1995-96 COL	ROB MCLEAN (sc)
McMahon,	1943-44 MC	MICHAEL McMAHON (sp)
Mike	1943-44 MC	MIKE MCMAHON (rep)
	1943-44 MC	MIKE MCMAHON (sc)
McManus,	1934-35 MM	S. MCMANUS (sp)
Sam	1934-35 MM	S MCMANUS (ret)
McMullen,	1994-95 NJ	DR. JOHN J. MCMULLEN (rep)
John	1994-95 NJ	DR. JOHN J. MCMULLEN (sc)
	1999-00 NJ	DR. J.J. MCMULLEN (rep)
	1999-00 NJ	DR. J.J. MCMULLEN (sc)
McMullen,	1994-95 NJ	PETER S. MCMULLEN (rep)
Peter	1994-95 NJ	PETER S. MCMULLEN (sc)
	1999-00 NJ	P.S. MCMULLEN (rep)
	1999-00 NJ	P.S. MCMULLEN (sc)
McNab,	1949-50 DET	MAX McNAB (re)
Max	1949-50 DET	MAX MCNAB (rep)
	1949-50 DET	MAX MCNAB (sc)
McNeil,	1952-53 MC	GERRY MCNEIL (re)
Gerry	1952-53 MC	GERRY MCNEIL (rep)
	1952-53 MC	GERRY MCNEIL (sc)
	1956-57 MC	G. MCNEIL (rep)
	1956-57 MC	G MC NEIL (sc)
	1957-58 MC	G. MCNEIL (rep)
	1957-58 MC	G MC NEIL (sc)
McPhee,	1985-86 MC	M. MCPHEE (ab)
Mike	1985-86 MC	M. MCPHEE (rep)
	1985-86 MC	M. MCPHEE (sc)
McQueen,	1998-99 DAL	J.J. MCQUEEN (rep)
J.J.	1998-99 DAL	J.J. MCQUEEN (sc)
McQueston,		
Harry	1949-50 DET	HARRY McQUESTON (re)
McReavy,	1938-39 BB	P. McREAVY (eb)
Pat	1938-39 BB	P MC REAVY (ret)
	1940-41 BB	PAT. MCREAVY (sp)
	1940-41 BB	PAT MCCREAVY (rep)
	1940-41 BB	PAT MCCEAVY (sc)
McSorley,	1986-87 EDM	M. MCSORLEY (ab)
Marty	1986-87 EDM	M. MCSORLEY (rep)
	1986-87 EDM	M. MCSORLEY (sc)
	1987-88 EDM	M. MCSORLEY (ab)
	1987-88 EDM	M. MCSORLEY (rep)
	1987-88 EDM	M. MCSORLEY (sc)
Meeker,	1946-47 TML	HOWARD MEEKER (re)
Howie	1946-47 TML	HOWARD MEEKER (rep)
	1946-47 TML	HOWARD MEEKER (sc)
	1947-48 TML	HOWARD MEEKER (re)
	1947-48 TML	HOWARD MEEKER (rep)
	1947-48 TML	HOWARD MEEKER (sc)
	1948-49 TML	HOWARD MEEKER (re)
	1948-49 TML	HOWARD MEEKER (rep)
	1948-49 TML	HOWARD MEEKER (sc)
	1950-51 TML	HOWARD MEEKER (re)
	1950-51 TML	HOWARD MEEKER (rep)
	1950-51 TML	HOWARD MEEKER (sc)
Meeking,	1924-25 VIC	H. MEEKING. (or)
Harry	1924-25 VIC	H. MEEKING (rep)
	1924-25 VIC	H. MEEKING. (sc)
Meger, Paul	1952-53 MC	PAUL MEGER (re)
	1952-53 MC	PAUL MEGER (rep)
	1952-53 MC	PAUL MEGER (sc)
Meilleur,	1975-76 MC	PIERRE MEILLEUR ASST. TRAINER (rep)
Pierre	1975-76 MC	PIERRE MEILLEUR ASST. TRAINER (sc)
	1976-77 MC	PIERRE MEILLEUR ASST. TRAINER (rep)
	1976-77 MC	PIERRE MEILLEUR ASST. TRA. (sc)

Name	Season	Engraving
	1977-78 MC	P. MEILLEUR A.T. (rep)
	1977-78 MC	P. MEILLEUR A.T. (sc)
	1978-79 MC	P. MEILLEUR A.T. (ab)
	1978-79 MC	P. MEILLEUR A.T. (rep)
	1978-79 MC	P. MEILLEUR A.T. (sc)
Melanson, Rollie	1980-81 NYI	R. MELANSON (ab)
	1980-81 NYI	R. MELANSON (rep)
	1980-81 NYI	R. MELANSON (sc)
	1981-82 NYI	R. MELANSON (ab)
	1981-82 NYI	R. MELANSON (rep)
	1981-82 NYI	R. MELANSON (sc)
	1982-83 NYI	R. MELANSON (ab)
	1982-83 NYI	R. MELANSON (rep)
	1982-83 NYI	R. MELANSON (sc)
Melnyk, Larry	1984-85 EDM	L. MELNYK (ab)
	1984-85 EDM	L. MELNYK (rep)
	1984-85 EDM	L. MELNYK (sc)
Meloche, Gilles	1990-91 PIT	GILLES MELOCHE GOALTENDING COACH & SCOUT (ab)
	1990-91 PIT	GILLES MELOCHE GOALTENDING COACH & SCOUT (rep)
	1990-91 PIT	GILLES MELOCHE GOALTENDING COACH &SCOUT (sc)
	1991-92 PIT	GILLES MELOCHE (rep)
	1991-92 PIT	GILLES MELOCHE (sc)
Merkosky, Glenn	2001-02 DET	GLENN MERKOSKY (rep)
	2001-02 DET	GLENN MERKOSKY (sc)
Merrick, Wayne	1979-80 NYI	W. MERRICK (ab)
	1979-80 NYI	W. MERRICK (rep)
	1979-80 NYI	W. MERRICK (sc)
	1980-81 NYI	W. MERRICK (ab)
	1980-81 NYI	W. MERRICK (rep)
	1980-81 NYI	W. MERRICK (sc)
	1981-82 NYI	W. MERRICK (ab)
	1981-82 NYI	W. MERRICK (rep)
	1981-82 NYI	W. MERRICK (sc)
	1982-83 NYI	W. MERRICK (ab)
	1982-83 NYI	W. MERRICK (rep)
	1982-83 NYI	W. MERRICK (sc)
Merz, Juergen	1986-87 EDM	JUERGEN MERZ (ab)
	1986-87 EDM	JUERGEN MERZ (rep)
	1986-87 EDM	JUERGEN MERZ (sc)
	1987-88 EDM	JUERGEN MERZ (ab)
	1987-88 EDM	JUERGEN MERZ (rep)
	1987-88 EDM	JUERGEN MERZ (sc)
	1999-00 NJ	J. MERZ (rep)
	1999-00 NJ	J. MERZ (sc)
	2002-03 NJ	J. MERZ (rep)
	2002-03 NJ	J. MERZ (sc)
Messier, Eric	2000-01 COL	ERIC MESSIER (rep)
	2000-01 COL	ERIC MESSIER (sc)
Messier, Mark	1983-84 EDM	M. MESSIER (ab)
	1983-84 EDM	M. MESSIER (rep)
	1983-84 EDM	M. MESSIER (sc)
	1984-85 EDM	M. MESSIER (ab)
	1984-85 EDM	M. MESSIER (rep)
	1984-85 EDM	M. MESSIER (sc)
	1986-87 EDM	M. MESSIER (ab)
	1986-87 EDM	M. MESSIER (rep)
	1986-87 EDM	M. MESSIER (sc)
	1987-88 EDM	M. MESSIER (ab)
	1987-88 EDM	M. MESSIER (rep)
	1987-88 EDM	M. MESSIER (sc)
	1989-90 EDM	M. MESSIER CAPT. (ab)
	1989-90 EDM	M. MESSIER CAPT. (rep)
	1989-90 EDM	M. MESSIER CAPT. (sc)
	1993-94 NYR	M. MESSIER CAPT. (rep)
	1993-94 NYR	M. MESSIER CAPT. (sc)
Metz, Don	1941-42 TML	DON METZ (sp)
	1941-42 TML	DON METZ (rep)
	1941-42 TML	DON METZ (sc)
	1944-45 TML	DON METZ (sp)
	1944-45 TML	DON METZ (rep)
	1944-45 TML	DON METZ (sc)
	1946-47 TML	DONALD METZ (re)
	1946-47 TML	DON METZ (rep)
	1946-47 TML	DON METZ (sc)
	1947-48 TML	DONALD METZ (re)
	1947-48 TML	DON METZ (rep)
	1947-48 TML	DON METZ (sc)
	1948-49 TML	DONALD METZ (re)
	1948-49 TML	DON METZ (rep)
	1948-49 TML	DON METZ (sc)
Metz, Nick	1941-42 TML	NICK METZ (sp)
	1941-42 TML	NICK METZ (rep)
	1941-42 TML	NICK METZ (sc)
	1944-45 TML	NICK METZ (sp)
	1944-45 TML	NICK METZ (rep)
	1944-45 TML	NICK METZ (sc)
	1946-47 TML	NICHOLAS METZ (re)
	1946-47 TML	NICK METZ (rep)
	1946-47 TML	NICK METZ (sc)
	1947-48 TML	NICHOLAS METZ (re)
	1947-48 TML	NICK METZ (rep)
	1947-48 TML	NICH METZ (sc)
Michayluk, Dave	1991-92 PIT	DAVE MICHAYLUK (rep)
	1991-92 PIT	DAVE MICHAYLUK (sc)
Mikita, Stan	1960-61 CHI	STANLEY MIKITA (rep)
	1960-61 CHI	STANLEY MIKITA (sc)
Millar, Peter	1983-84 EDM	P. MILLAR ATHLETIC THERAPIST (ab)
	1983-84 EDM	P. MILLAR ATHLETIC THERAPIST (rep)
	1983-84 EDM	P. MILLAR ATHLETIC THERAPIST (sc)
	1984-85 EDM	P. MILLAR ATH. THP. (ab)
	1984-85 EDM	P. MILLAR ATH. THP. (rep)
	1984-85 EDM	P. MILLAR ATH. THP. (sc)
	1986-87 EDM	PETER MILLAR (ab)
	1986-87 EDM	PETER MILLAR (rep)
	1986-87 EDM	PETER MILLAR (sc)
	1987-88 EDM	PETER MILLAR (ab)
	1987-88 EDM	PETER MILLAR (rep)
	1987-88 EDM	PETER MILLAR (sc)
Miller, Bill	1934-35 MM	W. MILLER (sp)
	1934-35 MM	W MILLER (ret)
Miller, Earl	1931-32 TML	MILLER (sp)
Miller, Joe	1927-28 NYR	J. MILLER (sp)
	1927-28 NYR	J MILLER (ret)
Miller, Mark	2000-01 COL	MARK MILLER (rep)
	2000-01 COL	MARK MILLER (sc)
Mironov, Dmitri	1997-98 DET	D. MIRONOV (rep)
	1997-98 DET	D. MIRONOV (sc)
Mitchell, John	1953-54 DET	JOHN MITCHELL , CHIEF SCOUT (re)
	1953-54 DET	JOHN MITCHELL CHIEF SCOUT (rep)
	1953-54 DET	JOHN MITCHELL CHIEF SCOUT (sc)
	1954-55 DET	JOHN MITCHELL , CHIEF SCOUT (re)
	1954-55 DET	JOHN MITCHELL CHIEF SCOUT (rep)
	1954-55 DET	JOHN MITCHELL CHIEE SCOUT (sc)
Mnatsakanov, Sergei	1996-97 DET	SERGEI MNATSAKANOV (rep)
	1996-97 DET	SERGEI MNATSAKANOV (sc)
	1997-98 DET	SERGEI MNATSAKANOV (rep)
	1997-98 DET	SERGEI MNATSAKANOV (sc)
Modano, Mike	1998-99 DAL	MIKE MODANO (rep)
	1998-99 DAL	MIKE MODANO (sc)
Modrzynski, Chris	2002-03 NJ	C. MODRZYNSKI (rep)
	2002-03 NJ	C. MODRZYNSKI (sc)
Mogilny, Alexander	1999-00 NJ	ALEXANDER MOGILNY (rep)
	1999-00 NJ	ALEXANDER MOGILNY (sc)
Molson, David	1964-65 MC	J. DAVID MOLSON PRESIDENT (rep)
	1964-65 MC	J DAVID MOLSON PRESIDENT (sc)
	1965-66 MC	J.D. MOLSON PRES. (rep)
	1965-66 MC	J D MOLSON PRESS (sc)
	1967-68 MC	J.D. MOLSON PRESIDENT (rep)
	1967-68 MC	J•D•MOLSON•PRESIDENT (sc)
	1968-69 MC	J. DAVID MOLSON PRESIDENT (rep)
	1968-69 MC	J DAVID MOLSON PRESIDENT (sc)
	1970-71 MC	J. DAVID MOLSON PRES. (rep)
	1970-71 MC	J. DAVID MOLSON. PRES. (sc)
Molson, Hartland	1957-58 MC	HON. SENATOR H. DE M. MOLSON PRESIDENT (rep)
	1957-58 MC	HON SENATOR H DE M MOLSON PRESIDENT (sc)
	1958-59 MC	HON. SENATOR H. DE M. MOLSON PRESIDENT (rep)
	1958-59 MC	HON SENATOR R DE M MOLSON PRESIDENT (sc)
	1959-60 MC	HON. SENATOR H. DE M. MOLSON PRESIDENT (rep)
	1959-60 MC	HON SENATOR H DE M MOLSON PRESIDENT (sc)
	1964-65 MC	HON. H. DE M. MOLSON CHAIRMAN OF THE BOARD (rep)
	1964-65 MC	HON H DE M MOLSON CHAIRMAN OF THE BOARD (sc)
	1965-66 MC	HON. H. DE M. MOLSON CHAIRMAN (rep)
	1965-66 MC	HON H DE M MOLSON CHAIR BOARD (sc)
	1967-68 MC	HON. H. DE M. MOLSON CHAIRMAN OF THE BOARD (rep)
	1967-68 MC	HON H DE M MOLSON CHAIRMAN OF THE BOARD (sc)
Molson, Peter	1968-69 MC	PETER B. MOLSON VICE PRES. (rep)
	1968-69 MC	PETER B MOLSON VICE PRES (sc)
	1970-71 MC	P.B. MOLSON VICE PRES. (rep)
	1970-71 MC	P.B. MOLSON VICE PRES. (sc)
Molson, William	1968-69 MC	WILLIAM M. MOLSON VICE PRES. (rep)
	1968-69 MC	WILLIAM N MOLSON VICE PRES (sc)
	1970-71 MC	WILLIAM M. MOLSON VICE. PRES. (rep)
	1970-71 MC	WILLIAM M. MOLSON• VICE. PRES (sc)
Mondou, Armand	1929-30 MC	ARMAND MONDOU. (sp)
	1929-30 MC	ARMAND MONDOU (ret)
	1930-31 MC	ARMAND MONDOU (sp)
	1930-31 MC	ARMAND HONDOU (ret)
Mondou, Pierre	1976-77 MC	PIERRE MONDOU (rep)
	1976-77 MC	PIERRE MONDOU (sc)
	1977-78 MC	PIERRE MONDOU (rep)

1977-78 MC PIERRE MONDOU (sc)
1978-79 MC P. MONDOU (ab)
1978-79 MC P. MONDOU (rep)
1978-79 MC P. MONDOU (sc)

Moog, Andy 1983-84 EDM A. MOOG (ab)
1983-84 EDM A. MOOG (rep)
1983-84 EDM A. MOOG (sc)
1984-85 EDM A. MOOG (ab)
1984-85 EDM A. MOOG (rep)
1984-85 EDM A. MOOG (sc)
1986-87 EDM A. MOOG (ab)
1986-87 EDM A. MOOG (rep)
1986-87 EDM A. MOOG (sc)

Moore, Alfie 1937-38 CHI ALFIE MOORE (sp)

Moore, Dickie
1952-53 MC DICKIE MOORE (re)
1952-53 MC DICKIE MOORE (rep)
1952-53 MC DICKIE MOORE (sc)
1955-56 MC D. MOORE (re)
1955-56 MC D. MOORE (rep)
1955-56 MC D MOORE (sc)
1956-57 MC DICKIE MOORE (rep)
1956-57 MC DICKIE MOORE (sc)
1957-58 MC R. MOORE (rep)
1957-58 MC R MOORE (sc)
1958-59 MC DICKIE MOORE (rep)
1958-59 MC RICHARD MOORE (sc)
1959-60 MC DICKIE MOORE (rep)
1959-60 MC RICH MOORE (sc)

Morenz, Howie
1923-24 MC H. MORENZ (or)
1923-24 MC H. MORENZ (rep)
1923-24 MC H. MORENZ (sc)
1929-30 MC HOWARD MORENZ. (sp)
1929-30 MC HOWARD MORENZ (ret)
1930-31 MC HOWARD MORENZ (sp)
1930-31 MC HOWARD MORENZ (ret)

Morris, Elwyn "Moe"
1944-45 TML ELWIN MORRIS (sp)
1944-45 TML ELWYN MORRIS (rep)
1944-45 TML ELVIN MORRIS (sc)

Morrow, Fred
1931-32 TML MR. F. K. MORROW (sp)

Morrow, Ken
1979-80 NYI K. MORROW (ab)
1979-80 NYI K. MORROW (rep)
1979-80 NYI K. MORROW (sc)
1980-81 NYI K. MORROW (ab)
1980-81 NYI K. MORROW (rep)
1980-81 NYI K. MORROW (sc)
1981-82 NYI K. MORROW (ab)
1981-82 NYI K. MORROW (rep)
1981-82 NYI K. MORROW (sc)
1982-83 NYI K. MORROW (ab)
1982-83 NYI K. MORROW (rep)
1982-83 NYI K. MORROW (sc)

Mortson, Gus
1946-47 TML ANGUS MORTSON (re)
1946-47 TML GUS MORTSON (rep)
1946-47 TML GUS MORTSON (sc)
1947-48 TML ANGUS MORTSON (re)
1947-48 TML GUS MORTSON (rep)
1947-48 TML GUS MORTSON (sc)
1948-49 TML ANGUS MORTSON (re)
1948-49 TML GUS MORTSON (rep)
1948-49 TML GUS MORTSON (sc)
1950-51 TML ANGUS MORTSON (re)
1950-51 TML GUS MORSTON (rep)
1950-51 TML GUS WORTSON (sc)

Mosdell, Ken
1945-46 MC KENNETH MOSDELL (re)
1945-46 MC KENNETH MOSDELL (rep)
1945-46 MC KENNETH MOSDELL (sc)
1952-53 MC KEN MOSDELL (re)
1952-53 MC KEN MOSDELL (rep)
1952-53 MC KEN MOSDELL (sc)
1955-56 MC K. MOSDELL (re)
1955-56 MC K. MOSDELL (rep)
1955-56 MC K MOSDELL (sc)
1958-59 MC KENNY MOSDELL (rep)
1958-59 MC KENN MOSDELL (sc)

Motter, Alex 1942-43 DET ALEX MOTTER (sp)
1942-43 DET ALEX MOTTER (rep)
1942-43 DET ALEX MOTTER (sc)

Mowers, Johnny
1942-43 DET JOHN MOWERS (sp)
1942-43 DET JOHNNY MOWERS (rep)
1942-43 DET JOHNNY MOWERS (sc)

Muckler, John
1983-84 EDM JOHN MUCKLER* (ab)
1983-84 EDM JOHN MUCKLER* (rep)
1983-84 EDM JOHN MUCKLER* (sc)
* see also Ted Green
1984-85 EDM JOHN MUCKLER* (ab)
1984-85 EDM JOHN MUCKLER* (rep)
1984-85 EDM JOHN MUCKLER* (sc)
* see also Ted Green
1986-87 EDM JOHN MUCKLER CO-COACH (ab)
1986-87 EDM JOHN MUCKLER CO-COACH (rep)
1986-87 EDM JOHN MUCKLER CO-COACH (sc)
1987-88 EDM JOHN MUCKLER CO-COACH (ab)
1987-88 EDM JOHN MUCKLER CO-COACH (rep)
1987-88 EDM JOHN MUCKLER CO-COACH (sc)
1989-90 EDM JOHN MUCKLER HEAD COACH (ab)
1989-90 EDM JOHN MUCKLER HEAD COACH (rep)
1989-90 EDM JOHN MUCKLER HEAD COACH (sc)

Muir, Bryan 2000-01 COL BRYAN MUIR (rep)
2000-01 COL BRYAN MUIR (sc)

Mulcahy, Charles
1969-70 BB CHARLES W. MULCAHY V.P. (rep)
1969-70 BB CHARLES W MULCAHY V P (sc)
1971-72 BB CHARLES W. MULCAHY JR. VICE PRES. GEN. COUNSEL (rep)
1971-72 BB CHARLES W. MULCAHY JR. VICE PRES. GEN. COUNSEL (sc)

Mullen, Joe 1988-89 CAL J. MULLEN (ab)
1988-89 CAL J. MULLEN (rep)
1988-89 CAL J. MULLEN (sc)
1990-91 PIT J. MULLEN (ab)
1990-91 PIT J. MULLEN (rep)
1990-91 PIT J. MULLEN (sc)
1991-92 PIT JOE MULLEN (rep)
1991-92 PIT JOE MULLEN (sc)

Muller, Kirk 1992-93 MC K. MULLER (rep)
1992-93 MC K. MULLER (sc)

Muni, Craig 1986-87 EDM C. MUNI (ab)
1986-87 EDM C. MUNI (rep)
1986-87 EDM C. MUNI (sc)
1987-88 EDM C. MUNI (ab)
1987-88 EDM C. MUNI (rep)
1987-88 EDM C. MUNI (sc)
1989-90 EDM C. MUNI (ab)
1989-90 EDM C. MUNI (rep)
1989-90 EDM C. MUNI (sc)

Munoz, Kenneth
1993-94 NYR KENNETH MUNOZ GOV. (rep)
1993-94 NYR KENNETH MUNOZ GOV. (sc)

Munro, Dunc
1925-26 MM D. MUNRO. (Capt.) (or)
1925-26 MM D. MUNRO (Capt) (rep)
1925-26 MM D. MUNRO (Capt) (sc)

Murdoch, Bob
1970-71 MC R. MURDOCH (rep)
1970-71 MC R. MURDOCH. (sc)
1972-73 MC ROBERT MURDOCK (rep)
1972-73 MC ROBERT MURDOCH (sc)

Murdoch, James
1931-32 TML MR. J. Y. MURDOCH (sp)
1944-45 TML J.Y. MURDOCK V.PRES. (rep)
1944-45 TML J.Y. MURDOCK (V PRES) (sc)
1946-47 TML J.Y. MURDOCH, K.C. DIRECTOR (re)
1946-47 TML J.Y. MURDOCH KC DIR. (rep)
1946-47 TML J Y MURDOCH KC (DIR) (sc)
1947-48 TML J.Y. MURDOCH, K.C. — VICE-PRESIDENT (re)
1947-48 TML J.Y. MURDOCH KC V.PRES. (rep)
1947-48 TML J.Y. MURDUCH KC (V PRES) (sc)
1948-49 TML J.Y. MURDOCH, K.C. VICE PRESIDENT (re)
1948-49 TML J.Y. MURDOCH KC V.PRES. (rep)
1948-49 TML J.V. MURDOCH KC (V PRES) (sc)
1950-51 TML J.Y. MURDOCH K C VICE-PRESIDENT (re)
1950-51 TML J.Y. MURDOCH KC V.PRES. (rep)
1950-51 TML J Y MURDOCH KC (V PRES) (sc)

Murdoch, Murray
1927-28 NYR M. MURDOCK (sp)
1927-28 NYR M MURDOCK (ret)
1932-33 NYR M MURDOCH (sp)
1932-33 NYR M MURDOCH (ret)

Murphy, Joe
1989-90 EDM J. MURPHY (ab)
1989-90 EDM J. MURPHY (rep)
1989-90 EDM J. MURPHY (sc)

Murphy, Joe
1993-94 NYR J. MURPHY TRAINER (rep)
1993-94 NYR J. MURPHY TRAINER (sc)

Murphy, Larry
1990-91 PIT L. MURPHY (ab)
1990-91 PIT L. MURPHY (rep)
1990-91 PIT L. MURPHY (sc)
1991-92 PIT LARRY MURPHY (rep)
1991-92 PIT LARRY MURPHY (sc)
1996-97 DET LARRY MURPHY (rep)
1996-97 DET LARRY MURPHY (sc)
1997-98 DET L. MURPHY (rep)
1997-98 DET L. MURPHY (sc)

Murphy, Ron
1960-61 CHI ROBERT MURPHY (rep)
1960-61 CHI ROBERT MURPHY (sc)
1969-70 BB R. MURPHY (rep)
1969-70 BB R MURPHY (sc)

Murray, Al 1988-89 CAL AL MURRAY ASST. TR. (ab)
1988-89 CAL AL MURRAY ASST. TR. (rep)
1988-89 CAL AL MURRAY ASST. TR. (sc)

Murray, Bill 1999-00 NJ B. MURRAY (rep)
1999-00 NJ B. MURRAY (sc)
2002-03 NJ W.J. MURRAY (rep)
2002-03 NJ W.J. MURRAY (sc)

Murray, Dr. James
1948-49 TML DR. JAMES MURRAY CLUB DOCTOR (re)
1950-51 TML DR. JAMES MURRAY CLUB DOCTOR (re)

Murray, Jim 1988-89 CAL JIM MURRAY TR. (ab)
1988-89 CAL JIM MURRAY TR. (rep)
1988-89 CAL JIM MURRAY TR. (sc)

Name	Season	Engraving
Murray, Lisa Ilitch	1996-97 DET	LISA ILITCH MURRAY (rep)
	1996-97 DET	LISA ILITCH MURRAY (sc)
	1997-98 DET	LISA ILITCH MURRAY (rep)
	1997-98 DET	LISA ILITCH MURRAY (sc)
	2001-02 DET	LISA ILITCH MURRAY (rep)
	2001-02 DET	LISA ILITCH MURRAY (sc)
Murray, Troy	1995-96 COL	TROY MURRAY (rep)
	1995-96 COL	TROY MURRAY (sc)
Murzyn, Dana	1988-89 CAL	D. MURZYN (ab)
	1988-89 CAL	D. MURZYN (rep)
	1988-89 CAL	D. MURZYN (sc)
Napier, Mark	1978-79 MC	M. NAPIER (ab)
	1978-79 MC	M. NAPIER (rep)
	1978-79 MC	M. NAPIER (sc)
	1984-85 MC	M. NAPIER (ab)
	1984-85 EDM	M. NAPIER (rep)
	1984-85 EDM	M. NAPIER (sc)
Naslund, Mats	1985-86 MC	M. NASLUND (ab)
	1985-86 MC	M. NASLUND (rep)
	1985-86 MC	M. NASLUND (sc)
Nattress, Ric	1988-89 CAL	R. NATTRESS (ab)
	1988-89 CAL	R. NATTRESS (rep)
	1988-89 CAL	R. NATTRESS (sc)
Nayler, Tommy	1950-51 TML	TOMMY NAYLOR ASSISTANT TRAINER (re)
	1950-51 TML	T. NAYLOR ASST. TR. (rep)
	1950-51 TML	T NAYLOR (ASS TR) (sc)
	1961-62 TML	THOMAS NAYLER ASST. TRAINER (rep)
	1961-62 TML	THOMAS NAYLER ASST TRAINER (sc)
	1962-63 TML	THOMAS NAYLER ASST. TRAINER (rep)
	1962-63 TML	THOMAS NAYLER ASST TRAINER (sc)
	1963-64 TML	THOMAS NAYLER ASST. TRAINER (rep)
	1963-64 TML	THOMAS NAYLER ASST TRAINER (sc)
	1966-67 TML	T. NAYLER ASST. TRAINER (sc)
	1966-67 TML	T NAYLER ASST TRAINER (sc)
Needham, Mike	1991-92 PIT	MIKE NEEDHAM (rep)
	1991-92 PIT	MIKE NEEDHAM (sc)
Nemchinov, Sergei	1993-94 NYR	S. NEMCHINOV (rep)
	1993-94 NYR	S. NEMCHINOV (sc)
	1999-00 NJ	SERGEI NEMCHINOV (rep)
	1999-00 NJ	SERGEI NEMCHINOV (sc)
Nesterenko, Eric	1960-61 CHI	ERIC NESTERENKO (rep)
	1960-61 CHI	ERIC NESTERENKO (sc)
Nevin, Bob	1961-62 TML	ROBERT NEVIN (rep)
	1961-62 TML	ROBERT NEVIN (sc)
	1962-63 TML	ROBERT NEVIN (rep)
	1962-63 TML	ROBERT NEVIN (sc)
Nicholls, David	1994-95 NJ	DAVI<u>D</u> NICHOLS (rep)
	1994-95 NJ	DAVID NICHOLS (sc)
Niedermayer, Scott	1994-95 NJ	SCOTT NIEDERMAYER (rep)
	1994-95 NJ	SCOTT NIEDERMAYER (sc)
	1999-00 NJ	SCOTT NIEDERMAYER (rep)
	1999-00 NJ	SCOTT NIEDERMAYER (sc)
	2002-03 NJ	SCOTT NIEDERMAYER (rep)
	2002-03 NJ	SCOTT NIEDERMAYER (sc)
Nieminen, Ville	2000-01 COL	VILLE NIEMINEN (rep)
	2000-01 COL	VILLE NIEMINEN (sc)
Nieuwendyk, Joe	1988-89 CAL	J. NIEUWENDYK (ab)
	1988-89 CAL	J. NIEUWENDYK (rep)
	1988-89 CAL	J. NIEUWENDYK (sc)
	1998-99 DAL	JOE NIEUWENDYK (rep)
	1998-99 DAL	JOE NIEUWENDYK (sc)
	2002-03 NJ	JOE NIEUWENDYK (rep)
	2002-03 NJ	JOE NIEUWENDYK (sc)
Nighbor, Frank	1914-15 VM	FRANK NIGHBOR (ib)
	1914-15 VM	FRANK NIGHBOR (rep)
	1914-15 VM	FRANK NIGHBOR (sc)
	1926-27 OTT	FRANK J. NIGHBOR (or)
	1926-27 OTT	FRANK J. NIGHBOR (rep)
	1926-27 OTT	FRANK J. NIGHBOR (sc)
Nilan, Chris	1985-86 MC	C. NILAN (ab)
	1985-86 MC	C. NILAN (rep)
	1985-86 MC	C. NILAN (sc)
Nill, Jim	1996-97 DET	JIM NILL (rep)
	1996-97 DET	JIM NILL (sc)
	1997-98 DET	JIM NILL (rep)
	1997-98 DET	JIM NILL (sc)
	2001-02 DET	JIM NILL (rep)
	2001-02 DET	JIM NILL (sc)
Nilsson, Kent	1986-87 EDM	K. NILSSON (ab)
	1986-87 EDM	K. NILSSON (rep)
	1986-87 EDM	K. NILSSON (sc)
Noble, Reg	1925-26 MM	R. NOBLE. (or)
	1925-26 MM	R. NOBLE (rep)
	1925-26 MM	R. NOBLE. (sc)
Nolet, Simon	1973-74 PHI	SIMON NOLET (rep)
	1973-74 PHI	SIMON NOLET (sc)
Noonan, Brian	1993-94 NYR	B. NOONAN (rep)
	1993-94 NYR	B. NOONAN (sc)
Norris, Bruce	1951-52 DET	BRUCE NORRIS — VICE PRESIDENT (re)
	1951-52 DET	BRUCE NORRIS V. PRES. (rep)
	1951-52 DET	BRUCE NORRIS (V PRES) (sc)
	1953-54 DET	BRUCE A. NORRIS, VICE PRESIDENT (re)
	1953-54 DET	B.A. NORRIS V. PRES. (rep)
	1953-54 DET	B A NORRIS (V PRES) (sc)
	1954-55 DET	BRUCE A NORRIS, VICE PRESIDENT (re)
	1954-55 DET	B.A. NORRIS V. PRES. (rep)
	1954-55 DET	B A NORRIS (V PRESS) (sc)
Norris, James	1935-36 DET	JAMES NORRIS/PRESIDENT (sp)
	1935-36 DET	JAMES NORRIS PRESIDENT (ret)
	1936-37 DET	JAMES NORRIS/PRESIDENT (sp)
	1936-37 DET	JAMES NORRIS PRESIDENT (ret)
	1942-43 DET	JAMES NORRIS PRESIDENT (sp)
	1942-43 DET	JAMES NORRIS PRES. (rep)
	1942-43 DET	JAMES NORRIS (PRESS) (sc)
	1949-50 DET	JAMES NORRIS, PRESIDENT (re)
	1949-50 DET	JAMES NORRIS PRES. (rep)
	1949-50 DET	JAMES NORRIS (PRES) (sc)
	1951-52 DET	JAMES NORRIS—PRESIDENT (re)
	1951-52 DET	JAMES NORRIS PRESIDENT (rep)
	1951-52 DET	JAMES NORRIS PRESIDENT (sc)
Norris, James D.	1935-36 DET	JAMES D. NORRIS/VICE-PRESIDENT (sp)
	1935-36 DET	J D NORRIS (VICE PRES) (ret)
	1936-37 DET	JAMES D. NORRIS/VICE-PRESIDENT (sp)
	1936-37 DET	JAMES D NORRIS (V PRES) (ret)
	1942-43 DET	LIEUT. J.D. NORRIS U.S.N.R. — V. PRES. (sp)
	1942-43 DET	LIEUT. J.D. NORRIS V. PRES. (rep)
	1942-43 DET	LIEUT J.D. NORRIS (V PRESS) (sc)
	1949-50 DET	JAMES D. NORRIS. VICE PRESIDENT (re)
	1949-50 DET	JAMES D. NORRIS V. PRES. (rep)
	1949-50 DET	JAMES D NORRIS (V PRES) (sc)
	1951-52 DET	JAMES D. NORRIS — VICE PRESIDENT (re)
	1951-52 DET	J.D. NORRIS VICE PRES. (rep)
	1951-52 DET	J D NORRIS (VICE PRES) (sc)
	1960-61 CHI	JAMES D. NORRIS CHAIRMAN (rep)
	1960-61 CHI	JAMES D NORRIS CHAIRMAN (sc)
Norris, Marguerite	1953-54 DET	MARGUERITE NORRIS, PRESIDENT (re)
	1953-54 DET	MARGUERITE NORRIS PRESIDENT (rep)
	1953-54 DET	MARGUERITE NORRIS PRESIDENT (sc)
	1954-55 DET	MARGUERITE NORRIS, PRESIDENT (re)
	1954-55 DET	MARGUERITE NORRIS PRESIDENT (rep)
	1954-55 DET	MARGUERITE NORRIS PRESIDENT (sc)
Northcott, Lawrence "Baldy"	1934-35 MM	L. NORTHCOTT (sp)
	1934-35 MM	L NORTHCOTT (ret)
Northey, William	1952-53 MC	W. NORTHEY-EXECUTIVE VICE PRES. (re)
	1952-53 MC	W. NORTHEY EX. VICE PRES. (rep)
	1952-53 MC	W NORTHEY EX(VICE PRES) (sc)
	1955-56 MC	W. NORTHEY, VICE-PRESIDENTS * (re)
		* refers also to D.C. Coleman
	1955-56 MC	W. NORTHEY V. PRES. (rep)
	1955-56 MC	W NORTHEY V PRES (sc)
	1956-57 MC	WM. NORTHEY PRESIDENT (rep)
	1956-57 MC	WM NORTHEY PRESIDENT (sc)
Nykoluk, Mike	1973-74 PHI	MIKE NYKOLUK ASST.C. (rep)
	1973-74 PHI	MIKE NYKOLUK ASST. C. (sc)
	1974-75 PHI	MIKE NYKOLUK ASST. COACH (rep)
	1974-75 PHI	MIKE NYKOLUK AS. COA. (sc)
Nyrop, Bill	1975-76 MC	BILL NYROP (rep)
	1975-76 MC	BILL NYROP (sc)
	1976-77 MC	WILLIAM NYROP (rep)
	1976-77 MC	WILLIAM NYROP (sc)
	1977-78 MC	WILLIAM NYROP (rep)
	1977-78 MC	WILLIAM NYROP (sc)
Nystrom, Bob	1979-80 NYI	B. NYSTROM (ab)
	1979-80 NYI	B. NYSTROM (rep)
	1979-80 NYI	B. NYSTROM (sc)
	1980-81 NYI	B. NYSTROM (ab)
	1980-81 NYI	B. NYSTROM (rep)
	1980-81 NYI	B. NYSTROM (sc)
	1981-82 NYI	B. NYSTROM (ab)
	1981-82 NYI	B. NYSTROM (rep)
	1981-82 NYI	B. NYSTROM (sc)
	1982-83 NYI	B. NYSTROM (ab)
	1982-83 NYI	B. NYSTROM (rep)
	1982-83 NYI	B. NYSTROM (sc)
O'Brien, Bill	1925-26 MM	W. O'BRIEN. / (Trainer.) (or)
	1925-26 MM	W. O'BRIEN / (Trainer) (rep)
	1925-26 MM	W. O'BRIEN / (Trainer) (sc)
	1934-35 MM	BILL O'BRIEN TRAINER (ret)
O'Connor, Frank	1931-32 TML	MR. FRANK P. O'CONNOR (sp)
O'Connor, Herbert "Buddy"	1943-44 MC	HERBERT O'CONNOR (sp)
	1943-44 MC	H. O'CONNOR (rep)
	1943-44 MC	H.O. CONNOR (sc)
	1945-46 MC	HERBERT O'CONNOR (re)
	1945-46 MC	HERB OCONNOR (rep)

	1945-46 MC	HERB OCONNER (sc)
Odelein,	1992-93 MC	L. ODELEIN (rep)
Lyle	1992-93 NYR	L. ODELEIN (sc)
Olausson,	2001-02 DET	FREDRIK OLAUSSON (rep)
Fredrik	2001-02 DET	FREDRIK OLAUSSON (sc)
Olczyk, Ed	1993-94 NYR	E. OLCZYK (rep)
	1993-94 NYR	E. OLCZYK (sc)
Oliver,	1928-29 BB	HARRY OLIVER (or)
Harry	1928-29 BB	HARRY OLIVER (rep)
	1928-29 BB	HARRY OLIVER (sc)
	1928-29 BB	H OLIVER (ret)
Oliwa,	1999-00 NJ	KRZYSZTOF OLIWA (rep)
Krzysztof	1999-00 NJ	KRZYSZTOF OLIWA (sc)
Olmstead,	1952-53 MC	BERT OLMSTEAD (re)
Bert	1952-53 MC	BERT OLMSTEAD (rep)
	1952-53 MC	BERT OLMSTEAD (sc)
	1955-56 MC	B. OLMSTEAD (re)
	1955-56 MC	B. OLMSTEAD (rep)
	1955-56 MC	B OLMSTEAD (sc)
	1956-57 MC	B. OLMSTEAD (rep)
	1956-57 MC	B OLMSTEAD (sc)
	1957-58 MC	B. OLMSTEAD (rep)
	1957-58 MC	B OLMSTEAD (sc)
	1961-62 TML	BERT OLMSTEAD (rep)
	1961-62 TML	BERT OLMSTEAD (sc)
O'Neill,	1944-45 TML	TOM O'NEILL (sp)
Tom	1944-45 TML	TOM O'NEILL (rep)
	1944-45 TML	TOM O'NEILL (sc)
Orlando,	1936-37 DET	JAMES ORLANDO DEFENSE (sp)
Jimmy	1936-37 DET	JAMES ORLANDO (ret)
	1942-43 DET	JAMES ORLANDO (sp)
	1942-43 DET	JAMES ORLANDO (rep)
	1942-43 DET	JAMES ORLANDO (sc)
Orr, Bobby	1969-70 BB	BOBBY ORR (rep)
	1969-70 BB	BOBBY ORR (sc)
	1971-72 BB	BOBBY ORR (rep)
	1971-72 BB	BOBBY ORR (sc)
Osgood,	1996-97 DET	CHRIS OSGOOD (rep)
Chris	1996-97 DET	CHRIS OSGOOD (sc)
	1997-98 DET	C. OSGOOD (rep)
	1997-98 DET	C. OSGOOD (sc)
Otto, Joel	1988-89 CAL	J. OTTO (ab)
	1988-89 CAL	J. OTTO (rep)
	1988-89 CAL	J. OTTO (sc)
Overton,	1998-99 DAL	DOUG OVERTON (rep)
Doug	1998-99 DAL	DOUG OVERTON (sc)
Owen,	1928-29 BB	GEORGE OWEN (or)
George	1928-29 BB	GEORGE OWEN (rep)
	1928-29 BB	GEORGE OWEN (sc)
Ozolinsh,	1995-96 COL	SANDIS OZOLINSH (rep)
Sandis	1995-96 COL	SANDIS OZOLINSH (sc)

Paek, Jim	1990-91 PIT	J. PAEK (ab)
	1990-91 PIT	J. PAEK (rep)
	1990-91 PIT	J. PAEK (sc)
	1991-92 PIT	JIM PAEK (rep)
	1991-92 PIT	JIM PAEK (sc)
Palangio,	1937-38 CHI	PETE PALANGIO (sp)
Pete	(I)1937-38 CHI	PALAGIO (ret)
	(II)1937-38 CHI	PETE PALANGIO (ret)
Palchak,	1967-68 MC	E. PALCHAK ASST. TR. (rep)
Eddie	1967-68 MC	E•PALCHAK ASST TR (sc)
	1968-69 MC	E. PALCHAK ASST. TR. (rep)
	1968-69 MC	E PALCHAK ASST TRAIN (sc)
	1970-71 MC	E. PALCHAK (rep)
	1970-71 MC	E. PALCHAK (sc)
	1972-73 MC	EDDY PALCHAK ASST. TRAINER (rep)
	1972-73 MC	EDDY PALCHAK. ASST. TRAINER (sc)
	1975-76 MC	EDDY PALCHAK TRAINER (rep)
	1975-76 MC	EDDY PALCHAK (sc)
	1976-77 MC	EDWARD PALCHAK TRAINER (rep)
	1976-77 MC	EDWARD PALCHAK H. TRA. (sc)
	1977-78 MC	ED PALCHAK H.T. (rep)
	1977-78 MC	ED. PALCHAK H.T. (sc)
	1978-79 MC	EDWARD PALCHAK H.T. (ab)
	1978-79 MC	EDWARD PALCHAK H.T. (rep)
	1978-79 MC	EDWARD PALCHAK H.T. (sc)
	1985-86 MC	E. PALCHAK TRAINER (ab)
	1985-86 MC	E. PALCHAK TRAINER (rep)
	1985-86 MC	E. PALCHAK TRAINER (sc)
	1992-93 MC	E. PALCHAK EQP. MGR. (rep)
	1992-93 MC	E. PALCHAK EQP. MGR. (sc)
Pandolfo,	1999-00 NJ	JAY PANDOLFO (rep)
Jay	1999-00 NJ	JAY PANDOLFO (sc)
	2002-03 NJ	JAY PANDOLFO (rep)
	2002-03 NJ	JAY PANDOLFO (sc)
Pappin, Jim	1963-64 TML	JAMES PAPPIN (rep)
	1963-64 TML	JAMES PAPPIN (sc)
	1966-67 TML	JIM PAPPIN (rep)
	1966-67 TML	JIM PAPPIN (sc)
Parent,	1973-74 PHI	BERNIE PARENT (rep)
Bernie	1973-74 PHI	BERNIE PARENT (sc)
	1974-75 PHI	BERNIE PARENT (rep)
	1974-75 PHI	BERNIE PARENT (sc)
Parker, Scott	2000-01 COL	SCOTT PARKER (rep)
	2000-01 COL	SCOTT PARKER (sc)
Paterson,	1990-91 PIT	RICK PATERSON (ab)
Rick	1990-91 PIT	RICK PATERSON (rep)
	1990-91 PIT	RICK PATERSON (sc)
	1991-92 PIT	RICK PATERSON (rep)
	1991-92 PIT	RICK PATERSON (sc)
Patrick,	1990-91 PIT	CRAIG PATRICK G.M. (ab)
Craig	1990-91 PIT	CRAIG PATRICK G.M. (rep)
	1990-91 PIT	CRAIG PATRICK G.M. (sc)
	1991-92 PIT	CRAIG PATRICK (rep)
	1991-92 PIT	CRAIG PATRICK (sc)
Patrick,	1914-15 VM	FRANK PATRICK (ib)
Frank	1914-15 VM	FRANK PATRICK (rep)
	1914-15 VM	FRANK PATRICK (sc)
Patrick,	1907 MW	L. PATRICK. (ib)
Lester	1907 MW	L. PATRICK (rep)
	1907 MW	L. PATRICK (sc)
	1924-25 VIC	L. PATRICK. (MGR.) (or)
	1924-25 VIC	L. PATRICK (MGR) (rep)
	1924-25 VIC	L. PATRICK (MCR) (sc)
	1927-28 NYR	LESTER PATRICK, (MGR.) (sp)
	1927-28 NYR	LESTER PATRICK (MGR) (ret)
	1932-33 NYR	LESTER PATRICK—MANAGER & COACH (sp)
	1932-33 NYR	LESTER PATRICK (MAN & COACH) (ret)
	1939-40 NYR	LESTER PATRICK. MANAGER (sp)
	1939-40 NYR	LESTER PATRICK (MAN) (ret)
Patrick,	1939-40 NYR	LYNN PATRICK (sp)
Lynn	1939-40 NYR	LYNN PATRICK (ret)
Patrick,	1939-40 NYR	MURRAY PATRICK (sp)
Muzz	1939-40 NYR	MURRAY PATRICK (ret)
Patterson,	1988-89 CAL	C. PATTERSON (ab)
Colin	1988-89 CAL	C. PATTERSON (rep)
	1988-89 CAL	C. PATTERSON (sc)
Patton,	1991-92 PIT	DONN PATTON (rep)
Donn	1991-92 PIT	DONN PATTON (sc)
Pavelich,	1949-50 DET	MARTY PAVELICH (re)
Marty	1949-50 DET	MARTY PAVELICH (rep)
	1949-50 DET	MARTY PAVELICH (sc)
	1951-52 DET	MARTY PAVELICH (re)
	1951-52 DET	MARTY PAVELICH (rep)
	1951-52 DET	MARTY PAVELICH (sc)
	1953-54 DET	MARTIN PAVELICH (re)
	1953-54 DET	MARTIN PAVELICH (rep)
	1953-54 DET	MARTIN PAVELICH (sc)
	1954-55 DET	MARTIN PAVELICH (re)
	1954-55 DET	MARTIN PAVELICH (rep)
	1954-55 DET	MARTIN PAVELICH (sc)
Pederson,	1990-91 PIT	B. PEDERSON (ab)
Barry	1990-91 PIT	B. PEDERSON (rep)
	1990-91 PIT	B. PEDERSON (sc)
Pelletier,	1973-74 PHI	MARCEL PELLETIER P.P.D. (rep)
Marcel	1973-74 PHI	MARCEL PELLETIER P.P.D. (sc)
	1974-75 PHI	MARCEL PELLETIER P.P.D. (rep)
	1974-75 PHI	MARCEL PELLETIER P.P.D. (sc)
Peluso,	1994-95 NJ	MIKE PELUSO (rep)
Mike	1994-95 NJ	MIKE PELUSO (sc)
Peplinski,	1988-89 CAL	J. PEPLINSKI C.C. (ab)
Jim	1988-89 CAL	J. PEPLINSKI C.C. (rep)
	1988-89 CAL	J. PEPLINSKI C.C. (sc)
Perron, Jean	1985-86 MC	J. PERRON COACH (ab)
	1985-86 MC	J. PERRON COACH (rep)
	1985-86 MC	J. PERRON COACH (sc)
Persson,	1979-80 NYI	S. PERSSON (ab)
Stefan	1979-80 NYI	S. PERSSON (rep)
	1979-80 NYI	S. PERSSON (sc)
	1980-81 NYI	S. PERSSON (ab)
	1980-81 NYI	S. PERSSON (rep)
	1980-81 NYI	S. PERSSON (sc)
	1981-82 NYI	S. PERSSON (ab)
	1981-82 NYI	S. PERSSON (rep)
	1981-82 NYI	S. PERSSON (sc)
	1982-83 NYI	S. PERSSON (ab)
	1982-83 NYI	S. PERSSON (rep)
	1982-83 NYI	S. PERSSON (sc)
Peters, Garry	1964-65 MC	GARRY PETERS (rep)
	1964-65 MC	GARRY PETERS (sc)
Peters, Jim	1945-46 MC	JAMES PETERS (re)
	1945-46 MC	JIM PETERS (rep)
	1945-46 MC	JIM PETERS (sc)
	1949-50 DET	JAMES PETERS (re)
	1949-50 DET	JIMMY PETERS (rep)
	1949-50 DET	JIMMY PETERS (sc)
	1953-54 DET	JAMES PETERS (re)

1953-54 DET JAMES PETERS (rep)
1953-54 DET JAMES PETERS (sc)

Peto, Len 1943-44 MC LEN PETO DIRECTOR (sp)
1943-44 MC LEN PETO DIRECTOR (rep)
1943-44 MC LEN PETO DIRECTOR (sc)

Pettinger, Eric 1928-29 BB E PETTINGER (ret)

Pettinger, Gord 1932-33 NYR GORDON PETTINGER (sp)
1932-33 NYR GORDON PETTINGER (ret)
1935-36 DET GORDON PETTINGER—CENTER (sp)
1935-36 DET GORDON PETTINGER (ret)
1936-37 DET GORDON PETTINGER—CENTER (sp)
1936-37 DET GORDEN PETTINGER (ret)
1938-39 BB G. PETTINGER (sp)
1938-39 BB G PETTINGER (ret)

Phillips, Bill 1925-26 MM M. PHILIPS. (or)
1925-26 MM M. PHILIPS (rep)
1925-26 MM M. PHILIPS. (sc)

Picard, Noel 1964-65 MC NOEL PICARD (rep)
1964-65 MC NOEL PICARD (sc)

Pickard, Jim 1979-80 NYI J. PICKARD A.T. (ab)
1979-80 NYI J. PICKARD A.T. (rep)
1979-80 NYI J. PICKARD A.T. (sc)
1980-81 NYI J. PICKARD A.T. (ab)
1980-81 NYI J. PICKARD A.T. (rep)
1980-81 NYI J. PICKARD A.T. (sc)
1981-82 NYI J. PICKARD A.T. (ab)
1981-82 NYI J. PICKARD A.T. (rep)
1981-82 NYI J. PICKARD (sc)
1982-83 NYI J. PICKARD A.T. (ab)
1982-83 NYI J. PICKARD A.T. (rep)
1982-83 NYI J. PICKARD A.T. (sc)

Pickett, John 1979-80 NYI JOHN O. PICKETT CHAIRMAN OF BOARD (ab)
1979-80 NYI JOHN O. PICKETT CHAIRMAN OF BOARD (rep)
1979-80 NYI JOHN O. PICKETT CHAIRMAN OF BOARD (sc)
1980-81 NYI JOHN O. PICKETT CHAIRMAN OF BOARD (ab)
1980-81 NYI JOHN O. PICKETT CHAIRMAN OF BOARD (rep)
1980-81 NYI JOHN O. PICKETT CHAIRMAN OF BOARD (sc)
1981-82 NYI JOHN O. PICKETT JR. CHAIRMAN (ab)
1981-82 NYI JOHN O. PICKETT JR. CHAIRMAN (rep)
1981-82 NYI JOHN O. PICKETT JR. CHAIRMAN (sc)
1982-83 NYI JOHN O. PICKETT JR. HAIRMAN (ab)
1982-83 NYI JOHN O. PICKETT JR. CHAIRMAN (rep)
1982-83 NYI JOHN O. PICKETT JR. CHAIRMAN (sc)

Pietrangelo, Frank 1990-91 PIT F. PIETRANGELO (ab)
1990-91 PIT F. PIETRANGELO (rep)
1990-91 PIT F. PIETRANGELO (sc)

Pike, Alf 1939-40 NYR ALFRED PIKE (sp)
1939-40 NYR ALFRED PIKE (ret)

Pilote, Pierre 1960-61 CHI PIERRE PILOTE (rep)
1960-61 CHI PIERRE PILOTE (sc)

Pilous, Rudy 1960-61 CHI RUDOLPH PILOUS COACH (rep)
1960-61 CHI RUDOLPH PILOUS COACH (sc)

Plamondon, Gerry 1945-46 MC GERARD PLAMONDON (re)
1945-46 MC GERRY PLAMONDON (rep)
1945-46 MC JERRY PLAMDNDON (sc)

Plante, Derek 1998-99 DAL DEREK PLANTE (rep)
1998-99 DAL DEREK PLANTE (sc)

Plante, Jacques 1952-53 MC JACQUES PLANTE (re)
1952-53 MC JACQUES PLANTE (rep)
1952-53 MC JACQUES PLANTE (sc)
1955-56 MC J. PLANTE (re)
1955-56 MC J. PLANTE (rep)
1955-56 MC J PLANTE (sc)
1956-57 MC JACQUES PLANTE (rep)
1956-57 MC JACQUES PLANTE (sc)
1957-58 MC JACQUES PLANTE (rep)
1957-58 MC JAC PLANTE (sc)
1958-59 MC JACQUES PLANTE (rep)
1958-59 MC JACQ PLANTE (sc)
1959-60 MC JACQUES PLANTE (rep)
1959-60 MC JACQUES PLANTE (sc)

Plasse, Michel 1972-73 MC MICHEL PLASSE (rep)
1972-73 MC MICHEL PLASSE (sc)

Pleau, Larry 1993-94 NYR LARRY PLEAU ASST. G.M. (rep)
1993-94 NYR LARRY PLEAU ASST. G.M. (sc)

Pocklington, Basil 1983-84 EDM XXXXX XXXXXXXXXXX (ab)
1983-84 EDM XXXXX XXXXXXXXXXX (sc)

Pocklington, Peter 1983-84 EDM PETER POCKLINGTON OWNER (ab)
1983-84 EDM PETER POCKLINGTON OWNER (rep)
1983-84 EDM PETER POCKLINGTON (sc)
1984-85 EDM PETER POCKLINGTON OWNER (ab)
1984-85 EDM PETER POCKLINGTON OWNER (rep)
1984-85 EDM PETER POCKLINGTON OWNER (sc)
1986-87 EDM PETER POCKLINGTON OWNER (ab)
1986-87 EDM PETER POCKLINGTON OWNER (rep)
1986-87 EDM PETER POCKLINGTON OWNER (sc)
1987-88 EDM PETER POCKLINGTON OWNER (ab)
1987-88 EDM PETER POCKLINGTON OWNER (rep)
1987-88 EDM PETER POCKLINGTON OWNER (sc)
1989-90 EDM PETER POCKLINGTON OWNER (ab)
1989-90 EDM PETER POCKLINGTON OWNER (rep)
1989-90 EDM PETER POCKLINGTON OWNER (sc)

Podein, Shjon 2000-01 COL SHJON PODEIN (rep)
2000-01 COL SHJON PODEIN (sc)

Poile, Norman "Bud" 1946-47 TML NORMAN POILE (re)
1946-47 TML BUD POILE (rep)
1946-47 TML BUD POILE (sc)

Poirier, Stewart 1989-90 EDM STUART POLRIER (ab)
1989-90 EDM STUART POIRIER (rep)
1989-90 EDM STUART POIRIER (sc)

Polich, Mike 1976-77 MC MICHAEL POLICH (rep)
1976-77 MC MICHAEL POLICH (sc)

Pollock, Sam 1958-59 MC SAM POLLOCK PERSONNEL DIR. (rep)
1958-59 MC SAM POLLOCK PERSONNEL DIR (sc)
1959-60 MC SAM POLLOCK PERSONNEL DIR. (rep)
1959-60 MC SAM POLLOCK PERSONNEL DIR (sc)
1964-65 MC SAM POLLOCK GEN. MANAGER (rep)
1964-65 MC SAM POLLOCK GEN MANAGER (sc)
1965-66 MC S. POLLOCK GEN. MGR. (rep)
1965-66 MC S POLLOK GEN MAN (sc)
1967-68 MC SAM POLLOCK VICE PRES. & GEN. MGR. (rep)
1967-68 MC SAM POLLOCK VICE PRES & GEN. MAN (sc)
1968-69 MC S. POLLOCK VICE PRES. GEN. MGR. (rep)
1968-69 MC S POLLOCK VICE PRES GEN MAN (sc)
1970-71 MC S. POLLOCK GEN. MGR. (rep)
1970-71 MC S POLLOCK. VICE PRES G. MAN (sc)
1972-73 MC SAM POLLOCK V.P. & G.M. (rep)
1972-73 MC SAM POLLOCK. V.P. & G.M. (sc)
1975-76 MC SAM POLLOCK V.P. & G.M. (rep)
1975-76 MC SAM POLLOCK V.P. & G.M. (sc)
1976-77 MC SAM POLLOCK V.P. & G.M. (rep)
1976-77 MC SAM POLLOCK V.P. & G.M. (sc)
1977-78 MC SAM POLLOCK V.P. & G.M. (rep)
1977-78 MC SAM POLLOCK V.P. & G.M. (sc)
1978-79 MC SAM POLLOCK D. (ab)
1978-79 MC SAM POLLOCK D. (rep)
1978-79 MC SAM POLLOCK D. (sc)

Portland, Jack 1938-39 BB J. PORTLAND (sp)
1938-39 BB J PORTLAND (ret)

Potvin, Denis 1979-80 NYI D. POTVIN CAPT. (ab)
1979-80 NYI D. POTVIN CAPT. (rep)
1979-80 NYI D. POTVIN CAPT. (sc)
1980-81 NYI D. POTVIN CAPT. (ab)
1980-81 NYI D. POTVIN CAPT. (rep)
1980-81 NYI D. POTVIN CAPT. (sc)
1981-82 NYI D. POTVIN CAPT. (ab)
1981-82 NYI D. POTVIN CAPT. (rep)
1981-82 NYI D. POTVIN CAPT. (sc)
1982-83 NYI D. POTVIN CAPT. (ab)
1982-83 NYI D. POTVIN CAPT. (rep)
1982-83 NYI D. POTVIN CAPT. (sc)

Potvin, Jean 1979-80 NYI J. POTVIN (ab)
1979-80 NYI J. POTVIN (rep)
1979-80 NYI J. POTVIN (sc)
1980-81 NYI J. POTVIN (ab)
1980-81 NYI J. POTVIN (rep)
1980-81 NYI J. POTVIN (sc)

Pouzar, Jaroslav 1983-84 EDM J. POUZAR (ab)
1983-84 EDM J. POUZAR (rep)
1983-84 EDM J. POUZAR (sc)
1984-85 EDM J. POUZAR (ab)
1984-85 EDM J. POUZAR (rep)
1984-85 EDM J. POUZAR (sc)
1986-87 EDM J. POUZAR (ab)
1986-87 EDM J. POUZAR (rep)
1986-87 EDM J. POUZAR (sc)

Powers, Eddie 1969-70 BB E.J. POWERS V.P. (rep)
1969-70 BB E J POWERS V P (sc)
1971-72 BB ED J. POWERS VICE PRES. TREAS. (rep)
1971-72 BB ED. J. POWERS V. PRES. TREAS. (sc)

Pradera, Gregorio 2000-01 COL GREGORIO PRADERA (rep)
2000-01 COL GREGORIO PRADERA (sc)

Pratt, Nolan 2000-01 COL NOLAN PRATT (rep)
2000-01 COL NOLAN PRATT (sc)

Pratt, Walter "Babe" 1939-40 NYR WALTER PRATT (sp)
1939-40 NYR WALTER PRATT (ret)
1944-45 TML BABE PRATT (sp)
1944-45 TML BABE PRATT (rep)
1944-45 TML BABE PRATT (sc)

Price, Noel 1965-66 MC NOEL PRICE (rep)
1965-66 MC NOEL PRICE (sc)

Priestlay,	1991-92 PIT	KEN PRIESTLAY (rep)
Ken	1991-92 PIT	KEN PRIESTLAY (sc)
Primeau, Joe	1931-32 TML	J. PRIMEAU (sp)
	1931-32 TML	J PRIMEAU (ret)
	1950-51 TML	JOSEPH PRIMEAU COACH (re)
	1950-51 TML	J. PRIMEAU COACH (rep)
	1950-51 TML	J PRIMEAU COACH (sc)
Pronovost,	1956-57 MC	A. PRONOVOST (rep)
Andre	1956-57 MC	A PRONOVOST (sc)
	1957-58 MC	A. PRONOVOST (rep)
	1957-58 MC	A PRONOVOST (sc)
	1958-59 MC	A. PRONOVOST (rep)
	1958-59 MC	A PRONOVOST (sc)
	1959-60 MC	ANDRE PRONOVOST (rep)
	1959-60 MC	ANDRE PRONOVOST (sc)
Pronovost,	1949-50 DET	MARCEL PRONOVOST (re)
Marcel	1949-50 DET	M. PRONOVOST (rep)
	1949-50 DET	M PRONOVOST (sc)
	1951-52 DET	MARCEL PRONOVOST (re)
	1951-52 DET	M. PRONOVOST (rep)
	1951-52 DET	M PRONOVOST (sc)
	1953-54 DET	MARCEL PRONOVOST (re)
	1953-54 DET	MARCEL PRONOVOST (rep)
	1953-54 DET	MARCEL PRONOVOST (sc)
	1954-55 DET	MARCEL PRONOVOST (re)
	1954-55 DET	MARCEL PRONOVOST (rep)
	1954-55 DET	MARCEL PRONOVOST (sc)
	1966-67 TML	MARCEL PRONOVOST (rep)
	1966-67 TML	MARCEL PRONOVOST (sc)
	1994-95 NJ	MARCEL PRONOVOST (rep)
	1994-95 NJ	MARCEL PRONOVOST (sc)
	1999-00 NJ	M. PRONOVOST (rep)
	1999-00 NJ	M. PRONOVOST (sc)
	2002-03 NJ	M. PRONOVOST (rep)
	2002-03 NJ	M. PRONOVOST (sc)
Provost,	1955-56 MC	C. PREVOST (re)
Claude	1955-56 MC	C. PREVOST (rep)
	1955-56 MC	C PREVOST (sc)
	1956-57 MC	CLAUDE PROVOST (rep)
	1956-57 MC	CLAUDE PROVOST (sc)
	1957-58 MC	C PROVOST (rep)
	1957-58 MC	C PROVOST (sc)
	1958-59 MC	CLAUDE PROVOST (rep)
	1958-59 MC	CLAUDE PROVOST (sc)
	1959-60 MC	CLAUDE PROVOST (rep)
	1959-60 MC	CLAUDE PROVOST (sc)
	1964-65 MC	CLAUDE PROVOST (rep)
	1964-65 MC	CLAUDE PROVOST (sc)
	1965-66 MC	CLAUDE PROVOST (rep)
	1965-66 MC	CLAUDE PROVOST (sc)
	1967-68 MC	CLAUDE PROVOST (rep)
	1967-68 MC	CLAUDE PROVOST (sc)
	1968-69 MC	C. PROVOST (rep)
	1968-69 MC	C PROVOST (sc)
Prysai,	1951-52 DET	METRO PRYSTAI (re)
Metro	1951-52 DET	METRO PRYSTAI (rep)
	1951-52 DET	METRO PRYSTAI (sc)
	1953-54 DET	METRO PRYSTAI (re)
	1953-54 DET	METRO PRYSTAI (rep)
	1953-54 DET	METRO PRYSTAI (sc)
Pulford, Bob	1961-62 TML	ROBERT FULFORD (rep)
	1961-62 TML	ROBERT PULFORD (sc)
	1962-63 TML	ROBERT PULFORD (rep)
	1962-63 TML	ROBERT PULFORD (sc)
	1963-64 TML	ROBERT PULFORD (rep)
	1963-64 TML	ROBERT PULFORD (sc)
	1966-67 TML	BOB PULFORD (rep)
	1966-67 TML	BOB PULFORD (sc)
Pushor,	1996-97 DET	JAMIE PUSHOR (rep)
Jamie	1996-97 DET	JAMIE PUSHOR (sc)

Quenneville,	1995-96 COL	JOEL QUENNEVILLE (rep)
Joel	1995-96 COL	JOEL QUENNEVILLE (sc)

Racicot,	1992-93 MC	A. RACICOT (rep)
Andre	1992-93 MC	A. RACICOT (sc)
Rafalski,	1999-00 NJ	BRIAN C. RAFALSKI (rep)
Brian	1999-00 NJ	BRIAN C. RAFALSKI (sc)
	2002-03 NJ	BRIAN C. RAFALSKI (rep)
	2002-03 NJ	BRIAN C. RAFALSKI (sc)
Ramage,	1988-89 CAL	R. RAMAGE (ab)
Rob	1988-89 CAL	R. RAMAGE (rep)
	1988-89 CAL	R. RAMAGE (sc)
	1992-93 MC	R. RAMAGE (rep)
	1992-93 MC	R. RAMAGE (sc)
Randolph,	2000-01 COL	DAVE RANDOLPH (rep)
Dave	2000-01 COL	DAVE RANDOLPH (sc)
Ranford,	1987-88 EDM	B. RANFORD (ab)
Bill	1987-88 EDM	B. RANFORD (rep)
	1987-88 EDM	B. RANFORD (sc)
	1989-90 EDM	B. RANFORD (ab)
	1989-90 EDM	B. RANFORD (rep)
	1989-90 EDM	B. RANFORD (sc)
Raymond,	1930-31 MC	ALP. RAYMOND (sp)
Alf	1930-31 MC	ALP RAYMOND (ret)
Raymond,	1925-26 MM	D. RAYMOND. (Dir.) (or)
Donat	1925-26 MM	D. RAYMOND (Dir) (rep)
	1925-26 MM	D. RAYMOND (Dir) (sc)
	1934-35 MM	HONOURABLE DONAT RAYMOND/PRESIDENT (sp)
	1934-35 MM	DONAT RAYMOND PRESIDENT (ret)
	1943-44 MC	SENATOR DONAT RAYMOND PRESIDENT (sp)
	1943-44 MC	SENATOR DONAT RAYMOND PRES. (rep)
	1943-44 MC	SENATOR DONAT RAYMOND (PRES) (sc)
	1945-46 MC	SENATOR DONAT RAYMOND PRESIDENT (re)
	1945-46 MC	SENATOR DONAT RAYMOND PRES. (rep)
	1945-46 MC	SENATOR DONAT RAYMOND (PRES) (sc)
	1952-53 MC	HON. DONAT RAYMOND - PRESIDENT (re)
	1952-53 MC	HON. DONAT RAYMOND PRESIDENT (rep)
	1952-53 MC	HON DONAT RAYMOND PRESIDENT (sc)
	1955-56 MC	HON. DONAT RAYMOND, PRESIDENT (re)
	1955-56 MC	HON. DONAT RAYMOND PRES. (rep)
	1955-56 MC	HON DONAT RAYMOND PRESS (sc)
	1956-57 MC	HON. DONAT RAYMOND CHAIRMAN (rep)
	1956-57 MC	HON DONAT RAYMOND CHAIR (sc)
Reardon,	1945-46 MC	KENNETH REARDON (re)
Ken	1945-46 MC	KEN REARDON (rep)
	1945-46 MC	KEN REARDON (sc)
	1955-56 MC	KENNY REARDON, ASS. MANAGER (re)
	1955-56 MC	KENNY REARDON ASST. MGR. (rep)
	1955-56 MC	KENNY REARDON ASS MAN (sc)
	1956-57 MC	KENNY REARDON VICE PRES. (rep)
	1956-57 MC	KENNY REARDON VICE PRES (sc)
	1957-58 MC	KENNY REARDON VICE PRES. (rep)
	1957-58 MC	KENNY REARDON VICE PRES (sc)
	1958-59 MC	KENNY REARDON VICE PRES. (rep)
	1958-59 MC	KENNY REARDON VICE PRES (sc)
	1959-60 MC	KENNY REARDON VICE PRES. (rep)
	1959-60 MC	KENNY REARDON VICE PRES (sc)
Reardon,	1938-39 BB	T. REARDON (sp)
Terry	1938-39 BB	T REARDON (ret)
	1940-41 BB	TERRY REARDON (sp)
	1940-41 BB	TERRY REARDON (rep)
	1940-41 BB	TERRY REARDON (sc)
Reay, Billy	1945-46 MC	WILLIAM REAY (re)
	1945-46 MC	WILLIAM REAY (rep)
	1945-46 MC	WILLIAM REAY (sc)
	1952-53 MC	BILLY REAY (re)
	1952-53 MC	BILLY REAY (rep)
	1952-53 MC	BILLY REAY (sc)
Recchi,	1990-91 PIT	M. RECCHI (ab)
Mark	1990-91 PIT	M. RECCHI (rep)
	1990-91 PIT	M. RECCHI (sc)
Reddick,	1989-90 EDM	E. REDDICK (ab)
Eldon	1989-90 EDM	E. REDDICK (rep)
"Pokey"	1989-90 EDM	E. REDDICK (sc)
Redmond,	1967-68 MC	M. REDMOND (rep)
Mickey	1967-68 MC	M REDMOND (sc)
	1968-69 MC	M. REDMOND (rep)
	1968-69 MC	M REDMOND (sc)
Reeves,	1989-90 EDM	ALBERT REEVES (ab)
Albert	1989-90 EDM	ALBERT REEVES (rep)
	1989-90 EDM	ALBERT REEVES (sc)
Reibel,	1953-54 DET	EARL REIBEL (re)
Earl	1953-54 DET	EARL REIBEL (rep)
"Dutch"	1953-54 DET	EARL REIBEL (sc)
	1954-55 DET	EARL REIBEL (re)
	1954-55 DET	EARL REIBEL (rep)
	1954-55 DET	EARL REIBEL (sc)
Reid, Dave	1998-99 DAL	DAVE REID (rep)
	1998-99 DAL	DAVE REID (sc)
	2000-01 COL	DAVID REID (rep)
	2000-01 COL	DAVID REID (sc)
Reid,	1989-90 EDM	DR. DAVID REID (ab)
Dr. David	1989-90 EDM	DR. DAVID REID (rep)
	1989-90 EDM	DR. DAVID REID (sc)
Reinprecht,	2000-01 COL	STEVEN REINPRECHT (rep)
Steve	2000-01 COL	STEVEN REINPRECHT (sc)
Reise,	1949-50 DET	LEO REISE (re)
Leo Jr.	1949-50 DET	LEO REISE (rep)
	1949-50 DET	LEO REISE (sc)
	1951-52 DET	LEO REISE (re)
	1951-52 DET	LEO REISE (rep)
	1951-52 DET	LEO REISE (sc)
Resch,	1979-80 NYI	G. RESCH (ab)
Glenn	1979-80 NYI	G. RESCH (rep)
	1979-80 NYI	G. RESCH (sc)
Rheaume,	2002-03 NJ	PASCAL RHEAUME (rep)
Pascal	2002-03 NJ	PASCAL RHEAUME (sc)
Ricci, Mike	1995-96 COL	MIKE RICCI (rep)

	1995-96 COL	MIKE RICCI (sc)
Richard, Henri	1955-56 MC	H. RICHARD (re)
	1955-56 MC	H. RICHARD (rep)
	1955-56 MC	H RICHARD (sc)
	1956-57 MC	HENRI RICHARD (rep)
	1956-57 MC	HENRI RICHARD (sc)
	1957-58 MC	H. RICHARD (rep)
	1957-58 MC	H RICHARD (sc)
	1958-59 MC	H. RICHARD (rep)
	1958-59 MC	H RICHARD (sc)
	1959-60 MC	H. RICHARD (rep)
	1959-60 MC	H RICHARD (sc)
	1964-65 MC	HENRI RICHARD (rep)
	1964-65 MC	HENRI RICHARD (sc)
	1965-66 MC	HENRI RICHARD (rep)
	1965-66 MC	HENRI RICHARD (sc)
	1967-68 MC	HENRI RICHARD (rep)
	1967-68 MC	HENRI RICHARD (sc)
	1968-69 MC	H. RICHARD (rep)
	1968-69 MC	H RICHARD (sc)
	1970-71 MC	H. RICHARD (rep)
	1970-71 MC	H• RICHARD (sc)
	1972-73 MC	HENRI RICHARD (rep)
	1972-73 MC	HENRI RICHARD (sc)
Richard, Maurice	1943-44 MC	MAURICE RICHARD (sp)
	1943-44 MC	MAURICE RICHARD (rep)
	1943-44 MC	MAURICE RICHARD (sc)
	1945-46 MC	MAURICE RICHARD (re)
	1945-46 MC	MAURICE RICHARD (rep)
	1945-46 MC	MAURICE RICHARD (sc)
	1952-53 MC	MAURICE RICHARD (re)
	1952-53 MC	MAURICE RICHARD (rep)
	1952-53 MC	MAURICE RICHARD (sc)
	1955-56 MC	M. RICHARD (re)
	1955-56 MC	M. RICHARD (rep)
	1955-56 MC	M RICHARD (sc)
	1956-57 MC	MAURICE RICHARD CAPTAIN (rep)
	1956-57 MC	MAURICE RICHARD CAPTAIN (sc)
	1957-58 MC	MAURICE RICHARD CAPTAIN (rep)
	1957-58 MC	MAURICE RICHARD CAPTAIN (sc)
	1958-59 MC	MAURICE RICHARD CAPT. (rep)
	1958-59 MC	MAURICE RICHARD CAPT (sc)
	1959-60 MC	MAURICE RICHARD CAPT. (rep)
	1959-60 MC	MAURICE RICHARD CAP (sc)
	1964-65 MC	MAURICE RICHARD ASST. TO PRES. (rep)
	1964-65 MC	MAURICE RICHARD ASS TO PRESS (sc)
Richer, George	1929-30 MC	GEO RICHER. (sp)
	1929-30 MC	GEO RICHER (PHYSS) (ret)
	1930-31 MC	GEO. RICHER (sp)
	1930-31 MC	GEO RICHER (ret)
Richer, Stephane	1985-86 MC	S. RICHER (ab)
	1985-86 MC	S. RICHER (rep)
	1985-86 MC	S. RICHER (sc)
	1994-95 NJ	STEPHANE J.J. RICHER (rep)
	1994-95 NJ	STEPHANE J.J. RICHER (sc)
Richter, Mike	1993-94 NYR	M. RICHTER (rep)
	1993-94 NYR	M. RICHTER (sc)
Rickard, Tex	1927-28 NYR	G. L. RICKARD, (DIR.) (sp)
	1927-28 NYR	G L RICKARD (DIR) (ret)
Rinfret, Fernand	1923-24 MC	F.RINFRET (or)
	1923-24 MC	F. RINFRET (rep)
	1923-24 MC	F. RINFRET (sc)
	1929-30 MC	HON.F.RINFRET. (sp)
	1929-30 MC	HON F RINFRET (ret)
	1930-31 MC	HON.F.RINFRET (sp)
	1930-31 MC	HON F RINFRET (ret)
Risebrough, Doug	1975-76 MC	DOUG RISEBROUGH (rep)
	1975-76 MC	DOUG RISEBROUGH (sc)
	1976-77 MC	DOUGLAS RISEBROUGH (rep)
	1976-77 MC	DOUGLAS RISEBROUGH (sc)
	1977-78 MC	DOUGLAS RISEBROUGH (rep)
	1977-78 MC	DOUGLAS RISEBROUGH (sc)
	1978-79 MC	D. RISEBROUGH (ab)
	1978-79 MC	D. RISEBROUGH (rep)
	1978-79 MC	D. RISEBROUGH (sc)
	1988-89 CAL	DOUG RISEBROUGH (ab)
	1988-89 CAL	DOUG RISEBROUGH (rep)
	1988-89 CAL	DOUG RISEBROUGH (sc)
Rivers, Gus	1929-30 MC	GUS RIVERS. (sp)
	1929-30 MC	GUS RIVERS (ret)
	1930-31 MC	GUS RIVERS (sp)
	1930-31 MC	GUS RIVERS (ret)
Roberge, Mario	1992-93 MC	M. ROBERGE (rep)
	1992-93 MC	M. ROBERGE (sc)
Roberto, Phil	1970-71 MC	P. ROBERTO (rep)
	1970-71 MC	P ROBRTO (sc)
Roberts, Gary	1988-89 CAL	G. ROBERTS (ab)
	1988-89 CAL	G. ROBERTS (rep)
	1988-89 CAL	G. ROBERTS (sc)
Roberts, Gord	1990-91 PIT	G. ROBERTS (ab)
	1990-91 PIT	G. ROBERTS (rep)
	1990-91 PIT	G. ROBERTS (sc)
	1991-92 PIT	GORD ROBERTS (rep)
	1991-92 PIT	GORD ROBERTS (sc)
Roberts, Jim	1964-65 MC	JAMES ROBERTS (rep)
	1964-65 MC	JAMES ROBERTS (sc)
	1965-66 MC	JAMES ROBERTS (rep)
	1965-66 MC	JAMES ROBERTS (sc)
	1972-73 MC	JIM ROBERTS (rep)
	1972-73 MC	JIM ROBERTS (sc)
	1975-76 MC	JIM ROBERTS (rep)
	1975-76 MC	JIM ROBERTS (sc)
	1976-77 MC	JIM ROBERTS (rep)
	1976-77 MC	JIM ROBERTS (sc)
Robertson, Earl	1936-37 DET	EARL ROBERTSON GOAL (sp)
	1936-37 DET	EARL ROBERTSON (ret)
Robertson, Fred	1931-32 TML	ROBERTSON (sp)
Robinson, Earl	1934-35 MM	E. ROBINSON (sp)
	1934-35 MM	E ROBINSON (ret)
Robinson, Larry	1972-73 MC	LARRY ROBINSON (rep)
	1972-73 MC	LARRY ROBINSON (sc)
	1975-76 MC	LARRY ROBINSON (rep)
	1975-76 MC	LARRY ROBINSON (sc)
	1976-77 MC	LARRY ROBINSON (rep)
	1976-77 MC	LARRY ROBINSON (sc)
	1977-78 MC	LARRY ROBINSON (rep)
	1977-78 MC	LARRY ROBINSON (sc)
	1978-79 MC	L. ROBINSON (ab)
	1978-79 MC	L. ROBINSON (rep)
	1978-79 MC	L. ROBINSON (sc)
	1985-86 MC	L. ROBINSON (ab)
	1985-86 MC	L. ROBINSON (rep)
	1985-86 MC	L. ROBINSON (sc)
	1994-95 NJ	LARRY ROBINSON (rep)
	1994-95 NJ	LARRY ROBINSON (sc)
	1999-00 NJ	L. ROBINSON (rep)
	1999-00 NJ	L. ROBINSON (sc)
	2002-03 NJ	L. ROBINSON (rep)
	2002-03 NJ	L. ROBINSON (sc)
Robitaille, Luc	2001-02 DET	LUC ROBITAILLE (rep)
	2001-02 DET	LUC ROBITAILLE (sc)
Rochefort, Leon	1965-66 MC	LEON ROCHEFORT (rep)
	1965-66 MC	LEON ROCHEFORT (sc)
	1970-71 MC	L. ROCHEFORT (rep)
	1970-71 MC	L ROCHEFORT (sc)
Rockstrom, Christer	1993-94 NYR	C. ROCKSTROM SCOUT (rep)
	1993-94 NYR	C. ROCKSTROM SCOUT (sc)
Rodden, Eddie	1928-29 BB	E RODDEN (ret)
Rogers, Alfred	1931-32 TML	MR. ALFRED ROGERS (sp)
Rollins, Al	1950-51 TML	ELWIN ROLLINS (re)
	1950-51 TML	ELVIN ROLLINS (rep)
	1950-51 TML	ELVIN ROLLINS (sc)
Rolph, Frank	1931-32 TML	MR. FRANK A. ROLPH (sp)
Rolston, Brian	1994-95 NJ	BRIAN ROLSTON (rep)
	1994-95 NJ	BRIAN ROLSTON (sc)
Romnes, Elwyn "Doc"	1933-34 CHI	ELWIN ROMNES (sp)
	1933-34 CHI	ELVIN ROMNES (ret)
	1937-38 CHI	DOC ROMNES (sp)
	1937-38 CHI	DOC ROMNES (ret)
Ronan, Ed	1992-93 MC	E. RONAN (rep)
	1992-93 MC	E. RONAN (sc)
Rooney, Steve	1985-86 MC	S. ROONEY (ab)
	1985-86 MC	S. ROONEY (rep)
	1985-86 MC	S. ROONEY (sc)
Ross, Art	1928-29 BB	ARTHUR H. ROSS V. PRES. •MGR. (or)
	1928-29 BB	ARTHUR H. ROSS V PRES. MGR. (rep)
	1928-29 BB	ART ROSS (MAN) (ret)
	1928-29 BB	ARTHUR H. ROSS V PRES. •MGR. (sc)
	1938-39 BB	ARTHUR H. ROSS/VICE-PRES. & MANAGER (sp)
	1938-39 BB	ARTHUR ROSS (V PRES) (ret)
	1940-41 BB	ARTHUR H. ROSS, VICE-PRES & MGR. (sp)
	1940-41 BB	ART H. ROSS VICE PRES. (rep)
	1940-41 BB	ART H. ROSS (V.PRESS) (sc)
Ross, Victor	1931-32 TML	MR. VICTOR ROSS (sp)
Ross, William	1931-32 TML	HON.W.D.ROSS (sp)
Rothschild, Sam	1925-26 MM	S. ROTHSCHILD. (or)
	1925-26 MM	S. ROTHSCHILD (rep)
	1925-26 MM	S. ROTHSCHILD (sc)
Roulston, Orville	1936-37 DET	ORVILLE ROULSTON DEFENSE (sp)
	1936-37 DET	ORVILLE ROULSTON (ret)
Rouse, Bob	1996-97 DET	BOB ROUSE (rep)
	1996-97 DET	BOB ROUSE (sc)
	1997-98 DET	B. ROUSE (rep)
	1997-98 DET	B. ROUSE (sc)
Rousseau, Bobby	1964-65 MC	ROBERT ROUSSEAU (rep)
	1964-65 MC	ROBERT ROUSSEAU (sc)
	1965-66 MC	R. ROUSSEAU (rep)

Name	Season	Inscription
	1965-66 MC	R ROUSSEAU (sc)
	1967-68 MC	R. ROUSSEAU (rep)
	1967-68 MC	R RQUSSEAU (sc)
	1968-69 MC	R. ROUSSEAU (rep)
	1968-69 MC	R ROUSSEAU (sc)
Roy, Patrick	1985-86 MC	P. ROY (ab)
	1985-86 MC	P. ROY (rep)
	1985-86 MC	P. ROY (sc)
	1992-93 MC	P. ROY (rep)
	1992-93 MC	P. ROY (sc)
	1995-96 COL	PATRICK ROY (rep)
	1995-96 COL	PATRICK ROY (sc)
	2000-01 COL	PATRICK ROY (rep)
	2000-01 COL	PATRICK ROY (sc)
Ruel, Claude	1968-69 MC	C. RUEL COACH (rep)
	1968-69 MC	C RUEL COACH (sc)
	1975-76 MC	CLAUDE RUEL D.P. (rep)
	1975-76 MC	CLAUDE RUEL D.P. (sc)
	1976-77 MC	CLAUDE RUEL D.P. (rep)
	1976-77 MC	CLAUDE RUEL D.P. (sc)
	1977-78 MC	CLAUDE RUEL D.P. (rep)
	1977-78 MC	CLAUDE RUEL D.P. (sc)
	1978-79 MC	CLAUDE RUEL D.P.D. (ab)
	1978-79 MC	CLAUDE RUEL D.P.D. (rep)
	1978-79 MC	CLAUDE RUEL D.P.D. (sc)
	1985-86 MC	C. RUEL PLYR. DEVL. (ab)
	1985-86 MC	C. RUEL PLYR. DEVL. (rep)
	1985-86 MC	C. RUEL PLYR. DEVL. (sc)
Ruotsalainen, Reijo	1986-87 EDM	R. RUOTSALAINEN (ab)
	1986-87 EDM	R. RUOTSALAINEN (rep)
	1986-87 EDM	R. RUOTSALAINEN (sc)
	1989-90 EDM	R. RUOTSALAINEN (ab)
	1989-90 EDM	R. RUOTSALAINEN (rep)
	1989-90 EDM	R. RUOTSALAINEN (sc)
Rupp, Mike	2002-03 NJ	MICHAEL P. RUPP (rep)
	2002-03 NJ	MICHAEL P. RUPP (sc)
Russell, Ernie	1907 MW	ERNIE RUSSELL. (ib)
	1907 MW	ERNIE RUSSELL (rep)
	1907 MW	ERNIE RUSSELL (sc)
Ruta, Thomas	1991-92 PIT	THOMAS RUTA (rep)
	1991-92 PIT	THOMAS RUTA (sc)
Rychel, Warren	1995-96 COL	WARREN RYCHEL (rep)
	1995-96 COL	WARREN RYCHEL (sc)
Sakic, Joe	1995-96 COL	JOE SAKIC (rep)
	1995-96 COL	JOE SAKIC (sc)
	2000-01 COL	JOE SAKIC (rep)
	2000-01 COL	JOE SAKIC (sc)
Saleski, Don	1973-74 PHI	DON SALESKI (rep)
	1973-74 PHI	DON SALESKI (sc)
	1974-75 PHI	DON SALESKI (rep)
	1974-75 PHI	DON SALESKI (sc)
Samis, Phil	1947-48 TML	PHILIP SAMIS (re)
	1947-48 TML	PHILIP SAMIS (rep)
	1947-48 TML	PHILIP SAMIS (sc)
Samuel, Sigmund	1931-32 TML	MR. SIGMUND SAMUEL (sp)
Samuelsson, Kjell	1991-92 PIT	KJELL SAMUELSSON (rep)
	1991-92 PIT	KJELL SAMUELSSON (sc)
Samuelsson, Ulf	1990-91 PIT	U. SAMUELSSON (ab)
	1990-91 PIT	U. SAMUELSSON (rep)
	1990-91 PIT	U. SAMUELSSON (sc)
	1991-92 PIT	ULF SAMUELSSON (rep)
	1991-92 PIT	ULF SAMUELSSON (sc)
Sanderson, Derek	1969-70 BB	D. SANDERSON (rep)
	1969-70 BB	D SANDERSON (sc)
	1971-72 BB	DEREK SANDERSON (rep)
	1971-72 BB	DEREK SANDERSON (sc)
Sands, Charlie	1938-39 BB	C. SANDS (sp)
	1938-39 BB	C SANDS (ret)
Sandstrom, Tomas	1996-97 DET	TOMAS SANDSTROM (rep)
	1996-97 DET	TOMAS SANDSTROM (sc)
Saraceno, Mario	1979-80 NYI	MARIO SARACENO SCOUT (ab)
	1979-80 NYI	MARIO SARACENO SCOUT (rep)
	1979-80 NYI	MARIO SARACENO SCOUT (sc)
	1980-81 NYI	MARIO SARACENO SCOUT (ab)
	1980-81 NYI	MARIO SARACENO SCOUT (rep)
	1980-81 NYI	MARIO SARACENO (sc)
Sather, Glen	1983-84 EDM	GLEN SATHER G.M. & COACH (ab)
	1983-84 EDM	GLEN SATHER G.M. & COACH (rep)
	1983-84 EDM	GLEN SATHER G.M. & COACH (sc)
	1984-85 EDM	GLEN SATHER G.M. & COACH (ab)
	1984-85 EDM	GLEN SATHER G.M. & COACH (rep)
	1984-85 EDM	GLEN SATHER G.M. & COACH (sc)
	1986-87 EDM	GLEN SATHER G.M. & COACH (ab)
	1986-87 EDM	GLEN SATHER G.M. & COACH (rep)
	1986-87 EDM	GLEN SATHER G.M. & COACH (sc)
	1987-88 EDM	GLEN SATHER G.M. & COACH (ab)
	1987-88 EDM	GLEN SATHER G.M. & COACH (rep)
	1987-88 EDM	GLEN SATHER G.M. & COACH (sc)
	1989-90 EDM	GLEN SATHER PRES. & G.M. (ab)
	1989-90 EDM	GLEN SATHER PRES. & G.M. (rep)
	1989-90 EDM	GLEN SATHER PRES. & G.M. (sc)
Savard, Denis	1992-93 MC	D. SAVARD (rep)
	1992-93 MC	D. SAVARD (sc)
Savard, Serge	1967-68 MC	S. SAVARD (rep)
	1967-68 MC	S SAVARD (sc)
	1968-69 MC	S. SAVARD (rep)
	1968-69 MC	S SAVARD (sc)
	1972-73 MC	SERGE SAVARD (rep)
	1972-73 MC	SERGE SAVARD (sc)
	1975-76 MC	SERGE SAVARD (rep)
	1975-76 MC	SERGE SAVARD (sc)
	1976-77 MC	SERGE SAVARD (rep)
	1976-77 MC	SERGE SAVARD (sc)
	1977-78 MC	SERGE SAVARD (rep)
	1977-78 MC	SERGE SAVARD (sc)
	1978-79 MC	S. SAVARD (ab)
	1978-79 MC	S. SAVARD (rep)
	1978-79 MC	S. SAVARD (sc)
	1985-86 MC	S. SAVARD G.M. (ab)
	1985-86 MC	S. SAVARD G.M. (rep)
	1985-86 MC	S. SAVARD G.M. (sc)
	1992-93 MC	SERGE SAVARD G.M. (rep)
	1992-93 MC	SERGE SAVARD G.M. (sc)
Sawchuk, Terry	1951-52 DET	TERRY SAWCHUK (re)
	1951-52 DET	TERRY SAWCHUK (rep)
	1951-52 DET	TERRY SAWCHUK (sc)
	1953-54 DET	TERRY SAWCHUK (re)
	1953-54 DET	TERRY SAWCHUK (rep)
	1953-54 DET	TERRY SAWCHUK (sc)
	1954-55 DET	TERRY SAWCHUK (re)
	1954-55 DET	TERRY SAWCHUK (rep)
	1954-55 DET	TERRY SAWCHUK (sc)
	1966-67 TML	TERRY SAWCHUK (rep)
	1966-67 TML	TERRY SAWCHUK (sc)
Scheinfeld, Lou	1974-75 PHI	LOU SCHEINFELD V.P. (rep)
	1974-75 PHI	LOU SCHEINFELD V.P. (sc)
Schmidt, Milt	1938-39 BB	M. SCHMIDT (sp)
	1938-39 BB	M SCHMIDT (ret)
	1940-41 BB	MILTON SCHMIDT (sp)
	1940-41 BB	MILTON SCHMIDT (rep)
	1940-41 BB	MILTON SCHMIDT (sc)
	1969-70 BB	M. SCHMIDT GEN.M. (rep)
	1969-70 BB	M SCHMIDT GE M (sc)
	1971-72 BB	MILT SCHMIDT GEN. MGR. (rep)
	1971-72 BB	MILT SCHMIDT G.MAN. (sc)
Schneider, Mathieu	1992-93 MC	M. SCHNEIDER (rep)
	1992-93 MC	M. SCHNEIDER (sc)
Schock, Danny	1969-70 BB	D SCHOCK (rep)
	1969-70 BB	D SCHOCK (sc)
Schriner, Dave "Sweeney"	1941-42 TML	DAVE SCHRINER (sp)
	1941-42 TML	DAVE SCHRINER (rep)
	1941-42 TML	DAVE SCHRINER (sc)
	1944-45 TML	DAVE SCHRINER (sp)
	1944-45 TML	DAVE SCHRINER (rep)
	1944-45 TML	DAVE SCHRINER (sc)
Schuch, Ted	1994-95 NJ	TED SCHUCH (rep)
	1994-95 NJ	TED SCHUCH (sc)
Schultz, Dave	1973-74 PHI	DAVE SCHULTZ (rep)
	1973-74 PHI	DAVE SCHULTZ (sc)
	1974-75 PHI	DAVE SCHULTZ (rep)
	1974-75 PHI	DAVE SCHULTZ (sc)
Schwab, Corey	2002-03 NJ	COREY A. SCHWAB (rep)
	2002-03 NJ	COREY A. SCHWAB (sc)
Sclisizzi, Enio	1951-52 DET	ENIO SCLISIZZI (re)
Scott, Joe	1973-74 PHI	JOE SCOTT PRES. (rep)
	1973-74 PHI	JOE SCOTT PRES. (sc)
	1974-75 PHI	JOE SCOTT PRES. (rep)
	1974-75 PHI	JOE SCOTT PRES. (sc)
Scurfield, Sonia	1988-89 CAL	SONIA SCURFIELD OWNERS* (ab)
	1988-89 CAL	SONIA SCURFIELD OWNERS* (rep)
	1988-89 CAL	SONIA SCURFIELD OWNERS* (sc)
		* refers also to Norman Kwong
Seaborn, Jim	1914-15 VM	JIM SEABORN (ib)
	1914-15 VM	JIM SEABORN (rep)
	1914-15 VM	JIM SEABORN (sc)
Seaman, Byron	1988-89 CAL	B.J. SEAMAN (ab)
	1988-89 CAL	B.J. SEAMAN (rep)
	1988-89 CAL	B.J. SEAMAN (sc)
Seaman, Daryl	1988-89 CAL	D.K. SEAMAN OWNERS* (ab)
	1988-89 CAL	D.K. SEAMAN OWNERS* (rep)
	1988-89 CAL	D.K. SEAMAN OWNERS* (sc)
		* refers also to Byron Seaman
Seibert, Earl	1932-33 NYR	EARL SEIBERT (sp)
	1932-33 NYR	EARL SEIBERT (ret)
	1937-38 CHI	EARL SEIBERT (sp)
	1937-38 CHI	EARL SEIBERT (ret)

Name	Season	Inscription
Seigneur,	1985-86 MC	F.X. SEIGNEUR (ab)
Francois-	1985-86 MC	F.X. SEIGNEUR (rep)
Xavier	1985-86 MC	F.X. SEIGNEUR (sc)
Selke, Frank	1931-32 TML	F. J SELKE, / — *ASST. MANAGER* (sp)
	1931-32 TML	F J SELKE (ASS MAN) (ret)
	1941-42 TML	F.J. SELKE ACTING MANAGER (sp)
	1941-42 TML	F.J. SELKE ACTING MGR. (rep)
	1941-42 TML	F J SELKE (ACTING MAN) (sc)
	1944-45 TML	F.J. SELKE ASSISTANT MANAGER (sp)
	1944-45 TML	F.J. SELKE ASST. MGR. (rep)
	1944-45 TML	F.J. SELKE (ASS MAN) (sc)
	1952-53 MC	FRANK J. SELKE - MANAGER (re)
	1952-53 MC	FRANK J. SELKE MANAGER (rep)
	1952-53 MC	FRANK J SELKE MANAGER (sc)
	1955-56 MC	FRANK J. SELKE, MANAGER (re)
	1955-56 MC	FRANK J. SELKE MANAGER (rep)
	1955-56 MC	FRANK J SELKE MANEGER (sc)
	1956-57 MC	FRANK SELKE MGR. DIR. (rep)
	1956-57 MC	FRANK SELKE MAN DIR (sc)
	1957-58 MC	FRANK J. SELKE MGR. DIR. (rep)
	1957-58 MC	FRANK J SELKE MAN DIR (sc)
	1958-59 MC	FRANK J. SELKE MGR. DIR. (rep)
	1958-59 MC	FRANK J SELKE MAN DIR (sc)
	1959-60 MC	FRANK J. SELKE MGR. DIR. (rep)
	1959-60 MC	FRANK J SELKE MAN DIR (sc)
Semenko,	1983-84 EDM	D. SEMENKO (ab)
Dave	1983-84 EDM	D. SEMENKO (rep)
	1983-84 EDM	D. SEMENKO (sc)
	1984-85 EDM	D. SEMENKO (ab)
	1984-85 EDM	D. SEMENKO (rep)
	1984-85 EDM	D. SFMENKO (sc)
Severyn,	1998-99 DAL	BRENT SEVERYN (rep)
Brent	1998-99 DAL	BRENT SEVERYN (sc)
Sevigny,	1978-79 MC	R. SEVIGNY (ab)
Richard	1978-79 MC	R. SEVIGNY (rep)
	1978-79 MC	R. SEVIGNY (sc)
Shack,	1961-62 TML	EDWARD SHACK (rep)
Eddie	1961-62 TML	EDWARD SHACK (sc)
	1962-63 TML	EDWARD SHACK (rep)
	1962-63 TML	EDWARD SHACK (sc)
	1963-64 TML	EDWARD SHACK (rep)
	1963-64 TML	EDWARD SHACK (sc)
	1966-67 TML	EDDIE SHACK (rep)
	1966-67 TML	EDDIE SHACK (sc)
Shanahan,	1996-97 DET	BRENDAN SHANAHAN (rep)
Brendan	1996-97 DET	BRENDAN SHANAHAN (sc)
	1997-98 DET	B. SHANAHAN (rep)
	1997-98 DET	B. SHANAHAN (sc)
	2001-02 DET	BRENDAN SHANAHAN (rep)
	2001-02 DET	BRENDAN SHANAHAN (sc)
Sheehan,	1970-71 MC	R. SHEEHAN (rep)
Bobby	1970-71 MC	R. SHEEHAN (sc)
Sheppard,	1933-34 CHI	JOHN HEPPARD (sp)
John	1933-34 CHI	JOHN SHEPPARD (ret)
Sherf, John	1936-37 DET	JOHN SHERF L.WING (sp)
	1936-37 DET	JOHNNY SHERF (ret)
Shero, Fred	1973-74 PHI	FRED SHERO COACH (rep)
	1973-74 PHI	FRED SHERO COACH (sc)
	1974-75 PHI	FRED SHERO COACH (rep)
	1974-75 PHI	FRED SHERO COACH (sc)
Shewchuk,	1938-39 BB	J. SHEWCHUK (sp)
Jack	1938-39 BB	J SHEWCHUK (ret)
	1940-41 BB	JACK SHEWCHUCK (rep)
	1940-41 BB	JACK SHEWCHUK (sc)
Shibicky,	1939-40 NYR	ALEX SHIBICKY (sp)
Alex	1939-40 NYR	A SHIBICKY (ret)
Shields,	1934-35 MM	A. SHIELDS (sp)
Allan	1934-35 MM	A SHIELDS (ret)
Shill, Jack	1937-38 CHI	JACK SHILL (sp)
	1937-38 CHI	JACK SHILL (ret)
Shipman,	1992-93 MC	J. SHIPMAN A. TRAINER (rep)
John	1992-93 MC	J. SHIPMAN A. TRAINER (sc)
Shore, Eddie	1928-29 BB	EDDIE SHORE (or)
	1928-29 BB	EDDIE SHORE (rep)
	1928-29 BB	EDDIE SHORE (sc)
	1928-29 BB	EDDIE SHORE (ret)
	1938-39 BB	E. SHORE (sp)
	1938-39 BB	E SHORE (ret)
Shutt, Steve	1972-73 MC	STEVE SHUTT (rep)
	1972-73 MC	STEVE SHUTT (sc)
	1975-76 MC	STEVE SHUTT (rep)
	1975-76 MC	STEVE SHUTT (sc)
	1976-77 MC	STEPHEN SHUTT (rep)
	1976-77 MC	STEPHEN SHUTT (sc)
	1977-78 MC	STEPHEN SHUTT (rep)
	1977-78 MC	STEPHEN SHUTT (sc)
	1978-79 MC	S. SHUTT (ab)
	1978-79 MC	S. SHUTT (rep)
	1978-79 MC	S. SHUTT (sc)
Siebert,	1925-26 MM	A.C. SIEBERT. (or)
Albert	1925-26 MM	A.C. SIEBERT (rep)
"Babe"	1925-26 MM	A.C. SIEBERT (sc)
	1932-33 NYR	A.C. SIEBERT (sp)
	1932-33 NYR	A C SIEBERT (ret)
Sim, Jon	1998-99 DAL	JON SIM (rep)
	1998-99 DAL	JON SIM (sc)
Simmons,	1961-62 TML	DONALD SIMMONS (rep)
Don	1961-62 TML	DONALD SIMMONS (sc)
	1962-63 TML	DONALD SIMMONS (rep)
	1962-63 TML	DONALD SIMMONS (sc)
	1963-64 TML	DONALD SIMMONS (rep)
	1963-64 TML	DONALD SIMMONS (sc)
Simon,	1995-96 COL	CHRIS SIMON (rep)
Chris	1995-96 COL	CHRIS SIMON (sc)
Simon,	1942-43 DET	CULLY SIMON (sp)
Cully	1942-43 DET	CULLY SIMON (rep)
	1942-43 DET	CULLY SIMON (sc)
Simon,	2002-03 NJ	PETER SIMON (rep)
Peter	2002-03 NJ	PETER SIMON (sc)
Simpson,	1987-88 EDM	C. SIMPSON (ab)
Craig	1987-88 EDM	C. SIMPSON (rep)
	1987-88 EDM	C. SIMPSON (sc)
	1989-90 EDM	C. SIMPSON (ab)
	1989-90 EDM	C. SIMPSON (rep)
	1989-90 EDM	C. SIMPSON (sc)
Sinden,	1969-70 BB	H. SINDEN COACH (rep)
Harry	1969-70 BB	H SINDEN COACH (sc)
Singleton,	1999-00 NJ	T.D. SINGLETON (rep)
Taran	1999-00 NJ	T.D. SINGLETON (sc)
	2002-03 NJ	T. SINGLETON (rep)
	2002-03 NJ	T. SINGLETON (sc)
Skinner,	1954-55 DET	JAMES D SKINNER, COACH (re)
Jimmy	1954-55 DET	JAMES D. SKINNER COACH (rep)
	1954-55 DET	JAMES D SKINNER COACH (sc)
Skoula,	2000-01 COL	MARTIN SKOULA (rep)
Martin	2000-01 COL	MARTIN SKOULA (sc)
Skov, Glen	1951-52 DET	GLEN SKOV (re)
	1951-52 DET	GLEN SKOV (rep)
	1951-52 DET	GLEN SKOV (sc)
	1953-54 DET	GLEN SKOV (re)
	1953-54 DET	GLEN SKOV (rep)
	1953-54 DET	GLEN SKOV (sc)
	1954-55 DET	GLEN SKOV (re)
	1954-55 DET	GLEN SKOV (rep)
	1954-55 DET	CLEN SKOV (sc)
Skrudland,	1985-86 MC	B. SKRUDLAND (ab)
Brian	1985-86 MC	B. SKRUDLAND (rep)
	1985-86 MC	B. SKRUDLAND (sc)
	1998-99 DAL	BRIAN SKRUDLAND (rep)
	1998-99 DAL	BRIAN SKRUDLAND (sc)
Slegr, Jiri	2001-02 DET	JIRI SLEGR (rep)
	2001-02 DET	JIRI SLEGR (sc)
Sloan, Blake	1998-99 DAL	BLAKE SLOAN (rep)
	1998-99 DAL	BLAKE SLOAN (sc)
Sloan, Tod	1950-51 TML	TOD SLOAN (re)
	1950-51 TML	TOD SLOAN (rep)
	1950-51 TML	TOD SLOAN (sc)
	1960-61 CHI	MARTIN A. SLOAN (rep)
	1960-61 CHI	MARTIN A SLOAN (sc)
Smehlik,	2002-03 NJ	RICHARD SMEHLIK (rep)
Richard	2002-03 NJ	RICHARD SMEHLIK (sc)
Smith, Alex	1926-27 OTT	ALEX SMITH (or)
	1926-27 OTT	ALEX SMITH (rep)
	1926-27 OTT	ALEX SMITH (sc)
Smith, Barry	1990-91 PIT	BARRY SMITH ASST. COACHES* (ab)
	1990-91 PIT	BARRY SMITH ASST. COACHES* (rep)
	1990-91 PIT	BARRY SMITH ASST. COACHES* (sc)
		* refers also to Rick Kehoe and Rick Paterson
	1991-92 PIT	BARRY SMITH (rep)
	1991-92 PIT	BARRY SMITH (sc)
	1996-97 DET	BARRY SMITH (rep)
	1996-97 DET	BARRY SMITH (sc)
	1997-98 DET	BARRY SMITH (rep)
	1997-98 DET	BARRY SMITH (sc)
	2001-02 DET	BARRY SMITH (rep)
	2001-02 DET	BARRY SMITH (sc)
Smith, Billy	1979-80 NYI	B. SMITH (ab)
	1979-80 NYI	B. SMITH (rep)
	1979-80 NYI	B. SMITH (sc)
	1980-81 NYI	B. SMITH (ab)
	1980-81 NYI	B. SMITH (rep)
	1980-81 NYI	B. SMITH (sc)
	1981-82 NYI	B. SMITH (ab)
	1981-82 NYI	B. SMITH (rep)
	1981-82 NYI	B. SMITH (sc)
	1982-83 NYI	B. SMITH (ab)
	1982-83 NYI	B. SMITH (rep)
	1982-83 NYI	B. SMITH (sc)

Name	Season / Team	Engraving
Smith, Bobby	1985-86 MC	R. SMITH (ab)
	1985-86 MC	R. SMITH (rep)
	1985-86 MC	R. SMITH (sc)
Smith, Brad	2000-01 COL	BRAD SMITH (rep)
	2000-01 COL	BRAD SMITH (sc)
Smith, Callie	1999-00 NJ	C. SMITH (rep)
	1999-00 NJ	C. SMITH (sc)
Smith, Clint	1939-40 NYR	CLINTON SMITH (sp)
	1939-40 NYR	CLINTON SMITH (ret)
Smith, Dallas	1969-70 BB	D. SMITH (rep)
	1969-70 BB	D SMITH (sc)
	1971-72 BB	DALLAS SMITH (rep)
	1971-72 BB	DALLAS SMITH (sc)
Smith, Dave	1993-94 NYR	D. SMITH TRAINER (rep)
	1993-94 NYR	D. SMITH TRAINER (sc)
	1998-99 DAL	DAVE SMITH (rep)
	1998-99 DAL	DAVE SMITH (sc)
Smith, Des	1940-41 BB	WES. SMITH (sp)
	1940-41 BB	DES SMITH (rep)
	1940-41 BB	DES SMITH (sc)
Smith, Geoff	1989-90 EDM	G. SMITH (ab)
	1989-90 EDM	G. SMITH (rep)
	1989-90 EDM	G. SMITH (sc)
Smith, R. Home	1931-32 TML	MR. R. HOME SMITH (sp)
Smith, Neil	1993-94 NYR	NEIL SMITH PRES. G.M. GOV. (rep)
	1993-94 NYR	NEIL SMITH PRES. G.M. GOV. (sc)
Smith, Normie	1935-36 DET	NORMAN SMITH — GOAL (sp)
	1935-36 DET	NORMAN SMITH (ret)
	1936-37 DET	NORMAN SMITH GOAL (sp)
	1936-37 DET	NORMAN SMITH (ret)
Smith, Reginald "Hooley"	1926-27 OTT	REG J. SMITH (or)
	1926-27 OTT	REG J. SMITH (rep)
	1926-27 OTT	REG J SMITH (sc)
	1934-35 MM	R. J. SMITH/CAPTAIN (sp)
	1934-35 MM	RJ SMITH CAPTAIN (ret)
Smith, Rick	1969-70 BB	R. SMITH (rep)
	1969-70 BB	R SMITH (sc)
Smith, Sid	1947-48 TML	SIDNEY SMITH (re)
	1947-48 TML	SID SMITH (rep)
	1947-48 TML	SID SMITH (sc)
	1948-49 TML	SIDNEY SMITH (re)
	1948-49 TML	SID SMITH (rep)
	1948-49 TML	SID SMITH (sc)
	1950-51 TML	SIDNEY SMITH (re)
	1950-51 TML	SID SMITH (rep)
	1950-51 TML	SID SMITH (sc)
Smith, Steve	1986-87 EDM	S. SMITH (ab)
	1986-87 EDM	S. SMITH (rep)
	1986-87 EDM	S. SMITH (sc)
	1987-88 EDM	S. SMITH (ab)
	1987-88 EDM	S. SMITH (rep)
	1987-88 EDM	S. SMITH (sc)
	1989-90 EDM	S. SMITH (ab)
	1989-90 EDM	S. SMITH (rep)
	1989-90 EDM	S. SMITH (sc)
Smythe, Conn	1931-32 TML	CONN SMYTHE, / — *MANAGER.* (sp)
	(I) 1931-32 TML	CONN SMYTHE MAN DIR (ret)
	(II) 1931-32 TML	CONN SMYTHE, *MANAGING DIRECTOR* (sp)
	1941-42 TML	MAJOR CONN SMYTHE, M.C. MANAGER (sp)
	1941-42 TML	MAJOR CONN SMYTHE MGR. (rep)
	1941-42 TML	MAJOR CONN SMYTHE (MAN) (sc)
	1944-45 TML	CONN SMYTHE MANAGING DIRECTOR (sp)
	1944-45 TML	CONN SMYTHE MGR. DIR. (rep)
	1944-45 TML	CONN SMYTHE (MAN DIR) (sc)
	1946-47 TML	CONN. SMYTHE GENERAL MANAGER (re)
	1946-47 TML	CONN SMYTHE GEN. MGR. (rep)
	1946-47 TML	CONN SMYTHE (GEN•MAN) (sc)
	1947-48 TML	CONN SMYTHE - PRESIDENT AND MANAGER (re)
	1947-48 TML	CONN SMYTHE PRES. & MGR. (rep)
	1947-48 TML	CONN SMYTHE (PRES & MAN) (sc)
	1948-49 TML	CONN SMYTHE PRESIDENT AND MANAGER (re)
	1948-49 TML	CONN SMYTHE PRES. MGR. (rep)
	1948-49 TML	CONN SMYTHE (PRES•MAN) (sc)
	1950-51 TML	CONN SMYTHE PRESIDENT AND MANAGER (re)
	1950-51 TML	CONN SMYTHE PRES. MGR. (rep)
	1950-51 TML	CONN SMYTHE (PRES MAN) (sc)
	1961-62 TML	CONN SMYTHE CHAIRMAN OF BOARD (rep)
	1961-62 TML	CONN SMYTHE BOARD CHAIRMAN (sc)
Smythe, Dick	1966-67 TML	RICHARD SMYTHE MASCOT (rep)
	1966-67 TML	RICHARD SMYTHE MASCOT (sc)
Smythe, Hugh	1941-42 TML	HUGH SMYTHE MASCOT (sp)
	1941-42 TML	HUGH SMYTHE MASCOT (rep)
	1941-42 TML	HUGH SMYTHE MASCOT (sc)
Smythe, Stafford	1931-32 TML	STAFFORD SMYTHE/MASCOT* (sp) * stamped sideways on Cup
	1931-32 TML	STAFFORD SMYTHE/MASCOT (ret)
	1961-62 TML	C. STAFFORD SMYTHE PRESIDENT (rep)
	1961-62 TML	C STAFFORD SMYTHE PRESIDENT (sc)
	1962-63 TML	C. STAFFORD SMYTHE PRESIDENT (rep)
	1962-63 TML	C STAFFORD SMYTHE PRESIDENT (sc)
	1963-64 TML	C. STAFFORD SMYTHE PRESIDENT (rep)
	1963-64 TML	C STAFFORD SMYTHE PRESIDENT (sc)
	1966-67 TML	C. STAFFORD SMYTHE PRESIDENT (rep)
	1966-67 TML	C ST FFORD SMYTHE PRESIDENT (sc)
Snider, Ed	1973-74 PHI	ED SNIDER CHAIRMAN OF BOARD (rep)
	1973-74 PHI	ED SNIDER CHAIR.OF BOARD (sc)
	1974-75 PHI	ED SNIDER CHAIRMAN OF BOARD (rep)
	1974-75 PHI	ED SNIDER CHAIR. OF BOARD (sc)
Soetaert, Doug	1985-86 MC	D. SOETAERT (ab)
	1985-86 MC	D. SOETAERT (rep)
	1985-86 MC	D. SOETAERT (sc)
Sokolowski, Matthew	1995-96 COL	MATTHEW SOKOLOWSKI (rep)
	1995-96 COL	MATTHEW SOKOLOWSKI (sc)
	2000-01 COL	MATTHEW SOKOLOWSKI (rep)
	2000-01 COL	MATTHEW SOKOLOWSKI (sc)
Somers, Art	1932-33 NYR	ARTHUR SOMERS (sp)
	1932-33 NYR	ARTHUR SOMERS (ret)
Sorrell, John	1935-36 DET	JOHN SORRELL L.WING (sp)
	1935-36 DET	JOHN SORREL (ret)
	1936-37 DET	JOHN SORRELL L.WING (sp)
	1936-37 DET	JOHN SORRELL (ret)
Speer, Bill	1969-70 BB	B. SPEER (rep)
	1969-70 BB	B SPEER (sc)
Stafford, Barrie	1983-84 EDM	B. STAFFORD TR. (ab)
	1983-84 EDM	B. STAFFORD TR. (rep)
	1983-84 EDM	B. STAFFORD TR. (sc)
	1984-85 EDM	B. STAFFORD TR. (ab)
	1984-85 EDM	B. STAFFORD TR. (rep)
	1984-85 EDM	B. STAFFORD TR. (sc)
	1986-87 EDM	B. STAFFORD TR. (ab)
	1986-87 EDM	B. STAFFORD TR. (rep)
	1986-87 EDM	B. STAFFORD TR. (sc)
	1987-88 EDM	BARRIE STAFFORD TR. (ab)
	1987-88 EDM	BARRIE STAFFORD TR. (rep)
	1987-88 EDM	BARRIE STAFFORD TR. (sc)
	1989-90 EDM	BARRIE STAFFORD TR. (ab)
	1989-90 EDM	BARRIE STAFFORD TR. (rep)
	1989-90 EDM	BARRIE STAFFORD TR. (sc)
Stanfield, Fred	1969-70 BB	F. STANFIELD (rep)
	1969-70 BB	F STANFIELD (sc)
	1971-72 BB	FRED STANFIELD (rep)
	1971-72 BB	FRED STANFIELD (sc)
Stanley, Allan	1961-62 TML	ALLAN STANLEY (rep)
	1961-62 TML	ALLAN STANLEY (sc)
	1962-63 TML	ALLAN STANLEY (rep)
	1962-63 TML	ALLAN STANLEY (sc)
	1963-64 TML	ALLAN STANLEY (rep)
	1963-64 TML	ALLAN STANLEY (sc)
	1966-67 TML	ALLAN STANLEY (rep)
	1966-67 TML	ALLAN STANLEY (sc)
Stanley, Barney	1914-15 VM	BARNEY STANLEY (ib)
	1914-15 VM	BARNEY STANLEY (rep)
	1914-15 VM	BARNEY STANLEY (sc)
Stanowski, Wally	1941-42 TML	WALLY STANOWSKI (sp)
	1941-42 TML	WALLY STANOWSKI (rep)
	1941-42 TML	WALLY STANOWSKI (sc)
	1944-45 TML	WALLY STANOWSKI (sp)
	1944-45 TML	WALLY STANOWSKI (rep)
	1944-45 TML	WALLY STANOWSKI (sc)
	1946-47 TML	WALTER STANOWSKI (re)
	1946-47 TML	WALTER STANOWSKI (rep)
	1946-47 TML	WALTER STANOWSKI (sc)
	1947-48 TML	WALTER STANOWSKI (re)
	1947-48 TML	WALTER STANOWSKI (rep)
	1947-48 TML	WALTER STANOWSKI (sc)
Stanton, Paul	1990-91 PIT	P. STANTON (ab)
	1990-91 PIT	P. STANTON (rep)
	1990-91 PIT	P. STANTON (sc)
	1991-92 PIT	PAUL STANTON (rep)
	1991-92 PIT	PAUL STANTON (sc)
Stark, Joe	1933-34 CHI	JOE STARK (sp)
	1933-34 CHI	JOE STARK (ret)
Stasiuk, Vic	1951-52 DET	VICTOR STASIUK (re)
	1951-52 DET	VIC STASIUK (rep)
	1951-52 DET	VIC STASIVK (sc)
	1954-55 DET	VICTOR STASIUK (re)
	1954-55 DET	VIC STASIUK (rep)
	1954-55 DET	VIC STASIUK (sc)
Steer, Fred	1985-86 MC	F. STEER VIPS.* (ab)
	1985-86 MC	F. STEER V.I.P.S.* (rep)
	1985-86 MC	F. STEER VIPS. * (sc) * refers also to Jean Beliveau and F-X Seigneur
Stemkowski, Pete	1966-67 TML	P. STEMKOWSKI (rep)
	1966-67 TML	P STEMKOWSKI (sc)

Name	Season / Team	Engraving
Stephenson, Bob	1907 MW	BOB. STEPHENSON. (ib)
	1907 MW	BOB STEPHENSON (rep)
	1907 MW	BOB STEPHENSON (sc)
Stephenson, Wayne	1974-75 PHI	WAYNE STEPHENSON (rep)
	1974-75 PHI	WAYNE STEPHENSON (sc)
Stevens, Kevin	1990-91 PIT	K. STEVENS (ab)
	1990-91 PIT	K. STEVENS (rep)
	1990-91 PIT	K. STEVENS (sc)
	1991-92 PIT	KEVIN STEVENS (rep)
	1991-92 PIT	KEVIN STEVENS (sc)
Stevens, Scott	1994-95 NJ	R. SCOTT STEVENS "C" (rep)
	1994-95 NJ	R. SCOTT STEFVENS "C" (sc)
	1999-00 NJ	SCOTT STEVENS (rep)
	1999-00 NJ	SCOTT STEVENS (sc)
	2002-03 NJ	R. SCOTT STEVENS CAPT. (rep)
	2002-03 NJ	R. SCOTT STEVENS CAPT. (sc)
Stevenson, Turner	2002-03 NJ	TURNER STEVENSON (rep)
	2002-03 NJ	TURNER STEVENSON (sc)
Stewart, Bill	1937-38 CHI	WILLIAM J. STEWART MANAGER (sp)
	1937-38 CHI	WM. J. STEWART MGR. (ret)
Stewart, Bob	1988-89 CAL	BOB STEWART EQUIP. MGR. (ab)
	1988-89 CAL	BOB STEWART EQUIP. MGR. (rep)
	1988-89 CAL	BOB STEWART EQUIP. MGR. (sc)
Stewart, Gaye	1941-42 TML	GAYE STEWART (sp)
	1941-42 TML	GAYE STEWART (rep)
	1941-42 TML	GAYE STEWARD (sc)
	1946-47 TML	GAYE STEWART (re)
	1946-47 TML	GAYE STEWART (rep)
	1946-47 TML	GAVE STEWART (sc)
Stewart, Jack	1942-43 DET	JOHN STEWART (sp)
	1942-43 DET	JACK STEWART (rep)
	1942-43 DET	JOHN STEWART (sc)
	1949-50 DET	JACK STEWART (re)
	1949-50 DET	JACK STEWART (rep)
	1949-50 DET	JACK STEWART (sc)
Stewart, Nels	1925-26 MM	N. STEWART. (or)
	1925-26 MM	N. STEWART (rep)
	1925-26 MM	N STEWART. (sc)
Stewart, Ron	1961-62 TML	RONALD STEWART (rep)
	1961-62 TML	RONALD STEWART (sc)
	1962-63 TML	RONALD STEWART (rep)
	1962-63 TML	RONALD STEWART (sc)
	1963-64 TML	R. STEWART (rep)
	1963-64 TML	R STEWART (sc)
St. Croix, Rick	1998-99 DAL	RICK ST. CROIX (rep)
	1998-99 DAL	RICK ST. CROIX (sc)
St. Laurent, Dollard	1952-53 MC	DOLLARD ST. LAURENT (re)
	1952-53 MC	DOLLARD ST LAURENT (rep)
	1952-53 MC	DOLLARD ST LAURENT (sc)
	1955-56 MC	D.ST.LAURENT (re)
	1955-56 MC	D. ST LAURENT (rep)
	1955-56 MC	D ST LAURENT (sc)
	1956-57 MC	D. ST LAURENT (rep)
	1956-57 MC	D ST LAURENT (sc)
	1957-58 MC	D. ST LAURENT (rep)
	1957-58 MC	D ST LAURENT (sc)
	1960-61 CHI	DOLLARD ST LAURENT (rep)
	1960-61 CHI	DOLLARD ST LAURENT (sc)
St. Pere, Eduard	1923-24 MC	ED. C. ST PERE (or)
	1923-24 MC	ED C ST. PERE (rep)
	1923-24 MC	ED. C. ST. PERE (sc)
	1929-30 MC	E.C.ST.PERE M.P. (sp)
	1929-30 MC	E C ST PERE M P (ret)
	1930-31 MC	E. C. ST. PERE, M.P. (sp)
	1930-31 MC	E C ST PERE M P (ret)
Strachan, Bert	1907 MW	BERT. STRACHAN. (ib)
	1907 MW	BERT STRACHAN (rep)
	1907 MW	BERT STRACHAN (sc)
Strachan, Bill	1907 MW	BILL STRACHAN (ib)
	1907 MW	BILL STRACHAN (rep)
	1907 MW	BILL STRACHAN (sc)
Strachan, James	1907 MW	JAMES STRACHAN (ib)
	1907 MW	JAMES STRACHAN (rep)
	1907 MW	JAMES STRACHAN (sc)
	1925-26 MM	JAS. STRACHAN. (Pres.) (or)
	1925-26 MM	JAS. STRACHAN (Pres) (rep)
	1925-26 MM	JAS. STRACHAN. (Pres) (sc)
Strong, Bill	1998-99 DAL	BILL STRONG (rep)
	1998-99 DAL	BILL STRONG (sc)
Stuart, Hod	1907 MW	HOD. STUART. (ib)
	1907 MW	HOD STUART (rep)
	1907 MW	HOD STUART (sc)
Stuchal, Dan	1998-99 DAL	DAN STUCHAL (rep)
	1998-99 DAL	DAN STUCHAL (sc)
Surprenant, Dave	1998-99 DAL	DAVE SURPRENANT (rep)
	1998-99 DAL	DAVE SURPRENANT (sc)
Suter, Gary	1988-89 CAL	G. SUTER (ab)
	1988-89 CAL	G. SUTER (rep)
	1988-89 CAL	G. SUTER (sc)
Sutter, Brent	1981-82 NYI	B. SUTTER (ab)
	1981-82 NYI	B. SUTTER (rep)
	1981-82 NYI	B. SUTTER (sc)
	1982-83 NYI	B. SUTTER (ab)
	1982-83 NYI	B. SUTTER (rep)
	1982-83 NYI	B. SUTTER (sc)
Sutter, Duane	1979-80 NYI	D. SUTTER (ab)
	1979-80 NYI	D. SUTTER (rep)
	1979-80 NYI	D. SUTTER (sc)
	1980-81 NYI	D. SUTTER (ab)
	1980-81 NYI	D. SUTTER (rep)
	1980-81 NYI	D. SUTTER (sc)
	1981-82 NYI	D. SUTTER (ab)
	1981-82 NYI	D. SUTTER (rep)
	1981-82 NYI	D. SUTTER (sc)
	1982-83 NYI	D. SUTTER (ab)
	1982-83 NYI	D. SUTTER (rep)
	1982-83 NYI	D. SUTTER (sc)
Sutton, Ken	1999-00 NJ	KEN W. SUTTON (rep)
	1999-00 NJ	KEN W. SUTTON (sc)
Svoboda, Petr	1985-86 MC	P. SVOBODA (ab)
	1985-86 MC	P. SVOBODA (rep)
	1985-86 MC	P. SVOBODA (sc)
Sydor, Darryl	1998-99 DAL	DARRYL SYDOR (rep)
	1998-99 DAL	DARRYL SYDOR (sc)
Sykora, Petr	1999-00 NJ	PETR SYKORA (rep)
	1999-00 NJ	PETR SYKORA (sc)
Taglianetti, Peter	1990-91 PIT	P. TAGLIANETTI (ab)
	1990-91 PIT	P. TAGLIANETTI (rep)
	1990-91 PIT	P. TAGLIANETTI (sc)
	1991-92 PIT	PETER TAGLIANETTI (rep)
	1991-92 PIT	PETER TAGLIANETTI (sc)
Talbot, Jean-Guy	1955-56 MC	J. G TALBOT (re)
	1955-56 MC	J.G. TALBOT (rep)
	1955-56 MC	J G TALBOT (sc)
	1956-57 MC	JEAN GUY TALBOT (rep)
	1956-57 MC	JEAN GUY TALBOT (sc)
	1957-58 MC	JEAN GUY TALBOT (rep)
	1957-58 MC	JEAN G TALBOT (sc)
	1958-59 MC	JEAN GUY TALBOT (rep)
	1958-59 MC	J GUY TALBOT (sc)
	1959-60 MC	JEAN GUY TALBOT (rep)
	1959-60 MC	JEAN GUY TALBOT (sc)
	1964-65 MC	JEAN GUY TALBOT (rep)
	1964-65 MC	JEAN GUY TALBOT (sc)
	1965-66 MC	JEAN GUY TALBOT (rep)
	1965-66 MC	JEAN GUY TALBOT (sc)
Tambellini, Steve	1979-80 NYI	S. TAMBELLINI (ab)
	1979-80 NYI	S. TAMBELLINI (rep)
	1979-80 NYI	S. TAMBELLINI (sc)
Tanguay, Alex	2000-01 COL	ALEX TANGUAY (rep)
	2000-01 COL	ALEX TANGUAY (sc)
Tardif, Marc	1970-71 MC	M. TARDIF (rep)
	1970-71 MC	M. TARDIF (sc)
	1972-73 MC	MARC TARDIF (rep)
	1972-73 MC	MARC TARDIF (sc)
Taylor, Billy	1941-42 TML	BILLY TAYLOR (sp)
	1941-42 TML	BILLY TAYLOR (rep)
	1941-42 TML	BILLY TAYLOR (sc)
Taylor, Bobby	1973-74 PHI	BOB TAYLOR (rep)
	1973-74 PHI	BOB TAYLOR (sc)
	1974-75 PHI	BOB TAYLOR (rep)
	1974-75 PHI	BOB TAYLOR (sc)
Taylor, Fred "Cyclone"	1914-15 VM	FRED TAYLOR (ib)
	1914-15 VM	FRED TAYLOR (rep)
	1914-15 VM	FRED TAYLOR (sc)
Taylor, Harry	1948-49 TML	HARRY TAYLOR (re)
	1948-49 TML	HARRY TAYLOR (rep)
	1948-49 TML	HARRY TAYLOR (sc)
Taylor, Tim	1996-97 DET	TIM TAYLOR (rep)
	1996-97 DET	TIM TAYLOR (sc)
Terreri, Chris	1994-95 NJ	CHRIS TERRERI (rep)
	1994-95 NJ	CHRIS TERRERI (sc)
	1999-00 NJ	CHRIS TERRERI (rep)
	1999-00 NJ	CHRIS TERRERI (sc)
Tessier, Orval	2000-01 COL	ORVAL TESSIER (rep)
	2000-01 COL	ORVAL TESSIER (sc)
Thayer, Skip	1990-91 PIT	SKIP THAYER TRAINER (ab)
	1990-91 PIT	SKIP THAYER TRAINER (rep)
	1990-91 PIT	SKIP THAYER TRAINER (sc)
	1991-92 PIT	SKIP THAYER (rep)
	1991-92 PIT	SKIP THAYER (sc)
Thiffault, Charles	1992-93 MC	CHARLES THIFFAULT A. COACH (rep)
	1992-93 MC	CHARLES THIFFAULT A. COACH (sc)
Thompson, Cecil "Tiny"	1928-29 BB	TINY THOMPSON (or)
	1928-29 BB	TINY THOMPSON (rep)
	1928-29 BB	TINY THOMPSON (sc)
	1928-29 BB	C THOMSON (ret)

Name	Season	Engraving
Thomson, Jim	1946-47 TML	JAMES THOMSON (re)
	1946-47 TML	JIM THOMSON (rep)
	1946-47 TML	JIM THOMSON (sc)
	1947-48 TML	JAMES THOMSON (re)
	1947-48 TML	JIM THOMSON (rep)
	1947-48 TML	JIM THOMSON (sc)
	1948-49 TML	JAMES THOMSON (re)
	1948-49 TML	JIM THOMSON (rep)
	1948-49 TML	JIM THOMSON (sc)
	1950-51 TML	JIM THOMSON (re)
	1950-51 TML	JIM THOMSON (rep)
	1950-51 TML	JIM THOMSON (sc)
Thomson, Paul	1927-28 NYR	PAUL THOMPSON (sp)
	1927-28 NYR	PAUL THOMPSON (ret)
	1933-34 CHI	PAUL THOMPSON (sp)
	1933-34 CHI	PAUL THOMSON (ret)
	1937-38 CHI	PAUL THOMPSON (sp)
	1937-38 CHI	PAUL THOMPSON (ret)
Tibbs, Bill	1951-52 DET	BILL TIBBS (re)
	1951-52 DET	BILL TIBBS (rep)
	1951-52 DET	BILL TIBBS (sc)
Tikkanen, Esa	1984-85 EDM	E. TIKKANEN (ab)
	1984-85 EDM	E. TIKKANEN (rep)
	1984-85 EDM	E. TIKKANEN (sc)
	1986-87 EDM	E. TIKKANEN (ab)
	1986-87 EDM	E. TIKKANEN (rep)
	1986-87 EDM	E. TIKKANEN (sc)
	1987-88 EDM	E. TIKKANEN (ab)
	1987-88 EDM	E. TIKKANEN (rep)
	1987-88 EDM	E. TIKKANEN (sc)
	1989-90 EDM	E. TIKKANEN (ab)
	1989-90 EDM	E. TIKKANEN (rep)
	1989-90 EDM	E. TIKKANEN (sc)
	1993-94 NYR	E• TIKKANEN (rep)
	1993-94 NYR	E. TIKKANEN (sc)
Timgren, Ray	1948-49 TML	RAYMOND TIMGREN (re)
	1948-49 TML	RAY TIMGREN (rep)
	1948-49 TML	RAY TIMGREN (sc)
	1950-51 TML	RAYMOND TIMGREN (re)
	1950-51 TML	RAY TIMGREN (rep)
	1950-51 TML	RAY TIMGREN (sc)
Tobin, Bill	1937-38 CHI	WILLIAM J. TOBIN/VICE PRESIDENT (sp)
	1937-38 CHI	WIL J TOBIN (V PRES) (ret)
Tocchet, Rick	1991-92 PIT	RICK TOCCHET (rep)
	1991-92 PIT	RICK TOCCHET (sc)
Todd, Dick	1993-94 NYR	DICK TODD A. COACH (rep)
	1993-94 NYR	DICK TODD A. COACH (sc)
Tonelli, John	1979-80 NYI	J. TONELLI (ab)
	1979-80 NYI	J. TONELLI (rep)
	1979-80 NYI	J. TONELLI (sc)
	1980-81 NYI	JO. TONELLI (ab)
	1980-81 NYI	J. TONELLI (rep)
	1980-81 NYI	J. TONELLI (sc)
	1981-82 NYI	J. TONELLI (ab)
	1981-82 NYI	J. TONELLI (rep)
	1981-82 NYI	J. TONELLI (sc)
	1982-83 NYI	J. TONELLI (ab)
	1982-83 NYI	J. TONELLI (rep)
	1982-83 NYI	J. TONELLI (sc)
Torrey, Bill	1979-80 NYI	WILLIAM A. TORREY PRES. & GEN. MGR. (ab)
	1979-80 NYI	WILLIAM A. TORREY PRES. & GEN. MGR. (rep)
	1979-80 NYI	WILLIAM A. TORREY PRES. & GEN. MGR. (sc)
	1980-81 NYI	WILLIAM A. TORREY PRES. & GEN. MGR. (ab)
	1980-81 NYI	WILLIAM A. TORREY PRES. & GEN. MGR. (rep)
	1980-81 NYI	WILLIAM A. TORREY PRES. & GEN. MGR. (sc)
	1981-82 NYI	WILLIAM A. TORREY PRES. & GEN. MGR. (ab)
	1981-82 NYI	WILLIAM A. TORREY PRES. & GEN. MGR. (rep)
	1981-82 NYI	WILLIAM A. TORREY PRES. & GEN. MGR. (sc)
	1982-83 NYI	WILLIAM A. TORREY PRES. & GEN. MGR. (ab)
	1982-83 NYI	WILLIAM A. TORREY PRES. & GEN. MGR. (rep)
	1982-83 NYI	WILLIAM A. TORREY PRES. & GEN. MGR. (sc)
Tory, John	1931-32 TML	MR. JOHN A. TORY (sp)
Toupin, Sylvain	1985-86 MC	S. TOUPIN ASST. TRAINER (ab)
	1985-86 MC	S. TOUPIN ASST. TRAINER (rep)
	1985-86 MC	S. TOUPIN ASST. TRAINER (sc)
Tremblay, Gilles	1964-65 MC	GILLES TREMBLAY (rep)
	1964-65 MC	GILLES TREMBLAY (sc)
	1965-66 MC	GILLES TREMBLAY (rep)
	1965-66 MC	GILLES TREMBLAY (sc)
	1967-68 MC	GILLES TREMBLAY (rep)
	1967-68 MC	GILLES TREMBLAY (sc)
	1968-69 MC	G. TREMBLAY (rep)
	1968-69 MC	G TREMBLAY (sc)
Tremblay, J.C.	1964-65 MC	JEAN CLAUDE TREMBLAY (rep)
	1964-65 MC	JEAN CLAUDE TREMBLAY (sc)
	1965-66 MC	JEAN CLAUDE TREMBLAY (rep)
	1965-66 MC	JEAN CLAUDE TREMBLAY (sc)
	1967-68 MC	JEAN CLAUDE TREMBLAY (rep)
	1967-68 MC	JEAN C TREMBLAY (sc)
	1968-69 MC	J.C. TREMBLAY (rep)
	1968-69 MC	J.C. TREMBLAY (sc)
	1970-71 MC	J.C. TREMBLAY (rep)
	1970-71 MC	J C TREMBLAY (sc)
Tremblay, Mario	1975-76 MC	MARIO TREMBLAY (rep)
	1975-76 MC	MARIO TREMBLAY (sc)
	1976-77 MC	MARIO TREMBLAY (rep)
	1976-77 MC	MARIO TREMBLAY (sc)
	1977-78 MC	MARIO TREMBLAY (rep)
	1977-78 MC	MARIO TREMBLAY (sc)
	1978-79 MC	M. TREMBLAY (ab)
	1978-79 MC	M. TREMBLAY (rep)
	1978-79 MC	M. TREMBLAY (sc)
	1985-86 MC	M. TREMBLAY (ab)
	1985-86 MC	M. TREMBLAY (rep)
	1985-86 MC	M. TREMBLAY (sc)
Trepeck, Carole Ilitch	1996-97 DET	CAROLE ILITCH TREPECK (rep)
	1996-97 DET	CAROLE ILITCH TREPECK (sc)
	1997-98 DET	CAROLE ILITCH TREPECK (rep)
	1997-98 DET	CAROLE ILITCH TREPECK (sc)
Trottier, Bryan	1979-80 NYI	B. TROTTIER (ab)
	1979-80 NYI	B. TROTTIER (rep)
	1979-80 NYI	B. TROTTIER (sc)
	1980-81 NYI	B. TROTTIER (ab)
	1980-81 NYI	B. TROTTIER (rep)
	1980-81 NYI	B. TROTTIER (sc)
	1981-82 NYI	B. TROTTIER (ab)
	1981-82 NYI	B. TROTTIER (rep)
	1981-82 NYI	B. TROTTIER (sc)
	1982-83 NYI	B. TROTTIER (ab)
	1982-83 NYI	B. TROTTIER (rep)
	1982-83 NYI	B. TROTTIER (sc)
	1990-91 PIT	B. TROTTIER (ab)
	1990-91 PIT	B. TROTTIER (rep)
	1990-91 PIT	B. TROTTIER (sc)
	1991-92 PIT	BRYAN TROTTIER (rep)
	1991-92 PIT	BRYAN TROTTIER (sc)
	2000-01 COL	BRYAN TROTTIER (rep)
	2000-01 COL	BRYAN TROTTIER (sc)
Trottier, Dave	1934-35 MM	D. TROTTIER (sp)
	1934-35 MM	DAVE TROTTIER (ret)
Trudel, Louis	1933-34 CHI	LOUIS TRUDEL (sp)
	1933-34 CHI	LOUIS TRUDEL (ret)
	1937-38 CHI	LOUIS TRUDELL (sp)
	1937-38 CHI	LOUIS TRUDELL (ret)
Tuele, Bill	1987-88 EDM	BILL TUELE DIR. P.R. (ab)
	1987-88 EDM	BILL TUELE DIR. P.R. (rep)
	1987-88 EDM	BILL TUELE DIR. P.R. (sc)
	1989-90 EDM	BILL TUELE DIR. P.R. (ab)
	1989-90 EDM	BILL TUELE DIR. P.R. (rep)
	1989-90 EDM	BILL TUELE DIR. P.R. (sc)
Turek, Roman	1998-99 DAL	ROMAN TUREK (rep)
	1998-99 DAL	ROMAN TUREK (sc)
Turner, Bob	1955-56 MC	B. TURNER (re)
	1955-56 MC	B. TURNER TRAINER (rep)
	1955-56 MC	B TURNER TRAINER (sc)
	1956-57 MC	ROBERT TURNER (rep)
	1956-57 MC	ROBERT TURNER (sc)
	1957-58 MC	R. TURNER (rep)
	1957-58 MC	R TURNER (sc)
	1958-59 MC	ROBERT TURNER (rep)
	1958-59 MC	ROBERT TURNER (sc)
	1959-60 MC	R. TURNER (rep)
	1959-60 MC	R TURNER (sc)
Tverdovsky, Oleg	2002-03 NJ	OLEG TVERDOVSKY (rep)
	2002-03 NJ	OLEG TVERDOVSKY (sc)

Name	Season	Engraving
Vachon, Rogie	1967-68 MC	ROGATIEN VACHON (rep)
	1967-68 MC	ROGATIEN VACHON (sc)
	1968-69 MC	R. VACHON (rep)
	1968-69 MC	R VACHON (sc)
	1970-71 MC	R. VACHON (rep)
	1970-71 MC	R. VACHON. (sc)
Vadnais, Carol	1967-68 MC	CAROL VADNAIS (rep)
	1967-68 MC	C VADNAIS (sc)
	1971-72 BB	CAROL VADNAIS (rep)
	1971-72 BB	CAROL VADNAIS (sc)
Vaisanen, Matti	1984-85 EDM	M. VAISANEN SCOUTS* (ab)
	1984-85 EDM	M. VAISANEN SCOUTS* (rep)
	1984-85 EDM	M. VAISANEN SCOUTS* (sc)
		* refers also to Garnet Bailey, Ed Chadwick, and Lorne Davis
	1986-87 EDM	M. VAISANEN SCOUTS* (ab)
	1986-87 EDM	M. VAISANEN SCOUTS* (rep)

Name	Season	Engraving
	1986-87 EDM	M. VAISANEN SCOUTS* (sc)
		* refers also to Garnet Bailey, Ed Chadwick, and Lorne Davis
	1989-90 EDM	MATTI VAISANEN SCOUTS* (ab)
	1989-90 EDM	MATTI VAISANEN SCOUTS* (rep)
	1989-90 EDM	MATTI VAISANEN SCOUTS* (sc)
		* refers also to Harry Howell and Albert Reeves
Van Impe,	1973-74 PHI	ED VAN IMPE (rep)
Ed	1973-74 PHI	ED VAN IMPE (sc)
	1974-75 PHI	ED VAN IMPE (rep)
	1974-75 PHI	ED VAN IMPE (sc)
Van Zant,	2001-02 DET	PIET VAN ZANT (rep)
Piet	2001-02 DET	PIET VAN ZANT (sc)
Vasalani,	1994-95 NJ	MIKE VASALANI (rep)
Mike	1994-95 NJ	MIKE VASALANI (sc)
	1999-00 NJ	M. VASALANI (rep)
	1999-00 NJ	M. VASALANI (sc)
	2002-03 NJ	M. VASALANI (rep)
	2002-03 NJ	M. VASALANI (sc)
Vasko,	1960-61 CHI	ELMER VASKO (rep)
Elmer	1960-61 CHI	ELMER VASKO (sc)
Verbeek, Pat	1998-99 DAL	PAT VERBEEK (rep)
	1998-99 DAL	PAT VERBEEK (sc)
Vernon,	1988-89 CAL	M. VERNON (ab)
Mike	1988-89 CAL	M. VERNON (rep)
	1988-89 CAL	M. VERNON (sc)
	1996-97 DET	MIKE VERNON (rep)
	1996-97 DET	MIKE VERNON (sc)
Vezina,	1923-24 MC	GEO. VEZINA (or)
Georges	1923-24 MC	GEO. VEZINA (rep)
	1923-24 MC	GEO. VEZINA (sc)
Voss, Carl	1937-38 CHI	CARL VOSS (sp)
	1937-38 CHI	CARL VOSS (ret)
Vyssokov,	1995-96 COL	LEO VYSSOKOV (rep)
Leo	1995-96 COL	LEO VYSSOKOV (sc)

Name	Season	Engraving
Waddell,	1997-98 DET	DON WADDELL (rep)
Don	1997-98 DET	DON WADDELL (sc)
Wakely,	1964-65 MC	ERNEST WAKELY (rep)
Ernie	1964-65 MC	ERNEST WAKELY (sc)
	1967-68 MC	ERNEST WAKELY (rep)
	1967-68 MC	ERNEST WAKELY (sc)
Walker,	1935-36 DET	FRANK “HONEY” WALKER—TRAINER (sp)
Frank	1935-36 DET	HONEY WALKER (TR) (ret)
“Honey”	1936-37 DET	FRANK “HONEY” WALKER—TRAINER (sp)
	1936-37 DET	HONEY WALKER TRAIN (ret)
	1942-43 DET	FRANK WALKER TRAINER (sp)
	1942-43 DET	FRANK WALKER TRAINER (rep)
	1942-43 DET	FRANK WALKER TRAINER (sc)
Walker,	1946-47 TML	G. E. WALKER CHIEF SCOUT (re)
George	1946-47 TML	G.E. WALKER CHIEF SCOUT (rep)
“Squib”	1946-47 TML	G.E. WALKER CHIEF SCOUT (sc)
	1947-48 TML	G. E. WALKER—CHIEF SCOUT (re)
	1947-48 TML	G.E. WALKER CHIEF SCOUT (rep)
	1947-48 TML	G.E. WALKER CHIEF SCOUT (sc)
	1948-49 TML	G. E. WALKER CHIEF SCOUT (re)
	1948-49 TML	G.E. WALKER CHIEF DIRECTOR (rep)
	1948-49 TML	G E WALKER CHIEF DIRECTOR (sc)
	1950-51 TML	G. E. WALKER CHIEF SCOUT (re)
	1950-51 TML	G.E. WALKER (rep)
	1950-51 TML	G E WALKER CH SC (sc)
Walker, Jack	1924-25 VIC	J. WALKER. (or)
	1924-25 VIC	J. WALKER (rep)
	1924-25 VIC	J. WALKER. (sc)
Walter,	1985-86 MC	R. WALTER (ab)
Ryan	1985-86 MC	R. WALTER (rep)
	1985-86 MC	R. WALTER (sc)
Walton,	1966-67 TML	MIKE WALTON (rep)
Mike	1966-67 TML	MIKE WALTON (sc)
	1971-72 BB	MIKE WALTON (rep)
	1971-72 BB	MIKE WALTON (sc)
Wamsley,	1988-89 CAL	R. WAMSLEY (ab)
Rick	1988-89 CAL	R. WAMSLEY (rep)
	1988-89 CAL	R. WAMSLEY (sc)
Ward, Aaron	1996-97 DET	AARON WARD (rep)
	1996-97 DET	AARON WARD (sc)
	1997-98 DET	A. WARD (rep)
	1997-98 DET	A. WARD (sc)
Ward,	1934-35 MM	J. WARD (eb)
Jimmy	1934-35 MM	J WARD (ret)
Wares,	1942-43 DET	EDDIE WARES (sp)
Eddie	1942-43 DET	EDDIE WARES (rep)
	1942-43 DET	EDDIE WARES (sc)
Waske, Ron	1979-80 NYI	R. WASKE H.T. (ab)
	1979-80 NYI	R. WASKE H.T. (rep)
	1979-80 NYI	R. WASKE H.T. (sc)
	1980-81 NYI	R. WASKE H.T. (ab)
	1980-81 NYI	R. WASKE H.T. (rep)
	1980-81 NYI	R. WASKE H.T. (sc)
	1981-82 NYI	R. WASKE H.T. (ab)
	1981-82 NYI	R. WASKE H.T. (rep)
	1981-82 NYI	R. WASKE H.T. (sc)
	1982-83 NYI	R. WASKE H.T. (ab)
	1982-83 NYI	R. WASKE H.T. (rep)
	1982-83 NYI	R. WASKE H.T. (sc)
Wasnie,	1929-30 MC	NICK WASNIE. (sp)
Nick	1929-30 MC	NICK WASNIE (ret)
	1930-31 MC	NICK WASNIE (sp)
	1930-31 MC	NICK WASNIE (ret)
Watkins,	1993-94 NYR	B. WATKINS DIR. COMM. (rep)
Barry	1993-94 NYR	B. WATKINS DIR. COMM. (sc)
Watson,	1964-65 MC	BRYAN WATSON (rep)
Bryan	1964-65 MC	BRYAN WATSON (sc)
Watson,	1942-43 DET	HARRY WATSON (sp)
Harry	1942-43 DET	HARRY WATSON (rep)
	1942-43 DET	HARRY WATSON (sc)
	1946-47 TML	HARRY WATSON (re)
	1946-47 TML	HARRY WATSON (rep)
	1946-47 TML	HARRY WATSON (sc)
	1947-48 TML	HARRY WATSON (re)
	1947-48 TML	H. WATSON (rep)
	1947-48 TML	H. WATSON (sc)
	1948-49 TML	HARRY WATSON (re)
	1948-49 TML	HARRY WATSON (rep)
	1948-49 TML	HARRY WATSON (sc)
	1950-51 TML	HARRY WATSON (re)
	1950-51 TML	HARRY WATSON (rep)
	1950-51 TML	HARRY WATSON (sc)
Watson, Jim	1973-74 PHI	JIM WATSON (rep)
	1973-74 PHI	JIM WATSON (sc)
	1974-75 PHI	JIMMY WATSON (rep)
	1974-75 PHI	JIMMY WATSON (sc)
Watson, Joe	1973-74 PHI	JOE WATSON (rep)
	1973-74 PHI	JOE WATSON (sc)
	1974-75 PHI	JOE WATSON (rep)
	1974-75 PHI	JOE WATSON (sc)
Watson, Phil	1939-40 NYR	PHILIP WATSON (sp)
	1939-40 NYR	PHILIP WATSON (ret)
	1943-44 MC	PHILLIP WATSON (sp)
	1943-44 MC	PHILLIP WATSON (rep)
	1943-44 MC	PHILLIP WATSON (sc)
Watt, Tom	1988-89 CAL	TOM WATT ASST. COACHES* (ab)
	1988-89 CAL	TOM WATT ASST. COACHES* (rep)
	1988-89 CAL	TOM WATT ASST. COACHES* (sc)
		* refers also to Doug Risebrough
Weiland,	1928-29 BB	COONEY WEILAND (or)
Ralph	1928-29 BB	COONEY WEILAND (rep)
“Cooney”	1928-29 BB	COONEY WEILAND (sc)
	1928-29 BB	C WEILAND (ret)
	1938-39 BB	RALPH C. WEILAND CAPTAIN (sp)
	1938-39 BB	RALPH WEJLAND CAPTAIN (ret)
	1940-41 BB	RALPH C. WEILAND, COACH (sp)
	1940-41 BB	RALPH C. WEILAND COACH (rep)
	1940-41 BB	RALPH C. WEILAND COACH (sc)
Welday,	1990-91 PIT	JOHN WELDAY STRENGTH & COND. COACH (ab)
John	1990-91 PIT	JOHN WELDAY STRENGTH & COND. COACH (rep)
	1990-91 PIT	JOHN WELDAY STRENGTH & COND. COACH (sc)
	1991-92 PIT	JOHN WELDAY (rep)
	1991-92 PIT	JOHN WELDAY (sc)
Wells, Jay	1993-94 NYR	J. WELLS (rep)
	1993-94 NYR	J. WELLS (sc)
Wentworth,	1934-35 MM	M. WENTWORTH (sp)
Cy	1934-35 MM	M WENTWORTH (ret)
Westerby,	1927-28 NYR	H. WESTERBY, / (TRAINER.) (sp)
Harry	1927-28 NYR	H WESTERBY (TRAINER) (ret)
	1932-33 NYR	HARRY WESTERBY — *TRAINER* (sp)
	1932-33 NYR	HARRY WESTERBY/TRAINER (ret)
	1939-40 NYR	HARRY WESTERBY. TRAINER (sp)
	1939-40 NYR	HARRY WESTERBY TRAIN (ret)
Westfall, Ed	1969-70 BB	E. WESTFALL (rep)
	1969-70 BB	E WESTFALL (sc)
	1971-72 BB	ED WESTFALL (rep)
	1971-72 BB	ED WESTFALL (sc)
Wharram,	1960-61 CHI	KENNETH WHARRAM (rep)
Ken	1960-61 CHI	KENNETH WHARRAM (sc)
Wharton,	1996-97 DET	JOHN WHARTON (rep)
John	1996-97 DET	JOHN WHARTON (sc)
	1997-98 DET	JOHN WHARTON (rep)
	1997-98 DET	JOHN WHARTON (sc)
	2001-02 DET	JOHN WHARTON (rep)
	2001-02 DET	JOHN WHARTON (sc)
White,	1999-00 NJ	COLIN WHITE (rep)
Colin	1999-00 NJ	COLIN WHITE (sc)
	2002-03 NJ	COLIN WHITE (rep)
	2002-03 NJ	COLIN WHITE (sc)
Wiebe, Art	1937-38 CHI	ART WIEBE (sp)
	1937-38 CHI	ART WIEBE (ret)

Name	Season	Inscription
Williams, Jason	2001-02 DET	JASON WILLIAMS (rep)
	2001-02 DET	JASON WILLIAMS (sc)
Williams, Robert	1972-73 MC	ROBERT WILLIAMS TRAINER (rep)
	1972-73 MC	ROBERT WILLIAMS. TRAINER (sc)
Wilson, Johnny	1949-50 DET	JOHN WILSON (re)
	1949-50 DET	JOHN WILSON (rep)
	1949-50 DET	JOHN WILSON (sc)
	1951-52 DET	JOHN WILSON (re)
	1951-52 DET	JOHN WILSON (rep)
	1951-52 DET	JOHN WILSON (sc)
	1953-54 DET	JOHN WILSON (re)
	1953-54 DET	JOHN WILSON (rep)
	1953-54 DET	JOHN WILSON (sc)
	1954-55 DET	JOHN WILSON (re)
	1954-55 DET	JOHN WILSON (rep)
	1954-55 DET	JOHN WILSON (sc)
Wilson, Larry	1949-50 DET	LARRY WILSON (re)
	1949-50 DET	LARRY WILSON (rep)
	1949-50 DET	LARRY WILSON (sc)
Wilson, Murray	1972-73 MC	MURRAY WILSON (rep)
	1972-73 MC	MURRY WILSON (sc)
	1975-76 MC	MURRAY WILSON (rep)
	1975-76 MC	MURRY WILSON (sc)
	1976-77 MC	MURRAY WILSON (rep)
	1976-77 MC	MURRY WILSON (sc)
	1977-78 MC	MURRAY WILSON (rep)
	1977-78 MC	MURRAY WILSON (sc)
Wilson, Rick	1998-99 DAL	RICK WILSON (rep)
	1998-99 DAL	RICK WILSON (sc)
Wilson, Ross "Lefty"	1951-52 DET	ROSS WILSON—ASS'T. TRAINER (re)
	1951-52 DET	ROS WILSON ASST. TR. (rep)
	1951-52 DET	ROS WILSON (ASS'T TR) (sc)
	1953-54 DET	ROSS WILSON, ASS'T. TRAINER (re)
	1954-55 DET	ROSS WILSON, ASS'T TRAINER (re)
	1954-55 DET	ROSS WILSON ASST. TRAINER (rep)
	1954-55 DET	ROSS WILSON ASS'T TRAINER (sc)
Winkler, Hal	1928-29 BB	HAL WINKLER (SUB GOALTENDER) (ret)
Wirtz, Arthur	1935-36 DET	ARTHUR M. WIRTZ/SEC.-TREAS. (sp)
	1935-36 DET	ARTHUR M WIRTZ (SEC TREAS) (ret)
	1936-37 DET	ARTHUR M. WIRTZ/SEC.-TREAS. (sp)
	1936-37 DET	ARTHUR M WIRTZ (SEC TREAS) (ret)
	1942-43 DET	A. M. WIRTZ SECT. TREAS. (sp)
	1942-43 DET	A.M. WIRTZ SECT. TREAS (rep)
	1942-43 DET	A M WIRTZ (SECT TREAS) (sc)
	1949-50 DET	ARTHUR M. WIRTZ, SEC'Y. — TREASURER (re)
	1949-50 DET	ART M. WIRTZ SEC. TREAS. (rep)
	1949-50 DET	ART M WIRTZ (SEC TREAS) (sc)
	1960-61 CHI	ARTHUR M. WIRTZ PRESIDENT (rep)
	1960-61 CHI	ARTHUR• M• WIRTZ PRESIDENT (sc)
Wirtz, Art Jr.	1960-61 CHI	A.M. WIRTZ JR. V.PRES. (rep)
	1960-61 CHI	ARTHUR M WIRTZ JR VICE PRESS (sc)
Wiseman, Eddie	1940-41 BB	EDDIE WISEMAN (sp)
	1940-41 BB	EDDIE WISEMAN (rep)
	1940-41 BB	EDDIE WISEMAN (sc)
Woit, Benny	1951-52 DET	BEN WOIT (re)
	1951-52 DET	BEN WOIT (rep)
	1951-52 DET	BEN WOIT (sc)
	1953-54 DET	BEN WOIT (re)
	1953-54 DET	BEN WOIT (rep)
	1953-54 DET	BEN WOIT (sc)
	1954-55 DET	BEN WOIT (re)
	1954-55 DET	BEN WOIT (rep)
	1954-55 DET	BEN WOIT (sc)
Wolanin, Craig	1995-96 COL	CRAIG WOLANIN (rep)
	1995-96 COL	CRAIG WOLANIN (sc)
Worsley, Lorne "Gump"	1964-65 MC	LORNE WORSLEY (rep)
	1964-65 MC	LORNE WORSLEY (sc)
	1965-66 MC	LORNE WORSLEY (rep)
	1965-66 MC	LORNE WORSLEY (sc)
	1967-68 MC	LORNE WORSLEY/GOALKEEPERS* (rep)
	1967-68 MC	LORNE WORSLEY/GOALKEEPERS* (sc)
		* refers also to Rogatien Vachon and Ernest Wakely
	1968-69 MC	L. WORSLEY (rep)
	1968-69 MC	L WORLSEY (sc)
Wregget, Ken	1991-92 PIT	KEN WREGGET (rep)
	1991-92 PIT	KEN WREGGET (sc)
Yelle, Stephane	1995-96 COL	STEPHANE YELLE (rep)
	1995-96 COL	STEPHANE YELLE (sc)
	2000-01 COL	STEPHANE YELLE (rep)
	2000-01 COL	STEPHANE YELLE (sc)
York, Marie DeBartolo	1990-91 PIT	MARIE DENISE DEBARTOLO YORK PRES. (ab)
	1990-91 PIT	MARIE DENISE DE BARTOLO YORK PRES. (rep)
	1990-91 PIT	MARIE DENISE DE BARTOLO YORK PRES. (sc)
		* see also Marie DeBartolo
Young, Doug	1935-36 DET	DOUG YOUNG CAPT. R.DEFENSE (sp)
	1935-36 DET	DOUG YOUNG CAPT (ret)
	1936-37 DET	DOUG YOUNG CAPT. R.DEFENSE (sp)
	1936-37 DET	DOUG YOUNG (CAPT) (ret)
Young, Scott	1990-91 PIT	S. YOUNG (ab)
	1990-91 PIT	S. YOUNG (rep)
	1990-91 PIT	S. YOUNG (sc)
	1995-96 COL	SCOTT YOUNG (rep)
	1995-96 COL	SCOTT YOUNG (sc)
Young, Wendell	1990-91 PIT	W. YOUNG (ab)
	1990-91 PIT	W. YOUNG (rep)
	1990-91 PIT	W. YOUNG (sc)
	1991-92 PIT	WENDELL YOUNG (rep)
	1991-92 PIT	WENDELL YOUNG (sc)
Yzerman, Steve	1996-97 DET	STEVE YZERMAN (rep)
	1996-97 DET	STEVE YZERMAN (sc)
	1997-98 DET	S. YZERMAN (rep)
	1997-98 DET	S. YZERMAN (sc)
	2001-02 DET	STEVE YZERMAN CAPT. (rep)
	2001-02 DET	STEVE YZERMAN CAPT. (sc)
Zeidel, Larry	1951-52 DET	LARRY ZEIDEL (re)
	1951-52 DET	LARRY ZEIDEL (rep)
	1951-52 DET	LARRY ZEIDEL (sc)
Zelepukin, Valeri	1994-95 NJ	VALERI ZELEPUKIN (rep)
	1994-95 NJ	VALERI ZELEPUKIN (sc)
Zubov, Sergei	1993-94 NYR	S. ZUBOV (rep)
	1993-94 NYR	S. ZUBOV (sc)
	1998-99 DAL	SERGEI ZUBOV (rep)
	1998-99 DAL	SERGEI ZUBOV (sc)

Number of names on the Stanley Cup

THE STANLEY CUP

ib inside original bowl
or original base
sp stovepipe (1930-31 to 1944-45)
re redesign (1945-46 to 1955-56)
ret retired band (1928-29–1939-40)
ab abandoned band (1978-79 to 1990-91)
rep replica Stanley Cup
sc Presentation Stanley Cup

ADDITIONAL TEAM ABBREVIATIONS

MSH Montreal Shamrocks
MV Montreal Victorias
OSS Ottawa Silver Seven
SM Seattle Metropolitans
TA Toronto Arenas
TB Tampa Bay Lightning
WIN Winnipeg Victorias

YEAR	TEAM	ib	ob	sp	re	or	rep	sc
1892-93	AAA	—	—	—	—	—	—	—
1893-94	AAA	—	—	—	—	—	—	—
1894-95	WIN	—	—	—	—	—	—	—
1895-96	MV	—	—	—	—	—	—	—
1896-97	MV	—	—	—	—	—	—	—
1897-98	MV	—	—	—	—	—	—	—
1898-99	MV	—	—	—	—	—	—	—
1898-99	MSH	—	—	—	—	—	—	—
1899-00	MSH	—	—	—	—	—	—	—
1900-01	WIN	—	—	—	—	—	—	—
1901-02	WIN	—	—	—	—	—	—	—
1901-02	AAA	—	—	—	—	—	—	—
1902-03	AAA	—	—	—	—	—	—	—
1902-03	OSS	—	—	—	—	—	—	—
1903-04	OSS	—	—	—	—	—	—	—
1904-05	OSS	—	—	—	—	—	—	—
1905-06	OSS	—	—	—	—	—	—	—
1905-06	MW	—	—	—	—	—	—	—
1906-07	KEN	—	—	—	—	—	—	—
1906-07	MW	20	—	—	—	—	20	20
1907-08	MW	—	—	—	—	—	—	—
1908-09	OTT	—	—	—	—	—	—	—
1909-10	OTT	—	—	—	—	—	—	—
1909-10	MW	—	—	—	—	—	—	—
1910-11	OTT	—	—	—	—	—	—	—
1911-12	QUE	—	—	—	—	—	—	—
1912-13	QUE	—	—	—	—	—	—	—
1913-14	TOB	—	—	—	—	—	—	—
1914-15	VM	9	—	—	—	—	9	9
1915-16	MC	—	—	—	—	—	—	—
1916-17	SM	—	—	—	—	—	—	—
1917-18	TA	—	—	—	—	—	—	—
1918-19		*Stanley Cup Not Awarded*						
1919-20	OTT	—	—	—	—	—	—	—
1920-21	OTT	—	—	—	—	—	—	—
1921-22	TSP	—	—	—	—	—	—	—
1922-23	OTT	—	—	—	—	—	—	—
1923-24	MC	—	21	—	—	—	21	21
1924-25	VIC	—	12	—	—	—	12	12
1925-26	MM	—	18	—	—	—	18	18
1926-27	OTT	—	—	—	—	—	—	17
1927-28	NYR	—	—	19	19	—	19	—
1928-29	BB	—	21	21	—	—	21	16
1929-30	MC	—	—	27	27	—	27	—
1930-31	MC	—	—	28	28	—	28	—
1931-32	TML	—	—	43	20	—	—	—
1932-33	NYR	—	—	17	17	—	—	—
1933-34	CHI	—	14	21	—	—	—	—
1934-35	MM	—	—	24	24	—	—	—
1935-36	DET	—	—	21	21	—	—	—
1936-37	DET	—	—	27	24	—	—	—
1937-38	CHI	—	—	23	20	—	—	—
1938-39	BB	—	—	24	24	—	—	—
1939-40	NYR	—	—	19	19	19	—	—
1940-41	BB	—	—	—	—	21	22	22
1941-42	TML	—	—	—	—	27	28	28
1942-43	DET	—	—	—	—	24	25	25
1943-44	MC	—	—	—	—	20	21	21
1944-45	TML	—	—	—	—	29	29	29
1945-46	MC	—	—	—	—	23	23	23
1946-47	TML	—	—	—	—	30	29	29
1947-48	TML	—	—	—	—	34	33	33
1948-49	TML	—	—	—	—	35	29	29
1949-50	DET	—	—	—	—	32	31	31
1950-51	TML	—	—	—	—	37	34	34
1951-52	DET	—	—	—	32	—	30	31
1952-53	MC	—	—	—	29	—	29	29
1953-54	DET	—	—	—	30	—	28	28
1954-55	DET	—	—	—	26	—	26	26
1955-56	MC	—	—	—	27	—	27	27
1956-57	MC	—	—	—	—	—	26	26
1957-58	MC	—	—	—	—	—	29	29
1958-59	MC	—	—	—	—	—	29	29
1959-60	MC	—	—	—	—	—	27	27
1960-61	CHI	—	—	—	—	—	30	30
1961-62	TML	—	—	—	—	—	31	31
1962-63	TML	—	—	—	—	—	28	28
1963-64	TML	—	—	—	—	—	27	27
1964-65	MC	—	—	—	—	—	32	32
1965-66	MC	—	—	—	—	—	27	27
1966-67	TML	—	—	—	—	—	32	32
1967-68	MC	—	—	—	—	—	28	28
1968-69	MC	—	—	—	—	—	28	28
1969-70	BB	—	—	—	—	—	36	36
1970-71	MC	—	—	—	—	—	31	31
1971-72	BB	—	—	—	—	—	27	27
1972-73	MC	—	—	—	—	—	29	29
1973-74	PHI	—	—	—	—	—	31	31
1974-75	PHI	—	—	—	—	—	33	33
1975-76	MC	—	—	—	—	—	29	29
1976-77	MC	—	—	—	—	—	34	34
1977-78	MC	—	—	—	—	—	35	35
1978-79	MC	—	—	—	—	—	36	36
1979-80	NYI	—	—	—	—	—	33	33
1980-81	NYI	—	—	—	—	—	33	33
1981-82	NYI	—	—	—	—	—	31	31
1982-83	NYI	—	—	—	—	—	31	31
1983-84	EDM	—	—	—	—	—	30	30
1984-85	EDM	—	—	—	—	—	38	38
1985-86	MC	—	—	—	—	—	41	41
1986-87	EDM	—	—	—	—	—	40	40
1987-88	EDM	—	—	—	—	—	34	34
1988-89	CAL	—	—	—	—	—	39	39
1989-90	EDM	—	—	—	—	—	46	46
1990-91	PIT	—	—	—	—	—	41	41
1991-92	PIT	—	—	—	—	—	52	52
1992-93	MC	—	—	—	—	—	41	41
1993-94	NYR	—	—	—	—	—	44	44
1994-95	NJ	—	—	—	—	—	43	43
1995-96	COL	—	—	—	—	—	41	41
1996-97	DET	—	—	—	—	—	52	52
1997-98	DET	—	—	—	—	—	55	55
1998-99	DAL	—	—	—	—	—	47	47
1999-00	NJ	—	—	—	—	—	52	52
2000-01	COL	—	—	—	—	—	48	48
2001-02	DET	—	—	—	—	—	52	52
2002-03	NJ	—	—	—	—	—	52	52
2003-04	TB	*Not Yet Engraved*						

This portrait of Lord Stanley hangs above a companion portrait of Stanley's wife, Constance, in the State Dining Room at Knowsley, the Earl of Derby's estate. It was executed by Sir Herbert von Herkomer (1849-1914), who was known for a realism in his portraits that rejected sentimentality. Some 15 of Herkomer's canvases are on permanent display at the National Portrait Gallery, London.
Courtesy the Earl of Derby Collection

Tampa Bay
LIGHTNING